Pathways to Power

Pathways to Power

The Domestic Politics of South Asia

Edited by
Arjun Guneratne and Anita M. Weiss

ROWMAN & LITTLEFIELD
Lanham • Boulder • New York • Toronto • Plymouth, UK

Published by Rowman & Littlefield
4501 Forbes Boulevard, Suite 200, Lanham, Maryland 20706
www.rowman.com

10 Thornbury Road, Plymouth PL6 7PP, United Kingdom

British Library Cataloguing in Publication Information Available

Library of Congress Cataloging-in-Publication Data

Pathways to power : the domestic politics of South Asia / edited by Arjun Guneratne and Anita M. Weiss.
    pages cm
  Includes bibliographical references and index.
  ISBN 978-0-7425-5685-0 (cloth : alkaline paper) — ISBN 978-0-7425-5686-7 (paperback : alkaline paper) — ISBN 978-1-4422-2599-2 (electronic) 1. South Asia—Politics and government. 2. Power (Social sciences)—South Asia. 3. Politics and culture—South Asia. 4. Social change—South Asia. 5. Human security—South Asia. I. Guneratne, Arjun, 1961– II. Weiss, Anita M.
  DS341.P375 2014
  320.954—dc23

                                                          2013034435

∞™ The paper used in this publication meets the minimum requirements of American National Standard for Information Sciences—Permanence of Paper for Printed Library Materials, ANSI/NISO Z39.48-1992.

Printed in the United States of America

Contents

Acknowledgments

We have recognized for a long time the need for a timely, engaging volume accessible to students on the varied paths taken by the governments and societies of the major countries in South Asia in the period following independence from Britain. Susan McEachern, editor at Rowman & Littlefield, approached us some years back about her desire for such a volume, and although we agreed, the challenge was to find authors to write comprehensively yet succinctly about the themes we wanted to explore. We were asking contributors to write not only about the more standard aspects of political and economic life, but also about themes they may not have otherwise considered: identity politics, the role of kinship and women's rights in political life, and the social costs of militarism. We also wanted them to describe in detail a case study that exemplifies the struggles over rights in the various countries of South Asia. We were fortunate in finding colleagues with intimate knowledge of the politics of the countries they wrote about, and who were sympathetic to our vision for this project. We are grateful to them for their contributions to this book.

This volume would not have been possible without the vision and constant encouragement of Susan McEachern, our editor at Rowman & Littlefield. Her recognition of the need for a volume of this sort—one which takes sociocultural and economic concerns into consideration when analyzing political paths—was the catalyst for this project. We appreciate the invaluable support provided by the entire editorial team at Rowman & Littlefield that helped bring this volume to fruition. We are grateful to Natalie Mettler, who translated most of the India chapter from the original French, and to Ashley Nepp, who revised and edited maps available in the public domain from the United Nations and the U.S. Central Intelligence Agency for use in the volume. We would also like to thank Patrick Jones for coming through with an invaluable index. Thanks are due to Camena Guneratne (Open University of Sri Lanka) for writing the section on the women's movement in Sri Lanka, to Virginie Dutoya (Université de Cergy) for the section on women in Indian politics, and to Isabelle Saint-Mezard (Université Paris 8) for the section on militarism in India. Aditi Sinha developed the India timeline. Chris Rodrigo brought his critical expertise to bear on the political economy section of the Sri Lanka chapter; the paragraphs on structural change and the evolution of exports, along with table 4.2 and the graph that accompanies it, are his work, and overall, the Sri Lanka chapter benefited from his close reading and comments. Arjun thanks his colleagues in the anthropology department at Macalester for their support during the many years this project was gestating: Jack Weatherford, Dianna Shandy, Ron Barrett, Olga Gonzalez, and Scott Legge. And my thanks especially to my wife, Kate Bjork, for her constant encouragement and support.

Since we began this book, major changes have continued to shape domestic politics in each of the countries, and their relationships with each other. Even so, there was a point where we had to declare the manuscript complete, despite new events (e.g., a newly elected PML-N government in Pakistan, the arrest of Jama'at-i-Islami leaders in Bangladesh for war crimes committed in 1971) that could have been included. We are satisfied with where we have concluded our discussion. We believe this book provides readers unfamiliar with the region with a worthwhile and useful introduction to the politics of the subcontinent and a base from which to expand their knowledge and understanding of the pathways to power its political actors have pursued since they won independence from Britain.

Arjun Guneratne and Anita M. Weiss
August 2013

Introduction

Situating Domestic Politics in South Asia

Arjun Guneratne and Anita M. Weiss

South Asia, one of the world's most important geopolitical areas and home to nearly one and a half billion people, is poorly known and little understood by many in the West. The region is dominated by India, which exceeds—in territory, size of economy, and population—the rest of the South Asian countries combined. India and its rival, Pakistan, which have fought three major wars since independence in 1947, continue in a state of nuclear-armed mutual hostility, with the status of Kashmir, divided between them, a continuing flashpoint. Although many of the poorest people in the world live in this region, it is home also to a rapidly growing middle class wielding much economic power. India, Pakistan, and Bangladesh, together the successor states to the British Indian Empire—the Raj—form the core of South Asia, along with two smaller states on its periphery: landlocked Nepal sprawling across the Himalaya and the island state of Sri Lanka. Many factors—cultural, historical, geographic, economic, and political—bring together the disparate countries of the region into important engagements with one another, forming an uneasy regional entity.

This volume explores the domestic politics of South Asia in the broadest possible sense, studying ongoing transformative social processes grounded in cultural forms. In doing so, it reveals the interplay between politics, cultural values, human security, and historical luck. While these are important correlations everywhere, nowhere are they more compelling than in South Asia, where such dynamic interchanges loom large on a daily basis. To take one example, religion is woven into politics throughout the region, a fact symbolized in the national flags of every

1

South Asian state. Even the flag of India, the most avowedly secular of the South Asian states, harkens back to India's cultural history with its representation of King Ashoka's wheel of righteousness (*dharma chakra*). Every other flag includes religious representations (see box I.1 on Sri Lanka's flag); where else in the world is political identity grounded in or shaped by religious identity in every state? Identity politics—not just of religion but also of caste, ethnicity, regionalism, and social class—infuses all aspects of social and political life in the subcontinent. Recognizing this complex interplay, this volume moves past conventional views of South Asian politics as it explicitly weaves the connections between history, culture, and social values into its examination of political life.

Box I.1. The Symbolism of the Lion Flag

The Lion Flag of Sri Lanka is derived from the royal standard of the last king of Kandy, and shows a lion (the symbol of the royal dynasty) against a deep red field. In its modern version, two stripes, one orange and the other green, have been added to the hoist (the side of the flag nearest the pole; the lion faces to the left, in the direction of the hoist). Conventionally, the lion against its red background represents the Sinhalese, the people of the lion, while the green and saffron stripes represent Sri Lanka's main ethnic minorities, the Muslims and the Tamils. The four Bo leaves at the corners of the flag represent the Buddhist values of loving kindness, compassion, joy in the happiness of others, and equanimity. The symbol of the lion signifies heroism, strength, and discipline, while the sword in its paw means that the country should be ruled righteously.

The Lion Flag can also be read in a very different way: It sums up the deep ethnic divides that plague Sri Lanka. This fact is symbolized in the flag's placing of minorities outside the border of the Lion Flag original. The net result is to maintain the integrity of the original standard, which represents the religion and the identity of the Sinhalese. What the flag symbolizes, then (the lion, sword drawn and at the ready, facing the saffron and green stripes) is the armed power of the Sinhala-dominated state confronting its minorities.

The view that the national flag of Sri Lanka symbolizes the fragmented nature of the country's national identity is not new. In January 1948, Sri Lanka's first prime minister, D. S. Senanayake, appointed a committee to advise the government on whether to adopt the Lion Flag of Kandy as the national flag. After meeting eleven times over two years, the committee, with one dissenting voice, decided to recommend that the Lion Flag, with the addition of two stripes in saffron and green, be the national flag of the country. The dissenting voice was that of Senator Nadesan, a Tamil whose views have proved to be remarkably prescient. Nadesan proposed a tricolor of yellow, red, and white, or of saffron, red, and green. This was unacceptable to the other members, on the grounds that such a flag would not be acceptable to the Sinhalese. The question then became how best to modify the Lion Flag, and the final decision (dissented to by Nadesan) was to add the stripes.

Nadesan had proposed instead to eliminate the yellow border that divides the saffron and green strips from the red field and its lion, and enclose the whole in one yellow border, thus the symbols representing the minorities with that representing the Sinhalese. As he noted, the consequences of the committee's decision would be that the minorities would see their position in the Lion Flag as being a subordinate one. He observed in summing up his dissent, "the suggestion that I have made does not entail the sacrifice of any vital part of the Lion Flag and thus cannot offend Sinhalese sentiments. At the same time it provides a method of evolving a flag which may be called 'national.'"[1]

We focus on the five major countries of the region—Bangladesh, India, Nepal, Pakistan, and Sri Lanka—as they are the primary political actors that influence regional power and power relations. We've chosen not to include Bhutan and the Maldives, tiny independent states whose combined populations are smaller than many small cities in the major countries of South Asia.[2] We have also excluded Afghanistan, which is not usually considered in academic discussions of the politics of the subcontinent, though it is increasingly now seen as having a growing role as an influential player in the politics between India and Pakistan.[3]

SOUTH ASIA AS A POLITICAL-CULTURAL SITE

The use of the term *South Asia* to refer to the cluster of states on the Indian subcontinent is relatively recent. Prior to World War II, this region was known simply as India, the "jewel in the crown" of the British Empire. The word *India* comes from the Sanskrit *Sindhu*, which means "the sea," and was applied in early historical times to the river Indus, which now flows through Pakistan. Through a process of linguistic evolution, *Sindhu* became *Hindu* in Persian, and the term was applied to the river, the land through which it flowed, and the people who inhabited that territory.[4] The India of the British Empire was split into two states at independence in 1947, one of which retained that name for itself, while the other called itself Pakistan. In 1971 East Pakistan broke away through a violent civil war to become the modern state of Bangladesh. Sri Lanka and Nepal were never part of British India; Sri Lanka, then known as Ceylon, was governed separately, as a crown colony, while Nepal retained its autonomy. Thus, part of the coherence of South Asia as a region or area derives from its immediate colonial antecedents—94 percent of modern South Asia's territory was governed or overseen from Delhi during the period of British colonial rule. We shall have more to say about this below and in chapter 1.

The division of the world into areas of study, such as South Asia, is a relatively recent phenomenon, dating from the close of World War II and the emergence of the United States as a superpower in competition with the Soviet Union for global influence. That required the production of knowledge of areas of the world about which Americans knew little. The intensive, interdisciplinary study of world areas began in this period, and with funding from the National Defense Education Act of 1958, expanded rapidly in U.S. universities.

Unlike many of the regions carved out for study that appear to lack organic unity, such as Southeast Asia, it is easier to see why the states of South Asia should be grouped together for study and analysis. They share cultural affinities deriving from a common past as well as the legacy of the British Indian Empire, which bequeathed to its successor states similar frameworks of constitutional governance, public administration, military organization, systems of law and, not least, a common elite language of English.

South Asia is far more populous and linguistically and culturally diverse than is Europe, and it is no easier to generalize about this region than about any other. Western images of the subcontinent have been shaped by the nature of the relations between them. In Greek and Roman times, and in the Middle Ages in Europe, "India"—in its original premodern sense—was thought of as a land of sages and ascetics, but also of opulence; it was the wealth of India that brought the British to Bengal, to trade. During colonialism, "India" became in the western imagination a land of surpassing spirituality, which could be contrasted with the materialism of the West, an image that coexisted with other notions: of pacifism; poverty; nonviolence; the home of Western Christianity's historical other, Islam; and also of "benighted heathens."[5] In contemporary times, the images have shifted: modern India has become an economic tiger, a major world power, and the world's largest democracy, while Pakistan, the other major successor to the Raj, has carved out an international niche as a moderate leader among Muslim states, although one often ruled by its military. These images have been shaped by various factors: trade in luxury goods from ancient times to the present; the conquests of Alexander the Great and of Western powers (the British, but also the French and Portuguese) in modern times; evangelism in the nineteenth century; and, most recently, economic globalization and the geo-political imperatives of the rise of the United States to world dominance.

Geography also contributes to the coherence of a concept of South Asia. Geographical factors not only create the boundaries of the region but have also helped to channel cultural and social processes within it. At the core of South Asia is the subcontinent, a vast peninsula extending south into the Indian Ocean. To the west, north, and east, South Asia is defined by mountain barriers: the Hindu Kush to the west and northwest, and the Himalaya (and adjacent mountain ranges) in a vast arc to the north, extending eastward until merging with the Patkai range that separates India from Myanmar. The Himalaya, with its high, snowbound passes, is not easily traversed, and few cultural influences or movements of population have come into India from the Tibetan plateau (although Buddhism was carried across those mountains, into Tibet and China). Nor, until the Japanese arrived in Burma during World War II, has South Asia been threatened by invasions from the east. People, however, have continually entered South Asia through the northwestern passes across the Hindu Kush, from what is now Afghanistan. Indo-Europeans (the

"Aryans"), arriving from their homeland in central Asia, brought with them the language that became the ancestor of the modern languages of north India, Sanskrit. The Greeks came under Alexander in 327 BCE, and the Hepthalites, or Huns, invaded in the fifth century CE, bringing to an end the Gupta empire. In the eleventh century came the first Islamic incursion from Central Asia, culminating in the invasion in 1526 of Babur, founder of the Mughal Empire. Until the arrival of Europeans, who came by sea, the daunting geographical features that obliged outsiders to enter India from the northwest also discouraged those invaders from maintaining links to their homeland. Instead, they were incorporated into the society that they found in India, and their cultural and social forms became woven into the tapestry of Indian civilization. Indic influence, meanwhile, flowed southeast, carrying Buddhism and Hinduism along the trade routes to Indo-China and the Indonesian archipelago.

Politically, South Asia has been characterized by numerous small or regional states, which were, from time to time, united by empires (the Mauryas, 321–185 BCE; the Guptas, fourth to sixth centuries CE; and prior to the advent of British rule, the Mughals, sixteenth to nineteenth centuries CE). However, these empires never united all of South Asia, although the Mughals came close, extending their control under the emperor Aurangzeb (reigned 1658 to 1707) almost to the southern tip of India. It is the institutions, customs, and practices set in place during Mughal rule that form the basis, in the contemporary imagination, of "traditional" India.[6]

The Mughals created an empire that covered most of modern South Asia. They gave to urban elites, both Hindu and Muslim, a model for a cosmopolitan culture, developed a road network to bind together their empire, standardized the currency as well as the systems of weights and measures, and reduced trade barriers within their dominions.[7] Although Muslim elites in urban centers were the descendants of Central Asian Muslim conquerors who had settled down in the lands they had acquired, and of the Persians who staffed the Mughal bureaucracy, the vast majority of Muslims in the subcontinent, including in Sri Lanka, are converts from Hinduism and share cultural and social forms and practices with their Hindu neighbors. Even in religious matters, it is common for Hindu devotees to visit the shrines of Muslim saints, and vice versa. Muslims in South Asia share far more with their non-Muslim neighbors—social forms such as caste, customary practices, institutions, beliefs, and languages— than they do with the peoples of the Middle East, with whom they share a world religion. South Asian societies are characterized by social and cultural processes that take foreign customs, practices, and institutions and rework them into the preexisting fabric of life so they come to be seen as local. Even foreign peoples have been incorporated as new castes in the system of castes, a process that has been ongoing for millennia.

The most important politico-historical factor that knits South Asia into a region appropriately to be isolated for study and description is, however, the shared experience of British rule. Although the British never directly controlled Nepal, the only major South Asian state to avoid being subjected to the Raj, they bequeathed to the region as a whole a language, English, that links its elites across the boundaries of ethnicity, religion, region, and nation. The Raj left to its successor states similar forms of civil administration, political and military organization, and legislative frameworks. It has even given to South Asia (including Nepal) cultural factors such as the game of cricket, whose role in giving the region a distinctive identity should not be underestimated.

One way to think about the politics of modern South Asia is to ask how the institutions and political forms that the region inherited from British rule have fared in the decades since. None of the modern states predate the British (although nationalists would differ); the political unity that each represents (with the exception of Nepal) is a legacy of empire. As we have noted, India, Pakistan, and Ceylon (now Sri Lanka) inherited state institutions (civil service, police and military, legislature and judiciary) modeled on British forms, and in the decades since, these have all been transformed in different ways that are specific to local cultures, histories, and political imperatives. Sri Lanka, ruled in the early years of its independence by a largely anglophile elite, preserved its dominion status and its political ties to Britain for much longer than its two giant neighbors. It became a republic only in 1972, but thereafter has moved in the direction of an increasingly authoritarian and undemocratic presidential system and the politicization of the relatively independent and professional state institutions the British had left behind. India and Pakistan swiftly became republics following independence, but while India has maintained its democratic and secular system, Pakistan became Islamicized, with the military the most powerful political actor. Bangladesh, since breaking away from Pakistan in 1971, has had similar experiences with Islamization and the military in politics, though these tendencies have been mediated by economic globalization and its status as one of the world's most aid-dependent economies.

Globalization has had a significant impact on the domestic politics of South Asia. The region was transformed into a peripheral dependency of the global economy in the nineteenth century. Colonialism played a provocative role in this process as South Asian market surpluses were exploited for the benefit of the imperial European powers. After the unsuccessful 1857 uprising against their rule, the British established various kinds of taxation and land tenure systems as well as a new infrastructure of rail lines, roads, postal services, printing and newspapers, and a bureaucracy to assist in running this infrastructure. The resultant new class of dependent, elite, English-speaking bureaucrats and professionals largely sided with the British against the old elites. The British Raj established cotton, indigo, and tea plantations, thereby transforming not only the economic base but also the social structure that existed around the economy. South Asian people were transported as indentured labor to other regions of the British Empire, and came to form significant sections of the population in the West Indies, Fiji, South Africa, the Straits Settlements (which later became part of modern Malaysia), and Hong Kong. The decennial censuses introduced by the British, especially given their insistence to list categories such as caste and religion, encouraged South Asians to think about their societies in new ways, and laid the basis for caste-based politics and such novel concepts as majority and minority communities. In other words, nearly all of South Asia was significantly transformed economically, politically, culturally, and socially due to the colonial encounter. Their economies were underdeveloped (i.e., experienced structurally limited development), and new economic conditions gave rise to new social classes: rural feudal elites whose properties were given to them by the British, a middle class, and an urban proletariat. The legacy of economic underdevelopment persists throughout the region today.

We can look at various institutions in British India as examples of this process: the rail system, which connected those cities that the British rulers alone chose; the civil service bureaucracy, which prepared local elites to serve the British but did not encourage participatory democracy or self-governance; and business, which emphasized the export of raw materials to Britain and other metropolitan areas but did little to build up a viable economic infrastructure serving local needs. As the Pakistani political scientist Khalid bin Sayeed argues, "The British must have been aware that the only justification for the kind of socially inequitable system that they had created in the rural areas was the furtherance of their own interests through a system of indirect rule."[8]

Strong indigenous new classes emerged that primarily served the economic and administrative needs of the colonizers. In doing so, they incorporated distinct characteristics of their colonial rulers into their lifestyles such as Western dress, the use of English, and Western education. The result was a sense of cultural subservience incorporated by many South Asians, which, the Indian social theorist Ashis Nandy argues, colonial rulers promoted to further subjugate their colonized populations.[9] South Asia also became the quintessential example of "orientalism" as British and other European scholars portrayed local culture through a Western lens. Wittingly or not, the result was that by emphasizing the social history of this great civilization—"the brightest jewel in England's Crown"—they also celebrated British power, as the empire that had defeated this civilization.[10]

The Indian economist J. S. Uppal[11] argued that when the British Raj finally pulled out of the subcontinent, the entire region was experiencing notable signs of underdevelopment:

- Excessive dependence on agriculture, fostered by the Raj opening up new markets in South Asia while simultaneously transforming existing industries to be dependent on the British;
- Deficiency in capital, thus precluding significant new investments either by states or by private investors;
- Low labor productivity, associated both with antiquated methods and tools as well as with high levels of unemployment and underemployment, preventing economies from absorbing qualified laborers;
- Unequal exchange when trading within the global economy—that is, it took longer to produce goods in South Asia than in South Asia's trading partners due, in large part, to the factors noted above;
- Lack of adequate infrastructure especially in communications, transportation, power, etc.;
- Marked unequal distribution of income and overall wealth;
- Low levels of consumption, given prevailing poverty.

Social crises resulted from these conditions throughout South Asia, notably the growing contradiction between increases in birth rates and diminishing death rates, the sluggishness of industrial development, and concentration of economies in agriculture. As discussed later in this book, the various countries of South Asia approached these crises in very different ways, ranging from India and Sri Lanka's experiments with quasi-socialist economies, Nepal and Bangladesh's dependence on foreign aid to keep governments and economies afloat, and Pakistan's devolution into military rule. The perpetuation of the various indicators of underdevelopment throughout the region today continues to have a significant impact on every country's economy, society, and political circumstances.

THE ORGANIZATION OF THE BOOK

Given the impact of South Asia's colonial past, this volume begins with an overview of its influence on domestic politics, thereby locating the historical foundations of contemporary politics in the subcontinent. The introductory chapter on the British Raj reveals the different ways in which the region was integrated into the global system and the substantive political transformations brought about by the colonial experience. Colonialism influenced such processes as local understandings of law and the administration of justice, transformations in prevailing distinct manifestations of power due to colonial legacies, the influence of various interpretations of Western common law brought by colonialists, and various codifications of customary practice, resulting in very different forms of postcolonial states.

The chapters that follow show how power has been distributed and contested since independence, how different social groups set out to acquire power, and the resources they draw upon to pursue their goals in each of the five major countries of the region. This book is structured so that each chapter stands alone as a comprehensive review of the domestic political history and power configurations of a distinct country in South Asia, while also allowing for thematic comparisons between countries. Each chapter also includes capsule biographies of important political actors and a timeline of significant events in the modern political history of each state.

Following an introduction to the country, each author then provides a comprehensive review of its political history since independence. We emphasize political eras, not chronological decades, as we pursue such issues as the development of the respective constitutions and resultant struggles over their creation, the political paths chosen, and how each country—despite having a common colonial heritage in government and administration—has diverged since independence under the pressure of local politics and cultural differences.

We then move on to a discussion of political economy, noting the interactions between persistent indicators of underdevelopment, political priorities, economic goals, and resulting realities. These overviews include discussions of development assistance and priorities, the effects of economic liberalization, and the importance of community development efforts and movements on the economy. Economic expansion that would benefit greater percentages of the population has been an elusive goal as high population growth rates undermine such efforts.

Identity Politics

Identity politics plays a central role in every South Asian country. As noted earlier, political identity is often grounded in and shaped by ethnic and religious identity, and identity politics infuses all aspects of social and political life. Ethnic, religious, caste, and class politics provoke groups to mobilize politically, igniting ethnic and civil wars in every country in the region. Language politics are a related phenomenon, which has resulted in new states and provinces in India and Pakistan and was a contributing factor in the 1971 dismemberment of Pakistan as well as in the nearly three-decade-long Sri Lankan civil war. Today, there is a movement in Pakistan to divide the largest province of Punjab and create a new province, Southern Punjab, on the basis of the linguistic distinctiveness of Saraiki—a dialect of Punjabi—that is spoken there.

Religion is equally used for political ends and affects social cohesion in remarkable ways, with the rise of the BJP in India, Islamization in Pakistan and Bangladesh, the consolidation of Buddhist nationalism in Sri Lanka, and the struggles over the place of Hinduism in Nepal. Although the growth of Hindu nationalism has challenged the foundations of India's secular democracy, India's nationalism, as the political scientist Srirupa Roy has argued, was predicated on the state seeing itself as the representative of all of India's many subnational groups; in so doing, it has cohered both as state and nation, surviving a number of secessionist movements, notably in the Punjab and in Kashmir.[12] In contrast, Nepal took a different tack, attempting to create a national identity based on imposing the language, culture, and religion of the dominant ethnic groups on a culturally highly heterogeneous population. This attempt ultimately failed, and what political form Nepal will ultimately take is still being worked out at the time of this writing. Sri Lanka's liberal democracy has been undermined by the forces of Sinhala Buddhist nationalism, which is closely identified today with the state. However, it would be a mistake to see political movements based on religion and culture as contemporary expressions of ancient forms of identity politics; as Lloyd and Susanne Rudolph have shown with respect to Muslim-Hindu tensions in India, and as Nissan and Stirrat argue with respect to Sri Lanka, they are very much the product of modern histories responding to contemporary political conditions and ideologies.[13]

The identity politics that have fractured South Asia also include deep divisions along ethnic, caste, and class lines, which have contributed, for instance, to Maoist insurgencies in India, Nepal, and Sri Lanka. The most successful of them all in recent years was the decade-long Maoist insurgency in Nepal that ultimately precipitated the fall of the monarchy, the emergence of Nepal as a republic, and the movement of the Maoists to the center stage of Nepali politics. The most decisive failure was in Sri Lanka, where the Maoist insurgencies of 1971 and 1987–1989 were crushed with heavy loss of life, while the three-decade-long civil war between the Sinhala-dominated state and the forces of Tamil separatism ended with the annihilation of the Tamil militant leadership and the further marginalization of the population they claimed to represent. These insurgencies were not only revolts against the state, but revolts also against the traditional caste order. The high-status Tamil Vellalar caste, traditionally dominant in Tamil politics in Sri Lanka, played little or no role in the leadership of the main Tamil secessionist organization, the Liberation Tigers of Tamil Eelam, while the JVP insurrections were, in great measure, uprisings of the subaltern, low-status castes against the domination of Sri Lankan politics by the traditional Sinhala caste elite.[14]

Women's Status

Each chapter also includes a section on the status of women, analyzing women's power and kinship networks and the interrelationship between gendered power relations and connections with political life. South Asia is justifiably seen as a region of the world in which patriarchal forms of power dominate and where women face significant social and cultural barriers to their advancement. The economist Bina Agarwal has attributed the low status that limits rural women in South Asia to the cultural and social barriers that prevent them from controlling land, despite legislation guaranteeing their right to do so.[15] The rights to land and the corresponding status that women possess varies across the subcontinent; women enjoy high status in the pockets of matrilineal descent in India's northeast, where property is inherited through the female line, and in Sri Lanka where bilateral inheritance is the norm. Elsewhere in South Asia, however, patrilineal forms of kinship organization and property inheritance dominate.

According to Agarwal, gender relations in rural South Asia exist within three principal areas where they are heavily contested: the household/family, the local community, and the state. Each of these interact to limit a woman's ability to own and dispose of land. There are social barriers to women claiming land even when the law allows it. Customs such as early marriage, village exogamy (obliging women to marry outside their natal villages, thus becoming strangers in their husbands' villages), patrilocal residence (in which a married couple reside with the husband's kin), and the general physical and economic vulnerability this confers on women, make them dependent on their natal homes (and their brothers) for support. They cannot afford to jeopardize this relationship by claiming their rights under the law, even were they aware of those rights, which is often not the case. There is also the cultural construction of gender, which militates against women participating in the public sphere. Women are also discriminated against by the male bias informing the decisions of bureaucrats and policy makers. In short, although there has been a clear trend in South Asia toward more progressive laws regarding bilateral inheritance, in actual practice, social custom dominates.

Despite the subaltern status of South Asian women generally, the region is remarkable in that all of its major countries (save Nepal) have produced major female political leaders and heads of state. Sri Lanka produced the world's first woman prime minister in Sirimavo Bandaranaike, whose daughter Chandrika subsequently became the country's fourth president by the widest margin to be recorded in a presidential election. India produced Indira Gandhi, and Pakistan followed with Benazir Bhutto, while both of Bangladesh's major political parties are led by women, Khaleda

Zia and Sheikh Hasina. Even so, women are woefully underrepresented in politics more generally, and when women do participate, they tend to be, like the women leaders mentioned here, the wives or children of major male political figures, and their entry into politics is through those links of kinship.

Every country in the region has tackled ways to empower women since independence. At the outset, women everywhere were entitled to vote and hold office, though *which* offices they could hold have been contested. Most countries have also reformed family laws, giving women the right of divorce; stipulating conditions for divorce, maintenance, and inheritance; removing intercaste barriers to marriage; outlawing child marriage; and raising the minimum marriage age. Family planning policies have had explosive implications throughout the region; the forced sterilization program in the mid-1970s resulted in the demise (albeit temporary) of the Congress Party's government in India, while Tehrik-e-Taliban militants have attacked family planning as a Western conspiracy to compromise women's honor in Pakistan. In Pakistan and Bangladesh, a cornerstone of Islamist groups' policies has rested on promoting gender segregation, limiting women's engagement with the larger society and promulgating laws limiting women's rights. Each country has grappled with how best to conform to the obligations they have agreed to fulfill by becoming a State Party to the UN Convention on the Elimination of Discrimination against Women (CEDAW). CEDAW requires States Parties—and every country in South Asia has become a Party to the Convention—to change laws, policies, and prevailing attitudes that condone discrimination. We can see this is indeed an uphill battle throughout South Asia when we consider how the Laws of Manu (Hindu canon law) portray the ideal role of women in society to be subservient to their husbands: "If a wife obeys her husband, she will, for that reason alone, be exalted in heaven."

Indeed, religion and other aspects of culture are impossible to disentangle throughout the region, and a great deal of confusion exists over where lines can be drawn between them. Many South Asians experience their religious identity as inseparable from other parts of their culture, and often conflate those things that are not in accordance with cultural norms, values, or practices as being in contradiction to religion. It is difficult, to say the least, to pass legislation or change policies to promote the empowerment of women when many constituents oppose the very concept of gender equality on religious grounds.

The Social Costs of Militarism

A further critical dimension of domestic politics in the region is the social costs of militarism. The excessive expenditures on armaments—in most cases, to fight against internal challengers, not international threats—has had an enormous influence on political and economic possibilities in the region. The most militarized country in South Asia, in terms of military personnel per capita, is Sri Lanka, followed by Pakistan; Bangladesh is the least militarized. The social cost of militarization includes not simply the scarce economic resources diverted to armaments, but also the general coarsening of civil society and the increase in crime and violence in society at large that often follows even when the guns have fallen silent. Nepal, Pakistan, and Sri Lanka are either recovering from prolonged conflict or remain immersed in it.

In South Asia, militarism often translates to a generalized politicization of religion in each country. Whether considering the Shiv Sena in India, the Pakistan Taliban, or the dynamics between Sinhalese Buddhists and Tamil Hindus during the decades-long civil war in Sri Lanka, we describe how politicized religion has transformed the local political horizon in each country. The chapters on India and Pakistan include discussions of the Kashmir dispute from different perspectives, and the ensuing nuclear proliferation resulting from the perception of each party that the other is a threat. The chapter on Nepal includes discussion of the Maoist rebellion, and the Sri Lanka chapter addresses the social cost of the Sinhalese/Tamil conflict. The "elephant in the room," however, is the ongoing conflict between India and Pakistan. The social costs of this conflict have not only harmed the economies and politics of the two belligerent countries but have affected the stability and growth prospects of the entire region.

Struggles over Rights

Each chapter concludes by highlighting one group or movement that has fought for rights in their respective country. In India, Christophe Jaffrelot interrogates ongoing struggles against caste discrimination. After discussing the doctrinal foundations of caste and hierarchy in Hinduism, he explores how social reforms since independence have replaced Sanskritization, the traditional process of "social climbing," with the ideology of egalitarian idealism. He shows how the process of instituting affirmative action and quotas has served to diminish the way Hinduism had previously been understood and practiced, thereby reducing the hold religion has over hierarchy and power relations. A very different scenario exists in Pakistan, as Anita Weiss shows in her discussion of the ideology and activities of the Tehrik-e-Taliban Pakistan (TTP) in Swat. The local faction of the TTP imposed their extreme views of Islamist practices in Swat, which the TTP in essence controlled between 2007 and 2009. The reverse of the promotion of the egalitarian idealism seen in India since independence is instead a new interpretation of religion's role and influence in society, thereby enhancing religion's hold over hierarchies and power. While the TTP differs from the usual kind of NGO that fights for rights—in Pakistan, such NGOs include the feminist Aurat Foundation, the Khyber Pakhtunkhwa-based community development NGO SUNGI, and the Human Rights Commission of Pakistan, all of which have been charged with being anti-Islamic by Islamist groups in the country—its influence on life in Pakistan is more compelling than any other group today. The TTP's interpretation of rights differs significantly from that held by most Pakistanis, hence the importance of understanding what that is.

Haroun er Rashid focuses on the eight priorities of the Nagorik Committee, a group of civil society members and groups, in the draft *Vision 2021* for Bangladesh:

1. To become a participatory democracy;
2. To have an efficient, publicly accountable, transparent and decentralized government;
3. To become a poverty-mitigated middle-income country;
4. To have a health-endowed nation;
5. To have a skilled and creative workforce;
6. To become a globally integrated regional economic and commercial hub;
7. To be environmentally sustainable;
8. To be a more inclusive and equitable society.

Notably, the Nagorik Committee, unlike the TTP in Swat, Pakistan, envisions a positive future for Bangladesh's people and polity more by reinforcing a secular system than emphasizing an Islamic one. Indeed, its goal of a more inclusive and equitable society harkens back to the struggles of many groups in India today to remove caste barriers.

Camena Guneratne, in her contribution to the chapter on Sri Lanka, describes the origin and development of the women's movement in Sri Lanka, from its inception in colonial times as a struggle for the franchise (which women achieved in 1931, at the same time as men) and over various other social issues, to their role in the civil war in opposition to state repression. Pratyoush Onta and Sierra Tamang's chapter on Nepal highlights the struggle of the Madhesis of Nepal's Tarai region to demand the same rights extended to Nepalis of hill origin. Because most Madhesis have kinship and other cultural connections with Indian populations across the border, the hill-centric Nepali state has always treated them as second-class citizens whose allegiance to Nepal was suspect. Today, however, they have become a potent force in politics whose demands can no longer be ignored.

EFFORTS TO PROMOTE REGIONAL COOPERATION

South Asian states have frequently played on the fear of an "external enemy" to promote internal nationalism. This has been particularly poignant in the cases of Pakistan and India. In addition, all smaller states are concerned about India as the regional hegemon, and their domestic politics are occasionally framed by concern over India's reaction to and occasional interventions in the internal affairs of its neighbors. These are most evident in conflicts between India and Pakistan over water treaties, and of India's fostering of Tamil insurgents in the 1980s to pressure the Sri Lankan government to follow a foreign policy better attuned to India's interests. India's willingness to coerce its smaller neighbors is also evident in its imposition of an economic embargo on Nepal in 1989–1990 to force the Himalayan kingdom to renew a treaty governing an open border and trade relations on terms favorable to India (although unfavorable to Nepal).

Given such contestations and rivalries, it is no surprise that efforts to promote regional cooperation remain problematic. Over the past five decades, there have been various efforts to initiate new programs and collaborations between South Asian states. These have taken such forms as economic accords, cultural gatherings, and grassroots peace efforts. None has had as much promise as SAARC—the South Asian Association for Regional Cooperation—nor has any fostered as much disappointment over its lack of impact.

SAARC was initially envisioned as the South Asian equivalent of ASEAN, the Association of Southeast Asian Nations. ASEAN has been very successful in its efforts to promote economic cooperation and regional trade within Southeast Asia, and the architects of SAARC had hoped for similar kinds of outcomes. There are two major differences between the two regions, however, that boded ill for South Asia: Southeast Asia has no regional hegemon like India that essentially has no need to trade with the other member states to promote its own economic development, and while there are minor, occasional disputes between Southeast Asian states, they are dwarfed in comparison to the ongoing, economically and politically dysfunctional conflict that persists between India and Pakistan.

SAARC has launched a number of initiatives, working bodies, and goals to promote regional collaboration on critical issues. The South Asian states—including Afghanistan, Bhutan, and the Maldives—have banded together to address various challenges such as agriculture and rural life, biotechnology, energy, human resource development, security and drug enforcement, and social development. The agriculture and rural life initiative was one of the first undertaken by SAARC given that "agriculture's role in the SAARC member states is projected to remain the key to driving overall national economic growth and well-being of its people."[16] Working through different technical committees, SAARC members have addressed, within this classification, such issues as food security, provision of clean water, and research extension to farmers. Other formal arenas of cooperation have included summits, accords, and other agreements to try and move forward to improved cooperation, but in practice SAARC has had a limited impact on regional integration and collaboration.

Despite the lofty goals of SAARC and the constant—if not incessant—meetings and congresses it continues to employ, its impact has been marginal on the South Asian subcontinent. There remain too many ongoing conflicts between the various states of South Asia that SAARC has not addressed, as the chapters of this volume make abundantly clear. ASEAN in Southeast Asia was able to become influential and, indeed, successful, after military conflicts in that region ceased. Despite SAARC's promotion of exchanges of journalists, civil society groups, and better understanding between states, the conflict over Kashmir continues to sideswipe these initiatives. Of equal importance is that South Asia has a regional hegemon, India, whose 2011 population (1.24 billion) is triple that of the combined populations (378 million) of the other four countries.[17] When India has professed a priority, it seems that SAARC takes it up and the result is generally in India's favor. Take, for example, SAARC's initiative to create a South Asia University. For many years, the idea was bandied about in conferences, meetings, and high-level summits. It was envisioned as an opportunity for SAARC to bring together the greatest minds of the subcontinent while also providing an outstanding higher-education opportunity for students from every South Asian country. But what was the final result? SAARC's South Asian University abuts Jawaharlal Nehru University in New Delhi, and its faculty consists mostly of JNU graduates. There is nothing particularly distinctive about the SAARC South Asian University except its focus on political economy; in essence, it is an Indian university with a political economy focus. Indeed, other SAARC proposals have shared similar fates: those that India wished to ignore dissipated, and those that India supported have essentially become Indian initiatives. India has been able to proceed with its own economic and political agenda without the need to collaborate with other states in the region. Until such time that India can be a partner rather than seek to be the regional chief executive, SAARC's prospects to promote economic and social collaborations within the region will remain problematic.

The politics of South Asia must be understood within the social and cultural matrix in which they exist. South Asia provides rich materials for a student of comparative politics. To map out the various pathways to power that South Asians have pursued, and to understand them in their context, students must draw on a range of disciplines: political science to be sure, but also anthropology, sociology, law, geography, and history. Consonant with that approach, the contributors to this volume are drawn from different fields, and their disciplinary backgrounds—political science, sociology, anthropology, history, and geography—shape their approach to their material.

India is a democracy that has survived despite its extraordinary cultural diversity, while Pakistan still seeks an accommodation between Islam, modernity, and its geostrategic location. Sri Lanka is a case study in how a liberal democracy can slide into authoritarianism and contrasts with Nepal, where a state and civil society emerging from centuries of authoritarian rule struggle to create a viable democracy. Bangladesh has opened its doors to global industrialists and donors alike, prioritizing economic over political solutions to its unrelenting poverty. This book is a guide to the politics of this major world region and serves as a springboard for further study.

NOTES

1. From the Report of the National Flag Committee, Parliamentary Series (House of Representatives) Fourth Session of the First Parliament, No. 5—tabled in the House of Representatives on February 27, 1951.

2. The World Bank estimates the current population of Bhutan at 725,940 and the Maldives at 315,885 (http://data.worldbank.org/country/).

3. Afghanistan is increasingly being considered as a state in South Asia, as seen by its inclusion as a founding member state in SAARC, the South Asian Association for Regional Cooperation, and its incorporation into the South Asia Council of the Association for Asian Studies in early 2011.

4. Bernard S. Cohn, *India: The Social Anthropology of a Civilization* (Delhi: Oxford University Press, 2000), 8.

5. See Milton Singer, *When a Great Tradition Modernizes* (New York: Praeger, 1972).

6. Cohn, *India: The Social Anthropology of a Civilization*, 68.

7. Cohn, *India: The Social Anthropology of a Civilization*, 75.

8. Khalid bin Sayeed, *Politics in Pakistan: The Nature and Direction of Change* (New York: Praeger, 1980), 7.

9. Ashis Nandy, *The Intimate Enemy: Loss and Recovery of Self Under Colonialism* (Oxford: Oxford University Press, 1989).

10. Bernard Cohn's essays in *An Anthropologist among the Historians* (New Delhi: Oxford University Press, 1987) and Thomas Metcalf's *Ideologies of the Raj* (New York: Cambridge University Press, 1994) are excellent introductions to the ways in which the British saw and understood India.

11. J. S. Uppal, *Economic Development in South Asia* (New York: St. Martin's Press, 1977).

12. Srirupa Roy, *Beyond Belief: India and the Politics of Postcolonial Nationalism* (Durham, NC: Duke University Press, 2007).

13. See Susanne Hoeber Rudolph and Lloyd I. Rudolph, "Modern Hate: How Ancient Animosities Get Invented," *New Republic* 208 (12), 1993, and Elizabeth Nissan and R. L. Stirrat, "The Generation of Communal Identities," in Jonathan Spencer, ed., *Sri Lanka: History and the Roots of Conflict* (London: Routledge, 1990).

14. The JVP, Janatha Vimukthi Peramuna, a leftist political party, led an insurrection in 1987–1989 in which 40,000 people are said to have been killed.

15. Bina Agarwal, *A Field of One's Own: Gender and Land Rights in South Asia* (Cambridge: Cambridge University Press, 1994).

16. See SAARC website: http://www.saarc-sec.org.

17. WorldBank,Data,"Population,Total,"http://data.worldbank.org/indicator/SP.POP.TOTL?cid=DEC_SS_WBGDataEmail_EXT.

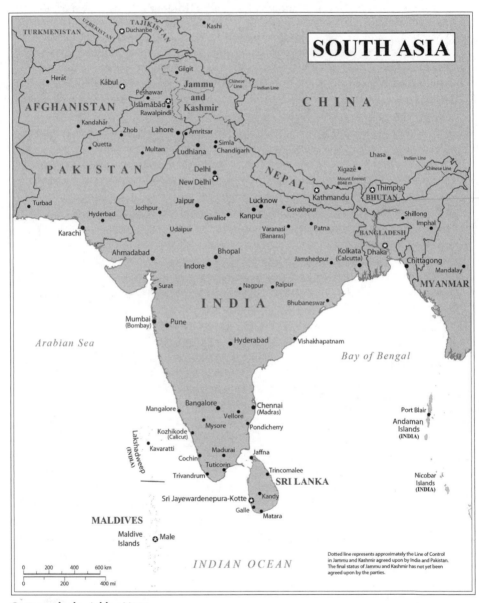

SOUTH ASIA

TURKMENISTAN
UZBEKISTAN
TAJIKISTAN
Duchanbe
Kashi

Herât
Kâbul
Peshawar
Gilgit
Jammu
and
Kashmir
Chinese
Line
Indian Line

CHINA

AFGHANISTAN
Islâmâbâd
Rawalpindi
Kandahâr
Zhob
Lahore
Amritsar
Quetta
Multan
Ludhiana
Simla
Chandigarh

PAKISTAN
Delhi
New Delhi

NEPAL

Lhasa
Indian Line

Xigazê
Chinese Line

Turbad
Hyderbad
Jodhpur
Jaipur
Lucknow
Mount Everest
8848 m
Kathmandu
Thimphu
BHUTAN

Karachi
Udaipur
Gwalior
Kanpur
Gorakhpur
Patna
Shillong
Imphal

Ahmadabad
Bhopal
Varanasi
(Banaras)
BANGLADESH

Indore
Jamshedpur
Kolkata
(Calcutta)
Dhaka
Chittagong
Mandalay

Surat
Nagpur
Raipur

INDIA

Bhubaneswar

MYANMAR

Mumbai
(Bombay)
Pune

Arabian Sea

Hyderabad
Vishakhapatnam

Bay of Bengal

Bangalore
Chennai
(Madras)
Port Blair

Mangalore
Vellore
Andaman
Islands
(INDIA)

Kozhikode
(Calicut)
Mysore
Pondicherry

Lakshadweep
(INDIA)
Kavaratti
Madurai
Jaffna

Cochin
Tuticorin
Trincomalee

Trivandrum
SRI LANKA

Nicobar
Islands
(INDIA)

Sri Jayewardenepura-Kotte
Kandy

Galle
Matara

MALDIVES

Maldive
Islands
Male

INDIAN OCEAN

Dotted line represents approximately the Line of Control
in Jammu and Kashmir agreed upon by India and Pakistan.
The final status of Jammu and Kashmir has not yet been
agreed upon by the parties.

0   200   400   600 km
0   200   400 mi

Cartography by Ashley Nepp

1

⟳

The Colonial Legacy

Shabnum Tejani

IMPERIAL CONQUEST

The British Empire in India and Ceylon can be dated from 1757 and 1796, respectively, with the annexation of Bengal, a wealthy province in eastern India, and the defeat of the Dutch on the coastal areas of Ceylon, to the creation of the modern, independent nation-states of India and Pakistan in 1947 and Ceylon (later Sri Lanka) in 1948. This chapter will focus on the political, economic, and social changes that took place during these two hundred years. While representing a short moment in history, colonial rule and the ways South Asians resisted or accommodated it had enormous implications for the kinds of states that emerged after independence.

Trade

The English did not come to India as colonizers looking to establish their power in distant lands: they came as traders to the Indian Ocean. Merchants from the Arabian Peninsula, China, and South and Southeast Asia had been trading in the Indian Ocean throughout the medieval period. It was the Portuguese who first established a major European presence in the Indian Ocean in the early sixteenth century with the control of port cities in India and Ceylon. Portugal's position was overtaken a hundred years later by the English, Dutch, and French East India Companies that were founded in 1600, 1602, and 1664, respectively.

TIMELINE: COLONIAL SOUTH ASIA, CA. 1600–1947

1600	English East India Company founded (EIC)
1602	Dutch East India Company founded
1619	English East India Company obtains permission to trade in India
1630	Portuguese invade Kandyan Kingdom, Sri Lanka
1658	Jaffna surrendered to the Dutch, Sri Lanka
1664	French East India Company founded
1730s–40s	Rise of regional states
1751	Robert Clive captures Arcot in south India
1757	Battle of Plassey, Clive defeats the nawab of Bengal
1762–66	Warfare between Kandyan Kingdom and the Dutch
1765	EIC forces expelled by Gurkhas in Nepal; EIC accepts the "Diwani," the right to rule, Bengal
1760–99	Haider Ali and son Tipu Sultan conquer large parts of south India
1770–80s	Maratha power in western India under Mahadaji Sindhia
1770	One-third of Bengal's population dies in a famine
1773	EIC Regulating Act, Warren Hastings becomes governor-general
1784	Second Regulating Act establishes a Board of Control in London
1785	Warren Hastings impeached; Lord Cornwallis becomes second governor-general; Cornwallis defeats Tipu Sultan, son of Haider Ali, annexing half his territory
1790–1839	Ranjit Singh controls Punjab; 1798 appointed Afghan governor; forges a Sikh kingdom
1792	Commercial treaty between Nepal and the British
1793	Permanent Settlement of land revenue in Bengal
1796	Colombo surrendered to the British
1798	Wellesley becomes third governor-general
1799	Defeat and death of Tipu Sultan in Mysore
1802	Sri Lanka ceded to the British becoming the Crown Colony of Ceylon
1803	British capture Delhi
1813	EIC's monopoly of trade ends
1817–18	Rebellion of Kandyan provinces suppressed, Sri Lanka

1818	British defeat the Marathas
1828–35	Bentinck becomes governor-general in an age of reform (Utilitarians)
1829	Abolition of sati (widow burning)
1833	Sri Lanka brought under unified government, administered through five provinces
1839–49	Anglo-Sikh wars; British annexation of territory across northern India; annexation of Punjab (1839) and Sind (1843)
1857	Mutiny/Revolt in the army of the EIC and popular revolts across northern and central India
1858	EIC disbanded; India comes under Crown rule; Queen Victoria's proclamation of Britain's "noninterference" in the customs and traditions of Indians
1858	Telegraph communication with India begins
1861	Imperial Legislative Council established with a few Indian representatives nominated by the viceroy
1872	The first all-India census
1877	Queen Victoria takes the title of Empress of India
1885	First session of the Indian National Congress
1890s	Plague and famine in western India
1899–1905	Viceroyalty of Curzon
1905–8	Partition of Bengal; Swadeshi movement
1906	Founding of the All India Muslim League
1909	Morley-Minto reforms introduce a "separate electorate" for Muslims
1911	Partition of Bengal revoked
1912	First election to Legislative Council in Sri Lanka
1915	M. K. Gandhi returns to India from South Africa
1916	Lucknow Pact between the Congress and the Muslim League
1919	Montagu-Chelmsford constitutional reforms
1919	Jallianwallah Bagh massacre; Gandhi's Rowlatt Satyagraha
1919–22	Khilafat movement
1920–22	Non-Cooperation movement
1927–28	Donoughmore Commission, Sri Lanka, 1931 constitution; Simon Commission and the Nehru Report, India
1929–31	Great Depression, the slump in the world economy hits agrarian prices

1930–33	Gandhi's Salt march; Civil Disobedience campaign; Round Table Conferences in London
1932	Communal Award; Gandhi's "fast unto death"; Poona Pact
1933	The name *Pakistan* is coined by Rahmat Ali
1935	Government of India Act: provincial autonomy
1937	Provincial elections, India, Congress wins majority seats. Burma separated from India; Sinhala Mahasabha founded by S. W. R. D. Bandaranaike, Sri Lanka
1939	Outbreak of Second World War
1940	Lahore Resolution ("Pakistan demand") of the Muslim League
1941	Foundation of Jama'at-i-Islami by Syed Abul Ala Maududi
1942	Quit India movement; Cripps Mission
1943	Bengal famine
1944	Gandhi-Jinnah talks; Tamil Congress founded in Sri Lanka
1945	Simla conference; failure to form national interim government
1946	A new constitution in Sri Lanka is ratified
1946	Elections: Muslim League wins the Muslim vote; Cabinet Mission plan; Direct Action Day and the great Calcutta killings; constituent assembly meets without the Muslim League
1947	Independence and partition, August 14 Pakistan, August 15 India
1947	First elections under dominion status for Sri Lanka (Ceylon), August 15; cabinet takes office and Parliament opens
1948	Independence in Sri Lanka (Ceylon), February 4; assassination of Gandhi; first Indo-Pak war

The English East India Company, founded in 1600 by a royal charter of Queen Elizabeth I, was granted the monopoly of England's trade in Asia and the right to arm vessels to ward off pirates and interlopers. Unable to break the Dutch control of the spice trade in Indonesia, the East India Company looked to India. India did not have spices but it had indigo for dye, and saltpetre for gunpowder. Moreover, after 1660, there was the emergence of a consumer economy in England. Thus, there began an increasing demand for fine Indian textiles such as muslin and chintz, as well as tea from China, and profits increased almost exponentially through the seventeenth and eighteenth centuries.

While the Dutch maintained control of the coastal areas of Ceylon into the early nineteenth century, the East India Company established fortified trading bases or "factories" along the coast—*factoring* being an old-fashioned term for trading. The main factories were the still undeveloped ports of Calcutta, Madras, and Bombay. It was from these points that British imperial rule would flow. Later in the nineteenth century, these three cities would become the capitals of the "presidencies," the main administrative units of the British Empire in India.[1]

Anglo-French Rivalry

The expansion of European trade in South Asia took place under the auspices of Mughal rule. Emperor Jahangir had given the English East India Company the license to trade in India in 1617. However, as the Mughal Empire began to crumble after 1707 with the death of the last great emperor, Aurangzeb, emergent regional powers that rose to challenge Mughal imperial control began to raid the Company's bases. It was in the context of the disintegration of this long-standing empire and the ensuing struggle for supremacy across the subcontinent that the East India Company sought to extend its position. It did this by intervening in interterritorial and succession disputes between rival regional princes, essentially supporting one against the other. Such interventions accelerated because of a struggle for power between the British and the French that was being played out across the globe; conflicts between Britain and France took place in Europe, North America, and South and Southeast Asia beginning in 1740 with the War of Austrian Succession in Europe until 1815 with the end of the Napoleonic Wars. The rivalry with Britain prompted a series of interventions between 1744 and 1748 where the British and the French became partners of Indian rulers who fought against each other. It was in this way that Europeans became increasingly drawn into Indian affairs and it was these rival wars with the French that initially drove British expansion.[2]

Annexation of Bengal

The English East India Company successfully secured their position against the French in south India but it was the province of Bengal in eastern India, with its promise of huge wealth, that Company officials had their eye on. The trade in Bengal grew increasingly lucrative in the eighteenth century and by 1750 it accounted for 75 percent of the

Company's acquisition of Indian goods. Keen to multiply their profits in Bengal, Company officials had been trading well beyond what their license from the emperor allowed. They also began to extend the fortifications in Calcutta to ward off the possibility of a French attack. The ruler of Bengal, the young Mughal prince Nawab Siraj ud-Daula, ordered them to dismantle these fortifications in 1756, but in a clear challenge to his position, they did not.

The nawab stormed the garrison in Calcutta in June 1756, defeating the Company. Furious at this humiliation, Robert Clive, a colonel who had shown his mettle in the wars in the south, swore he would recover the Company's trading privileges, which he did in February 1757. Not satisfied with this success, Clive entered into a conspiracy with two wealthy native merchant bankers to persuade Mir Jaffar, a general in the nawab's army, to defect, in return for which they promised to install him as Bengal's ruler. At the battlefield in Plassey in 1757, Mir Jaffar ordered his troops to do nothing as the East India Company defeated the rest of Siraj ud-Daula's army. The Company killed the nawab and installed Mir Jaffar as a puppet ruler.

With victory at Plassey came the annexation of Bengal, one of the most fertile and prosperous provinces in India. The year 1757 is generally taken as the date at which the East India Company moved from mercantile trade to beginning a period of political, albeit informal, rule. Mir Jaffar ceded the right to collect land revenue across the fertile districts south of Calcutta. Subsequently, the Company defeated another regional ruler in 1764 at the Battle of Buxar and won from the Mughal Emperor the "Diwani" of Bengal. This was the right to collect the entirety of revenue across the region.

The East India Company had functioned as a trading outfit for one hundred fifty years. It is striking that it would opt for political conquest and the control of land as a way to continue. Historians have long debated the intentions of East India Company officials: to what extent had the Company *intended* to conquer Bengal? It is easy to read history backward, to see British colonialism as inevitable or to attribute Company officials with a coherent master plan. But there is little evidence for this. Clive was unwilling to take on a political role. The Company's control of land revenue happened almost by accident, or as has been said, "in a fit of absence of mind." Yet, this should not diminish the implications of Bengal's annexation. The administration of the province continued under the Mughal Emperor, but Bengal was his in name only. Moreover, once granted the Diwani, Clive believed that there was such wealth to be gained from the land that it could pay for the trade in Asia, which until now had been financed by importing silver bullion from Britain. However, in order for this strategy to be viable, the Company would need to continue to expand its territory through annexing land. Thus began Britain's conquest of South Asia.[3]

Subsidiary Alliance System

The Company's expansion of territorial control of the subcontinent continued through the eighteenth and into the nineteenth century. It rapidly became the norm for military power to be brought in to protect profit, something known as "military fiscalism." Conquest was piecemeal and annexation came about through the "subsidiary alliance system." Company officials would lend a regional ruler military "protection" in return for a subsidy or tribute. They would then increase the rate of the subsidy, thereby creating a stranglehold on the nawab in question, who would be forced to raise the extra revenue by bearing down on his subjects: landowners, peasants, sometimes even his soldiers. Alienated from these groups and in an increasingly hopeless debt trap, the nawab's land would be annexed as collateral payment. Officials worked closely with Indian intermediary groups—financiers, traders, revenue farmers, and so on—to make this happen.

Indigenous Opposition

Nevertheless, annexation of territory did not happen easily or without resistance. Through the eighteenth and early nineteenth centuries, the Company was engaged in a number of expensive military campaigns at any one time. The regional powers that succeeded the Mughals proved difficult to subdue. In particular the great warrior states succumbed only after protracted battles: Mysore in south India (1799), the Marathas in the west (1818), and the Sikhs in the north (1849).[4] The Company was roundly defeated in Afghanistan in 1842, losing 16,000 men. There were three wars in Burma (1824–1885), and Sind was taken in 1843. The Anglo-Nepalese war (1814–1816) fought between the kingdom of Nepal and the East India Company can also be attributed to aggressive expansionism, as can the conquest of Ceylon (1815–1818).[5] The East India Company took control of the coastal regions of Ceylon from the Dutch in 1796. Ceylon's interior had remained independent of European influence throughout, ruled by various indigenous polities and, from the 1590s, solely by the monarchs of Kandy. However, after a number of smaller wars in the early nineteenth century and an uprising of Kandyan chiefs in 1817, the kingdom lost its autonomy to become a "crown colony" of the British Empire in 1818.[6] These ventures drained the treasury and forced the annexation of more land. When Awadh, a large and prosperous province in northern India, was taken in 1856 with a bounty of 5 million pounds sterling, the Company controlled territory across the length and breadth of South Asia.[7] However, it is important not to see this as a story of heroic natives resisting mercenary and grasping colonials or the inevitable forward march of imperial power. Rather, it was a far more complex unfolding, having to do with shifting alliances and interlocking interests and rivalries.

THE EARLY COLONIAL STATE

The wealth generated through land revenue made the Company's servants hugely wealthy with many living like quasi-native princes themselves. The Company became surrounded by controversy toward the end of the eighteenth century for its practices were seen as corrupt by many in London. When the military and administrative costs mounted beyond control, Parliament passed a series of Regulating Acts to bring the Company under closer scrutiny. A governor-general was appointed to rein in their activities, the first being Warren Hastings in 1772. It fell to him and his successors to create an ordered system of government, what is called "Company rule." It was during the period of Company rule that the cornerstones of a colonial state were set up—the codification of law, stabilizing land revenue, and organizing the civil and military administration.

Codification of Law

When Hastings took up his post (1773–1785) the Company's people were still essentially traders. They knew little about governance and less about India. Setting up an administration to govern in India, then, was a huge experiment. Hastings argued that British rules had to be adapted to "the Manners and Understandings of the People and the Exigencies of the Country, adhering as closely as we are able to their ancient uses and Institutions." In other words, British rule had to be tailored to Indian conditions: it could not be transported wholesale.

However, there was a tension here. The British believed that their predecessors, the Mughals, had ruled despotically. In contrast, they understood their own society as being regulated by a rule of law whose values it was their duty to impart. Thus, Hastings saw the role of the new state to bring about a regime that reflected the values of Britain while not disrupting the balance of power of indigenous institutions—be they landed, political, or religious. This was a deeply pragmatic approach. Conservative opinion in Britain would see the social chaos ensuing from the French Revolution in 1789 as a result precisely of turning the traditional structures of society upside down. This was not a risk they were willing to take in India. Laws that were drawn up would have to reflect as well as systematize existing practices while somehow introducing modes of British justice.

Hastings assumed that India already had in existence a fixed body of laws that were long established but that had been eroded and corrupted over time, and which could be recovered and reinstituted in their "original" form. Like many Europeans, he also believed that India was divided into two great communities: Hindus and Muslims. He—erroneously—considered them to be two distinct sets of people with separate laws by which they lived. It was up to the British to discover what these were, to document and codify them in order that they could be used in matters of adjudication.

Hastings drew on the expertise of those he believed were best qualified to advise on matters of law and custom: the *maulvis*—Muslim legal and religious scholars of the Quran and the Hadith—and the pandits—Brahman priests trained in the study of Vedic texts, the philosophical treatises of early India. The problem with Hastings's approach was twofold. First, the "Digests of Hindoo and Muhammadan Laws" that he drew up relied on textual traditions that reflected orthodox and Brahmanical interpretations. Second, they codified and sought to systematize practices that varied across region, through time, and by context.

The Hindus and Muslims in South Asia are hugely diverse populations characterized by a variety of sects whose customs and beliefs are heterodox and often overlap with those of other religious sects in the same region. A Muslim and Hindu in the Punjab, for instance, often had more in common than a Muslim from Punjab and another from Bengal. The codification of law under the early colonial state overlooked this diversity and saw only two distinct strands. Moreover, it made static practices that had previously been more flexible and preferred orthodox and upper-caste interpretations of law.[8]

In Ceylon, East India Company officials believed there was little by way of native laws in place as compared with India. The Roman-Dutch law prevailed on the coast and after 1796 was supplemented with English Common Law. Muslims were also ruled by Roman-Dutch law, while the Tamil population in Jaffna in the north adhered to customary laws of Indian origin. After the final annexation of the kingdom of Kandy in 1815, however, a process similar to that conducted in India was undertaken whereby British officials sought to compose digests of laws and customs based on accounts of "native experts." This led to a code of law applicable to the Sinhala population. The compilation of such digests sought to reflect as well as rationalize indigenous modes of adjudication. But, as in India, the move to standardize customary practice meant that the diversity of such practices was no longer recognized by the state. Furthermore, while native laws continued, after 1833 it was English law that provided the inspiration for the system of justice applied in Ceylon, and this introduced some significant departures from local custom. For instance, where Sinhala and Tamil law recognized a woman's independent legal status and the right to own property, colonial legislation on matrimonial property rights introduced the idea of a wife's inferior status in relation to her husband, the inferior legal position of the widow, and the unity of personality of husband and wife. Thus, as in India, colonial codification of law in Ceylon sought to maintain indigenous customs but while doing so fundamentally altered those very customs by introducing innovations based on English law. Moreover, ideas about particular communities—Sinhala, Tamil, Sunni, Shi'a, Hindu—coalesced around these processes of codification.[9]

Land Revenue Administration

The main imperative for governing India was to continue the flow of land revenue. This paid for the army and the administration and was the source of wealth for the Company. The second governor-general, Lord Cornwallis (1786–1793), introduced measures that would ensure the stability of revenue collection. These, in turn, fundamentally altered the shape of the economy and rural society. The most important among these was the introduction of the Permanent Settlement in 1793.

In the eighteenth century, Britain's political classes widely believed that private property in land created social stability and progressive, forward-looking societies. Officials looked to India and saw what they thought was a parallel elite to their own aristocracy among the large landlords of Bengal, the *zamindars*, and proceeded to transfer ownership rights to them. It was thought that giving zamindars property rights would ensure their loyalty and therefore social stability, but also that it would create an incentive to make the land more productive and efficient.

The permanent settlement of land revenue in Bengal is fundamental to the history of the colonial state, for it created an idea of private property in India where previously one did not exist. Zamindars were a prominent rural elite under the Mughals, but they did not have property rights as the British conceived of them. They could sell or transfer their own revenue collecting rights but not the land itself. Moreover, the entitlements to the land were not held solely with the zamindars but were distributed across the range of people who were associated with the land and forests: smaller landlords, peasant cultivators, pastoralists, and tribals. Under the Company, zamindars were turned into landowners. Individual titles were documented and property rights were systematized in accordance with a legal framework. In this new system, peasants and others who had

had customary entitlements to the land found their status reduced to that of mere tenants. Zamindars, if they failed to meet the high revenue demand, found their estates liable to sale—something that began happening with increasing frequency.

In the early nineteenth century, Thomas Munro, the governor of Madras, instituted another form of revenue collection known as *ryotwari*. He argued that the permanent settlement had not encouraged enterprise among zamindars and, in fact, there were large areas in India where zamindars did not exist at all. Munro believed that the *ryots*, peasant cultivators, were more deserving of property rights and that responsibility over their land would encourage the spirit of industriousness that was lacking among the zamindars. Ryotwari established a direct revenue relationship between the state and the peasant or village, circumventing intermediary groups.[10]

Civil and Military Administration

Company officials had relied on the Mughal administrative structure to conduct the business of revenue collection. However, Cornwallis was scathing about the trustworthiness of Indian officials and began the process of placing Company servants in senior positions. The first among these, and on which the smooth functioning of this emerging administration hinged, was the collector. He was a Company official charged with collecting the tax revenue of a district. He also behaved as magistrate and head of the police and often decided cases in court. He was the local face of the colonial government, supervising a number of Indians in his own employ but subordinate to the hierarchy of the Company's administration above him. The collector received a large salary and pension and was banned from engaging in private trade. These reforms sought to create a class of civil servants who were incorruptible executors of Company affairs and marked the beginning of a distinctively colonial form of administration.

It became increasingly important for the Company to train its own experts and administrators. Thus, the third governor-general, Lord Wellesley (1798–1805), established a civil service corps to service the growing administrative needs of the state. He founded the College at Fort William in Calcutta (1802) where civil servants were taught local languages before taking up their posts. In England, Company directors set up Haileybury College (1804) where civil servants would spend two years in preparation before their departure. The Indian Civil Service (ICS) became the "steel frame" of the British Empire and continues in a similar form today as the Indian Administrative Service (IAS). Ceylon had its administrative counterpart in the Ceylon Civil Service (CCS). However, its status as a crown colony meant that there were significant differences with India. Crown colonies were under the direct legislative control of the crown and thus did not have their own representative governments. Normally they were administered through executive and legislative councils nominated or elected by the governor. The crown colony of Ceylon had a governor appointed by the secretary of state in London and a legislative council comprising nine official (crown-appointed) and six unofficial (locally elected) members, three of whom represented the three main ethnic groups—one low-country Sinhala, one Tamil, and one Burgher. Over time, however, various constitutional reforms allowed Ceylonese even greater participation in the colony's government.

As the civil service expanded, so too did the military bureaucracy. After Plassey, Robert Clive began recruiting Indian soldiers, known as "*sepoys*," to fight for the Company's army. Soldiers were recruited from high-caste peasant communities from the plains of north India and Bihar. Respecting caste restrictions on inter-dining and foreign travel, officials did not require sepoys to do either. Company troops were sent across South Asia to secure the annexation of land. By 1789 it had become one of the largest European-style standing armies in the world. It expanded dramatically during the Napoleonic Wars, reaching 155,000 in 1805. In Ceylon, in contrast, there was no significant military force, with only a parade ground army in existence at independence.[11]

MUTINY AND REBELLION

The Company controlled India from 1757 until 1857. This was a period of informal rule—India was not officially a colony of Britain despite an increasingly complex structure of governance. The Mutiny/Revolt of 1857 was a moment of huge upheaval for the British in India and marked the transition from Company to Crown rule. In 1858, India became part of the British Empire and would remain so until independence in 1947.

Disaffection and Social Unrest

The early colonial state was qualitatively different from previous regimes in its ambition to unify South Asia legally as well as territorially through a centralized bureaucratic structure. What also set it apart was the degree of intervention into the lives of individual communities. Weavers were squeezed by the state bringing production more directly under its control. Peasants found their earlier mobility restricted and many became impoverished due to high revenue demand. Earlier social restraints on the exploitation of labor by landlords and merchants were diminished as the state's emphasis on private property and its increased control of the economy removed these safeguards.

There was a growing tide of social and cultural as well as economic grievances against the Company's policies in the period before 1857. Recruitment patterns to the army, for instance, initially respected caste prohibitions on inter-dining and traveling abroad. However, after the 1840s, troops were increasingly being sent to fight in Southeast Asia, North Africa, and China. And the expansion of recruitment into the military after the defeat in Afghanistan forced different communities together, offending the sensibilities of the high-caste groups that formed the core of the Bengal army.

Annexation of land and high revenue demand also provoked resentment. These had a profound effect on how Indians saw themselves. The annexation of Awadh in 1856, for instance, was a humiliation for north Indian society. The rural elite of this wealthy province experienced a great sense of fallen pride as their lands were taken over and they were reduced to tax collecting bureaucrats. At times the revenue demand forced them onto the land as cultivators and into a position well below their social standing. The period before 1857, then, was characterized by greater state control of the cultivating population and erosion of the privileges of the rural elite.

Resistance and Rebellion

Rebellion against the policies of the Company was a key feature of early colonial society. Peasant cultivators resisted the revenue demand imposed on them and revolted against the state, zamindars, and moneylenders. Tribal communities rebelled as the state took control of large swathes of forests for commercial ventures such as logging and intensive agriculture. There were zamindar revolts in the 1830s against high land-revenue demand and the erosion of their traditional privileges. Grain riots took place in urban areas, and artisans such as weavers protested against the loss of their livelihoods. There had also been a number of mutinies in the army before 1857: the Madras army in Vellore (1807), the Bengal army in Java (1815).[12]

Mutiny

The rebellion began as a military mutiny in Meerut, a garrison town in the United Provinces in the plains of northern India. The immediate trigger for the revolt was the introduction of the Lee Enfield rifle, the cartridges of which were greased with a combination of beef and pork fat. This was taken as a profound insult to their religious sensibilities and, together with the sepoys' multiple other grievances—the annexation of Awadh being the most painful with one-third of the Bengal army drawn from high-caste and landed families in that province—proved the final straw. On May 10, 1857, after eighty-five sepoys had been led off in chains for refusing to load the rifles, the others rose up in the night, massacring the English residents of the town, and marched to Delhi. There they found the aged Mughal emperor, Bahadur Shah Zafar, whom they sought to return to the throne as a symbol of Indian authority.

The rebellion quickly spread to different regions that witnessed numerous civil uprisings. Before long, the British had lost control over large swathes of northern and central India. A whole range of social groups came into the fray: landlords, peasants, princes, and merchants, each aggrieved for their own reasons, took up arms against the British. The revolts were particularly bloody in certain parts. In Kanpur (Cawnpore), in northern India, the resistance was led by Nana Saheb, the heir to the Maratha kingdom who had lost his lands to the British. Nana Saheb defeated the garrison at Kanpur. He offered safe passage to the troops as they sought to leave but reneged on his pledge murdering over four hundred, including women and children. The siege at Lucknow, the capital of the annexed region of Awadh, was a crucial center of the rebellion where, in a long-fought struggle, the rebels controlled the city from May 1857 until March 1858.

However, the rebellions were brought under control within the space of a year, albeit at great cost to Britain, and the conflict was over by July 1858. The state had never encountered anything like the challenge presented in 1857, and the retribution that followed was deliberately brutal. There were mass public executions: rebels were caught and hanged and thousands were blown live from cannons. Much of Delhi, one of the centers of the uprising, was destroyed. Hundreds of villages were torched because of their proximity to rebel areas.

The history of 1857 has been interpreted in a myriad of different ways and served a number of ideological agendas. For colonials who chronicled this moment it was a "sepoy mutiny" limited to recalcitrant soldiers who were correctly shown their place. For a later generation of Indian nationalists it was the "first Indian war of independence," a moment when Indians fought together against illegitimate rule. The truth lies somewhere in between.[13]

HIGH NOON OF COLONIALISM, 1858–1914

The rebellion of 1857 marked a significant turning point in the history of the state in South Asia. On August 2, 1858, the British Parliament passed the Government of India Act, transferring all authority of the East India

Company to the British crown. A viceroy replaced the governor-general, and a secretary of state for India with cabinet status was appointed. The transfer of power from Company to crown signals the moment when India formally became a colony of the British Empire. Officials of the Government of India—as the administration of the colonial state was called—introduced a series of reforms that consolidated this new structure of governance, accelerating a process of centralization and bureaucratization that had begun in the 1820s. It is also during this period that South Asia developed the characteristics of a classical colonial economy, with India and Ceylon producers of agricultural raw materials for export and net importers of manufactured goods. This section will examine the political economy of South Asia in the period from the transition to crown rule until the outbreak of World War I, when the power of the colonial state was at its zenith.

Consolidation of Territory

In the transition to crown rule, Indian territories came under the jurisdiction of the Government of India and were the "dominions" of the British monarch. "British India," the area directly administered as a colony, was composed of three main administrative units called "presidencies"—Bengal, Bombay, and Madras—and comprised two-thirds of the subcontinent. The rest remained as large and small principalities under Indian rulers, the *maharajas* (kings), nawabs (governors), and *sardars* (chiefs). These were the so-called native or princely states. They numbered over five hundred in total and were spread across South Asia. The princely states were administered through what was known as "indirect rule": they were semiautonomous, tributary states under the suzerainty of Queen Victoria. The princes managed their internal affairs but the colonial state retained overall control of foreign relations. Some of the more important native states included Kashmir in the north, Hyderabad in the south, and Bhopal in central India. Administrative reorganization had taken place much earlier in Ceylon. A Royal Commission in 1829 recommended the end of regional divisions based on ethnic and cultural lines that organized the island into low-country Sinhalese, Kandyan Sinhalese, and Tamil areas. Instead, it introduced a uniform administrative system based on five provinces, later expanded to nine.[14]

Restructuring the Civil and Military Administration

As important was setting in place the state's bureaucratic apparatus. The army was restructured to preserve a high European-to-Indian ratio. This was set at 1:2—a level that was maintained until 1914—to ensure that any hint of rebellion in the future could be quickly quashed. The army changed its recruitment patterns and began to draw from new social groups: Sikhs and Muslims from Punjab, Pathans from the North West Frontier, and Gurkhas from Nepal. Officials had developed theories about the racial characteristics of Indians from different regions and backgrounds: Gujaratis were "entrepreneurial," Bengalis were "effete," wandering tribes were "criminal," and so on. Punjabis, Pathans, and Gurkhas were believed to have warrior-like qualities. Accordingly, they were called the "martial races" and recruitment to the army drew heavily from these communities.[15] The British Indian army was also sent to protect and further imperial interests across the globe: to subdue the Mahdi uprisings in Sudan (1896), to China during the Boxer Rebellion (1900), and to South Africa during the Boer War (1899–1902). Sixty thousand Indian troops died fighting for Britain during World War I.

The civil service expanded dramatically after the transition to crown rule. The ICS conducted the colonial state's day-to-day business with representatives at every level of Indian society, beginning with the viceroy and continuing right down to the district collector and the district magistrate who were the most senior officials that Indians would ordinarily encounter. After 1857, lines between colonials and natives became much more starkly drawn and racial discrimination in the administration was institutionalized. All the senior posts in the civil service were composed of British officials who were recruited through entrance exams that were held exclusively in London. Indians were employed in the lower ranks of the administration, but even those from elite backgrounds educated in colonial schools faced open discrimination, something that was equally true in Ceylon.

The bureaucratic and legal framework of the Government of India was highly elaborate. Law courts were established in each province and brought under a centralized set of legal procedures. The laws of British India rested on the laws of the British Parliament and were drafted under the advice of an official council in London. Detailed records about a relatively limited range of subjects such as matters of administration, land transfers, marriages, and so on were maintained at every level of the administration. Statistical data on all matters of political and economic activity were published in annual reports. Governors of each presidency wrote fortnightly summary reports. Duplicate copies of everything were returned to London and held in the India Office Library, under the direction of the secretary of state for India.

Economy and Technology

Land revenue was the basis of economic wealth creation during the period of early colonial rule. The Company bolstered its profits with the trade in cotton and opium, but in 1833 Parliament ended the Company's monopoly of the trade in Asia and, following the industrial revolution, Indian artisanal textiles could no longer compete with the cheaper machine-made cotton from Lancashire. The loss of overseas markets for woven goods was devastating for weaving communities, particularly in Bengal, where many were forced to leave their traditional occupations to work on the land as cultivators.

The nineteenth century saw a fundamental shift in the nature of the colonial economy in South Asia with revenue increasingly being generated through trade. Scholars have argued that in the eighteenth century, European trade in India was "an age of partnership": Indian merchants were central to the Company's success in trade as well as its expansion of power often providing the necessary financial backing for military ventures. However, by the 1820s, European entrepreneurs had cut Indian merchants out of these partnerships and began to dominate overseas trade. The import of manufactured goods was accompanied by the expansion of commercial agriculture with India becoming a primary producer of cash crops such as indigo, jute, and cotton for export. This shift in the balance of trade, with the colony becoming a producer of cheaper agricultural raw materials while providing the market for more expensive manufactured products, established the foundations for a classically colonial economic relationship that became fully established in the second half of the nineteenth century.

It was through the intensification of commercial agriculture that India and Ceylon became increasingly drawn into the world capitalist economy that had Britain at its center. Commercial agriculture, in turn, was made possible by capital investment in infrastructure and technology. In the years immediately following the transition to crown rule, there was a huge flow of capital into India: one-fifth of British investments abroad were in India. Of these, 70 percent were in the new technologies of transport and communication, particularly the railways. This proved crucial to the massive expansion of the imperial economy from the late nineteenth century into the early twentieth. International trade increased exponentially through the nineteenth century increasing tenfold between 1800 and 1870. By 1870, Britain had become an industrial giant producing half the world's iron and steel and half the world's cotton textiles. Its production was greater than the next two industrial powers—the United States and Germany—combined.[16]

Public Works: Railways and Irrigation

The idea to develop new ports and a railway system in South Asia, along with postal and telegraph services and a canal system, was introduced in the 1840s to facilitate the integration of different provinces and spread British power. Railways would also enable the easy movement of troops. At the same time, British entrepreneurs had been pushing for Indian markets to be opened up to their products. Textile merchants looked to reduce their dependence on cotton produced in the American South and saw Egypt and the Bombay presidency in western India as possible alternative sources of raw cotton. It was the railway that would provide the transport for these goods.

The construction of the railway was part of an imperial vision that was pushed forward by British capitalist enterprise. It was funded by private companies—the Great Indian Peninsular Railway and the East India Railway—but government kept control of the construction and management. Investors were guaranteed a 5 percent return so investment was completely without risk. The layout of the track reflected economic interests that focused on transport routes from the interior to the ports of Calcutta, Bombay, Madras, Karachi, Cochin, and Colombo, from where goods could be shipped out. The railways provided a market for British manufactured goods: rails, locomotives, sleepers, British coal, even the points, were all exported to India despite the existence of railway workshops turning out competitively priced products at least initially. The expertise—engineers, drivers, and plate layers—was also brought from Britain. By the end of the nineteenth century nearly five thousand miles of rail had been laid and the Indian railway was the fifth-longest system in the world. However, the railway profits, rather than financing India's development, were returned to the bank accounts of investors in Britain. India was also subject to "home charges." These covered a range of expenses incurred by the state for running India: the costs of wars at home and abroad, the secretary of state's office in London, pensions for civil and military officials, and banking and shipping services. The largest of these charges was the guaranteed 5 percent return for the railways. These charges provided the basis for the "drain of wealth" theory—an important argument made by early nationalists that profits were being siphoned back to Britain and impoverishing India in the process.[17]

Along with the railways, the irrigation canals were the most important public works projects. Canal irrigation expanded rapidly after 1857, and in the 1870s the Government of India began a series of irrigation projects in the Punjab. The state made land grants to Sikh and Jat communities to reward their loyalty during the uprising of 1857 and created large tracts of farmland out of arid regions previously used by pastoral nomads. The images of Punjab as a green and fertile land and its inhabitants as traditional farmers are thus relatively recent, emerging from this period. Irrigation enabled the production of large agricultural surpluses for export.[18]

Other major public works projects included the postal service and telegraph. In 1854 the "penny post" was introduced allowing mail to be sent anywhere in India, even to the remotest villages, at the same cost. Moreover, the improvement of transport and the opening of the Suez Canal meant that a letter that would have taken two years to reach London in the early nineteenth century took only one month by 1870. There was also the construction of a dense network of telegraph lines and cables below the sea that linked major cities in South Asia with financial centers in London. By 1880, 25,000 miles of cables had been laid that facilitated the transmission of a range of information: market information on prices and orders as well as details to do with internal security and political activity.[19]

Colonials saw the public works projects as vital to India's moral as well as material development. They argued that the Government of India would be a modernizing force bringing enlightenment, "civilization," to the colony. Technology was seen as central to this. Technological innovation, it was believed, had the power to lift people out of their traditional ways of life, in India and elsewhere. In this sense, it was seen as an *improving* force, raising the overall standard of living and introducing Indians to the values of scientific rationality, progress, and industry. The railways were to open up the interior to new markets. Irrigation would make arid land fertile. Farmers would bring common and scrub land into cultivation and tame wild jungle landscapes. In this, the land would be transformed and made productive, all of which would benefit the state in no small measure.[20]

An Export Economy: Cash Crops and Labor

The railways and irrigation technology facilitated the commercialization of agriculture. By the 1880s, cash cropping had become established. Different regions were now used for the production of different crops. Ceylon was transformed into a plantation economy in the 1830s, with coffee, rubber, and coconut plantations; after a leaf disease destroyed the coffee plants, investors switched to tea and, with India, Ceylon replaced China for tea production. All tea was now grown in Assam, Darjeeling, and the highlands of Sri Lanka. The Deccan, in western India, became prime cotton country. Wheat was produced in Punjab and the western United Provinces in northern India. Coke, ore, and minerals were mined from Jharkhand in Bihar. Jute came from eastern Bengal, today's Bangladesh, and rice from Burma. By 1914, almost all goods arriving at ports were raw materials for export.

Labor also became an important export, something that was enabled by better steam transport. With the abolition of slavery, Britain needed a new source of labor in the colonies and began a system of indenture. From the 1870s, often faced with economic uncertainty, Indians went abroad in large numbers—from eastern India to the Caribbean, Mauritius, and Fiji; from Gujarat in western India to southern and eastern Africa. Tamils, meanwhile, left Madras for the Malay peninsula and Ceylon.[21]

Indian Industrialists

Those who did best out of this new colonial economy were the trading castes from Rajasthan and Gujarat: the Marwari Jains, Memons, and Parsis. The railways, cotton, and mineral mining made possible the growth of Indian-owned industry. Two families were most closely associated with this, the Tatas and the Birlas. Jamsetji Tata, a Parsi, opened his first cotton mill in central India in 1877 followed by two more in Bombay and Gujarat. In 1907 he established Tata Iron and Steel in Bihar. The Birlas, Marwaris from Rajasthan, were trading across north India and moved into textile and steel production during World War I.[22]

Colonial Knowledge

It is a truism to say that British colonial officials needed to "know" their colonies in order to rule them. Yet it is important to emphasize that *how* they gathered information and the manner in which they interpreted it had a great bearing on the character of this rule. British colonialism fundamentally altered the economies of India and Ceylon. It also integrated these territories into political units under a centralized framework of law. However, colonialism was as much an epistemological and ideological intervention as it was a political and economic one.

In the early colonial period, the generation of data and information was driven by the revenue, military, and judicial requirements of the East India Company. Officials were appointed to report on the leading families of different districts, as this had a bearing on revenue collection. Likewise, knowledge of a region's history as well as of the customs and occupations of those who worked in each district and subdivision was important for recording agricultural activity. Thomas Munro saw the village as the institution around which rural society was organized, and thus it became a basic unit for data collection under the Company. Local surveys listed the number of households in each village and officials estimated population on the basis of these. "Caste" became a significant unit of analysis in these early population estimates, as officials thought that household sizes differed according to caste ranking. Maps also provided vital information. Maps were drawn up under the Company to record the size and distribution of cultivable, common, scrub, and forest land. They documented new boundaries as well as areas of strategic importance. The Great Trigonometrical Survey begun in 1818 sought to map the whole of South Asia and was the most extensive survey of its kind in the world at the time.[23] Moreover, Company officials were required to learn about Indian social institutions in order to adjudicate appropriately. They relied on local informants to discover the intricacies of indigenous legal systems, and language learning became crucial for the translation and administration of these laws.

During the period of colonial rule, caste and religion became important categories through which officials sought to understand South Asian societies. For colonials, caste and religion marked the basic difference between India and Britain. Many Europeans saw the so-called traditional identities such as caste and sect as the foundations of Indian social organization. Identities were communal rather than individual and the state was epiphenomenal: even as dynasts and regimes changed, society did not. In their view, it was this stagnancy and resistance to change that ensured India remained "backward." Such an understanding, or "knowledge," of Indian society was crucial for shaping future policies of the administration. It also justified colonial intervention in a range of social, judicial, and other matters, as introducing Indians to the values of modernity, rationality, and the institutions of the European state became a core ideological element of British rule.[24] This is something we will address in further detail as we proceed through the chapter.

Statistical records proliferated after 1858. These went well beyond simple administrative necessity and dealt with all aspects of Indian economy, society, and environment. Detailed information as diverse as land surveys and irrigation methods was produced alongside police reports on "criminal tribes" and censuses. Anthropological information on ethnic groups was amassed in a manner that was thought to be as "scientific" as data on regional flora and fauna. Together, this became part of an attempt at producing a systematic empirical map of India. These data were compiled in the series of imperial gazetteers and annual reports that were published through the late nineteenth and early twentieth century.

Census

Comprehensive census operations began in 1871 and took place every ten years after that. The census counted and sorted the population by ethnic group, caste, religion, sect, gender, age, location, and occupation. It took some time before they were systematized from region to region. There was also much uncertainty around the categories to be employed and how they would be defined. A village, for instance, was defined as having a population below five thousand. But, quite often, a "village" had

the characteristics of a "town" and vice versa. Moreover, population estimates were done according to household. There were also difficulties in
defining age and adulthood. At what age was a boy considered an adult?
In the Delhi district this was twelve and a girl was considered an adult at
ten. But it was also recognized that there were many who considered even
younger people as adults.

However, the most complex and important question for census takers
was caste. Officials believed that caste, along with religion, race, and sect,
were the basic units of South Asian society. This assumption had profound implications for the ways in which the army and bureaucracy were
restructured in the mid-nineteenth century and provided the basis of a
range of colonial policies into the twentieth. For instance, reform of the
army incorporated assumptions about "martial races"—the Sikhs, Gurkhas, Jats, and Rajputs. It was from these groups that the state began to
recruit in large numbers. In the civil service, questions were raised about
the balance of Hindus and Muslims and there were concerns that upper-
castes, Brahmans in particular, were enjoying disproportionate access to
government schools and civil service employment. In the Ceylon census,
"race" came to have a greater prominence, as caste was not seen to have
the same social meaning and role as it did in India.

Census enumerators believed that a system of classification of castes
could be developed that transcended regional specificities and attempted
to categorize the thousands of different castes into larger blocks. Thus,
lists prepared for the 1881 census sought to standardize the way in which
information was recorded from region to region and used standard names
for the various castes and races. In India, in 1881 there were five main
categories: Brahmans, Rajputs, Castes of Good Social Position, Inferior
Castes, and Non-Hindus or Aboriginal Castes (Tribals). Mostly, though,
there was an attempt to tally a person's *jati*, a term meaning "subcaste"
that defines one's occupation, with their *varna*, a term for caste denoting
one of the four hierarchically arranged categories (Brahman, Kshatriya,
Vaishya, Shudra) into which all Hindus are, in theory, supposed to fit.
In Ceylon, a similar attempt to systematize the process of categorization
was in evidence. In 1881, it was decided to reduce the number of races
to just seven: Europeans, Sinhalese, Tamils, Moormen, Malays, Veddas,
and others, although these were further divided into subcategories in the
early twentieth century.

But clearly, society was more complex than these categories. In the case
of caste, within each varna category there are hundreds of *jati* but not all
jati fit neatly into *varna* groupings. There was, and continues to be, a great
deal of fluidity between them. For instance, we think of Brahmans as a
literary caste of priests and teachers. But Brahmans were often landowners and moneylenders. Vaishyas are theoretically merchants and money-

lenders but there were instances of Vaishya *jati* in positions of political authority as advisers or administrators, technically the role of Kshatriyas. The attempt to create a system of classification of caste, race, and community did not solve this problem of categorization. There were many cases where enumerators simply could not decide where a particular *jati* fit in the bigger picture. Indeed, in 1881, there were close to two and a half million "vague and indefinite" entries. Administrators also found it difficult to decide whether certain sects were Hindu or Muslim, as very often through the ages, a Muslim sect would have adopted the customs and culture of its neighboring Hindus and vice versa.

In instances of indeterminacy, administrators turned to the "natural leaders," those they identified as representatives of different communities, to make the judgment. But this in turn proved its own source of conflict when caste representatives deemed their *varna* position higher than the state had decided. In the process of census enumeration, many castes and sometimes whole villages sought upward caste mobility, arguing a higher *varna* status for their community. The state's documentation of castes was a means to create a detailed register of Indian society. However, the very process of recording made these categories more coherent. It made previously porous and fluid boundaries more rigid and often created clear distinctions where few had existed. In Ceylon, for example, the racial category of Sinhala was further subdivided into the low-country and Kandyan Sinhalese, on the basis of their differential exposure to Europeans. The census recognized their distinct histories but, in doing so, preserved these differences. Crucially, census classification enabled the longevity of caste, race, and community identities as South Asians themselves came to embrace them. Significantly, these classifications made possible the creation of "majority" and "minority" populations—Hindu and Muslim, Sinhala and Tamil—which would be later mobilized for political gain.[25]

Creating Legitimacy

In 1911, at the peak of imperial power, British residents in India numbered only one hundred eighty-five thousand. This was barely 1 percent of Britain's population and a much tinier fraction of India's. How did so few manage to direct the wealth and destiny of such complex and highly variegated societies? The stability and legitimacy of British colonialism was sustained through the collaboration of Indian elites and by creating avenues of patronage that rewarded their loyalty.

On the one hand was the patronage of a range of "traditional" elites: officials conferred titles, land grants, and honors on the rural landed gentry—Kandyan chiefs; religious leaders such as the Sufi pirs of Sind, who had enjoyed immense political authority under the Mughals; and the native princes who still controlled large populations across India. These forms of public recognition gave such groups a stake in the continuity of the new imperial system.[26] On the other was the emergence of "new elites." The state had created a bureaucracy that was populated largely by upper-castes who had been educated in colonial schools. Many experienced social mobility through employment in the colonial administration.

Dominance without Hegemony

Before we move forward, it is important to recognize that colonialism was not fully dominant in South Asia. It is too easy to look at the vast sweep of British rule and assume that there was a complete break with the past in terms of how ordinary people lived their lives. The social historian Ranajit Guha has argued that the colonial state was dominant but not hegemonic. It was dominant in that it succeeded in restructuring the political, social, and economic institutions of the state and the ways in which people engaged with them procedurally. However, it was not hegemonic in that it did not fundamentally alter people's day-to-day lives. There was a great deal of continuity with the past in terms of how South Asians related to each other and to authority and how they understood their social duties and responsibilities.[27]

CULTURAL REFORM AND POLITICAL
CHANGE UNDER THE RAJ, 1800–1900

So far we have addressed the political and economic foundations of the colonial state. We have looked at the mechanisms by which British rule was established in South Asia and some of the ways in which it was sustained and resisted. Colonialism was not simply an imposition of power from above by people who did not belong: it was an *encounter*. And in that encounter, South Asians were as important a set of players as colonials. Landlords and chieftains resisted, often violently, the Company's efforts to annex land. Pastoral and tribal populations did the same in the face of the state's attempts to confine their movements and define their occupations. However, rebellion was only one aspect of how South Asians responded to the experience of colonialism. In this section, we examine the reactions of a tiny but politically and culturally important group that emerged under British rule: the Western-educated elite.

The respect for Indian tradition that had characterized European attitudes in the eighteenth century gave way to the reformist zeal of the Utilitarians in the early nineteenth. Convinced of the superiority of British values, colonial officials and Christian missionaries launched trenchant criticisms against Indian society. They argued that it was stagnant and unchanging as well as hierarchical and corrupt, unlike the progressive, civilized societies of Enlightenment Europe. Utilitarians believed it was their duty to inculcate Indians in the values of liberalism. Thus, they introduced a range of social and economic reforms that sought to demonstrate the rational rule of law and the importance of scientific innovation and encouraged a moral industriousness.[28] Such harsh denunciations had a profound effect on these new elites, prompting what one historian has called a "crisis of cultural legitimacy."[29] In response, many pursued a liberal reform agenda while many others took up questions of religious reform. All sought to fashion a reply to the challenge posed by Christianity and the encounter with colonial modernity.

New Elites

The "old" elites of Indian society can broadly be identified as the princes, chiefs, zamindars, and gentry classes, as well as religious authorities such as the pundits and maulvis. Imperial society created new arenas of social and political engagement and a new, primarily urban, professional "class" of people. Central to the emergence of this group, sometimes referred to as "middle class," were colonial educational institutions and employment in the administration. In 1833, the Company replaced Persian with English as the language of the administration in India. In Ceylon, English was introduced as the language of the courts everywhere except the Tamil north. In 1835, Thomas Babington Macaulay, a Whig politician and lawyer, and adviser to the East India Company, argued that education in English would create a class of men who were "English in taste, in opinions, in morals and in intellect." Colonial education was thus central to a liberal vision of reform.

Colleges, built in grand, neo-classical styles, were established in the major cities rather than evenly spread across India, and little importance was given to primary education. Literacy in English became a mark of social standing and an avenue of social mobility for the elite. English literacy was concentrated in cities. In the late 1830s there were several thousand learning English in Calcutta alone. By 1911, Delhi and Calcutta together had more residents literate in English than there were British citizens in South Asia. In Ceylon, the 1911 census showed 88 percent of those at school received a purely vernacular education. Only about 9 percent of those literate were also able to read and write in English. The figures were rather similar in India. Overall literacy was about 6 percent, with less than 10 percent literate in English, a tiny fraction of the population at 0.5 percent.

It is striking that those who took most easily to Western education were Brahmans. By the late nineteenth century, 90 percent of students at Deccan College, one of the premier colleges in the Bombay presidency, were Brahmans. They also held two-thirds of government administrative posts. When municipal boards were expanded in the 1880s to open up some positions through election to Indians, Brahmans dominated these also. This was significant, as municipal boards established the framework for local government, later becoming the provincial legislative councils. The urban educated upper-castes were also numerous in professions like journalism and law. This was something that was replicated across British India. Muslims, on the other hand, particularly those in northern India whose families had served Mughal administrations for generations, did not make a similar transition. After the eclipse of Mughal power in the early nineteenth century, many of the Muslim gentry lost their positions under the new regime and experienced a great sense of loss. The decline of Persian as the language of government represented another blow to their already diminished status. Thus, we see a differential engagement with the new institutions of the state among the upper-castes and aristocratic classes of India.

While there was a rapid expansion of numbers of Indians in the colonial administration, there remained a ceiling on their promotion to higher positions in the army and the civil service. ICS and CCS exams could only be taken in London, which meant that access was restricted to the very wealthy. In 1880, there were still only a dozen Indian ICS officers. However, the growing complexity of administrative needs and moral pressure from Indians resulted in one-fifth of posts being opened to Indians in 1887. These came to be taken up largely by upper-castes, primarily Brahmans.[30]

In the encounter with colonial education, most South Asians sought to achieve a balance between "tradition" and "modernity"—between the mores of the culture in which they had been raised and the ideas they encountered during their education: of science and rationality; individualism, equality, and social class; nationalism, citizenship, and historical progress; and the place of women in society, what today we would call *modern* ideas. In what follows we explore the more significant nineteenth-century reform movements.

Hindu Reform Movements

Christian missionaries had not succeeded in converting many Indian elites. However, their severe criticisms of Hinduism—that it was hierarchical, idolatrous, and irrational and that it treated women poorly—prompted many pundits and learned men to reflect closely on their own society. One of the most prominent early examples of someone who grappled with these criticisms was Raja Ram Mohan Roy.

Ram Mohan Roy and the Brahmo Samaj

Ram Mohan Roy (1772–1833) was a Bengali scholar learned in Sanskrit, Arabic, Persian, and English, who had been in the employ of the Company for some time. He accepted the criticism that caste was hierarchical and superstitious, and he was attracted to the monotheistic religions of Islam and Christianity as well as scientific insights on the natural world, which he sought to combine with new interpretations of ancient Hinduism. In 1828 Roy founded the Brahmo Samaj, a society that brought together issues of religious reform and social criticism. The stated goal of the Samaj was to promote "improvement" and "enlightenment." Roy was drawn to the circle of Utilitarian liberal reformers and supported their campaign to abolish *sati* (widow burning) in 1829. He called on the government to promote enlightened education, mathematics, science, and natural philosophy. The Brahmo religion reflected reformist ideas of the time: it sought to create a modern, rational version of Hinduism, a new religion for the modern age. However, it is important to recognize that while Ram Mohan Roy promoted social and religious reform, he did not reject his culture or repudiate the Indian past. Rather, he sought to reread them to suit the contemporary moment.[31]

Swami Vivekananda and the Defense of Hinduism

Ram Mohan Roy's response to the criticism of his society was to embrace Western knowledge and incorporate the values of other religious traditions to create a composite worldview. Later reformers took a different tack. Many launched a passionate defense of Hinduism. Swami Vivekananda (1863–1902), for instance, was a Brahman reformer preaching in the last third of the nineteenth century. He argued that Hinduism, like Christianity, was a revealed religion, the various deities being simply reflections of a divine whole. Moreover, caste as it existed was a departure from its true form. In ancient India, he maintained, caste was by merit rather than birth. Thus, women and low-castes could, by virtue of their actions, ascend the ritual order. It was not hierarchical, for each varna outlined a set of social duties and responsibilities that were equally valuable: the work of a sweeper or a farmer was as important as that of a teacher or a priest. In this sense, the varna system represented an organic unity and was the perfect social order for India. Such reformers argued that they should not reject caste but rather restore the original spirit of its practice.

However, Vivekananda took this defense of Hinduism further. He argued that Hindus should not apologize for their religion. Hindus, he maintained, had become spiritually and morally weakened as a result of hundreds of years of foreign invasion. It was this that ultimately led to their colonization. Colonialism had deprived Indians of their self-respect, something that could only be recovered through *swaraj*, or self-rule. Thus, Vivekananda advocated spiritual self-strengthening relating it to social and national unity.[32]

The Arya Samaj and an Indigenous Identity

It was with the Arya Samaj that Hindu reform became explicitly political. The Samaj was founded by Swami Dayanand Saraswati (1824–1883), a Brahman from Gujarat who had been preaching a radically reformed Hinduism since the mid-1870s. Dayanand argued that Hindu society had degenerated since the wars of the Mahabharata. Superstitions had crept in, caste had become fragmented, and Hindus eventually fell before the proselytizing religions of Islam and Christianity. He sought to purge what he saw as Hinduism's adulterations. These included idolatry, caste, child marriage, pilgrimages, horoscopes, restrictions on foreign travel, the ban on widow remarriage, and temple worship—in essence, the majority of Hindu rituals. He argued that once these were cleared away only the pure kernel of Hinduism would be left, which would be reminiscent of the ancient days of the glorious Vedic past.

The Samaj's calls to dismantle much of Hindu ritual practice as well as its support for the equality of women and low-castes challenged the edifice of orthodox Hinduism. However, even as Dayanand sought to re-work Hindu traditions to fit a changing world, he defended a traditional rather than modern ethics. Dayanand believed that a revival of what he saw as the truths of the Vedic past could provide the cultural and spiritual foundation for Hindus in the present. It was an attempt to devise a response to the criticisms put forward by the British that lay outside Western intellectual influence, to create an identity that had indigenous, authentically "Indian" roots.

But this indigenous turn contained the seeds of a deeply reactionary political ideology. Dayanand related the "decline" of Hinduism with the arrival of "foreigners" from central Asia and Europe, with their religious dogmas and violent conversions. He argued that Islam and Christianity, having originated from elsewhere, could never be properly "Indian" religions. Despite their having been present in South Asia for well over a thousand years, Indian Muslims and Christians were, in the language of the Aryas, "lost Hindus" as their ancestors had been converted from Hinduism. The implication of this for the politics of the Arya Samaj, and later Hindu nationalists, was significant. Muslim and Christian conversions in earlier generations meant that converts were from the same racial, ethnic, and cultural stock as Hindus and could be "reclaimed." In this reading of India's past, Muslims and Christians could never be considered properly "Indian" until they had been "returned" to the Hindu fold—they would have to be reconverted or remain outsiders.[33]

The Woman Question

The "woman question" was as central to the concerns of Hindu reformers in the nineteenth century as caste. Colonials had been severe in their assessment of the status of women in India. It was widely believed that the position of women was an indicator of a society's advancement. Observing Hindu society, James Mill had concluded, "nothing can exceed the habitual contempt which the Hindus entertain for their women. . . . They are held, accordingly, in extreme degradation." Utilitarians saw it as their mission to reform Indian society and uplift the status of women: they intervened in *sati*, banning it in 1829, as well as in debates on child marriage, the prohibition of widow remarriage, polygyny, and female education. Similarly, missionaries in the mid-nineteenth century held that Indian weakness and disunity had to do with the low status of women.

Upper-caste Hindu reformers debated these issues endlessly between themselves as well as with colonial officials. Most supported the reform of women's position, arguing in favor of widow remarriage and women's education. Dayanand, among others, maintained that during the Vedic period, the Golden Age of Indian culture, women and men had been equal: it was only with foreign invasion and the weakening of these cultural mores that women became subjected to brahmanical patriarchy. Historians have argued that Indian "tradition" was reconstituted under colonial rule and women often became the ground on which this took place. Women were central to these nineteenth-century reform agendas, for they were seen as repositories of tradition: they reflected and embodied cultural, religious, and later national identities. Thus the reworking of ideas about tradition and identity was regularly conducted through debating the role and behavior of women. However, those who conducted the debates and set their terms were not women but men. After 1858, such public debate was overtaken by concerns about colonial political and economic policies. Social and religious reformers gave way to a new generation of self-styled nationalists who argued that the state's promise of "noninterference" in matters of tradition and religion meant that attempts to reform the position of women was off limits. The "nationalist resolution of the woman question," as Partha Chatterjee has called it, was precisely this move to deem certain arenas "public" or "political" and others "private" or "domestic."[34]

Buddhist Revival in Ceylon

The Buddhist revival in Ceylon in the nineteenth century reflected many similar characteristics of the Hindu reform movements in India. Spearheaded by Western-educated Sinhalese Buddhists and monks from the Sinhala low country, the movement began in 1860 as a response to the aggressive proselytizing of Christian missionaries. In this sense, it was a protest movement that articulated a response to European power in a language of religious, ethical, and cultural reform. The movement sought to counter missionary claims of the superiority of Christian values. It found its voice through a range of public associations and their publications: pamphlets, journals, and newspapers. Activists established Buddhist schools and an indigenous education system to resist the spread of Western knowledge. In the move to overturn missionary criticism, Buddhist reformers in Ceylon returned to Buddhism's ancient texts. Like upper-caste reformers in India revisiting the *Vedas*, Buddhists reread these texts, arguing that they showed Buddhism in its "original" form. The Buddhism of early India was a fundamentally "rational" religion and thus, they argued, compatible with a modern, scientific outlook. It did, not have the devotional, cultish, or mythical elements that were so much a part of contemporary practice. These were later adulterations or "accretions" that had weakened the faith from within, laying them open to missionary attack and political conquest.

Buddhist reformers of the late nineteenth and early twentieth centuries sought to purge the syncretic elements, "streamlining" Buddhism for a new age. The development of this "intellectual Buddhism" had been pushed forward by Colonel Olcott, a Theosophist from New York. Anagarika Dharmapala, one of the leading figures of the Buddhist revival, appealed to middle-class followers to study Buddhist doctrine more closely and reject the worship of deities. Reformers also introduced a set of rituals around which a shared identity could grow: new communal practices around Vesak, for instance, modeled themselves on the celebration of Christmas with the exchange of gifts and cards commemorating the birth, death, and enlightenment of the Buddha. This modern Buddhism was thus not simply about countering the religious claims of missionaries but an avenue through which an increasingly assertive middle class could mobilize an authentic, indigenous identity.[35]

Muslim Reform Movements

Sir Sayyid Ahmad Khan and the Muhammadan Anglo-Oriental College

British supremacy in the eighteenth and nineteenth centuries had brought a steep decline in the position of the Muslim elite. Unlike Hindu elites, Muslims tended to remain aloof from government education and the new spheres of employment in the bureaucracy. Sir Sayyid Ahmad Khan (1817–1898) was a Muslim reformer who advocated engagement with the new regime and became an important figure on the intellectual landscape of generations of nationalist Indian Muslims. He argued that Indian Muslims had stagnated under the British and maintained that education would provide a way out of what he saw as a traditionalist outlook. Sir Sayyid thus sought to persuade upper-class north Indian Muslims of the values of Western education. He developed the idea of creating a

---

Box 1.1. Begum Rokeya Sakhawat Hossein (1880–1932)

Rokeya Sakhawat Hossein was a reformer of Muslim women's education. She was born in the Rangpur district in today's Bangladesh to a landed, highly literate family. Her eldest brother, Ibrahim, supported her education in English and Bengali, where other upper-class Muslims at the time learned Arabic. At sixteen, Rokeya was married to Syed Sakhawat Hossein, the deputy magistrate of Bhagalpur in Bihar. A widower, Sakhawat Hossein had been educated in the West and wanted a companion in his young wife. He continued her English lessons and urged her to write. Very soon, Begum Rokeya was publishing articles on the condition of women. She wrote novels and short stories on women's oppression and the role of education in overcoming this. One essay on the *burquah*, "The Veil," commented on women's unequal development and their confinement for male honor. Another, *Sultana's Dream* (1905) depicted a world where women ruled and men hid indoors. Soon after her husband's death in 1909, Begum Rokeya opened the Sakhawat Memorial Girls' School, moving it to Calcutta in 1911. The school emphasized literacy as well as craftwork, gardening, and home science. It maintained rules of *purdah*, female seclusion, when transporting the women between their homes and the school. Begum Rokeya still wrote satirical pieces on the tragedy of female seclusion, arguing that there was no basis for it in the Quran or Shariah. Her ideas were unpopular, too radical, perhaps, for the time, but her school continued, attended by Muslim girls from well-established families.

"modern Islam," founding a Scientific Society in 1864. In 1875, he established the Muhammadan Anglo-Oriental College in Aligarh in the United Provinces, today's Uttar Pradesh. It was an English-style institution intended as a place for aristocratic Muslims to immerse themselves in the learning of the West while maintaining knowledge of their own religious codes. His interpretation of Islam emphasized the similarities between Quranic revelation and the laws of nature discovered by modern science. Like Hindu and Buddhist reformers, this was an attempt to accommodate new and old forms of knowledge. The college at Aligarh became an important center of Muslim intellectual life, educating the sons of landlords and service families for entry into the bureaucracy. In the early twentieth century, it became a place of nationalist protest and pan-Islamist activity.

Sir Sayyid was criticized by traditional Muslim scholars for his attempts to reinterpret some of the fundamental aspects of Islam. Despite this, he enjoyed widespread respect among British officials and by the 1880s was acknowledged as the spokesperson of Indian Muslims. Sayyid Ahmad Khan was a pivotal figure in the character of Muslim engagement with the colonial state. He encouraged employment in the civil service and, in contrast with upper-caste Hindus who had begun to question the legitimacy of the British presence in India, insisted that Muslims would be loyal subjects of the crown. He also maintained that Muslims and Hindus in India were equal but separate communities, and it was with him that the "Indian Muslim" became a political category.[36]

The Dar al-Ulm at Deoband, 1867

Another Muslim response to British rule was to pull away from modern institutions, to shore up "tradition," even as these very traditions were being rewritten and recreated for modern times. The position of the Muslim religious elite had also undergone a reversal under colonialism. The *Ulema*, religious scholars trained in Islamic law, had been a powerful group in medieval India enjoying both religious and political authority. However, while many retained their titles and land grants under British rule, they lost their authority and influence with the state. The colonial state took over Muslim charitable endowments for schools and Muslim judges who had sat as advisers on the Quran, lost their positions. In response, many *Ulema* strove to retain their niche, arguing that they had the sole right to interpret the *Shariat*. Moreover, they argued that Muslims had to reorganize their educational institutions (*madrasas*) to prevent the influx of morally inferior ideas, to protect Islam against what they called "contemporary times."

The Dar al-Ulum, or "place of knowledge," at Deoband in the United Provinces, was founded in 1867, ten years after the revolt of 1857. The founders of the seminary at Deoband were heirs to the tradition of Shah Waliullah, the eighteenth-century Islamic reformer who had emphasized reform of the traditional curriculum and a regeneration of the Islamic social order. At the outset the seminary was strictly apolitical. The first generation concentrated on creating an educational institution that would return the Indian Muslim community to the correct religious path. Its founders emphasized quiet reflection on the state of Muslim society. Their aim was to educate men of all classes in the traditional Islamic curriculum, to create a new generation of *Ulema*. But Deoband was also quite modern. It was modelled on an English institution: it ran courses within academic departments that were taught by experts in the field. It held examinations, awarded degrees and prizes, and had its own in-house publication. However, the curriculum was taught in Urdu, Arabic, and Persian, rather than English, and focused on Islamic knowledge. Subjects were in revealed science, philosophy, astronomy, logic, and jurisprudence. A close study of Islamic religious texts formed a core part of the curriculum.[37]

A Reform of Islam in South Asia?

Deoband and Aligarh were not opposed to each other. They both addressed the condition of Muslim society under colonialism but filled different needs. One sought to preserve knowledge of the traditional sciences and prepare men for religious service. The other provided upper-class Muslim men with Western education so they could enter government service. Muslim reform movements took place across South Asia and were concerned with the protection and renewal of the position of Indian Muslims and of Islam. They were concentrated in northern and eastern India, regions with large Muslim populations, and relied on the inculcation of textual knowledge. Those we have touched upon had specific and quite narrow audiences in mind. However, there were other movements across the subcontinent that also emphasized reform and renewal of the knowledge and practice of Islam which took a more popular approach. Such movements promoted a scriptural idea of Islam with Arabic and Urdu rather than the local vernacular as the language of the religion. Muslim missionaries also proselytized among low-caste and untouchable Hindus in rural areas where Hinduism in one form or another was dominant. These were all efforts to reshape Muslim piety in a changing social context. Different in individual approaches, what these movements shared was their attempts to overwrite the syncretic, heterodox practices of Islam that were prevalent across the subcontinent with more unitary, orthodox interpretations of the faith. This is something that they had in common with Hindu reform movements like the Arya Samaj.

Out of the multifarious variegated practices of different Hindu and Muslim communities and sects, combined with a reinterpretation of the past, Hindu and Muslim missionaries sought to carve out a "true practice" of their respective religions.

Non-Brahman Movements

Non-Brahmans or low-caste Hindus were Shudras (i.e., the lowest rung of the *varna* system) and, broadly speaking, were laborers, craftsmen, and farmers. Non-Brahmans were not drawn to Hindu reform movements like the Arya Samaj whose appeal remained largely confined to upper-caste Hindus. In contrast with upper-caste reformers who challenged the legitimacy of colonial rule, non-Brahmans expressed their loyalty to the state, appealing to the progressive nature of British rule and petitioning for places to be reserved for their communities in the government's administration and the army. Colonial officials often gave tacit support to non-Brahman movements but tended to stay away from instituting any reforms to promote their upliftment. This was especially true after 1858, when the state pledged a policy of "noninterference" in the customs and religions of Indians.

The most prominent non-Brahman movement in nineteenth-century India was led by Jyotirao Phule (1827–1890) who was central to the articulation of a modern anti-Brahman philosophy and for politicizing non-Brahman identity. Phule came from a gardening caste in western India. He had attended a Scottish missionary school in the 1840s, where he was deeply influenced by the religious radicalism of nineteenth-century Europe, being particularly affected by Thomas Paine's *Age of Reason*. Phule founded a school in Poona for Shudra girls in 1849 and began promoting the education of low-caste, untouchable, and Muslim communities soon after. He developed a scathing critique of Brahmanism during the 1850s and 1860s, arguing that it was a form of slavery, responsible for the social and mental degradation of non-Brahmans and untouchables. In 1873, he founded the Satyashodhak Samaj, or Truth-seeking Society. The Samaj sought to "free Shudras from subjugation to Brahmans." It focused on education, starting a night school for farmers, and petitioned the state for greater resources to be directed toward non-Brahman education.

Education and employment continued to be a central concern of non-Brahman politics into the twentieth century. Many also campaigned for rituals and ceremonies to be performed without Brahmans. However, while they opposed Brahman dominance, they continued to accept caste as a principle of social organization. It was not until the late 1920s that this would change to a call for the abolition of caste altogether. A range of caste associations emerged alongside the Satyashodhak Samaj in the early twentieth century, concerned largely with their varna classification. Many challenged census classifications that ranked them as Shudras, arguing they were Vaishyas or Kshatriyas. To this end, a number of non-Brahman communities demonstrated reformist impulses, pledging to refrain from behavior that was associated with low-castes such as meat-eating, animal sacrifice, and alcohol consumption. They took up the cause of widow remarriage and avoidance of dowry; some began to cremate rather than bury their dead. Thus, low-caste movements combined political attacks on upper-castes with social reform agendas that had every appearance of mimicking the habits associated with upper-caste status and abandoning those thereby associated with the "unclean."[38]

Public Associations

The last third of the nineteenth century witnessed a flourishing of new spheres of shared activity through the emergence of public associations that recorded and reflected the great social change of this period. These included religious reform and caste associations and literary societies that addressed questions about the origins and structure of the various South Asian languages as well as creating new literary and dramatic forms. Political associations with a range of competing and overlapping goals emerged. Print became a vital medium of communication for all such activity with the proliferation of newspapers, journals, and pamphlets debating a range of contemporary issues. Such societies were overwhelmingly founded in urban centers by people who were removed in some way from their "traditional" occupations and surroundings through colonial education, government service, or by a range of new professional activities. Some scholars argue that this marked the beginning of "modern" forms of social and political engagement and the emergence of a bourgeois urban "middle class" in the mold of Europe that led "public opinion."[39] Let us consider the most politically significant of these organizations before taking up the question of whether there was indeed a new South Asian middle class.

The Indian National Congress

In 1885 a group of seventy Western-educated men came together in Bombay to form an association called the Indian National Congress. They were led, initially, by Allan Octavian Hume, a British ICS officer sympathetic to Indian aspirations for professional mobility and employment in the civil service. The core leadership came from Bombay and Calcutta. They were largely men who had met in London in the 1860s and 1870s while studying for the ICS exams under the mentorship of Dadabhai

Box 1.2. Mahadev Govind Ranade (1842–1901)

M. G. Ranade was a scholar, liberal social reformer, high court judge, and early nationalist. He studied at Bombay University for his BA (1862) and the Government Law College for his LLB (1866), serving on the Bombay Legislative Council and then as a judge in the Bombay High Court from 1893. He was also a journalist and historian who wrote in his mother tongue Marathi, publishing the monumental *Rise of Maratha Power* in 1900. Ranade was of the highest caste of Brahmans in Maharashtra and profoundly committed to the social and political reform movements of the nineteenth century. He was one of the early members of the Prarthana Samaj (1867), a movement, like the Brahmo Samaj in Bengal, which sought to reform hierarchy and idol worship in Hinduism. In 1870, Ranade, along with a group of like-minded Brahmans in Poona, founded the Poona Sarvajanik Sabha, a society that debated issues of local government taxation, rural poverty, and public health. He was also a founding member of the Indian National Congress (1885). Ranade joined the Widow Remarriage Association in 1869. When his own wife died, his colleagues expected he would marry a widow. However, his father, a conservative, quickly found a child bride, aged eleven, for Ranade, who was thirty-one at the time and did not dispute the choice. But Ranade became mentor and teacher to his wife, Ramabai, who became an important social reformer in her own right. Perhaps his most important contribution to reform was the National Social Conference (1887), an institution that brought individuals and organizations from around India together to learn from each other's initiatives. Ranade believed that India was better suited to evolutionary rather than revolutionary change and advocated slow reform, adaptation, and argumentation as his methods, although if all else failed, he said, rebellion would be unavoidable.

Naoroji (1825–1917), a Parsi social reformer and the first Indian member of the British Parliament. On their return to India those who did not enter the civil service formed associations of the kind outlined above. This moment is conventionally taken as the beginning of the Indian nationalist movement, the end being independence and the transfer of power in 1947. However, we must be careful not to read history backward. The popular mass nationalism that emerged after 1920 was far from anyone's imagination in 1885, least of all the founders of the Congress. It is important to see the organization as simply one among many public associations at the time.

The early Congress was essentially a debating society for elite, Western-educated men. They formulated three types of demands: political, administrative, and economic. The first petitioned to make the legislative councils more representative. This was not an egalitarian demand but reflected the aspirations of this new elite, who maintained that political rights should be for the "natural leaders" of Indian society: the educated and those of good social standing. They argued that British rule in India had been simply "un-British" and that all who were able to compete for positions should be allowed to. There was an expectation that an expansion of political rights could be introduced gradually through constitutional reform, an approach that came to be known as "constitutional gradualism." The administrative demand argued for "Indianization" of the services: greater opportunities for Indian promotion in the bureaucracy and army, and for ICS exams to be held simultaneously in India and Britain. The economic demand focused on the "drain of wealth" theory. Nationalist economists such as Romeshchandra Dutt argued that the growing poverty of India was a direct result of British rule, and demanded a reduction in "Home Charges" and an end to unfair trade tariffs.[40]

The Congress was self-consciously middle class, cosmopolitan, and secular, open to men of all faiths and backgrounds. However, while there were a few prominent Muslim members in the initial years, there was not a sustained Muslim membership into the twentieth century. The Aligarh Muslim elite felt they had a great deal to lose by participating in elected councils, believing that Brahmans would dominate because of their lead in English education. And the hugely influential Sayyid Ahmad Khan, while advocating Western education, opposed Muslim membership of Congress and Western forms of political representation arguing that they were unsuited to India. His point was that Western representation was "territorial," that is to say, by district, region, or state, rather than communal or by one's identity. But Hindus and Muslims were the two great communities of India and should be represented in substantial measure. His fear was that Muslims, a numerical minority and lagging behind in Western education, would always be at a disadvantage in such a system.

The Ceylon National Congress was formed in 1919 in a similar manner to the INC, drawing together an indigenous, English-educated elite from different ethnic and regional backgrounds. They were notables, similarly "moderate" in their demands, emphasizing "gradualism and constitutionalism" and seeking to expand the role of native Sri Lankans in government rather than independence from the empire. As with the INC, at the outset there were members from numerically minor communities: the president of the CNC was a leading member of the Tamil community,

Sir Ponnambalam Arunachalam, and for a time the well-heeled Tamil and Sinhalese worked together for political reform. In 1921, however, Tamil members left the CNC over a change in the form of political representation. Hitherto, members had been elected on the basis of both territorial and communal electorates, with a few nominated by the governor. But Sinhalese members advocated territorial-only elections to which Tamils were opposed. Although Tamils figured well among the elite, they were still a numerically minor population on the island and believed their interests would be marginalized.[41]

The political methods of the early Congresses were "moderate" on account of their reliance on petitions and belief in the force of persuasive argument. Moderates tended to be anglicized in their outlook and successful in their professions. They advocated social reforms and a model of political participation in line with European liberalism. In India in the 1890s, a younger generation of Congress nationalists emerged with a strong critique of this approach. These "extremists" as they came to be known, argued that moderates followed a politics of "mendicancy": self-government would never be achieved by asking for it politely or by aping the values of the colonizers. Rather, they pursued a more militant, confrontational approach. The most well-known extremists came from Bengal, Punjab, and Maharashtra: Bipin Chandra Pal, Lala Lajpat Rai, and Bal Gangadhar Tilak. They argued that Indians should not imitate the West but should find an identity based on their own history and traditions. They defended autonomy over Indian customs arguing that the British had no right to interfere in these. Instead of petitions and debates, this generation of politicians developed a new range of political methods. They advocated the use of only *swadeshi*, or Indian-made, goods, founded "national" schools that emphasized knowledge of Indian history and science, employed vernacular languages rather than English, and emphasized the need for dedicated work in the villages.[42]

A New Middle Class?

Scholarship on this period has seen the emergence of public associations, the use of print and the proliferation of English as a cosmopolitan language of the urban elite as evidence of a bourgeois middle class articulating "public opinion" through modern forms of political organization that were autonomous of the state or traditional institutions. Conventional understandings have represented the "old" elites—landlords, princes, and so on—as resistant to change, "collaborators" loyal to the state. Those who participated in these new public spheres became publicists, lawyers, and civil servants and campaigned in municipal elections. They have been seen as the new "moderns," the groups from which critiques of colonialism and eventually full-blown nationalism developed.

However, we must be careful not to assume they were exactly like the European bourgeoisie. They may have been urban professionals but most came from a predominantly non-bourgeois social base. Many of this new middle class had strong ties to the land as hereditary landlords as well as holding a privileged position in caste society. These ties to "traditional" society often constrained more radical political aspirations. Moreover, it was not only those educated in English who became involved in these new arenas of politics. A range of overlapping public arenas—mostly in vernacular languages—emerged during this time, and the arenas of representative politics were arguably far less important at this stage than these others.[43]

Conclusion: Tradition or Modernity?

Historical scholarship has tended to separate cultural, religious, and political innovations in nineteenth-century south Asian society into two categories: the "reformers," or modernizers, on the one hand, and the "revivalists," or traditionalists, on the other. Reformers are represented as those who adopted liberal values on the questions of social and political change. Thus Ram Mohan Roy is the classic example of a reformer, as are the men of the early Congress. They supported a formulation of rights, justice, and political representation in line with the West. Revivalists rejected this approach as inappropriate. They emphasized the importance of drawing on India and Ceylon's own traditions rather than aping the values of the West. Thus, they sought to "revive" what they argued were the ancient fundamental truths of their respective religions, before they had been corrupted by external influence.

However, the stark distinction scholars have drawn between reformers and revivalists is misleading. Far from being static, traditions are always evolving through time and in different contexts. The so-called revivalists reinterpreted Hindu, Muslim, and Buddhist traditions and recast them for the contemporary moment. In this sense, they were as modern as the reformers. Each of these movements represented attempts to come to terms with the condition of South Asian societies under colonialism. It is important, then, to understand all such movements as reformist and contemporary even as we acknowledge that the kind of change each advocated worked within different philosophical idioms.[44]

NATIONALISM

In considering nationalism in South Asia we are faced with a number of complex questions. When can we say that nationalism emerged? Narratives of Indian and Sri Lankan nationalisms have customarily begun with the respective National Congresses. Yet we saw in the previous section that members of the early INC promoted an elite interest-group politics that was far removed from any popular broad-based movement advocating a shared national identity. And we will see that the politics of the CNC never moved beyond elite negotiation into the arena of mass anti-colonial nationalism. What, then, did it mean to be a nationalist? Did this change over time? And did it mean the same thing to everyone? Did the freedom and independence of "India" mean the same to Jawaharlal Nehru, the charismatic, urbane, leader of Congress and first prime minister of independent India as it did to a mill worker from Bombay or an *adivasi* (indigenous person) from the forests of Assam? What did "freedom" and independence mean to an upper-class Tamil or Sinhalese? If we argue that nationalism could not possibly have meant the same to everyone, how can we explain the mass nature of the movement we see emerging in India after 1920? What made it possible for so many thousands from urban and rural society, from different regional, caste, linguistic, and class backgrounds and of both sexes to rally around the banner of nationalism? Similarly, how can we understand what nationalism meant in Ceylon in the absence of such a movement? This section will explore some of these questions. We will examine how nationalism came to be defined in a range of different contexts as well as how South Asian politicians sought to build the constitutional framework for a new state.

Patriotism: The Swadeshi Movement, 1905–1911

The new generation of congressmen rejected the "moderate" constitutional methods of their predecessors. They were more confrontational in their approach, mobilizing popular campaigns around tenants' rights and the boycott of foreign goods while arguing that colonialism was illegitimate and should be opposed unequivocally. Many sought to undo the intellectual colonialism of government schools by founding alternate educational institutions. Opposition also came in more violent forms: in 1897 two brothers in Poona assassinated Walter Rand, the plague commissioner who had overseen the state's invasive policies during the epidemic in western India in 1896. Extremism in Congress was pushed forward by the Viceroy's aggressive policies. Lord Curzon was of the opinion that India would be best served if ruled by an autocratic hand.

In 1905, in the name of administrative efficiency, Curzon partitioned Bengal into two smaller provinces: East Bengal and Assam, with its capital in Dacca (Dhaka), and the rest of Bengal province, which included Bihar and Orissa, with Calcutta as the main city. East Bengal had a Muslim majority population and the western province a Hindu majority. The decision was clearly political and made with a full understanding of the demographics of the province. Many prominent Muslim families in East

Bengal who had seen their fortunes decline welcomed the partition since it created a province where they were in a clear majority and thus appeared to protect their interests. The urban professional elite, Hindu and Muslim alike, saw it as an attempt to "divide and rule" Bengalis.

The partition precipitated the Swadeshi movement, the first mass mobilization of political protest that called itself nationalist. Swadeshi, meaning "one's own country," comprised different approaches, from the moderates who petitioned against the partition, to the extremists who promoted a "doctrine of passive resistance" that included the boycott of British goods and institutions and the founding of National Schools, to a band of revolutionary terrorists. Swadeshi activists urged merchants to give up trade with the British, students to leave their colleges, and lawyers to leave their practice. They composed national anthems, performed poetry, distributed pamphlets and published journals. The mood of this early patriotism was to combine religion and politics. Literature and plays written during this period were infused with religious imagery often equating the mother country with the mother goddess.

The movement was nationalist in name but remained geographically confined to Bengal in the east and Maharashtra in the west. It also had a narrow social base: the main participants were urban, educated, upper-caste men with Muslims, non-Brahmans, and the rural population remaining largely outside. Swadeshi nationalists had succeeded in creating a sense of anxiety among colonial officials, but the boycott of government institutions and trade, especially around Lancashire cotton, did not last long. The differences between moderates and extremists had been bitter, resulting in a split in Congress in 1907. Many extremists, including Tilak, were imprisoned for sedition, and the state succeeded in co-opting the essential self-interest of merchants and industrialists. In 1911 the state revoked the partition, by which time the movement had petered out.[45]

Politics during Wartime, 1914–1918

A range of developments in the period 1914–1918 laid the foundations for the first truly broad-based anticolonial movement—Non-Cooperation—which would be launched in 1920. World War I affected Indians in a variety of ways: it impacted the urban and rural poor through massive recruitments; heavy taxes affected those in trade and industry; and spiraling inflation meant that the price of basic goods—kerosene, oil, salt, and staples such as barley and millet—increased exponentially, in some cases by 400 percent. With rising prices, food scarcity, and artisan unemployment, urban centers witnessed food riots. The war multiplied a range of existing grievances and this combined with a new mood for change after 1918.

The first two decades of the twentieth century also saw the increased strength of peasant movements, many of which were organized around no-tax and anti-landlord campaigns. In the princely state of Mewar, for instance, peasants were forced to pay some eighty-six different types of cesses and experienced some of the worst forms of exploitation. In 1905 and again in 1913, many protested by collectively refusing to cultivate lands and attempted to migrate to neighboring areas. Peasant movements in Bihar (1900–1916) and Gujarat (1918) contributed substantially to the early success of Gandhian nationalism.[46]

The Home Rule Leagues founded in 1916 revitalized Congress politics during the war. They sought to mobilize the growing sense of anger and disaffection, and their leaders—Tilak after his release from prison, Annie Besant, a liberal English woman living in India, and Muhammad Ali Jinnah, who became the first prime minister of Pakistan—organized demonstrations in cities and towns across South Asia. In public meetings they spoke about the illegitimacy of British rule, the poverty and degradation it had engendered, and of the need for national self-government. The audiences were still urban, largely around Bombay, Calcutta, and Madras, but the scale and intensity of the demonstrations, as well as the demography of the participants, was far broader than during the Swadeshi movement. This time there was considerable participation of non-Brahman traders and other non-Brahman laboring castes.[47]

The year 1916 was also significant for the first campaign of the Gujarati lawyer Mohandas Karamchand Gandhi, who had returned from twenty years in South Africa. Gandhi was not well known in India. He was viewed with suspicion by Congress moderates who saw him as a radical for his opposition to the racism of the South African state and by extremists who viewed him as a conservative for his steadfast loyalty to the British during the war. Gandhi was thus isolated from Congress but spent 1916–1919 testing the methods of civil disobedience he had developed in the years away. In India he called these methods *satyagraha,* or "truth-force." They involved winning over the opposition through nonviolent noncooperation, simply with the power of truth. He was invited to Chamaparan in Bihar to lead a campaign among indigo workers who had been agitating for their rights for many years. The satyagraha was hugely successful. Gandhi won some measure of success in further satyagrahas among peasant and factory workers in Kheda and Ahmedabad in Gujarat. But the real turning point came after the war.[48]

Gandhi and Nonviolent Non-Cooperation, 1919–1922

Two events in 1919 provided the springboard to the Non-Cooperation movement in 1920. First was the introduction of the Rowlatt Bills that would continue wartime restrictions on civil rights including detention without trial for two years. Second was the peace treaty following the war that proposed to portion out the lands of the defeated Ottoman Empire to the successful European powers. In this event, the Caliph of Turkey, the temporal head of the Muslim world, would lose his position and the Muslim Holy Places would come under British rule.

Having heard of Gandhi's new political methods, people turned to him to lead a protest against the Rowlatt Bills. The Rowlatt Satyagraha began in April 1919. Gandhi had called for *hartals* (work stoppages) across India. The protests were massive but peaceful affairs. In Punjab, the satyagraha was intense, with agitators attacking symbols of the colonial state: banks, post offices, a town hall, a railway station. On April 13, 1919, a large number of civilians, unaware that martial law had been imposed, gathered in Jallianwala Bagh, a park near Amritsar, to celebrate the spring festival. Without warning or provocation, a military unit under General Dyer began firing on the crowd, killing hundreds and injuring more. Dyer later said that his only regrets were that he had run out of ammunition and the streets were too narrow to bring in armored vehicles.

After Amritsar, the protests continued with greater intensity. At the same time, Gandhi sought out an alliance with Muslim leaders, for he had long believed that Hindu-Muslim unity was necessary to oppose the British. He felt that supporting Muslims in the Khilafat movement was important for this, and in turn, Muslim leaders, the Ali brothers, Mohamed Ali and Shaukat Ali in particular, were eager to make alliances with Hindu politicians. The social, economic, and political conditions were ripe for a more radical politics, and Gandhi's act of genius was to align the Rowlatt Satyagraha and the Khilafat movement—two events not obviously connected—within the same domain of anticolonial protest. In doing so, he was able to lift them out of their particular contexts and give them a broader meaning. This ability to bring the apparently unconnected together around a symbol would characterize Gandhi's political strategy in the coming years.[49]

By 1920 the Non-Cooperation movement took off fully. It had two strands. One was the formal campaign organized by Gandhi and Congress politicians. The other was the increasing politicization of the population through labor and peasant organizations at the grass roots. The formal campaign involved the boycott of titles, schools, and government employment and the nonpayment of taxes. Gandhi was adamant that protest should be nonviolent and called on everyone to take up spinning Indian cotton or *khadi*. He saw spinning as the way to bring Indians from all backgrounds together: urban and rural, professional and farmer, rich and poor. Spinning did not challenge the hierarchies in Indian society, thus there was no risk of pitting people against each other. Rather, it was a symbol that Gandhi believed would bring people together.

Demonstrations took place all over India with people walking side-by-side, chanting slogans of Hindu-Muslim unity. The tide of support for Gandhi was overwhelming, and even moderate constitutionalists who had grumbled about his tactics were silenced. The support allowed Gandhi to restructure Congress to transform it from an elitist to a potentially mass-based organization. Committees were established at the local level. Provincial Congress Committees were reorganized along linguistic lines, proportionate representation was established, and there was a fifteen-member working committee that would be the executive head.

Political mobilization at the grass roots was momentous. There was an incredible strike wave during these years, with jute workers coming out in Calcutta, mill workers in Bombay, and railway workers in Jamalpur. There was a general strike in Bombay in January 1920 that reported 200,000 men out. In Bengal there were 110 strikes reported in the second half of 1920 alone. Labor leaders inaugurated the first All India Trade Union Congress in 1920 in Bombay. Peasant movements took off around the country, in Rajasthan, Bihar, the United Provinces, and elsewhere. In the United Provinces, a peasant by the name of Baba Ramchandra was associated with widespread agrarian riots in the province in the early months of 1921. Rioters targeted the houses and crops of large landowners as well as merchant property. There were several clashes with the police and instances where peasants had set up their own "courts" to dispense local justice. There were others who followed the lead of Baba Ramchandra and preached the nonpayment of rent and land to the landless, all in the name of Gandhi. Hill tribes were also rebellious during this period burning down thousands of acres of reserved forests.

The anticolonial message presented by elite nationalists from the cities was clearly far removed from the concerns of nonliterate peasants demonstrating against their landlords. Yet, in a study of what such a population made of Gandhi during the Non-Cooperation period, the historian Shahid Amin argued that peasants had heard of Gandhi, even if most had not seen him, and they constructed him in their imaginations as an almost mythical, godlike figure. He would liberate them from the drudgery of their labor, bring rain when it had not come, and with his powers he could reduce their payments to landlords. Thus, by connecting with Gandhi, peasants somehow hooked in to the wider movement and Congress nationalists claimed their movements under the same banner of Non-Cooperation. Nevertheless, peasants interpreted Gandhi *in their own terms*. The central point being that Gandhi's call for 'Swaraj' or Home Rule meant very different things to different people depending on their immediate needs and aspirations.[50]

Studies of this period depict an almost elemental upheaval. Khilafat leaders were calling for independence even if it meant taking up arms.

People seemed to be on the verge of mass revolt. However, while Gandhi spearheaded the movement he also acted as a brake on its radicalization. He called for boycott but wanted to retain control over what form this took. He did not encourage industrial strikes, fearing they would slip into militancy and Marxism. He called for nonviolence but was concerned that Indians were not adequately disciplined for this. Thus, he had not yet sanctioned full-scale civil disobedience despite being urged to do so. When in February 1922 news came of a horrific instance of violence in the United Provinces where peasants had locked twenty-two policemen in their station burning all of them alive, Gandhi immediately called a halt to the all-India campaign. He went on a fast of atonement for his role in the violence, and the rest of the anticolonial movement went into a tail spin. The trajectory of Non-Cooperation—a mass movement followed by an abrupt stop—was to initiate a pattern that would come to characterize Indian nationalism right up to independence.

A Political Society: Socialism, Communalism and Anti-Untouchability, 1923–1933

The abrupt suspension of Non-Cooperation brought a huge sense of anti-climax. Many were angry at what they felt was a whimsical decision that had prevented a real challenge to the state. The period 1923–1928 was marked by a lack of direction in the Congress agenda. Gandhi withdrew from public life, traveling around India preaching his "constructive program": Hindu-Muslim unity, ending untouchability, and khadi. Moreover, after the strong alliance between Congress and Muslim leaders, 1923 onward witnessed increasing outbreaks of violence between Hindus and Muslims in different regions, something that came to be termed "communalism." Nevertheless, this apparent disarray allowed a range of other movements to come to the fore.

Student activism and communist politics became an important part of nationalism in this period. This was a decade after the Russian Revolution, whose inspiration was clear in the politics of this new generation. Middle-class youth participated in urban demonstrations and some began to turn to revolutionary terrorism. There were fewer industrial strikes between 1923 and 1927, most likely due to the moderate politics of the AITUC, but those that did take place were significant. In April 1923 in Ahmedabad, Gujarat, fifty-six out of sixty-four textile mills were shut down by a massive strike against a 20 percent wage cut. Gandhi, never a supporter of industrial action, urged the workers against further action saying: "faithful servants serve their masters even without pay." There were signs of an autonomous grassroots movement that had started in the Bombay mills from 1923 with the Girni Kamgar Mahamandal, led by two communist activists who had been mill hands themselves, in contrast with the liberal politics of the Bombay Textile Labour Union. Thus, in 1923 and 1924, labor militancy and organization among Bombay textile workers had been able to push wages significantly higher than in Calcutta's jute mills. The Indian labor movement became increasingly militant in the late 1920s and into the 1930s with the emergence of a communist leadership agitating for a more broadly radical approach.[51]

Communism

Indian Communism sprang from within the national movement itself as people became disillusioned with the Congress leadership's resistance to a sustained confrontation with the state. Revolutionaries, Non-Cooperators, Khilafatists, and labor and peasant activists sought new avenues to political and social emancipation. The Communist Party of India was founded by M. N. Roy in 1920. A Marxist political theorist from Bengal, Roy was one of the founders of the Communist Party of Mexico in 1919. He traveled to Russia in 1920 where he entered into a famous debate with Lenin about the strategy of Communists in the colonial world. Lenin urged support of the predominantly bourgeois-led nationalist movements in colonies such as India. But Roy disagreed, arguing that the Indian masses were disenchanted with bourgeois leaders like Gandhi and were ready for a revolution independent of them.

Colonial officials wrote about what they called "Bolshevism" in India, with some anxiety. But the threat posed by Communism was minimal: Communists were relatively few in number and concentrated in urban centers. The Workers and Peasants Parties established in Calcutta in 1925 and Punjab in 1927 were significant in the Left politics of the interwar years for their aim to forge a broad front between labor and peasants. However, they too had little influence, particularly in rural areas, despite their manifestos calling for the abolition of large landowners. Nevertheless, there were several important Communist-led strikes among industrial workers in 1927–1928. With the world in economic depression, the power of the labor movement as a whole declined after 1930. Moreover, Communists were weakened by government repression as well as by a change in their approach: until this point they had worked with Congress, despite many differences on strategy and ideology. After 1930, Indian Communists took a sharp left turn, ferociously attacking Congress leaders such as Gandhi and Jawaharlal Nehru, calling them the "running dogs of imperialism." A revival of labor activity supported by Communists would be seen in the years after 1933.

Congress also witnessed a challenge to its moderate politics from within. Two young socialists, Jawaharlal Nehru and Subhas Chandra

Bose, joined Congress during Non-Cooperation. Both saw anti-imperialism and socialism as integrally linked. They spoke at many rallies and took youth groups into the countryside to address gatherings of thousands of peasants. Nehru presided over the Socialist Youth Congress in 1928, which called for independence as "a necessary preliminary to communistic society." Bose addressed another Youth Congress, hailing youth movements in "Germany, Italy, Russia, and China."

A concerted move to push Congress leftward emerged in 1933 when a group of Congress members who had been imprisoned during the Civil Disobedience movement came together to form the Congress Socialist Party (CSP). The ideology of the founders ranged from radical nationalism to more well-developed ideas of Marxian scientific socialism. However, Gandhi and conservatives within Congress detested the socialist ideas of class war and calls for the confiscation of private property, feeling such radicalism went against the tenets of nonviolence. Yet, the CSP enjoyed great success for a time. CSP activists developed close connections with the emerging farmers' movements, particularly in Bihar and Andhra Pradesh. They trained cadres of farmers in the United Provinces and succeeded in pushing Congress to begin thinking about questions of agrarian reform.[52]

Communal and Caste Identities

The mid-1920s were significant years for Hindu nationalism. There were a number of organizations that came about during this time aimed at politicizing Hindu and Muslim community identities. The Hindu Mahasabha, an explicitly Hindu nationalist organization founded in 1915 and revived in 1923, led a *shuddhi*, or "purification" campaign together with the Arya Samaj to convert or "reclaim" Muslims in northern India into the Hindu fold. In 1923, V. D. Savarkar coined the term *Hindutva*, a term that incorporated ideas about blood, culture, and territory and provided the ideological core for Hindu nationalism. The Rashtriya Swayamsevak Sangh (RSS), a paramilitary organization that would go on to become the institutional center of Hindu nationalism in the postindependence period, was founded in 1925. On the other side, *tabligh* and *tanzim* movements sought to strengthen Muslim identity in the face of what was seen as aggressive Hindu mobilizing. The Jamiat-ul-Ulema-i-Hind, an organization of Ulema founded in 1919 by the pan-Islamist Abdul Bari, took the lead in responding to the shuddhi campaigns, organizing a protest meeting in Bombay in 1923 to revive religious knowledge among Muslims. Again, this was a form of "purification" and "self-strengthening" whose intellectual roots can be traced back to the reform movements of the nineteenth century.[53]

Non-Brahman and untouchable movements also gained momentum in the 1920s under the leadership of Bhimrao Ramji Ambedkar (1891–1956) in Maharashtra and E. V. Ramasami Naicker, or "Periyar" (1879–1973) in Tamil Nadu. Ambedkar, who came from an untouchable community in Maharashtra, had studied in Columbia University in New York, where he was awarded his PhD in 1917, and then later at the London School of Economics, where he earned an LLM and passed the English bar, a truly remarkable education for someone of his social background. On his return to India, Ambedkar became politically involved. He supported anti-landlord movements and led agitations to open public places to untouchables, particularly tanks and wells. Ambedkar steadfastly resisted Congress politicians' attempts to appropriate the movement for untouchable rights, feeling that the upper-caste composition of the Congress leadership would dilute the strength of their demands.

Periyar was from a merchant family. He had been inspired by Gandhi's leadership during the Non-Cooperation movement, and was elected president of the Madras Congress Committee. However, he soon became disheartened by what he saw as Congress's Brahman leadership. In Madras, Periyar had supported reservations in government jobs and educational institutions for non-Brahmans but was defeated by a predominantly upper-caste vote. Brahman members of the committee also opposed his attempts to end caste discrimination around temple entry. Disillusioned, Periyar resigned from Congress in 1925. He called for the destruction of Brahman domination of Congress as a necessary condition for the country to win freedom. In 1926 he founded the Self-Respect Movement, which initiated a sharp break with Hinduism. It opposed Brahman priesthood, worked to abolish caste, and supported the liberation of women. What is striking about the movements that emerged during the 1920s is that while maintaining a nationalist position they were often deeply critical of Congress's formulation of nationalism.[54]

The Salt Satyagraha and Civil Disobedience, 1930–1931

Congress was not a political party with any ideological coherence but an anticolonialist platform representing a range of interest groups with divergent political positions. Some of the more powerful interests within Congress were the wealthy landlords and industrialists, who did not welcome any talk of land or labor rights. Thus the will to support peasant and workers' movements was constrained by these vested interests. Nevertheless, by 1928 peasant satyagrahas had begun again, especially in Gandhi's home region of Gujarat, and the pressure was on for another round of mass struggle.

Although the more radical end of Congress wanted to call for a huge round of civil disobedience that would culminate in strikes across the country and demand immediate independence, Gandhi was reluctant to unleash forces over which he had no control. His demands were moderate and included the release of political prisoners, lowering the rupee-sterling exchange rate, and a reduction in land revenue rather than calls for redistribution or independence. When the viceroy rejected these, Gandhi, angered, agreed to another campaign, this time around the issue of salt. The salt tax amounted to about 4 percent of total revenue. This was a brilliant choice of symbol: it linked Swaraj with a concrete grievance that affected vast numbers of people. It was also a way to emphasize the plight of the poor without challenging the hierarchies of Indian society. Gandhi led a group of his followers on a 241-mile march to the coast. There he bent down to take a handful of salt, in violation of the salt law saying: "With this I am shaking the foundations of the British Empire." The image of this slight figure, dressed only in a loin cloth, so defiant of the power of the British Empire, was electrifying.

Thus began the next round of civil disobedience. Almost as soon as the march had begun, village officials along Gandhi's route started resigning their posts. People around the country began making their own salt along with other civil disobedience campaigns. Civil disobedience in 1930 was more disciplined than it had been in 1920. There were a few instances of violence but there was a remarkable discipline in the practice of nonviolence even in the face of brutal police attacks against protesters.

Impressive numbers of people confronted the state, seemingly with one voice, and tens of thousands were sent to prison. However, the success of civil disobedience as a "national" campaign was qualified. Many congressmen supported Gandhi not because of his ideals but because they felt that without him no mass campaign was possible. Moreover, Congress contained such a motley group of interests—labor and peasant groups, industrialists, liberals, socialists, Gandhians—that there could be no shared consensus on what constituted "freedom" beyond getting the British out. Furthermore, Muslims and Sikhs were conspicuous by their absence, increasingly criticizing Congress as working for Hindu rather than national interests.

As with Non-Cooperation, Gandhi abruptly called off the movement and for similar reasons: to manage its radical elements. At the outset of the civil disobedience campaign, thousands of middle-class activists and well-off peasants were arrested and imprisoned very quickly. After this, support seemed to decline as businesses became impatient with the ban on foreign trade. At the same time, the movement was radicalized from below with tribal rebellions, peasants resisting arrest, and seizures of property, presenting dangerous forms of protest that went beyond the bounds of Gandhi's influence. In return for calling off the movement, the viceroy offered some measure of self-government in matters relating to defense, external affairs, and financial credit for India. Gandhi, seeing the movement in decline, agreed. This marked a real climb down on the main issues: the Gandhi-Irwin Pact of 1931 kept the salt tax on the books and made no mention of independence to the dismay of a wide range of nationalists inside and outside Congress.[55]

Constitutional Issues

In November 1930, as the civil disobedience movement was starting to wane, King George V inaugurated the Round Table Conferences in London, chaired by the Labour prime minister, Ramsay MacDonald. These meetings, held over three sessions between 1930 and 1932, brought together representatives of a range of Indian parties—members of the All India Muslim League, the Hindu Mahasabha, Indian Liberals, leaders of the Sikh and Depressed Classes, as well as representatives of the princely states—to frame a constitution for when power was devolved to India. Several important leaders were absent. Congress boycotted the meetings, seeing them as too great a compromise, and many others had been imprisoned during civil disobedience. After the 1931 pact with the viceroy, Gandhi joined the conferences in their second session as Congress's representative.

It is important to put these conferences in context. Indian nationalists had pushed for greater influence in government policy since the late nineteenth century. The first series of constitutional reforms had been introduced in 1909 and were to be reviewed every ten years. At the first review in 1918, British officials made a commitment to what they called "progressive self-government" or, more specifically, "the gradual development of self-government institutions with a view to the progressive realization of responsible government in India as an integral part of the British Empire."

The Montagu-Chelmsford Reforms of 1919, named after the viceroy and secretary of state at the time and from which the above quote is taken, introduced "diarchy," or a two-tier system of governance. They created some provincial autonomy, devolving responsibility for certain departments to the provincial governments: education, health, agriculture, and municipal issues, for instance. However, these powers were limited, as British officials retained control of the politically weightier departments such as law and order, security, and finance, and they held a veto on any changes sought by Indians through the new reforms. Far from sharing power, such measures were a way for the state to retain control and, by co-opting the political ambitions of Indian politicians, quell potential radicalism.[56]

The second review came in 1927 with the Simon Commission, named after its chairman. There were no Indian representatives on this committee, which incensed the Indian political elite. Instead, they arranged an alternative forum to discuss how power would be shared after the British were gone. The Nehru Report that resulted was published in 1928 but did not represent a consensus among the different parties. On the contrary, many have argued that the report sidelined the concerns of minority representatives. Leaders of the Muslim League, for instance, had agreed to forgo separate electorates, a provision introduced in 1909 for under-represented communities, in return for guaranteed representation for Muslims in regions where they were the majority population. They were particularly embittered when it became clear that a possible agreement had been stifled by the Hindu Mahasabha. The Round Table Conferences in London were to reopen negotiations that had failed before.[57]

The Communal Question

The reason it was so difficult to reach a consensus on constitutional representation between different Indian parties had to do with the so-called "communal" or "minority" question. Elections to municipal councils introduced in the late nineteenth century had been held on so-called "territorial" lines: representatives were elected from a region or district rather than on the basis of religious, caste, or ethnic community. Colonial officials believed that this had resulted in the professional classes, largely upper-caste Hindus, coming to the fore. It was only a very thin sliver of Indian society who had taken to the new forms of political institutions introduced by the British, and their interests were now disproportionately represented. Concerned that their mechanisms for representation were not properly representative of Indian society, officials at the highest levels of the colonial administration began discussions in 1906 about formulating a constitution for India that did not fall prey to these earlier problems.

The response of Muslim leaders, who went in deputation to the viceroy in 1906, was that modern systems of representation were inappropriate for a society such as India, for with each vote equally weighted, those populations that were numerically smaller would be marginalized. Muslims were numerically a minority in India, but to treat them as such would be wrong: they had, over hundreds of years, contributed significantly to the culture and mores of India. Any constitutional reforms should therefore ensure that their status and interests were protected. The deputation continued that in future constitutional reforms, Muslims should be allowed to choose their own representatives: they should be granted a "separate" or "communal" electorate comprised only of Muslims. It was from this initial deputation that the All India Muslim League was founded in 1906.

Representatives of the professional classes vehemently opposed these proposals arguing that creating separate categories on the basis of religion undermined the whole exercise of political representation, which was responsible to general rather than particular interests. But the viceroy agreed. European intellectuals and colonial officials had long seen India as a society made up not of individuals but of sects, castes, and religious communities. These were water-tight social identities that allowed little mobility between them. Moreover, Indians were so bound by these identities, they argued, that they were unable to act in a general interest. Any constitution for India had to consider these social conditions and reflect the range of communities. On the basis of these arguments, the first constitutional reforms of 1909 created a separate electorate for Muslims with seats reserved on the executive and legislative councils specifically for members of this community. These reforms were extremely limited, serving mainly to appoint elite representatives to various advisory councils. However, their implications were far-reaching: the arguments about the uniqueness of the minority community and its need to be protected through separate electorates formed the basis of all future arguments about minority, or "communal," representation.[58]

Ceylon

In Ceylon, the issue of communal representation proved equally contentious. Sinhala and Tamil political leaders had worked together in the Ceylon National Congress, petitioning the state for greater recognition in various arenas of colonial society. In 1921, Tamil members left the CNC over the issue of territorial elections, which its Sinhala members now demanded. Until this point, members had been elected on a combination of territorial representation and communal electorates, with some nominations from the governor. Although well represented among the professional and upper classes, Tamils were a minority community in the island, approximately 11 percent of the population in 1921, and feared being marginalized if the method of representation changed.

The Donoughmore Commission of 1927 came with the aim of providing a draft constitution for Ceylon. The All-Ceylon Tamil Conference had been founded to oppose territorially based electorates. Despite this, the resulting reforms abolished communal representation and established territorial elections to a State Council held first in 1931. While retaining control of security and foreign affairs, the reforms devolved executive power over Ceylon's internal affairs to those elected and introduced a committee system of governance designed to prevent any one ethnic group from dominating. Each of the seven committees was responsible for a different area of administration and consisted of members drawn from all the ethnic groups represented in the State Council. The reforms introduced universal suffrage, much to the dismay of the political elite, who would much rather have had the franchise restricted to men of property and education. The conservative Tamil leadership was particularly opposed to extending it to women. Significantly, the ACTC boycotted the elections to the State Council.[59]

Securing a Majority: The Round Table Conferences, 1931–1932

Likewise in India, minority community representatives opposed the normative, liberal model of representation. At the second session of the Round Table Conferences in 1931, spokesmen for Muslims and depressed classes, Christians, Sikhs, and European commercial interests argued that a representative framework of one-person-one-vote would fail to protect minority interests. What they needed was separate representation. Ambedkar maintained that a separate electorate for untouchables was the only way for this population to establish itself in a new political arena. This was a population that was overwhelmingly poor and illiterate. It had for centuries suffered grievous caste discrimination and continued to carry the psychological scars of generations. A separate electorate and reservations in education and employment would begin to level the playing field until such time as they were ready to compete. At this stage, open, or so-called democratic, competition was disingenuous, for it would simply result in the success of the most privileged, those best equipped to compete.[60]

Congress, the Hindu Mahasabha, Indian Liberals, and others vehemently opposed the demand for separate representation in the new constitution, arguing that this would fragment the general electorate and reduce India to a series of minorities. Separate electorates for each minority community would undermine national unity and the democratic process. Centrally, opponents argued that the constitutional and communal questions were separate—the former political, the latter, social—and must not be confused. But therein lay the problem: for minority representatives, determining their place in a future independent India lay at the center of constitutional considerations; the two were inseparable.

Gandhi opposed separate electorates for untouchables on religious rather than political grounds. Sikhs and Muslims were entitled to community representation to make them feel secure, he said, but untouchables were a part of Hinduism. Discrimination against them was a crime against humanity and must end, but to create a separate political category was tantamount to what he called a "vivisection of Hinduism." Gandhi threatened to "fast unto death" if untouchables were granted a separate electorate. In contrast, Ambedkar argued that untouchables were outside the caste system and had never been treated as Hindus. Social reform had not worked, and to rely on the good will of upper-castes to end discrimination was pure folly. Separate electorates were necessary to ensure that a person was chosen who would work in the interests of the group rather than in the interests of a powerful majority.

The Communal Award of 1932 granted separate electorates to all the minority groups. Gandhi went on his fast as promised, and there was enormous pressure from around India for Ambedkar to revoke the claim for separate representation for untouchables. He ultimately acceded, calling this a cynical "defense of caste." The upshot of this was that Sikhs and Muslims retained their minority status, although ironically, as we shall see in the following section, leaders of the Muslim League had begun to argue that Muslims should be considered not a minority but a nation within India. Seats were reserved for untouchables but in a joint rather than a separate electorate. This undermined the entire argument for a measure of autonomy and protection for a historically disenfranchised community. Perhaps the most important legacy of this moment for the postcolonial period is that it determined majority and minority populations. Untouchables were effectively appropriated as Hindus and became part of a democratic majority. As Indians moved toward a transfer of power, their leaders had deemed a liberal democracy the most appropriate framework for governing. In the constitutional debates of 1909 and 1918, reservations for minority groups were made on the basis that the landscape of India's communities, large and small, were equally entitled to representation. By 1932, a spectrum of nationalist opinion, excluding minorities, had come to see separate representation as undemocratic and antinational. It was the voice of the majority that would carry the day.[61]

Government of India Act 1935

The Simon Commission and the Round Table Conferences became the basis for the 1935 Government of India Act, which extended the franchise from 6.5 to 35 million people. It granted full provincial autonomy: Indian politicians now controlled all matters related to governance in their respective regions. However, the Government of India retained the most important powers of defense, finance, and law and order at the center. Colonial officials presented these reforms as a significant step toward Indian self-rule, but Indian nationalists were scathing, calling it a "charter of slavery." Historians have tended to agree, arguing that devolving power into the hands of Indian politicians was less an act of imperial beneficence and more a strategy to co-opt their political ambitions and stem a potentially violent challenge to the state. Most of the provisions of the 1935 Act made their way unchanged into the constitution of independent India and remain there today.[62]

INDEPENDENCE AND PARTITION, 1937–1948

The years 1947 and 1948 saw the culmination of powerful nationalist movements and arduous constitutional negotiations. Three independent national states were created in South Asia as colonial subjects became citizens in their own right. This was a time of enormous upheaval. Partition and the creation of Pakistan resulted in the migration of millions across borders that had not yet been defined. Equally, these migrations ruptured families and communities, people who had lived side by side for generations, in the most brutal ways. Between one and two million were killed and tens of thousands of women were abducted. This was a moment of great tragedy, causing untold pain, the scars of which remain in plain view today. It was also a moment of great joy. People across South Asia held a great sense of possibility and optimism for the future of their countries.

In contrast to the period of nationalist struggle that preceded the independence of India and Pakistan in 1947, that of Ceylon was the culmination of a process of negotiation and constitutional reform. The leadership of the Ceylon National Congress had passed to the conservative wing led by D. S. Senanayake (1884–1952), who advocated dominion status rather than full independence. The other wing was led by S. W. R. D. Bandaranaike (1899–1959), the scion of a powerful family under the British. Thus, there was no mobilization for self-rule: decisions about the future governance of the colony were taken by a small coterie of people to which the vast majority of Sri Lankans were, at best, spectators. The Soulbury Commission of 1944 introduced the independence constitution. Its primary goal was to ensure the protection of minority interests while ensuring that the majority Sinhala population had a "proportionate share in all spheres of Government activity to which their numbers and influence entitle them."[63] Power was transferred on 4 February 1948 when the crown colony became a dominion within the Commonwealth with the British monarch remaining as the head of state, represented in the island by a governor-general and a prime minister as the head of government. The Dominion of Ceylon became the Republic of Sri Lanka in 1972. It could be argued that the absence of an anticolonial movement and the shared sacrifice that would have brought had a significant bearing on independent Sri Lanka's failure to create a national identity that could transcend ethnic and regional identities.[64]

The events of the decade that preceded the creation of the independent nation-states of India and Pakistan have been the subject of heated debate. Historians still disagree about the answers to questions they pose students: Why did the British quit India? Was the partition of India inevitable? In what sense were Gandhi, Jinnah, and Nehru national leaders? How important was the nationalist movement in winning freedom? How far was religious identity the basis for the foundation of Pakistan? This section provides a context for these and other related questions about one of the most extraordinary periods in twentieth-century world history.

Depression and the World Economy

The interwar years were marked by economic decline, which fuelled nationalist agitation. The Great Depression resulted in a dramatic collapse of prices. Between 1929 and 1932 the prices of India's major cash crops more than halved as the overseas markets for these dried up. However, revenue payments for agriculturalists remained the same, making the effective burden of debt greater. The result was a breakdown of the circuits of rural credit. Intermediate moneylenders were unable to recover their loans and, as bigger creditors pulled out, their liquidity dried up. The rupture of credit relations profoundly destabilized existing social relationships in the countryside. The balance, however unequal, that had existed between moneylender and peasant cultivator, was gone as the rural elite lost their principal mode of social control—debt collection. The effect of the Depression in urban centers was more mixed as the construction and manufacturing industries did better than agriculture. Industry was a small but growing proportion of the overall economy. It was in this context that Gandhi launched the civil disobedience movement in 1930.[65]

Devolution: 1937 Provincial Elections

The Government of India Act of 1935 extended the franchise and created a number of new ministerial positions in provincial governments. Elections to these posts were held in 1937. Despite its limitations, the act was the clearest signal that the British intended to cede power to Indians at the center. For this to be transferred to Congress, its leaders needed to demonstrate that they were a properly representative body of Indians. After their strident criticisms of the act, Congress leaders eventually campaigned on the basis that they would wreck the councils from within. About half of all those eligible to vote did so, and Congress won overwhelmingly in eight out of eleven provinces. However, they failed to win support in Muslim-majority areas. Muslim League leaders thus opposed Congress's claim to represent the nation, arguing that they stood for sectional rather than national interests. Furthermore, a gulf had opened up in Congress between a leftist camp led by the socialist and militant nationalist Subhas Chandra Bose and the Gandhian right-wingers represented by the industrialist G. D. Birla. Gandhi anointed Jawaharlal Nehru president of Congress in 1936 to stave off a leftist challenge. Nehru's inauguration speech pointed to socialism as heralding a new civilization, with the Soviet Union providing a model for the way forward. His caveat was that he was not willing to force this philosophy on Congress. At the outbreak of World War II, then, Congress was divided from within and faced a serious challenge to its legitimacy from without.

World War

Congress leaders offered full cooperation with the war effort in return for a postwar discussion on the political structure of an independent India. In addition, they insisted on the immediate formation of something approaching responsible government at the center. They were refused on both counts, and it became clear that despite the gestures toward Indian self-rule, the British had little intention of dissolving the Government of India. On the contrary, the government extended restrictions on civil liberties and retained "emergency powers"—the ability of the center to suspend a provincial government at will. When war broke out, the viceroy, Lord Linlithgow, declared unilaterally that India would be part of the Allied forces and fight alongside Britain against Hitler. Moreover, Winston Churchill, as head of the national coalition, declared in November 1942: "I have not become the King's First Minister in order to preside over the liquidation of the British Empire." Churchill consistently opposed Labour leaders such as Clement Atlee and Stafford Cripps who supported a complete transfer of power.[66]

During the 1930s there had been much negotiation between Indian leaders and British officials about how to part company. Once war broke out, all those discussions ended. Britain required enormous human and material resources to fight the war and a large proportion of these came from India. The size of the Indian army increased tenfold as troops were sent to the Middle East and Southeast Asia, as well as to protect India's borders against the alarming progress of Japanese troops through Burma toward Assam. Between 1939 and 1945 nearly 3.5 billion rupees was spent on defense in India. War expenses were funded by generating a vastly increased money supply. This, in turn, created high rates of inflation and high prices for basic commodities especially food. Wartime inflation hit the rural poor hard. The tragic famine in Bengal in 1943–1944 where over three million agricultural laborers and tenant farmers starved was created not by a shortage of food but by a lack of affordability. A dramatic result of these years of enormous expense, high inflation, and global conflict was a reversal in the balance of payments between Britain and India. London had agreed that India would be reimbursed after the war. By 1945 Britain was in debt to the Government of India to the tune of 1.3 billion pounds sterling. Scholars have argued that Britain's economic policies in the interwar period were unsuited to deal with the changes wrought by World War II. Moreover, it was their economically weak position at the end of the war as much as a strong nationalist movement that finally forced them to relinquish their Indian empire.[67]

Nationalist Agitation: Quit India, 1942

Nationalist agitation was fragmented and weak in the early years of the war, marked only by sporadic acts of resistance. Congress ministers resigned their posts *en masse* in 1940 in protest at the viceroy's announcement that India would join the war effort. Gandhi was not willing to sanction an all-out campaign calling instead for individual satyagrahas. The Indian Left was split around a response to the war: the Communists and hard Left contingent argued that there should be a united effort against fascism, while the Socialists and other left-wing parties were opposed, supporting militant, antiwar demonstrations. Nationalist opposition was also muted as certain sections of Indians benefited economically. The war provided a stimulus to Indian industry: employment in factories increased by one-third as the cutting off of imports forced a reliance on Indian-made products and labor unrest was kept in check by subsidies for basic goods. Moreover, spiraling prices for agricultural commodities brought some profit to the better-off agrarian classes after the years of depression. For Indian businessmen the war meant an opportunity for quick profits.

However, with the early success of the Axis Powers, Britain's hold on its empire in South Asia looked tenuous. Britain's weak position combined with the government's failure to agree on how to transfer power (see below) spurred nationalists into action. In the summer of 1942 Gandhi made a number of uncharacteristically militant speeches. The time had come, he said, for the British to go and urged: "Let every Indian consider himself to be a free man. . . . Mere jail going would not do."[68] Britain had suffered huge losses in Southeast Asia and, in 1942, began a retreat. Indian troops stationed there were essentially left to make their own way back from Burma to India on foot, through jungles and over mountains, in appalling conditions. Gandhi picked up on the groundswell of anger from demobilized troops and their families and called for mass struggle.

The Quit India campaign was launched on August 8, 1942. This was not civil disobedience but a huge uprising, and presented the greatest threat to British power since 1857. The entire Congress leadership was imprisoned the following day. It began in urban centers led by student and labor activists who spearheaded strikes and clashed with police. The revolt quickly spread to the countryside, where agricultural workers attacked communications networks and symbols of colonial authority. From September, students and peasant squads conducted terrorist activity. The center of the uprising was in Bihar and eastern United Provinces, where the colonial administration collapsed in a number of districts and militants set up parallel governments.

A largely unarmed population gave way under a brutal response from British forces. The viceroy ordered machine gunning from the air against agitators breaking up communication lines in Patna. Public flogging and torture were widespread. By the end of 1943, over 90,000 people had been arrested. The growing intensity showed the nationalist movement to be a movement properly from below. Gandhi put his name to it, but it went substantially beyond anything that he would have envisioned. He was the undisputed leader of a movement over which he had no control. This paradox reflected a particular relationship between the people and the nationalist elite who claimed to lead them. It demonstrates how the meaning of nationalism was refracted through myriad lenses. Congress sought to take the credit for the Quit India movement, but in many ways the different uprisings were autonomous of its leaders.[69] At the same time, its leaders strove to have Congress recognized as the only legitimate representative of an emergent Indian nation. The demand for Pakistan forwarded by Muhammad Ali Jinnah and the All India Muslim League posed the greatest challenge to Congress's claims to legitimacy. It is to this that we now turn.

The Demand for Pakistan

The creation of Pakistan leaves many questions unanswered. How was it that the idea for Pakistan, which had so little currency in 1940, became powerful enough to create a new nation-state by 1947? How do we explain why people who had lived side by side for generations if not centuries, who shared customs, traditions, and languages, participated in such a profound separation? Had they really come to see themselves as fundamentally different? And if Pakistan was to be a homeland for India's Muslims, why did so many remain behind?

We address these questions by looking at four interrelated issues: first, the relationship between the center of power in Delhi and the various provinces; second, Jinnah's argument for Pakistan; third, the emergence of the Pakistan movement as a mass movement; and finally, the role of the British. This section presents two arguments. First, that the Pakistan demand was not for the creation of a separate state—it only became so very late in the day as all other possibilities failed. Second, that it was not a religious demand. Jinnah, who formulated the demand for Pakistan and is seen as its founding father, argued that Pakistan should be a secular state. His argument was one for the protection of minorities that was mapped onto the geography of the subcontinent.

Majority and Minority Provinces

In British India, Muslims were a numerical majority in only two provinces, Punjab in the northwest and Bengal in the east. Muslims constituted 70 percent of the population in Sind, a neighboring province of Punjab but administratively a part of the Bombay Presidency. One of the Muslim League's central demands in 1928 was for the separation of Sind and its creation as a Muslim-majority province, in return for forgoing separate electorates. Elsewhere in British India the Muslim population was a tiny minority. In the plains of the United Provinces, Muslims were a significant but numerically minor presence. Across South Asia, Muslims were a sociological minority—that is, in business, education, politics, civil service, and the professions of law and journalism, Muslims were present in small numbers, even in regions where they were a numerical majority. However, the existence of separate electorates for Muslims meant that in elections to provincial and central legislative assemblies, Muslims constituted a corporate bloc that could choose Muslim candidates without competition from elsewhere. They continued, then, as a separate political category.

Separate electorates rendered Muslims a permanent minority. Those seeking to represent "Muslims" competed for votes within their own constituencies but did not seek to engage—either through alliance or opposition—beyond this narrowly defined category. Thus, where by 1942 people were rallying around the Congress banner in increasingly large numbers, there was no all-India Muslim organization that could claim such mass support.

Provincial autonomy was good for regions like Punjab and Bengal, as it allowed for the development of local politics with scant regard for what was happening in Delhi. It was not so good for the All India Muslim League, whose exclusively Muslim-identity politics held no meaning for leaders in the Muslim majority provinces. This explains why, in the 1937 elections, the Muslim League did so poorly, gaining only 4.4 percent of the Muslim vote. However, despite the limitations of the 1935 Act, it seemed to promise the beginning of the end to British rule. It was in this context that some Muslim politicians from minority provinces approached Jinnah, a lawyer trained in England who led the Muslim League.

Jinnah and the Constitutional Argument for Muslim Protection

Jinnah's central concern for Indian Muslims was to ensure their constitutional protection in a future independent India. Jinnah argued that if India was to adopt liberal democracy after independence, Muslim interests in the provinces in which they were a minority would be swamped by a majority population that was, within a world of political categories identified by religion, Hindu. Democratic principles would thus lead to undemocratic results. He drew up his famous "Fourteen Points" in 1929 after what he saw as the failures of the Nehru Report to ensure such protection. The central demands were: a federal constitution with residuary powers vested in the provinces; legislatures constituted with adequate minority representation assured in each province; one-third representation for Muslims in the central legislature; provisions in the constitution for Muslims to attain, alongside other Indians, a share in state institutions and local government; and the separation of Sind from the Bombay Presidency. Congress rejected these out of hand, maintaining that the nationalist movement embraced Indians of all castes and religious backgrounds and would protect minorities after a successful transfer of power.

But the 1937 elections marked a turning point. The 1935 Government of India Act had outlined a federation that kept the unitary center of the colonial state intact. After 1937, the political leadership in Punjab and Bengal became concerned at the fate of their regional autonomy if Congress controlled the central legislature. It was in this context that they approached Jinnah. Jinnah agreed to broker the majority provinces' position in negotiations. However, this did not address the divergent political concerns of Muslims elsewhere who were concerned not for their autonomy but for protection as a minority. "Muslim" was a constitutional category and a catch-all term but it did not reflect a convergence of interests among India's diverse population of Muslims. And ultimately, even in the unlikely event of such a convergence, their absolute numbers in the central legislature meant Muslims would be unable to overturn a majority Congress vote.

The fundamental question was how to get around the problem of being a minority. In 1930, Maulana Muhammad Iqbal (1877–1938), a poet, philosopher, and politician who worked closely with Jinnah, made his presidential address at the League's annual meeting, where he called for the creation of a "North West Indian Muslim state" to include Punjab, Sindh, Baluchistan, and the North West Frontier. Iqbal's call for a Muslim state did not go far, but soon after, a number of other similar ideas began to circulate. The name "Pakistan" appears to have its origins in a pamphlet written in 1933 by a Punjabi student at Cambridge, Chaudhri Rahmat Ali, who saw a series of contiguous Muslim provinces reaching from Punjab,

Box 1.3. Sir Muhammad Iqbal (1877–1938)

Sir Muhammad Iqbal, also known as Allama Iqbal, poet, philosopher, and politician, is widely seen as the philosophical inspiration of Pakistan. Born in Sialkot, Punjab province, in today's Pakistan, to humble beginnings, he was an important figure in Urdu and Persian literature. Iqbal's ancestors were Kashmiri Pundits, Brahmans who converted to Islam in the nineteenth century. He studied philosophy, English literature, and Arabic in Lahore, where he gained a BA (1897) and MA (1899), before traveling to Trinity College, Cambridge, on a scholarship in 1905. Graduating with his BA the following year, he was called as a barrister to the bar at Lincoln's Inn. In 1907, influenced by the work of Nietzsche, Goethe, and Henri Bergson, Iqbal moved to Germany for a doctorate in Persian metaphysics. He returned to India in 1908. Politically, Iqbal was active in the Muslim League and critical of the Indian National Congress, seeing it as dominated by Hindus. He advocated cooperation between Muslim countries and envisioned separate Muslim provinces within India. Muslim identity, he believed, would suffer under a central Indian government: secularism would weaken the spiritual strength of Islam, and a Hindu majority would dilute the political and cultural influence of Muslims. In 1930, Iqbal famously argued for an autonomous grouping of Muslim-majority provinces in the northwest of India. Critical of the factionalism within the League, Iqbal believed Jinnah was the man to lead it. Iqbal published a series of lectures, *The Reconstruction of Religious Thought in Islam* (1934), where he argued that Islam provided a legal and political philosophy for the modern age and could provide the basis for an Indian Muslim state. He continued to publish poetry and political commentary until his death in 1938.

through the Afghan province, Sind, and Kashmir into central Asia. Neither Iqbal's nor Rahmat Ali's proposals were taken seriously. However, by the late 1930s, a number of schemes had been proposed that claimed "nationhood" for Indian Muslims. Most stopped short of complete independence, proposing the formation of distinct autonomous Muslim blocs within a loose Indian confederation.

Two Nations: The Lahore Resolution, 1940

In 1939 the British had declared that they would not transfer power to any system whose authority was explicitly denied by what they called "large and powerful elements in India's national life." This conceded the League's claim to represent India's Muslims and its right to a veto on future constitutional proposals. In 1940, at the Muslim League's annual session in Lahore, Jinnah forwarded a bold idea: Muslims were not a minority but a nation. There were two nations in India, Hindu and Muslim. The Lahore Resolution demanded "that the areas in which the Muslims are numerically in a majority as in the north-western and eastern zones of India should be grouped to constitute 'Independent States,' in which the constituent units shall be autonomous and sovereign."

This came to be known as the "Pakistan Demand" and a call for a separate state. However, to see this as a call for partition is to read history backward. The resolution was vague. Neither Pakistan nor partition was explicitly mentioned, nor was the form that "independence" and "sovereignty" should take clearly defined. Historians have argued that the assertion that Muslims were a nation held out the possibility of parity in negotiations, with Hindus allowing Indian Muslims to circumvent the obstacles presented by their minority status. It was a bargaining tool to be used in a postwar settlement.

Supporting this is the striking fact that even by 1940 few Muslim leaders took the Pakistan idea very seriously. Sikander Hayat Khan of the Punjab Unionist Party declared that he was opposed to Pakistan if it implied Muslim Raj in the northwest and Hindu Raj elsewhere. In the early 1940s some Muslim politicians even argued that it was the Hindu press and politicians who had misinterpreted the Resolution in order to block more moderate Muslim demands. As remarkable, in retrospect, was the opposition on the part of many religious leaders to the creation of a separate state. Many ulema, especially from Deoband, aligned with Congress and sought to promote religious rejuvenation among Muslims rather than a separate political space for them.

The implication of arguing that Muslims were a nation was that when the Government of India was dissolved, the center as it had existed under colonial rule would have to be reconstituted and power would be transferred to two responsible bodies rather than one. Jinnah was pushing for Congress and the British to accept the principle that Muslim provinces would be regrouped into a political unit. Whether this would be as part of a confederation with the majority Hindu provinces or as an entirely separate state would be negotiated later along with the future of the princely states. The crucial point was that there would be a new constitutional arrangement in which Muslims would have an equal share of power.

The Lahore Resolution had been vague, but as time went on, Jinnah elaborated what "Pakistan" would comprise. The key areas were Punjab and Bengal, where the majority of India's Muslims lived. These provinces were separated by over a thousand miles of land, potentially posing a huge structural problem if a new state were to be created. What Jinnah seemed to be arguing for was not separation but the autonomy of these provinces *within* an all-India configuration. Furthermore, he was clear that the territorial boundaries of these states would remain intact, that is, that Punjab and Bengal would remain *undivided*. Jinnah's concern had always been for the constitutional protection of the Muslim minority. His solution was to create Pakistan and Hindustan as sovereign states within India. Each would have its own internal minorities—Hindustan would have Muslims and Pakistan Hindus—which each would be equally bound to protect.

The Pakistan Movement, 1942–1946

The only way that Jinnah's proposal could be adopted was if there was demonstrable popular support for "Pakistan." The fundamental problem lay in the contradictory positions of Muslims in majority and minority provinces and, more precisely, the diversity of India's Muslims as a whole. A single political program was thus impossible.

So how did the Pakistan idea—conceived and discussed in small elite circles—become a mass movement? In short: by rallying around the banner of Islam. To be sure, the League had made some headway. Where Sikander Hayat Khan and Fazl ul-Haq had remained ambivalent toward the League's politics, changes in leadership in Punjab and Bengal after the former died and the latter was ousted, paved the way for greater support for Jinnah's position. With the entire Congress leadership imprisoned during the Quit India movement, an election in 1943 saw the League win in more provinces: Assam, Sind, and the North West Frontier. Moreover, the League's leadership had initiated the formation of a volunteer corps, the National Guard, to mobilize at the grass roots in Muslim communities, with volunteers playing a crucial part in relief efforts during the Bengal famine. By 1944, Jinnah and the League enjoyed much more support in the majority provinces, but there was still a long way to go and the call to religion appeared the only way to mobilize support for an idea whose constituents were divided in every other way. We know, of course, that Muslims are far from unified in the practice of their faith and profoundly opposed in many of their beliefs. Yet, the mass character of the Pakistan movement took shape around the cry of "Islam in Danger!"

This call was inflected in different ways. To peasants in Punjab and Bengal, Pakistan was presented as the end of exploitation by Hindu landlords and moneylenders. In Bengal, one member of the Muslim League promised the abolition of rent. These were slogans for the rural poor. Pakistan also held appeal for a nascent Muslim business and professional class offering to create a space free of competition from the well-established Hindu industrial houses and the stranglehold an upper-caste elite seemed to have in government employment. This appealed especially to well-heeled Muslims in Bombay and the United Provinces. The call to a separate identity was less potent in Punjab and Bengal, where a shared regional culture held sway. "Pakistan" for the middle classes in these provinces would have appeared disruptive, endangering well-established centers of trade and education such as Amritsar and Calcutta. The financial backing for the Pakistan movement came not only from landlords but from these emergent industrial classes. A Federation of Muslim Chambers of Commerce and Industry was founded in April 1945, and Muslim banks and an airline company were planned soon after the war. Partition did provide a major economic boon for these groups, insulating them from competition with the long-established Hindu-owned business houses.

Constitutional Negotiations, 1942–1946

Cripps Mission, 1942

The colonial government's arrogance in declaring that Indians would fight alongside Britain during the war engendered great resentment in India and prompted the resignation of the entire Congress leadership at the outbreak of World War II. However, as the Axis forces moved ever closer to India—Singapore, Rangoon, and the Andaman Islands fell in February and early March 1942—British leaders sought the cooperation of Indians in recruiting more troops into the British Indian army to counter Japanese imperialism in Southeast Asia and German Fascism in Europe. They sent Sir Stafford Cripps, a Labour minister, member of the cabinet and supporter of Indian independence, at the end of March 1942 to negotiate. He offered dominion status after the war with the option to leave the Commonwealth and gain full independence as well as a constituent assembly elected by the provincial legislatures. Significantly, individual provinces were offered the ability to opt out of the proposed federal structure to form a political unit autonomous of the Indian union.

Cripps's proposal died a quick death. Congress saw the provincial option as a tacit acceptance of the Pakistan principle and rejected it. The opt-out clause was also a problem for Jinnah, as it brought the contradictions of his argument to the fore. This was a proposal for the representation of provinces, not religious minorities for whom there was still no provision in the central government. For Punjab and Bengal to opt out, non-Muslims in these provinces would also have to agree not to join the federation—something which Jinnah knew was unlikely. But the support of Hindus was central to his formulation of Pakistan, as this was the only way, in Jinnah's view, for Muslims to be properly protected in the regions and at the center. Thus he joined Congress in opposing the Cripps scheme. There were a number of other obstacles to agreement, which led ultimately to Cripps returning to London in April 1942 without success. And Congress passed the Quit India resolution in August.

The Beginning of the End Game

Elections in Britain in July 1945 returned a Labour government to power with Clement Atlee replacing Churchill as prime minister. Atlee was more sympathetic to Indian self-rule than his Conservative counterpart had been. Labour's priority was to create housing and jobs for postwar Britain rather than reassert its imperial presence in the face of widespread opposition throughout Indian society. Moreover, there were also a large number of educated men working as politicians or in the civil administration who had begun to look ahead to national self-government. Provincial elections in India in 1946 resulted in Congress winning massively in non-Muslim ministries (91 percent of the non-Muslim vote) and forming majority governments in all provinces barring Bengal, Punjab, and Sind. The Muslim League made dramatic gains in Muslim areas. As compared with its poor showing in 1937, it won all thirty seats reserved for Muslims at the center and 75 percent of Muslim votes polled. By this point, Britain had lost both the will and the ability to continue its rule. Archibald Wavell (Linlithgow's successor) understood that his role was now to oversee a transfer of power.

Jinnah argued that the League's success in the elections demonstrated that it was now the legitimate voice of India's Muslims. At one level he was right. Despite a limited franchise, those who were eligible to vote did. And they voted for a Pakistan that fused the secular idea of a nation with the sacred ideal of spiritual purity, a land that was Dar al-Islam. On the other hand, the political campaign appealed to the emotions—there was still no clarity on exactly what "Pakistan" would look like or where its boundaries would lie. Furthermore, while the League won big in terms of numbers, it had done so in coalition with local leaders: it had little by way of organizational infrastructure at the grass roots. In Punjab in particular—the cornerstone of Pakistan—there was no League presence. Rather, a coalition of congressmen, Punjab Unionists, and Sikhs held sway, and a simmering communal tension threatened to blow Jinnah's hopes for an undivided province apart.

Cabinet Mission Plan, 1946

In the face of League-Congress intransigence, three cabinet ministers were sent to India between March and June 1946 to work out a solution. The Cabinet Mission Plan proposed a three-tiered federation. The second tier—the most significant innovation of the plan—involved a compulsory grouping of provinces. Two of these would be the Muslim-majority provinces in the northwest and the northeast and the third would be the Hindu-majority provinces of central and southern India, each with its own legislature. The first tier would comprise a weak center, responsible for defense, foreign affairs, and currency. This scheme sought to preserve a united India while accommodating the core idea of Jinnah's Pakistan. And indeed, the grouping of provinces came closest to Jinnah's aspirations, avoiding the partition of Punjab and Bengal and retaining a measure of power for their regional leaders. Jinnah had unequivocally rejected the liberal democratic formulation of governance that projected the idea of "minority" and "majority" populations onto the social landscape of South Asia. He consistently argued for parity between Pakistan and Hindustan, saying that these were separate but equal communities. The League agreed to the Cabinet Mission Plan, and it was then for Congress to do the same.

However, Congress plans for the rapid industrial and social development of the postindependence state involved clear direction dispensed from a strong center at the all-India level; provinces pursuing their own agendas would pull in different directions. In a speech in July 1946, Jawaharlal Nehru dismissed the compulsory grouping, saying that provinces should be free to join either group or none at all. He took a "we'll see" approach, deferring agreement on the final formulation until after independence. Without any guarantee that the provincial arrangement would stick, Jinnah pulled out of the deal, and with this any hope of a united India disappeared.[70]

Constituent Assembly, 1946–1950

The Cabinet Mission proposed that an interim government be formed until a constitution was in place. Representatives would be chosen on the basis of the provincial legislative assemblies elected in 1946; each province would be allotted seats in proportion to their population, approximately 1 to 1 million. Communities would also be represented in proportion to their population and would be elected by members of that community in the legislative assembly. Despite their rejection of the Cabinet Mission Plan, the League joined the interim government. When it was announced that a constituent assembly would be formed in December 1946, the

League was warned that it could join only if it accepted the long-term plan. Congress had thrown out the compulsory grouping of provinces and the League had rejected anything other than that. The government of India pushed forward with the meetings of the constituent assembly, which was convened in the absence of the League.[71]

Communal Violence

In a desperate bid to achieve a Pakistan with its own sovereign center, Jinnah called for a campaign of "direct action" on August 16, 1946. Widespread nationalist fervor—for Pakistan as well as India—combined with huge uncertainty to produce the terrible communal violence that foreshadowed independence. The Great Calcutta Killing began on Direct Action Day and continued until August 20. Around four thousand were killed and ten thousand injured by mobs in the city. This was followed in October by around seven thousand Muslims murdered in Bihar and a smaller number of Hindus killed in the district of Noakhali in east Bengal. Both Wavell and Sardar Patel noted that the larger proportion of those who died were Muslims. The violence spread across the United Provinces in early 1947 and into Punjab, which witnessed some of the worst atrocities. This was a truly bleak moment in the history of modern South Asia where the darkest sides of humanity came to the fore. Murder and rape seemed to be the objectives of this violence, not, as had been seen in previous communal conflict, the desecration of sacred places. Nothing seemed to be able to stem the violence until Mahatma Gandhi, in his finest hour, stepped forward.

The Mahatma had remained aloof from the constitutional wrangling and was increasingly alienated from Congress, unhappy with what he saw as a self-interested vying for power between the different parties. He had total disdain for all conventional forms of political power and a passionate anti-communalism which made him say to a League leader "I want to fight it out with my life. I would not allow the Muslims to crawl on the streets in India. They must walk with self-respect." On hearing of the violence, at the age of seventy-seven, Gandhi made his way to Noakhali, then Bihar, then to the slums of Calcutta and Delhi. From January 1947, he walked barefoot through burning, riot-torn villages, singing a hymn by Rabindranath Tagore: "If there is none to heed your call, walk alone, walk alone." He called on Muslims and Hindus to put down their arms and went on a fast unto death for communal brotherhood. This act of pure sacrifice seemed to touch a chord as a semblance of peace descended upon Calcutta on the eve of independence.

Punjab was not so fortunate. There, the communal equation was not simply between Hindus and Muslims but also involved Sikhs who formed a significant political and religious minority, numerically 13 percent of the population. Sikhs had settled largely in Punjab's central districts, around Lahore and Amritsar. They were adamantly opposed to a partition, for in such an event, the boundary line would be drawn through the heart of their community splitting it in two, greatly diminishing their influence in the province. Moreover, they were deeply suspicious of Muslims, thus remaining in Pakistan if it was created was not an option. In March 1947, the Unionist party, although whittled down, was still in office in alliance with Congress and Akali Sikhs. As Jinnah campaigned to bring down the government in favor of the League, a communal holocaust ensued. The violence created enormous insecurity, leaving people with the sense that their physical safety would only be guaranteed by "their own" community. Certainly, neighbors of different religious backgrounds protected each other. But the fear of being attacked was overwhelming. This fear went a great distance to consolidating a sense of communal difference among people whose cultures and histories were so intertwined.[72]

Independence and Partition, 1947

Fearing communal violence would become civil war, Britain's main priority was to quit India as quickly as possible. Peasant rebellions were being reported in southern and eastern India at the same time. In February 1947 Clement Atlee announced that the British would depart India on June 30, 1948, with Lord Mountbatten, as the last viceroy, to oversee the transfer of power. The Hindu Mahasabha demanded the partition of Punjab and Bengal and was supported by the Congress high command. Mountbatten moved the date of departure forward to August 15, 1947, even as he was still deciding whether to devolve power to two or more states and where their boundaries would lie. Unwilling to tie their fate to Punjab, Bengali Muslims put forward a plan for a united Bengal that would remain independent of India and Pakistan, while Nehru proposed power should be transferred on the basis of the 1935 Government of India Act to two dominions within the Commonwealth. Research has shown that the "united Bengal" plan disappeared when the Congress in Bengal supported partition—something their predecessors had wholeheartedly opposed in 1905—if it guaranteed control over the western part including Calcutta. Without the port city of Calcutta, an independent province in the east was not considered economically viable.

Under enormous pressure to finalize a solution, Mountbatten told Jinnah to accept the partition of Punjab and Bengal or lose everything. And so he did, in defeat rather than victory, agree to the "mutilated and moth-eaten" Pakistan he had rejected just three years earlier, a nation made up of two half provinces separated by a thousand miles of Indian territory. And so too did Nehru, along with the other congressmen, reluctantly raise their hands in June 1947, to vote for partition. Jinnah was warned that now the Muslim majority provinces had become Pakistan, he should not attempt to try to secure any further provisions for Muslims remaining within India: this was a final settlement. At midnight on 15 August 1947 Nehru made his famous "tryst with destiny" speech in the constituent assembly. And Pakistan became, for Congress and later within Indian nationalist ideology, a secessionist state breaking away from the Indian union rather than the culmination of arguments and ideals about how the Muslims of India would be represented after the end of colonial rule.[73]

Crossing Borders

Communal violence continued as people crossed into their new homelands. It is estimated that somewhere between one and two million people lost their lives during this time. Partition also brought about one of the largest transfers of population in modern history. Over twelve million people migrated across frontiers still undefined. They went by foot and by bullock cart in endless streams, to be housed in makeshift refugee camps on either side of the borders. In late 1947, in a period of a few months, five million Hindus and Sikhs crossed from west Punjab into India and five and a half million Muslims went in the other direction. Indian Punjab was now 60 percent Hindu and 35 percent Sikh, and Pakistan Punjab was almost entirely Muslim. Migrations on the eastern side were more protracted, less violent and left a sizeable Hindu minority (about 23 percent) within East Pakistan.

Strikingly, many accounts reveal that those who left their homes did not see these departures as permanent. Rather, these were supposed to be temporary measures until the insecurity passed. Property was left in the care of neighbors and often some family members remained behind. But there was no returning. Families were torn apart, many of whom would not meet each other again for several decades, if at all. Agreements between India and Pakistan to hold evacuee property in Bengal in trust until owners returned never came to pass. Muslims were unable to reclaim their homes, finding them occupied usually by Hindu refugees from east Bengal. Most felt they had no choice but to make their way back to Pakistan. The new Indian and Pakistani governments moved quickly to resettle refugees. Hindus and Sikhs arriving in Delhi were compensated for their loss of property and housed. However, Muslims and Hindus on the "wrong" side of the border continued to be viewed with extreme suspicion.

One disturbing aspect of this time was the abduction of women. Between forty and fifty thousand women were taken as part of the spoils of war rather than murdered. Some were sold, others raped and abandoned, and yet others married to their abductors. Soon after 1947 the two governments began a policy of forcibly repatriating women to the nations where they were seen to "belong." The power of communal logic was overwhelming: if families could not be found, Muslim women were sent to Pakistan, Hindu and Sikh women to India. The act of returning was complex. Some women were welcomed by their families, but others were rejected by fathers and brothers who saw them as having lost their honor. Sometimes women themselves were filled with shame and were reluctant to return. Others had settled into new homes with new families and did not want to lose everything again. It was only in 1954 that forcible repatriation was abandoned as a policy of the state.[74]

National Histories

The emergence of India and Pakistan produced, to use David Ludden's term, new geographies of belonging. Almost one-third of all Indians in 1946 had become Pakistanis in 1948. In 1946, one in five Indians—100 million people—was Muslim. Of these, about 60 million would live in Pakistan, East and West, making it the largest Muslim state in the world. At the same time, nearly 40 million Muslims remained in India making them the largest group of Muslims in a non-Muslim state.

This notion that religious community characterized the people of South Asia recalibrated the ways in which national histories were written. Before 1947 "India" referred to a geographical entity as well as a region of shared culture and history. After partition, national histories obscured these common pasts. Jinnah, once hailed as the "Ambassador of Hindu-Muslim unity," was the founder of Pakistan and came to be represented in India as anti-Indian. The things that had divided Muslims before Pakistan—region, language, politics, culture, sect, caste, and so on—continued to do so after its creation. Jinnah had used religion as a mobilizing and unifying ideal, never really defining what Pakistan meant. But nationalist propaganda on both sides of the border politicized the meaning of partition, giving India and Pakistan identities defined, in part, from the experience of separation. In Pakistan, whatever his intentions, Jinnah is heralded as the savior of South Asia's Muslims and the man who gave concrete expression to the vision of an Islamic state. Partition is thus seen as the ultimate victory. In India, on the other hand, the commonsense understanding of Pakistan, as well as its representation in a range of media publications is as the expression of narrow-minded communalism:

the product of a secessionist, regressive, and fundamentally illegitimate movement.

Yet, despite the trauma suffered in the process in which India and Pakistan achieved independence, there were also elation, excitement, and celebrations. Together with Sri Lanka, three nations were born mid-century, and a great sense of possibility heralded a new dawn.

NOTES

1. Sudipta Sen, *Empire of Free Trade: East India Company and the Making of the Colonial Marketplace* (Philadelphia: University of Pennsylvania Press, 1998); Sinnappah Arasaratnam, *Ceylon and the Dutch, 1600–1800: External Influences and Internal Change in Early Modern Sri Lanka* (Brookfield, VT: Variorum, 1996); Lakshmi Subramanian, *Indigenous Capital and Imperial Expansion: Bombay, Surat and the West Coast* (New Delhi: Oxford University Press, 1996); Om Prakash, *The Dutch East India Company and the Economy of Bengal, 1630–1720* (Delhi: Oxford University Press, 1988); Ashin Dasgupta and M. N. Pearson (eds.), *India and the Indian Ocean, 1500–1800* (Calcutta: Oxford University Press, 1987); M. N. Pearson, *The Portuguese in India*, The New Cambridge History of India (Cambridge: Cambridge University Press, 1987); Sanjay Subrahmanyam, *Improvising Empire: Portuguese Trade and Settlement in the Bay of Bengal, 1500–1700* (Delhi: Oxford University Press, 1987); Blair B. Kling and M. N. Pearson, *An Age of Partnership: Europeans in Asia before Dominion* (Honolulu: University of Hawai'i Press, 1979); K. N. Chaudhuri, *The Trading World of Asia and the English East India Company, 1660–1760* (Cambridge: Cambridge University Press, 1978); P. E. Pieris, *Ceylon and the Portuguese, 1505–1658* (Tellippalai, Ceylon: American Mission Press, 1920).

2. Catherine Asher and Cynthia Talbot, *India before Europe* (Cambridge: Cambridge University Press, 2006); John F. Richards, *The Mughal Empire*, The New Cambridge History of India (Cambridge: Cambridge University Press, 1996); C. A. Bayly, *Indian Society and the Making of the British Empire*, The New Cambridge History of India (Cambridge: Cambridge University Press, 1988); Muzaffar Alam, *The Crisis of Empire in Mughal North India: Awadh and the Punjab, 1707–1748* (Delhi: Oxford University Press, 1986).

3. Michael Fisher (ed.), *The Politics of British Annexation in India, 1757–1857*, Themes in Indian History series (Delhi: Oxford University Press, 1993); P. J. Marshall, *Bengal: The British Bridgehead: Eastern India, 1740–1828*, The New Cambridge History of India (Cambridge: Cambridge University Press, 1988).

4. Stewart Gordon, *Marathas, Marauders and State Formation in Eighteenth Century India* (Delhi: Oxford University Press, 1994); J. S. Grewal, *The Sikhs in the Punjab*, The New Cambridge History of India (Cambridge: Cambridge University Press, 1990); Hasan Mohibbul, *History of Tipu Sultan* (Calcutta: World Press, 1971).

5. John Whelpton, *A History of Nepal* (Cambridge: Cambridge University Press, 2005).

6. Patrick Peebles, *A History of Sri Lanka* (Westport, CT: Greenwood Press, 2006); Chandra R. De Silva, *Sri Lanka: A History* (Delhi: Vikas, 1997) and his *Ceylon under the British Occupation, 1795–1833* (Navrang: Lake House, 1996).

7. Richard Barnett, *North India between Empires: Awadh, the Mughals and the British, 1720–1801* (Berkeley: University of California Press, 1980).

8. Jon Wilson, *The Domination of Strangers: Modern Governance in Eastern India, 1780–1835* (Basingstoke, UK: Palgrave Macmillan, 2008); Robert Travers, *Ideology and Empire in Eighteenth-Century India: The British in Bengal* (Cambridge: Cambridge University Press, 2007); Nicholas Dirks, *The Scandal of Empire: India and the Creation of Imperial Britain* (Cambridge, MA: Harvard University Press, 2006); Durba Ghosh, *Sex and the Family in Colonial India* (Cambridge: Cambridge University Press, 2006); Radhika Singha, *A Despotism of Law: Crime and Justice in Early Colonial India* (Delhi: Oxford University Press, 1998); Neeladri Bhattacharya, "Remaking Custom: The Discourse and Practice of Colonial Codification," in R. Champakalakshmi and S. Gopal (eds.), *Tradition, Dissent and Ideology: Essays in Honour of Romila Thapar* (Delhi: Oxford University Press, 1996); Bernard Cohn, "Law and the Colonial State in India," in B. Cohn, ed., *Colonialism and Its Forms of Knowledge: The British in India* (Princeton, NJ: Princeton University Press, 1996); Thomas Metcalf, *Ideologies of the Raj*, The New Cambridge History of India (Cambridge: Cambridge University Press, 1994); David Washbrook, "Law, State and Agrarian Society in Colonial India," *Modern Asian Studies* 15, no. 3 (1981): 649–721.

9. John D. Rogers, "Early British Rule and Social Classification in Sri Lanka," *Modern Asian Studies* 38, no. 3 (July 2004): 625–47; Nira Wickramasinghe, *Sri Lanka in the Modern Age: A History of Contested Identities* (London: Hurst, 2006); Patrick Peebles, *Social Change in Nineteenth Century Ceylon* (Delhi: Navrang, 1995); John D. Rogers, *Crime, Justice and Society in Colonial Sri Lanka* (London: Curzon, 1987); L. B. Clarence, "Application of European Law to Natives of Ceylon," *Journal of the Society of Comparative Legislation* 1 (1896–1897): 227–31.

10. Peter Robb, *Peasants, Political Economy and Law* (Delhi: Oxford University Press, 2007); Sugata Bose, *Peasant Labour and Colonial Capital: Rural Bengal since 1770*, The New Cambridge History of India (Cambridge: Cambridge University Press, 1993); Peter Robb (ed.), *Rural India: Land, Power and Society under British Rule* (Delhi: Oxford University Press, 1992); David Ludden, "World Economy and Village India, 1600–1900: Exploring the Agrarian History of Capitalism," in S. Bose and A. Jalal (eds.), *South Asia and World Capitalism* (Delhi: Oxford University Press, 1990); Burton Stein, *Thomas Munro: The Origins of the Colonial State and His Vision of Empire* (Delhi: Oxford University Press, 1989); Robert E. Frykenberg (ed.), *Land Control and Social Structure in Indian History* (Madison: University of Wisconsin Press, 1969); Ranajit Guha, *A Rule of Property for Bengal: An Essay on the Idea of Permanent Settlement* (Paris: Mouton, 1963).

11. Nile Green, *Islam and the Army in Colonial India: Sepoy Religion in the Service of Empire* (Cambridge: Cambridge University Press, 2009); Clive Dewey, *The Mind of the Indian Civil Service* (Delhi: Oxford University Press, 1996); Seema Alavi, *The Sepoys and the Company* (Delhi: Oxford University Press, 1995); Javed

Majeed, "James Mill and the History of British India and Utilitarianism as a Rhetoric of Reform," *Modern Asian Studies* 24, no. 2 (1990): 209–34; C. A. Bayly, *Rulers, Townsmen and Bazaars: North Indian Society in the Age of British Expansion, 1770–1870* (Cambridge: Cambridge University Press, 1983); B. B. Misra, *The Bureaucracy in India: An Historical Analysis of Development up to 1947* (Delhi: Oxford University Press, 1977).

12. Sanghamitra Misra, *Becoming a Borderland: Space and Identity in Colonial Northeastern India* (Delhi: Routledge, 2011); Peter Robb, "From Law to Rights: The Impact of the Colonial State on Peasant Protest in Bihar," in W. Pinch (ed.), *Speaking of Peasants: Essays on Indian History and Politics in Honor of Walter Hauser* (Delhi: Manohar, 2008); in Ajay Skaria, *Hybrid Histories: Forests, Frontiers and Wildness in Western India* (Delhi: Oxford University Press, 1999); Mahesh Rangarajan, *Fencing the Forest: Conservation and Ecological Change in India's Central Provinces, 1860–1914* (Delhi: Oxford University Press, 1996); Neeladri Bhattacharya, "Pastoralists in a Colonial World," in D. Arnold and R. Guha (eds.), *Nature, Culture, Imperialism: Essays on the Environmental History of South Asia* (Delhi: Oxford University Press, 1995).

13. William Dalrymple, *The Last Mughal: The Fall of a Dynasty, Delhi 1857* (Delhi: Penguin, 2006); David Omissi, *The Sepoy and the Raj* (Basingstoke, UK: Macmillan, 1994); Gautam Bhadra, "Four Rebels of Eighteen-Fifty-Seven," in R. Guha and G. Spivak (eds.), *Selected Subaltern Studies* (New York: Oxford University Press, 1988); Rudrangshu Mukherjee, *Awadh in Revolt: A Study of Popular Resistance* (Delhi: Oxford University Press, 1984); Ranajit Guha, *Elementary Aspects of Peasant Insurgency* (Delhi: Oxford University Press, 1983); Eric Stokes, *The Peasant Armed: The Indian Revolt of 1857*, ed. C. A. Bayly (Oxford: Clarendon, 1986); Thomas Metcalf, *The Aftermath of the Revolt: India: 1857–1870* (Princeton, NJ: Princeton University Press, 1964); V. D. Savarkar, *The Indian War of Independence, 1857* (Bombay: Phoenix, 1947, orig. pub. 1909).

14. Barbara Ramusack, *The Indian Princes and Their States* (Cambridge: Cambridge University Press, 2004); Manu Bhagavan, *Sovereign Spheres: Princes, Education and Empire in Colonial India* (Delhi: Oxford University Press, 2003); Mridu Rai, *Hindu Rulers, Muslim Subjects: Islam, Community and the History of Kashmir* (London: Hurst, 2003); Ian Copland, *The British Raj and the Indian Princes: Paramountcy in Western India, 1857–1930* (Bombay: Orient Longman, 1982).

15. Heather Streets, *Martial Races: The Military, Race and Masculinity in British Imperial Culture, 1857–1914* (Manchester, UK: Manchester University Press, 2004); Mrinalini Sinha, *Colonial Masculinity: The "Manly Englishman" and the "Effeminate Bengali" in the Late Nineteenth Century* (Manchester, UK: Manchester University Press, 1995).

16. On the economic history of this period, see J. L. A. Webb, *Tropical Pioneers: Human Agency and Ecological Change in the Highlands of Sri Lanka, 1800–1900* (Athens: Ohio University Press, 2002); Mike Davis, *Late Victorian Holocausts: El Nino Famines and the Making of the Third World* (London: Verso, 2001); Rajnarayan Chandavarkar, *The Origins of Industrial Capitalism in India: Business Strategies and the Working Classes in Bombay, 1900–1940* (Cambridge: Cambridge University Press, 1994); Tirthankar Roy, *Artisans and Industrialization: Weavers in Twentieth-Century*

India (Delhi: Oxford University Press, 1994); B. R. Tomlinson, *The Economy of Modern India, 1860–1970*, The New Cambridge History of India (Cambridge: Cambridge University Press, 1993); Sumit Guha (ed.), *Growth, Stagnation and Decline? Agricultural Productivity in British India* (Delhi: Oxford University Press, 1992); Rajat Kanta Ray, *Entrepreneurship and Industry in India, 1800–1947* (Delhi: Oxford University Press, 1992); S. Bose and A. Jalal (eds.), *South Asia and World Capitalism* (Delhi: Oxford University Press, 1990); Neil Charlesworth, *Peasants and Imperial Rule* (Cambridge: Cambridge University Press, 1985); Amiya Kumar Bagchi, *Private Investment in India: 1900–1939* (Cambridge: Cambridge University Press, 1972); Sarvepalli Gopal, *British Policy in India, 1858–1905* (Cambridge: Cambridge University Press, 1965).

17. Laura Bear, *Lines of the Nation: Indian Railway Workers, Bureaucracy and the Intimate Historical Self* (New York: Columbia University Press, 2007); Ian Kerr, *Building the Railways of the Raj, 1850–1900* (Delhi: Oxford University Press, 1995).

18. David Gilmartin, "Scientific Empire and Imperial Science: Colonialism and Irrigation Technology in the Indus Basin," *Journal of Asian Studies* 15, no. 4 (1994): 1127–49; Elizabeth Whitcombe, "The Environmental Costs of Irrigation in British India: Waterlogging, Salinity, Malaria," in D. Arnold and R. Guha (eds.), *Nature, Culture, Imperialism: Essays on the Environmental History of South Asia* (Delhi: Oxford University Press, 1995, 237–59).

19. Deep Kanta Lahiri Choudhury, *Telegraphic Imperialism: Crisis and Panic in the Indian Empire, c. 1830–1920* (Basingstoke, UK: Palgrave Macmillan, 2010); A. K. Bagchi, D. Sinha, and B. Bagchi (eds.), *Webs of History: Information, Communication and Technology from Early to Postcolonial India* (Delhi: Indian History Congress, 2005); C. A. Bayly, *Empire and Information: Intelligence Gathering and Social Communication in India, 1780–1870* (Cambridge: Cambridge University Press, 1996).

20. David Arnold, *Science, Technology and Medicine in Colonial India* (Cambridge: Cambridge University Press, 2000); Robert Kubicek, "British Expansion, Empire and Technological Change," in A. Porter (ed.), *The Oxford History of the British Empire: The Nineteenth Century* (Oxford: Oxford University Press, 1999), 247–69; Daniel R. Headrick, *Tentacles of Progress: Technology Transfer in the Age of Imperialism, 1850–1940* (New York: Oxford University Press, 1988).

21. Clare Anderson, *Subaltern Lives: Biographies of Colonialism in the Indian Ocean World: 1790–1920* (Cambridge: Cambridge University Press, 2012); N. Jayaram and Yogesh Atal (eds.), *The Indian Diaspora: Dynamics of Migration* (New Delhi: Sage Publications, 2004); Patrick Peebles, *Plantation Tamils of Ceylon* (London: Leicester University Press, 2002); Crispin Bates, "Tribal Migration in India and Beyond," in Gyan Prakash (ed.), *The World of the Rural Labourer in Colonial India* (Delhi: Oxford University Press, 1992); N. Shanmugaratnam, "Impact of Plantation Economy and Colonial Policy on Sri Lanka Peasantry," *Economic and Political Weekly* 16, no. 3 (January 17, 1981): 69–71, 73–80; Haraprasad Chattopadyaya, *Indians in Sri Lanka: A Historical Study* (Calcutta: O.P.S. Publ., 1979).

22. Anne Hardgrove, *Community and Public Culture: The Marwaris of Calcutta* (Delhi: Oxford University Press, 2004); Asiya Siddiqi, "The Business World of Jamsetjee Jejeebhoy," in A. Siddiqi (ed.), *Trade and Finance in Colonial India,*

1750–1860 (Delhi: Oxford University Press, 1995); D. Tripathi (ed.), *Business Communities of India: A Historical Perspective* (Delhi: Oxford University Press, 1984); Thomas Timberg, *The Marwaris: From Traders to Industrialists* (Delhi: Vikas, 1978).

23. Ian Barrow, *Surveying and Mapping in Colonial Sri Lanka, 1800–1900* (Delhi: Oxford University Press, 2008); Ian Barrow, *Making History, Drawing Territory: British Mapping in India, 1756–1905* (Delhi: Oxford University Press, 2003); Matthew Edney, *Mapping an Empire: The Geographical Construction of British India, 1765–1843* (Chicago: Chicago University Press, 1997.

24. See James Mill, *The History of British India* (London: James Madden, 1858); Javed Majeed, *Ungoverned Imaginings: James Mill's "History of British India" and Orientalism* (Oxford: Clarendon, 1992).

25. Ishita Bannerjee-Dube (ed.), *Caste in History* (Delhi: Oxford University Press, 2007); John Rogers, "Caste as a Social Category and Identity in Colonial Lanka," *Indian Economic and Social History Review* 61, no. 1 (2004); Nicholas B. Dirks, *Castes of Mind: Colonialism and the Making of Modern India* (Princeton, NJ: Princeton University Press, 2001); Susan Bayly, "Caste and 'Race' in the Colonial Ethnography of India," in P. Robb (ed.), *The Concept of Race in South Asia* (Delhi: Oxford University Press, 1997); Arjun Appadurai, "Number in the Colonial Imagination," and David Ludden, "Orientalist Empiricism: Transformations in Colonial Knowledge," in C. Breckenridge and P. Van der Veer (eds.), *Orientalism and the Postcolonial Predicament: Perspectives on South Asia* (Philadelphia: University of Pennsylvania Press, 1993); Bernard Cohn, "The Census, Social Structure and Objectification in South Asia," in B. Cohn (ed.), *An Anthropologist among the Historians and Other Essays* (Delhi: Oxford University Press, 1990); N. G. Barrier (ed.), *The Census in British India: New Perspectives* (Delhi: Manohar, 1981); André Beteille, "Homo-Hierarchicus, Homo-Equalis," *Modern Asian Studies* 13 (October 1979): 529–48.

26. See Sara Ansari, *Sufi, Saints and State Power: The Pirs of Sind, 1843–1947* (Cambridge: Cambridge University Press, 1992); Bernard Cohn, "Representing Authority in Victorian India," in E. Hobsbawm and T. Ranger (eds.), *The Invention of Tradition* (Cambridge: Cambridge University Press, 1983).

27. Ranajit Guha, *Dominance without Hegemony: History and Power in Colonial India* (Cambridge, MA: Harvard University Press, 1997).

28. Avril A. Powell, *Scottish Orientalists and India: The Muir Brothers, Religion, Education and Empire* (Woodbridge, UK: Boydell, 2010) and her *Muslims and Missionaries in Pre-Mutiny India* (Richmond, UK: Curzon, 1993); S. N. Mukherjee, *Sir William Jones: A Study in 18th-Century British Attitudes to India* (Cambridge: Cambridge University Press, 1968); K. Jones (ed.), *Religious Controversy in British India: Dialogues in South Asian Languages* (Albany: State University of New York Press, 1992); Eric Stokes, *The English Utilitarians and India* (Delhi: Oxford University Press, 1959).

29. Rosalind O'Hanlon, *Caste, Conflict and Ideology: Mahatma Jotirao Phule and Low-Caste Protest in Nineteenth-Century Western India* (Cambridge: Cambridge University Press, 1985).

30. Sanjay Seth, *Subject Lessons: The Western Education of Colonial India* (Durham, NC: Duke University Press, 2007); Sumit Sarkar, "The City Imagined: Calcutta of the Nineteenth and Early Twentieth Centuries," in *Writing Social History* (Delhi:

Oxford University Press, 1997); Partha Chatterjee, *The Nation and Its Fragments: Colonial and Postcolonial Histories* (Princeton, NJ: Princeton University Press, 1994), ch. 3; Gauri Viswanathan, *Masks of Conquest: Literary Studies and British Rule in India* (London: Faber, 1990); M. W. Roberts: *Caste Conflict and Elite Formation: The Rise of a Karava Elite in Sri Lanka, 1500–1931* (Cambridge: Cambridge University Press, 1982); David Washbrook, *The Emergence of Provincial Politics: The Madras Presidency, 1870–1920* (Cambridge: Cambridge University Press, 1976); C. A. Bayly, *The Local Roots of Indian Politics: Allahabad, 1880–1920* (Oxford: Clarendon, 1975); E. Leach and S. N. Mukherjee (eds.), *Elites in South Asia* (Cambridge: Cambridge University Press, 1970); R. J. Moore, *Liberalism and Indian Politics, 1872–1922* (London: Edward Arnold, 1966).

31. Amiya Sen (ed.), *Social and Religious Reform: The Hindus of British India* (Delhi: Oxford University Press, 2003); Kenneth Jones, *Socio-Religious Reform Movements in British India* (Cambridge: Cambridge University Press, 1989); Stephen Hay (ed.), *Sources of Indian Tradition*, vol. 2 (New York: Columbia University Press, 1992). Both Jones and Hay provide excellent summaries of a range of reform movements in the nineteenth and twentieth centuries. David Kopf, *The Brahmo Samaj and the Shaping of the Modern Indian Mind* (Princeton, NJ: Princeton University Press, 1979). On Sikh reform movements, see W. H. Mcleod, *Essays in Sikh History, Tradition and Society* (Delhi: Oxford University Press, 2007); Tony Ballantyne, *Between Colonialism and Diaspora: Sikh Cultural Formations in an Imperial World* (Durham, NC: Duke University Press, 2006).

32. Andrew Nicholson, *Unifying Hinduism: Philosophy and Identity in Indian Intellectual History* (New York: Columbia University Press, 2010); Shamita Basu, *Religious Revivalism as Nationalist Discourse: Swami Vivekananda and New Hinduism in Nineteenth-Century Bengal* (Delhi: Oxford University Press, 2002).

33. Kenneth Jones, *Arya Dharm: Hindu Consciousness in Nineteenth Century Punjab* (Berkeley: University of California Press, 1976).

34. S. Sarkar and T. Sarkar (eds.), *Women and Social Reform in Modern India*, vols. 1 and 2 (Delhi: Oxford University Press, 2007); Geraldine Forbes, *Women in Modern India* (Cambridge: Cambridge University Press, 1996); Uma Chakravarti, "Whatever Happened to the Vedic Dasi? Orientalism, Nationalism and a Script for the Past," Partha Chatterjee, "The Nationalist Resolution of the Women's Question," and Lata Mani, "Contentious Traditions: The Debate on *Sati* in Colonial India," in K. Sangari and S. Vaid (eds.), *Recasting Women: Essays in Indian Colonial History* (Delhi: Kali for Women, 1989).

35. Anne Blackburn, *Locations of Buddhism: Colonialism and Modernity in Sri Lanka* (Chicago: Chicago University Press, 2010); R. F. Young and G. P. V. Somaratna, *Vain Debates: The Buddhist-Christian Controversies of Nineteenth-Century Ceylon* (Vienna: Institute for Indology for the University of Vienna, 1996); Richard Gombrich and Gananath Obeyesekere, *Buddhism Transformed: Religious Change in Sri Lanka* (Delhi: Motilal Banarsidass, 1990); G. D. Bond, *The Buddhist Revival in Sri Lanka Religious Tradition: Reinterpretation and Response* (Columbia: University of South Carolina Press, 1988).

36. Ayesha Jalal, *Partisans of Allah: Jihad in South Asia* (Cambridge, MA: Harvard University Press, 2008); S. I. Habib, "Reconciling Science with Islam in 19th-Century India," *Contributions to Indian Sociology* 34, no. 1 (2000): 63–92; Ayesha

Jalal, *Self and Sovereignty: Individual and Community in South Asian Islam since 1850* (London: Routledge, 2000); Jones, *Socio-Religious Reform Movements*; David Lelyveld, *Aligarh's First Generation: Muslim Solidarity in British India* (Princeton, NJ: Princeton University Press, 1977); Peter Hardy, *The Muslims of British India* (Cambridge: Cambridge University Press, 1972). On women's social reform see Gail Minault, *Secluded Scholars: Women's Education and Muslim Social Reform in Colonial India* (Delhi: Oxford University Press, 1998); Rokeya Sakhawat Hossein, *Sultana's Dream and Selections from "The Secluded Ones,"* ed. and trans. Roushan Jahan (New York: Feminist Press, 1988).

37. Barbara Daly Metcalf, *Islamic Revival in British India: Deoband, 1860–1900* (Princeton, NJ: Princeton University Press, 1982).

38. Masao Naito, "Anti-Untouchability Ideologies and Movements in Maharashtra from the Late Nineteenth Century to the 1930s," in H. Kotani (ed.), *Caste System, Untouchability and the Depressed* (Delhi: Manohar, 1997); O'Hanlon, *Caste, Conflict and Ideology*; Gail Omvedt, *Cultural Revolt in a Colonial Society: The Non-Brahman Movement in Western India, 1873–1930* (Bombay: Scientific Socialist Education Trust, 1976). On non-Brahman movements in south India, see V. Geetha and S. V. Rajadurai, *Towards a Non-Brahmin Millennium: From Iyothee Thass to Periyar* (Calcutta: Samya, 1998).

39. Tithi Bhattacharya, "A World of Learning: The Material Culture of Education and Class in Nineteenth-Century Bengal," in C. Bates (ed.), *Beyond Representation: Colonial and Postcolonial Constructions of Indian Identity* (Delhi: Oxford University Press, 2006); Riho Isaka, "Gujarati Elites and the Construction of a Regional Identity in the Late Nineteenth Century," in Bates, *Beyond Representation*; Veena Naregal, *Language Politics, Elites and the Public Sphere: Western India under Colonialism* (London: Anthem Press, 2002); J. C. Masselos, *Towards Nationalism: Group Affiliations and the Politics of Public Associations in Nineteenth-Century Western India* (Bombay: Popular Prakashan, 1974); Christine Dobbin, *Urban Leadership in Western India: Politics and Communities in Bombay City* (Oxford: Oxford University Press, 1972).

40. Romesh Chunder Dutt, *The Economic History of India, vol. 2: In the Victorian Age* (New York: A. M. Kelley, 1904, 1969); Dadabhai Naoroji, *Poverty and Un-British Rule in India* (Delhi: Publications Division, Government of India, 1901, 1962).

41. Peebles, *History of Sri Lanka*, ch.7; Wickramasinghe, *Sri Lanka in the Modern Age*, ch. 4; and Nira Wickramasinghe, *Ethnic Politics in Colonial Sri Lanka, 1927–1947* (Delhi: Vikas, 1995).

42. Sanjay Joshi, *Fractured Modernity: The Making of a Middle Class in Colonial North India* (Delhi: Oxford University Press, 2001); M. Tori, "'Westernized Middle Class': Intellectuals and Society in Late Colonial India," in J. L. Hill (ed.), *The Congress and Indian Nationalism: Historical Perspectives* (London: Curzon, 1991); John McLane, *Indian Nationalism and the Early Congress* (Princeton, NJ: Princeton University Press, 1977; Richard Cashman, *Myth of the Lokamanya: Tilak and Mass Politics in Maharashtra* (Berkeley: University of California Press, 1974); J. Gallagher, G. Johnson, and A. Seal (eds.), *Locality, Province, Nation: Essays on Indian Politics, 1870–1940* (Cambridge: Cambridge University Press, 1973); Stanley Wolpert, *Tilak*

and Gokhale: Revolution and Reform in the Making of Modern India (Berkeley: University of California Press, 1962).

43. Sanjay Joshi (ed.), *The Middle Class in Colonial India* (Delhi: Oxford University Press, 2010).

44. Partha Chatterjee, "Our Modernity," in *The Present History of West Bengal: Essays in Political Criticism* (Delhi: Oxford University Press, 1997).

45. Shabnum Tejani, *Indian Secularism: A Social and Intellectual History, 1890–1960* (Delhi: Permanent Black, 2007), ch. 2; C. A. Bayly, *Origins of Nationality in South Asia: Patriotism and Ethical Government in the Making of Modern India* (Delhi: Oxford University Press, 1998), chs. 4 and 6; Aurobindo Ghose (Sri Aurobindo), *Bande Mataram, Early Political Writings* (Pondicherry: Sri Aurobindo Ashram, 1995); Sumit Sarkar, *The Swadeshi Movement in Bengal, 1903–1908* (Delhi: Oxford University Press, 1983); J. H. Broomfield, *Elite Conflict in a Plural Society: Twentieth Century Bengal* (Berkeley: University of California Press, 1968); Bipin Chandra Pal, *Swadeshi and Swaraj: The Rise of the New Patriotism* (Calcutta: Yugayatri Prakashak, 1954); Aurobindo Ghose, *The Doctrine of Passive Resistance* (Calcutta: Arya Publishing House, 1948); Lala Lajpat Rai, *Unhappy India: Being a Reply to Miss Katherine Mayo's "Mother India"* (Calcutta: Banna Pub. Co., 1928); Bipin Chandra Pal, *The Soul of India: A Constructive Study of Indian Thoughts and Ideals* (Calcutta: Choudhury & Choudhury, 1911); Bal Gangadhar Tilak, *The Arctic Home in the Vedas* (Poona: n.p., 1903).

46. Vinayak Chaturvedi, *Peasant Pasts: History and Memory in Western India* (Berkeley: University of California Press, 2007); David Hardiman (ed.), *Peasant Resistance in India, 1858–1914* (Delhi: Oxford University Press, 1992); Sumit Sarkar, *Modern India, 1885–1947* (Delhi: Macmillan, 1983), ch. 4; Sumit Sarkar, "The Conditions and Nature of Subaltern Militancy: Bengal from Swadeshi to Non-cooperation, c. 1905–22," in R. Guha (ed.), *Subaltern Studies III* (Delhi: Oxford University Press, 1984); David Arnold, "Rebellious Hillmen: The Guden-Rampa Risings, 1839–1924," in R. Guha (ed.), *Subaltern Studies I* (Delhi: Oxford University Press, 1982).

47. Cashman, *Myth of the Lokamanya*; H. F. Owen, "Towards Nationwide Agitation," in D. A. Low (ed.), *Soundings in Modern South Asian History* (London: Weidenfeld & Nicholson, 1968).

48. M. K. Gandhi, *An Autobiography: The Story of My Experiments with Truth* (London: Penguin, 2007); David Hardiman, *Gandhi in His Time and Ours: The Global Legacy of His Ideas* (London: Hurst, 2003); David Arnold, *Gandhi* (New York: Longman, 2001); M. K. Gandhi, *Hind Swaraj and Other Writings*, A. Parel (ed.) (Cambridge: Cambridge University Press, 1997); Jacques Pouchepadass, *Champaran and Gandhi: Planters, Peasants and Gandhian Politics* (Delhi: Oxford University Press, 1999); Judith Brown, *Gandhi's Rise to Power: Indian Politics, 1915–1922* (Cambridge: Cambridge University Press, 1972).

49. M. Naeem Qureshi, *Pan-Islamism in Indian Politics: A Study of the Khilafat Movement, 1918–1924* (Leiden, Netherlands: Brill, 1999); Mushirul Hasan, *Nationalism and Communal Politics in India, 1885–1930* (Delhi: Manohar, 1991); Gail Minault, *The Khilafat Movement: Religious Symbolism and Political Mobilization in India* (New York: Columbia University Press, 1982); M. Hasan (ed.), *Communal*

and Pan-Islamic Trends in Colonial India (Delhi: Manohar, 1981); R. Kumar (ed.), *Essays in Gandhian Politics: The Rowlatt Satyagraha of 1919* (Oxford: Clarendon, 1971).

50. Shahid Amin, "Gandhi as Mahatma: Gorakhpur District, Eastern UP, 1921–2," in Guha (ed.), *Subaltern Studies III*; Rajat K. Ray, "Masses in Politics: The Non-Cooperation Movement in Bengal," *Indian Economic and Social History Review* 11, no. 4 (1974): 343–410.

51. Chandavarkar, *Origins of Industrial Capitalism in India.*

52. Satyabrata Rai Chowdhuri, *Leftism in India, 1917–1947* (Basingstoke, UK: Palgrave Macmillan, 2007); Shashi Joshi, *Struggle for Hegemony in India, 1920–1947*, vols. 1–3 (Delhi: Sage, 1992–1994); K. Kumar (ed.), *Congress and Classes: Nationalism, Workers and Peasants* (Delhi: Manohar, 1988); B. Chandra (ed.), *The Indian Left: Critical Appraisals* (Delhi: Vikas, 1983); D. N. Dhanagare, *Peasant Movements in India, 1920–1950* (Delhi: Oxford University Press, 1983); K. N. Panikkar (ed.), *National and Left Movements in India* (Delhi: Vikas, 1980). On Nehru and Bose in this earlier period, see Jawaharlal Nehru, *An Autobiography* (Delhi: Oxford University Press, 1991); Subhas Chandra Bose, *An Indian Pilgrim: An Unfinished Autobiography and Collected Letters, 1897–1921* (New York: Asia Pub. House, 1965).

53. Chetan Bhatt, *Hindu Nationalism: Origins, Ideologies and Modern Myths* (Oxford: Berg, 2001); Pradeep Datta, "Dying Hindus: The Production of Hindu Communal Commonsense in Early Twentieth-Century Bengal," in B. Pati (ed.), *Issues in Modern Indian History: For Sumit Sarkar* (Mumbai: Popular Prakashan, 2000); John Zavos, *The Emergence of Hindu Nationalism in India* (Delhi: Oxford University Press, 2000); Peter van der Veer, *Religious Nationalism: Hindus and Muslims in India* (Berkeley: University of California Press, 1994); Ayesha Jalal, "Exploding Communalism: The Politics of Muslim Identity in South Asia," in S. Bose and A. Jalal (eds.), *Nationalism, Democracy and Development: State and Politics in India* (Delhi: Oxford University Press, 1997); Gyan Pandey, *The Construction of Communalism in Colonial North India* (Delhi: Oxford University Press, 1990); Sandria Freitag, *Collective Action and Community: Public Arenas and the Emergence of Communalism in North India* (Berkeley: University of California Press, 1989); C. A. Bayly, "A Pre-history of Communalism? Religious Conflict in India, 1700–1860," *Modern Asian Studies* 19 (April 1985): 177–203; Francis Robinson, *Separatism among Indian Muslims: The Politics of the United Provinces' Muslims, 1860–1923* (Cambridge: Cambridge University Press, 1974). See also V. D. Savarkar, *Hindutva, Who Is a Hindu?* (Delhi: Hindi Sahitya Sadan, 2003).

54. Ramnarayan S. Rawat, *Reconsidering Untouchability: Chamars and Dalit History in North India* (Bloomington: Indiana University Press, 2011); Anupama Rao, *The Caste Question: Dalits and the Politics of Modern India* (Berkeley: University of California Press, 2009); M. S. S. Pandian, *Brahmin and Non-Brahmin: Genealogies of the Tamil Political Present* (Delhi: Permanent Black, 2007).

55. David Hardiman, *Peasant Nationalists of Gujarat: Kheda District, 1917–1934* (Delhi: Oxford University Press, 1981); Judith Brown, *Gandhi and Civil Disobedience, 1928–1934* (Cambridge: Cambridge University Press, 1977); Sumit Sarkar, "The Logic of Gandhian Nationalism: Civil Disobedience and the Gandhi-Irwin Pact, 1930–31," *Indian Historical Review* 3, no. 1 (1976): 114–46.

56. Peter Robb, *The Government of India and Reform: Policies Towards Politics and the Constitution, 1916–1921* (Oxford: Oxford University Press, 1976).

57. S. R. Bakshi, *Simon Commission and Indian Nationalism* (Delhi: Munshiram Manoharlal, 1977); All Parties Conference, 1928, *The Nehru Report: An Anti-Separatist Manifesto* (Delhi: Michiko & Panjathan, 1975).

58. Tejani, *Indian Secularism*, ch. 3; David Page, *Prelude to Partition: The Indian Muslims and the Imperial System of Control, 1920–1932* (Delhi: Oxford University Press, 1982); M. N. Das, *India under Morley and Minto: Politics behind Revolution, Repression and Reforms* (London: Allen & Unwin, 1964).

59. M. W. Roberts (ed.), *Documents of the Ceylon National Congress and Nationalist Politics in Ceylon 1929–50*, vols. 1–4 (Colombo, Sri Lanka: Dept. of National Archives, 1977).

60. B. R. Ambedkar, "Evidence before the Southborough Committee, 1919," in *Dr. Babasaheb Ambedkar, Writings and Speeches*, vol. 1 (Bombay: Education Dept., Govt. of Maharashtra, 1979); Indian Round Table Conference, *Proceedings of Federal Structure Committee and Minorities Committee* (London, 1932).

61. Tejani, *Indian Secularism*, ch. 5; Bidyut Chakrabarty, "The Communal Award of 1932 and Its Implications in Bengal," *Modern Asian Studies* 23, no. 3 (1989): 493–523; Trilok Nath, *Politics of the Depressed Classes* (Delhi: Deputy, 1987).

62. David Washbrook, "The Rhetoric of Democracy and Development in Late Colonial India," in Bose and Jalal (eds.), *Nationalism, Democracy and Development*.

63. E. F. C. Ludowyk, *The Story of Ceylon* (London: Faber & Faber, 1967), 279.

64. Peebles, *History of Sri Lanka*, chs. 8 and 9; Wickramasinghe, *Sri Lanka in the Modern Age*, ch. 5.

65. Dietmar Rothermund, *India and the Great Depression, 1929–1939* (Delhi: Manohar, 1992); David Washbrook, "South Asia, the World System and World Capitalism," *Journal of Asian Studies* 49, no. 3 (August 1990): 479–508; Claude Markovits, *Indian Business and Nationalist Politics, 1931–1939: The Indigenous Capitalist Class and the Rise of the Congress Party* (Cambridge: Cambridge University Press, 1985); Rajat K. Ray, *Industrialization in India: Growth and Conflict in the Private Corporate Sector, 1914–1947* (Delhi: Oxford University Press, 1979); Amiya Bagchi, *Private Investment in India, 1900–39* (Cambridge: Cambridge University Press, 1969).

66. D. A. Low, *Britain and Indian Nationalism: The Imprint of Ambiguity, 1929–42* (Cambridge: Cambridge University Press, 1997); D. A. Low (ed.), *The Congress and the Raj: Facets of the Indian Struggle, 1917–47* (London: Arnold-Heinemann, 1977).

67. B. R. Tomlinson, *The Political Economy of the Raj, 1914–1947: The Economics of Decolonization in India* (London: Macmillan, 1979). On the Bengal famine, see Sugata Bose, "Starvation Amidst Plenty: The Making of Famine in Bengal, Honan and Tonkin, 1942–45," *Modern Asian Studies* 24, no. 4 (October 1990): 699–727; Amartya Sen, *Poverty and Famines: An Essay in Entitlement and Deprivation* (Oxford: Clarendon, 1981).

68. Sumit Sarkar, *Modern India, 1885–1947* (Madras: Macmillan India Press, 1983), 388.

69. Leonard Gordon, *Brothers against the Raj: A Biography of Indian Nationalists Sarat and Subhas Chandra Bose* (New York: Columbia University Press, 1990); Gyan Pandey (ed.), *Quit India: The Indian Nation in 1942* (Calcutta: Bagchi, 1988).

70. Yasmin Khan, *The Great Partition: The Making of India and Pakistan* (New Haven, CT: Yale University Press, 2007); Vazira Zamindar, *The Long Partition and the Making of Modern South Asia: Refugees, Boundaries, Histories* (New York: Columbia

University Press, 2007); David Gilmartin, "Partition, Pakistan and South Asian History: In Search of a Narrative," *Journal of Asian Studies* 57, no. 4 (November 1998): 1068–95; Joya Chatterji, *Bengal Divided: Hindu Communalism and Partition, 1932–47* (Cambridge: Cambridge University Press, 1994); Mushirul Hasan (ed.), *India's Partition: Process, Strategy and Mobilization* (New Delhi: Oxford University Press, 1993); David Gilmartin, *Empire and Islam: Punjab and the Making of Pakistan* (Berkeley: University of California Press, 1988); Ayesha Jalal, *The Sole Spokesman: Jinnah, the Muslim League and the Demand for Pakistan* (Cambridge: Cambridge University Press, 1985).

71. Rochana Bajpai, *Debating Difference: Group Rights and Liberal Democracy in India* (Oxford: Oxford University Press, 2011); Granville Austin, *The Indian Constitution: Cornerstone of a Nation* (Oxford: Clarendon, 1966).

72. Ravinder Kaur, *Since 1947: Partition Narratives among Punjabi Migrants of Delhi* (Delhi: Oxford University Press, 2007); I. Talbot and D. Singh (eds.), *Epicentre of Violence: Partition Voices and Memories from Amritsar* (Delhi: Permanent Black, 2006); Gyan Pandey, *Remembering Partition: Violence, Nationalism and History in India* (Cambridge: Cambridge University Press, 2001); Ian Talbot, *Freedom's Cry: The Popular Dimension in the Pakistan Movement and Partition Experience in North-West India* (Karachi: Oxford University Press, 1996); Dennis Dalton, *Mahatma Gandhi: Non-Violent Power in Action* (New York: Columbia University Press, 1993), ch. 5. Literature has been better able to capture the experience of partition violence. See *Memories of Madness: Stories of 1947* (Delhi: Penguin, 2002), especially stories by Saadat Hasan Manto, "Toba Tek Singh," and Khushwant Singh, "Train to Pakistan"; Amitav Ghosh, *The Shadow Lines* (London: Bloomsbury, 1988).

72. Ian Copland, *The Princes of India in the Endgame of Empire, 1917–1947* (Cambridge: Cambridge University Press, 1997); R. J. Moore, *Escape from Empire: The Attlee Government and the Indian Problem* (Oxford: Clarendon, 1983).

73. Ritu Menon and Kamla Bahsin, *Borders and Boundaries: Women in India's Partition* (Delhi: Kali for Women, 1998); V. Das (ed.), *Mirrors of Violence: Communities, Riots and Survivors in South Asia* (Delhi: Oxford University Press, 1990).

SUGGESTED READINGS

Bayly, C. A. *Indian Society and the Making of the British Empire.* Cambridge: Cambridge University Press, 1988.

Chatterjee, Partha. *The Nation and Its Fragments: Colonial and Postcolonial Histories.* Princeton, NJ: Princeton University Press, 1993.

Cohn, Bernard S. *Colonialism and Its Forms of Knowledge: The British in India.* Princeton, NJ: Princeton University Press, 1996.

Hardiman, David, *Gandhi in His Time and Ours: The Global Legacy of His Ideas.* London: Hurst, 2004.

Metcalf, B. D., and T. Metcalf. *A Concise History of Modern India.* Cambridge: Cambridge University Press, 2006.

Metcalf, Thomas. *Ideologies of the Raj.* Cambridge: Cambridge University Press, 1995.

Sangari, K., and S. Vaid (eds.). *Recasting Women: Essays in Indian Colonial History.* Delhi: Kali for Women, 1989.

Sisson, Richard, and Stanley A. Wolpert. *Congress and Indian Nationalism: The Pre-independence Phase.* Berkeley: University of California Press, 1988.

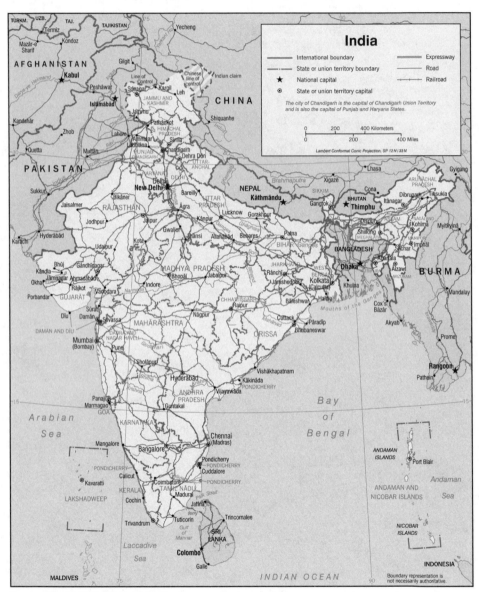

Source: **Central Intelligence Agency**

2

✤

India

Christophe Jaffrelot

POLITICAL HISTORY SINCE INDEPENDENCE

Upon achieving independence in 1947, India emerged as a federal union with a parliamentary system modeled on that of Great Britain, a state-controlled economy, and a strict policy of nonalignment. In the domain of politics, India has been "the largest democracy in the world" since 1950—except during the Emergency from 1975 to 1977—but its institutions and the party system remained dominated by elite groups until the more recent rise of the lower castes. This phenomenon reached a point of no return in the 1990s, when a major pillar of India's democracy, its secular character, came under attack because of the Hindu nationalist mobilization. The rise of the lower castes and the assertion of communal forces then affected the electoral prospects of the Congress, a broad coalition of groups that found it increasingly difficult to bring together citizens from all castes and creeds. Soon after, regional parties also developed at the expense of the former dominant party. Not only did Congress lose ground in the 1990s, but the socialist model introduced by Nehru was questioned at the same time, leading to a more liberal approach to the economy. In terms of foreign affairs, the country also distanced itself from Moscow after the demise of the Soviet Union, and turned to the United States. The post–1990 India, on which this chapter will focus, definitely marks the end of an era.

TIMELINE: INDIA

August 15, 1947	End of British rule and birth of India as a sovereign nation
1948	Mahatma Gandhi assassinated by a Hindu extremist (January 30); integration of Princely states; first war with Pakistan over Kashmir
1949	Cease-fire in Kashmir
January 26, 1950	India becomes a Sovereign Democratic Republic and the Constitution of India comes into force
1951	First five-year plan launched
1952	First general elections of the Lok Sabha; the Congress Party wins the first general elections under leadership of Jawaharlal Nehru
1956	Second five-year plan launched
1957	Second general elections; decimal coinage introduced
1962	Third general elections in India; Chinese attack on India; India loses brief war
May 4, 1964	Death of Jawaharlal Nehru
1965	Second Indo-Pak War fought over Kashmir, April–September
1966	Indira Gandhi is appointed as India's first woman prime minister at the end of a bitter leadership battle with former finance minister Morarji Desai
December 1971	Third Indo-Pak War precipitated by secession of East Pakistan with India supporting its independence efforts
July 1972	Shimla agreement signed between Prime Minister Indira Gandhi and Pakistan prime minister Zulfiqar Ali Bhutto; Line of Control (LOC) established as the de facto border (albeit not a legally recognized international boundary) between India and Pakistan
1974	India detonates first nuclear device in Pokhran, Rajasthan
1975	Indira Gandhi declares state of emergency after being found guilty of electoral malpractice
1976	India and China establish diplomatic relations
1977	Sixth general elections; Indira Gandhi's Congress Party loses elections and the Janata Party gets a majority in the Lok Sabha

1979	Morarji Desai resigns as prime minister and Charan Singh becomes prime minister; Charan Singh resigns; Sixth Lok Sabha dissolved
1980	Congress (I) comes to power; Indira Gandhi sworn in as prime minister
June 1984	Indira Gandhi launches Operation Blue Star in Punjab to flush out militants from the Golden Temple
October 31, 1984	Indira Gandhi assassinated by Sikh bodyguards; Rajiv Gandhi becomes prime minister
1987	Rajiv Gandhi sends Indian troops for peacekeeping operation in Sri Lanka's ethnic conflict
November 1989	Rajiv government loses poll and resigns
December 1989	Janata Dal leader V. P. Singh sworn in as seventh prime minister, new cabinet sworn in; ninth Lok Sabha constituted
1990	Janata Dal splits; BJP withdraws support to the government after L. K. Advani takes out Rath Yatra and is arrested; Mandal Report implementation announced by V. P. Singh
May 21, 1991	Rajiv Gandhi assassinated; P. V. Narasimha Rao becomes prime minister in June
December 6, 1992	Violence in Ayodhya due to Ram Janam Bhoomi-Babri Masjid dispute culminating in destruction of the mosque by Hindu extremists, resulting in rioting and thousands of deaths; Janata Dal coalition government falls; Parliament dissolved
1993	The infamous Bombay bomb blasts: a wave of bombings leave 300 dead in Bombay
1998	Atal Bihari Vajpayee becomes Indian prime minister; India detonates its second nuclear device (Pokhran II)
1999	"Operation Vijay" launched by the Indian Army to flush out Pakistani infiltrators inside Line of Control in the Kargil sector of Jammu and Kashmir
2001	Failed "Agra Summit" between India and Pakistan in July 2001
2004	National Democratic Alliance (NDA) government ousted by the Congress and its allies in the General Election; Congress president Sonia Gandhi opts against becoming prime minister of India; Congress and its allies form government at the center under Prime Minister Manmohan Singh

2005	Bus services, the first in sixty years, operate between Srinagar in Indian-administered Kashmir and Muzaffarabad in Pakistan-administered Kashmir
2007	Pratibha Patil becomes first woman to be elected president of India (July)
November 2008	Nearly 200 people are killed and hundreds injured in a series of coordinated attacks by gunmen in the main tourist and business area of India's financial capital, Mumbai
July 2009	Resounding general election victory gives governing Congress-led alliance of Prime Minister Manmohan Singh an enhanced position in Parliament, only eleven seats short of an absolute majority
September 2009	Allahabad High Court rules that disputed holy site of Ayodhya should be divided between Hindus and Muslims
August 2011	Prominent social activist Anna Hazare stages twelve-day hunger strike in Delhi to protest state corruption, after government proposals to tighten up anti-graft legislation fall short of his demands
March 2012	State assembly polling in the states of Uttar Pradesh, Punjab, Goa, and Uttarakhand; Mulayam Singh's Samajwadi Party ousts Maaywati's BSP in UP and his son Akhilesh is sworn in as new chief minister. Akali Dal–BJP alliance retains Punjab and BJP and Congress win Goa and Uttarakhand, respectively; Anna Hazare holds an anti-graft rally in New Delhi again after a lull of seven months and announces resumption of his campaign; BRICS countries (Brazil, Russia, India, China, and South Africa) summit held in New Delhi

Compiled by Aditi Sinha.

The Making of a Model (1947–1991)

The Nehru Years—"The Largest World Democracy"

The "Republic, sovereign and democratic" that is the Indian Union officially came into being with the proclamation of its Constitution on

January 26, 1950. This document, largely shaped by the Dalit leader B. R. Ambedkar, built upon the British parliamentary model, which had begun to be introduced earlier under colonialism. Dominant authority was granted to the office of prime minister, whose strength derived from majority support in the Lower House of Parliament. The Lower House or Lok Sabha (the House of the People), is the ruling arm of the two-chamber Parliament, which also comprises the Rajya Sabha, or the Council of States.

India is a union of states, the importance of which was expanded by the reform of 1956 that made many regional borders coincide with linguistic areas. Henceforth, states would form linguistically homogenous entities, their idioms being recognized in the Constitution, which acknowledges fourteen official languages.

According to the Constitution, the states act only marginally as a counterbalance to the federal center, located in New Delhi, the capital of the Union, and the real counter-authority must be sought in the judiciary. The Supreme Court is endowed with a notable independence, decides on lawsuits between federal states and is the ultimate court of appeal. All issues relating to interpretations of the Constitution are decided by the Supreme Court, and the high courts (tribunals of federal states) frequently turn to the Supreme Court for arbitration. Another key element of the law is the electoral commission that oversees the voting process. In addition to these official counterbalances, the press plays an essential role and is protected by Article 19 of the Constitution. Newspapers sustain political debates, particularly around the times of elections, which occur every five years, since universal suffrage was granted in 1952.

At the end of 1951, 171 million voters, the majority of whom were illiterate, were called upon to exercise their right to vote in an unprecedented election so far as the number of voters was concerned. An ingenious plan was undertaken to surmount this obstacle: each candidate was associated with a pictographic symbol that was printed next to his or her name on the voting slip so voters could mark their selections with their fingers after pressing them onto inked stamp pads. This solution partially explains the encouraging percentage of participation (45.7 percent), which kept increasing during the era of Nehru (see box 2.1), until it peaked at 55.4 percent in 1962.

During the period following independence, the memory of partition made national unity an imperative objective. Nehru, who was prime minister from 1946 until his death in 1964, wanted to build a multicultural nation. He wanted to reassure religious minorities, who were uneasy in the shadow of the Hindu community, which made up 84.1 percent of the population in 1951. This was particularly worrying to the 9.8 percent of the population who were Muslim and had opted to stay in India rather

Box 2.1. Jawaharlal Nehru (1889–1964)

Jawaharlal Nehru was born in 1889 in Allahabad where his father, a longtime Congress Party leader, was a respected lawyer. He studied law in Cambridge and joined his father's law firm on returning to India in 1912.

He admired Mahatma Gandhi and became his "spiritual son," but his Western mannerisms made him quite different from Gandhi. President of the Congress Party in 1929, 1936, and 1946, Nehru made many personal sacrifices for independence, including spending more than nine years in prison. Often referred to as Panditji, Nehru became India's first prime minister in 1947.

Nehru favored a quasi-socialist economic system, and he set up a strong Planning Commission to direct India's economic development with centralized five-year plans. The "Licence Raj" was created to centralize the private sector: every business had to be granted the administration's authorization before increasing or diversifying production. The last pillar of Nehru's system was protectionism, with importation taxes and quotas that allowed for self-centralized development.

Although Nehru chose to keep India within the Commonwealth and retain strong relationships with Britain, he also sought to make India, the first Asian nation to achieve independence, the leader of the anticolonial struggle. Nehru admired Chinese culture as much as he hated Japanese militarism and Western imperialism. India officially recognized the People's Republic of China in January 1950 and supported its admission to the UN. In 1954 Nehru and Zhou Enlai framed the Doctrine of Five Principles (Panchashila), which allowed China to recognize its sovereignty in Tibet.

In April 1955, the Bandung Conference championed by Nehru enabled many formerly colonized countries, which refused to align with either the capitalistic West or with the Soviet Union, to become the Non-Aligned Movement. Nehru's health began to decline in 1962, attributed by many scholars to his dismay over the Sino-Indian war, given his earlier regard for China. He died on May 27, 1964. His daughter, Indira Gandhi, succeeded him as prime minister two years after his death.

than become part of Pakistan, and who therefore required reassurance. In response, however, the Hindu traditionalists in the Congress Party (Indian National Congress), led by Vallabhbhai Patel, the deputy prime minister and minister of the interior who considered the Muslim minority to be a "fifth column" that could not be trusted, aggressively pursued a policy of cultural homogenization.

The choice of national language was the principal point of friction. The most militant Hindu deputies wanted to elevate Hindi, spoken by a plurality of Indians (42 percent of the population), into the national language. The populations in the south of the country refused. In the end, Nehru insisted on a compromise: Hindi was declared the national language, but the regional use of vernacular dialects was reaffirmed, and English remained the official language for a transitory period of fifteen years, which would be extended through the 1960s.

In religious matters, the Nehru and Ambedkar option also prevailed. India is "secular," meaning that the state recognizes all religions. Furthermore, Article 30 authorizes religious and linguistic minorities to maintain their own schools and to request subsidies from the State to sustain these institutions.

Although untouchability was officially abolished (Article 17), along with forced labor (Article 29), Indian voters elsewhere demonstrated their great conservatism. For example, the guarantees on property rights in Article 32 weakened agrarian reform. Most of the states were even sued by landed property owners, many of whom won their cases and the right to considerable compensations.

The victory of the Congress Party in the 1951–1952 elections nevertheless reinforced Nehru's position as leader, and a period of setting up of institutions followed.

Domination without Division of the Congress Party

Nehru, who since youth had been influenced by English socialism and the Soviet model, sought to commit India to a socialist path. In 1959, the Congress Party adopted a resolution advocating for the creation of a system of agricultural cooperatives inspired by China's experimental policies.

This project, however, was not carried out by the state governments, which were all, or almost all, under the influence of the Congress Party. The explanation is that although the Party continued to be dominated by the intelligentsia and liberal professionals, it also counted a growing number of conservative notables among its members. The Party needed to attract industrialists and landed property owners to finance its election campaigns and win elections by making use of the popularity of local leaders. Therefore, the Party did not hesitate to solicit the support of former princes (maharajahs or nawabs) who had partly retained their prestige as well as their revenues.

At the same time, the opposition was handicapped because some of its constituent parties were descended from the Congress Party. The ambivalence of the Socialist Party, which had emerged *within* the Congress Party in 1934 and only left its ranks in 1948, was particularly evident. Although the socialists made up a third parliamentary group after the 1952 elections, beginning in 1953, Jayaprakash Narayan, one of the socialist leaders, pledged to negotiate with Nehru, whereas another socialist leader, Ram Manohar Lohia, criticized this initiative, which eventually failed.

The Indian Communists were plagued by lesser, but still comparable, ambiguities. The Communist Party of India (CPI), which opted for integration into parliamentary politics in 1951, became the first opposition party in 1952, and had made the transition fully by 1957. This party split in 1964, with the emergence of the Communist Party of India (Marxist), the CPI(M), from the pro-Chinese faction. From the mid/late–1960s, the CPI (largely because of Indira Gandhi's secular and socialist credentials, was inclined to collaborate with the Congress Party, which deprived the opposition of any party of substance.

On the right, the Bharatiya Jana Sangh (BJS, Indian People's Alliance), created in 1951, was the embodiment of a rare subset of Indian politics, having never been part of the Congress Party, because it was the political face of the Rashtriya Swayamsevak Sangh (RSS, National Volunteer's Union), the leading force in Hindu nationalism since its emergence in 1925. The BJS believed India to be a Hindu nation and that minority groups should assimilate themselves into the dominant Hindu culture. The Muslims were their main target because of their alleged transnational allegiance. In the elections of 1952, the BJS won only 3.1 percent of the vote.

After being broken up, the opposition was proportionally less significant in the political game, yet this decline was not of the magnitude of the weakening of the Congress Party. The image of moral rigor and of sacrifice in which the Party was forged under the influence of Mahatma Gandhi declined. This is one of the reasons why Nehru implemented, in 1963, the "Kamaraj Plan," named after the Indian chief minister (the head of government) for the state of Tamil Nadu. This plan sought the resignation of six ministers and six chief ministers in states under the authority of the Congress Party, in order to devote themselves to revitalizing the Party, which had become complacent and dysfunctional because of its long hold on power. The impact of this measure was, however, cut short by the death of Nehru on May 27, 1964, which, moreover, exacerbated the internal conflict at the heart of the Party.

After independence, India opted for a policy of nonalignment that led it to reject the Cold War logic of "bloc against bloc," in the name of Gandhian values of pacifism and a Third Worldism praising Afro-Asiatic solidarity. This approach was made official by the 1955 Bandung Conference, and manifested in the strengthening of ties between India and China, which climaxed with the visit of Zhou Enlai to New Delhi in 1954. When the Dalai Lama fled to India in 1959, however, relations between the two countries became so poisoned that Nehru came to mistrust China. Nehru's reputation was tarnished by a disastrous war with China in 1962, over areas in the Himalayas to which China laid claim but that were then under Indian control. The Indian defenses were overcome and two important tracts of territory fell under the control of Beijing. This war was traumatizing for the Indians, more so because China was still one of their allies during the 1950s.

The weakening of India, following the war of 1962 and the demise of Nehru, convinced Pakistan that the context was favorable for an attack in 1965. Since 1947, the two countries had clashed on the issue of Muslim-majority Kashmir, a region bordering the "country of the pure" (Pakistan), that Islamabad claimed but that India controlled. This issue had already led to a war in 1948–1949, originally over the problem of dividing the province. In 1965, the Pakistani offensive was attributed, wrongfully, to an uprising of Kashmiri Indians. The war was won, however, by India.

Indira Gandhi: From Populism to Authoritarianism

Upon Nehru's death, Lal Bahadur Shastri, a veteran of the Congress Party, became the head of government. He revealed himself to be a true leader in directing the war of 1965, but he died in January 1966 in Tashkent of a heart attack, at the time of the peace negotiations. The Congress Party establishment, which the press called "the Syndicate," looked to Indira Gandhi, the daughter of Nehru, to succeed him. She seemed easy to manipulate and her popularity, based on her family background, seemed a guarantee of success in the 1967 elections. She did, in fact, win the elections and became prime minister.

Still, the election results confirmed the erosion of the Party, which lost power in nine states where, most often, the "anti-Congress" coalitions that took power did not have anything in common apart from their shared opposition to the dominant party. The elections served as an indicator of the average citizen's discontent, especially in the North, where a veteran of the Congress Party named Charan Singh, left the Party at election time to form his own party, the Bharatiya Kranti Dal (Indian Revolutionary Party), in Uttar Pradesh with opposition support.

The Naxalite (Communist) wave reflects the same variation on a revolutionary method. This was another consequence of the 1967 elections, since it began in West Bengal after the CPI(M)'s decision to join hands with Congress dissidents in order to form a coalition government. The Party seemed, therefore, in the eyes of certain militants, to renounce the revolution for the benefits of power. Its actions led to the radicalization of some of its erstwhile followers that prepared the ground for Naxalism. This movement takes its name from Naxalbari, a village in West Bengal where, from May 1967, members of the CPI(M) drew inspiration from Mao Zedong's techniques of insurrection. The CPI(M) expelled the first Naxalites from its ranks, but when they received support from Beijing, the Naxalites allied with militant Communists in applying comparable methods in Andhra Pradesh. In April 1969, these two groups founded the Communist Party of India (Marxist-Leninist) and called for an intensification of guerrilla activity. This violence reached its peak in 1970–1971. The principal leaders of the CPI(M-L) were then captured by the army. Naxalism did not survive after that time, except in certain isolated rural areas, from Bihar to Andhra Pradesh to Madhya Pradesh.

Reverses suffered by the Congress Party at the time of the 1967 elections aroused criticism in party ranks, including from Morarji Desai, the defeated opponent of Indira Gandhi at the time of the succession to Shastri, who had become finance minister and deputy prime minister. As Desai represented the conservative face of the Congress Party, the prime minister decided to rely on the party's left wing, which had as its principal mouthpiece the Congress Forum for Socialist Action, whose leaders were baptized "Young Turks" by the press.

The conflict between Indira Gandhi and Desai exploded publicly after the death of the president of the Republic, Zakir Hussein, on May 3, 1969. Desai proposed Sanjiva Reddy as successor. Reddy belonged to the rightist wing of the party against which Mrs. Gandhi was fighting. Indira Gandhi, whose chosen candidate was the outgoing vice president, Varahagiri Venkata Giri, responded on July 16 by taking away Desai's finance portfolio; he left the government. Five days later, she announced the nationalization, by presidential ruling, of the fourteen biggest banks in the country. She then supported Giri to succeed Hussein; he campaigned as an "independent" and was elected on August 16, 1969, with 51 percent of the vote on the second round of voting. Soon after, the fight for control of the apparatus of the Congress Party led to a split—Desai and the rest of the "Syndicate" remained at the head of the Congress Party (O) [O for *Organization*], whereas Indira Gandhi launched the Congress Party (R) [R for *Ruling*].

The prime minister then emphasized the socialist dimension of her program. All the same, the judiciary hampered her actions. The Supreme

Court ruled against the abolition of privileges and pensions accorded to former princes. In response, Indira Gandhi called for a snap election to attempt to reinforce her mandate and receive a clearer majority in Parliament. On December 27, 1970, she announced the dissolution of the Lok Sabha and led a particularly intense campaign to forge a slogan that personalized the stakes in a new way: "Some say let's rid ourselves of Indira. I say let's rid ourselves of poverty" (*garibi hatao*). The Congress Party (R) took back two-thirds of the seats—350 of 518—with 43 percent of the vote and Indira Gandhi was able to restart her program of reforms, relying on the Party's left. The Twenty-Fourth Amendment to the Constitution was passed to curtail the Supreme Court's power to rule on Parliament's right to amend the Constitution, and the Twenty-Fifth abolished the privileges and pensions of princes. Indira Gandhi, however, did not redistribute lands as she had pledged, because she feared alienating herself from the landowners, who still controlled a good part of the rural vote.

Elsewhere, Indira Gandhi modified the foreign policy she inherited from her father. In 1971, the support she gave to the Bengalis of East Pakistan triggered a war between Delhi and Islamabad. India prevailed again—thus facilitating the birth of Bangladesh—and dictated the terms of the peace agreement to Zulfiqar Ali Bhutto at the Shimla conference, where it was notably decided that thenceforth, the issue of Kashmir would only be discussed bilaterally. Furthermore, the support that the United States gave to Pakistan during the conflict induced India to draw closer to the USSR and sign a treaty of friendship in 1971. Moscow thereby became India's primary ally—particularly at the UN—and its main arms supplier. Not satisfied with turning her back on Nehru's policy of nonalignment, Indira Gandhi also deepened the questioning of pacifism, as inherited from Gandhi, while carrying out the nation's first nuclear test in 1974.

The "JP Movement" and the Emergency

The discontinuity between Indira Gandhi's election promises and the accomplishments of her government was readily exploited by the opposition. In January 1974, demonstrations erupted in Ahmedabad, Gujarat, where students marched in the streets demanding the dissolution of the Legislative Council (the upper house of the state Parliament). The movement acquired a national dimension when, in April, the main trade union of railwaymen, organized by George Fernandes, went on a general strike: 1.7 million railway employees paralyzed India. The government put an end to this movement by putting 20,000 strikers in temporary detention. The repression led a veteran of the independence movement, Jayaprakash Narayan (nicknamed JP), to return to politics at the age of seventy-two. From March to November, this socialist Gandhian led mass demonstrations in Bihar, in which the participants adhered to the principles of non-violence in the face of police clubs.

The apoliticism proclaimed by the "JP Movement" was blurred as the repression intensified. Jayaprakash Narayan finally called for the resignation of the government of Bihar in addition to that of Indira Gandhi. The JP Movement was then salvaged by the opposition parties. In November, the Congress Party (O), the Socialist Party, the Jana Sangh, the Bharatiya Lok Dal (BLD) of Charan Singh, and the Akali Dal (the Sikh party of Punjab) formed a committee of national coordination to support the Gandhian "total revolution" of JP.

Soon afterward Indira Gandhi suffered a serious reversal of fortune when, on June 12, 1975, the High Court of Allahabad invalidated her election to Parliament in 1971 on account of illegal practices such as the use of materials belonging to the state (jeeps, megaphones) during her election campaign. She responded by asking the president of the republic, Fakhruddin Ali Ahmed, to proclaim a state of emergency under the terms of Article 352 of the Constitution, which authorizes the president to do so in cases of external aggression or internal problems. This period of emergency rule allowed Indira Gandhi, with the support of the Communist Party of India (CPI), to put democracy on hold. On June 26, many dissidents of the Congress Party (R) as well as leaders of the opposition were arrested. Three days later, a series of presidential decrees curtailed judicial protection of basic rights and authorized the government to detain any political opponent, without charge or representation, for two years. In total, about one hundred thousand people were put in prison during the state of emergency. Although most political parties were not prohibited outright, their leaders were incarcerated or prevented from speaking freely because of censorship. Moreover, twenty-six organizations, from the RSS to the CPI(M-L) and the Jama'at-i-Islami, a fundamentalist Muslim group, were banned.

On July 21, 1975, the two chambers of Parliament not only approved the declaration of a state of emergency, but also voted for a constitutional amendment (the Thirty-Ninth) that facilitated the use of these exceptional proceedings and amended the provisions of the Representation of the People Act (1951) under which Indira Gandhi had seen her 1971 electoral win invalidated. In November 1976, the Forty-Second Amendment markedly reduced the role of the Supreme Court, allowing Parliament to amend the basic nature of the Constitution by requiring that the invalidation of any law be henceforth confirmed by a two-thirds majority of the Court.

Indira Gandhi justified the state of emergency with the need to put out of action right-wing forces, in particular the Hindu nationalists, who had begun to coalesce around the JP movement. In 1976, an amendment added two significant adjectives to the preamble of the Constitution: India, from that time on, became a secular and socialist republic. Starting on July 1, 1975, a twenty-point program promised, among other things, to redistribute lands by carrying out significant agrarian reform. Even though the Congress Party (R) did not have the network of cadres necessary to put such a plan into effect, the land ceilings were somewhat better enforced, as those who lost land were unable to bring the issue to court.

The excesses of the government weakened its public support. A good example of this was the new policy on birth control. This policy was above all the work of Sanjay Gandhi, the youngest son of Indira, who had become her right-hand man during the Emergency, a critical period when she mistrusted anyone not in her immediate circle. In 1976, Sanjay stated it was necessary to reduce the birth rate from 3.5 per 100 to 2.5 per 100 by 1984. The state authorities in charge of family planning received increasingly demanding sterilization quotas to fill, the escalation of which was fueled by overzealousness: the figure for the sterilized people grew from 2.6 million in 1975–1976 to 8.1 million in 1976–1977. The majority of sterilizations were forcefully carried out on those without the means to protect themselves, particularly in the North, where population growth was highest.

Hostility to the regime was kept alive by opponents who had avoided arrest and fled underground. They distributed pamphlets and organized acts of sabotage targeting mostly the railway. But it was in prison that their leaders prepared for the future. The incarceration of opposition leaders in fact promoted their regrouping. Charan Singh, the oldest partisan of the opposition, unveiled the idea of a single party in February 1976. JP, freed the following month for health reasons, supported this idea, and the parties concerned began negotiations.

On January 16, 1977, Indira Gandhi announced, to everyone's surprise, that general elections would be held in March. This decision can probably be explained by the prime minister's conviction that she remained popular and that the opposition would not succeed in organizing in time, but also by the fact that Pakistan was getting ready to hold legislative elections and India did not want to seem less democratic than its greatest enemy.

At stake in the 1977 elections was nothing less than the future of democracy in India, as the state of emergency marked the end result of a process of degradation that had been set in motion in the 1960s by the erosion of the Congress and confirmed at the beginning of the 1970s by the personalization of power in an increasingly populist and authoritarian mold.

The Janata Episode

In the week following Indira Gandhi's announcement about the upcoming elections, the Congress Party (O), the Bharatiya Lok Dal, the Jana Sangh (the principal Hindu nationalist party), and the Socialist Party fused into the Janata Party. Soon after, this new party, which had Morarji Desai as president and Charan Singh as vice president, received the support of Jagjivan Ram, a dissident of the Congress Party (R) and interior minister during the state of emergency, who had recently founded the Congress for Democracy (CFD).

The Congress Party (R) suffered a historic defeat and, with 34.5 percent of the vote, won only 154 Parliament seats out of 542. The Janata Party secured 295 seats, with 41.3 percent of the vote. Support for Indira Gandhi had remained fairly strong in the south, but had collapsed in the north, where the state of emergency had been more severe. Indira Gandhi and her son Sanjay were even attacked by their constituents in Uttar Pradesh. Among those elected to Parliament from the Janata Party, 31 percent were former members of the Jana Sangh, and the rest came from the ex-BLD (19 percent), the Socialists (17 percent), the former Congress Party (O) (15 percent), the CFD (10 percent), as well as other dissidents of the Congress Party, such as Chandra Shekhar's breakaway faction of the Congress (R) (2 percent). The new government took up its duties on March 24, 1977. With only two representatives in important ministerial positions, Atal Bihari Vajpayee in External Affairs (Foreign Affairs) and Lal Krishna Advani in Information and Broadcasting, the Hindu nationalists clearly accepted some underrepresentation since they had considerable weight among the newly elected parliamentarians. The choice of head of government was a more delicate matter, as Morarji Desai, Charan Singh, and Jagjivan Ram were all possible candidates. Finally, at the age of eighty-one, Desai attained the position for which he had tried to challenge Indira Gandhi in 1966. Charan Singh had to be content with the position of deputy prime minister.

The Desai government began by erasing the most visible traces of the Emergency. Censorship and laws allowing preventative detention were repealed. Those organizations banned in 1975 were legalized. The Forty-Fourth Amendment granted to state High Courts and the Supreme Court the power to appraise the constitutionality of laws. However, the Janata Party did not succeed in repealing the Forty-Second Amendment, which authorized Parliament to modify the fundamental nature of the Constitution, because the Congress Party, which still made up the majority of the Rajya Sabha, opposed this effort. The government was also unable to both retract Article 31, which called into question the primacy of basic rights, and to reestablish the Supreme Court's domain to defend these rights.

Above all, the government failed to condemn those responsible for the state of emergency. Starting May 19, 1977, Parliament created a commission of inquiry whose leadership was entrusted to a retired judge, but his report held little weight, as Indira Gandhi did not respond to his summons.

The victors of 1977 had little in common other than their visceral opposition to the increasing power of the state orchestrated over thirty years by Nehru and his daughter. These victors were made up of the Bharatiya Lok Dal (BLD, Indian People's Party) of Charan Singh, the defender of smallholders; the Jana Sangh (Indian People's Alliance), which was close to the business world and committed to free trade; and the Gandhians—the socialist version in JP and the conservative version in Desai—who traditionally favored the decentralization of power down to the village level. The five-year plan of 1978–1983 therefore encouraged the artisanal and agricultural sector, and Charan Singh, who was named minister of finance in January 1979, submitted, the following month, a budget favoring the peasants.

The rift that deeply split the Janata Party, and pitted the former members of the Congress Party (O) and the JS against those of the BLD and the Socialist Party, was the question of secularism. The debate over school textbooks provides a particularly revealing example. Starting in 1977, Desai declared a ban on school textbooks that the Hindu nationalists had already been clamoring against, mostly because the authors were left-wing academics who did not portray the Muslim invaders of the medieval period in a sufficiently unfavorable light. This minor concern was the seed of an important controversy at the heart of the Janata Party. Another dispute erupted the following year when an ex-Jana Sangh member of Parliament proposed a law that sought to prevent religious conversions obtained through deception, often in return for payment or by coercion. This plan was directed primarily at Christian missions that, according to Hindu nationalists, were responsible for a part of the erosion (in relative numbers) of the demographic (Hindu) majority. It was supported for a time by the Desai government and gave rise to fears on the left that the religious freedoms of minorities would be threatened.

The coming together of Desai and the former JS stirred up criticisms by the opposition and other parts of the Janata Party. These criticisms were amplified when Hindu nationalists were implicated in numerous anti-Muslim riots in 1978–1979 in which militants attacked minorities all the more violently if they were believed to be protected in high places. In response, Charan Singh launched a grand campaign against the prime minister and his ex-Jana Sangh allies in the name of defending secularism. His attitude reflected his personal ambitions, but also the growing tension between the states and the ex-Jana Sangh in government. The ex-BLD ruled with the support of the ex-Jana Sangh in Uttar Pradesh, Bihar, and Haryana. They used their power to establish employment quotas for the administration of "their" states. These quotas favored members of lower castes, who were mostly peasants and who constituted the natural political base for Charan Singh. But the ex-Jana Sangh, represented more by the urban high-caste middle class, was hostile to these measures and the institutionalization of divisions among castes in favor of unity and the "Hindu nation."

Charan Singh left the government to become the head of a new party, the Janata Party (S) [S for Secular], and accused Desai of compromising himself by associating with Hindu nationalists. The schism deprived the Janata Party of its majority. Desai resigned, and the president of the republic, Sanjiva Reddy, asked Charan Singh to turn to Indira Gandhi for support in forming a new government. Yet Indira Gandhi refused to support him, and the president decided to hold a snap election by dissolving the Assembly. In this way, the Janata episode concluded prematurely in late 1979; the heterogeneity of the coalition in power had condemned it to fail during this first phase of non-Congress government.

The Test of National Unity against the Gandhis

The elections of January 1980 consecrated the return to power of Indira Gandhi, at the head of a new party that she created in 1978, the Congress Party (I)—I for Indira—that won 353 seats with 42.7 percent of the vote. The Janata Party held on to only 31 seats with 19 percent of the vote, while the Janata Party (S) of Charan Singh secured 41 seats with 9.4 percent of the vote. As a result, the Janata Party experienced another split, with the ex-Jana Sangh members leaving to found the Bharatiya Janata Party (BJP, Indian People's Party) in May 1980.

Indira Gandhi's second regime began with a new round of questions about institutions because of, once again, an excessive centralization of power. In February 1980, Indira imposed President's Rule—a formerly exceptional procedure that quickly became commonplace—in nine states that were either governed by the opposition or had not held elections in one or two years. This allowed the Congress Party (I) to retake power in these areas, except in Punjab and Tamil Nadu. Indira Gandhi no longer subscribed to the secularism that she once had written into the Constitution. Not only was she driven to seek consolation from Hindu spiritual guides possibly because of the loss of her son Sanjay, who died while flying his plane in 1980, but she also ostentatiously attended a large number of Hindu temples. Moreover, she stressed her Hindu identity in this way because the mobilization of this majority community seemed to her the best way to preserve national unity.

Separatist tensions multiplied at the beginning of the 1980s and, in a historical irony, they resulted partly from the Hindu undertones of Indira Gandhi's politics. In this vein, Sant Bhindranwale, one of the leaders of the Sikh separatists who took up arms in Punjab in 1983, benefited from the protection of Delhi because the Congress Party (I) was trying to weaken the moderate Sikhs of the Akali Dal, their main rivals for power in Punjab. The same determination to not lose a grip on any aspect of power could also be found in the Party's approach to Assam. In this northeastern state, the Assam Gasom Student Party had demanded, since 1979, the elimination of Bengalis from electoral lists, because these people were natives of West Bengal, or Bangladesh, rather than of Assam. The Bengalis, however, in exchange for the protection of New Delhi, pledged their support to the Congress Party (I), which therefore refused to sacrifice this "votebank." At the time of the 1983 elections to the state legislative assembly, ethnic Assamese boycotted voting and massacred large numbers of non-Assamese at the polls, but Congress received a solid majority (91 seats out of 109) in the state assembly, which radicalized Assamese separatists in the United Liberation Front of Assam.

In Punjab, the situation was also rapidly decaying. At the start of 1984, Sant Bhindranwale's followers occupied the Golden Temple in Amritsar, the main Sikh holy site. In July, the central government authority gave orders to retake the temple by force, which outraged the Sikh community. On October 31, Indira Gandhi was assassinated in Delhi by two Sikh bodyguards. The reprisals, orchestrated by members of the Congress Party, killed thousands of Sikhs, particularly in New Delhi.

While Indira Gandhi's second regime did very little to contribute to the popularity of the Congress Party (I), her death evoked a wave of sympathy in its favor. The party consequently won an unprecedented 48.1 percent of the vote (securing 415 seats out of the available 517) at the time of the general elections in December 1984, which were prompted by the dissolution of the Lok Sabha. The first to benefit in the wake of this tidal wave of change was none other than Rajiv Gandhi, Indira's oldest son, who had taken over as head of government after her death. The new prime minister proclaimed his determination to modernize India so that it could "enter into the twenty-first century," a slogan buoyed up by his youth—he was forty-one—and the fact that this airline pilot was a novice to politics: he was a new kind of politician.

On the international level, this manifested in various daring and refreshingly different actions. In 1988, Rajiv Gandhi made an official visit to China, the first such visit of a significant Indian politician since the affront inflicted on Vajpayee, then Indian external affairs minister, who found himself in Beijing in 1979 when the People's Liberation Army attacked New Delhi's friend, Vietnam. Rajiv Gandhi's visit to China allowed the renewal of negotiations about border disputes between the two countries. The following year in Islamabad, even though his talks were with another young political heir, Benazir Bhutto, no concrete gains were made.

In terms of internal politics, in 1985, Rajiv Gandhi concluded a settlement with the Sikh leader Sant Longowal and those Assamese responsible for the violence, which demonstrated that he was more flexible than his mother. He sought in other respects to clean up politics by introducing a law to dissuade elected parliamentarians from changing parties during the course of their time in office, which they frequently did, often for dishonest reasons. On the occasion of the centenary of the Congress Party on December 30, 1985, he gave a forceful speech in which he deplored corruption and the absence of discipline at the heart of the Party. Yet it was not too long before Rajiv Gandhi himself succumbed to the kinds of political expediency that he had denounced. The most significant example of this is the Shah Bano case, which intensified the erosion of secularism set in motion by his mother. Shah Bano, a sixty-two-year-old Muslim woman who had been repudiated by her husband under Quranic law, had obtained the right to alimony from the courts, despite opposition from Muslim organizations, which saw this case as questioning Shariat as a legitimate source of Indian law. On February 27, 1986, Rajiv Gandhi secured passage of a law that would exempt the Muslim community from the provisions in the civil code invoked by the Supreme Court during this case, with the goal of retaining the support of Muslim opinion leaders. This tactic served to further increase the importance of religious factors in political life.

In 1987, Rajiv Gandhi was suspected to have accepted bribes from a Swedish armaments company, Bofors, which hoped to acquire an important contract with India. The press pounced on the story, and the man who took charge of what was to become a veritable anticorruption crusade was none other than Rajiv Gandhi's defense minister, Vishwanath Pratap Singh.

V. P. Singh and the Second Janata Episode

V. P. Singh left the Congress Party to found the Jan Morcha (the People's Front), which then incorporated the Lok Dal of Charan Singh and the Janata Party led by Chandra Shekar, who had assumed its presidency in 1977. This new party, named the Janata Dal (the People's Party), became the rallying point of a bigger but looser formation, the National Front, which also comprised regional parties. At the time of the 1989 general elections, the Congress Party only retained 197 elected parliamentarians, with 37.2 percent of the vote; the Janata Dal, which came in second with 27 percent of the vote and 143 seats, and with the support of the BJP and the Communist MPs, became a crucial component of a new parliamentary majority.

Named prime minister, V. P. Singh began to take action under the banner of social reform. He announced that the recommendations of the Mandal Commission would be implemented, which marked both a political and social turning point. This commission, which took its name from its president, B. P. Mandal, had been established in 1978 to study the needs of Other Backward Classes (OBC), a category recognized by the Constitution but one whose contours were imprecisely defined. According to the Mandal report, the OBC corresponded to castes that, although of inferior status to those deemed high castes, were higher than untouchables, and essentially defined by their occupation of working the land. According to the report, the OBC represented 52 percent of the population. The report recommended that 27 percent of jobs in government administration and public universities should be set aside for members of the OBC in order to help elevate them.

V. P. Singh's decision to implement the recommendations of the Mandal report triggered high-caste opposition. Students protested vigorously against the reduction of their career prospects implied in the new administrative quotas, which until then had always been the privileged domain of high castes. Some even set themselves on fire. The Supreme Court suspended V. P. Singh's decision for long enough to examine its constitutionality. The coalition in Parliament was also threatened, as the BJP opposed the politics of V. P. Singh who, in their eyes, had rekindled caste divisions. Anxious to counter the "Mandal effect," the BJP decided to participate in the resurgence of the conflict over Ayodhya.

This controversy resurfaced in the middle of the 1980s, when Hindu nationalists began to demand the restoration of a site in the town of Ayodhya (in Uttar Pradesh) on which the founder of the Mughal dynasty had built a mosque, but which they considered the birthplace of the Hindu deity Ram and on which they wanted to construct a temple. In 1989, the BJP ran their campaign on this issue and experienced a great electoral success, with their presence in Parliament growing from two seats in 1984 to eighty-eight in 1989.

In the autumn of 1990, the president of the BJP, L. K. Advani, turned once again to the Ayodhya debate to protest the fallout from the Mandal report. He led a procession across North India intending to end at the site of the mosque where they would build a temple (*mandir* in Hindi) dedicated to Ram. The procession covered around ten thousand kilometers, but the authorities arrested Advani and he never crossed into Uttar Pradesh. The mosque was thereafter seized in an attack by militants, which compelled the forces of order to respond with a counterstrike that

left around fifteen dead. These events were followed by numerous disturbances between Hindus and Muslims across the country.

When the BJP withdrew its support of the V. P. Singh administration,
the government collapsed and early elections were organized for the
spring of 1991, after an attempt to patch up relations allowed Chandra
Shekhar to become prime minister for a few months. India had had three
prime ministers in less than twenty months, and no one dared to take the
unpopular measures necessary to address glaring problems, which precipitated the external payments crisis of the summer of 1991.

India Post-1991

In India, the early 1990s were a milestone in many different ways. The
growing influence of the lower castes—evident from the electoral victory of V. P. Singh in 1989—and the rise of the BJP—whose Hindu
nationalist militancy was fostered by the corresponding apprehensions
of its upper-caste supporters—precipitated the decline of the Congress,
whose electoral prospects were already affected by the development of
regional parties. In terms of public policies, the advent of a new India
was epitomized by a pathbreaking liberalization policy in the economy
and a diplomatic rapprochement with the United States in the domain of
international relations.

The Rao Years, a Turning Point for India

The general elections of June 1991 allowed the Congress Party (I) to retake
power on the back of a wave of sympathy generated by the assassination
of Rajiv Gandhi by the Tamil Tigers of Sri Lanka, at the end of the election
campaign period. Yet the party never regained an absolute majority; they
won 232 out of 515 available seats, with 36.5 percent of the vote. Moreover, P. V. Narasimha Rao owed his promotion to prime minister to the
fact that he did not ally himself with any of the factions in the Congress
Party. Even though his position was fragile, he set India on a path to
economic liberalization, which was primarily orchestrated by Manmohan
Singh, the finance minister. The "Licence Raj," a system of administrative
authorizations by which all private businesses that wanted to diversify or
increase production had to get permission from the state, was dismantled.
In addition, protectionist barriers were curtailed and multinational companies were welcomed with open arms in numerous sectors.

The Rao government had little experience in both economic and international affairs. At the same time that he turned his back on socialism,
the prime minister distanced himself from Russia, the heir to an empire
in full-blown decay. Although Moscow remained an important ally, par-

ticularly as the arms supplier for India, New Delhi began to explore new diplomatic horizons. Narasimha Rao inaugurated a "Look East" policy aimed at securing a place for India in the Asian economic miracle. India was accordingly admitted to ASEAN as a sectoral dialogue partner, and then as a full dialogue partner in 1995. Similarly, the Rao government opened an embassy in Israel, and Tel Aviv did the same in India, both to form ties with a country from which Delhi hoped to buy arms (and, in fact, in a few years Israel became India's number two arms supplier) and because this set India on the path to a durable relationship with the United States.

In internal matters, the politics of liberalization were accompanied by a period of decline for the Congress. Narasimha Rao was also losing the trust of such important social groups as lower castes, to whom the Congress Party had been loath to grant the recommendations of the Mandal report before the Supreme Court obliged them to in 1992, and Muslims, who were alienated when he allowed Hindu nationalists to demolish the mosque in Ayodhya on December 6, 1992. As a result, he had fiery internal critics and suffered major defections. Arjun Singh, the number two in government, left his position in 1994 to form a new party with Nayaran Dutt Tiwari, until then the head of the Congress Party in Uttar Pradesh. In this context, the 1996 elections marked an unmatched reversal of fortune for the Congress Party, whose representation fell to 141 seats.

Conquest of Power by the BJP

The main beneficiary of the decline of the Congress Party was the BJP, which became the leading party in the Lok Sabha with 160 seats, but which lacked the means to shape the government administration. Power therefore fell to a third group, the United Front (UF), created by the merging of the National Front of 1989–1990 with the Left Front dominated by the CPI and the CPI(M). All the same, no one could govern without the support of the Congress Party in Parliament. This coalition approved Deve Gowda, a former leader of the Janata Dal, as prime minister. His plan sought to defend secularism, which the BJP was accused of threatening, and to reintroduce decentralization.

In the autumn of 1996, the government succeeded in organizing elections in the Jammu and Kashmir Assembly, a state that had been under President's Rule since 1990. In February 1997, the government repeated this success in Punjab, a region long caught up in Sikh separatism, where the level of participation rose from 24 percent in 1992 to 69 percent.

The government experienced its greatest success in foreign affairs. Inder Kumar Gujral, the external affairs minister, wanting to improve India's relations with its neighbors, negotiated a treaty with Bangladesh to share the waters of the Ganga-Brahmaputra, organized the visit of Chinese president Jiang Zemin to India for the first time, and renewed dialogue with Pakistan.

The Congress Party, which had no interest in allowing the power of the UF to grow, forced Deve Gowda to resign. After that, in December, it withdrew its support from the government of his successor, I. K. Gujral, prompting early elections.

The Congress Party did not benefit from the 1998 general elections, and once again found itself behind the BJP in number of seats (141 to 171). Moreover, this election signaled a new stage in the process of political decomposition that had started at the beginning of the decade: the national parties occupied only 387 seats in the Lok Sabha, down from 462 in 1991. In the same period, regional party representation had gone from 38 to 143 seats. Under these conditions, the formerly dominant parties had to resign themselves to forming coalitions. Called upon to establish the new administration, the BJP formed an alliance of 24 parties that lost power only a few months later, when one of the parties defected. They regained control, however, in the 1999 elections, and this time for longer. This BJP-dominated coalition, the National Democratic Alliance (NDA), was the first coalition to govern without any major hitches throughout its full term, until 2004. The BJP was thus able to capitalize on its decade of growing popularity, resulting from the Ayodhya debate and the rallying of higher-caste and middle-class voters, who rejected V. P. Singh's policy of affirmative action and a Congress Party marred by both corruption and factionalism.

Based on its success in elections, the BJP painted itself as a disciplined and patriotic party. Furthermore, it profited from the "Kargil victory" in 1999, Kargil being the name of the town in Indian-controlled Kashmir where India defeated Pakistani troops that had infiltrated the area. This triumph was largely attributed to Prime Minister Atal Bihari Vajpayee, who had gained power in 1998. As a result, this party, whose existence had long been limited to the Hindi-speaking north, began to attract a following in the south (Karnataka) and especially in the west (Gujarat).

Once in power, the BJP set to work on a more moderate program than the one it had espoused in the opposition. This reflected the Party's participation in a coalition that, during its election campaign, promised to respect a moratorium on significant issues such as the Ayodhya temple, the autonomy of Jammu-Kashmir—which the BJP wanted to abolish—and the introduction of a uniform civil code that would call into question the status of Shariat as a source of Indian law. The BJP thereby unfettered itself from three major symbols of its Hindu nationalism. It also reverted to an economic patriotism, based on the pursuit of a policy of self-sufficiency rather than globalization. This was a surprising (re)presentation of the BJP as a liberal party, which bore out its support of a reduction of the state's role in the economy.

The BJP remained loyal to its program, even when it proceeded to carry out nuclear tests starting in May 1998, a few weeks after Vajpayee took power and selected his confidantes for key positions in the education system to rewrite history textbooks. He did the same in the states he controlled, like Gujarat, where Narendra Modi gave control of the administration to Hindu militants, which explains the government's lack of concern with repressing communal violence. In February 2002, such violence exploded in the town of Godhra in Gujarat, leaving almost two thousand Muslims dead, according to the most reliable unofficial estimates; the official figure was five hundred fifty victims. The government's failure in communal relations was compounded by its lack of attention to the poorest segments of the population, particularly in rural areas. As a result, the NDA lost its support in these areas, which enabled the surprising return of the Congress Party in the 2004 elections.

On the international level, the Vajpayee years were marked by important nuances in Indian politics. The nuclear tests propelled India onto the global scene, and its desire for power was finally recognized. Initially, these tests elicited criticisms and sanctions, especially by large Asian countries like China (against which the tests would mostly have been directed) and Japan, but also by the United States. But India derived more advantages than inconveniences, notably because the international respect gained fanned nationalism.

Moreover, the events of September 11, 2001, in the United States rapidly changed the situation. From that moment, the United States became victim to the same kind of terrorism that India had suffered in Kashmir, and even beyond, so New Delhi was able to join the global coalition instituted by Washington and finger Pakistan as having sheltered Al-Qaeda and aided the Taliban. This solidarity of democracies against international jihadism extended readily to include Israel, in the spirit of which the BJP compared the situation of the Hindus—surrounded by Muslims—with that of the Jews.

The strengthening of relations between India and the United States also accelerated between 1998 and 2004 for economic reasons. The politics of liberalization of the Vajpayee government attracted increasing American investment and lubricated commercial exchanges. Furthermore, the Indian diaspora in the United States (around two million people) served as a link between the two countries, not only because of the large numbers of Indian data processing specialists who live in Silicon Valley but also because the formidable economic success of this minority group (the richest in terms of income per capita) made it a model community in American eyes.

The Return of the Congress Party, and of the Gandhis

The return of the Congress Party in 2004 cannot be explained solely by the unpopularity of the BJP, which was only relative. The fact that Sonia Gandhi, Rajiv's widow (see box 2.2), had accepted the presidency of the party after the repeated election disasters of the 1990s, and had been active in the countryside, played a great part. The Party's decision to work as part of a coalition, to present itself as a party of the poor, and to try to win back all its dissidents, were also important factors in its successful recovery.

In 2004, the Congress Party made significant, though not considerable, electoral gains. Although their representation did increase to 145, from 112 in 1999, this still gave them only a seven-seat lead over the BJP, and their win in terms of votes cast remained unimpressive (26.7 percent). The contrast between the Party's poor performance in votes and its gain in seats can be explained by the preelection formation of coalitions.

Immediately after the elections of spring 2004, the parties involved settled on an electoral agreement with the Congress Party and formed

---

Box 2.2. Sonia Gandhi (1946–)

Sonia Gandhi was born in 1946 in Italy, near the town of Vicenza. She met Rajiv Gandhi at Cambridge, and the couple married in 1968. They settled in India, as part of the Nehru/Gandhi household, among whom Sonia raised her two children, Rahul (born in 1970) and Priyanka (born in 1972). Sonia gained Indian citizenship in 1983.

She entered Indian politics in 1984, shortly after Rajiv, when she campaigned for him against the widow of Sanjay Gandhi, Maneka, in the state of Amethi. Her name appeared in newspapers again for less noble reasons when one of the suspects in the Bofors affair (linked to the bribes that the armaments firm paid to Rajiv) was confirmed to be an Italian friend of Sonia, Ottavio Quattrocchi.

Following Rajiv's assassination in 1991, and after refusing for seven years, she accepted the leadership of the Congress Party in 1998, after it had suffered repeated election losses. She became the leader of the opposition in the Lok Sabha in 1999, and led the Congress to victory in 2004. She refused, however, to become prime minister, because of the BJP opposition to a foreigner becoming head of government. Even so, she played a key role in presiding over the ruling coalition, the United Progressive Alliance (UPA), by maintaining the association between the UPA and the Communist left until 2008.

the United Progressive Alliance (UPA), which then negotiated an agreement with the Communists, who finally consented to support the UPA government without taking part in it. The Congress Party in Parliament elected Sonia Gandhi as its head, but she preferred to leave the position of prime minister to Manmohan Singh, whose reputation for integrity and competence could not be doubted by anyone. She chose not to accept the position because of the concern that her foreign origins—she was born in Italy—might give rise to additional arguments by the Hindu nationalist opposition. Named as the head of the UPA's coordinating committee, and of the committee charged with smoothing over relations between the UPA and the left, she was still a major political player.

Manmohan Singh continued the policy of economic liberalization by opening up new sectors to foreign investors, by reducing customs barriers to better insert India into global trade, and by favoring business. But the government's dependence on Communist parliamentarians led them to abandon privatization, to shy away from labor law reforms, and to adopt a more interventionist policy. It is for this reason that the 2005 budget has a provision that provides payment of a hundred days of minimum wages per annum to any rural family struck by unemployment. The government moreover extended its policy of affirmative action favoring lower castes, giving them increased access to higher education. From then on, 27 percent of all spots in universities were reserved for the OBC.

In the international context, the Manmohan Singh government continued trends started by its predecessors. It added a Chinese dimension to its "Look East" policy, as a result of which economic and commercial relations between the two countries intensified and by 2006–2007, China had become second only to the United States as one of India's most important commercial partners. The United States was also India's primary strategic ally, as testified in 2006 by the Bush administration's decision, validated by Congress, to transfer civil nuclear engineering technology to New Delhi. This was contrary to the rules applied by Washington, up to that point, to countries that had not signed the Nuclear Non-Proliferation Treaty.

Renationalization or Regionalization of Indian Politics?

The 2009 general elections, which started on April 13, 2009, and ended more than a month later on May 16, broke one more record since 714 million people were eligible to vote and about 58 percent exercised that right. Although these elections were interpreted as a sign of renationalization of Indian politics, in fact, they accelerated the regionalization process.

Certainly, the national ruling leaders were reconfirmed at the helm of the country: for the first time since 1984, the ruling party escaped the

Table 2.1. Congress Performance (1977–2009)

Year	1977	1980	1984	1989	1991	1996	1998	1999	2004	2009
Number of seats	154	353	415	197	232	140	141	140	145	206
Share of the valid votes	34.3%	42.7%	48.1%	39.5%	36.5%	28.80%	25.82%	28.30%	26.53%	28.52%
Total number of seats	492	492	517	517	529	521	543	543	543	543

Source: Election Commission of India.

anti-incumbency reflex that had become almost systematic. In fact, no prime minister in office for a full term of five years had fought elections successfully since Jawarharlal Nehru in 1962.

But the success of the Congress must not be overrated, nor the renationalization of Indian politics that it was supposed to reflect according to many commentators. The Congress Party had won sixty-one seats more than in 2004, but it has improved its score in terms of votes polled by only 2 percent. In fact, the Party won approximately 27 percent of the votes polled since 1996 (see table 2.1).

In 2009 the two largest national parties continued to lose ground vis-à-vis the other parties in terms of votes (see table 2.2). Parties making an impact in one or two states only, on the contrary, have continued to rise. These parties may be officially classified among the "national parties" by the Electoral commission,[1] but four of the six official national parties have, in fact, a regionalized profile: the BSP got twenty of its twenty-one seats in Uttar Pradesh, the CPI(M) got sixteen of its twenty-four seats in Kerala and West Bengal, the NCP did the same in Maharashtra and the RJD in Bihar and Jharkhand. In other words, there is no "renationalization" of politics in India, but a constant trend toward regionalization.

The Congress benefited from the rise of the regional parties for two reasons. First, the new regional parties—giving a clear indication of the increasing fragmentation of Indian politics—helped the Congress by cutting out the votes of its main opponent parties in many states. Second, the Congress benefited from the regionalization of politics in the sense that its state's allies were rather successful.

In 2009, the first loser of the elections was the BJP. With about 19 percent of the votes polled, the BJP fell below its 1991 score. Yet, the BJP lost only 3.3 percent of the valid votes and it resisted very well in a half dozen states, like Karnataka, where it had recently won the state elections and where the BJP performed remarkably with 19 seats out of 28 (with 7 percent more votes than in 2004). L. K. Advani, at age eighty-two, whom the BJP had projected as its prime ministerial candidate, announced his

Table 2.2. Performances of the BJP, the Congress, and Other Parties (1991–2009 Lok Sabha Elections) in Percent of Valid Votes

Parties	1991	1996	1998	1999	2004	2009
Congress	36.26	28.80	25.82	28.30	26.53	28.52
BJP	20.11	20.29	25.59	23.75	22.16	18.84
Total	56.37	49.09	51.41	52.05	48.59	47.36
Other parties	43.63	50.71	48.59	47.95	51.41	52.54
Grand Total	100	100	100	100	100	100

Source: Election Commission of India, http://eci.nic.in/.

resignation from the post of leader of the opposition immediately after the elections. He remained until the end of the year, when a rather un-known regional leader—Nitin Gadkari, still then the chief of the BJP in Maharashtra—was appointed party president.

If the BJP was the biggest loser of the elections because it was plausibly expected that it would be back in office, the most dramatic defeat was that of the Communists, who had never won so few seats, only twenty-four. In West Bengal, this setback was partly a sequel of Nandigram and Singur, two issues that the Trinamool Congress had been very good at exploiting.[2]

The two OBC (Other Backward Caste) leaders, Mulayam Singh Yadav and Laloo Prasad Yadav, who had refused to remain associated with the Congress in order to form a fourth front, were the other big losers. The Samajwadi Party of Mulayam Singh Yadav saved twenty-four seats out of the thirty-six it had in the United Provinces, whereas Laloo Prasad Yadav's Rashtriya Janata Dal was routed in Bihar, from twenty-three to only three seats.

The Bahujan Samaj Party got only twenty seats, whereas it thought it would get fifty and be the king maker. But the BSP made progress com-pared to the 2004 Lok Sabha elections (twenty-one seats against nineteen) and was still, by far, the first party in terms of votes polled, 27.4 percent, which was 3 percent more than in 2004 and 10 percent more than the Con-gress. As a result, with more than 6 percent of the valid votes, it became the third national party of India, ahead of the CPI(M).

The regionalization of Indian politics was reconfirmed during the state elections that followed. Although national parties retained a few states—like Andhra Pradesh, Maharashtra (two states that remained with the Congress in 2009–2010) and Karnataka (won by the BJP in 2010)—many others were won (or retained) by state parties. In May 2011 the CPI(M)—a shrinking national party—lost power to Mamta Banerjee's Trinamool Congress in West Bengal, a state the Communists had ruled since 1977. In February/March 2012, a state party—the Samajwadi Party—replaced another one—the BSP—at the helm of India's largest state, Uttar Pradesh, after winning (like the BSP in 2007) a clear majority in terms of seats—and in spite of the mobilization of national leaders of the BP and the Congress, including Rahul Gandhi. The SP and the BSP won about 55 percent of the valid votes, while the Congress and the BJP got only 29 percent.

Conclusion

India prides itself on the claim that it has been "the greatest democracy in the world" since the 1950s; and the democratization of the political sys-tem since the 1990s gives more credit to this assertion. It has moved away from the authoritarian tendencies shown by Indira Gandhi and seen the emergence of bipartisan coalitions that allowed for rotations of power in which players could complete their full terms of office. More important, the rise to power of the lower castes, who are increasingly well represented in the ruling class, particularly through parties that rely on them, has added a new social dimension to Indian politics that was previously largely ignored. However, the plebeianization process has developed in tandem with the regionalization of politics. Indeed, the rising groups often come from large castes and communities that identify themselves with regions, or even states—and that form the driving forces of state parties. For instance, the Yadavs, an important OBC caste group in northern India, have played a major role in the successes of the Samajwadi Party in Uttar Pradesh. National cohesion will clearly be one of the problems of India in the near future—as evident from the resistance of several state governments vis-à-vis the antiterrorist policies of the Home minister, P. Chidambaram.

However, the rise of corruption, and even more so the criminalization of politics, undoubtedly constitute an even more important challenge that Indian democracy today has to address. In this respect, the rule of law was proof of a real capacity by the government to react to these challenges. The electoral commission, which was led by T. N. Seshan from 1990 to 1997, launched an offensive against unscrupulous politicians, to ensure that voting progressed fairly. In addition, the Supreme Court was engaged, during 1990, in a phase of "judicial activism" necessitated by the degradation of political practices. It also increasingly intervened in the governance of the country, as testified by its efforts to engender respect for the environment, an issue that had been largely ignored by the political parties. But "judicial activism" has not dissuaded politicians from indulging in malpractices. In February 2012 the telecommunications minister, A. Raja, was arrested because he underpriced licenses in exchange for bribes, resulting in a loss of $38 billion for the Indian state.

The judiciary looking not effective enough (and more and more tainted itself), an anticorruption movement has been started by a Gandhian veteran, Anna Hazare. This movement—which is supported by opposition parties (including the BJP) and is especially popular among the urban middle class of India—asks for the institution of a Lok Pal (citizen's ombudsman) before whom everybody, from bureaucrats to the prime minister, should be accountable. Understandably, the political class at large is reluctant to implement such a reform.

If the democratization of India's democracy has endowed it with a more convincing social content, it now needs to avoid another problem: that of becoming an illiberal democracy.

POLITICAL ECONOMY

India's economic reform of 1991 is often presented as a radical shift. Certainly, the country never before explicitly decided to dedicate much importance to market logic. Yet the liberalization of the economy had already started in the 1980s, under Indira Gandhi, and later, especially by her son Rajiv. The withdrawal of the state from economic affairs needs to be explained, which will be the subject of this section, after an initial discussion of the most significant features of the reforms in India.

The Reaffirmation of Free-Market Logic

India had existed for half a century with a mixed economy, a system characterized, as its name suggests, by the marriage of the private and public sectors. The latter took on successively more importance following the program of nationalization instituted by Nehru and later by his daughter, Indira Gandhi, which was much more interventionist than that of her father, as evidenced by the submission of all the banks and insurance schemes to state control during the years 1960–1970. In what is today recognized as the "Nehruvian system," the private sector not only coexisted with an increasingly dominant public sector, but was also forced to accept the logic of a managed economy. Even if economic planning was less rigorous than in the Soviet system, the five-year plans remain rather indicative of the level of government intervention, which was further supported by the Planning Commission's longtime status as one of the most powerful institutions in the country. It had the role of optimizing the allocation of resources so as to address both town and country planning, and supervising production so it would remain balanced. The principal instrument of the state in this political economy was, however, the "Licence Raj"—which meant that for any increase or diversification of its production, a company was required to obtain administrative authorization from a qualified civil servant. This bureaucratization of procedures, which unquestionably allowed for differences in development among regions to be limited, exerted a strong constraint on the Indian business environment and brought about endemic corruption, as those who could afford it sought to accelerate the granting of licenses with bribes. This economic system had also been characterized, since the 1950s, as backing away from the worldwide market: following a development plan of import substitution, independent India closed itself off to multinational firms—which could not control more than 50 percent of the shares of a joint venture in India—and to other potential threats to its industries. Not only were certain products, like cars, subjected to exceptionally high customs duties—certain tariffs exceeded 400 percent—India also imposed import quotas.

This system made it possible to limit social and regional inequalities with subsidies dedicated to redistribution, through the creation of a civil service, with balanced values, drawn largely from the middle class. Furthermore, the desire for national independence would also lead India to endow first-rate educational institutions—starting with the Indian Institutes of Technology—which, over time, would allow the country to assert itself as a leader in space exploration, nuclear expertise, and information technology. On the negative side, the economic system set up by Nehru and "hardened" by his daughter suffered from low productivity in the public sector and weak competitiveness of companies, both public and private, which were not subjected to competition on the international level. This prevented the development of economies of scale by limiting their production capacity. India's weak insertion into the global economy quickly resulted in a mediocre capacity to export: the share of Indian exports decreased from 1.9 percent of the total economy in 1950 to 0.6 percent in 1973. However, India needed to export because it relied on certain imports, in particular oil, a resource that it possessed too little of to sustain its enormous energy needs.

Rajiv Gandhi, Indira's son, attempted to modernize the system in the 1980s, notably with the slackening of the "Licence Raj," but remained very hostile to multinational companies. So, rather than accepting foreign direct investments (FDI), which nourished the Chinese economy, India modernized with credit. By 1991, it had accumulated $72 billion in debt and was facing a veritable balance of payments crisis by June of that year, when the totality of its available funds comprised the equivalent of four weeks' worth of foreign exchange reserves.

The government's reaction to the resulting IMF structural adjustment plan for India is particularly revealing. The finance minister at the time, Manmohan Singh, who later became prime minister in 2004, was the first to recognize that his country's economic model was on its last legs. He could back up this conclusion with force and credibility because he had worked at the UNDP and the Asian Development Bank, and therefore knew enough about the economies of East Asia and Southeast Asia to understand the "miracle" of a growth rate in the double digits. He reminded his fellow Indians that South Korea and India had had the same income per capita at the end of the 1940s. Like many others, Manmohan Singh was also concerned by China's rapid rise to power. In this context, the government agreed to follow a number of the IMF recommendations. Among these was the dismantling of the Licence Raj and of the well-known Monopolies and Restrictive Trade Practices Act, which required large firms to have a special permit in order to invest in certain areas. The list of the spheres of activity restricted to the public sector that had covered eighteen industries (including the iron and steel industries, mines, air transportation, telecommunications, and electric production) was reduced to three: the production of planes and warships, rail-bound transports, and nuclear energy. Furthermore, multinational corporations were allowed to hold a majority in joint ventures in many sectors (such as automobile, transportation infrastructure, pharmaceutical, tourism, telecommunications,[3] etc.), and even to establish subsidiary companies, which they wholly controlled, in certain priority sectors. Finally, import quotas were decreased little by little,[4] and tariff barriers dropped dramatically, peaks declining from 400 percent in 1990 to 35 percent in 2000, while average customs duties fell from 79 percent to 20 percent in 2004.[5] The failure of customs duties to drop significantly can be explained by their considerable importance to public revenue, of which they accounted for 38 percent in 1991. The government combined this policy of relying on customs duties with the creation of special economic zones, based on the Chinese model. In these areas, factories and service providers benefited from a more liberal regulation (particularly in terms of labor laws) and functioned exclusively for export production. There were twelve such zones in India in the 1990s, of which three—Positra in Gujarat, Gopalpur in Orissa, and Nanguneri in Tamil Nadu—attracted many private businesses.[6]

Those in business circles whose companies had thrived under the old protectionism were initially anxious about the liberalization process, but they were quick to accept the new economic course. Freed from an economic regulation that many saw as a yoke inhibiting their initiatives, historically dominant Indian capitalist families once again had room to maneuver and new captains of industry emerged. Those from political families were also attracted to the world of business by the promise of large profits. Sons of senior officials and soldiers earned MBAs and began to create their own companies, or to make careers for themselves elsewhere in the Indian economy. By the turn of the twenty-first century, 35 million such businessmen earned $1,000 per month, which in terms of purchasing power, makes them the "new rich" of India. However, this group, which grows at the rate of 10 percent per year, also profits from a new tax code that is part of the "supply policy": the maximum rate of income tax was decreased from 56 percent to 30 percent, and that of corporate tax from more than 50 percent to 35, and then 30 percent.

Another sign of change has been that the "new rich" show a certain ostentation that former generations of industry leaders never demonstrated, either because they adhered to the traditional values of discipline and austerity so valued by the merchant castes, from which the majority of India's first industrialists were recruited, or they were discouraged from displaying their wealth by the socialist spirit of the time. Luxury—formerly the prerogative of princes, maharajahs, and other nawabs—became the trademark of Indian capitalists, both those who inherited companies and those who founded their own businesses.

This reaffirmation, one might even say revenge, of free-market logic can only really be understood by taking into account the influence of nonresident Indians (NRIs), particularly among the Indian diaspora in the United States. This group has doubled in size over the last ten years, and today amounts to 2.5 million people. Currently, the numbers of legal Indian immigrants to the United States is second only to that of the Chinese. Many of these migrants come to the United States to further their studies, so that today, Indians constitute one of the most populous communities on American college and university campuses.[7] Their number increased from 30,000 in 1996–1997 to 75,000 in 2003–2004 (it doubled in the five years between 1998–1999 and 2002–2003). Since 2002–2003, when they already accounted for 13 percent of the total (74,603 out of 586,323), Indian students have made up the most significant share of the foreign student population in the United States. These students—like their relatives back home—have done well for themselves in the United States. Indeed, the U.S. census of 2000 showed that Indian Americans had an average income per capita of $60,093 compared with the national average of $38,885 (only 6 percent of Indian Americans live below the poverty line). An important part of the explanation for this success is the fact that three quarters of the members of this community attend university.

This diaspora has been a major factor in changing the image of India in the United States, and in establishing a link between the two countries, as much from an economic position (especially through data-processing companies) as from a political standpoint (the U.S. Congress and the Senate have cultivated an "India Caucus," a veritable ethnic lobby group that promises to benefit Indian diplomatic efforts). The strategic, political, economic, and even social coming together of these two countries evident in the last twenty-two years suggests that India is headed to emulate the market democracy championed by the United States. In reality, although India has been busy liberalizing its economy, and even though the urban middle class is contributing to the Americanization of the country, India is still far from meeting the criteria of the Washington Consensus.[8]

The Resistance of the Regulatory State

The role of the Indian State's inner sanctum, although limited, is still very substantial. Public authorities continue to play a significant role in internal regulation, even though the Licence Raj was dismantled, and the protectionism of the past is no longer the norm in Indian relations to the outside world.

In spite of the questioning of the government's economic policies, which continued through the beginning of the 1990s, the state still intervened at all levels of the economy. The World Bank warned against the persistence of this bureaucratic phenomenon when it stressed to India that it took ninety days to get a factory off the ground (compared to thirty days in China).[9] In response, the government objected that state intervention was designed to defend the most vulnerable social groups. Indeed, this is the stated objective of the policy of Small Scale Industries (SSI). These SSIs—which are defined by a limited ability to invest (less than US$250,000 annually)—are the only ones to be authorized to operate in certain sectors, and the state has drawn up a list of products reserved for them.[10] In this way, the toy industry succeeded in eluding control by large companies, unlike in China. SSIs continue to account for 45 percent of industrial production, yet the strength of this policy has eroded, and the list of the products reserved for SSI status declined from 821 in 1998 to 605 ten years later.[11] In this case, the power of the state corresponds to a strictly Gandhian point of view, which advocates protection of small-scale family and artisanal enterprises from competition with large companies, even though many SSIs today operate in the "high tech" sector.

In the same way, the privatization of businesses that were nationalized between 1950 and 1980 is not a priority of the Indian government. Besides, the word "privatization" is taboo in India, where one speaks instead about "disinvestment"—the Indian government even created a "Ministry of Disinvestment" at the end of the 1990s. This gave weight not only to the power of the trade unions, but also to the importance traditionally attached to state action in the economic sphere. In 1950, India had only five public national companies, which accounted for 290 million rupees of annual investments. In the 2000s, India has 240 public national companies that represent more than 2,525,000 million rupees ($399 million) of investment. In July 1991, the government released a document titled "The Industrial Policy Statement" to detail its intended reforms. It forecast initial disinvestments, for which control remained in the hands of public officials, that were intended to increase the state treasury and were therefore distinct from privatization that occurred later. From 1991 to 2000, the state thus reduced its direct participation in thirty-nine companies, which accounted for 3 percent of the government's shares in public companies.[12] After 2000, the coalition government led by the BJP that was in power from 1998 to 2004, sought to commit itself to what Prime Minister Atal Bihari Vajpayee called "strategic sales." These required that at least 26 percent of all shares of a public firm be held by a private operator, who thereby gained veto power and possibly even the majority of the firm's shares, if he or she were already an important shareholder.

Over the following three years, thirty-five companies were subjected to "strategic sales." Some of these firms granted veto power to private companies, as in the case of the telecommunications company VSNL and also that of Indian Petrochemicals, the second-largest Indian petrochemical firm. Others transformed themselves from public firms to private, as in the cases of Bharat Aluminium Company (BALCO), the third-largest aluminum producer; Modern Food (sold to Hindustan Lever); and Maruti, which became a subsidiary of Suzuki. These companies accounted for only 1.13 percent of the state's interests in public firms, but these developments gave rise to sharp criticism by the trade unions. Moreover, the Supreme Court was presented with the BALCO case and generated a crucial judgment that validated the policy still called "disinvestment," even if the focus had shifted to privatization.[13] Still, the opposition to these policies multiplied and took a political turn, foreshadowing that the "strategic sales" in two leading companies of the Indian economy (Hindustan Petroleum and Bharat Petroleum) desired by Arun Shourie, Vajpayee's minister of disinvestment, would not be able to occur because of resistance that penetrated even into the heart of the coalition government.

The changes of 2004 that brought the Congress Party back into power, at the head of a parliamentary coalition in which the Communists played a crucial role, resulted in a freezing of the "strategic sales" policy. In June 2004, the members of this new political alliance developed a National Common Minimum Program that forcefully affirmed the government's commitment to defending a large part of the public sector, specifically that part whose objectives were social, and to not privatize those state enterprises that generated profits. In fact, even the concept of "disinvestment" was called into question when the Communists opposed the sale of a minimal number of state shares in the electric company BHEL in spring 2005. As a result, India continues to have a strong public sector that constitutes a quarter of the GNP, nearly a third of the capital investments to the Indian economy, and approximately nineteen million employees (out of the twenty-eight million that work in the formal sector).[14]

Another domain that the state continues to dominate relates to labor laws. Decades of co-administration of the Indian economy by the Congress Party and the trade unions—in particular the trade union of the Congress Party, the National Indian Trade Union Congress (INTUC)—allowed a small minority of workers in the formal sector—employees—to put in place a remarkable legislative mechanism, or "labor laws," to protect their interests. Only companies employing fewer than a hundred people can, for example, dismiss any of them without first obtaining government authorization. The Vajpayee government prepared a bill proposing that this threshold be raised to one thousand employees, but the

Communist partners of the Congress Party were very attached to these "labor laws." Economic liberals interpreted the absence of an "exit policy" for companies to be an entry barrier, because foreign investors would be wary of becoming involved in a country from which it is objectively so difficult to withdraw. In practice, however, multinational companies have resorted to recruiting workers on contracts of limited duration.

Lastly, the state continues to play a major role in the agricultural sector, which dominates the Indian economy and which employs more than 60 percent of the population even though it contributes less than one-fifth of the total GNP. In this sector, the prices of both initial inputs and finished products are managed by the government. For example, peasants may be charged minimally for the electricity powering the water pumps that facilitate the irrigation of their fields. Likewise, the cost of fertilizers is systematically reduced by government subsidies. These measures, which follow the same logic as the exemption of income tax for peasants, were meant to be supplemented by the new government's "National Rural Employment Guarantee Act."[15] This arrangement is consistent with the platform on which the Congress won the election in 2004. In reaction to the effects of the economic liberalization exacerbated by Vajpayee's policies, opposition Congress members denounced the widening of inequalities and proposed a return to greater state intervention. The inequalities in question are naturally social, since the few dozens of thousands of people earning $1,000 per month in income contrast with the 450 million living on $1.50 a day, but they are also geographical, as the regions of India that benefited the most from economic modernization, the south and west, also profited from an average income per person three times higher than the rest of the country.[16]

The 2004 victory of the Congress Party resulted primarily from the electoral mobilization of the most underprivileged, who were increasingly unhappy with the Vajpayee government's economic policy. Indeed, the immense survey carried out by the Center for the Study of Developing Societies shows that among those who voted for the National Democratic Alliance (NDA), which was the coalition that supported Vajpayee, 35 percent thought that their financial position had improved under the outgoing government. Only 22 percent of those who voted for the Congress Party felt the same way. Moreover, this investigation showed a perfectly linear relationship between the index of dis/satisfaction with the Vajpayee government and one's socioeconomic category: the poorer the voters were, the more they perceived their living conditions as having worsened, and vice versa.[17] These underprivileged groups had always seen the state as their protector, and they came to see the Congress Party as the viable alternative to the BJP.

Furthermore, historical anthropology suggests that the Hindu king-doms and the empires that succeeded them, including the British Empire, were traditionally perceived as institutions of social control, but also as protective powers from which their subjects expected much. The most familiar name for the state was "ma-bap" (literally, "mom-dad"). The persistence of this role of the state, therefore, reflects a national consensus beyond the mission with which it is officially entrusted in the Constitu-tion. As Granville Austin writes in his pioneering work about the Indian Constitution: "[It] is first and foremost a social document [of which] the majority of its provisions are either directly aimed at furthering the goals of the social revolution or attempt to foster this revolution by establishing the conditions necessary for its achievement."[18]

In 2004, the elections made it possible for the voices of those who feared the continued erosion of the state and an acceleration of the eco-nomic liberalization that had victimized them to be heard. These groups brought to power a Congress Party that promised them it would revive certain aspects of the Nehru/Gandhi era. The Party's election campaign promised not only the National Rural Employment Guarantee Act and the implementation of official support mechanisms for artisanal enter-prises ("small-scale industries") threatened by liberalization, but also to give priority to agriculture by doubling the credit available for this sector over three years and significantly reducing interest rates on agricultural loans. This policy of redistribution also included new affirmative ac-tion programs in favor of religious and linguistic minorities, women, untouchables, and indigenous peoples. Also included in these promises was an increase in the percentage of the GNP set aside for the budgets of the public education (from 2 percent to 6 percent) and public health (3 percent) systems.

This program relied on election demagogy because the state treasury, which remains unfilled because of privatization, is not able to support such extra costs (the public deficit is close to double-digit percentage of the GNP if the states' deficits are included). Still, the 2004 elections al-lowed the Indian masses to issue a warning that the political community could not ignore. In such a way, India benefits greatly from democracy, a system that not only allows its citizens an "anti-incumbency reflex" but also, in so doing, the ability to amend the policies followed. In fact, the appointments of Manmohan Singh to head the government and of P. Chidambaram to head the Ministry of Finance indicated that the policy of economic liberalization would continue. The government's dependence, however, on the mandate of its voters, and on Communist members of Parliament, led it to de-emphasize privatization and to once again espouse an interventionist policy. The budget report of March 2005 suggested that a compromise had been reached, behind closed doors, between the Congress Party and the Communists. It addressed two key points: on the one hand, India opens to external investors, and on the other, privatization and the reform of labor law is excluded from the political agenda.

ঌ

India is without doubt one of the most remarkable democracies to have been developed outside the West. For the past twenty years, its political liberalism has coexisted with a new kind of economic liberalism. By deregulating and opening its economy to the worldwide market, India entered into globalization, helped by undeniable sectoral assets—particularly in the field of data processing—and a diaspora of entrepreneurs. This liberalization goes hand in hand with the democratization mentioned above, in that power shifts from the hands of yesterday's elites to the private sector, thereby giving a significant voice in the public sector to the new middle class that is emerging from the general populace. The liberalization process, however, has had a clearly negative impact on the social fabric of India. Inequalities have increased, not only geographically (the northern states are lagging behind) but also in socio-economic terms. The Gini coefficient for these inequalities has risen from 0.260 in rural India and 0.342 in urban India in 1999–2000 to, respectively, 0.291 and 0.382 in 2009–2010.

This development has taken place even though the state persists in playing a crucial role in the economy. Public enterprises thus continue to serve a paramount role in many domains, and those that the government classifies as "small-scale industries" enjoy considerable protections. This government intervention is essential to the (dynamic) equilibrium of India today. A rapid withdrawal of this government role would render directionless the current policy of affirmative action. Even so, the decrease in the number of jobs reserved for the Scheduled Castes and Scheduled Tribes due to the decline of the public sector aggravates a more general problem: high growth in recent years has not created many jobs. This issue may worsen if the growth rate continues to decline—from below 6 percent in 2012–2013 to possibly around 5 percent in 2013–2014.

IDENTITY POLITICS

India is multiple. Its continental mass (3.9 million square kilometers) and its demographic power (1.2 billion inhabitants) obviously contribute to this, but its neighbor China, which is comparatively huge in terms of surface area and population, is much more homogeneous.

India has an atypical cultural diversity. This country is above all the place of all religions. Admittedly, Hinduism accounts for 80 percent of the total population but, besides the fact that Hinduism is divided into many sectarian currents, there are still more than 250 million who belong to other faiths. Islam, in particular, is one of the great religions of India. This is not only because the size of the Muslim population, composed of nearly 180 million believers, makes the Indian Union the second Muslim country in the world, equal to Pakistan, but because of the traces of Islam that mark Indian history, as evident, for example, in Persian-style miniature paintings and monuments inherited from the Mughal Empire, as well as the observable syncretism of cultural elements in music and, of course, spirituality.

Beyond this, even though they make up only 2 percent of the population, Christians constitute a very important Indian minority. On the one hand, they call themselves "sons of the soil," because Saint Thomas evangelized the country before he died and was buried there in 52 CE. On the other hand, even though they number only 25 million, Christians play an important role in education and health care (as testified by the work of Mother Teresa), and in theological matters (both in India and abroad, as evident in the impact of Indian inculturation theorists, particularly in Jesuit circles). Sikhs also constitute 2 percent of the Indian population yet their social, political, economic, and cultural weight is not reflected by this small percentage: they are still overrepresented in the army because of their status as a "martial race" that was ascribed to them by the British, and they dominate the economy of Punjab, one of the richest states in terms of per capita revenue and the only state where Sikhs are in the majority. Next on the list are those communities that do not account for even 1 percent of the population, which, however, do not have a negligible importance. Buddhism was born in India, and even though it was driven out of the country during the medieval period, it is still such a part of the national heritage that it appears on the Indian flag as the wheel of Dharma that decorates the flag's center (the ochre, white, and green bands each refer to one of the other religions mentioned above).

Zoroastrianism has even fewer followers than Buddhism—especially since the installation of the Dalai Lama in India in 1959 and the conversion of thousands of Dalits since 1956. Its followers, the Parsis, number only 65,000 as of the 2001 census. Yet this handful of people exert themselves prominently in the Indian economy through old family firms like Godrej and, especially, Tata. Jews number fewer still, particularly since the departure of thousands of Indian Jews to Israel after the creation of the Hebrew state. Still, New Delhi can pride itself on the fact that the country has never known anti-Semitism, for which it offers as proof the synagogue of Cochin, dating from the fourteenth century.

The incredible religious efflorescence just covered (and which would not be complete unless one added Jainism, the forms of animism cultivated by indigenous populations, and Muslim subgroups such as Shi'ism, Ismailism, etc.) has, in fact, given rise to a relatively peaceful coexistence. This does not necessarily confirm the irenic perspective that underestimates the conflicts between Hindus and Muslims (that underlay Partition in 1947).[19] Although not ignoring the recurring riots of which Muslims today are victims, it is nevertheless necessary to recognize India as a success meriting praise for its efforts to transcend religious pluralism and maintain diversity in unity. This is embodied in the idea of secularism, an "ism" that is not the same as American secularism, because it is not about the separation of the state and church(es), but rather an equal benevolence of the state for the various religious communities. There is no state religion in India, but the recognition of several religions by the state. This principle (of unity) is recognized by the Indian Constitution in Article 30, which states that any denominational school can request public allocations.

Multiculturalism vs. Ethno-Nationalism

Jawaharlal Nehru, who led the government of India from 1947 to his death in 1964, interpreted secularism in a truly multicultural sense that made it possible for religious minorities to feel at home in India. Nehru sought especially to integrate the Muslims who had chosen to remain in India—when others had left to Pakistan—but who might wonder whether they had made a mistake. For them, Nehru deferred *sine die* the introduction of a uniform civil code and accepted Shariat as a source of law, whereas Hindu traditional laws were reformed to fit a Western logic as relating to divorce, inheritance, and adoption. From the start, Indian secularism has therefore been biased, a fact that has driven Hindu nationalists to attack it.

In the eyes of the Hindu nationalists, the party of Nehru, the Congress Party, is pseudo-secularist because it favors Muslims, their number one public enemy, and a minority who represents a "fifth column" that they claim is pan-Islamic and pro-Pakistani, and to which Congress Party members pander in exchange for their votes in elections.

During the 1980s, Hindu nationalists could, for the first time, mobilize public opinion on this topic against Rajiv Gandhi, Nehru's grandson and Indian prime minister from 1984 to 1989, specifically regarding the Shah Bano case. This case was named for a Muslim woman who, repudiated by her husband based on Islamic law, demanded alimony in a court of justice. She won her case, but her husband appealed to the Supreme Court, which confirmed the earlier judgment. Furthermore, its verdict disapproved of the Muslim attachment to their traditional laws. Islamic leaders responded without delay by taking to the street, shouting the slogan "Sharia in danger!" Rajiv Gandhi changed the law in Parliament to remove the Muslim community from the clauses of the Code of Criminal Procedure that the judges invoked to justify alimony payments for Shah Bano. The Hindu nationalists were in an ideal position to be indignant at this political maneuver, which was dictated by electoral interests. They launched a counter offensive to prevent Hindus from becoming "second-class citizens in their own country," as they themselves phrased it.

This mobilization of Hindu nationalists also pivoted on the Ayodhya debate. In this town in the north of India, a mosque had been built in the sixteenth century on a site considered by Hindus to be the birthplace of the god Ram. The riots caused by Hindu nationalists polarized the electorate: as Hindus were the majority, their confrontations with Muslims led them to feel increased support for the tenets of the BJP and to thereby vote for it. Indeed, these violent incidents supported the rise of the Hindu nationalist party, the BJP.

Communal Violence and the BJP's Rise to Power

Since 1989, all general elections provided the opportunity for Hindu nationalists to lay claim to the site of Ayodhya with an increasing aggressiveness for (re)building a temple there dedicated to Ram. Their party, the Bharatiya Janata Party (BJP—Indian People's Party), grew systematically.

In June 1991, the BJP won 120 seats in Parliament with 20.1 percent of the votes cast, which propelled it to second place among the Indian political parties. The BJP also obtained a majority of the seats in the Uttar Pradesh state assembly, which, when added to its recorded regional successes in 1990 in the states of Madhya Pradesh, Rajasthan, and Himachal Pradesh, enabled it to control key aspects of the governments of the Hindi-speaking north. The BJP's rise can largely be explained by the mobilization of many Hindus within the framework of the Ayodhya movement; the districts where communal riots occurred elected many more BJP parliamentarians than elsewhere.

The BJP did not, however, manage to transform itself in a way that convinced and mollified protesting factions within the governing party. This was evident in the Party's difficulties in dealing with Uttar Pradesh, where they hesitated between building a temple dedicated to Ram in Ayodhya—which would cause a violent reaction by Muslims and harm the Party's image—or to wait, which risked alienating militant Hindu nationalists. The latter put an end to this dilemma when they took the Ayodhya mosque by force and razed it to the ground on December 6, 1992. This coincided with a planned event—a ceremony organized by the RSS, the implications of which were intended to be entirely symbolic. This destruction was followed by many communal riots that were caused either by Hindu demonstrations of joy or by Muslim protests. The violence—to which police repression added additional victims—left approximately twelve hundred dead and was particularly deadly in Bombay. The New Delhi government reacted by imprisoning Hindu nationalist leaders, banning the RSS, and subjugating the four BJP-controlled states to President's Rule. The first two measures were flexibly applied, and were even occasionally called into question by the courts; as for the last one, it dealt a crushing blow to the BJP but failed to substantially limit its growth, as demonstrated by the Party's electoral success in 1996 and 1998.

Already ahead of the Congress Party in parliamentary seats since 1996, the BJP, for the first time, won practically the same number of votes cast in 1998 (the BJP won 25.6 percent, the Congress Party 25.8). Although the election results of 1999 did not confirm this phenomenon as an actual trend, they are open to more than one interpretation. The BJP seemed to be the clear winner, the more so as it experienced a further gain in seats. Yet, with 183 representatives in Parliament, it was still far from holding the majority, for which 272 seats are needed.

The BJP's electoral success was also based on its image, that of a party less corrupt and more disciplined than the others, and above all better able to ensure law and order. This idealized representation corresponds only crudely with the historical reality that allowed the BJP to replace the Congress Party, which, in the eyes of the middle class, was synonymous with authority, even of authoritarianism under Indira Gandhi. This image of the Congress Party was further deepened by the "Kargil victory" (named for the city in Indian-administered Kashmir where India crushed Pakistani infiltrators in the spring of 1999), which was largely attributed, by middle-class social circles, to Vajpayee's cold-bloodedness.

The Test of Power

Once in power, the BJP implemented a more moderate program than that which it endorsed as the opposition. This is a classical effect of having to deal with political responsibilities, but, in this case can also be attributed to the fact that the party had become part of a coalition, the National Democratic Alliance (NDA), whose electoral proclamation declares commitment to respecting a moratorium on the Ayodhya debate, as well as the relative autonomy of Jammu and Kashmir, as articulated in Article 370 of the Constitution (the removal of which was continually advocated by the BJP), and the imposition of a uniform civil code that would, in particular, weaken the status of Shariat as a special source of law for Muslims.[20]

On the other hand, the education minister, M. M. Joshi, sought to appoint men close to the RSS (or its ideas) to key posts, such as the directorship of the Indian Council for Historical Research, the Indian Council for Social Research Science, and the National Council for Education and Research Training, which is the institution in charge of preparing school textbooks. These appointments would have made it possible for Hindu nationalists to rewrite history textbooks in order to refute the Aryan invasion theory (which they wrongly counter with the theory that Aryans were Hindu immigrants), to underline the atrocities of the Muslim invasions (through exaggeration), and to rehabilitate their founding fathers at the expense of the figures who continually outshine them, like Gandhi and Nehru. For the RSS, this rewriting of history and of the education sector in general is more significantly important because they imagine that such biases will allow them to refashion the spirit of India.

In matters of defense, the efforts authorized by the Vajpayee government, since it took power in 1998, also fit with RSS expectations. The NDA's first budget increased the appropriations going to defense by more than 30 percent. Moreover, the RSS was the first to approve nuclear tests that spring, justifying them with the argument that only the atomic bomb would allow India to ensure its own safety.

The government in New Delhi also "covered up" the machinations of BJP chief ministers, who benefited from having an absolute majority. This was especially true with respect to Gujarat, the state in the Indian Union longest under continuous BJP control since 1995, when the Party won power there. Narendra Modi, chief minister of Gujarat since his appointment by the government in 2001, and an active member of the RSS, dedicated his administration to the service of Hindu militancy, as evidenced by the communal violence that erupted in Godhra in February 2002 and lasted several weeks. The mortality count based on the official, but reliable, estimate was of nearly two thousand Muslim victims, a figure unparalleled by any wave of violence between Hindus and Muslims since the pogroms of Partition. Prime Minister Vajpayee was alarmed by this violence, but did not take any significant action against Modi, who benefited from the polarization of the local population by dissolving the Gujarat Assembly and triumphantly winning in the planned elections at the end of 2002. In 2004, the BJP lost effective power, in particular because their policy of economic liberalization was perceived as "pro-rich." Yet, in 2007 and 2012 Modi once again dominated in Gujarat thanks to a considerable election win.

WOMEN'S POWER AND KINSHIP
NETWORKS IN POLITICAL LIFE

By Virginie Dutoya

In 1947, when India became independent, women were granted the same political rights as men, and the principle of nondiscrimination on the ground of sex was inscribed in the Constitution.[21] However, if women were equal citizens by law, this formal equality did not translate into equal political participation, not to speak of equal access to political power. In terms of women's access to political power, two indicators seem particularly relevant: presence and leadership in political parties, and capacity to secure elected and/or executive positions. One could argue that such a formal definition of political power centers on institutional and party politics, whereas women are often more keen to participate in so-called "un-formal" politics. It is true that, especially since the eighties, Indian women have engaged in a large array of movements, from Hindu nationalism to the Naxalite movement, including, of course, feminist or women's movements.[22] And these movements have given some women access to political agency. However, the fact that all these movements engage at some point with the state to get a decision made, or to replace one, suggests that political power is still mainly located in the state and its institutions.

Women and Political Power in India: Major Trends since Independence

Women are present in most, if not all, Indian political parties and many parties have a women's wing. However, these women's wings are not conceived as real places of power and decision making. Indeed, the most powerful female politicians usually do not belong to these women's wings. But even in the mainline party, women are increasingly present, and four major parties (including the ruling Congress) were led by women at the 2009 general elections. Many parties are nowadays engaged in giving more positions to women in the party structure; for instance, the BJP amended its constitution in January 2008 to reserve 33 percent of the party positions for women. However, women are still often underrepresented, as is the case in the Congress Working Committee, in which women represented only 18 percent of the members (four out of twenty-two) in 2009.[23] In many parties, women are hardly represented in decision making. This battle for inclusion in parties[24] is necessary, as big parties remain the easiest way for women to get elected at the state and federal levels.

The underrepresentation of women in elected bodies further demonstrates that women are still not at par with men in terms of access to political power. Until the ninth Lok Sabha (elected in 1989), women represented between 4.5 percent and 6.5 percent of the members, with the exception of the eighth Lok Sabha, in which women's presence increased to 8.3 percent.[25] This has slightly but regularly increased in the nineties and the early years of this century, and at the time of writing 59 of the 545 members of the Lok Sabha were women, making women's representation in the Lok Sabha cross the 10 percent line for the first time. In the Rajya Sabha, women were generally slightly more numerous, and women have represented between 7 percent and 15.5 percent of the members since independence.[26] In state legislatures women have also been widely underrepresented. It is only in local bodies that women have been able to form a substantial part of the members in the last two decades. This is because the same constitutional amendments that in 1992 reformed local governments and made them compulsory in all states of the federation also promulgated a 33 percent quota for women. And in 2005, they represented more than 40 percent of the representatives in the Panchayati Raj institutions.[27]

As for executive functions, some women have reached the highest position in India. Indira Gandhi became prime minister in 1966, which sets India ahead of many Western democracies. However, she remains more of an exception, and apart from her, most portfolios and positions as chief minister or governor have been held by men. For instance, only 6 percent of the cabinet ministers were women between 1997 and 2006. Moreover, women usually get "soft ministries"—that is, ministries concerned with issues considered "feminine" and/or less prestigious, such as tourism, women's development, health, and so on, even though there are some exceptions. But if women are often confined to "soft domains," because of stereotypes about "female qualities," this does not mean that they feel compelled to act as women and for women. As a matter of fact, according to Stéphanie Tawa Lama-Rewal, most female politicians have avoided making feminist statements or taking up feminist issues.[28]

The profile of high-level women politicians in India is more varied than the cliché of the urban middle-class and upper-caste (and "Westernized") woman suggests. However, many of them come from privileged backgrounds and do not have much in common with the average Indian woman. Among the eighty-two women who were elected to at least one of the last three Lok Sabha, sixty-three had a university degree, and only two of them were below matriculation. However, almost 27 percent of these women belonged to Scheduled Castes or Scheduled Tribes categories, which shows a real diversity of social profiles. On the other hand, few women from religious minorities reach political power. For instance, since independence, only eighteen Lok Sabha seats have been held by Muslim women, for a total of only fourteen Muslim women members of the Lok Sabha, some having been elected several times.

Hurdles and Resources in Women's Pursuit of Political Power

Women's unequal access to power has many roots. First, it is linked to their underrepresentation in political parties, which results in a low percentage of female candidates. For instance, women represented only 7 percent of the candidates in 2009.[29] The impact of socioeconomic factors is quite ambiguous. The Indian social structure is largely male dominated and women lack autonomy in many ways. According to the 2001 census, only 47.8 percent of women above fifteen years old are literate, against 73.4 percent of men. About one-third of the married women have experienced marital violence, and almost 50 percent of them do not participate in household decisions.[30] Northern India also has an ancient culture of segregation of men and women, summarized in the concept of purdah (from the Persian word for curtain), a practice that while concerning only a minority of the population sets as an ideal for the whole society the seclusion of women inside the home and their submission to the men of the family. This suggests a social setup in which women have few opportunities to access political power. However, there seems to be no correlation between the condition of women in a state or constituency (in terms of literacy, access to health, etc.) and the capacity of women to be elected from that place. As a matter of fact, states considered as "backward" and patriarchal have usually fared better in terms of women's representation than states where the situation of women is reputedly better, such as Kerala.[31] When interrogated about the difficulties of politics for women, most (female) politicians insist on the lack of direct access to economic resources as well as the challenge of upholding traditional social duties (especially toward the family) while pursuing a political career. But they usually admit that they are not themselves concerned with these types of issues.[32]

Moreover, if there are many hurdles to women's access to power, they also have some resources. First, women have played an important role in the nationalist struggle, and female politicians do not hesitate to highlight this heritage (and especially the engagement of women behind Gandhi) to legitimize their presence in the public sphere. Moreover, women can use the double image of womanhood in Indian culture and project themselves as loving and caring mothers and/or as forceful goddesses,[33] thus going beyond the usual association of women with softness and altruism, qualities that are usually considered as nonpolitical.

Family support is another very crucial element for women who want to get involved in political life. It is often said that most female politicians belong to the "beti-biwi brigade" (the daughters and wives brigade) and are mere proxies. This is particularly the case for local governments, in which women are well represented because of the above-mentioned 33 percent reservations. It is said that men unable to present themselves because of the reservations have given the ticket to their wives, but are still the ones exercising the actual power. A new word has even been invented to refer to these men: *sarpanchpati* (a combination of the words for "mayor" and "husband").

Kinship Networks and Female Political Power

The interlinking of female political power and family is not a new phenomenon, and Gail Minault had already underlined it in her studies of
women in politics from the colonial period to the seventies, presenting the
model of the "extended family" to expose the intricacies between the roles
of women in private and public sphere.[34] In the case of female politicians
at national and state levels, there are many examples of women benefiting
from kinship. For almost 75 percent of the women sitting in the fifteenth
Lok Sabha, one can easily point to one or several powerful men among
their kin. However, this is also true of many men. Indira Gandhi and Sonia Gandhi of course benefited from their position of daughter or wife of
powerful men, but as mothers they also transmitted this power to some
men of their family. Political dynasties are a widespread phenomenon in
South Asia, and it is not clear to what extent women benefit more from
it. Moreover, reducing women's political power to a simple phenomenon
of nepotism tends to minimize women's capacity to hold (and give)
power independently of the way they accessed it. Many women, like Su-
shma Swaraj of the BJP or Mamata Banerjee of the Trinamool Congress,
achieved political power independently, and many others benefited from
their families, but created their own political space, like Meira Kumar,
speaker of the Lok Sabha or Jayalalitha, leader of the AIADMK.

Nevertheless, it remains that kinship is an important resource for
women, and though it is not certain that men do not benefit from it as
much as women, the impact of kinship on political power is gendered
in the sense that it affects women *qua* women. One of the difficulties in
understanding the role played by kinship lies in the multiple forms it can
take. Some women benefit from the kinship network in which they were
born, while some others benefit from the one into which they married, as
wife or as daughter-in-law. Even if there are exceptions, "blood kinship"
is not typically feminine, whereas it is less frequent for a man to directly
and politically benefit from the kinship contracted by marital alliance.
Kinship can also be much more distant or informal. For instance, Jayalalitha benefited from her "affair" with M. G. Ramachandran (but also from
her own status of movie star), and eventually defeated his widow, who
had a firmer kinship connection with him. Caste can also be considered as
a form of kinship that some women can also mobilize, as Mayawati, the
leader of the BSP is doing. However, this is not typically feminine.

One must also underline the difference between getting concrete political support from a kinsman and benefiting from his or her reputation
and legacy. Many women have actually used their connections with dead
politicians more to strengthen their legitimacy than as a concrete material
support (though both aspects are of course linked, as kinship ties may

help to secure support from a party, even if the kin is deceased). Moreover, women have always used kinship as a symbolic tool to justify their presence in the political sphere. The use of fictive kinship ties enables them to overcome social constraints such as male-female segregation by presenting themselves as fictive mother/sister of the men they meet in the realm of their political activities. Thus kinship, in its many dimensions, can be conceived as a useful tool for women (but also for men) wishing to secure power. However, in the case of women it reinforces the impression that they are "proxies" and not able to stand for themselves. From that perspective, the proposed bill to extend reservations beyond the local-governments level up to Parliament could be a way to grant more autonomy in women's political participation.

Reservations for Women: A New Path toward Political Power?

Since 1992 and the Seventy-Third and Seventy-Fourth Amendments, one out of three constituencies in local bodies is reserved for women (with a rotation at every election). Since 1996, a draft law has regularly been presented to the Parliament to extend this reservation to Vidhan Sabhas (state legislative assemblies) and to the Lok Sabha. This "Women's Reservation Bill" is supported by most of the important parties of India, among them the Congress and the BJP. It has, however, some fierce opponents, mainly from the Samajwadi Party, the Janata Dal, and the Rashtriya Janata Dal, three parties that rely widely on (low) caste mobilization, and who, so far, have been able to block the vote on the bill.

Debates on this bill have revolved around the question of kinship and identity. Most detractors of the bill argue that they do not oppose women getting a bigger share of political power, but want to make sure that "their" women will benefit from reservations, whether based on caste or religion. Thus, they insist on the necessity to have "reservations within reservations" for OBC women and women belonging to religious minorities (Muslims mainly). They sometimes support their claim by arguing that in the case of local bodies, reservations have led merely to "proxies" and not to the emergence of an autonomous female leadership.

Apart from this debate, feminists themselves do not all agree on the issue of reservations for women. Historically, women's organizations opposed such quotas, claiming that they wanted equality and not favoritism. But this claim faded in the eighties, as it appeared that several decades of independence had not given women a fair share of political power. Moreover, the women's movement was receptive to the rhetoric of female empowerment developed by Congress (especially Rajiv Gandhi) in the eighties and early nineties, and saw the point in engaging with formal politics.[35] Thus a majority of Indian "feminists" and women's groups support the bill. But the question of whether reservations will undermine women's credibility and autonomy remains. As noted before, the outcome of reservations in local bodies is for the least contested and contrasted, and it is difficult to predict what would be the impact of reservations at national and state level. But the fact that the Women's Reservation Bill guarantees that reservations would be filled by elections gives a better prospect of autonomy than, for instance, in Pakistan, where "women's seats" in National Assembly are filled by a system of quasi nominations. And it seems that reservations for women have a future in India, as the government recently announced its will to pass the Women's Reservations Bill during the fifteenth Lok Sabha and to raise the 33 percent quota in local bodies to 50 percent.[36]

THE SOCIAL COST OF MILITARISM

By Isabelle Saint-Mezard

India's approach to military affairs has been somewhat ambiguous. In the initial years after Independence, many nationalist leaders did not think highly of the armed forces.[37] Having served under British rule, they were regarded with a certain level of distrust. As a result, they were allocated only limited resources, especially as Prime Minister Nehru wanted to promote a pacifist foreign policy, devoid of any strong military dimension. It took a decade and a half and the military defeat by China in 1962 for India to change tack. India's armed forces have since expanded substantially and India stands today as a major military power in Asia. With more than 1.3 million active-duty personnel, its military comes third, after China and the United States, as the largest land force in the world. It is also a matter of pride to many Indians that their country has entered the restricted club of nuclear-weapon states. In point of fact, many in the Indian elite see military strength as a critical component of India's global rise to power.

While they are regarded by the leadership and the public at large as a symbol of India's rise, on a day to day basis the armed forces remain faced with a challenging security situation. Their prime mission is to defend the integrity of the country in a hostile neighborhood, which requires protecting a 9,320-mile-long land border and a 4,722-mile-long coastline. In addition, they have been increasingly tasked with internal security duties, including fighting terrorism and insurgencies. Thus, despite the fact that India has growing strategic ambitions in the world, its armed forces are constrained by immediate threats to the domestic situation, with heavy demands on them to help maintain internal security. This predicament partly results from the increasing proclivity on the part of civilian authorities to resort to military force as a management tool in the face of domestic conflicts. This "civilian militarism" also explains why the number of paramilitary forces has expanded exponentially, with about 1.3 million today in their ranks.

Reforming and Modernizing the Indian Military

In keeping with the British legacy, the Indian armed forces have had a tradition of service to the nation and they have always been under full civilian control. Very early on, they have also come to be dominated by the powerful bureaucracy of the Defence Ministry. However, their growing marginalization from the decision-making process has been a source of tension and mismanagement. The 1999 Kargil war episode against Pakistan starkly revealed the lapses in India's security and defense preparedness. India has since tried to reform its higher defense planning, with a view to giving more voice to the military brass in the decision-making process, while improving institutional coordination between the military establishment and the Defence Ministry bureaucracy. However, India's defense reforms have not yet proved very successful, and its higher defense management is still found wanting.

In comparison with its Pakistani neighbor, India's defense expenditure has not impacted so much on social and development sectors. To be brief, there were two major phases of massive military expansion: the first one followed the 1962 defeat by China, as the leadership realized that there was no getting away from military affairs; the second one took place in the 1980s when India aimed at securing its predominance over the South Asian region. A new cycle of military modernization has been ongoing since the late 1990s. According to the IISS Military Balance, "between 2000 and 2009 the defense budget will have increased by 50 percent in real terms."[38] As a share of the GDP, however, India's defense spending has proved rather reasonable, as it has been kept below 3 percent.[39] In other words, the ongoing phase of military modernization has benefited from a higher rate of economic growth, rather than a reallocation of funds away from social sectors.

Because the major threats to India's security have come from Pakistan and China, India's military tradition has been imbued with a continental mind-set and the army has always dominated the two other services (securing more than 50 percent of the defense budget for itself). However, the air force and the navy have received more attention and funding as Indian authorities realized that these two services would spearhead India's higher geopolitical ambitions. In recent years, the air force has benefited from major investments, as reflected by a massive plan to acquire 126 medium multirole combat aircraft, an extraordinary acquisition plan even by international standards, while the navy has carved out an ambitious role for itself in the Indian Ocean.

Indeed, a major drive in India's recent military modernization has been to induct force-projection capabilities such as aircraft carriers, nuclear-propelled submarines, and long-range jetfighters with mid-air refuelling capability. A related objective has been to develop a "nuclear triad," with each of the three armed services—the army, the air force, and the navy—working on its own delivery systems, so as to provide India with a credible deterrent capability that would guarantee both its security and its independence (given that it does not belong to any alliance system).

However, there is a growing tension between India's higher strategic ambitions and the reality on the ground, as the armed forces have to make do with an increasing quantity of obsolete equipment. Many modernization and expansion programs are behind schedule, because of bureaucratic inertia and corruption, rather than just financial constraints. Indeed, the Defence Ministry suffers from a well-known dysfunctional procurement system, and the replacement of obsolete equipment is not proceeding fast enough. Moreover, funding priorities have usually been given to counterterrorism and internal security rather than long-term modernization programs. This trend has been reinforced after the November 2008 Mumbai attacks, with additional funding being allocated primarily to India's Special Forces, coast guards, and police forces.

The Pressure of Internal Security Campaigns

Despite the fact that internal policing is not its primary mission, the army has been deployed to maintain internal stability and security since the early days of independent India. This trend was reinforced in the 1980s in response to the Sikh upsurge in Punjab, and then in the 1990s because of the outburst of violence in Jammu and Kashmir and in the northeast. To this day, the army is still heavily involved in counterterrorism and counterinsurgency operations in Kashmir and in the northeast (Assam, Nagaland, and Manipur). In this respect, some observers, such as Sunil Dasgupta, point to a growing trend toward civilian militarism in India: "Today the core of the Indian state—politicians, bureaucrats, and the public generally—have become militaristic."[40] In other words, civilian authorities have become prompt to use force and to deploy troops as a response to domestic trouble and contestation, instead of considering other options that would involve a political or developmental approach.

Being intense and complex, counterinsurgency operations in Kashmir and the northeast have been a source of tension in the army's interactions with the local communities. Instances of extra-judicial killings, of torture and fake encounters, and more generally of gross human rights abuse have alienated local populations and stained the image of the forces in the country. In this context, a long-standing controversy has developed over the Armed Forces Special Powers Act, which grants security forces extraordinary powers of search, arrest, and detention in insurgency-hit areas, such as Kashmir and in the northeast. Local authorities and pressure groups have demanded the suppression of the act, but the center has so far resisted repealing it.

At the same time, a malaise has grown within the rank and file, as reflected by a growing number of suicides. At the officers' level, the army is faced with serious manpower shortage. Military careers are not as attractive as they used to be, as the younger generations are lured away by the private sector, which offers higher salaries and better career opportunities.

The Exponential Growth of the Paramilitaries

India has a large paramilitary force of about 1.3 million men. While the Rashtriya Rifles (65,000) and Assam Rifles (63,000) come under the supervision of the Ministry of Defence, all other paramilitaries are supervised by the Home Affairs Ministry, among which are the Central Reserve Police Force (230,000) and the Border Security forces (208,000). These forces are focused on internal security, including counterinsurgency, post-disaster relief, riot control, and election security duties. Like the army, they are heavily involved in Kashmir and the Northeast. But their situation appears even more difficult than that of the army, especially in terms of training and equipment, as well as rotation and posting in conflict zones (with many paramilitaries spending their entire career in combat zones).[41] This fact has been starkly brought out in their fight against the Naxalites.

The battle against the Maoist rebellion was for a long time left to the state armed police (law and order is indeed a state responsibility). But the failure of the local police to counter the expanding rebellion finally led the central authorities to decide on the deployment of federal forces. Being all too familiar with the pressure of internal security campaigns, the army has so far resisted being involved in the fight against Maoism. As a result, the paramilitaries, especially the Central Reserve Police Force (CRPF), have been at the forefront of the anti-Naxalite battle, and more often than not, they have fought under dire conditions against highly motivated militants.

If anything, the massive anti-Naxalite operation (Green Hunt) announced in October 2009 has led to an escalation in the level of violence, with the paramilitary paying a heavy toll. In April 2010, a unit of the CRPF was ambushed in the Dantewada district of the Chhattisgarh state, leaving seventy-six out of eighty-two troops dead. The report submitted following the "Dantewada massacre," pointed to well-known loopholes such as "leadership failure" and "lack of coordination between the CRPF and the state police."[42] Against this background, it comes as no surprise that the paramilitary feels destitute: being underresourced and under-trained, their mission gets often embroiled in center-state tensions, especially as there is a lack of coordination with the local police and administration. Thus, the example of the anti-Naxalite operations confirms the trend toward "civilian militarism" in the Indian leadership. It is crystal clear, however, that a militaristic approach to such an issue will only result in further violence, especially if the Indian authorities underestimate the social, economic, and political dimensions of the Naxalite movement.

STRUGGLES OVER RIGHTS: A CASE STUDY

Being a democracy, India has always made a point to cultivate the rule of law by endowing its citizens with scores of rights. The first section of its Constitution, promulgated in 1950, is a list of "Fundamental Rights." The problem, for the virtual beneficiaries of these rights, has traditionally been how to have them implemented. The Dalits (ex-untouchables) are probably the group that has been in a position to gradually make the laws passed for them enforced. One of the reasons for this partial success (this is still a work in progress) lies in political activity: since B. R. Ambedkar (1891–1956), the first Indian Dalit leader (see box 2.3), the ex-untouchables have organized themselves on the political scene, through the creation of parties among other things.

The Caste System at the Crossroads

The caste system is inseparable from Hinduism, even though it is not limited by the same religious parameters. The oldest traces of this system appear in the first of the Vedas—the pioneering texts of Sanskrit litera-ture—that dates back to approximately 2000 BCE. One of the stanzas in this text—Rig Veda 90.X—relates a myth of origin, a cosmological account in which the world is said to derive from the sacrificial dismemberment of a primordial man—Virat Purush—whose mouth gave rise to the Brah-mans, his arms to the Kshatriyas, his hands to the Vaishyas, and his feet to the Shudras. Thus, in the beginning was the group, and not the individual of Judeo-Christian Genesis, in which Eve stems from a rib of Adam and all of humanity descends from this lone couple.

The fourfold division of society given by the Rig Veda is hierarchical: the mouth is naturally higher than the feet, and in the same way, below

Box 2.3. Bhimrao Ramji Ambedkar (1891–1956)

Bhimrao Ramji Ambedkar, an untouchable of the Mahar caste, was born in Madhya Pradesh on April 14, 1891. He entered the prestigious Elphinstone College in Bombay, later receiving his MA from Columbia University in 1916 and his PhD from the London School of Economics in 1922. He studied law in England and was called to the bar.

In 1924, Ambedkar founded the Bombay Bahishkrit Hitakarini Sabha (Association of Victims of Ostracism). The British appointed him in 1927 to the Legislative Council of the Presidency of Bombay. Although unsuccessful in his efforts to end discrimination against untouchables, his work brought him to public notice. As head of the Independent Labor party, which he founded in 1936, Ambedkar was elected to the Provincial Assembly of Bombay in the elections of 1937. During World War II, Ambedkar, who believed that British rule had benefited the lower castes, cooperated with the British, being appointed minister of labour in 1942. In 1942, he founded the Scheduled Castes Federation, but was unable to win a seat in the 1946 elections.

After independence, Ambedkar became minister of justice, and president of the Constitution Drafting Committee. He ensured respect for fundamental rights—the first part of the constitutional text—and the involvement of government in the reform of society. Untouchability and other forms of discrimination were abolished, and he sought to reform practices associated with marriage, divorce, adoption, and inheritance. Opposed by the more conservative elements of Congress, he resigned from the government in September 1951.

Failing to win a seat at the general election in 1952, Ambedkar was appointed to the Upper House of Parliament, where he remained until his death. He converted to Buddhism, along with hundreds of thousands of untouchables—mainly Mahars—in 1956, just weeks before his death on December 6.

even the Shudras, is a group that dates back to Indian antiquity, the so-called untouchables, whose origin has been the subject of countless theories. The very name of this fifth category reflects a cardinal principle of caste hierarchy, the relationship between pure and impure. The Brahman personifies purity par excellence, while contact with the untouchable is polluting. Between these two, there is a whole range of purity/impurity divided by two thresholds: Brahmans, Kshatriyas, and Vaishyas form a higher group, those of the "twice-born," and the male children of these castes receive a new name at age six during the *upayanaya* ritual; Shudras are clearly lower, but still well above untouchables. In an Indian village, this social segmentation traditionally results in a separation of spaces, with each caste living in a distinct neighborhood, and the untouchables sometimes even confined to a separate hamlet.

To define caste, socioeconomic function is added to the criteria of pure and impure, and it of course goes hand in hand with status. The Brahman specializes in the work of the spirit, as a priest serving in a temple—which is far from being the most prestigious—or as a government official (as senior officials to the prime minister, Brahmans more or less monopolized higher public office in Hindu kingdoms for centuries). The Kshatriya is the quintessential warrior. His calling is to defend society and to conquer territories. Kings were drawn from the Kshatriya class and, as *primus inter pares* (first among equals), depended on lieutenants also derived from the same caste. Their descendants—whether maharajahs or minor landowning village leaders—developed their fiefs to become notable local or regional figures, and later became landowners when the British introduced the concept of land as private property. The Vaishyas were originally craftsmen and tradesmen. Over time, this first function passed over to the Shudras, and Vaishyas retained only the second occupation. As merchants and usurers above all, they are able to handle money without any inhibition, even to accumulate it. The emergence of India as a capitalist power, following colonization, caused many Vaishyas to go into industry and today still, a significant number of companies listed in the Bombay Stock Exchange are in the hands of members of castes belonging to this category (for example, the firm Laxmi Mittal). The Shudras are the craftsmen—ranging from blacksmith to jeweler to weaver—but more of them are farmers and stockbreeders. They are the castes whose demographic weight is by far the most important. The Shudras who possess the most land and are the most numerous make up the dominant castes and can, in fact, exert local authority. As for the untouchables, their economic functions are naturally in agreement with their status. The most degrading tasks thus belong to their station, such as tanning and shoe manufacture, as leatherworking is particularly stigmatized in Hindu society, which reveres the cow as the preeminent sacred animal.

There is a third and final structuring principle of caste to consider, in addition to the pure/impure ratio and socioeconomic function, and that is endogamy. Endogamy logically completes this social model as the mixing of castes must naturally be banned for this system of inequality to be perpetuated. The boundaries of endogamy define caste in a strict sense of the term. In fact, Brahmans, Kshatriyas, Vaishyas, and Shudras are presented as castes only in name: they are *varnas* (colors) and resemble the "estates" of prerevolutionary France rather than sociological units; as the Indian anthropologist M. N. Srinivas has observed, they provide a shared idiom through which people all over India can determine their relative status. The true caste is the endogamous unit, *jati*, a word derived from the verb *jana*, meaning "to be born." Among the Brahmans, to take one example from among a hundred (and there are even more!), one distinguishes among castes based on knowledge from the four Vedas, the Chaturvedi, that blend into a coherent work and whose status is higher than that of the Trivedi (three Vedas), which in turn is more prestigious than the Dwivedi (two Vedas). Matrimonial unions were the business of parents, who generally committed their children, while still very young, to socially legitimate weddings, taking into account their astrological birth charts. Even today, endogamy remains the rule in villages and, in a looser form, in the city, except among a small cosmopolitan elite.

From Sanskritization to Egalitarian Idealism

Caste society defines the overall social system—which itself comes from the idea of a caste *system*—because the dominant values, which are Brahmanic, are perceived as socially universal. From this assumption diffuse the mechanisms of Sanskritization, a social practice that the Indian anthropologist M. N. Srinivas defines as "the process by which a 'low' Hindu caste, or tribal or other group, changes its customs, ritual, ideology and way of life in the direction of a high, and frequently, 'twice-born' cast [Brahmans, Kshatriyas or even Vaishyas]."[43] Members of low-castes adopt, for example, the most prestigious features of the Brahman food regimen and thus become vegetarians. Such a process shows the enactment of social coherence, since all the groups look upon the values of the high castes—and exclusively of the Brahman—as the legitimate values of society. Still, coherence does not equal cohesion. In fact, Sanskritization in itself testifies to the aspiration of low-castes to rise socially.

All the same, such social climbing has not really been possible since colonial times because of the combined effect of introduced individualistic values and policies of affirmative action. The missionary schools of the nineteenth century were the first channel through which the values of equality and freedom reached Indian society. Men of high caste deduced the need to modernize their society. Individuals from low-castes were also influenced, although fewer in number, and built up a reformatory, even revolutionary, zeal based on these ideas, as illustrated by Ambedkar, the first leader of the untouchables, whom he preferred to call Dalits (broken men), in Maharashtra.

Social reform became the official policy of the Indian Republic shortly after independence in 1947. Untouchability was abolished and any discrimination based on caste criteria made punishable by law. This formal equality did not, however, prevent the continuation of segregation, albeit unseen; for example, the law granting untouchables access to temples was hardly ever respected. Circumstances would only really change with an affirmative action policy that would be carried out with exceptional determination.

Welfare through Affirmative Action for Dalits

The British instituted the practice of affirmative action at the end of the nineteenth century, which aimed to support the education of untouchables. In 1892, they established schools reserved for untouchables in the state of Madras, as their access to public schools had been limited because of the attitudes of teachers and other pupils' parents. A policy of scholarships was also gradually developed. Untouchables—renamed *Depressed Classes*—were not managing to find employment after graduation, so the British went further in introducing administrative recruitment quotas. In 1934, 8.5 percent of vacant posts in the civil service were reserved for them. This figure was increased to 12.5 percent in 1946. Lastly, the British also reserved seats in elected assemblies for *Scheduled Castes*, another bureaucratic euphemism used for untouchables, starting in 1935. This legal framework favoring Dalits—the name by which untouchables generally prefer to be known—was maintained in the Constitution adopted in 1950, with a small difference: under the terms of proportionality, the State determined the percentage of the places reserved for Dalits at universities, their quota of positions in the civil service, and the percentage of parliamentary seats reserved for them (15 percent). These figures are based on the ratio of Scheduled castes to the rest of the Indian population, and began with the census of 1951. Dalits constitute the only castes whose numbers are measured every ten years in new census takings so that the government can adjust quota levels accordingly.

It took a long time for the effects of the affirmative action policy in favor of untouchables to be felt, because of the delay imposed by the social environment and the authorities' reluctance to fill the quotas, particular in the civil service. Since the 1980s, however, these quotas have been observed at all the levels and the overall system has improved by also taking promotions into account. As a result, this policy has given rise to a small elite out of which have come true Dalit leaders, who have created associations and political parties. The formation of such a circle is not, however, only due to affirmative action. The movement for social transformation launched in the 1920s by Ambedkar also bore fruit. In fact, Ambedkar urged his caste brothers, with a certain degree of success, to convert to

Buddhism, a religion that gave Dalits a renewed identity outside of the caste system.

In order that the quotas continue to support the rise of Dalits, three problems will have to be solved. First, the parties concerned wish to see this policy extended to the private sector, which today is growing much faster than the public sector. The business world, however, has resisted this, arguing that merit remains the only criteria by which employees are selected. The tensions resulting from this resistance worry the public authorities and it can be expected that they will try, possibly through legislation, to make businesses change their hiring practices. Second, Dalit elites appear sometimes to be easily co-opted by the establishment, which can buy their cooperation by offering them high positions in public administration or universities. Third, the children of Dalits, who have already benefited from affirmative action measures, tend to monopolize the quotas in universities and the civil service at the expense of other Dalits: having been given a privileged home environment in which they grew up as the children of the new elite that arose from the quotas, they easily win in contests against less favored competitors. Some observers think that it is necessary to exclude them from access to quotas that their parents have already benefited from. On the other hand, one then risks not having sufficient qualified candidates, and it is possible that the sons of the Dalit elite—educated as they are—will suffer from segregation.

The Lower Castes Take Over?

Although the policy of the quotas was implemented without much difficulty for Dalits, this was not the case for the castes located just above them, the Shudras. When this group saw conditions improving for untouchables, thanks to the quotas, they requested the same kind of advantage. The Nehru government refused, officially because it was dedicated to a socialist system in which caste differences would be dissolved, and semi-officially because the high-caste elites feared being dislodged from power by peasants who were already politically significant because of their economic and demographic importance.

Some states in the south of the country had early on applied social programs favoring groups described as Other Backward Classes (disadvantaged caste groups that are not Dalit), but they had to wait until 1990 to know whether the federal government would implement the recommendations of a commission that dated back to 1978. This was the Mandal Commission, named after its president, which had identified 3,743 castes as OBC, accounting for 52 percent of the national population. Their report noted that these OBCs occupied only 12.5 percent of civil service posts, and it recommended that this figure be raised to 27 percent. When this quota was announced in 1990, members of high castes, especially students, protested vehemently about the reduction of their job prospects, and called into question the sociopolitical order that they still dominated. The Supreme Court suspended its decision before validating the recommendations of the Mandal Commission in 1992 with a slight twist: the children of the OBC elite could not profit from the quotas. Still, high-caste resistance had provoked an OBC countermovement to defend the quota of which the high castes wanted to deprive them. New political parties claiming large OBC membership turned the tide and nominated greater numbers of candidates from low-castes, starting in the elections of 1991. This was an increasingly successful strategy, because the OBCs—which constitute at least a relative majority throughout India—voted from that point on for candidates from their own castes, rather than from high castes. They thus seized power in the great states of northern India, Bihar and Uttar Pradesh. Today, a staggering majority of chief ministers are from the OBCs, and only four out of twenty-eight are of Brahman background.

The most recent episode to date in the OBCs' rise to power occurred in April 2008 in the domain of higher education. The low-caste leaders desired to extend the quota policy for OBCs to universities, in their eyes a necessary measure to prepare these castes for the responsibilities that awaited them in the civil service. The Congress Party–led government had agreed to this demand in 2007, but the Supreme Court had immediately suspended this decision under the pretext that no statistics supported the theory that OBCs were underrepresented in higher education. It kept its arguments up the following year, specifying that the OBC elites could not benefit from quotas and that the establishments concerned should increase their capacity by 54 percent so as not to reduce the number of places open to those without affirmative action support.

The concept of caste is much transformed since one and a half centuries ago. It is no longer only the organizing element of a vertical social system: it exists more importantly on its own. It is better connected to an interest group with commendable values—not only limited to those of the Brahmans—and endowed with associations that defend corporatism, even that of political parties. Although caste still exists, there is no more caste *system*, at least in urban areas, but in rural areas, hierarchy remains strongly internalized. So even though the caste system has metamorphosed, caste continues to be one of the basic units of Indian life, as evidenced by the importance that some families still attach to endogamy within the *jati* group, as well as in the new, but relative, freedom of varnas and even of the varna "twice born."

NOTES

1. The Electoral Commission recognizes as national parties those that have been in existence for at least five years and have been recognized as state parties in at least four states. A party is recognized a state party when it has sent at least 4 percent of the state's quota to the Lok Sabha or 3.33 percent of members to that state's assembly.

2. Singur and Nandigram were villages where the West Bengal state government wanted to expropriate land to build industrial plants. Tata wanted to manufacture the Nano in Singur, and the government wanted to set up a Special Economic Zone in Nandigram. In both instances, peasants were able to resist the projects successfully, in the case of Nandigram after violent clashes with the police that left fourteen people dead.

3. The liberalization of the telecommunications sector started in 1994 with initial efforts to introduce competition into a sphere formerly dominated by state enterprises. This policy only really advanced, however, with the New Telecom Policy launched by the Vajpayee government in 1999.

4. The decline of these quotas accelerated after the WTO determined, in 1997, that the justification of these quotas put forth by New Delhi, based on the problems of balance of payments, was unfounded. In April 2001, India removed the last remaining quotas.

5. S. Chauvin and F. Lemoine, "India in the World Economy: Traditional Specialisations and Technology Niches," CEPII Working Paper no. 9 (2003), 16; Baldev Raj Nayar, "India in 2004: Regime Change in a Divided Democracy," *Asian Survey* 45, no. 1 (2005): 72.

6. N. Bajpai, "A Decade of Economic Reforms in India: The Unfinished Agenda," Center for International Development at Harvard University, Working Paper no. 89 (2002), 8.

7. In May 2005, the United States Citizenship and Immigration Services (USCIS) announced that they would grant 20,000 additional H1B visas (on top of the 65,000 visas in this category already decided upon at the beginning of the year) to foreigners holding diplomas from American universities, at the master's level or higher, and specialized in state-of-the-art technologies. This step aimed primarily to meet the needs of American computer science engineering firms, which would profit greatly from Indian students eager to find employment in the United States.

8. To curb any premature enthusiasm encouraged by these figures, it is worthwhile to read: S. Khagram, M. Desai, and J. Varughese, "Seen, Rich but Unheard? The Politics of Asian Indians in the United States," in Gordon H. Chang (ed.), *Asian Americans and Politics*, 258–84 (Washington, DC: Woodrow Wilson Center/ Stanford University Press, 2001).

9. World Bank, *India—Sustaining Reforms, Reducing Poverty* (Washington, DC: Author, 2003), 56.

10. Montek S. Ahluwalia, "Economic Reforms in India since 1991: Has Gradualism Worked?" *Journal of Economic Perspectives* (Summer 2002): 3.

11. In 1998–1999, three industries were withdrawn from the system of obligatory licenses: sugar, coal, and oil (for products other than crude oil). In 1999–2003,

seventy-three products followed suit, among which leather goods and toys were the most important. In 2004, eighty-five items that had been on the list of the products reserved for SSI were removed in the name of economic efficiency (particularly those produced in economies of scale); Government of India, *Economic Survey 2004–2005* (New Delhi: Author, 2005), 166.

12. S. Kaur, "Privatization and Public Enterprise Reform: A Suggestive Action Plan," Australia South Asia Research Centre, Working Paper no. 8 (2004), 2.

13. P. Meyer, "The Hindu Rate of Reforms: Privatisations under the BJP—Still Waiting for That *Bada Kadam*," *South Asia Studies* 25, no. 3 (December 2002).

14. Employees in the formal sector represent less than 5 percent of the working-age population in India.

15. This electoral promise has proven difficult to keep; it is possible that the government is satisfied to offer this guarantee to one person of age per family.

16. According to the UNDP, 35 percent of the Indian population lives on less than $1 a day, and 80 percent on less than $2 a day; S. Chauvin and F. Lemoine, "The Indian Economy: Structural Changes and Long-Term Prospects," CEPII, Working Paper no. 4 (2005), 31.

17. K. C. Suri, "Reform: The Elites Want It, the Masses Don't," *The Hindu*, May 20, 2004 (supplement titled "How India Voted"), AE7.

18. G. Austin, *The Indian Constitution—Cornerstone of a Nation* (Bombay: Oxford University Press, 1972), 50.

19. I refer to this subject in my book: *Les nationalistes hindous* (Paris: Presses de Sciences Po, 1993).

20. See: T. B. Hansen and C. Jaffrelot, eds., *The BJP and the Compulsions of Politics in India* (Oxford: Oxford University Press, 2001).

21. Article 15 of the Indian Constitution prohibits discrimination on the ground of sex (among others) but authorizes special provisions for women and children. Nevertheless, many provisions of Indian law remained discriminatory for women especially in the field of family law.

22. There is a rich literature on Indian feminism. One can, for instance, refer to Maitrayee Chaudhuri (ed.), *Feminism in India* (New Delhi: Kali for Women & Women Unlimited, 2004) and Nandita Gandhi and Nandita Shah, *The Issues at Stake: Theory and Practice in the Contemporary Women's Movement in India* (New Delhi: Kali for Women, 1992).

23. Source: Congress Party's website: http://www.congress.org.in/cwc.php (accessed January 20, 2009).

24. An example of this battle was the much publicized resignation of Brinda Karat from the Central Committee of the CPI(M) in 1998 to protest against the very low representation of women in the party's decision-making bodies. She eventually agreed to join the Politburo in 2005, when five women were integrated in the Central Committee.

25. This exception is usually explained by the strength of the women's movement during this period and also by the assassination of Indira Gandhi in 1984, which generated a "sympathy wave" in favor of women in the following elections. Unless stated otherwise, the data on members of Parliament and Lok Sabha elections come from the Lok Sabha's Who's Who (http://164.100.47.132/

LssNew/members/lokprev.aspx) and the Election Commission Reports (http://
eci.nic.in/eci_main1/ElectionStatistics.aspx).

26. Updated with Rajya Sabha Who's Who: http://164.100.47.5/Newmembers/
alphabeticallist_all_terms.aspx (accessed January 20, 2010).

27. Ministry of Woman and Child Development, *A Handbook of Statistical Indicators on Indian Women* (New Delhi: Author, 2007), 22. Available at http://wcd.nic
.in/stat.pdf.

28. Stéphanie Tawa Lama-Rewal, "Les femmes et le pouvoir exécutif en Inde,"
Histoire@Politique: Politique, culture et société 1 (2007): 15–16.

29. On women candidates, it is interesting to note that women always had a
better winning rate than men (almost 50 percent of women candidates won the
seat in 1957), but it has sharply decreased and is now around 10 percent (in Lok
Sabha elections), which shows that being a candidate is no longer reserved to
women with strong winning chances and that the profile of candidates is diversifying.

30. Unless stated otherwise, all statistical data come from Ministry of Woman
and Child Development, *A Handbook of Statistical Indicators on Indian Women*. The
data used in this handbook come mainly from the 2001 census and the National
Family Health Survey, especially the third one (2005–2006).

31. This was noted by the National Committee on the Status of Women, *The
Status of Women in India* (Delhi: Indian Council of Social Science Research, 1974),
293, and is confirmed in the present Lok Sabha, in which no woman is elected
from Kerala (against twelve in Uttar Pradesh.

32. This information was gathered through interviews held in Delhi between
September 2009 and September 2011.

33. Lama-Rewal, "Les femmes et le pouvoir exécutif en Inde," 13–14.

34. Gail Minault, *The Extended Family: Women and Political Participation in India
and Pakistan* (Columbia, MO: South Asia Books, 1981), 13–14.

35. Stéphanie Tawa Lama-Rewal, *Femmes et politique en Inde et au Népal: Image et
présence* (Paris: Karthala, 2004), 219.

36. As of this writing in August 2013, the Rajya Sabha had passed the Women's
reservation bill, but the Lok Sabha was yet to vote on it. The quota for women in
local bodies has been increased to 50 percent in many states, but no bill has been
passed by the Parliament in that regard.

37. Stephen Cohen, *India: Emerging Power* (Washington, DC: Brookings Institution Press, 2001).

38. International Institute for Strategic Studies, *The Military Balance 2010*
(London: Routledge, 2010), 349. In comparison, Pakistan's defense budget was
estimated by the IISS to be above 3 percent of the GDP at least until 2006 (see also
SIPRI Military Expenditure Database, http://milexdata.sipri.org/).

39. A number of defense analysts think that the defense budget should hover
around 3 percent of the GDP if India is to seriously meet its military needs. But the
leadership has not yet shown itself willing to allocate such a share, with its focus
on the development and social needs of the country.

40. Sunil Dasgupta, "India: The New Militaries," in Muthiah Alagappa, *Coercion and Governance: The Declining Political Role of the Military in Asia* (Stanford, CA:
Stanford University Press, 2001), 92–117.

41. Raman Kirpal, "Soldiers of Misfortune," *Tehelka Magazine* 7, no. 18 (August 2010).

42. Brijesh Pandey, "Hard Battles, Harder Lifes," *Tehelka Magazine* 7, no. 29 (July 24, 2010).

43. M. N. Srinivas, *Social Change in Modern India* (New Delhi: Orient Longman, 1995), 6.

SUGGESTED READINGS

Austin, G. *The Indian Constitution: Cornerstone of a Nation.* New Delhi: Oxford University Press, 2010.

Brass, P. *The Politics of India since Independence.* Cambridge: Cambridge University Press, 1990.

Frankel, F., and M. S. A. Rao (eds.). *Dominance and State Power in Modern India.* 2 vols. Delhi: Oxford University Press, 1989–1990.

Jaffrelot, C. *Religion, Caste and Politics in India.* New Delhi: Primus, 2011.

—— (ed.). *India since 1950: Society, Politics, Economy and Culture.* New Delhi: Yatra Books/Foundation Books, 2011.

Kohli, A. *Poverty amid Plenty in the New India.* Cambridge: Cambridge University Press, 2012.

Mahajan, G. *Identities and Rights: Aspects of Liberal Democracy in India.* Delhi: Oxford University Press, 1998.

Malone, David M. *Does the Elephant Dance?* New York: Oxford University Press, 2011.

Rudolph, Lloyd, and Susanne Hoeber. *In Pursuit of Lakshmi: The Political Economy of the Indian State.* Chicago: University of Chicago Press, 1987.

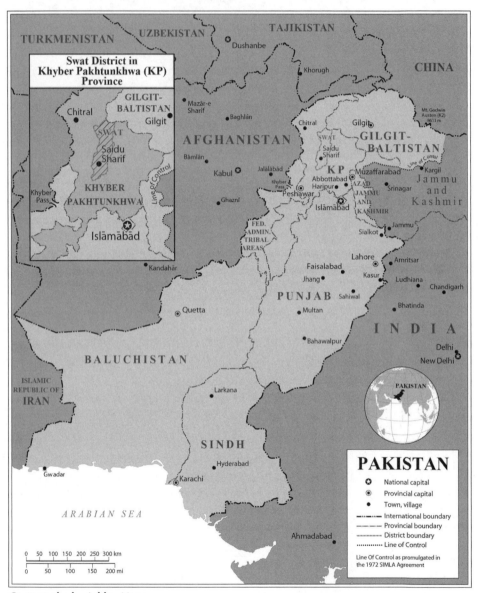

Cartography by Ashley Nepp

3

۶

Pakistan

Anita M. Weiss

Over sixty years since independence from Britain, the political state of affairs within Pakistan has arguably never been worse. Violence permeates social life on a daily basis, as suicide bombings have become more common than anyone could ever have imagined. Equally disturbing is that instead of a popular social interrogation into the myriad domestic reasons behind this violence, there is a commonly held belief that external forces—India's RAW, the U.S. security contractor Blackwater among others, even the U.S. government's drone attacks on Pakistan—are responsible for it. These reasons are not solely associated with the "Pandora's box" of politicized Islam opened by Zia ul-Haq thirty years ago, but are tied as well to the inequities of provincial power relations (Khyber Pakhtunkhwa[1]—formerly the Northwest Frontier Province—feeling exploited by the center for low hydroelectric power payments, and Baluchistan Province feeling equally exploited for low natural gas payments); infrastructural decline (daily electrical outages, limited investment in education and health care resulting in highly weakened systems, massive destruction, and displacement due to July/August 2010 floods); flagrant abuse of power by official entities; and an overall sense of social malaise grounded in the average person's access to legal, economic, political, and social justice being compromised on a daily basis. There is no national consensus on such things as how to share water, the rights women inherently have, what comprises a "good education" aside from having served time as a student, or an ideal vision of civil-military relations. We read nothing about social investment aside from base numbers of literates, and no interrogation of the contours of what are the necessary

TIMELINE: PAKISTAN

March 24, 1940	Adoption of Lahore Resolution, the demand for a separate homeland for the Muslims of British India
August 14, 1947	Declaration of Independence from British India; Muhammad Ali Jinnah becomes first governor-general and Liaqat Ali Khan becomes first prime minister
September 11, 1948	Death of Quaid-e-Azam Muhammad Ali Jinnah
March 1949	Constituent Assembly passes the Objectives Resolution
October 16, 1951	Assassination of Prime Minister Liaqat Ali Khan
March 23, 1956	First Constitution declares the country the Republic of Pakistan; Iskander Mirza becomes first president
October 1958	Mirza abrogates the Constitution and declares martial law; soon sent into exile and Field Marshal Muhammad Ayub Khan becomes Chief Martial Law Administrator (CMLA) and later president
1961	Passage of Muslim Family Laws Ordinance (MFLO), which regulates marriage and provides women with unprecedented legal rights in marriage and divorce
June 8, 1962	Second Constitution declares the country the Islamic Republic of Pakistan
1965	Second war between Pakistan and India over Kashmir
March 25, 1969	Yahya Khan declares martial law, abrogates 1962 Constitution and becomes president
1969	The princely states of Swat, Dir, and Chitral—the final ones to sign instruments of accession—join the Islamic Republic of Pakistan
1971	East Pakistan secedes, prompting civil war; India intervenes. Bangladesh declares itself independent as Pakistan military surrenders to Indian armed forces; Yahya Khan resigns, and PPP Chairperson Zulfiqar Ali Bhutto becomes head of state
1972	Bhutto and Indian prime minister Indira Gandhi agree to new Line of Control (LOC) in Kashmir
August 14, 1973	Inauguration of third (and prevailing) Constitution; Bhutto becomes prime minister
July 5, 1977	General Zia ul-Haq overthrows Bhutto in a coup d'état and proclaims martial law
February 2, 1979	Introduction of Nizam-e-Mustafa, Zia's Islamization program, which introduced a new series of penal laws based on Islam
April 4, 1979	Zulfiqar Ali Bhutto hanged by Zia's government on the charges of being an accomplice to murder
November 21, 1979	U.S. Embassy attacked in Islamabad, a marine guard is killed in attack; U.S. Consulate and American Center attacked in Lahore

December 26, 1979	Soviet invasion into Afghanistan results in Pakistan becoming a Frontline State in the U.S. proxy war with the USSR, resulting in over three million Afghans seeking refuge in Pakistan and longtime implications for U.S. development assistance
1985	General elections held; Zia becomes president supposedly with 98 percent of the vote
Spring 1988	Zia dismisses Prime Minister Mohammad Khan Junejo's government and orders new elections
August 17, 1988	Zia ul-Haq and U.S. ambassador Arnie Raphael die in a plane crash returning from Multan; investigation concludes it was a result of a "criminal act of sabotage"
November 1988	National elections held
December 2, 1988	Benazir Bhutto, head of the PPP, becomes prime minister and forms the government
August 6, 1990	Bhutto government dismissed on grounds of corruption
November 6, 1990	Nawaz Sharif becomes prime minister as his Pakistan Muslim League (PML-N) forms the government
July 18, 1993	Sharif government dismissed on grounds of corruption
October 19, 1993	Benazir Bhutto's PPP wins by slim margin in October elections and she becomes prime minister for the second time
November 6, 1996	Bhutto's second government dismissed on grounds of corruption
February 17, 1997	Sharif's PML-N party wins February national election and he becomes prime minister for the second time
October 12, 1999	General Pervez Musharraf overthrows Nawaz Sharif and declares martial law; both Sharif and Bhutto go into exile abroad
October 2001	U.S. invasion of Afghanistan, having significant long-term ramifications for Pakistan
October 2002	National elections held; Musharraf's PML-Q forms the national government. The MMA, a coalition of six Islamist political powers, forms the government in NWFP, the first time an Islamist party comes to power anywhere in Pakistan. The MMA heads the opposition at the national level.
October 8, 2005	Major earthquake destroys large parts of NWFP and Azad Kashmir
March 2007	President Pervez Musharraf dismisses chief justice of the Supreme Court, Iftikhar Muhammad Chaudhry, prompting the creation of the Lawyer's Movement clamoring for his reinstatement (which occurs in July)
October 2007	Benazir Bhutto returns to Pakistan where her cavalcade is attacked in Karachi
November 2007	Pervez Musharraf declares martial law (on his own government); dismisses the Chief Justice of the Supreme Court and the higher judiciary; reverses many of his actions by the end of the month (except the restoration of the chief justice) and resigns from the military

December 28, 2007	Assassination of Benazir Bhutto in Rawalpindi
March 25, 2008	Following February 18 elections, PPP is invited to form the government, resulting in Syed Yousaf Raza Gillani, a little known politician from Multan, becoming prime minister
August 18, 2008	Pervez Musharraf resigns as president of Pakistan
September 9, 2008	Asif Ali Zardari, now head of the PPP, is elected president
March 16, 2009	Restoration of Iftikhar Muhammad Chaudhry as chief justice
May 2009	Pakistan military proclaims full curfew in Swat as it attacks Fazlullah-led Tehrik-e-Taliban Pakistan (TTP)
April 15, 2010	NWFP is officially renamed Khyber Pakhtunkhwa (KP)
July 8, 2010	The Gilgit–Baltistan Empowerment and Self-Governance Order 2009 (August) results in the Northern Areas being declared Pakistan's fifth province, Gilgit-Baltistan, in July
Summer 2010	Heavy monsoon rains cause devastating floods, resulting in death and destruction in many parts of KP and Punjab
June 25, 2012	Raja Pervez Ashraf becomes new prime minister after Gilani is disqualified by the Supreme Court on June 19, 2012
March 25, 2013	Mir Hazar Khan Khoso appointed car taker prime minister by the Election Commission of Pakistan to oversee the upcoming national election.
May 11, 2013	Following the first time an elected government finished its term in Pakistan, national elections held. Nawaz Sharif's PML-N party is successful nationally while Imran Khan's PTI party wins the majority vote in KP and forms the provincial government in alliance with the Jama'at-i-Islami. Nawaz Sharif sworn in for the third time as prime minister on June 5, 2013.
July 30, 2013	Mamnoon Hussain, PML-N candidate, elected new president of Pakistan; sworn in on September 9

components to being a member of Pakistani society fully engaged in the life of the country.

Yet these issues are critical to our understanding of Pakistan's domestic political scrimmages and the international role it is playing in today's world. What transpires in the domestic political terrain is now intrinsically related to myriad global concerns in a variety of ways and for a variety of reasons. For example, the persistent uneasy relationship between inhabitants of Baluchistan (demanding a greater share of proceeds from the sale of natural gas) and the federal government culminated in explosions that wracked gas pipelines near Sui in January 2005, and such violence continues today. The animosity toward the federal government over this matter added essentially just another layer to the preexisting antagonistic relationship that harkens back to the 1970s provincial separatist movement. Context, however, is important. While the global community had the luxury to ignore the divisiveness that existed here in the 1970s, it can no longer do so today as U.S. and allied forces seek to hunt down insurgents who have ostensibly retreated from Afghanistan and taken refuge in the province of Baluchistan and in the tribal areas of Pakistan. The October 2001 U.S. attack on and ultimate overthrow of the Taliban government in neighboring Afghanistan has served to further exacerbate preexisting tensions; those same tensions have concomitantly fueled local anti-U.S. resentment, as the national government has been seen as a staunch ally of the United States and terrorist attacks proliferate daily.

POLITICAL HISTORY SINCE INDEPENDENCE

Pakistan was formed as an independent state in the partition of British India that took effect on August 14, 1947. This division was the result of demands by the Muslim League, led by Muhammad Ali Jinnah, which was seeking a homeland for Muslims where they would not be at risk of discrimination or persecution by a Hindu majority in postindependence India. Based principally on where Muslims were in the majority, the new country initially comprised the northeast sector of the subcontinent as well as the northwest. The name of the new country, which in Urdu (the national language) means "land of the pure," is actually an acronym and was formulated to represent its constituent parts:

P	Punjab (the populous eastern province)
A	Afghania (previously NWFP, now Khyber Pakhtunkhwa, KP)
K	Kashmir (from the outset, perceived as a component part of Pakistan)
I	(short vowel that doesn't exist in Urdu)
S	Sindh (the southern province)
TAN	final part of Baluchistan (the southwestern province)

What is missing from this acronym is a *B* for Bengal, whose eastern half made up East Pakistan from 1947 to 1971. Separated from West Pakistan by about sixteen hundred kilometers of Indian territory and huge linguistic and cultural differences, East Pakistan became the independent state of Bangladesh in December 1971. Importantly, too, when Kashmir was not included as a part of Pakistan in 1947, Pakistan set out to liberate the area in the 1948 war with India and hence annexed the now quasi-autonomous Azad ("Free") Kashmir and parts of what now comprises the new province (Pakistan's fifth) of Gilgit-Baltistan (formerly the Northern Areas).

It is sobering to reflect on how Pakistan has transformed since 1947, when British India became independent and a homeland for Muslims was carved out of its northern corners. Questions, debates, and mistrust of a shared vision by its leaders arose from the outset. Muhammad Ali

Box 3.1. Muhammad Ali Jinnah (1876–1948)

Widely regarded as the leader of Pakistan's independence movement, the Quaid-e-Azam, Jinnah, building on the inspiration of Allama Iqbal, played a pivotal role in mobilizing the Muslim community of South Asia to demand a homeland when the British quit the subcontinent. He practiced law in Bombay upon his return to India from studying in England and joined the Muslim League and the Congress Party. Working for greater Hindu-Muslim unity, he brokered an agreement between the two in 1916, the Lucknow Pact, in which Congress finally accepted the Muslim demand for a separate electorate. Convinced that Congress stood only for the rights of Hindus and fearing that Gandhi's method of mass struggle would lead to divisions between the two communities, he broke with Congress in 1920.

Jinnah became the head of the Muslim League in 1935, and under his leadership the Muslim League passed the Pakistan Resolution on March 23, 1940. It called for the formation of a separate state to be carved out of the Muslim-majority regions of the subcontinent. Jinnah could now transform the Muslim League into a popular movement. With the birth of Pakistan on August 14, 1947, Jinnah became the country's first governor-general, advocating that while Pakistan would be a homeland for Muslims, members of all religions would be welcome in the new country. On September 11, 1948, at the age of seventy-one, he died at Karachi after a protracted illness. His birthday, December 25, is celebrated annually as a national holiday.

Jinnah—a British-trained lawyer who rose to be the founding father of the country, the *Quaid-e-Azam*—and other Western-oriented professionals envisioned a multiethnic, pluralistic, democratic state free from the hegemony of any one group (see box 3.1). The hope for this is evident in Jinnah's inaugural presidential address to the Constituent Assembly of Pakistan three days prior to independence, when he declared that "If we want to make this great State of Pakistan happy and prosperous we should wholly and solely concentrate on the well-being of the people, and especially of the masses and the poor."[2] Jinnah encouraged the rise of a vigorous civil society, one in which ethnic and religious divides would be set aside so as to promote the overall well-being of the new country, exhorting his new compatriots,

[If you] work together in a spirit that every one of you, no matter to what community he belongs, no matter what relations he had with you in the past, no matter what is his colour, caste or creed, is first, second and last a citizen of this State with equal rights, privileges and obligations, there will be no end to the progress you will make. . . . You are free; you are free to go to your temples, you are free to go to your mosques or to any other places of worship in this State of Pakistan. You may belong to any religion or caste or creed—that has nothing to do with the business of the State.[3]

Jinnah regarded Pakistan as the culmination of what had finally become a mass-based grassroots movement, expanded to consist of partisans from a range of ethnic, class, regional, and religious backgrounds, a profusion of groups working together for the overall well-being of the state regardless of their divisions. Jinnah and other leaders of the new state expected that differences would be resolved within a republican context as a popular consensus existed on the state's necessity, viability, and structure. Most citizens of the new state, whether originally hailing from areas deemed in the 1947 partition to become part of Pakistan or the hordes of migrants (*muhajirs*) who left everything behind in those areas ceded to India as they boarded trains for Pakistan, shared a conviction that they had achieved something pivotal for the Muslims of South Asia. The havoc and social chaos that became the legacy of partition kindled a unifying spirit among many of the citizenry of the new state. Pakistan's future held great promise, according to the mainstream, populist narrative. While substantive political and economic challenges confronted the new state, most Pakistanis believed that these would be surmounted over time.

Alternative viewpoints, however, also existed from the outset. Distinct groups initially wanted no part of Pakistan, but for different reasons. Supporters of the Punjab Unionist Party had placed their loyalties with the British; their successors still identify with global culture as they educate their children in British-style schools, speak English among themselves, and tend to value indigenous aesthetics only as quaint historic relics. Many Pakhtuns, from the outset, refused to accept the international boundary between Pakistan and Afghanistan as the Durand Line had been determined by the British, while most Baluch weren't sure what the new country held for them. Distinct *madrasas*,[4] particularly those run by the Deobandis[5] in India, initially recoiled from the demand for Pakistan on the grounds that Islam could not be limited by the borders of a nation-state (on the argument that a Muslim's identity is first and foremost with the religion, which has no sentient boundaries). After Partition many Indian Muslims, however, soon migrated to Pakistan out of necessity. Once arriving there, many then viewed Pakistan's possibilities as limitless, creating a *dar-ul-Islam* (abode of Islam), once their new compatriots would understand their message.

It was in the character of the country's founder, Muhammad Ali Jinnah, where a semblance of unity was able to exist among the myriad contesting political stakeholders. This was short-lived, however, as he died on September 11, 1948, barely a year after the country's birth. While succeeded by the country's first prime minister, Liaqat Ali Khan, as the nation's leader, consensus on key political issues now became far more elusive. This transformed into a disastrous precedent when Liaqat Ali Khan was assassinated on October 16, 1951.

The State's Initial Focus

The state's focus was initially on basic survival. Following the first war with India in 1948, many Pakistanis feared that without a strong military, the country could be decimated by India. The delay in framing a constitution certainly didn't help alleviate these fears. As a temporary fix, the government adapted the Government of India Act of 1935 as its working constitution. Consensus on a number of important concerns was difficult to achieve. Safdar Mahmood argues that six issues were the most problematic at the outset;[6] these remain so today (see table 3.1).

In the quest to find consensus on a constitution, the Constituent Assembly passed the Objectives Resolution in March 1949 (see box 3.2). Articulating the broad objectives and goals of the future constitution, the Constituent Assembly pledged to incorporate the principles of democracy, freedom, equality, and social justice. Fractious views emerged from both West and East Pakistan on what structure the state should take. Finally, nine years later, on March 23, 1956, Pakistan had a constitution—its first of three.

There were other contentious disputes in the country's first decade of existence, especially concerning the raison d'être of the new country that, in turn, led to disputes of groups' rights. In the wake of anti-Ahmediyya demonstrations and the imposition of martial law in the Punjab provincial capital of Lahore in 1953, the federal government commissioned the Munir Report to inquire into the cause of the riots. Hamid Khan, author of the most comprehensive constitutional history of Pakistan to date, notes that the Report's observations of the role being played by politicized Islam then and the sectarian factionalism it fomented is foreboding when considering the state of the country fifty years later: "The committee also found from the interviews with leaders of various sects and schools of Islam that they could not stand one another and called each other *kafirs* [nonbelievers] as well. According to the Barelvi *ulema*, Deobandis and Wahabis were outside the pale of Islam . . . [and] according to a *fatwa* [religious edict] of the Deobandis, all Asna Ashari Shias were *kafirs*."[7]

The year the first constitution was framed proved to be politically disastrous for the country and laid a foundation for the fractious, unrepresentative politics that would characterize much of Pakistan's future. Two weak governments lacking a majority led to serious uncertainty and

Table 3.1. Constitutionally Disputed Issues at the Outset and Their Current Status

Initial disputed issue	Current status of disputed issue
The character of the proposed constitution, and especially the place that Islam should occupy in it.	The argument over the Eighteenth Amendment—who has the right to appoint the judiciary, among other issues—has been resolved by the Supreme Court, although the role Islam should play in the state remains in dispute.
Geographical division of the country and the question of quantum of representation in the federal legislature	The Northern Areas finally became a province in January 2010. When NWFP became KP in March 2010, it was accompanied by riots in the non-Pakhtun parts of the province. Pakistan's census is a perennial dispute, given how redistricting might affect ethnic groups (e.g., more Pakhtuns than Baluch in Baluchistan due to migration from Afghanistan)
Distribution or allocation of powers between the federal government and the provinces, especially regarding provincial autonomy	The issue of which laws are to be determined by the federal or provincial governments was largely resolved in early 2010 when the Federal List and Concurrent List was finally eliminated (due to the Eighteenth Amendment), but the dispute is not yet fully resolved.
Identification of a national language	While no longer under dispute, since government-run schools became Urdu medium in the early 1980s, this has resulted in practical discrimination against the masses who no longer know English well (and thus cannot be competitive for jobs)
The question of the relationship between the executive and the legislature, especially the question of whether Pakistan should adopt a parliamentary or presidential form of government	This remains under dispute as was evident in the legal battle over the Eighteenth Amendment. Prior military governments had elevated the power of the president over the prime minister; many stakeholders are trying to reverse that relationship.
Provincial and parochial power tussles.	This dispute manifests daily in violent attacks and suicide bombings, especially targeting government institutions and symbols.

Source: Safdar Mahmood, *Pakistan: Political Roots and Development, 1947–1999* (Oxford University Press, 2007), 36.

Box 3.2. The Objectives Resolution

Whereas sovereignty over the entire universe belongs to Allah Almighty alone and the authority which He has delegated to the State of Pakistan, through its people for being exercised within the limits prescribed by Him is a sacred trust;

This Constituent Assembly representing the people of Pakistan resolves to frame a Constitution for the sovereign independent State of Pakistan;

Wherein the State shall exercise its powers and authority through the chosen representatives of the people;

Wherein the principles of democracy, freedom, equality, tolerance and social justice as enunciated by Islam shall be fully observed;

Wherein the Muslims shall be enabled to order their lives in the individual and collective spheres in accordance with the teachings and requirements of Islam as set out in the Holy Quran and the Sunnah;

Wherein adequate provision shall be made for the minorities to profess and practice their religions and develop their cultures;

Wherein the territories now included in or in accession with Pakistan and such other territories as may hereafter be included in or accede to Pakistan shall form a Federation wherein the units will be autonomous with such boundaries and limitations on their powers and authority as may be prescribed;

Wherein shall be guaranteed fundamental rights including equality of status, of opportunity and before law, social, economic and political justice, and freedom of thought, expression, belief, faith, worship and association, subject to law and public morality;

Wherein adequate provisions shall be made to safeguard the legitimate interests of minorities and backward and depressed classes;

Wherein the independence of the Judiciary shall be fully secured;

Wherein the integrity of the territories of the Federation, its independence and all its rights including its sovereign rights on land, sea and air shall be safeguarded;

So that the people of Pakistan may prosper and attain their rightful and honored place amongst the nations of the World and make their full contribution towards international peace and progress and happiness of humanity.

instability, culminating in President Iskander Mirza declaring the first Martial Law in the country on October 7, 1958. He was soon sent into exile by Ayub Khan, who had been commander in chief of the army since 1951, more recently defense minister, and now as chief martial law administrator declared himself president three weeks later (see box 3.3).

Pakistan's first foray into having a constitution was a short-lived accomplishment on two fronts. Not only was Pakistan's first constitution soon abrogated by the declaration of martial law, but it would also be replaced twice, in 1962 and 1973; the latter remains in force today. Key factors that differentiated these constitutions was the role of the president (the 1962 constitution having it at its strongest), the degree of centralization of power, the extent to which the National Assembly enjoyed substantive powers, and the role and influence of local legislative structures.

The "Golden Age of Development," 1958–1968

The decade of Ayub Khan's rule (1958–1968) is popularly remembered as having been Pakistan's "Golden Age of Development," especially by the industrial elite of the country. Industrial and financial power became highly centralized as the "Twenty-Two Families" came to control Pakistan's economy.[8] During this era, Pakistan's economy grew substantially. Feudal families that embraced innovation became successful; those that did not, along with the vast majority of the country that was poor to begin with, saw their options diminish over the years, resulting in exaggerated ethnic and class divisions. Industrialists emerged as a key class in this era and, given the unprecedented expansion of their economic clout along with their newfound alliances with the military, were able to contest the political might of the feudal groups.

Despite the relative economic prosperity during this era, public dissatisfaction with unrepresentative democracy, a deteriorating law-and-order situation, and Ayub's authoritarian control resulted in demonstrations throughout the country in late 1968. India and Pakistan had fought another war over Kashmir in 1965 in which Pakistan ostensibly suffered a humiliating defeat, and the army fell out of favor with the people. The ensuing political chaos resulted in Ayub Khan's resignation and his handing over power to General Yahya Khan, his army chief. Yahya Khan summarily abrogated the 1962 constitution and declared martial law on March 25, 1969.

The Breakup of Pakistan and Emergence of the PPP

The national elections held the following year in 1970 proved decisive—and disastrous—for Pakistan: the Awami League of East Pakistan won 167 seats and the Pakistan People's Party (PPP), emerging as the majority

Box 3.3. Muhammad Ayub Khan (1907–1974)

Muhammad Ayub Khan rose to the highest echelons of power in Pakistan's military, then president of the country, and finally was one of Pakistan's only leaders to die a peaceful death in retirement. Born in Haripur, a non-Pakhtun area of Khyber Pakhtunkhwa, he received his early education there before studying in Aligarh. Shortly before completing his degree, he was selected in 1926 to attend the Royal Military College at Sandhurst in England. Commissioned in the Indian Army in 1928, he was the senior-most Muslim officer, a Brigadier, at Pakistan's Independence in 1947. On October 7, 1958, Iskander Mirza imposed Pakistan's first Martial Law and designated Ayub as chief martial law administrator. Ayub soon dismissed Mirza, assumed the position of president, and later gave himself the rank of field marshal.

Ayub's focus was on modernizing Pakistan, promoting economic growth, implementing land reforms, and ridding the country of myriad imbedded social problems. He introduced Basic Democracies, whereby local leaders were elected through an indirect system, albeit these reforms were not extended to the higher levels of governance. By the end of the 1960s, following the 1965 war with India and criticisms of Ayub's handling of the truce, the Tashkent Declaration, his popularity had waned. On March 25, 1969, General Muhammad Yahya Khan, the commander in chief of Pakistan's army, proclaimed martial law and assumed the presidency. Ayub retired from public life, remaining with his family in the area of Islamabad, the national capital that he had founded, until his death on April 19, 1974.

party in West Pakistan, won just more than half that number, 86 seats. Powerful forces in West Pakistan, including the influential leader of the PPP, Zulfiqar Ali Bhutto, refused to accept the outcome that the majority party and prime minister of the country could hail from East Pakistan. Thus, East Pakistan seceded from the republic, India quickly came to its aid, a third horrific war was fought between India and Pakistan, and the result was the dismemberment of the country. East Pakistan officially seceded in December 1971 and became the independent country of Bangladesh.

The political fallout of this action was immediate: the Pakistan army—the one institution most Pakistanis considered worked well in the country—was now disgraced, Yahya Khan resigned, and PPP chairperson Zulfiqar Ali Bhutto became the head of state. Soon afterward, Bhutto and Indian prime minister Indira Gandhi agreed to a new boundary in Kashmir, the Line of Control. While still officially disputed, it has become the de facto international border between these two states in Kashmir.

Having campaigned on a platform of Islamic Socialism, Bhutto initiated a series of policies promoting nationalization of vital industries and greater integration of Islamic practices into the activities of the state and social life. On August 14, 1973—twenty-six years after achieving independence—Pakistan inaugurated its third constitution, which despite having been amended numerous times since then, remains the paramount foundation of law in the country. Bhutto made many promises, especially to unions and to rural workers, most of which were never implemented, but importantly, some of them were. He nationalized a number of industries and industrial units, especially in banking, food, steel rerolling, and other critical arenas. Many workers were heartened that they were now in charge. However, this nationalization was not the result of a workers' struggle but rather was done for political gain (on the part of the PPP), which saw industrial units of Bhutto's opponents nationalized, but not those of Bhutto's allies. Without the necessary internal discipline in the labor force that results from a workers' struggle, production faltered and economic turmoil ensued.[9]

Bhutto's government also implemented land reforms. Similar to the implementation of the first land reform, the West Pakistan Land Reforms Regulation of 1959 under Ayub Khan, it was the government's political opponents who lost land and its allies were hardly affected. Most of this land, too, was of marginal use for cultivation. However, the land reform under Ayub Khan had scant impact on affecting local power relations, as the allowable land ceilings remained very high and excessive land holdings reverted to the government (not to other individuals). Bhutto's 1972 land reform was different in that it redistributed some of the seized land to landless rural laborers (albeit the numbers were very limited); *some* poor farmers actually did get land put into their own names. The end result of this action, coupled with the PPP support of industrial unions and workers' rights, was for the PPP to be associated in the popular imagination with supporting the rights of the poor. Whether born out in fact or not, this ideology persists to this day.

Prime Minister Bhutto called for national elections to be held in early spring 1977. From all accounts, he and his PPP party would have won that election, but it appears that Bhutto was determined to have a landslide victory. Amid charges of rigging the elections and popular protests, Chief of the Army Staff Zia ul-Haq, on July 5, 1977, overthrew Bhutto in what became Pakistan's third coup d'état. Charged with abetting the murder of a political rival in Lahore, Bhutto was thrown in prison and ultimately killed there, in April 1979, on those charges. It is popularly understood, however, that Zia had been determined to eliminate his former leader.

Pakistan Again under Military Rule, Zia Introduces Islamization

Zia vowed to hold elections quickly, but after a number of such promises it became apparent he was determined to stay in power. On February 2, 1979, Zia took an unprecedented action: he promulgated his Islamization program, an act that would have long-lasting implications for state and society in Pakistan for years to come. While the Islamization program affected the political landscape in general, its most serious implications were on the rights and roles of women. (See further discussion of this in the section on "Women's Power and Kinship Networks in Political Life" below.)

No substantive policies for Islamic reforms had existed in Pakistan prior to Zia's Islamization program.[10] The country had not even been declared to be an Islamic republic until its second constitution in 1965. Eight years later, the third constitution finally included other references to Islam and the supremacy of Islamic laws and had mandated the establishment of the Council of Islamic Ideology to ensure that no laws in Pakistan are in contradiction to the Shariat (law). Islamic laws in Pakistan are generally based on Hanafi interpretations—widely considered to be the most liberal in the Muslim world—though on occasion the state has turned to decisions based on other schools of *fiqh* (Islamic jurisprudence) as well.

Zia's Islamization program consisted of establishing a *zakat*-based welfare/taxation system, a profit-and-loss banking option in accordance with Islam's prohibitions against usury (*riba*), and an Islamic penal code entitled the Hudood Ordinances. Selectively gleaned from fiqh, the Hudood Ordinances focused on enforcing punishments for three kinds of crimes explicitly outlined in Islamic Shariat (law): theft of private property, the consumption of intoxicants, and adultery and fornication (*zina*). The most controversy swirled around the latter, the zina clause, both because the ordinance governing it made no legal distinction between adultery and rape and its enforcement was highly discriminatory against women, as it became relatively easy for a woman to be charged with (and hence arrested for) adultery. If a woman made a claim of rape but could not prove it, she could also be imprisoned. It is not surprising, therefore, that uneducated women with no experience of how a legal system operates or funds for legal defense came to populate Pakistan's prisons.[11]

The Law of Evidence, promulgated four years later in 1983 and subsequently upheld only in cases concerning economic transactions, would have restricted women from providing evidentiary testimony in certain kinds of cases and require corroboration by another woman in other kinds of cases. Regardless, the law clearly gives men and women different legal rights and, at the least, underscores that the state does not regard women and men as equal economic actors.

The one component of his Islamization program that Zia ul-Haq had been unable to implement was his proposed Shari'at Bill, which would have required *all* laws in the country to be in conformity with Islam. A highly diluted version was passed by the Nawaz Sharif government three years after Zia's death, in April 1991. There are many ways in which this Shari'at Law can be interpreted. Women's groups in particular were concerned that the reforms made in the Muslim Family Laws Ordinance (MFLO) of 1961 would be jeopardized if more conservative forces could convince the courts that it was not in conformity with religious precepts. The constitutionally mandated Council for Islamic Ideology had undertaken review of the Ordinance, but would not publicly release its assessment—written in the 1980s—until recently, as more conservative groups would have lambasted the fairly liberal opinions expressed in the report and further polarized the country around the issues of women's rights.

The Islamization program was pursued in a rather complicated ideological framework. His stance contradicted popular culture in which most people were "personally" very religious but not "publicly" religious. An untoward outcome was that by relying on an Islamically based policy, the state fomented factionalism: by legislating what is Islamic and what is not, Islam itself could no longer provide unity, as it was now being defined to exclude previously included groups. Importantly, too, the state had attempted to dictate a specific ideal image of women in Islamic society—*chador aur char divari*, "remaining veiled and within the four walls of one's home"—which was largely antithetical to that existing in popular sentiments and in everyday life.

Who can predict the fate of Zia's government had the USSR not invaded Afghanistan that fateful day of December 26, 1979? While Pakistan had essentially fallen off of U.S. "radar," its importance was suddenly rejuvenated as it quickly became a frontline state in the U.S. proxy war over Afghanistan with the USSR. The U.S. government put together a nonmilitary aid package to Pakistan for $3.2 billion dollars for 1982–1987; this was followed with an allocation of $4.1 billion for 1988–1993. Full details on the total amount of the military support given to Pakistan remain unclear, but it was far greater than nonmilitary.

The Democratic Interregnum, 1988–1999

On August 17, 1988, Zia ul-Haq—along with then U.S. ambassador Arnold Raphael—died in a plane crash whose cause has never been fully established. That November, elections were finally held once again in Pakistan, and Benazir Bhutto, now leader of the PPP, was able to form a government. In December 1988, she became the first female prime

minister of any Muslim country (see box 3.4).[12] The ensuing eleven-year
democratic interregnum saw Benazir Bhutto and the PPP jockeying for
power with Nawaz Sharif, scion of an industrial family who had revived
the Pakistan Muslim League (PML). Social conditions continued to deteriorate while each government was dismissed twice on charges of corruption, culminating in General Pervez Musharraf declaring martial law on
October 12, 1999.

What are these eleven years best known for? While limited in making
substantive transformations, three things stand out in particular:

- Nawaz Sharif promulgated the Shariat Law during his first tenure,
  albeit this was a far more "'watered-down'" version than the one Zia
  had tried to pass;

Box 3.4. Benazir Bhutto (1953–2007)

With a name that is synonymous with the Pakistan People's Party,
Benazir Bhutto served twice as Pakistan's prime minister (1988–
1990, and 1993–1996), and was the first female prime minister of a
Muslim country. Born in Sindh and educated at Radcliffe and Oxford, she returned to Pakistan shortly before the July 5, 1977, coup
d'état that overthrew her father, Zulfiqar Ali Bhutto. Following his
execution in April 1979, she spent the ensuing five years in and out
of prison, finally able to leave the country in 1984. She returned to
Pakistan in April 1986 amid rampant antigovernment demonstrations and became a symbol of the hope for the reestablishment of
democracy in the country. She became prime minister when the PPP
was invited to form the government in December 1988.

Her time in power was problematic: although the PPP's rhetoric
included the lofty goals of universal education, human rights, and
women's empowerment, her first administration was characterized by
efforts to appease entrenched powerful leaders while her second administration was characterized largely by efforts to remain in power.
Both of her governments were dismissed on charges of corruption and
mismanagement. Benazir returned to Pakistan in October 2007, campaigning to contest the national elections slated for January 2008. She
never saw the new year: she was assassinated as a campaign rally was
concluding on December 27 in Rawalpindi. Her "political will" named
her husband, Asif Ali Zardari, as her successor until such time her son,
Bilawal, can undertake the leadership of the PPP.

- Benazir Bhutto developed a government-wide National Plan of Action (NPA) to implement the Beijing Platform for Action in the time period following the 1995 United Nations Fourth World Conference for Women, during her second tenure, and had Pakistan ratify the UN CEDAW Convention;
- Nawaz Sharif, in his second tenure during the summer of 1999, posted the Pakistan army in Kargil, in the high mountains of Kashmir, where the conflict just nearly "got out of control" (see discussion in "Social Costs of Militarism" below)

There were no major political transformations, alliance building efforts, or even major catastrophes during this time period, other than Pakistan's detonating a nuclear weapons test in May 1998 and the Kargil incident getting out of control in the summer of 1999. It soon became evident that the military was fed up with the democratic experiment.

Another Foray into Military Rule, 1999–2008

When Pervez Musharraf, Pakistani chief of the army staff, was flying back to Pakistan from Sri Lanka on October 12, 1999, Nawaz Sharif gave the ill-fated order that Musharraf's aircraft not be allowed to land in Pakistan, apparently out of fear of an impending coup d'état. This quickly became an international incident, especially as Musharraf was flying on a passenger aircraft and everyone onboard suddenly became in-flight hostages. When the aircraft finally landed in Karachi, Nawaz was arrested and Musharraf's eight-year rule began.

Instead of self-anointing himself as the chief martial law administrator (CMLA), as previous military rulers had done, he declared himself the chief executive (CE), in line with the idea that he would lead the country onto a more solid economic footing. He appointed a number of civil society activists to key positions in his cabinet. In the first week of September 2001, Musharraf launched a new "Task Force on Human Development" initiative, whose goals were to undertake a universal primary education plan and an adult literacy program, primary health care plan, skills training and microcredit programs, and the like.[13]

Yet events of the following week—September 11, 2001—placed Pakistan squarely into a frontline position in U.S. efforts to thwart al-Qaeda and other terrorist entities. The assistance Musharraf's government offered the United States in its war in Afghanistan put his administration into direct confrontation with many Pakistanis, especially those who opposed the U.S. invasion and the ensuing raids within Pakistan in search of Taliban and al-Qaeda personnel. Violent attacks within Pakistan escalated amid fears that extremist groups were expanding their spheres of influence (see discussion in "Social Costs of Militarism" below). In December 2001, the violent attack on the Indian Parliament in New Delhi allegedly by Pakistan-based Kashmiri militants resulted in a worldwide condemnation of the limited power exhibited by the Pakistan government to prevent its nationals from committing terrorist attacks domestically and internationally. The United States government, in particular, was furious with its ally, Musharraf, for not doing more to contain these groups.

Merely a month later, in January 2002, Musharraf banned a number of extremist Islamist groups for having terrorist connections, including Lashkar-e-Jhangvi, TNSM, and Sipah-e-Sihaba. However, these and many other banned organizations have reappeared with new names and have continued their vitriolic tirades and violent attacks. Suddenly Pakistan, too, was witnessing something that had never happened there before: violent suicide attacks, which continue today.

In preparation for the October 2002 national elections, Musharraf substantially revised the local government structure. Seeking to preserve his political power, he called for a Referendum to be held on April 30, 2002. It is widely considered to have been fraudulent and indeed farcical, as it asked the electorate to vote yes or no:

> For continuation of the system of local government, establishment of democracy, continuation and stability of reforms, elimination of sectarianism and extremism and attainment of the ideals of Quaid-i-Azam. Do you want to make General Pervez Musharraf President for the next five years?[14]

Four months later, Musharraf promulgated the heavily debated and problematic Legal Framework Order (LFO) 2002, which made a number of constitutional changes, including reinstating reserved seats for women (to mandate women's parliamentary participation, which had expired under Benazir's first government) and placing minimal educational requirements on candidates running for office (the equivalent of a high school degree if running for local level elections, and a university degree if running for national level elections). Importantly, too, the LFO reinserted the highly contested Constitutional Article 58(2)(b), giving the president the right to dissolve the National Assembly at his discretion and set in place new processes of appointing provincial governors and judges. Hamid Khan argues that the LFO was "an attempt to rewrite the Constitution by a military ruler to perpetuate himself in power under dubious authority conferred upon him by an emaciated Supreme Court."[15] Pakistan had woefully been there before.

Musharraf's newly created political party, the PML-Q, was able to assemble a government following the October 2002 elections. But in a significant way, this was a problematic victory: for the first time in Pakistan's fifty-five-year history, an Islamist political party had success at the ballot box. The Islamist coalition, the Muttahida Majlis-i-Amal (MMA), won a majority of the vote in the NWFP provincial elections and became leader of the opposition at the national level.

The MMA was a coalition of six Islamist parties: Jama'at-i-Islami, Jamiat Ulema-e-Islam (Fazlur Rehman group), Jamiat Ulema-e-Islam (Sami ul-Haq group), Jamiat Ulema-e-Pakistan, Markazi Jamiat Ahle Hadith, and Tehrik Nifaz Fiqah Jaferiya (a Shi'a party). These parties had joined together in early 2000 as the Pakistan-Afghanistan Defense Council to support the Taliban regime in response to global criticism of the government in Afghanistan. Following the early October 2001 U.S. attack on Afghanistan, the constituent parties decided to make an alliance "to implement an Islamic system and to protect Islamic values" with the objective of ensuring the "supremacy of Islamic Law and enactment of legislation according to the recommendations of the Islamic Ideological Council" and became the MMA.[16] In particular, it was seeking to cross lines where it could pass legislation to structure an individual's degree of religious piety, though indeed this would be the MMA's interpretation of piety.

While the provincial MMA government tried to pass a variety of laws that they could tout as helping to "Islamify" the area, these efforts were short-lived. The most important result of their tenure was that they enabled violent, militant groups euphemistically known as "the Pakistan Taliban"—including the TNSM and the Tehrik-e-Taliban Pakistan (TTP), which are profiled in the final section of this chapter—to gain a foothold in the province. Providing a space to these groups has been done at great social cost, as discussed below in "Social Costs of Militarism" section.

At the national level, Musharraf's government was increasingly under siege. Militant groups targeted institutions of the state (e.g., schools, police academies, even toll collectors on the Motorway) and attempted to assassinate Musharraf at least twice. Elites were critical of Musharraf's failure to move Pakistan's economy forward and through the never-ending gridlocks unbridled terrorism was causing in the country. Importantly, too, the U.S. government kept stating publicly that Musharraf could be doing a lot more to support "the global war on terrorism." However, the more the U.S. government would state this, the more the average Pakistani winced at the implication that the Pakistan government was just to do the United States' bidding. This did not go down well with the majority of the population, and Musharraf's popularity declined rapidly.

In the course of Musharraf's tenure, there was much criticism of his holding two offices simultaneously, one appointed (employed as an army general) and one elected (president). Indeed, there was a constitutional requirement that the country's president not only could not be employed by the state, but that two years had to elapse before an individual could ascend to that office. In March 2007, anticipating that the seated Chief Justice of the Pakistan Supreme Court would uphold this requirement and force him from office, Musharraf unilaterally dismissed Iftikhar Chaudhry. This act provoked an unprecedented mass-based movement that has come to be called the "Lawyer's Movement."

While the Lawyer's Movement was agitating first to have Chief Justice Iftikhar Chaudhry reinstated and then to have him make a decision about the constitutionality of Musharraf holding the two offices, Musharraf decided to act for his own political preservation. National elections were scheduled to be held in January 2008; defying precedent, Musharraf declared that the seated Parliament would first be asked to elect the president on October 6, 2007.[17] By now, Iftikhar Chaudhry had been reinstated as chief justice of the Supreme Court. The day before the presidential election was to be held, Musharraf promulgated the "National Reconciliation Ordinance (NRO), 2007"[18] with the goal of facilitating the return of Benazir Bhutto to participate in politics in Pakistan. It is popularly assumed, though with no actual evidence, that Musharraf had reached an agreement with the United States that he would remain president if he assented to Benazir becoming prime minister. Two important clauses of the NRO state thusly,

Amendment of section 494, Act V of 1898:

(2) Notwithstanding anything to the contrary in sub-section(1), the Federal Government or a Provincial Government may, before the judgment is pronounced by a trial court, withdraw from the prosecution of any person including an absconding accused who is found to be falsely involved for political reasons or through political victimization in any case initiated between 1st day of January, 1986 to 12th day of October, 1999 and upon such withdrawal clause (a) and clause (b) of sub-section (1) shall apply.

Insertion of new section, Ordinance, XVIII of 1999: In the said Ordinance, after section 33, the following new section shall be inserted, namely:

33A. Withdrawal and termination of prolonged pending proceedings initiated prior to 12th October, 1999.

(1) Notwithstanding anything contained in this Ordinance or any other law for the time being in force, proceedings under investigation or pending in any court including a High Court and the Supreme Court of Pakistan initiated by or on a reference by the National Accountability Bureau inside or outside Pakistan including proceedings continued under section 33, requests for mutual assistance and civil party to proceedings initiated by the Federal Government before the 12th day of October, 1999 against holders of public office stand withdrawn and terminated with immediate effect and such holders of public office shall also not be liable to any action in future as well under this Ordinance for acts having been done in good faith before the said date.

The NRO essentially allowed Benazir's return to Pakistan by declaring an amnesty on any pending charges against her. However, by declaring the cutoff date as October 12, 1999, a similar amnesty was *not* given to Nawaz Sharif who was accused of attempted murder on that date (for not allowing Musharraf's plane to land in Karachi that day, when the coup occurred).

Benazir returned to Pakistan from her home in Dubai thirteen days after the passage of the NRO, on October 18, 2007. A cavalcade of supporters greeted her—but as they marched through the serpentine streets of Karachi, a suicide bomber attacked her jubilant supporters, killing 115 people and injuring countless more. This foreboding incident occurred while Nawaz Sharif was attempting—unsuccessfully—to return to Pakistan and the Supreme Court announced they would soon determine the constitutionality of the October 6 presidential election.

Merely two weeks later, just as the Supreme Court was about to announce its verdict about the presidential election, Musharraf took an unprecedented step: he essentially launched a coup d'état on himself on November 3 when he proclaimed an Emergency (as chief of the army staff) and ordered the constitution would be in abeyance. He claimed various reasons for his actions, including suicide bombings, terrorist attacks, judicial interference, and the judiciary overstepping its authority. Most analysts conclude, however, that Musharraf knew the Supreme Court verdict on the constitutionality of the election was imminent and that it would not be in his favor. In promulgating the Provisional Constitutional Order (PCO), he suspended certain constitutional rights (in Articles 9, 10, 15, 16, 17, 19, and 25) and proclaimed that the Supreme Court and the provincial high courts were "deprived of the power to make any order against the President and the Prime Minister" and that no judgment, order or process "could be made or issued by any court or tribunal against the President or the Prime Minister."[19] The government placed strict controls on the press and shut down transmission on private television channels; these channels lamented at the time that they were not even allowed to transmit cricket matches during that period.

Were the Emergency and the PCO necessary, and did they even improve Musharraf's position in the country? Apparently not, as he was unable to prevent Nawaz Sharif from returning to Pakistan on November 25. He resigned from the military November 28 (thereby making the Supreme Court verdict on the constitutionality of his holding two offices irrelevant) and lifted martial law on December 15. The entire judiciary *except* for the chief justice was reinstated.

The drama that unfolded in Pakistan throughout 2007 was not to end on December 15. Amid national campaigning, many politicians were targeted by terrorists. Then on December 27, as Benazir Bhutto was waving to the crowd from the sunroof of her car while departing from a campaign appearance in Rawalpindi, a suicide bomber blew himself up right beside her. Benazir Bhutto, heir to the legacy of Zulfiqar Ali Bhutto, the first woman prime minister of a Muslim country and an enduring symbol of democratization in Pakistan, was now dead at age fifty-four.

The Return of Democracy to Pakistan

National elections were postponed to February 18, 2008, both to observe a national period of mourning for Benazir as well as to enable the PPP to reposition itself as a political party, given the assassination of its leader. As the PPP won a third of the 242 contested seats in the National Assembly and Nawaz Sharif's PML-N won 27 percent (Pervez Musharraf's PML-Q won only 16 percent of the vote), they joined forces and formed a PPP-led coalition government and on March 25, 2008, Syed Yousuf Raza Gilani became Pakistan's prime minister.

Things were shaky within the coalition from the outset. Nawaz Sharif—who had been prevented from contesting the election himself because of outstanding legal problems—had vowed his party would prioritize reinstatement of the chief justice of Pakistan, Iftikhar Chaudhry. Hailing from the southern Punjab city of Multan, Gilani had limited experience in national politics. The prevailing view was that PPP chairman, Asif Ali Zardari, widower of Benazir Bhutto, was actually at the helm of power, an assessment that rang even truer when Zardari was elected president of Pakistan by the national and four provincial legislatures on September 9, 2008, following the August 18 resignation of Pervez Musharraf. By the time he resigned, Musharraf was floundering politically: he had resigned from the military (his main base of support in the country), had been the target of repeated assassination attempts, and was facing impeachment proceedings. Yet after his departure and Zardari's election, the course of government in Pakistan hardly changed. One of the key foci of the election campaign had been the reinstatement of Chief Justice Iftikhar Chaudhry, but Zardari hemmed and hawed over taking that step. Popular opinion surmised that *his* concern was that Chaudhry would reopen the many corruption cases that loomed against Zardari, thus forcing him to resign from office. It was only after a second nationwide strike led by the Lawyer's Movement that Zardari, on March 16, 2009, finally acceded to pressure and reinstated the chief justice of the Supreme Court—over a year after his party had come to power in the national election.

Alliances within Zardari's government waxed and waned, with one political party leaving the PPP-led coalition while another joined it. The Supreme Court disqualified Prime Minister Gilani—declaring him ineligible to hold office—when he was found in contempt for refusing to contact the government of Switzerland about bank funds being held there in President Zardari's name. He was quickly replaced by Raja Pervez Ashraf, who himself was under attack for corruption by the court, but who was able to finish his term when the entire government resigned in March 2013 to make way for a caretaker government that was tasked by the Election Commission of Pakistan to oversee the upcoming national election.

While there are real threats challenging Pakistan today and jeopardizing its future, as discussed in the following sections of this chapter, there are also promising signs that democracy is becoming entrenched in the operation of the state. The PPP government became *the very first* in Pakistan's checkered political history to serve out its term. It unsuccessfully contested reelection, winning a majority only in the province of Sindh, in nationwide elections held on May 11, 2013. The result at the national level was a victory for Nawaz Sharif's PML-N party, which formed a national government in early June with Nawaz Sharif at its helm, his third time as prime minister. Imran Khan's populist opposition party, the PTI (Pakistan Tehrik-i-Insaf), using the slogan of a "Naya Pakistan" (New Pakistan), won the majority of seats in KP and formed a provincial coalition government with the Jama'at-i-Islami. The PML-N candidate, Mamnoon Hussain, was easily elected by the national and provincial legislatures as the new president of Pakistan and sworn in on September 9, 2013. The national government has been heavily criticized in its first one hundred days in office for being weak, unimpressive, and hardly concerned with the needs of the masses, but with its promises to unveil new national security and energy policies, popular sentiment appears to be that the people in Pakistan are willing to wait a while before passing judgment on its effectiveness.

POLITICAL ECONOMY

The Government of Pakistan's consistent lack of investment in human capital in the over sixty-five years since independence reverberates throughout the country in myriad ways. Uneven growth, especially in the 1950s and 1960s, resulted in conditions for Pakistan's poorest classes to hardly change or get worse. Jinnah's pluralistic view of Pakistani society was shaken further in the mid-1960s and 1970s as divisions and distinctions between different ethnic and class groupings became more conspicuous. Animosity grew between muhajirs and Punjabis, the two most powerful economic-ethnic groups in the country. The end result of that era was the dismemberment of the country in 1971, separatist movements in Baluchistan and KP in the ensuing decade, and sectarian feuds overflowing into the national arena that remain to the present time.

Pakistan's development history was to have been the modernization theorists' "example to the world" of what could occur with large infusions of foreign capital. The idea behind this was that the gap between rich and poor was greater in poor countries than in wealthier ones, so large infusions of capital into an economy would then serve to lessen the gap, and hence development would occur. Such development would enable poor countries to replicate the developed parts of the world as they shed their traditions and adopted the economic, political, and social trappings of modernity.[20]

Economic growth and development priorities in Pakistan during the Ayub Khan administration are salient examples of this orientation. Economists from the Harvard Advisory Group exerted unparalleled influence over economic policies in the late 1950s and early 1960s in Pakistan. They argued that Pakistan's economy could take off if given large injections of capital, either in the form of joint ventures or loans. But who actually benefited from this assistance? Who could qualify for the loans or participate in joint ventures? While the industrial elite benefited in the aforementioned Golden Age (1958–1968), ethnic and class divisions became exaggerated in this era due to such uneven growth, with the rich getting much richer and the lot of the poor either hardly changing or getting worse.

Growing poverty in the country has exacerbated ethnic differences. Pakistan lags behind countries with comparable per capita income in most social indicators. According to the World Bank, while the "poverty headcount fell in Pakistan during the 1980s, from 47 percent in 1985 to 29 percent in 1995, more recently, it has been increasing." and that "poverty remains a serious concern in Pakistan. . . . More importantly, difference in income per capita across regions have persisted or widened."[21] Over a third of children under age five are inappropriately underweight, a telling statistic of the failure of development efforts to promote equity in development and opportunity.[22] Over two-thirds of Pakistan's population currently lives on less than $2 per day; over a third live below the national poverty line. The World Bank's country update for Pakistan in 2004 saliently argued—which still applies today—that it is Pakistan's failure to address social development adequately that is responsible for the growing impoverishment in the country:

> Pakistan has grown much more than other low-income countries, but has failed to achieve social progress commensurate with its economic growth. The educated and well-off urban population lives not so differently from their counterparts in other countries of similar income range. However, the

poor and rural inhabitants of Pakistan are being left behind. For example, access to sanitation in Pakistan is 23 percent lower than in other countries with similar income.[23]

Pakistan's economy has grown far more than that in many other low-income countries, but then it has had more natural resources to exploit—including fertile agricultural land, hydroelectric power opportunities, and natural gas—than do many others. Benefits from economic growth have been markedly skewed between rich and poor. Land reforms, too, have had a negligible role in affecting rural poverty. The kinds of high growth rates in agriculture that would be necessary to overcome the very high population growth rates in rural areas and result in reducing rural poverty have not occurred.

Indeed, Pakistan has failed to achieve social progress commensurate with its economic growth potential, or even with its base economic growth. The educated and well-off urban population lives not so differently from their counterparts in other countries of similar income range. However, the poor and rural inhabitants of Pakistan have been left with limited resources, clamoring for jobs, decent schools for their many children, plagued by inflation, and living—quite literally—in the dark. Pakistan's ranking in the UNDP's Human Development Index slipped from 120 in 1991 to 138 in 2002 and is now tied with Bangladesh at 146 in 2013, worse than Lao PDR (138), Swaziland (141), and Democratic Republic of the Congo (142) and only just above Angola (148) and Myanmar (149), all countries with *far* weaker natural resources and economies.[24]

The sixth most populous country in the world, Pakistan had a 2013 population estimated at 184 million, with one of the world's highest population growth rates.[25] Its land area, however, is only thirty-second in size. Pakistan's population is not evenly distributed throughout the country, ranging dramatically from sparsely populated Baluchistan to some of the highest densities in the world in parts of Karachi and the old city of Lahore.

Greater numbers of people are demanding goods and services in the country and most of them are living in densely populated cities difficult to navigate (physically as well as politically). Electricity, sanitation, water, and food are now priced at a premium that seem unaffordable to many. While the majority of Pakistan's inhabitants still live in rural areas, the country's urban population is now over 50 million people (see table 3.2).

The urban population in Sindh has nearly surpassed the province's rural population, due in large part to migration to the city of Karachi where the population surpassed 13 million in 2007 (see table 3.3). Pakistan's urban annual growth rate has averaged 3.82 percent since 1950, with slower growth experienced only recently.[26]

Table 3.2.   Population by Province and Urban-Rural Residence (in millions)

	Total pop.	Urban pop.	% urban	Rural pop.	% rural
National	147.1	51.9	35.3%	95.2	64.7%
Baluchistan	8.5	2.0	23.5%	6.5	76.5%
KPK	20.9	3.4	16.3%	17.5	83.7%
Punjab	84.8	31.1	36.7%	53.7	63.3%
Sindh	32.9	15.4	46.8%	17.5	53.2%

Source: Federal Bureau of Statistics, *Pakistan Demographic Survey* 2006, Table 1, pp. 39–43.

Pakistan's cities continue to experience significant growth: seven other cities (Faisalabad, Gujranwala, Hyderabad, Lahore, Multan, Peshawar, and Rawalpindi) have populations of over a million; Lahore's population is well over 5 million. The international think tank City Mayors now projects Karachi, in 2010, to have become the largest city in the world with a population of 15.5 million (although its total metropolitan area of 18 million puts it smaller than a number of others in this comparison).[27] Roughly a third of all urban dwellers live either in Karachi or Lahore.

Pakistan's cities have tremendous infrastructure problems. At least one-third of urban residents live in *katchi abadis* and other slums lacking basic services.[28] Urban transportation is a nightmare everywhere, and nowhere greater than in Lahore. There, the deterioration of public transit networks and the proliferation of automobiles and private minibuses have caused unprecedented traffic congestion, bottlenecks, and pollution. The Ravi River receives so much hazardous and untreated waste on a daily basis that the city of Lahore is essentially encircled now by poison.[29]

Table 3.3.   Population of Major Pakistani Cities (thousands)

	2000	2005	2010	2015
Faisalabad	2,140	2,482	2,833	3,260
Gujranwala	1,224	1,433	1,643	1,898
Hyderabad	1,221	1,386	1,581	1,827
Karachi	10,019	11,553	13,052	14,855
Lahore	5,448	6,259	7,092	8,107
Multan	1,263	1,445	1,650	1,906
Peshawar	1,066	1,235	1,415	1,636
Quetta	614	725	836	971
Rawalpindi	1,519	1,762	2,015	2,324

Source: Population Division of the Department of Economic and Social Affairs of the United Nations Secretariat, "World Population Prospects: The 2006 Revision" and "World Urbanization Prospects: The 2007 Revision," accessed at http://esa.un.org/unup.

Indeed, politics uses poverty extensively in Pakistan. The end result is a narrow view of community, a divisive cleavage that pits Western-oriented, wealthy groups (which have embraced the information super-highway and other advantages globalization has brought) against poor, disempowered groups—those who cannot afford a government education and who know that receiving one won't help their state. These are the people who identify with their groups wholly, be it tribal identity, sectarian identity, kinship, locale, and the like.

The recent PPP-led coalition government considered the Shaheed Benazir Bhutto Income Support Fund (BISF) to be the cornerstone of its policies to alleviate poverty in the country, allocating 34 billion rupees to it in the 2008–2009 budget. It was anticipated that up to three million "economically vulnerable families" with monthly incomes of less than 6,000 rupees would receive 2,000 rupees every other month under the BISF.[30] Members of the National Assembly and the Senate were provided with eight thousand application forms to be distributed in their constituencies for poor families to complete. The completed forms needed to be verified by the Union Councillor at the local level, then by the area MNA, who would submit the applications to NADRA for verification and final approval. Payment was made only to the female family head, which the PPP government argued ensured women's empowerment and would certainly be used to support children. Thus far, the PML-N government has not announced any alternative policy, so it is presumed the BISF will continue but under a new name.

Many concerns have been voiced about this program: the targeting method (self-targeting mechanisms that involve an application process are known to deter the neediest from participating, and this would be especially true in Pakistan's prevailing patronage systems); that those without identity cards would at least initially be at a disadvantage (and it is the poorest who tend to lack them); that it doesn't strengthen the institutional infrastructure but rather is dependent on the largesse of individual parliamentarians; and that provincial representatives have been bypassed by focusing solely on national ones, who perhaps are less in touch with local needs in their constituencies. The BISF was also con-troversial if considering it as a poverty alleviation effort. It was instead a new form of subsidy program that focuses on shoring up income instead of providing food subsidies (which inadvertently provide more assistance to the rich than to the poor because they consume more). While purchas-ing power of daily essentials increased for some disadvantaged families, it was not linked to any educational, development, or income-generating programs. Critics contend that substantial monies from the BISF have gone "missing," while the PPP government praised it as a cornerstone of their poverty alleviation strategy, to the extent that they requested the fund be increased to 70 billion rupees in the 2009/2010 budget.[31]

IDENTITY POLITICS

Despite the assumptions of the Two Nations theory,[32] Pakistan's formidable Muslim population came from diverse practices and heritages. These ranged among Sunnis from the austere Deoband school, the Sufi-oriented Berelvi school,[33] the orthodox Ahle Hadith, to the modernist Aligarh school, and among Shi'as from the followers of the Twelve Imams, the disciples of the Aga Khan, to members of the *Dawoodi Bohra* and *Memon* communities. Notwithstanding these formal divisions, Sufi teachers who had spread Islam throughout the subcontinent still had their followings, and most Bengali Muslims, accustomed to a more syncretic Islamic tradition, found little in common with the rest.

Sectarian differences have become particularly compelling not only in the ways various groups are negotiating—sometimes violently—changing power dynamics between them, but also in the ongoing process of constructing civil society in the country. The vision of a Muslim majority state in which religious minorities would share equally in its development also came under question shortly after independence (and persists today). The pluralistic perspective was definitively discarded in 1979 when Zia ul-Haq's administration left no question that some interpretations of Islam were to wield unprecedented influence in the state.

Notwithstanding the imperial loyalists and divisions within Muslim factions, there were also considerable regional and cultural divides at the outset. Punjabi, Pakhtun, Sindhi, Baluchi, and Bengali orientations toward kinship, power, the role of the state, and citizenship differ substantially. The roughly seven million muhajirs who migrated to Pakistan after Partition emerged as an additional ethnic group, manifesting later as a political group, the MQM—Muhajir Qaumi Movement—as well. The critical challenge of identity politics in Pakistan became how to create a shared sense of being Pakistani that could overcome the compelling local cultural orientations and political conflicts. In the case of Bengal, physically ensconced at the other end of the subcontinent and sharing very few sociocultural similarities with the major ethnic groups of western Pakistan, this was ultimately not possible and East Pakistan seceded. The remainder of Pakistan is still engaged in this task.

Despite 97 percent of its population being Muslims, Pakistan still seeks to find an appropriate role for Islam in civic and political life. What it means to be a Muslim is intrinsically tied to local cultural traditions that, to many adherents, are inextricably intertwined. Indeed, there exists substantial confusion over where the lines are drawn between what is Islamic, what is codified tradition, and how (if at all) to delineate their separate jurisdictions. In other words, many Pakistanis experience their identity as Muslims as inseparable from other component parts of their culture and often confuse those things that are not in accordance with cultural norms, values or practices as being in contradiction with Islam. Alternatively, other groups (e.g., those promoting human rights, women's rights, business interests, and many political parties) question Islam's jurisdictional space in the contemporary political sphere and whether state-sanctioned Islamic injunctions should have a role to play in socioeconomic domains in Pakistan.

The country is divided politically into five provinces: Baluchistan, Khyber Pakhtunkhwa (previously the Northwest Frontier Province), the Punjab, Sindh, and the newest province, Gilgit-Baltistan. There are a number of other political entities that are administered directly by the federal government but which enjoy a great deal of local autonomy—FATA (Federally Administered Tribal Agencies), the autonomous district consisting of the capital city of Islamabad, and the largely autonomous Azad Jammu and Kashmir (AJK).

Along Pakistan's northeast border with Afghanistan lies a legacy of British colonialism, the seven tribal agencies and six frontier regions that comprise the somewhat autonomous FATA.[34] Here, tribal leaders' power holds sway over their members' lives to a considerable extent, and federal institutions and laws are essentially irrelevant. Political agents, representatives of the federal government, rarely wield even limited influence; they are essentially couriers. A common sentiment in FATA is the disdain with which most residents regard the federal government. Development projects that have sought to build modern roads, schools, and new kinds of economic enterprises are often viewed locally as insidious efforts to dominate the tribal areas. It is erroneous to assume that the federal government of Pakistan maintains effective power and influence in FATA.

The semiautonomous Azad Kashmir (the common moniker for Azad Jammu and Kashmir) consists of those parts of the princely states of Jammu and Kashmir that Pakistan annexed in the 1948 war with India. It shares some features with the federally administered areas in that its external relations are under the protection and control of the government of Pakistan though its internal affairs enjoy a great degree of political autonomy. Azad Kashmir has its own constitution and prime minister and, unlike FATA, does not send representatives to the federal Parliament (National Assembly) in Islamabad.

Political identity is closely associated with ethnicity. Separatist movements and ethnic crises have plagued Pakistan since its inception, though the nature and composition of such conflict has changed over time. At independence, there was a definable fear that Pakistan might cease to exist; East Pakistan's secession in 1971 further aggravated that anxiety. More recently, separatist movements in the Khyber Pakhtunkhwa (KP), Baluchistan and Sindh have given way to demands for greater power and autonomy.

Ethnicity is a key influence in political attitudes. Ethnic identity is the primary foundation of provincial divisions in Pakistan, albeit residence in a province is by no means an exclusive domain of only one distinct ethnic group. Indeed, some of the greatest initial political divisiveness occurred surrounding which province distinct districts should join. For example, many Baluchis had championed having Dera Ghazi Khan be a part of Baluchistan, although it ended up being in Punjab. Numerous Pakhtuns live in villages abutting GT (Grand Trunk) Road between Rawalpindi and Attock, but one does not enter Khyber Pakhtunkhwa until the bridge is crossed. One of the key reasons for the delay in enumerating the 1981 census (it was finally held in 1998, seventeen years later) is that popular knowledge held that with the influx of millions of Afghan Pakhtun refugees into Baluchistan, the majority ethnic group in the province had changed; stating definitively that Baluchis no longer comprised the majority ethnic group in Baluchistan would provide further fuel for open provocation between groups in the province.

These are not symbolically imagined communities either. Ethnic orientations toward social hierarchies, toward the state, even toward Islam differ markedly between some groups. Being cognizant of the most salient ways that ethnicity influences political and economic stances enables us to gain a fuller view of how the different segments that comprise Pakistan interact. There are significant cultural differences between major ethnic groups in Pakistan that contribute to interprovincial misunderstandings and very real tensions.

Punjab

Punjab is the most populous province in Pakistan, comprising more than half of the country's population. Reciprocity is a central cultural value in the agrarian base of village Punjabi society. This is quite rational, as the Punjab has a long history of settled agriculture, and maintaining age-old alliances within farming communities is essential. This results in a range of social networks based on local solidarities of group necessity. There is, consequently, a great deal of social pressure to share and pool resources (e.g., income, political influence, personal connections) among Punjabis. In other words, when Punjabis have risen to positions of power and wealth, they have tended to include other Punjabis in the process, either by preference or social pressures. Punjabis often regard their actions in which they have used their influence to benefit others in their networks—finding jobs, promoting them, helping others acquire a passport so as to be able to work abroad—as a normal part of the cultural requirement of mutual obligation and reciprocity. This practice, however, has led to frequent charges by non-Punjabis of favoritism, corruption, and nepotism.

Zamindars, feudal rural landlords whose class was created by the British colonialists, have long wielded unquestioned power alongside local religious icons, *pirs*. Each had only the other to fear as viable adversaries. The landlords, who had owned and controlled large tracts of land for centuries, were granted additional land by the British in the nineteenth century in return for favors, when the latter set out to document land ownership in the province. While the influence of zamindars has been mitigated by the growing power of industrialists in the province, patronage relations (particularly in rural areas) remain strong. Villagers ardently campaign for the local zamindar—or the candidate the zamindar supports—in elections, knowing that only with access to someone who has access to power can they be successful in asking for a water line to be connected, a job to be found for a relative, or to lobby for a government subsidy. Such ties take generations to build and both sides—zamindars and villagers alike—distrust those who shift allegiances for temporary gain.

On May 3, 2012, the National Assembly adopted a resolution in support of dividing the province of Punjab into two smaller entities, Punjab and Southern Punjab, the latter consisting of the Seraiki-speaking areas. At the same time, the creation of three other provinces was proposed: Bahawalpur (a former princely state in southern Punjab), Hazara (the Hindko-speaking area of Khyber Pakhtunkhwa) and FATA (which would resolve the legacy of the British frontier area addressed earlier). However, with the change of government as a result of the May 2013 elections, the status of moving forward with these changes is unclear.

Sindh and Muhajirs

Sindhi identity politics, while rooted in similar agrarian values as in Punjab, manifest quite differently in part due to historical circumstances. Unlike in most of the Punjab, where large agrarian landholdings are a relatively new phenomenon (the past hundred years or so), in Sindh land—and hence power—has historically been concentrated around only a few large landholding families, *waderas*, who enjoyed essentially absolute rule over their very impoverished subjects.

Partition caused the creation of a new ethnic community in Pakistan when a great number of migrants from India shifted to Karachi (the national capital at that time) and created a new self-reference group, muhajirs. The first clashes between resident Sindhis and Punjabis with muhajirs emerged soon after partition when the new state gave the latter replacement housing and land for what muhajirs claimed to have left behind in India. Some questioned the parity involved when those who had fought for the country but remained within it could not also be compensated with abandoned property. These refugees, generally better educated than most native Sindhis, filled a vacuum in the province's commercial life, but not without social cost. Over time, muhajirs created new institutions to care for the needs of their community members, culminating with their own political party, the MQM. Oskar Verkaaik argues that many youth in the MQM (Muhajir Qaumi Movement) joined the party as a way to transgress ethnic categorizations and gain a sense of agency and collectivity, presumably in an environment in which they perceived they had neither precisely because of their ethnicity.[35] The hostility and resentment that has emerged from both groups—indigenous Sindhis and muhajirs in the MQM—toward each other is unprecedented: Sindhis decrying an outside group that now dominates the economy of the province, while muhajirs claim they wield no political influence in the province, and the more recent pitting of Sunnis against Shi'as in incalculable acts of violence. Violent kidnappings have become common throughout the province, and especially in the city of Karachi, most with political provocation while others without.

Khyber Pakhtunkhwa, Baluchistan, and FATA

The remaining two original provinces, Khyber Pakhtunkhwa and Baluchistan, have incurred tumultuous changes in the past twenty-five years. It is these locales that served as the frontline areas initially in the U.S. proxy war against the former Soviet Union in Afghanistan, then as recruiting ground for the religious seminaries that ultimately manifested as the Taliban in Afghanistan, then since October 2001 as enclaves of resistance to official Pakistani collaboration with the United States on a variety of fronts, and more recently as violent sites of contestation themselves. Among both Pakhtun and Baluch tribespeople, these irredentist groups— recognizing only the legitimacy of their own local leaders—have seen everything that mattered to them, within their families, their communities, their tribes, shattered in this time period. We must be cognizant that these are the same groups that *didn't* want roads to connect to their villages, or modern schools, and have been reluctant to embrace Western health care systems. Their communities have undergone incredible upheavals, not the least of which was the in-migration of some three million refugees from Afghanistan over time. It is grossly misleading to essentialize these groups, to assume that since they are irredentists they speak with one voice; indeed, the sectarian divides between groups are as compelling as the differences existing between them and nontribal Pakistanis.

The province of Khyber Pakhtunkhwa and the Federally Administered Tribal Areas (FATA) are closely identified with Pakhtuns, who now are popularly assumed to account for the majority of the population in Baluchistan as well. It is difficult to ascertain an accurate figure of the Pakhtun population, as questions about women in a household are, in the Pakhtun view, an invasion of privacy, while the numbers of men in a household are often overstated, as they are a source of strength. Pakhtuns, who constitute one of the largest tribal groups in the world, do not perceive their tribe as being bound in any way by the Durand Line, the literal "line in the sand" that had been drawn by Sir Mortimer Durand in 1893 delineating the boundary between British India and independent Afghanistan, and which remains today the international boundary between Pakistan and Afghanistan.

The provincial capital, Peshawar, is a quintessentially Pakhtun city: the crowded commercial center is constantly in motion, propelled by bearded, turbaned men with hardly a woman in sight. Compelling archways reveal bazaars where goods and currencies from throughout the world are traded. Commercial transactions, consistent with all forms of transactions among Pakhtuns, are negotiated through tribal and clan lenses. These are marked by complex, shifting patterns of allegiances, alliances, and antagonisms that can last for generations. Hospitality is a major virtue: once someone is an invited guest, the same obligations and allegiances exist toward them as if they were family or clan members.

A cultural trait among Pakhtuns that differs significantly from Punjabis or Sindhis is the intensely egalitarian ethos that traditionally exists among Pakhtun men, placing the tribal leader as but the first among equals.[36] Any attempt at coercion is considered a serious insult and risks precipitating a feud. Many Pakhtuns today are frustrated by what they perceive as a creeping "Punjabification" of social hierarchies that has been growing in Khyber Pakhtunkhwa in the past twenty years; the Pakhtun concept of a leader being "first among equals" has been eclipsed by Punjabi practices of elites considering their constituents as inferiors who should serve them. This has elicited noticeable resentment against many incumbent politicians, particularly in the provincial elections held in October 2002 that resulted in the coming to power of the MMA, a coalition of six Islamist political parties.

Pakhtun social life is significantly informed by *pakhtunwali*, often referred to as the Pakhtun Code of Honor. Pakhtunwali demands that an individual offer hospitality to guests consisting of food, shelter, and the provision of security under all circumstances. Some people have argued that the relatively minimal tension that initially existed between Pakistani Pakhtuns and the large number of Pakhtun refugees from Afghanistan following the Soviet invasion of Afghanistan in 1979 can be attributed to a heightened sense of kinship with fellow Pakhtuns along with the deeply felt obligation to obey the customary dictates of hospitality. An extension of the norms of hospitality implies that even if the person seeking shelter is an enemy, he must be well treated. However, to receive hospitality consistently from someone implies that the recipient is under his protection, a subservient relationship that Pakhtuns shun. The level of frustration among Pakistani Pakhtuns with the refugees escalated after the former Soviet Union withdrew from Afghanistan in the early 1990s, and many felt the internecine violence resulting from warring clans in the conflict was overflowing into their borders.[37] Following the U.S. attack on the Pakhtun-dominated Taliban government in Afghanistan in 2002, many Pakhtuns once again sought shelter from their fellow tribespeople on the other side of the Khyber Pass, in Pakistan.

Vendettas and feuds are an endemic feature of social relations and often span many generations. A popular perception among Pakhtuns is that if the vendetta is not successful this generation, it will be successful in the next. In tribal areas, where government control only erratically contains violence and the level of wealth is generally limited, perennial feuding remains persistent. The proliferation of guns—including clones of AK47s, Uzis, and Kalishnikovs made in the town of Dara Adam Khel—has exacerbated much of the violence. Once a feud becomes resolved, a common practice has been that the aggrieved clan is given a female for marriage, under the assumption that the children of that union will ensure peaceful, long-lasting ties between the clans. This practice of *swara*, however, has been criticized for having girls as young as six years old taken away, and a female given in swara—in actuality a sentence she must pay because of a crime committed by a male family member—is essentially condemned to a life of mental and physical torture.

The government of Pakistan has established numerous schools—including ones devoted exclusively to girls—in an effort to imbue Pakhtuns with a sense of Pakistani nationalism and to ward off separatist movements as well as to promote development and alleviate poverty. Numerous development projects in the past two decades have sought to provide diverse employment opportunities for Pakhtuns in Khyber Pakhtunkhwa given limited prevailing economic and commercial options. In particular (and with ample support from international donor agencies), the government has sought to develop comprehensive development projects in areas of opium poppy cultivation that include roads, schools, and incentives for industrial investment. But this has been challenging, for what kinds of incentives are realistic when the amount of opium poppy that can fit onto two donkeys is sufficient to support financially an entire village for a year? Given their irredentist traditions and resistance to become integrated in wider Pakistani socioeconomic networks it is not surprising, therefore, that Pakhtuns have largely resisted efforts to replace opium poppy crops with tomatoes or onions. In the mid-1990s, after the Taliban came to power in Afghanistan and banned opium poppy cultivation, it proliferated once again in the northwest parts of Pakistan.

As mentioned earlier, the National Assembly in May 2012 tabled a resolution for the creation of four new provinces, two of which would directly affect KP. Hazara would be carved out of the Hindko-speaking areas of eastern Khyber Pakhtunkhwa, where most people do not identify as being ethnic Pakhtuns or speak Pashto. The second would transform the Federally Administered Tribal Areas, FATA, into a formal province, in which its citizens would have all the rights, privileges, and obligations that all citizens in Pakistan enjoy. No timetable yet exists for when this might occur.

Ethno-nationalist politics are of the greatest importance in the remaining province to discuss, Baluchistan. Over two-thirds of all Baluch people in the world are said to reside in Pakistan, and the majority live in this province (the remainder live in Iran and Afghanistan). It is an exceedingly inhospitable habitat. Visiting foreign geologists have characterized the landscape as similar to that found on Mars: barren, rocky—reminiscent of lava flows—and dry.

Baluchistan has long served as a crossroads with fluid borders until the British Raj and later the government of Pakistan demarcated distinct boundaries. For example, Dera Ghazi Khan (now in Punjab) and Dera Ismail Khan (in southern KP) are said to have been founded by Baluch cousins, though neither is located within the contemporary province of Baluchistan.[38]

Baluch tribal structure, as irredentist as that of Pakhtuns, concentrates power in the hands of local tribal leaders, *sirdars*. In marked contrast to that of the neighboring Pakhtuns, Baluch society is highly stratified, with *sirdars* holding the most power, followed by *hakims* (lower-level tribal leaders) and then by a lower level of tenant farmers and former slaves. Clans formed through patrilineal descent, however, are significant mostly for the sirdars and hakims. The basic exchange traditionally underlying this elaborate system was the leader's offer of booty or property rights in return for support in battle. In more recent years, various favors are generally traded for votes, but the structure of the system—the participation of the lower echelons through patron-client ties—remains essentially the same.[39]

As with Pakhtun tribes to the north—and virtually throughout the subcontinent—the British played local rivals against each other in a policy of indirect rule. They offered subsidies and promises of autonomy to local rulers in exchange for access to the strategic border with Afghanistan. Local leaders today maintain this policy as far as they can, continuing to exploit the endemic anarchy, be it regarding local, provincial, or national affairs. Governments change, natural resources are commodified (e.g., *sui* gas, petroleum, and precious minerals), but the key players—or their descendants—remain the same.

The Baluch people have been long accustomed to indirect rule, a policy that leaves local elites with a substantial measure of autonomy. Decisions have traditionally been made by the sirdar in consultation with elders in a tribal *jirga* (a form of local court); such decisions were absolutely binding. The federal government, in an effort to wield more control over the population through its own judiciary, abolished the jirga system in the 1970s. The results of this effort, however, according to many Baluch, have been tenuous, at best.

There have been sporadic separatist movements in Baluchistan since independence. Indeed, the political fissures between Baluchistan and the Pakistan federal government periodically manifest in provocative, destabilizing insurrections. Violent confrontations between Baluch insurgents and the Pakistani government in the mid-1970s were particularly brutal and have had long-lasting repercussions; nearly every Baluch was affected in some way, and most began to identify with the opposition. What were initially demands for greater regional autonomy escalated into a full-scale movement aimed at restructuring the government of the country. Zulfiqar Ali Bhutto's overthrow by Zia ul-Haq in 1977 was welcomed by many in Baluchistan, in contrast to popular sentiment in the rest of the country, which was appalled by yet another military takeover.

The violence that characterized demands for autonomy in Baluchistan have returned, though focused more on control of natural resources (and adequate payment thereof), especially natural gas. Sectarian strife has also hit Baluchistan hard, with attacks on Shias, Christians, and Hindus frequently making headlines since 2012.

Implications of Military Encounters in Afghanistan for Pakistan

Just as relations with the central government began to improve, the Soviet Union invaded Afghanistan, engendering nearly the entire northern border of Baluchistan to be placed on alert as a frontline area. Baluchistan's landscape in the 1980s changed markedly as Afghan refugee camps were established throughout the northern parts of the province. Within a decade, traditional divides had declined in importance as Baluch increasingly thought of themselves as a unified group in opposition to Pakistani or Punjabi hegemony. Today, many Baluch, in contrast to the vast majority of Pakistanis, are relatively ambivalent over the matter of Kashmir. Many consider the government of Pakistan's stance on Kashmir to be a convenient ploy to deflect attention away from its exploitation of their province. They cite that while Baluchistan supplies the rest of the country with natural gas and other valuable resources, there has been little development in Baluchistan outside of its capital city, Quetta. Since 2004, explosions—attributed to Baluch angry with the federal government over what is perceived as minimal payment for Baluch supplies of natural gas—have destroyed natural gas pipelines and railroad tracks in the interior of the province.

The ongoing political turmoil in neighboring Afghanistan has had a weighty impact on Pakistan's demographics. Areas of Khyber Pakhtunkhwa and Baluchistan that previously had been uninhabited were settled by Afghan refugees in the 1980s and continue to be dominated by their descendants. Temporary mud housing was transformed into cement structures in many instances. This has also caused the demographic balance to change as ethnic Pakhtuns, many being refugees from Afghanistan, have settled in Baluchistan and, through their political party, Pakhtunkhwa Milli Awami, have been demanding a political voice in the province. Aside from the environmental effects of populating desert areas, the social impact has been profound. The escalation of animosity between refugees and Pakistanis, particularly in the Punjab, caused the government of Pakistan to restrict the refugees' free movement in the country in the mid-1980s. While Pakistan had tried to extend assistance to its neighbors at a time of need, many Pakistanis, hurt by the resultant inflation, lack of lower-paying jobs which had been taken by refugees, and the proliferation of weapons especially in urban areas (which many felt had been smuggled by refugees to pay for the war effort in Afghanistan), felt their friendship had gone far enough.

The United Nations High Commissioner for Refugees (UNHCR) facilitated the Pakistan government's efforts to keep the refugees separate from the local population by placing restrictions on disbursements of food and other goods from its refugee camps in the then NWFP and Baluchistan. Following the October 2001 attack by the United States against the Taliban-led government in Afghanistan, the UNHCR, the Pakistan government, and an array of NGOs have encouraged the refugees to return to Afghanistan. However, until internecine fighting stops and substantive rebuilding in Afghanistan commences, chances for this to occur at any significant rate are slim.

An unusual alliance emerged during the past decade with the ascent of the Muttahida Majlis-e-Amal (MMA), a coalition of various Islamist political parties which won the October 2002 provincial elections in what was then NWFP (today Khyber Pakhtunkhwa) and also wielded considerable influence in Baluchistan.[40] The influence of separatist provincial political parties appears to have receded in both provinces, as Pakhtuns and Baluch alike became increasingly receptive to the more religious and socially orthodox message of the MMA. It did not, however, fare as well in the February 2008 elections, more likely due to the overall political changes in the country as well as the challenges of incumbency. However, the major party in the MMA, the Jama'at-i-Islami, became the junior partner (to the

PTI) in the coalition government in Khyber Pakhtunkhwa following the May 2013 elections.

While in power holding a majority of seats in the Khyber Pakhtunkhwa provincial legislature (2002–2008), the MMA's goal was to purge non-Islamic traditions and practices and bring provincial laws into conformity with the dictates and edicts of Islam. Important, too, was its rhetoric—and practice—to support Pakhtuns and Baluch seeking shelter in Pakistan from U.S. troops in Afghanistan. It also facilitated opening a political space for the TNSM (Tehreek-e-Nafaz-e-Shariat-e-Mohammadi, or Movement for the Enforcement of Islamic Law) in the province to gain influence. Toward the end of the MMA's time in power, in December 2007, the Tehrik-i-Taliban Pakistan was founded by Baitullah Mahsud, whose then assistant, Maulana Fazlullah, started his own branch in Swat (discussed further below in "Social Costs of Militarism").

Regardless of existing political parties and alliances, we should bear in mind that the defining relationship between groups in the eastern part of Pakistan is tribal affiliation, and no government (national or foreign), political party, alliance, or group, can supersede that potent affinity.

Other Areas

The Northern Areas, composed of Baltistan, Gilgit, and Hunza, are Pakistan's fifth province, Gilgit-Baltistan, as a result of the Gilgit-Baltistan Empowerment and Self-Governance Order of August 2009. Consisting of vestiges of early princely states that had acceded to Pakistan at independence, this remote, mountainous area consists largely of self-sufficient, homogenous communities that have remained mostly free of the ethnic and sectarian strife that has plagued other parts of Pakistan. It is only now being brought into the national discourse through expansion of roads and telecommunication networks, which also facilitates tourism, the area's largest income-generating activity, as mountain climbers converge here from throughout the world. A sizeable portion of the population in Gilgit comprises followers of the Aga Khan, and they have benefited from development interventions funded by the Aga Khan Development Network.

Azad Jammu and Kashmir, an autonomous region in Pakistan, is today known more for its political predicament than for any other reason. While the origins of the conflict are clear, the subsequent history and ongoing violent encounters that resulted in two wars (1948 and 1965) and nearly escalated into a nuclear confrontation in the high mountains of Kargil in July 1999 are highly contested. The state of Jammu and Kashmir was one of 584 princely states that, in August 1947, were given the option of joining either India or Pakistan. While the population was overwhelmingly Muslim, the state's Hindu prince, Maharaja Hari Singh, opted to have his state join India. Kashmir was subsequently annexed into the Indian

Union on October 27, 1947, despite objections by many of its Muslim residents as well as by the government of Pakistan. Shortly afterward, the Pakistan government brought a formal complaint to the United Nations that decreed that India was to hold a referendum in Kashmir to ensure the right of self-determination for the people of Kashmir. The events that followed—from Pakistan's "liberation" of parts of northwestern Kashmir in 1948, the 1965 war, the escalation of what was initially East Pakistan's secession in 1971 to a full-blown war with India over Kashmir, and the militant uprising in the province that has escalated in the past decade—have resulted in the widespread assertion within Pakistan that resolution of the territorial boundaries of Kashmir is central both to the integrity of the republic of Pakistan and to Muslims throughout the world as well as to improving political, economic, and social relations with India.

A final issue of political identity concerns provincial rights. There is an ongoing debate between the provinces and the federal government on the kinds of laws that provinces can legislate and the kinds of laws that remain the domain of the federal government. This was disputed in the initial development of the first constitution, and was addressed more thoroughly in the 1973 constitution. This determined that laws on the Federal List (the domain of the federal government) could only be made in the National Assembly and laws on the Concurrent List (the domain of provinces) would be made either by the National Assembly or a Provincial Assembly (with priority of the former over the latter). This arrangement, however, was to last only ten years (i.e., until 1983), after which time responsibility for laws pertaining to national defense, foreign policy, and international agreements would remain on the Federal List, and responsibility for most other matters on the Concurrent List would devolve solely to the provincial governments. This debate on states' rights was finally resolved on April 8, 2010, with the passage of the Eighteenth Constitutional Amendment. The resultant devolution process has now seen the establishment of numerous provincial ministries to oversee what was once solely the domain of the federal government.

WOMEN'S POWER AND
KINSHIP NETWORKS IN POLITICAL LIFE

Pakistani social life revolves around family and kin. For most people, family loyalty overrides other obligations; the overwhelming importance of family ties retains its significance even among the most Westernized members of the elite. The family is the basis of social organization and provides its members both identity and protection. The honor or shame of individual members—particularly of female members—affects the general standing of a family in the greater community. An isolated individual living apart from relatives is uncommon; even male workers who have migrated to cities will usually prefer to live with a relative or a friend of a relative. Adults who do not have their own households usually join that of a relative.

The household is the primary kinship unit. In its ideal form, it includes a married couple, their sons, their sons' wives and children, and unmarried offspring. Daughters live with their parents until marriage; it is expected that sons will live with their parents their whole lives in the joint family system. Sons often establish separate households after their father's death, though this depends on the preferences of the individuals involved and financial circumstances. Limited resources, quarrels, and divisiveness are the main reasons behind the premature dissolution of a household.

Descent is traced patrilineally, and the *biradari* (patrilineage) plays a significant role in social and political relations. The biradari is not an economic entity, as its members neither hold property in common nor share earnings. Biradari members often live in close proximity in rural areas, although land fragmentation and generations of out-migration have led to the dispersal of many members. Patrilineally related families continue to maintain ties with their natal village and are supposed to enjoy the legal right of first refusal in any biradari land sale.

Members of a biradari celebrate life events together and, whenever possible, retain political alliances between them. This network of extended families has traditionally served as a sort of mutual aid society cum welfare agency, contributing food and assisting with guests at ceremonies and major religious holidays, arranging loans to members, assisting in finding employment, and contributing to the dowries of poorer families. An important social change that has occurred as Pakistan moves from a society based on ascription to one based on achievements is that close kin from one's mother's family now also actively participate in the above to the extent that individual members urge them to consider themselves as close kin.

Marriage

There is considerable pressure for patrilineal kin to maintain good relations with one another so as to present a unified public front, which has important political and economic ramifications. Those with sons and daughters of marriageable age recognize the strategic necessity to maintain good relations because a child whose family is at odds with his or her biradari is considered a poor marriage prospect.

Marriage serves as a means of cementing alliances between extended families. There remains a preference for marriage to one's patrilineal cousin, otherwise to kin from within the biradari. Some groups allow for marriage of cousins related through one's mother, although all Pakistanis do not accept this practice. The pattern of continued intermarriage coupled with the occasional marriage of nonrelatives creates a convoluted web of interlocking ties of descent and marriage, resulting in the perception by many non-Pakistanis that everyone who they know is related to one another.

Social ties are defined in terms of giving away daughters in marriage and receiving daughters-in-law. To participate fully in social life, a person must be married and have children, preferably sons. Women overwhelmingly get married and have children in Pakistan; 98 percent of all women between the ages of thirty-five and forty-nine have been married. However, fertility rates are finally declining. Two generations ago, an average family consisted of eight to ten children; a generation ago, it was six to eight children; and today, the norm is two to four, even among many rural families.[41]

Parents and their siblings become actively involved in arranging marriages for their children. The assumption is that elders are more worldly and experienced, and that they know the temperament of their own child very well, and hence are in a better position to decide a good match than their child. Older siblings arrange marriages for younger ones in the event of their parents' early deaths or if the older sibling becomes particularly successful in business or politics. Traditionally, a husband and wife would only meet each other after they signed the *nikah nama*, the Muslim marriage contract, unless they were already related and knew each other. Even then, in most families, once the marriage had been agreed upon, a female cousin would no longer meet with her male cousin/fiancé, until the marriage. Today, the vast majority of marriages are still arranged, though among some elite and some highly educated families (still a minority of both of these, however), a son may suggest with whom he would like for the parents to arrange his marriage.

An extreme form of arranged marriage referred to as exchange marriages—*watta satta*—is also common in parts of the Punjab and Sindh: a sister and brother are married to a brother and sister (respectively). Traditionally, this is thought as being a kind of "insurance" for daughters, in that her brother would know that if he mistreats his wife, his wife's brother will in turn mistreat his sister (the brother's wife), and hence the women would receive better care. However, this practice has been raised repeatedly in recent years as a human rights abuse, for women are often victimized or divorced not because of their own actions, but because of something that has happened in some other marital unit.

In most families (except for the poorest), the process of arranging a marriage (i.e., securing an agreement between two families for a male and female to be married), having an engagement ceremony, and all of the functions leading up to the actual wedding celebration take a lot of time and entail numerous gifts being exchanged between the two extended families. The financial hardship of marrying a daughter off, in particular, leads some poor families to agree to a match with a much older man, often a widower, which would not require as many gifts or as much dowry.

Dowry—*jahez*—is the gift a family gives to their daughter when they marry her off. There is no association between dowry and Islam, as the religion calls for a bride price (*haq mehr*, discussed below) but not for a dowry. Instead, this is a cultural tradition common in the Punjab and most parts of Sindh, but practiced far less in Khyber Pakhtunkhwa and Baluchistan. Families save up their entire lives for their daughters' dowries, and both the daughter and other female family members sew, knit, and embroider various goods she will take with her to her in-laws' home. In addition, it is expected that the dowry will include a bedroom set (bed, dresser, etc.), cooking utensils, clothes, and extra *charpais* (string beds) for guests. The government of Pakistan periodically tries to restrict the cost of marriages (e.g., banning serving a meal at functions; restricting the extra lighting used), and has outright banned dowries, but with little practical success. These cultural traditions run deep, and while people may discuss the various merits of less grandiose functions or eliminating dowries, no one wants his own daughter to have to be demeaned by the fact that her family did not adequately provide for her at the time of her marriage. A rich dowry confers prestige on the young married woman, and its contents—household goods, furniture, clothing, jewelry, and a car or motorcycle, if at all possible—are to remain the property of the bride (albeit this too does not always happen in practice).

The haq mehr, a dower established under Islamic law, is a stipulated figure between the two families that would be paid to the wife in the event of divorce or her husband's early death. While some families set a symbolic *mehr* of 32 rupees—in accordance with the traditions of the Prophet—it may also be a substantial figure; many wealthy families demand hundreds of thousands of rupees before finalizing a marriage agreement.

A married woman's lot is often difficult in the early years of marriage. The young bride has very little status in her husband's household. She is subservient to her mother-in-law and has little influence on her husband's activities. A wife gains status and power as she bears sons. Sons will care for her in her old age, while daughters are a liability, to be given away in marriage with their virginity intact. Therefore, mothers favor their sons, often nursing them longer than daughters. In later life, the relationship between mother and son remains intimate, with the mother retaining far more influence over her son than most wives ever have.[42]

Gender Relations in Pakistan

Two principles characterize the basic understanding of gender relations in Pakistan: women are subordinate to men (and therefore must adhere to their wishes and commands) and men's honor resides in the actions of the women of his family. Throughout the country, gender relations differ more by degree than by type.

Space is allocated to and used differently by men and women in Pakistan. Traditionally, a woman was seen as needing protection from the outside world where her respectability—and therefore that of her family—is at risk. Women in many parts of the country live under traditional constraints associated with *purdah*, which necessitate the separation of women from the activities of men, both physically and symbolically, thereby creating very differentiated male and female spheres. Purdah is practiced in various ways, depending on family tradition. While gender relations are somewhat more relaxed among most people in Punjab and Sindh, nowhere (traditionally) do unrelated men and women mix freely.

Most women spend the bulk of their lives physically within their homes; they go outside only when there is a substantive purpose. The culture outside the home generally revolves around the actions of men. In most parts of the country—perhaps Islamabad, Karachi, and wealthier parts of a few other cities being the exception—people consider a woman (and by extension, her family) to be shameless when there are no restrictions placed on her mobility.

Two important factors differentiate the degree to which women's mobility is restricted: class and rural/urban residence. Poor rural women in Punjab and Sindh have traditionally enjoyed a great degree of mobility if for no other reason than sheer necessity. These women characteristically are responsible for transplanting seedlings and weeding crops, and are often involved in activities such as raising chickens (and selling eggs) and stuffing wool or cotton into local blankets (*razais*). When a family's level of prosperity rises and it begins to aspire for a higher status, often the first social change that occurs is putting a veil on its women and placing them into some form of purdah.

Poor urban women in close-knit communities, such as the old cities of Lahore and Rawalpindi, will generally observe some form of purdah and wear either a *burqa* (fitted body veil) or *chadar* (loosely draped cotton cloth) when they leave their homes. In such localities, large living areas had originally been constructed so as to accommodate many levels of extended kin living together. For purposes of economy today, these former *havelis* have been sectioned off into smaller living units, so now there is often one family—consisting on average of seven members—living in one or two rooms on each small floor. In areas of lower density where people generally do not know their neighbors, there are fewer restrictions on women's mobility.

Legal Reforms and Women's Rights

The issue of women's rights is compelling in Pakistan as different constituencies are deeply divided over what constitutes women's social roles and rights, what activities and privileges are acceptable and unacceptable for women, who is to define what these social roles and rights are, and where responsibility lies for ensuring these rights.[43] The prevailing conflict is, in a very important way, the culmination of domestic political events that began with Zia's Islamization program in 1979. As discussed earlier, these have been instrumental in transforming both state and society in Pakistan in many visible and subtle ways.

While laws and the legal environment have certainly changed—the *Hudood* laws, the federal Shariat Bill, and the growing influence of the federal Shariat court and Council on Islamic Ideology—the even more compelling transformation has been the concomitant rise in overall conservatism throughout the country. This conservatism has been fueled by a number of factors including political and economic policies (at least during Zia's tenure, and periodically since then), the rise of Islamist politics worldwide, and the growing number and influence of madrasas (religious schools), *deeni madaris* (residential religious schools), and the various *tabliqh* groups,[44] which are teaching a far more orthodox interpretation of Islam than that commonly adhered to in the country in the past. The shift from *personal* piety to *public articulations* of piety continues to be susceptible to a great deal of misrepresentation and emotional manipulation. This conservatism has been overly absorbed with gender concerns.

The government of Pakistan has long been a formal defender of women's rights. Prior to 1979, there had been two major issues around which the state had acted affecting women's position: (1) the question of an accommodation between Muslim family law and civil, democratic rights; and (2) the extent of women's political representation. The outcome of the first was the passage of the Muslim Personal Law of Shariat (1948), which recognized a woman's right to inherit all forms of property, and the 1961 Muslim Family Laws Ordinance (MFLO) to regulate marriages and restrain polygamy. This legislation was the first time a controversial bill in the arena of gender politics was promulgated in Pakistan. Efforts on behalf of the second (to promote women's political representation) can be seen in the futile attempt to have the government include a Charter of Women's Rights in the first constitution, the argument around Fatima Jinnah (a woman) being allowed to contest the national election for the presidency in 1965 (for which a fatwa was issued condoning her candidacy), and the reservation of seats in the National Assembly for women in 1973.

Pakistan had become a State Party to a number of gender-focused UN human rights instruments, beginning with the 1953 Convention on the Political Rights of Women. While Pakistan never ratified the subsequent UN Convention on the Consent to Marriage, Minimum Age for Marriage, and Registration of Marriage, it claimed it went further than that Convention's requirements when it promulgated the MFLO. Still in force, the MFLO requires the registration of all marriages and provides a number of safeguards for women in the event of a divorce or a husband's second marriage. The Jama'at-i-Islami and other Islamist groups have opposed the MFLO on the grounds that Islamic law does not require the registration of marriages (among other concerns).

The 1973 Constitution affirms that the state is committed to eliminating exploitation and guarantees that "all citizens are equal under the law and are entitled to equal protection of law," and that there is to "no discrimination on the basis of sex alone." It promises that "steps shall be taken to ensure full participation of women in all spheres of national life" and that it is the responsibility of the state to "secure the well-being of the people, irrespective of sex, caste, creed or race, by raising their standard of living." Given that women's rights are clearly constitutionally enshrined, it is apparent that identity politics are the driving force behind the debate over women's rights in Pakistan. Indeed, after Zia's demise and Benazir Bhutto and Nawaz Sharif jockeyed for power, no pivotal legislation was passed that further affected the rights of women, one way or the other. The 1991 Sharia Bill, greatly watered down from what both Zia and Nawaz had initially proposed, was promulgated, declaring Islam as the Supreme law in the country but without any further stipulations. The mandate to reserve seats for women in parliamentary elections expired, and neither Benazir nor Nawaz resurrected it, a big disappointment for women's rights activists.[45] They clamored for the Hudood Ordinances—and particularly the *zina* clause—to be repealed, but that didn't happen either. Pakistan became a States Party to the UN Convention on the Rights of the Child in 1990, the 1993 Vienna Declaration (which recognized "women's rights as human rights"), the 1994 Cairo Population and Development conference's Programme of Action, and the 1995 *Platform for Action* in preparation for the 1995 Fourth World Conference on Women (FWCW) in Beijing.

When Benazir Bhutto spoke at the FWCW in Beijing, she (as did many other heads of state speaking there) pledged that her government would become a party to the UN CEDAW Convention.[46] Through ratification of CEDAW, Pakistan assumed the obligation to review the impact of existing laws on women, change those laws that discriminate against women, and submit periodic reports to the UN Division for the Advancement of

Women on its progress. CEDAW's principle of State Obligation requires States Parties not only to bring their domestic laws in line with the Convention, but also to ensure the practical realization of rights by undertaking extra measures to implement enabling conditions so that women's capacity to access the opportunities provided is enhanced.[47]

The Musharraf government, after coming to power in a coup in October 1999, revived the issue of women's empowerment as a key component of its policies to promote Pakistan's progress. It established distinct quotas to promote women's greater participation in public arenas of society: 5 percent for women in government service (now 10 percent); 17 percent for women in the national and provincial parliaments; and 33 percent for women in most tiers of local government. It formalized the National Commission on the Status of Women, sought national consensus on a National Policy on Women, and overall set in motion a series of reforms to promote women's rights consistent with globalized norms articulated in the CEDAW Convention.

The first law Musharraf's government promoted to address women's rights explicitly was the Criminal Law (Amendment) Act of 2004 (enforced in early 2005), popularly referred to as the "honor killing law" as it enhanced punishments for honor killings as a deterrence.[48] This was followed by the federal government's efforts to modify the problematic Hudood Laws. Now a States Party to CEDAW, the government of Pakistan still needed to address these laws that clearly discriminated against women. However, only after the Council of Islamic Ideology in spring 2006 weighed in and recommended that the state rewrite the Hudood Ordinances "to conform with the intents of Qur'an, Sunnah and Sharia"[49] and incorporate the reframed law in the Pakistan Penal Code and the Criminal Procedure Code was there political momentum to revise them. A general consensus emerged that the laws had to be reformed: too many poor, illiterate women had been imprisoned under zina charges.[50] The federal government tabled the bill—the Protection of Women Bill 2006—in August 2006. The MMA lodged an immediate outcry against the suggested reforms, charging that as it stood the Hudood Ordinances were a viable Islamic document and that the reforms "would encourage adultery in society and would further increase obscenity, vulgarity, and western culture in Pakistan."[51] While the bill was implemented in November 2006, the various constituent parties within the MMA remain opposed to it.

A third bill on women's rights—the Prevention of Anti-Women Practices (Criminal Law Amendment) Bill 2006—sought to end the "social, political and religious excesses against women"[52] by banning practices as forced marriages, marriage in exchange for vengeance, and deprivation of women's inheritance. The National Assembly decided to cease its review of the Bill, first submitted in February 2007, two years later in spring 2009 (a year after the PPP came to power), claiming that it was insufficient, poorly scripted, and that other legislation would instead be forthcoming.

Soon after coming to power in February 2008, the PPP government declared that it would promulgate a national domestic violence act and address sexual harassment at the workplace. Women's rights activists were heartened when the National Assembly passed the Domestic Violence (Prevention and Protection) Bill 2009 on August 4, 2009, but were soon dismayed that the Senate did not take up the bill for discussion in a timely manner and allowed it to expire. Nearly three years later, in late February 2012, Senator Nilofar Bakthiar reintroduced an identical bill, now termed the Domestic Violence (Prevention and Protection) Act 2012, and it passed with support from all political parties represented in the upper house, including the JUI-F, which had earlier deferred the initial bill in the Senate that had caused it to lapse.[53]

A second initiative signed into law January 29, 2010, the Protection against Harassment for Women at the Workplace Act 2009, makes provisions for the protection against sexual harassment of women in public space. While concerned with women, importantly, it is not restricted to women. Another bill, passed in tandem, amends Pakistan's penal code so that sexual harassment is finally recognized as a crime. This is a seminal step because as more women enter public space as workers, addressing women's legal right to work in a safe environment is critical to their continuing engagement in the formal sector of the economy, polity, and society.

Two additional laws affecting women's rights were promulgated in December 2011: the first rectifies the abandonment of the Anti-Women Practices Bill in 2009 by listing specific punishable offenses against compelling women to marry as well as depriving women from inheriting property and other "anti-women practices." The second law, to prevent acts of acid-throwing as a way to subjugate women, cites explicit penalties punishable by long imprisonment and fines of up to a million rupees.[54] Another act of legislation promises to make perhaps the greatest difference of all to affect women's rights and empower them in the future: the elevation of the National Commission on the Status of Women (NCSW) in early February 2012. The NCSW has been granted greater administrative autonomy to review laws, make recommendations, liaise with provincial governments, and overall gain greater scope, funding, and effect in redressing violations of women's rights.

The momentum to move forward on changing laws to ensure women's rights was clearly championed by the PPP-dominated national government. Now that the PML-N is in power, women's rights activists are concerned that the rights already won are in jeopardy of being reversed.

Few anticipate that new legislation to promote women's rights will be introduced under the current regime.

SOCIAL COSTS OF MILITARISM

The social costs of militarism in Pakistan are woefully evident wherever one looks.

From the outset, the new state had to rebuild roads, buildings, rail lines, and other parts of its infrastructure that had been shattered by the violence that accompanied partition. Shortly afterward, its efforts to "liberate" Kashmir resulted in the first of three wars against India. But it wasn't the wars that had so much of a debilitating social cost for Pakistan; rather, it was the diversion of strategic resources, human capital, and funding that could have been used instead to strengthen schools, health care, sanitation, water systems, and the overall economy. Pakistan has been mobilized as a country awaiting military conflict for much of its history; that perhaps has been the greatest social cost of militarism of all.

Through most of its history, Pakistan's government has been controlled by the military. Muhammad Ali Jinnah, the Quaid-e-Azam (founding father) of the country, envisioned a secular democracy that would take root in the country, but the influence of parliamentary processes has been limited, and the current debates underway regarding combatting terrorism continue to compromise them. With the deaths of both Jinnah and Liaqat Ali Khan within three years of Pakistan's birth, the ensuing political chaos combined with the absence of a charismatic civilian leader with strong national standing and the military threat from India created an opening for military rule to be widely condoned, at least for a while. Indeed, the fundamental political issue in Pakistan has been between civilian politics and the military; from the military standpoint, it has been a question of keeping civilian politics at bay.

The influence of the military in governing Pakistan remains a potent concern. Hasan-Askari Rizvi, a Pakistani political scientist who has researched the military extensively, contends that its influence extends far beyond the barracks in Pakistan:

> The long years of direct and indirect rule have enabled the military to spread out in the civilian administration, semi-government institutions, the economy and the major sectors of the society. Its clout no longer depends on controlling political power. It is derived from its organizational strength and its significant presence in the polity and the society. The military has acquired a formidable position and role over time. It is the crystallization of the importance and centrality it has enjoyed in the state structure from the beginning. . . . The survival of the state became the primary concern of

the rulers of Pakistan who equated it with an assertive federal government, strong defense apparatus, high defense expenditure and a state-directed monolithic nationalism. The imperatives of state security and survival gave primacy to state building over nation building.[55]

These "imperatives of state security" resulted in four instances of direct military rule (1958–1962, 1969–1972, 1977–1985, and 1999–2008) and two phases of indirect "civilianized" military rule following martial law (1962–1969 and 1985–1988). Political parties continue to fear the military's return to power, as was evident in Nawaz Sharif's strong reaction in late August 2010 to Muttahida Qaumi Movement (MQM) leader Altaf Hussain's controversial call for Pakistani "army generals to act against corrupt politicians" in Sharif's demand for a parliamentary action against the MQM chief, allegedly for inviting the army to impose martial law in the country.[56]

The nagging legacy of the dispute over Kashmir has contributed to the military's political influence, as it remains the critical antagonist in Pakistan's problematic relationship with neighboring India. This defining dispute—where jurisdiction for Kashmir's governance lies—has prompted a wide range of rethinking Pakistan's historical legacy and contemporary place in the South Asian subcontinent and the wider global economy. The military, for historical reasons, had long ago become a class in itself, serving its own interests foremost. It holds a unique class position in the country as it postures itself as the sole defender of Pakistan. Hostility with India has been an integral element of how the military has fashioned itself and created an identity. In the 1990s, the conflictual relationship with India over Kashmir became a much more proactive policy, though this is now waning in part due to the events at Kargil in the summer of 1999, in part because of the languishing economy, and in part because of events affecting Pakistan and its military emerging from the catastrophe of September 11, 2001.

Following the October 2001 invasion of Afghanistan, the repercussions on Pakistan have been enormous. There is a sizeable segment of the population that disavows the official view that the Taliban are terrorists, and hence disdain the support that the Pakistan government has given to the United States in their war effort. There is a smaller faction—largely consisting of those who have joined extremist groups but also composed of more loosely knit groups—that actively undertake terrorist acts against the state of Pakistan, be it targeting police stations, government offices, schools and universities, mosques at prayer time, or even toll collection kiosks on the national highways. Pakistan had previously (before 2001) never experienced suicide bombings, and today they are commonplace. Fear grips everyday society as people wonder how the wave of terrorist aggression can be stopped.

There is widespread opposition with one policy resulting from the federal government and the army's alliance with the West's "war on terror": CIA-directed drone attacks bombarding FATA, allegedly targeting Afghan Taliban supporters seeking refuge in the area or militant sympathizers living in the area. Within FATA, the cities of Wana, Darra Adam Khel, and Miranshah have become virtual pounding blocks while the North Waziristan, Orakzai, and Khyber agencies have been particularly hard hit. A September 2010 survey found that more than three-quarters of FATA residents oppose the drone strikes: only 16 percent think these strikes accurately target militants, while 48 percent think they largely kill civilians and another 33 percent feel they kill both civilians and militants; 81 percent conclude that innocent civilians are being killed by the drone attacks.[57]

Outside of FATA in Pakistan, a strong majority of the population concurs with FATA's residents on what is seen as a misguided policy of allowing the drone attacks. Many consider that anger over the drone attacks—as well as the government of Pakistan support of the ongoing military occupation of Afghanistan—is the reason behind terrorist attacks in the country. A July 2010 survey conducted by the Pew Global Attitudes Project found that "nearly all Pakistanis describe terrorism as a very big problem."[58] The despondency over the unrelenting terrorist attacks—as well as Pakistan's lackluster economy—is resulting in an overwhelming majority of Pakistanis dissatisfied with national conditions, unhappy with the nation's economy, and concerned about political corruption and crime.

STRUGGLES OVER RIGHTS: CASE STUDY OF THE TEHRIK-E-TALIBAN PAKISTAN (TTP) IN SWAT

This case study is somewhat different from those highlighted in other chapters in this volume. It is not focused on a group using democratic principles to assert their rights because, while some groups like this indeed do exist in Pakistan, their influence is limited. Instead, the TTP operating in the Provincially Administered Tribal Area (PATA) of Swat in KP is reviewed here because the reverberations of its actions have had an earth-shattering impact throughout Pakistan. The TTP in Swat are seeking to assert their right to be governed solely under Islamic law, and to create what they consider to be an ideal Islamic society, despite that this interpretation is not shared by the majority of the population of Pakistan.

Swat had remained a semi-autonomous princely state, along with Dir and Chitral, until 1969 when it finally acceded to Pakistan. Its ruler, the Wali of Swat, had governed the area through a combination of Islamic law (*shariah*) and paternalistic decrees. When Field Marshal Ayub Khan, whose two daughters had married two of the wali's sons, was overthrown in a coup d'état in 1969, Swat's fate was sealed as well. The wali and his family realized they could not militarily contest the Pakistan state and finally acceded, thereby ending their royal state.

For roughly twenty years, Swat underwent a period of adjustment. The two most significant changes included the arrival of numerous government bureaucrats—people who were not indigenous to the area, didn't know the local people and practices, took seemingly forever to effect change, and could be bribed, in contrast to the wali's retinue—and of the British-based system of law, a legacy of the Raj used throughout the Republic of Pakistan. The key reason people in Swat resort to the legal system is over property disputes; the newly imposed system was slow to adjudicate matters. Gradually, Swatis began to miss the "speedy justice" of the days of the wali's rule, albeit it had been autocratic. The longer land disputes remained unresolved, the more they festered and prompted violent clashes between groups.

Sufi Mohammad and a small group of supporters founded the Tehreek-e-Nafaz-e-Shariat-e-Mohammadi (TNSM) in Dir in 1989 with the goal to reinstate Shariat as the primary legal system in Malakand Division (which includes Swat) and the Kohistan District of PATA. Within a few years, the movement had gained support in Swat and was beginning to destabilize governance in the area. In response to TNSM's provocations, the government promulgated new regulations twice in the 1990s—1994 and 1999—to enhance the scope of the Shariat courts in PATA, but with limited impact. Legal delays remained incessant and outcomes became widely perceived as influenced more by bribery than by justice.

Two years later, in October 2001, in the wake of the U.S. invasion of Afghanistan, Sufi Mohammad and many of his supporters left for Afghanistan to fight alongside the Taliban government there. Both he and his son-in-law, Maulana Fazlullah, were imprisoned upon returning to Pakistan in January 2002; while he remained in jail until 2008, Fazlullah was released in 2003.

Fazlullah, a cable operator (someone who transports people across rivers via a cable for a fee) in the Mamdherai/Imamdherai area of Swat, took up the leadership of TNSM. He began broadcasting programs on Islam and how to live "as a good Muslim" via FM radio in 2004. Women became his most enthusiastic supporters, allegedly donating large quantities of gold jewelry to help build Fazlullah's madrasa (religious school).

Within a few years, the TNSM was targeting police stations and other official offices for violent attacks. Decapitations, especially of police in outlying areas, became a primary, formidable tactic in their quest to get Shariat declared the legal system in Malakand Division. People were confused about the seemingly mixed messages emanating from the FM station, and were reluctant to act against Fazlullah.

Key leaders within the TNSM are said to have disagreed with Fazlullah's violent activities and officially disowned his policies although some members, mostly from Swat, remained with him. In December 2007, he and his followers helped found the *Tehrik-i-Taliban Pakistan* (TTP, often referred to as "the Taliban" by Swatis), headed overall by Baitullah Mahsud but headed locally—in Swat—by Fazlullah.

As the influence of the TTP and Maulana Fazlullah grew, three things occurred: the *bazaar*—all public trading areas—was closed; they demanded that women had to be in full purdah; and girls were discouraged from going to school, especially past fourth grade (age ten). A climate of fear had clearly been created. In this environment, people were fearful of attracting the Taliban's attention. Between the beheadings, school bombings, and the closing of most bazaars, the impetus to fight back eluded the Swatis. The fear of beheading led many people to give up activities the Taliban disallowed, despite their utility for the larger society.

In addition to the psychological pressure there was the physical devastation wreaked by the Taliban. Their power had built up over a period of roughly three years. In February 2009, the federal government capitulated to their demand to institute Shariat law throughout the district. This agreement, the Malakand Accord, was widely criticized throughout Pakistan as being akin to "giving into the terrorists' demands." It called for the withdrawal of the Pakistani army from Swat, the release all Taliban prisoners, the withdrawal of any criminal cases against Taliban leaders and fighters, and the imposition of Shariat. In mid-April, the Taliban launched a cavalcade from Swabi headed toward Swat, openly brandishing all sorts of guns and military weapons; the government now had no option but to act. Swat, previously nicknamed "the Switzerland of Pakistan," was devastated, and now the Taliban were openly challenging the writ of the state.

The Pakistan military had periodic incursions into Swat to root out the Taliban in the years leading up to its wholesale attack against them in spring 2009. There were food and petrol shortages, and medicine was scarce. Women were disproportionately affected, in part because of the traditional gender segregation in this area and in part because now many male family members were absent, either killed by the Taliban or having joined them. The crisis escalated in May and people were told to leave, overnight. Over 1.5 million people departed Swat for refugee camps in Mardan, Nowshera, and Peshawar. The Pakistan military launched a major offensive against the TTP on May 6, complete with artillery attacks and helicopter onslaughts. However, pushing the Taliban out of the valley proved to be harder than the government had anticipated. Swatis only began to return to the valley in September 2009.

Today, the threat of a return of the Taliban is a reality in Swat. The movement exists right under the surface: everyone knows someone who had joined the TTP. The growing alienation from the federal government, the ongoing drone attacks in nearby FATA, and the continuing war in Afghanistan all serve to animate Taliban supporters to believe they will eventually succeed at their cause.

NOTES

1. The Northwest Frontier Province (NWFP) was officially renamed Khyber Pakhtunkhwa, or KP, in March 2010.

2. Reprinted in C. M. Naim (ed.) *Iqbal, Jinnah and Pakistan: The Vision and the Reality*, South Asian series no. 5 (Syracuse, NY: Syracuse University Maxwell School of Citizenship and Public Affairs, 1979), 212.

3. Ibid., 212–13.

4. Madrasas are Islamic religious schools often centered around the teachings of a charismatic leader.

5. This sect emerged when Sunni Muslims, opposed to British rule in South Asia, established a religious school, the Dar-Ul-Ulom, in 1867 in the northern Indian city of Deoband. Deobandi teachings espouse a highly literal interpretation of Islam.

6. Safdar Mahmood, *Pakistan: Political Roots and Development, 1947–1999* (Oxford University Press, 2007), 36.

7. Hamid Khan, *Constitutional and Political History of Pakistan*, 2nd ed. (Karachi: Oxford University Press), 72. This detailed 800-page tome is an outstanding resource for substantive research.

8. See Anita M. Weiss, *Culture, Class and Development in Pakistan: The Emergence of an Industrial Bourgeoisie in Punjab* (Boulder, CO: Westview Press, 1991) for an extensive discussion of the concentration of wealth and power that occurred during this era.

9. Ibid.

10. The Islamization program focused on four areas: economic programs, judicial reforms, an Islamic penal code, and a new education policy. A discussion of particular details of Zia's Islamization program is in Anita M. Weiss, (ed.), *Islamic Reassertion in Pakistan: The Application of Islamic Laws in a Modern State* (Syracuse: Syracuse University Press, 1986), 10–17; for an updated discussion refer to Anita M. Weiss and S. Zulfiqar Gilani (eds.), *Power and Civil Society in Pakistan* (Oxford: Oxford University Press, 2002), 586–90.

11. Under Zia's Law of Evidence, if a woman who has been raped does not have enough witnesses to prove her innocence, she can be charged with adultery (*zina bil jabr*, adultery without consent). A former Superintendent of Police (SP) of Sargodha district, one of the most populous in Punjab, told me that he estimated that over 90 percent of women imprisoned in his district had been charged with adultery. He also estimated that nearly all of them were innocent.

12. The eldest of four children, Benazir was born in Karachi on June 21, 1953. Educated in Pakistan at various convent schools (where children of the elite generally studied), she went abroad to Radcliffe (in Cambridge, Massachusetts) in 1969 to pursue a BA. She went on to graduate school at Oxford where she was studying when the contentious March 1977 election was held in Pakistan, resulting in riots by the opposition against her father. She returned to Pakistan ten days before her father was overthrown by Zia ul-Haq. For further reading about Benazir Bhutto, refer to her autobiography *Daughter of the East* (London: Hamish Hamilton, 1988).

13. Refer to http://www.hdtaskforce.com for further elaboration of the task force's goals and subsequent activities.

14. As reproduced in Hamid Khan, *Constitutional and Political History of Pakistan*, 2nd ed. (Karachi: Oxford University Press, 2009), 658.

15. Ibid., 662.

16. MMA, "Islamization in NWFP Draft Document," issued Fall 2003, in Urdu (translated by author); no page numbers.

17. In Pakistan's parliamentary arrangement members of the National Assembly, along with members of each of the four provincial assemblies, elect the president of the republic. The precedent had been that the newly elected assemblies would elect the president.

18. The NRO was declared "null and void" by the Supreme Court of Pakistan on December 16, 2009.

19. Khan, *Constitutional and Political History of Pakistan*, 701.

20. For an extended discussion of this, with particular reference to Pakistan, refer to Weiss, *Culture, Class and Development in Pakistan*.

21. The World Bank first expressed its concern about this in its "Pakistan Country Update," 2004. Updated details can be found at World Bank, "Data: Pakistan," http://data.worldbank.org/country/pakistan.

22. United Nations Development Programme, *The Real Wealth of Nations: Pathways to Human Development*, Human Development Report 2010 (New York: UNDP, 2010).

23. World Bank, "Data: Pakistan."

24. United Nations Development Programme, "Table 1: Human Development Index and Its Components," in *The Rise of the South: Human Progress in a Diverse World*, Human Development Report 2013 (New York: UNDP, 2013), 146.

25. As no national census has been held since 1998, estimates differ widely. On August 10, 2013, the Population Census Organization, Government of Pakistan, estimated the country's population on that date at 183,948,763. However, the UNDP in 2010 (UNDP, *The Real Wealth of Nations*, 186, table 11) had already estimated the population at 185 million, while the *CIA World Factbook* estimated the July 2013 population as 193.2 million. The UN Population Division estimated Pakistan's 2012 population at 173 million, while the World Bank (World Bank, "Data: Pakistan") estimated it at 179.2 million for that year. Figures in the Ministry of Population Welfare's draft "National Population Policy 2010" estimated Pakistan's population at 171 million.

26. Population Division of the Department of Economic and Social Affairs of the United Nations Secretariat, "World Population Prospects: The 2006 Revision"

and "World Urbanization Prospects: The 2007 Revision," accessed at http://esa .un.org/unup.html.

27. City Mayors Statistics "The Largest Cities in the World and Their Mayors," accessed at http://www.citymayors.com/statistics/largest-cities-mayors–1.html.

28. Government of Pakistan, Planning Commission, T*en Year Perspective Development Plan 2001–11 and Three Year Development Programme 2001–04*, Islamabad, 2001, 249.

29. Ali Raza, "Ravi Receives 1,307 Tonne Toxic Waste Daily," *The News*, April 20, 2010, accessed at http://www.thenews.com.pk/daily_detail.asp?id=235023.

30. Associated Press of Pakistan news release, November 2, 2008, accessed at http://www.app.com.pk/en.

31. A summary of the main forecasts, measures, and plans presented to the National Assembly by then Minister of State for Finance Hina Rabbani Khar, on June 13, 2009, for the 2009/2010 budget can be accessed at www.brecorder.com/ latestindex.php?latest_id=10276&cindex=29&current_ page=4.

32. Allama Iqbal, in the early twentieth century, reasoned that two distinct nations—now manifest as Hindus and Muslims—have existed simultaneously in South Asia, with different historical backgrounds, traditions, cultures, and social orders. The Two Nations theory was one of the foundations of the demand for Pakistan at independence.

33. Barelvi Sunnis comprise about half of Pakistan's population; their greatest concentration is in the Punjab. Founded in the early nineteenth century, Barelvi teachings espouse a *pir*-focused, populist understanding of Islam, prioritizing communal practices over reading texts.

34. Robert Nichols provides extensive documentation and commentary on the Frontier Crimes Regulation Act, which led to the formation of FATA. See Robert Nichols (ed.), *The Frontier Crimes Regulation: A History in Documents* (Karachi: Oxford University Press, 2013).

35. Verkaaik discusses this phenomenon of joining the MQM "for fun" in his chapter "Fun and Violence," in Verkaaik, *Migrants and Militants: Fun and Urban Violence in Pakistan* (Princeton, NJ: Princeton University Press, 2004), 111–36. Further discussion of the development of ethnic politics and conflicts in Sindh is in Stanley Tambiah, "Ethnic Conflict in Pakistan," in Tambiah, *Leveling Crowds: Ethnonationalist Conflicts and Collective Violence in South Asia* (Berkeley: University of California Press, 1996), 163–212; and Oskar Verkaaik's earlier book, *A People of Migrants: Ethnicity, State and Religion in Karachi* (Amsterdam: VU University Press, 1994).

36. The most comprehensive study of Pakhtun traditional social life can be found in Louis Dupree, *Afghanistan* (Princeton, NJ: Princeton University Press, 1980). See also Fredrik Barth, *Political Leadership among Swat Pathans* (London: University of London, Athlone Press, 1959).

37. For further discussion, refer to Asif Ashraf and Arif Majid, *Economic Impact of Afghan Refugees in NWFP* (Peshawar: Pakistan Academy for Rural Development, 1988).

38. Spelling of the tribe and province is also commonly "Baloch" and "'Balochistan,'" respectively.

39. This view was shared with me by Sirdar Zulfiqar Khan Khosa, October 2003.

40. The MMA has been essentially defunct since the 2008 elections, but groups within the Jama'at-i-Islami and the Jamiat Ulema-e-Islam have recently begun negotiations to revive it.

41. Government of Pakistan, *Pakistan Integrated Household Survey 2002*, x, and UNDP, *Human Development Report 2009, Overcoming Barriers: Human Mobility and Development* (Table L, Demographic Trends) (Basingstoke, UK: Author), 193.

42. For an interesting discussion of the social implications of relationships between sons and parents in Pakistan, refer to S. Zulfiqar Gilani, "Personal and Social Power in Pakistan" in Anita M. Weiss and S. Zulfiqar Gilani, eds., *Power and Civil Society in Pakistan* (Oxford: Oxford University Press, 2001), 49–63.

43. For an extensive discussion of legal reforms and women's rights in Pakistan, refer to Anita M. Weiss, *Moving Forward with the Legal Empowerment of Women in Pakistan*, Special Report No. 305 (Washington, DC: U.S. Institute for Peace, 2012).

44. The *Tabligh Jama'at* was founded in Delhi in 1920 with the goal of educating Indian Muslims about the fundamental beliefs and practices of Islam, *da'wah*. See Vahiduddin Khan, *Tabligh Movement* (New Delhi: Islamic Centre, 1986); Muhammad Khalid Masud, *Travellers in Faith: Studies of the Tablighi Jama'at as a Transnational Islamic Movement for Faith Renewal* (Leiden, Netherlands: Brill, 2000); and Nicholas Howenstein, "Islamist Networks: The Case of Tablighi Jamaat" (USIP Briefing, October 2006).

45. The Pervez Musharraf government reinstated the policy of reserving seats for women in the 2002 national elections.

46. Convention on the Elimination of All Forms of Discrimination against Women, which Pakistan ratified in early 1996.

47. I have elaborated on various constitutional points that have important gendered implications in "Interpreting Islam and Women's Rights: Implementing CEDAW in Pakistan," *International Sociology* 18, no. 3 (September 2003): 586.

48. A fuller discussion of this Act can be found in Zubeida Mustafa, "A Long Way to Go," *Dawn*, May 31, 2007, accessed at http://archives.dawn.com/weekly/review/archive/070531/review2.htm.

49. As reported by Anwar Mansuri, "CII Wants Hudood Law Reformed," *Dawn* June 28, 2006, accessed at http://beta.dawn.com/news/198972/cii-wants-hudood-law-reformed.

50. An editorial in *Dawn* reported that because of the *zina* ordinance (in the Hudood Ordinances), the number of women imprisoned climbed drastically. It noted that there were merely 70 women imprisoned in Pakistan in 1979; by 1988, there were 6,000 women in Pakistan jails, 80 percent of whom were imprisoned under the zina laws. In 2002, 80 percent of adultery-related Hudood cases were filed without supporting evidence. *Dawn*, August 14, 2006, accessed at http://www.dawn.com/2006/08/14/ed.htm.

51. This quote by MMA MNA Razia Aziz captures the tone of rhetoric used by MMA members once the Hudood reforms were tabled in the National Assembly. *Dawn*, August 27, 2006, accessed at www.dawn.com/2006/08/27/local20.htm.

52. This is discussed in Amir Wasim, "Bill Seeks to End Anti-Women Practices," *Dawn*, February 14, 2007, accessed at www.dawn.com/2007/02/14/top1.htm.

53. See Amir Wasim, "Domestic Violence No More a Private Affair," *Dawn*, February 21, 2012, at http://beta.dawn.com/news/697039/domestic-violence-no-more-a-private-affair-2 (accessed March 24, 2012).

54. "Acid Control and Acid Crime Prevention Bill 2010," accessed at www .na.gov.pk/uploads/documents/1302318969_628.pdf.

55. Hasan-Askari Rizvi, "The Military," in Anita M. Weiss and S. Zulfiqar Gilani, eds., *Power and Civil Society in Pakistan* (Karachi: Oxford University Press, 2001), 186.

56. Amir Wasim, "PML-N Seeks Parliament's Action against MQM Chief," accessed at http://dawnnews.tv/wps/wcm/connect/dawn-content-library/ dawn/the-newspaper/front-page/pmln-seeks-parliaments-action-against-mqm -chief-580.

57. The FATA poll was conducted with the locally based Community Appraisal and Motivation Programme from June 30 to July 20, 2010, with face-to-face interviews of 1,000 residents and a margin of error of +/- three percentage points. Funding for the poll was provided by the United States Institute of Peace (USIP). CNN's analysis of the poll is accessible at: http://www.friendskorner.com/ forum/f137/news-u-s-led-drone-war-self-defeating-shows-fata-poll-funded-us -congress-202813/. The poll itself is at: http://counterterrorism.newamerica.n..s/ FATApoll.pdf.

58. Reported in "Public Opinion in Pakistan: Concern about Extremist Threat Slips," July 29, 2010, accessed at http://pewresearch.org/pubs/1683/pakistan -opinion-less-concern-extremists-america-image-poor-india-threat-support -harsh-laws.

SUGGESTED READINGS

Cohen, Stephen P. *The Idea of Pakistan.* Washington, DC: Brookings Institution Press, 2004.

Cohen, Stephen P., et al. *The Future of Pakistan.* Washington, DC: Brookings Institution Press, 2011.

Khan, Hamid. *Constitutional and Political History of Pakistan.* 2nd ed. Karachi: Oxford University Press, 2009.

Lieven, Anatol. *Pakistan: A Hard Country.* New York: Public Affairs, 2011.

Naim, C. M. (ed.) *Iqbal, Jinnah and Pakistan: The Vision and the Reality.* South Asian series #5. Syracuse, NY: Syracuse University Maxwell School of Citizenship and Public Affairs, 1979.

Nelson, Matthew J. *In the Shadow of Shari'ah: Islam, Islamic Law, and Democracy.* New York: Columbia University Press. London: Hurst.

Talbot, Ian. *Pakistan: A Modern History.* London: Hurst & Company, 2005.

Weiss, Anita M. "Crisis and Reconciliation in Swat through the Eyes of Women." In *Beyond Swat: History, Society and Economy along the Afghanistan-Pakistan Frontier,* edited by Magnus Marsden and Benjamin Hopkins, 179–92. New York: Columbia University Press, 2012.

———. "Moving Forward with the Legal Empowerment of Women in Pakistan." USIP Special Report 305. Washington, DC: USIP, May 2012.

Weiss, Anita M., and S. Zulfiqar Gilani (eds.). *Power and Civil Society in Pakistan.* Oxford: Oxford University Press, 2001.

SRI LANKA

⊗ National capital
◉ Provincial capital
● Town, village
–·–·– Provincial boundary

INDIA

Palk Strait

Kankesanturai
Point Pedro
Kayts
Jaffna
Jaffna Peninsula
Elephant Pass
Kilinochchi
Nanthi Kadal
Puthukkudiyiruppu
Mullaittivu
Vellankulam

NORTHERN

Talaimannar
Mannar
Mannar I.
Puliyankulam

Pamban I.
ferry

Gulf of Mannar

Kokkilai Lagoon

Bay of Bengal

Vavuniya
Nilaveli
Trincomalee

Kalpitiya

Anuradhapura

NORTH CENTRAL

Mutur
Kantalai

Puttalam

Habarane

Polonnaruwa

NORTH

Dambulla
Valachchenai

WESTERN

Chenkaladi
Batticaloa

Maduru Oya Reservoir

Chilaw
Kurunegala

CENTRAL

Matale

EASTERN

Maha Oya
Kalmunai

Kandy
Mahiyangana
Amparai
Tirrukkovil

Negombo
Kegalla
Victoria Falls Reservoir
Randenigala Reservoir
Bibile
Senanayake Samudra

Nuwara Eliya
Badulla

WESTERN

Avissawella

Colombo
UVA
Pottuvil

Mount Lavinia
Sri Jayewardenepura Kotte
Moratuwa
Haputale
Monaragala

Panadura
Ratnapura
Balangoda

Kalutara
SABARAGAMUWA
Pelmadulla

Beruwala
Kataragama

Embilipitiya
Ambalangoda
Tissamaharama

SOUTHERN
Hambantota

INDIAN OCEAN

Galle
Matara
Tangalla

SRI LANKA

0   20   40   60   80 km
0   10   20   30   40   50 mi

Cartography by Ashley Nepp

4

౨౨

Sri Lanka

Arjun Guneratne

Sri Lanka's modern political history is dominated by the tensions, dating to the colonial period, characterizing relations between the country's two major ethnic groups, the Sinhalese and the Tamils. It is also the story of the transition from a liberal democratic form of government with an independent judiciary and an independent civil service to a strongly authoritarian system characterized by a strong executive, a weak legislature and judiciary, and a civil service entirely dominated by the executive. The movement toward authoritarianism has coincided with (and contributed) to the increasingly violent divide that has separated the two major ethnic groups, a divide born not of immemorial hatreds, as some commentators like to think, but from the jockeying for power in a modern democracy. Sri Lanka's politics must be understood, then, in terms of these two factors.

In 1948, Sri Lanka, then known as Ceylon, achieved its independence from Britain with a liberal Westminster style constitution. Despite a democratic tradition dating to 1931, a long history of social conflict has brought into being a strongly authoritarian state. Most of the institutions necessary for good government that it had at independence, including a public service insulated from political interference, an independent judiciary, a free media, and a professional police force, have been largely dismantled over the last forty years and along with them, the rule of law in public life. Violence is endemic in politics. The current constitution, adopted in 1978, provides for a powerful presidency as the strongest institution of the state, and leaves the power of Parliament greatly diminished. This transformation in governance and in political life dates from the 1972

TIMELINE: SRI LANKA

1931	Donoughmore Commission introduces constitutional reforms, including universal franchise
February 4, 1948	Sri Lanka, then known as Ceylon, becomes independent as a dominion in the Commonwealth
1948	Citizenship Act deprives plantation workers of Indian descent of their citizenship
1951	SWRD Bandaranaike founds the Sri Lanka Freedom Party (SLFP)
1956	Mahajana Eksath Peramuna, coalition led by the SLFP, comes to power, with SWRD Bandaranaike as prime minister
1958	Bandaranaike-Chelvanayakam Pact is signed and then abrogated later the same year; anti-Tamil riots follow.
1959	Sinhala made official language; Bandaranaike assassinated by a Buddhist monk
July 1960	Mrs. Bandaranaike becomes world's first elected woman prime minister
1965	United National Party wins elections; Dudley Senanayake becomes prime minister
1970	Sirimavo Bandaranaike returns to power
1971	First Janatha Vimukthi Peramuna (People's Liberation Front) insurgency
1972	First Republican Constitution introduced; Tamil New Tigers formed in Jaffna
1976	Liberation Tigers of Tamil Eelam (LTTE) founded by Velupillai Prabhakaran (successor to earlier organization, Tamil New Tigers); TULF adopts Vaddukoddai Resolution
1977	UNP wins power in a landslide; J. R. Jayawardene becomes prime minister
1978	Second Republican Constitution introduced; J. R. Jayawardene becomes president with executive power
July 1983	Anti-Tamil pogrom in retaliation for the ambush of an army patrol; thousands are killed. Civil war may be dated from this year.

1987	India intervenes to prevent defeat of Tigers in Jaffna. Indian Peace Keeping Force (IPKF) lands in Sri Lanka. Sri Lanka signs accord with India. Second JVP insurgency; war breaks out between India and the Tigers.
June 1990	LTTE breaks off peace talks and begins Second Eelam War.
1991	Rajiv Gandhi assassinated by a Tiger suicide bomber
May 1993	President Premadasa assassinated by a Tiger suicide bomber
November 1994	Chandrika Kumaratunga elected president in a landslide; initiates peace talks with the Tigers
April 1995	Peace talks fail and war resumes (Third Eelam War)
December 1999	Attempted assassination of President Kumaratunga; she is reelected to a second term
April 2000	The Sri Lanka army suffers a major debacle when the Tigers capture the Elephant Pass army camp
December 2001	The UNP comes to power, with Ranil Wickremasinghe as prime minister
February 2002	Wickremasinghe signs a cease-fire agreement with the Tigers; both sides enter into peace talks facilitated by the Norwegian government
April 2003	Tigers withdraw from peace talks, but cease-fire holds
February 2004	Kumaratunga dismisses Wickremasinghe, and following her party's victory in the subsequent general election, appoints Mahinda Rajapakse as prime minister. The Tiger commander, Karuna Amman, defects to the government. The Indian Ocean tsunami kills over 30,000 people and possibly delays Tiger plans to resume the war.
2005	Sri Lanka's foreign minister assassinated by LTTE on August 12; Mahinda Rajapakse elected president of Sri Lanka in November
2006	Peace talks fail; war resumes on July 26 (Fourth Eelam War)
2009	War ends, with the final defeat of the Tigers and the death of its leader in May. Around 300,000 Tamils held hostage by the Tigers are put in internment camps by the state. General Fonseka announces his candidacy for president.

Arjun Guneratne

2010	Rajapakse wins reelection in January. Fonseka arrested in February on charges of corruption and jailed. Parliament approves Eighteenth Amendment to Constitution, removing term limits on the president and giving him control over various public service commissions.
August 2012	The Supreme Court rules the Divi Neguma bill unconstitutional. The Bill is intended to bring development funds administered by the Provincial Councils under the control of the president's brother, Basil Rajapakse.
January 2013	Chief Justice Shirani Bandaranayake is impeached by Parliament and replaced by former attorney-general Mohan Pieris

Constitution, but gathered force as a result of the 1978 Constitution. In addition to politicizing the public service, the 1978 Constitution centralized all state power in the hands of the president of the republic, with virtually no checks on his (or her) exercise of that authority and no countervailing force in either the legislature or the judiciary.

Sri Lanka's modern political history has also been shaped by deepening estrangement between its two major ethnic communities, the Sinhalese and the Tamils, which resulted in a civil war lasting from 1983 to 2009, when Tamil aspirations to a separate state were decisively defeated. Sinhalese nationalists have sought since independence to consolidate their hold on the island's politics, remaking an ethnically plural state into a Sinhala Buddhist one. The Tamil elite, on the other hand, sought to preserve the relatively privileged position it had achieved under British rule, which was threatened by the majoritarian politics of postindependence Sri Lanka. This it proved unable to do, and the recourse of Tamil youth to militancy culminating in civil war has had disastrous consequences for the country in general and its Tamil population in particular. The resistance of the Tamil population to Sinhala Buddhist nationalism led to the rise of the national security state in Sri Lanka and created the context in which the largely untrammeled powers given to the executive could be used to erode a democratic tradition dating to 1931.

POLITICAL HISTORY SINCE INDEPENDENCE

Sri Lanka is the only one of the four successor states to Britain's Indian Empire that was not ruled from Delhi. The country's independence on

February 4, 1948, came not as the outcome of a long struggle against colonialism but as the culmination of a lengthy process of negotiation and constitutional reform that saw control over Britain's model colony transferred to a small, anglicized native elite. Ceylon, as the country was known under colonial rule, remained a dominion within the Commonwealth, retaining the British monarch as its head of state (represented in the island by a governor-general, with a prime minister as head of government) until 1972, when it became a republic under the name of Sri Lanka, the name by which its Sinhala speaking majority know it. This lack of a national struggle and the absence of shared sacrifice probably contributed to the failure of independent Sri Lanka to forge a national identity that could transcend the particularities of ethnicity and religion.

Sri Lanka became independent with a relatively liberal constitution. The 1948 Constitution gave to Sri Lanka a form of government modeled on that of Britain, with a Parliament of ninety-five members representing territorial constituencies elected by popular vote, an additional six members appointed by the governor-general, and an upper house of thirty members (the Senate), half of whom were elected by members of the lower House and the remainder appointed by the governor-general on the cabinet's recommendation. The Senate was relatively weak, with little power to oppose legislation; those appointed to it tended to be party loyalists or "members of ethnic, religious or caste groups chosen to attract the political support of the groups to which they belonged."[1] The governor-general was appointed by the queen on the advice of the prime minister and continued in office essentially at the prime minister's pleasure.[2] Executive power was vested in a cabinet of ministers under the prime minister, and both prime minister and cabinet were answerable to Parliament.

For the Soulbury Commission, the main question the Constitution had to address was that of protecting minority rights while ensuring that the majority had a "proportionate share in all spheres of government activity to which their numbers and influence entitle them."[3] The constitution achieved this by guaranteeing under section 29 "the free exercise of any religion" and prohibiting discrimination both positive and negative on grounds of religion or community.

The civil service at independence was relatively insulated from political pressure by an independent Public Service Commission responsible for the appointment and discipline of public servants. The administration was organized by district, each of which was administered by a senior member of the Civil Service known as a government agent (GA). Government departments were organized under the various ministries and answered to the minister in charge, who was an elected member of the legislature. An important aspect of the history of public administration in

Sri Lanka has been the erosion of the relative autonomy of the civil service; the thrust of both legal and extralegal developments in the country has been to politicize the public administration and bring it more directly under the control of politicians.

The constitution laid down the basic structures of governance but made no pronouncements about ideology or the direction that government policy should take; it allowed both conservatives and socialists to pursue their policies with equal latitude and similar constraints. Its key positive features were the protection from political interference it gave the public service, which included the police, and the independence it provided to the judiciary; the untrammeled right to judicial review of legislation; the protection it sought to provide minority communities from unbridled majoritarian rule; and the vesting of executive power, following the Westminster model, in a prime minister and cabinet answerable to Parliament and depending on its confidence to continue in office.

1948–1956: The Old Elite in Power

The United National Party, which came to power with the support of independents in the first parliamentary elections of 1947, was not yet a party in the modern sense of the word. Rather, it was a coalition of local elites who were united by their fear of the rising power of the left. Independent candidates played a major role in the first decade after independence, and it took several elections before political parties in the modern sense—organized institutions with a mass base and a political program—emerged.

At the onset of independence the political class was drawn mainly from large landowning families that had prospered under colonial rule. They were the source of support and patronage for village elites, who, by their position in local administrative structures or as providers of employment, had power over poorer villagers. These patronage networks were the basis on which electoral support was mobilized. As traditional systems of patronage eroded in the years after independence, access to the resources mobilized by the state became a crucial way to construct patron-client networks. The only way to do this was through political parties, which further marginalized independent candidates and helped to consolidate the party system over time.[4]

The only political parties as such at independence were those of the left, primarily the Lanka Sama Samaja Party (Equal Society Party, or LSSP), the Communist Party, and the old Labor Party, now in decline. Founded in 1928, the Labor party was influenced by British liberal ideals, and was social-reformist rather than Marxist in its outlook; it was eventually pushed aside by the more radical Marxist parties. The LSSP had been formed in 1935 and the Communist Party in 1944 by radicalized members of the elite, and both parties were well organized among the Colombo working class, as well as the mostly Tamil workforce in the plantations, which had been brought from India as indentured labor during colonial rule. One of the first legislative acts of the new government was to deprive plantation workers of Indian descent of their citizenship (the Citizenship Act of 1948 provided for citizenship by descent or by registration, and most plantation workers were eligible for neither). The UNP and even high caste Tamil members of Parliament from Jaffna saw this as a way to weaken the LSSP and the CP, but it also altered the ethnic balance of the electorate and thereby transformed the distribution of power in a way detrimental to Tamil interests.[5]

Three groups competed for the Tamil vote in the areas where Tamils were in a majority. There were those who argued for integrating Tamils into a national party, those who wished to return independent candidates who would be free to take advantage of whatever opportunities were available to maximize Tamil influence, and finally those, organized under the banner of G. G. Ponnambalam's All Ceylon Tamil Congress (ACTC), who advocated an organized party to fight for Tamil rights. Ponnambalam eventually prevailed and cooperated with the newly formed UNP government. In 1949 a faction of the ACTC that disagreed with the policy of cooperation broke away to form the Federal Party, seeking to make Sri Lanka a federal state. Although its leader, S. J. V. Chelvanayakam, lost in a landslide in the 1952 elections to the candidate of the ACTC, the Federal Party emerged as the dominant party representing Tamil interests after the elections of 1956.

The UNP represented landed and business interests, with a commitment to maintain, as a guarantee of social stability, the welfare state that had emerged during the colonial period, with food subsidies, free education, and a national health system. Much of the development effort of the government was devoted to the promotion of peasant settlement schemes in the sparsely populated region known as the Dry Zone, which covers two-thirds of the country. The aim was to expand rice production while providing land to landless rural people.

D. S. Senanayake died in 1952 and was succeeded by his son Dudley. Dudley resigned within a year following island-wide demonstrations protesting cuts in the food subsidy, which was becoming unsustainable due to deterioration in Sri Lanka's terms of trade. He was in turn followed by D. S. Senanayake's nephew, Sir John Kotelawela (prime minister from 1953 to 1956). The elder Senanayake's death had weakened the fractious coalition of notables that was the UNP, and Kotelawela, who was arrogant, elitist, and deeply unpopular, weakened it further. Many members of the UNP left the party, and the alienation of the UNP's social base helped bring about its defeat in 1956.

Independence did not bring dramatic changes to the way the population at large experienced government. The country continued to be administered in English, and politics and the civil service continued to be dominated by members of the anglicized elite that had emerged during colonial rule. Although the political class shared to some degree the values on which the Westminister-style political system was founded, these values were remote from the experience and concerns of the Sinhala and Tamil-speaking majority in the country.

Educated sections of the rural Sinhalese middle classes, monolingual in Sinhala and resentful of the continued dominance of the "English educated," found their champion in S. W. R. D. Bandaranaike. Bandaranaike had aspired to leadership of the UNP but saw his route to power blocked by the dynastic tendency of the Senanayake family. He left the UNP in 1951 to found the Sri Lanka Freedom Party (SLFP), which quickly became the vehicle for the aspirations of the Sinhala-educated middle class. In 1956, with the backing of Buddhist monks, schoolteachers, ayurvedic physicians (i.e., practitioners of traditional medicine), and other members of the educated rural Sinhala society that had been marginalized in the postindependence years, the SLFP was swept to power as the dominant partner in a coalition government.

1956 to 1971: The Intensification of the Sinhala-Tamil Divide

The year 1956 is a watershed in the history of modern Sri Lanka, for it marks the entrance to center stage of those who had been waiting in the wings of Sri Lankan politics. They were the monolingual, Sinhala-educated members of the rural elite, Buddhist and deeply nationalist, who resented the political dominance of the anglicized class that had negotiated Sri Lanka's independence. They came together under the banner of the Mahajana Eksath Peramuna (MEP), or People's United Front, a coalition under the leadership of Bandaranaike's new Sri Lankan Freedom Party (SLFP). This victory heralded the emergence of a competitive two-party system, with power oscillating henceforth between the UNP and the SLFP and its leftist (and in later years, nationalist) allies.

The MEP government's most consequential legacy to Sri Lanka was its language policy, which did great damage to inter-ethnic relations and set in motion a train of events that would lead to civil war twenty-five years later. It made Sinhala the sole official language of the country, thereby marginalizing both the Tamil language and its speakers. The law required all government officials to learn Sinhala in order to retain their jobs, which placed Tamil officers at a disadvantage. Government service had been a major avenue of advancement for Tamils from Jaffna during the colonial era and in the first decade after independence, and this legislation was the most serious threat yet to their position in the country. Although they had been coeval partners in nationalist politics under British rule, the Sinhala Only Act underscored their marginalization in the polity that was taking shape.

In response, the Federal Party demanded a federal constitution providing autonomy to the two Tamil-language majority provinces and equal status for Sinhala and Tamil.[6] In an attempt to defuse tensions, Bandaranaike formally agreed to provide for official status for Tamil in the Northern and Eastern Provinces, to provide for regional councils, and to refrain from settling Sinhalese in those areas. This came to be known as the Bandaranaike-Chelvanayakam Pact. It was met with vigorous opposition by the UNP—Dudley Senanayake called it "an act of treachery"—which seized the opportunity to attack the government by playing on Sinhala chauvinism.[7] This subsequently became the favored tactic of the party in opposition, whether UNP or SLFP: to discredit every agreement the government in power might arrive at to respond to Tamil aspirations and grievances, thus contributing to Tamil disillusionment with the political process. Caving to pressure, Bandaranaike abrogated the agreement on April 10, 1958.

Tamil protest was met with violence by thugs linked to government politicians. In June 1956 and May 1958, major riots broke out between the two communities, requiring the deployment of the military to restore order. These were the first in a series of riots over the years that punctuated the deterioration of relations between the Sinhalese and the Tamils and led in this instance to the first major out-migration of Tamils, mostly to the West, and the creation of a diaspora that would be augmented over the years by people fleeing violence and repression in their homeland. Bandaranaike himself attempted to rectify matters somewhat by introducing a bill to make Tamil a regional language; this was passionately resisted by the nationalist forces he had helped to unleash, particularly sections of the Buddhist clergy. He was eventually assassinated by a Buddhist monk in 1959, the victim of a conspiracy led by the chief prelate of an important temple, who resented that the prime minister had thwarted his business ambitions and denied him the policy-making role to which he believed himself entitled.[8]

On the economic front as well, the MEP introduced a major change of direction. Where the UNP had essentially maintained the system friendly to private enterprise it had inherited from the British, the MEP, in line with its more socialist orientation, gave a much bigger role to the state sector. The economic restructuring and reorientation that began under Bandaranaike lasted until 1977, and is discussed in detail below (see "Political Economy").

Bandaranaike's successor, W. Dahanayake, was unable to hold the MEP coalition together, and following the general election of March 1960, the UNP formed a minority government that lasted about a month, with Dudley Senanayake as prime minister. At the general election of July 1960, the SLFP under Sirimavo Bandaranaike, the widow of the former prime minister, who had succeeded to the leadership of the party, won with an absolute majority. Mrs. Bandaranaike became prime minister—the first woman anywhere in the world to hold that office (see box 4.1). The Federal Party emerged as the dominant political force among Tamils, winning ten of the thirteen seats at stake in the north. Her government lasted until 1964, and fell when some of her own supporters crossed over to the opposition to protest her entering into a coalition with the Trotsky-ite LSSP.

Sirimavo Bandaranaike was far more hardline in her approach to inter-ethnic relations than her husband. He had been, as one biographer rather

---

Box 4.1. Sirimavo Bandaranaike (1916–2000)

The daughter of one of Sri Lanka's old feudal families, Sirimavo Bandaranaike was thrust into politics when her husband, S. W. R. D. Bandaranaike, was assassinated in 1959, and the party he had founded coalesced around her. Although she had not been involved in politics up to the time of his death, she went on to win the July 1960 general election, becoming the modern world's first female head of government; she became prime minister twice more, in 1970–1977 and again in 1994–2000, this time in the shadow of her powerful daughter, President Kumaratunga. Among them, the Bandaranaikes, parents and daughter, provided leadership to Sri Lanka for twenty-six of its first sixty-five years since independence.

Mrs. Bandaranaike was committed to furthering the populist policies of her late husband; her nationalization of British and American oil companies earned her the hostility of those powers and pushed her to forge close relationships with the Soviet Union and China, and to pursue a policy of nonalignment in world affairs. Even so, she succeeded in mobilizing military aid from a broad range of countries across the ideological and political divide—the United States, Britain, India, Pakistan, the Soviet Union, Yugoslavia, and China—to suppress the first JVP insurrection of 1971. A staunch Sinhala Buddhist nationalist, she did much to deepen the ethnic divide; she made no effort to negotiate a political compromise with the Tamil minority, and was vigorous in enforcing the provisions of the Sinhala Only Act in Tamil areas.

kindly put it, a "complex, inconstant, visionary,"[9] but his wife subscribed sincerely to the tenets of Sinhala chauvinism, and viewed the Tamils and their aspirations as a threat to Sinhala hegemony. During her tenure as prime minister, according to one commentator, "Tamils and Christians found recruitment to Government Departments and State Corporations next to impossible."[10] She enforced the official language policy, requiring courts in Tamil-majority areas to issue decisions in Sinhala only, and providing for government administration throughout the country to be in Sinhala with no concessions for the use of Tamil. Although the language policy is usually associated with the SLFP, both major parties had been playing the language card since the 1956 election, and indeed, the UNP had charged during the July 1960 campaign that the SLFP had a secret pact not to implement the Sinhala-only policy.

But the government was weakened by internal dissension between the progressive and conservative wings of the SLFP. For its part, the UNP had reorganized following its defeat at the polls, and adopted an ideology of "democratic socialism" that had more popular appeal; the return of the popular Dudley Senanayake to party leadership also gave it a boost (see box 4.2). For the first time also, the UNP was able to form a coalition with other parties to contest the elections.

Following the general election of March 1965, the UNP returned to power at the head of a coalition led by Dudley Senanayake. Senanayake sought to resolve matters with the Federal Party, which supported him from outside the coalition, by agreeing to make Tamil the language of administration in the Northern and Eastern Provinces and by devolving a certain amount of responsibility to District Councils that would help to meet Tamil aspirations for self-governance (this was known as the Senanayake-Chelvanayakam Pact), but like Bandaranaike before him, he abandoned the agreement under severe pressure from Sinhala nationalists. Even so, despite the vigorous opposition of the SLFP, the language provisions Senanayake had agreed to became law in 1966.

Senanayake inherited an economy in crisis, largely due to the fall in the price of tea, the single most important commodity for the country's economy, resulting in a severe shortage of foreign exchange. In response, the government focused its attention on the development of agriculture (rice production). However, the balance-of-payments problem that the UNP had inherited persisted, as did high unemployment. In particular, the government's focus on agriculture did not create jobs for the country's university graduates, and the government's failure to solve the problem of unemployment in addition to its decision to cut the rice subsidy, made it vulnerable at the next polls in May 1970, which it lost by a landslide to a coalition of the SLFP, the LSSP (the Trotskyites), and the Communist Party.

Box 4.2. Dudley Senanayake (1911–1973)

Of all of Sri Lanka's heads of state and government, Dudley Senanayake is the only one to be remembered as a politician of liberal
and democratic tendencies. Born into the first of Sri Lanka's two major political dynasties, the Senanayakes (whose extended family has
produced four of the country's prime ministers), Dudley Senanayake, the eldest son of D. S. Senanayake, was four times prime minister, and from 1965 to 1970 headed the first government to serve its
full term of office. On his return from Cambridge University in 1936,
he was elected to the second State Council, and after independence,
became minister of agriculture and lands in his father's cabinet. The
sudden death of his father thrust him into the prime ministership,
a position he did not greatly want. He was the preferred choice of
the party leadership, which distrusted D. S. Senanayake's arrogant
and unpopular nephew, Sir John Kotelawela, who had the greater
claim to the position (not for nothing was the UNP known as the
Uncle-Nephew Party). Senanayake died in 1973; it is likely that had
he lived, Sri Lankan politics might have followed a very different
course, for although he would have endorsed the economic reforms
introduced by J. R. Jayawardene, he lacked the latter's authoritarian
streak and was opposed to the centralization of power in an executive presidency. Well over a million people attended his funeral, an
outpouring of grief unprecedented in the country's history.

1970–1977: The First Republic

The return of Mrs. Bandaranaike to power is significant for several reasons: her policies deepened the country's economic crisis, and the period
of her rule saw the first violent challenge to state power mounted by
radicalized Sinhala youth, as well as the beginnings of a much graver
challenge to the integrity of the state mounted by their disaffected Tamil
counterparts. For the first time also, authoritarianism, in the aftermath of
the failed insurgency mounted by the People's Liberation Front (Janatha
Vimukthi Peramuna, or JVP), was introduced to independent Sri Lanka's
politics, and severe restrictions were placed on media freedom. Most important, with a two-thirds majority in Parliament, she set out to consum-
mate the unfinished agenda of 1956 by adopting a new Constitution that
severed the island's last ties to Britain and declared it to be a republic,
with a president (in a ceremonial role) replacing the governor-general as

head of state, the prime minister retaining executive authority. Constitution making in this case and again in 1978 were essentially exercises in majoritarian power; the Constitution represented the ruling party's vision of what the state should be like, and was not a document arrived at by consensus or with input from the minority communities.

The most politically significant changes in the Constitution were the following. It abolished the upper house of Parliament and created a National State Assembly of 168 members, who, as before, would continue to be elected on a first-past-the-post system. Over the protests of the Tamil representatives, it discarded the 1948 Constitution's protection for minority rights and gave to Buddhism "the foremost place," while reaffirming Sinhala as the sole official language of the country. It also abolished the Public Services Commission and the Judicial Service Commission, both of which, in the earlier Constitution, had served to safeguard the independence and integrity of the civil service and the judiciary. Finally, by explicitly prohibiting judicial review of legislation, the position of the legislature as the supreme branch of government was reinforced.

Interethnic relations continued to deteriorate, with no meaningful steps being taken to address the grievances of the increasingly marginalized Tamil population. Nor was Mrs. Bandaranaike, as leader of the political party responsible for the language laws of 1956, interested in addressing them. Indeed, the adoption of the 1972 Constitution had been a provocation as far as the Tamil leadership was concerned. Eventually, in May 1976, the Tamil United Liberation Front, the successor of the Federal Party, meeting at its national convention in the parliamentary constituency of Vaddukoddai, took the extreme step of adopting a resolution seeking full independence for the Tamil-majority provinces[11] in a new state to be called Tamil Eelam. The resolution set out at length the grievances of the Tamils, including the disenfranchisement of half the Tamil population in 1948 (for which, ironically, many Tamil representatives themselves had voted); the state-sponsored settlement by Sinhalese of the Tamil-majority provinces; the language policy; the primacy accorded to Buddhism in the Constitution; the denial of equality of opportunity to Tamils in public employment, education, and economic life in general; discriminatory policies toward Tamil language and culture; state-sponsored violence toward Tamils; and finally, the removal of the constitutional safeguards for minorities guaranteed by the 1948 Constitution. The resolution also noted the failure of several attempts by Tamil political leaders to resolve those grievances by parliamentary means within a united Sri Lanka, attributing those failures to the callous disregard of the government in power.[12]

The formal declaration by the Tamil political leadership of the goal of secession contributed to the growth of a small-scale but containable insurgency in the Northern Province by a few hundred youth impatient with the parliamentary tactics of their elders. It took the advent in 1977 of a new government, however, for the insurgency to balloon into a full-scale civil war. It was the frustrations of Sinhala youth that reached the boiling point first, providing the Sri Lankan state with its first major military challenge.

In April 1971, the JVP launched an insurgency against the government fueled by the frustrations of educated but unemployed youth drawn disproportionately from the rural lower-middle class and lower-status castes among the Sinhalese. Although the insurgency was crushed and the JVP banned for a time, the party survived to become a significant force in the island's politics. Founded in 1967, the JVP was in part a response of rural lower-middle-class youth to perceived shortcomings in the traditional left. Chief among these was the privileged background of the leaders of the LSSP and the Ceylon Communist Party, who were drawn from among the English-educated Colombo elite that the JVP despised. Nor did the Old Left's commitment to parliamentary politics, their orientation toward the urban working class and neglect of the rural population from which the JVP drew its strength have much appeal for the party's leadership, which was committed to the violent seizure of state power.

The JVP began as a Marxist-Leninist organization, working in the tradition of Mao and rejecting tactics based on the urban working class and its institutions, stressing instead the role of the peasantry. The cultural environment that formed the outlook of the JVP's cadre, however, was the Sinhala-Buddhist ideology of the rural intelligentsia that had propelled S. W. R. D. Bandaranaike to power in 1956. It later evolved, post-1971, into a chauvinistic Sinhala-nationalist party.

The Origins of Authoritarianism, 1977–2005

In 1977, rejecting the economic austerity, mismanagement, and corruption of Mrs. Bandaranaike's years in power, the electorate dealt the United Front coalition an overwhelming defeat at the general election. The UNP, under the leadership of J. R. Jayawardene, who had succeeded Dudley Senanayake on the latter's death in 1973, won 50.9 percent of the vote and a lopsided 140 of 168 seats. Mrs. Bandaranaike's Sri Lanka Freedom Party was reduced to 8 seats (despite its 29.7 percent of the popular vote) in the first-past-the-post contest, while her former coalition partners, the Communist Party and the Trotskyist Lanka Sama Samaja Party or Equal Society Party (LSSP) were completely eliminated from the legislature. For the first time in Sri Lanka's modern history, a party representing the interests of the Tamil community, the Tamil United Liberation Front (TULF), emerged as the principal opposition party, with 18 seats (6.75 percent of the vote) in Parliament.

The Jayawardene era is the second watershed in Sri Lankan politics (the first being the election of 1956) and merits close examination. Although the 1972 Constitution had set the stage for the dismantling of Sri Lanka's liberal democratic system, much of what came later—the development of an authoritarian state, the escalation of the Tamil insurgency into a full-scale civil war, the erosion of democratic practices and respect for the rule of law by state agents, and the constraints placed on civil liberties—can be traced to practices of rule introduced by his government, and most significantly the provisions of Sri Lanka's third constitution in thirty years, for which he was responsible.

Jayawardene, like all of his predecessors a member of Sri Lanka's anglicized elite, had come to power intending to adopt a new constitution to consolidate UNP rule and create a stronger executive, which he believed to be more conducive to achieving economic development. This constitution, adopted in 1978 and amended several times, is a curious hybrid of the British parliamentary system and the French "imperial" presidency; the Sri Lankan political scientist A. J. Wilson called it "the Gaullist system in Asia."[13] Under the 1972 Constitution, the president's functions were ceremonial, executive power being vested in a prime minister and a cabinet answerable to Parliament. Although the newly defined office of president in the 1978 Constitution is answerable to the people at elections every six years, the president is not answerable to Parliament, and indeed, once the president has been elected, there are few constraints on executive power. In addition, the president selects the prime minister and appoints the cabinet of ministers, thereby significantly reducing the role and power of both, and he appoints all secretaries to ministries (the highest office in the public administration service), thereby ensuring his absolute control over the machinery of government. The appointment of other senior public servants is vested in the cabinet of ministers, which can choose to delegate the responsibility to a vestigial public services commission with few powers. This allows for the continuing politicization of the public service, including the police, a process that began with the Constitution of 1972 and that has achieved complete fruition under the regime of Mahinda Rajapaske (2005 to the present).

The 1978 Constitution provides for a president who may be elected to a maximum of two six-year terms (since amended to provide for unlimited terms), who is head of state, head of government, and commander in chief of the armed forces. The president appoints the prime minister and cabinet from among the members of Parliament but is not answerable to that body. The Constitution also provides for a referendum, to allow the president to submit any bill rejected by Parliament directly to the people.

Jayawardene's Constitution made some concessions to Tamil grievances, but they were insufficient to satisfy Tamil aspirations. Sinhala was made the official language of administration and the courts, while Tamil was given the status of a national language. What "national" meant was not defined in the Constitution, but Tamil was permitted, along with Sinhala, in public administration and judicial proceedings in the Northern and Eastern Provinces, although Sinhala remained the language of record.

Neither the Supreme Court nor Parliament provide adequate counterbalance to the power of the Sri Lankan presidency, although when the legislature is controlled by the opposition, which has rarely been the case, some constraint on presidential power is possible. Even then, the president may dissolve Parliament after one year has lapsed from its election, and call for a new election, a provision that limits the power of uncooperative legislatures.

The Supreme Court was dissolved with the promulgation of the new Constitution, and a new one constituted with justices regarded as more sympathetic to the ruling party. In no other instance did the Constitution terminate and reconstitute any other public institution. The Constitution now gave the president the sole right to appoint superior court justices. However, one provision of the Constitution that has become important for civil society was the fundamental rights provisions, which have been used by ordinary citizens, as well as government servants, to seek redress from the abuses of state power.

Under the 1978 Constitution, a system of proportional representation replaced the first-past-the-post system, and it seemed unlikely that any single political party would in the future be able to get the two-thirds majority needed to amend or replace the Constitution. The UNP's landslide win of 1977 had been achieved with 51 percent of the vote; at no general election until the SLFP's sweeping victory in 2010 has any political party equaled or exceeded that figure. All but two of the amendments to the 1978 Constitution came before the general election of 1989, when the UNP lost its five-sixths majority. The Seventeenth Amendment was passed in 2001 to establish a number of independent commissions to oversee elections, the public service, the police, human rights, corruption, finance, and the delimitation of constituencies. In addition, a constitutional council was created by the amendment to oversee the appointment of members to these commissions. However, this amendment was never fully implemented and was subsequently repealed by passage of the Eighteenth Amendment in 2010 (see below).[14]

The UNP's rule was characterized by a degree of routine authoritarianism not seen before in the island's politics. Jayawardene, who became the first executive president, allowed little space for democratic dissent;

his policies contributed to the rise of militant resistance to state power by both Tamil and, in 1987–1989 with the second insurrection of the JVP, Sinhala youth. He stifled democratic opposition in various ways. For example, thugs were routinely used to intimidate opponents, including Supreme Court judges whose rulings on important matters did not favor the government, and the police were routinely deployed to harass the democratic opposition.

The government broke with the populist economic policies of the past. Restrictions on imports were relaxed, foreign exchange transactions liberalized, investment encouraged, and the private sector encouraged to grow. A free trade zone was set up near Colombo. The state, however, became more dependent than it had been on massive inflows of foreign aid to subsidize its economic reforms. Indeed, without the massive infusions of foreign funds, mostly for infrastructural development, the UNP's economic agenda would have foundered. On social policy, although the UNP could not dismantle the welfare system that had grown up since the 1930s, it sought, in line with its neo-liberal agenda, to reduce its size, a process accelerated by the outbreak of war. The demands of military expenditure became a rationale for reductions in social spending undertaken by every government up to the present.

On foreign policy, the UNP took a pro-Western stance very different from Mrs. Bandaranaike's nonaligned approach. The UNP's Westward tilt led India, which was close to the Soviet Union, to provide covert support for the Tamil insurgency; although India had no wish to see an independent Tamil state emerge in Sri Lanka, it believed that the insurgency could be used to pressure the Jayawardene regime. The UNP responded to the development of the Tamil insurgency by promulgating the draconian Prevention of Terrorism Act (PTA), which gave sweeping powers to the state security forces to detain people without trial. This act laid the groundwork for the systematic torture that has become normative in the way the security forces and police in Sri Lanka deal with ordinary criminals as well as insurgents making war on the state.[15] While the law was ostensibly intended to combat the Tamil insurgency, it proved just as useful later on in repressing political opposition among the population at large.

By depriving her of her civic rights for seven years for alleged abuse of power as prime minister, Jayawardene ensured that Mrs. Bandaranaike could not stand against him in the presidential election of 1982, which he won against the little-known candidate put up by the SLFP. The next general election would have had to take place under the system of proportional representation, and it was clear that the government could not expect to receive a two-thirds majority. Jayawardene, therefore, used the constitution's provisions for a referendum (the only time it has ever been used) to keep intact the parliamentary majority that he had used so effectively to consolidate his rule. The referendum of 1982 asked the electorate to extend the life of Parliament for another six years. It was characterized by widespread fraud, intimidation, and impersonation of voters by the UNP machine to ensure its passage; fraud and violations of election law have since become endemic in Sri Lankan elections, which were relatively clean before. The referendum won by almost 55 percent of the vote, although voter participation declined from 6.6 million at the presidential polls to 5.8 million in the referendum.[16]

The Beginnings of Civil War

While Jayawardene was consolidating his power, insurgency had been growing in the ranks of militant Tamil youth. At its inception, the insurgency never consisted of more than a few hundred armed youth, organized into a number of different militant groups. Beginning in the mid-1970s, these groups escalated their activities with bank robberies, assassinations, and attacks on police and military personnel, culminating in the ambush in July 1983 of a military patrol that killed thirteen soldiers. In response to this attack, a violent pogrom was unleashed against the Tamil people throughout the island, in which leading figures in the government were implicated, and which for several days the government did nothing to stop. Thousands of Tamils died and many thousands more fled the south to take refuge among their kin in the north. The pogrom radicalized Tamil opinion and generated thousands of recruits for the separatist cause.

The Sri Lankan civil war can be conventionally dated from July 1983. In the first phase, the Liberation Tigers of Tamil Eelam (LTTE), one of the dozen or so different Tamil militant groups, eliminated several rival organizations and absorbed the cadre of others into its own ranks. On the military front with the government, however, after peace talks held in Thimphu, Bhutan, failed to bring about a settlement, a campaign launched by the state security forces put the LTTE on the defensive and led eventually to intervention by India, ostensibly on humanitarian grounds.

On July 29, 1987, facing the threat of Indian military intervention, the government signed the Indo-Sri Lanka Peace Accord. Under the terms of the accord, Sri Lanka agreed to merge, subject to a future referendum, the Tamil-dominated Northern and Eastern Provinces, to devolve power to the provinces (formalized in the Thirteenth Amendment to the Constitution), to return the Sri Lanka army to barracks, and to invite an Indian Peace-Keeping Force (IPKF) to maintain order in the north and east. However, the Tamil parties, in particular the LTTE, were not consulted about the accord, and the LTTE agreed to what was, in effect, a *fait accompli* with great reluctance. An uneasy peace lasted for three months, and the LTTE then resumed their armed struggle, but this time against the Indian army, which was in occupation of the territory it claimed for its own.

Although it was the threat of Indian military intervention that obliged Jayawardene to agree to the Indo-Lanka Accord (which was opposed by many in his government, including his prime minister), the treaty gave him breathing space to address the JVP insurgency that was brewing in the south. This was the second coming of the JVP; following its debacle of 1971, it had been banned for some years, then allowed to reemerge as a political party, and then was banned once again and forced underground by Jayawardene, who made it the scapegoat for the July 1983 pogrom. The JVP had begun its campaign early in 1987, with assassinations of political opponents, bank robberies, and raids on army barracks to obtain arms. Sinhala anger over the Indian intervention helped to boost the JVP's insurgency, which until then had been a low-intensity conflict.

The erosion of the welfare state that had taken place during this period had increased the hardship of ordinary people, while, at the same time, the economic policies pursued by the government had led to a sharp rise in income inequality. The share of the total national income of the highest 10 percent of Sri Lankan households rose from 28 percent in 1973 to 37.3 percent in 1981,[17] and almost half the population of Sri Lanka lived below the official poverty line of 350 rupees (about US$10) per household per month. Forty percent of the working age population was unemployed in those areas in the South where the JVP was active.[18] At the same time, the government had closed off all democratic avenues of political expression and dissent, and protest had been met with repression. It is hardly surprising then that the JVP, whose candidate received only 4 percent of the vote in the presidential election, had achieved a substantial degree of popular support, particularly in its stronghold in the Southern Province, for its uprising.

The JVP's goal was the achievement of state power through the collapse of the Sri Lankan state. It unleashed a reign of terror, targeting not only members of the ruling party but also those of the Old Left and SLFP organizers in the south, as well as ordinary people who disobeyed its edicts. Because of the brutality of its tactics, and its refusal to compromise, public opinion eventually turned against the JVP, and it was defeated by a concerted campaign of counterterror by the state, in which death squads operated freely throughout the country. By November 1989, the JVP insurgency was over, its top leadership wiped out; at least 40,000 people may have died.

The Premadasa Years and Eelam War II

Jayawardene had chosen Ranasinghe Premadasa to be prime minister because his humble origins and his natural rapport with the Sinhala masses
served to counterbalance the view of the UNP as the party of Colombo-
based elites. A member of the low status Hena caste, Premadasa had the
distinction of being the first and last non-Goyigama (the dominant caste
in Sinhala society) to be either prime minister or president. Premadasa
became the UNP's candidate at the presidential election of 1988. His victory was razor thin in what was, because of the opposition of the JVP, the
most violent election in Sri Lanka's history—more than eight hundred
people were killed in the run-up to it and voter turnout fell precipitously
to 55.3 percent.

Premadasa's years in office were also the most violent in Sri Lanka's
modern history. In the north and east the LTTE was waging war against
the Indian Peacekeeping Force (IPKF) and its Tamil militant allies, while
in the south, during the first year of Premadasa's presidency, the JVP
waged a savage war against both the state and the mainstream political
parties, to which the state responded with even greater savagery. With
the presence of Indian troops in the island a continuing provocation to
southern sentiment, Premadasa demanded in June 1989 that the IPKF
be withdrawn, but this only happened in March 1990 after V. P. Singh
became prime minister of India.

Unlike Jayawardene, Premadasa was a populist who had spent his
years as prime minister developing a number of programs intended to
help the poor, including a housing program and village development
program known as Gam Udawa (Village Awakening), and the Janasaviya
scheme, a program under which every family under the poverty line
was given 25,000 rupees over a two-year period, to subsidize both consumption and investment. It was intended, Premadasa told Parliament,
"to transform a population that subsisted on food stamps into persons
engaged in productive livelihood and enterprises."[19] Premadasa was
also responsible for establishing two hundred garment factories around
the island, in part to address the grievances of unemployed rural youth.
These programs directly addressed the needs of the poorest sections of Sri
Lankan society, and undermined their support for the JVP.

Premadasa sought to resolve the ethnic issue by engaging the Tigers in
peace talks, but barely three months after the IPKF left, the LTTE resumed
the war. It had, during the thirteen-month period of peace talks, and sea-
soned by its campaign against the IPKF, become a much more formidable
organization than before, capable of engaging the Sri Lanka army in
conventional warfare and overrunning fortified military positions. During this period, it carried out a number of political assassinations, most

significantly that of Rajiv Gandhi, whose return as India's prime minister it feared. On May 1, 1993, Premadasa himself was murdered by an LTTE suicide bomber as he participated in a May Day rally. He was succeeded by his prime minister, D. B. Wijetunge, a mild man with no ambition for the presidency. The UNP chose Gamini Dissanayake, a powerful former cabinet minister who had been Premadasa's rival, to be its candidate for president, but he was assassinated by the LTTE.

Kumaratunga and Eelam War III

In November 1994, Chandrika Kumaratunga, daughter of two prime ministers, S. W. R. D. Bandaranaike and Sirimavo Bandaranaike, became president of Sri Lanka in the most decisive presidential election victory in the country's history. Kumaratunga came to power repudiating the politics of Sinhala chauvinism her parents had embraced. For the first time, Tamils and Muslims voted in large numbers for a political party that had, since its inception, been associated with Sinhala-Buddhist nationalism. She received 62 percent of the vote and majorities among every ethnic community in the country, sweeping all but one of the country's 160 polling divisions. True, she ran against a political novice, the widow of Gamini Dissanayake, who had been nominated in his stead, but a large part of her appeal was that she held out the promise of peace after more than a decade of war. After seventeen years of UNP rule, the country wanted change.

Kumaratunga began with a commitment to negotiate peace with the LTTE, based on a devolution of power. Great hopes were raised among the people, but her efforts came to nothing due to both the intransigence of the LTTE, which was prepared to settle for nothing short of an independent state of Tamil Eelam, and the intransigence of the parliamentary opposition led by the UNP, which opposed her proposals for a federal solution to the ethnic issue. War broke out again in April 1995 when the LTTE withdrew from talks and attacked the military.

Kumaratunga had campaigned on the promise of abolishing the powerful executive presidency, which was widely seen as a threat to democratic governance, but the power of the presidency proved too attractive once she was in office. In the context of an impasse with the opposition UNP over constitutional reforms to devolve power to the provinces, the matter was shelved. Her successor, Rajapakse, also made the same promise during his reelection campaign in 2010, but the levers of power that the institution provides have proved too valuable to give up.

Kumaratunga, narrowly escaping an assassination attempt by the LTTE during the election campaign, won reelection in 1999 with 51 percent of the vote over the UNP candidate Ranil Wickremasinghe, in an election fought over how to resolve the ethnic conflict. Two years later, however, Wickremasinghe's UNP, which had formed a coalition to contest the general elections of December 2001 with dissident members of Kumaratunga's People's Alliance, the Sri Lanka Muslim Congress and the Sri Lanka Workers Congress, won the general election, and he became prime minister. In the interim, the government had suffered a number of reverses on the battlefield, including the fall of its most important garrison in the north, the army camp at Elephant Pass. Although the government had been able to stave off the fall of Jaffna itself, both sides were exhausted by the fighting, and the September 11 attacks in the United States had served to create a more hostile international climate for the LTTE. With the facilitation of Norway, the new prime minister was able to enter into a cease-fire with the LTTE in February 2002 and began talks toward a negotiated solution.

The LTTE had no more interest in negotiating peace in 2002 than it had in 1995. Its goal was always the establishment of a separate state, an aim it would not compromise. In March 2003, after six rounds of negotiations on a federal solution to resolve the crisis, it abruptly withdrew from the talks, citing the failure to invite it to Washington to participate in a conference of Sri Lanka's aid donors. Although the cease-fire held through the end of Kumaratunga's term, the LTTE took advantage of it to organize in areas under government control as well as to carry out a campaign of assassination and intimidation against its opponents, culminating in the assassination of Sri Lanka's foreign minister, Lakshman Kadirgamar, in August 2005 (see box 4.3). The Sri Lanka Monitoring Mission, an observer group from the Scandinavian countries entrusted with the task of monitoring the ceasefire, recorded 3,830 violations of the cease-fire by the LTTE as of 2005, with 351 violations by the government.[20] In November 2003, in the face of the LTTE's mounting violations of the cease-fire, the president took over the defense, interior, and information ministries. In February 2004, she dissolved Parliament, four years before its term was to expire, and called for fresh elections. The People's Alliance was returned to power, and in 2005, at the end of her term, the country prepared for a new presidential election.

The Rajapakse Era: Authoritarianism Triumphant

The presidential election of 2005 was a contest between the former prime minister, Ranil Wickremasinghe of the UNP, and Mahinda Rajapakse, the scion of an old political family from the Southern Province, who had been the prime minister in President Kumaratunga's last cabinet. The Sinhalese component of the electorate had grown disenchanted with the UNP and the failure of the peace process Wickremasinghe had champi-

Box 4.3. Lakshman Kadirgamar (1932–2005)

Lakshman Kadirgamar, born into a Tamil Christian family in Colombo, was the most successful foreign minister Sri Lanka has had. Serving twice in that role, from 1994 to 2001 and again from 2004 to August 2005, when he was assassinated by the LTTE, he succeeded in getting the LTTE banned in many of the western countries where they had been allowed to organize and raise funds for their war against the Sri Lankan state. Kadirgamar believed to the end of his life that it was possible to be both Sri Lankan and Tamil, and he worked toward that goal; that conviction also led to his death. He was one of the few public figures in Sri Lankan life at whose door a charge of narrow nationalism could not be laid; he believed very firmly in the possibility, indeed the necessity, of a plural society, and worked toward a united Sri Lanka where Tamils could live with dignity as equal citizens. He might have been prime minister in 2004, but for the opposition of the pro-Rajapakse faction of the SLFP to giving him the post.

An outstanding athlete—he played cricket and rugby, and was an all-India hurdles champion—Kadirgamar studied law at Oxford, where he became only the second Sri Lankan to be elected president of the Oxford Union. He authored the first country report for Amnesty International (on Vietnam, in 1963), and worked for the International Labor Organization (ILO) and the World Intellectual Property Organization, before returning to Sri Lanka to resume his law career and eventually enter politics as a member of the People's Alliance.

oned. Kumaratunga was opposed to Rajapakse who posed a threat to the power of the Bandaranaikes in the SLFP, but Rajapakse, a Sinhala Buddhist nationalist himself, and an outsider to the Westernized Colombo elite that has provided almost all of the country's other prime ministers and presidents (save Premadasa), was strongly backed by the Sinhala nationalist parties, including the National Heritage Party of certain Buddhist monks and the JVP, now a significant force of Sinhala chauvinism. Although Kumaratunga's achievement had been to move the SLFP away from its Sinhala Buddhist chauvinism, Rajapakse returned the party to its Sinhala nationalist roots.

The 2005 election was different from previous presidential elections in that the winner won by appealing to just one community (the Sinhalese); in every prior election, the winning candidate had won only by appealing across ethnic and religious divides. Rajapakse won by a sliver: 50.29 percent of the vote. The LTTE prevented the Tamils in the territory they controlled from voting; most of those votes would probably have gone to Ranil Wickremasinghe.

Winning the War

President Rajapakse's term in office is characterized by two significant and related developments. The first is the ending of the country's long civil war. Rajapakse and his advisers concluded, following a series of provocations by the LTTE (including the attempted assassinations of the army commander and the secretary to the Defense Ministry, who is the president's brother), that there was no prospect for a negotiated solution to the civil war. The total defeat of the LTTE and the annihilation of its leadership, following a military campaign lasting almost three years, are due to the collective leadership of the president; his army commander, Sarath Fonseka; and his brother, the defense secretary, Gotabhaya Rajapakse. In May 2009 the war ended with the death of Velupillai Prabhakaran and the complete destruction of the LTTE.

Neither the United States and Europe, which lobbied for a negotiated solution to the war, nor successive governments in Colombo, which were to varying degrees responsive to Western concerns and pressure, fully accepted that Prabhakaran and his more militant and committed supporters in the Tamil diaspora would settle for anything short of an independent state of Tamil Eelam. This made negotiations an exercise in futility and simply set the stage for a resumption of fighting; the LTTE had always regarded peace negotiations as a tactic rather than a strategy to help them achieve their state of Eelam. Rajapakse opted instead for a military solution regardless of the cost to human lives or to the economy, and he proved impervious to Western pressure to end the war and resume negotiations, a stance that also burnished his nationalist credentials. The support extended by China, the country's largest aid donor, has allowed the government to resist the pressure placed on it by its traditional aid donors in the West.

Consolidating Power

The second development is the ruthless consolidation of the most authoritarian regime in the country's modern history; under President Rajapakse and his brothers, the Constitution's potential for authoritarianism has been fully realized. This is not to downplay the authoritarianism of the presidencies of Jayawardene and Premadasa, but there were countervailing forces against them that no longer exist. A confluence of events made Rajapakse's authoritarianism possible. First, the Sri Lankan government's victory made the president and his regime immensely popular in the aftermath of the war, which translated into convincing victories in both the presidential election of 2010 and the general election that followed soon thereafter, in which the president's coalition received nearly two-thirds of seats in Parliament—an accomplishment that the proportional representation system was supposed to preclude. Second, he was confronted by a singularly weak opposition, in disarray under a weak leader. Ranil Wickremasinghe, who had led his party, the UNP, to a series of defeats at presidential, general, and provincial elections (nineteen by one count), continues to cling to his position despite several efforts by more competent people in the UNP to remove him. Third, state power has been consolidated within the Rajapaske family; one brother is the president, another is the Speaker of the House, a third is the powerful defense secretary, and the last is a powerful minister. Among them, they control over 70 percent of the national budget.[21] Fourth, repression of the media reached unprecedented levels during the war and continued into the peace. More than twenty journalists critical of the government have been murdered; dozens of others have fled abroad; and countless others have been threatened, kidnapped, or disappeared. Fifth, in the context of a Parliament that has been severely weakened by the extent of presidential power, political support can be readily garnered by the lavish distribution of material privileges, particularly those that come with cabinet rank; Rajapakse's cabinet includes almost every member of the government benches, and members of the opposition have been readily lured across the aisle with offers of cabinet positions and monetary incentives.

The penultimate act in the consolidation of power was the passage of the Eighteenth Amendment to the Constitution in September 2010. The government's soaring popularity in the immediate aftermath of the war as well as the opposition's ineptitude and liberal violations of the election laws allowed the SLFP and its allies to come close to acquiring a two-thirds majority in the parliamentary election of 2010. It was able to put together enough votes to pass the controversial Eighteenth Amendment on an urgent basis, after only a day of debate and without allowing time for public discussion. The amendment removes the two-term limit on holding presidential office, and repeals the Seventeenth Amendment to the Constitution; it now gives the president the authority to directly appoint all of the members of certain key commissions, including the Election Commission, the Public Service Commission, the Police Commission, the Human Rights Commission, and the Commission to Investigate Bribery.

The president is also given the power to appoint all judicial officers of the higher courts, including the Supreme Court, the attorney-general, and the auditor-general, among others. These appointments do not require confirmation or oversight by any other body of state, such as Parliament. The Eighteenth Amendment thus effectively politicizes all of these institutions and officers crucial to good governance, and brings them directly under the president's control.

Finally, in a highly controversial move, the chief justice, Shirani Bandaranayake, was impeached by Parliament in 2013, following a series of Supreme Court rulings inimical to the government's interests, even though the Supreme Court found the procedure adopted for the impeachment unconstitutional. She was replaced by a man widely perceived to be a loyalist of the Rajapakses,' the former attorney-general Mohan Pieris. With this move, the modicum of independence enjoyed by the judiciary was removed, leaving the president and his brothers to exercise almost untrammelled power.

Compromising the Peace

Although Rajapakse won the war, he squandered a rare opportunity to win the peace and move Sri Lanka to a new track in interethnic relations. The LTTE fought behind the shield of the hundreds of thousands of Tamil civilians it took hostage as they fled before the advancing Sri Lankan army. At the war's end, these people were further victimized by being forcibly interned in camps by the government. The regime suspected the loyalty of the civilian Tamil population of the Vanni, which had lived for two decades under LTTE rule, and the government feared that LTTE cadre had hidden themselves among the civilians, there to resume the fight another day. The government insisted that these internally displaced people could not be allowed to return to their homes until remnants of the LTTE were weeded out and their villages demined. Although there is something to this argument, by keeping children, the elderly, and the sick, as well as those who had families to go to outside the camps, detained for months under squalid conditions, the government not only violated their rights as citizens of Sri Lanka but also confirmed the negative view held of it by its critics. More than four years after the war ended, no progress has been made toward a political solution to Tamil grievances. In addition, there has been land grabbing in the north and east by government-backed Sinhalese settlers and commercial interests in the aftermath of the war. The government has also indulged in pointlessly petty actions, such as forbidding the singing of the national anthem in Tamil, and requiring citizens of Tamil origin in a neighborhood in Colombo to register with the police. The Rajapakse regime clearly believes that its military victory rules out need for political accommodation of any sort, which is the position of the extreme nationalists in its ranks.

The political culture of the regime rivals and perhaps exceeds the regimes of Jayawardene and Premadasa in its lack of tolerance for democratic opposition. It goes beyond it in its use of the military and military intelligence to buttress its power. It is intolerant of dissent and has little use for a free media; murders of opposition figures and critics of the government are seldom if ever investigated.[22] Having been developed mainly as a paramilitary auxiliary to the military during the long decades of war against the LTTE, the police today are in any case poorly trained in police work, and their ability to act independently to investigate crimes, especially political ones, is virtually nonexistent. Following on the successful silencing of the press, the government moved to bring the Internet more securely under its control by blocking a number of independent and dissident sites covering news of Sri Lanka (such as Tamilnet.com and lankanewsweb.com) located abroad and by shutting down independent sites located in the island.

Threats to the Regime

At the end of the war, President Rajapakse dominated the political stage in Sri Lanka and his chances of reelection seemed assured. The opposition had no credible candidate to oppose him, but found one in the ambitious army commander, who had fallen out with the Rajapakses after being sidelined by them after the war's end. Sarath Fonseka was as entitled as the president to the mantle of war hero, or so the opposition hoped. The main platform on which the opposition supported Fonseka was a promise to abolish the executive presidency and return power to Parliament, a promise that Rajapakse himself made (and then ignored after he was reelected). The consequence of an ugly electoral campaign in which election laws were routinely violated and the state's resources used for partisan politicking (by the government in power, in keeping with tradition) was that Fonseka lost by a wide margin, gaining only 40 percent of the vote (ironically, he won overwhelmingly in the Tamil- and Muslim-dominated Northern and Eastern Provinces, thus underscoring the deep ethnic divide in the island's politics). Thereafter, the Rajapakses moved swiftly to consolidate their victory; the defeated opposition candidate was accused of corruption in military procurements and tried and convicted by a court martial consisting of officers junior to him in rank whom he had disciplined when commander in chief of the army. Although the real purpose of the Rajapakses in having their rival arrested was to remove from the scene a dynamic figure who had rejuvenated a dispirited opposition and united it against difficult odds, it also sent a clear message to alienated members of their own party of the folly of opposing them. Fonseka was subsequently pardoned by the president after spending time in prison, but stripped of his right to hold elected office or vote.

The other major threat to the regime comes from outside the country. The LTTE's supporters in the diaspora have pursued a relentless campaign against the government to seek redress for the abuses committed by the military in the final months of the war, including the alleged shelling of hospitals and the summary executions of prisoners. The government so far has resisted pressure to investigate these allegations, and has failed to implement the measures suggested by its own much criticized commission of inquiry into the causes of the breakdown of the 2002 cease-fire (the Lessons Learnt and Reconciliation Commission).

POLITICAL ECONOMY

Sri Lanka is a paradox. A small Asian state with fairly high levels of poverty and, for most of its modern history, relatively low per capita income had nevertheless achieved by the 1970s a human development profile that far exceeded what might be expected of its level of economic development, which placed it well ahead of its neighbors in South Asia (see table 4.1). This achievement can be attributed to a focus on social welfare beginning before independence and intensifying thereafter, albeit at the expense of investment in other areas. Contrary to the assumptions of economists that social development follows economic growth, in Sri Lanka the rise in social indicators came before significant economic growth had been achieved.

Table 4.1. Selected Social Development Indicators for South Asia

	India	Pakistan	Bangladesh	Nepal	Sri Lanka
Life expectancy at birth	65 (2011)	65 (2010)	69 (2011)	69 (2011)	75 (2010)
Infant mortality per 1,000 live births in 2011	47	59	37	39	11
Adult literacy rate	74 (2011)*	55 (2009)	56 (2009)	60 (2010)	91(2010)
Total fertility rate	2.6 (2011)	3.4 (2010)	2.2 (2011)	2.7 (2011)	2.3 (2010)
Population growth in 2011	1.4	1.8	1.2	1.7	1.0

Source: Except where indicated, data is from the World Bank (http://data.worldbank.org/), for the years indicated in parentheses.

* Census of India, http://www.censusindia.gov.in/2011-prov-results/indiaatglance.html.

The main components of this welfare state, which continued to expand into the 1970s, were food subsidies (which became increasingly difficult to maintain but politically impossible to dispense with), free education through the university level, and free health care through a network of hospitals and clinics that reached into every district in the island. In addition, much attention and resources were channeled into smallholder agriculture, which benefited the poorer sections of the population. Between 1956 and 1977, the cost of the three pillars of the welfare state (health, education, and food subsidies) amounted to approximately 10 percent of GNP.[23] The welfare state produced admirable outcomes in comparison with the rest of South Asia, creating a highly literate population with better health and longevity than its neighbors (see table 4.1), but critics have argued that the diversion of resources to support this system came at the expense of investment in the country's development. As the economist Joan Robinson observed, "Ceylon has tasted the fruit before she has planted the tree."[24]

At its inception, the welfare state was funded by high commodity prices for the country's major export crops, which together accounted for about 90 percent of the country's foreign-exchange earnings. It continued even after the decline in commodity prices and after the opening up of the economy, even though overall expenditures on social welfare declined. All the major political parties were committed to social welfare policies, and more important, so was the electorate at large, which mattered in the context of democratic, competitive politics. At the height of the welfare state, between 1970 and 1977, the country allocated between 20 and 25 percent of its national budget to social welfare.[25] From the point of view of the UNP, the welfare state also blunted the edge of revolutionary left-wing politics by giving a large swathe of the population an investment in the state.

The Evolution of the Economy

Sri Lanka's economic development has gone through three phases. From independence until 1956, the UNP governments in power were content to maintain the structures of the economy they had inherited from British rule, which depended for its export earnings primarily on tea, rubber, and coconut. This was an agriculturally based economy with a very weak industrial and public sector. The emphasis was on private enterprise. From 1956 to 1977, a series of left-leaning governments pursued a strategy of import substitution, with protection for state-led industrialization and strong financial controls. From 1977 onward, governments have pursued a strategy of economic liberalization, in which state assets were privatized, exchange controls loosened, and private enterprise given the leading role. The welfare state has survived, albeit in an attenuated form; the lion's share of the budget now goes not to health, education, and food subsidies but to Sri Lanka's defense institutions, in keeping with the rise of the national security state.

The Colonial Economic Legacy, 1948–1956

During the eight years that followed independence, the agricultural, fisheries, and forestry sector contributed about 50 percent of GDP; the challenge for the governments that came later was how to diversify and modernize the economy. The economy during this first phase was dominated by a mainly mercantilist private sector with a poorly developed industrial component and a private sector with little capacity to invest in industrialization. The country's politics was dominated by a conservative, land-owning, and anglicized elite under the banner of the United National Party (UNP), whose principal political concern was to keep in check a vigorous and dynamic left movement led by two major political parties, the Trotskyist Lanka Sama Samaja Party (Equal Society Party) and the Communist Party. Furthermore, the government of the time, dominated by commercial interests and the propertied classes, had little interest in industrialization, which would have "caused dislocation to the trade of the former and discomfort to the consumption of the latter," as well as strengthening the base of the Marxist parties in the industrial working class.[26] This indifference may have been shaped by the plantation-owning elite that were in power, who believed that "revenue from plantation exports would continue indefinitely into the future and industrial goods could continue to be imported."[27] Such views were buttressed by the boom experienced by the country during the Korean War, when rubber prices were at a premium.

The economy was dominated by the plantation sector, which had originated in the 1840s with the establishment first of coffee plantations, and then, after coffee was destroyed by a blight, of tea, as well as rubber and coconut. The tea plantations were mainly owned by the British, but many Sri Lankans owned coconut and rubber plantations, which formed the basis of the wealth of many prominent families. Despite the importance of rice cultivation—both ideologically and economically—the country imported two-thirds of its food. This economic system has been succinctly portrayed in the following terms: "[It] was predominantly agricultural, with a large service sector developed largely to meet the trade and finance needs of the plantation sector and very little industrial activity. The export plantation sector earned the foreign exchange used for the importation of a variety of consumer, intermediate and investment goods and through the taxation of that sector the government raised a major part of its revenue to be used for normal governmental activities and to maintain a widespread welfare state system."[28] The small manufacturing sector received a boost during World War II, when it expanded to provide substitutes for imported consumer goods that could no longer be brought into the country, but it quickly collapsed at war's end when imports resumed.

Sri Lanka at independence was favorably positioned, vis-à-vis many of its neighbors in the region, to develop a strong industrial base, but the transition from a primarily agrarian society to one with a more diversified economy, including sustained expansion of manufacturing, had to wait for the economic reforms of the post-1977 Jayawardene era. The UNP governments in power from 1948 to 1956 did not favor state promotion or ownership of industry, and gave free rein to the private sector. Continuing a trajectory put into place during the time of the pre-independence State Council, and championed by D. S. Senanayake, the state's development activities during this period emphasized the expansion of rice agriculture mainly through the restoration of ancient irrigation works and the construction of new ones to settle a landless (and mostly Sinhala) population in the sparsely settled northern and eastern regions of the country. These efforts did manage to expand domestic agriculture, especially rice production.

The Closed Economy: 1956–1977

The second phase of Sri Lanka's economic development was a period of statism, which began soon after 1956, when the coalition led by S. W. R. D. Bandaranaike's Sri Lanka Freedom Party (SLFP) came to power. It lasted until 1977, when the government led by his widow, Sirimavo Bandaranaike, fell to a rejuvenated United National Party. Economic policy during this period was characterized by "import substitution, state control and protection,"[29] although UNP governments during this period allowed for a relatively greater role for the private sector. Bandaranaike's government, and the SLFP governments that followed, significantly expanded basic industries under the public sector and gave the state a much greater role in the management of the economy than before. SLFP governments closed the economy to outside investment, with stringent restrictions imposed on the remittance of capital and profits. A wave of nationalizations—of the ports, bus companies, domestic banks, and foreign oil companies (which prompted Britain and the United States to cut off aid)—took place between 1956 and 1965. There were more nationalizations during Mrs. Bandaranaike's second term in the 1970s (when tea plantations, most of which were owned by British trading companies, were nationalized as part of a comprehensive land reform that restricted private ownership of land by individuals to fifty acres). In order to conserve scarce foreign exchange, import of goods was curtailed. Al-though the UNP government of 1965–1970 reversed some of these changes by expanding the private sector and privatizing some state en-terprises, the SLFP-led United Front government that succeeded it from 1970 to 1977 returned to a strict import substitution policy, with high tariffs and few consumer goods imports. A policy of state-led industrial-ization, which saw the establishment of a number of public corporations, especially during the 1970–1977 period of the United Front government, emphasized an import-substitution strategy.

Economic policy during this period was shaped by the SLFP's socialist allies, the Trotskyist LSSP and the Communist Party, and facilitated by the existence of a powerful socialist bloc centered on the Soviet Union and China, to which the SLFP had close ties. The welfare state was expanded and consolidated, and the state played a much larger role in the economy. In 1958, the MEP passed the Paddy Lands Act, which guaranteed security of tenure to tenants and constrained the authority of landlords over them. The act was also intended to prevent fragmentation of paddy lands and provide a means to consolidate fragmented holdings.[30] The MEP govern-ment (1956–1959) had an activist approach to economic planning, and in 1959 introduced a ten-year plan for the economy, which was subsequently abandoned as the government began to face a balance of payments crisis. In fact, the government began to run deficits in 1957 following the end of the world rubber boom.

The government introduced an industrial policy based on promoting import substitution and protective tariffs; manufacturing's share of GDP rose from 3.9 to 5.2 in the decade ending in 1960. The UNP government of 1965–1970 continued with essential aspects of this policy, but in milder form; in an effort to get industry moving, foreign direct investment (FDI) was encouraged with "tax holidays, duty free import of capital and in-termediate goods and waiving of domestic taxes on exports."[31] But like its predecessor, the UNP's focus was on the development of agriculture rather than of industry, and most of its energy and resources were de-voted to that end.

The return of the UNP to power between 1965 and 1970 did not end the statist policy in place, although the UNP was friendlier to private enter-prise than the SLFP had been. In large part, the UNP won power because of voter opposition to the scarcities of the closed economy, but it had no real answer to the problem other than borrowing from abroad to finance consumption and maintain the welfare state. Foreign funds as a source of financing for imports rose from 8 percent in 1964 to 49 percent in 1970, and the country's foreign debt went from 730 million rupees when the UNP came to power to 2,968 million rupees in 1970. By the end, the UNP was borrowing from commercial banks, at commercial rates of interest. Nor did its principal achievement—the success of its green revolution— yield it much in political dividends. The green revolution, in Sri Lanka, as elsewhere, was focused on removing technical barriers to increasing agricultural production, such as the introduction of tractors, chemical fertilizers, and new high-yielding varieties of rice, as well as expanding the credit available for agriculture; these benefits, however, disproportionately benefited the large farmers (with better access to capital) at the expense of other strata of rural society. Consequently, at the election of 1970, the rural vote went overwhelmingly against the UNP. As the country slid deeper into debt, the situation was worsened by the continuing decline in the price of tea and rubber, the two mainstays of the country's foreign exchange earnings.

The last iteration of the closed economy policy came during the period of the United Front government, in 1970–1977. The United Front rolled back the pro-business policies pursued by the UNP when it was in power from 1965 to 1970, and passed the Business Takeover Act, allowing it to nationalize business enterprises. However, the continuing crisis in the balance of payments, exacerbated by the world oil-price hike, forced it to cut the food subsidy at the heart of Sri Lanka's welfare state (the very issue on which it had once campaigned against the UNP), and impose stringent austerity measures on the people. Much of the country's budget went to maintaining the welfare state and to food imports. Here, too, the UF had made the mistake of dismantling Senanayake's agricultural development thrust, which had made the country almost self-sufficient in rice (Mrs. Bandaranaike's left-wing allies subscribed to the idea that development could only come through industrialization and that emphasis on agriculture was misguided). Other factors contributing to the failure of the closed economy model included the oil crisis of the early 1970s and the floating exchange rate, which along with the government's left-wing orientation limited access to credit on the international financial markets dominated by the United States. The public sector industries were inefficient, in large part because of poor management and overstaffing deriving from political interference in their management, and the general political climate was not friendly to private enterprise. Finally, plantation agriculture continued to dominate export earnings, in the context of falling commodity prices. Popular reaction to the austerities imposed during this period, as well as anger over public corruption (albeit a pale shadow of the corruption and misrule that was to come later) brought about the end of this phase in Sri Lanka's economic development, and the introduction of the next phase, which prevails to this day.

The Open Economy: From 1977

The third phase was inaugurated by the sweeping victory of the UNP at the polls in 1977. The UNP has traditionally been the representative of business interests, and the more cosmopolitan of the two major parties. But the reforms it introduced were not simply economic, they were also political. The chief architect of those reforms, J. R. Jayawardene, was a strongly conservative leader, who believed that Sri Lanka needed a strong, centralized, and stable government (along Singaporean lines), which the volatility of the parliamentary system could not provide. The economic reforms were therefore part and parcel of a much larger authoritarian political project to centralize power in a strong presidency free of constraints; to weaken trade unions; and, not least of all, to entrench the UNP as the dominant political force in the island—which it became for seventeen years.

There were three aspects to the economic policies Jayawardene pursued, but all were linked or shaped by noneconomic factors. The first was economic liberalization. Backed by multilateral agencies like the World Bank and the IMF, and by Western countries, Jayawardene was determined to stimulate the private sector to play a major role in the economy by promoting foreign investment and encouraging the growth of export-led industries, primarily in garment manufacture, that would employ semiskilled labor. The banking sector was opened up to foreign banks, while local banks were pushed to expand into rural areas. The new government also encouraged migration of Sri Lankan labor abroad; by 1983, some 200,000 people, or 1.3 percent of the population, were working in the Middle East (a rate much higher than the rest of South Asia). Trade liberalization, however, was not uniform or across the board but was influenced by considerations of ethnicity and class. For instance, rice production, the mainstay of Sinhala farmers, was protected, but trade in chilies and onions, which are the main crops produced by Tamil farmers in Jaffna, was liberalized.

The second aspect involved "massive capital expenditures on agriculture, industry, housing, and infrastructure, financed with foreign aid" to catalyze economic growth.[32] Public sector investment also provided sources of patronage, including jobs for party members and contracts for the party's business supporters—patronage is crucial in extending political power and entrenching it—as well as opportunities for politicians with oversight of key areas (such as irrigation, highways, power) for personal enrichment. Consequently, the state sector grew rather than contracted during the early period of liberalization.

The biggest part of the government's investments was the expansion of the multipurpose irrigation system around Sri Lanka's largest river, the Mahaweli. This was a continuation of the UNP's traditional concern with irrigation and agricultural production. The accelerated Mahaweli program provided water to large parts of the central and north-central regions of the country, and facilitated small-scale agriculture, including resettlement of landless farmers on a scale much larger than before. The project was a success in boosting agriculture, but demand for agricultural products in the country did not expand sufficiently to sustain prices, on account of the insufficient growth of other sectors of the economy. Nor could food products be exported, because they were not competitive in international markets, except in the form of processed food, which took off much later.

The third aspect was the cuts to food subsidies; these were at least partly motivated by a strong free-market ideology. Jayawardene opposed food subsidies on principle (although he supported public expenditures on health and education), and as finance minister, he had been responsible for the cuts to food subsidies that had led to Dudley Senanayake's resignation in 1953. The reduction in the food subsidy mainly affected the urban working class, who were traditionally supporters of the left; it raised food prices, which benefited farmers, who had supported the UNP in 1977. Jayawardene responded forcefully to trade union actions against this move; the Essential Public Services Act passed in 1979 outlawed union action in the public sector, and the unions were subjected to a mixture of legislative action, violence, and repression to bring them into line.

The open economy survived the election of the People's Alliance in 1994 under President Kumaratunga, which had initially committed itself to reversing it but which soon retreated from that position after winning the election. The economic policies the PA inherited had been in place for seventeen years, and the demise of the Soviet Union and the rise of China as a capitalist economic power had eliminated from the world scene a "visible socialist alternative."[33] Acceptance of the neoliberal model gave access to capital markets and the prospect of foreign investment; resistance to it, on the other hand, had no rewards. Economic liberalization has also expanded the scope for corruption, and the opportunities for rent seeking by cabinet ministers and ordinary politicians was not to be foregone. In the case of the regime currently in power, it has contributed to the emergence of a kleptocratic state, completely dominated by a family oligarchy for whom the resources of the state, linked to their near total control of state power, has provided vast opportunities for the accumulation of private wealth.

President Kumaratunga was also forced to tack to the right because of a decline in economic growth and investor confidence, provoked in large part by the SLFP's reputation. She hewed more closely to market-oriented policies favored by the World Bank and the IMF, and stepped up the pace of privatization of state-owned assets. Commitments made to workers in the run-up to the election were abandoned. But she also continued President Premadasa's welfare program, which subsidized almost a third of Sri Lankan households.

Structural Change and Evolution of Exports

The transformation in the Sri Lankan economy is shown in table 4.2. The biggest change is the decline of the importance of agriculture and the corresponding rise in the importance of industrial goods as percentages of GDP. In 1960–1964, agriculture had been under 50 percent of GDP, and industry had been about 10 percent; by 2007, agriculture's share of GDP had declined to 12 percent and that of industry had risen to almost 30 percent. The manufacturing sector had expanded to around 18 percent of GDP. The most significant part of manufacturing is the production of apparel and garments for export.

Figure 4.1 shows a dramatic change in Sri Lanka's export mix over the period 1970 to 2010. Since exports are an infallible indicator of a country's international competitiveness, it is clear that right up to 1970, the plantation crops of tea, rubber, and coconut, which accounted for over 90 percent of total exports, were the only qualifiers, apart from precious

Table 4.2. Sector Composition (Percent Relative to GDP) and Average Growth; 1960–2007

Sector size	1960–1964	1970–1977	1984–1989	1991	1995	1999	2003	2007
Agriculture	46.1	36.8	27.2	22.2	20.0	17.0	13.7	11.9
Industry total	10.3	16.5	21.4	27.2	30.2	27.5	27.7	28.5
Mining				1.0	1.1	1.1	1.3	1.9
Manufacturing	5.6	9.1	12.9	17.8	20.0	17.8	18.1	17.7
Utilities				1.8	2.1	2.0	2.2	2.5
Construction	2.4	4.9	7.3	6.6	7.1	6.7	6.0	6.4
Services	43.6	46.7	51.4	45.1	45.0	55.4	58.6	59.6

Average growth	1960–1964	1970–1977	1984–1989	1990–2000		2000–2003		2003–2007
Industry	7.6	1.0	3.9	7.2		1.9		7.3
Manufacturing	10.1	2.3	5.7	7.9		0.8		5.8
GDP at factor cost	4.1	2.9	2.6	5.3		2.8		6.5

Source: G. Chris Rodrigo, "Manufacturing Industry," in Ajitha Tennakoon, ed., *Sri Lankan Economy in Transition* (Colombo: Vijitha Yapa Publications, 2009).

stones and spices, that were exported even before the dawn of the colonial era in 1505. By the turn of the century, industrial exports, consisting largely of garments, had expanded to take up almost 80 percent of total exports. By 2010, this fraction has declined to around 70 percent, which is still quite commendable for a low-income country. What is even more commendable is that Sri Lanka's garments, which are now to be found in almost every retail store in the U.S. market, have found a relatively secure, high-quality, high-value niche in the now intensely competitive global market for garments in the face of competition from very low-wage countries such as India, Bangladesh, and Vietnam. This success is attributed to the relatively high literacy levels of the country's garment workers (mostly women), who can be trained to skill levels superior to international norms. Such skill levels are particularly important in items such as women's undergarments, which require intricate work. The only negative side of the garment industry is that it requires fairly large expenditures on imported inputs, which reduce the net export effect.

While exports of textiles and garments have slowed in recent time, other sectors have picked up strongly, with double-digit year-on-year growth. These include the export of processed food products, which though currently small compared to, say, Thailand, has tremendous growth potential on account of Sri Lanka's more favorable climatic and soil conditions. In fact, the processed food industry employs a larger number of workers than the textile and garment sector overall. Other

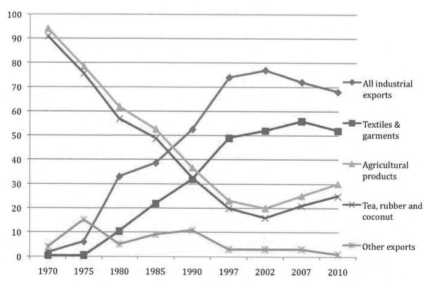

Figure 4.1. Evolution of Sri Lanka's export mix from 1970 to 2010, relative to total exports (in percent). Courtesy of Chris Rodrigo.

successful export sectors include electrical goods and software services (which are not included in manufactures exports).

Overall, though, Sri Lanka's industries and the economy as a whole have done much less well than would be expected given the human and natural resource endowments. This shortfall is often attributed to the twenty-six-year civil war that ended in 2009. The World Bank claims that "Sri Lanka is now transitioning to middle-income-country status." However, the country is now facing further challenges as a consequence of the world economic crisis.

IDENTITY POLITICS

The dominant form of identity politics in Sri Lanka during the latter half of the twentieth century and into the first decade of this one has been the struggle between Sinhala and Tamil nationalisms, which has overshadowed the political significance of other forms of identity, including caste, region, and religion. Sri Lanka's twenty million people are ethnically very diverse. Linguistically, they are divided into two main groupings, the Sinhalese and the Tamil-speaking people. Four of the world's major religions have substantial numbers of followers in Sri Lanka: Buddhism (the overwhelming majority), Hinduism, Christianity, and Islam.

The Sinhalese, who comprise about 75 percent of the population, are mostly Buddhist, and as a legacy of colonialism are divided regionally and culturally into two groups. The Kandyan Sinhalese live in the interior and resisted European rule until 1815. The Low-Country Sinhalese occupy the coastal areas and lived under Portuguese, Dutch, and British colonial rule for over four hundred years; consequently there are substantial cultural differences that distinguish them from the Kandyans. As late as the first half of the twentieth century, the Kandyans regarded themselves as distinct from the Sinhalese of the low country, and their political leaders were the first to demand (in the 1920s) that Sri Lanka be made a federal state, long before Tamils raised the same demand after independence.

A substantial minority of the Low-Country Sinhalese are Roman Catholic, and there have been tensions between them and Buddhists in the past, most notably the riots between Catholics and Buddhists in 1883. In modern Sri Lanka, their Catholic identity is subordinated to their Sinhala one, however, which separates them from those of their coreligionists who are Tamil. In addition to divisions by region and religion, the Sinhala population is also divided by caste, with the Goyigama caste politically and numerically dominant. While caste was important in politics during the colonial period when elections to the State Council often invoked caste considerations and support for a candidate was mobilized along caste lines, in contemporary Sri Lanka patron-client networks cutting across caste lines have proved to be more significant.

The Tamil-speaking population is similarly diverse. First of all, they are divided between those whose ancestors have, like the Sinhalese, been settled in the island for centuries, and those who have arrived relatively recently, beginning in the nineteenth century, to work in the tea plantations. The latter call themselves Hill Country Tamils, and they have sometimes been referred to as Plantation Tamils or Indian Tamils. The former are regionally divided into Jaffna Tamils hailing from the traditional seat of Sri Lankan Tamil culture, the Jaffna peninsula and its hinterland, and the Batticaloa Tamils of the Eastern Province. While most Tamils are Hindu, a minority is Christian and preponderantly Catholic. In addition to these regional and religious divisions, Tamil society is also splintered along caste lines, and caste relations in Tamil society tend to be more oppressive and conservative in their values than they are among the Sinhalese. An important form of political mobilization among Tamils prior to the rise of separatist politics was the anti-caste movement of low castes against the domination of the high-caste Vellalas (the analogue in Tamil society of the Sinhala Goyigama). Identity politics within the Tamil community has pitted region against region and caste against caste, and it is the shared threat of Sinhala domination that has papered over these fissures today.

The third important ethnic category in the Sri Lankan population are the Muslims. Although they are mostly Tamil speakers, their identity coheres around their religion. Islam was introduced to Sri Lanka by Arab traders, whose descendants still comprise an important component of the modern Muslim population, but most Muslims, especially those of the Eastern Province, are the descendants of Tamil-speaking converts. That Sri Lankan Muslims have resisted attempts by Tamil nationalists to include them in the Tamil fold and have generally aligned themselves with Sinhala majority parties has been a source of tension and conflict between the two communities.

In addition to these three major divisions in the island's population, there are numerous smaller ethnic groups, of whom the most significant are the Malays, the descendants of Malayan and Javanese soldiers of colonial armies stationed in the island, and the Burghers, descendants of unions between the Portuguese and Dutch and local women. Despite the diversity of the population, the vast majority of the people who inhabit the island of Sri Lanka have their origins in the mainland of India. Over millennia, waves of immigrants, mostly from the southern cone, settled on the island and crystallized over the centuries into the communities we know today, a process of ethnic formation that became politicized under colonial rule.

Identity became politically relevant during the colonial period, when the British sought to classify the population in order to govern it. The incremental steps toward self-rule taken during the nineteenth and early twentieth centuries was based on communal electorates, in which different communities (Sinhala, Tamil, Burgher) would elect their own representatives to the colonial Legislative Council. Nor was the numerical preponderance of Sinhalese in the population reflected in the allocation of seats. It is in this context, for instance, that Muslim identity began to crystallize, as the Muslim elite sought representation on the council in the teeth of claims by the Tamil elite that Muslims were ethnologically Tamil and should not be treated as a distinct group. The British in the event did not buy the argument, and created a "Mohammedan" seat in 1889.[34]

The Tamil elite of Jaffna had prospered under colonial rule and played a role in public and professional life quite disproportionate to their numbers. They saw themselves not as a minority but as an integral and, with the Sinhalese leaders, a coeval part of the Sri Lankan polity. They were, in fact, the initial leaders of the Ceylon National Congress, which sought self-rule from Britain. Unlike in British India, however, there was no attempt on the part of Tamil leaders to demand that the British partition the island prior to independence. Alarmed by the realization that universal franchise and noncommunal electorates (which they opposed) would inevitably benefit Sinhala politicians to their detriment, the Tamil elite made a number of attempts to secure their position, beginning with the unsuccessful demand put forward by G. G. Ponnambalam that 50 percent of all seats in Parliament be reserved for minorities.

The existential threat to the position of Tamils in Sri Lankan society came from three policies pursued by governments since 1956 (in one case since the 1930s). The land policy pursued since 1931 by D. S. Senanayake and governments since independence opened up jungle land in the northern and eastern regions of the country for settlement by mostly landless Sinhalese from the south and the hills. This was motivated in part by practical consideration (that was where land was available), but also by ideological considerations. These areas were regarded as the heartland of the historic civilization, which the Sinhalese claimed as their own, that had flourished there for fifteen hundred years until it ended in the fourteenth century. Tamils, however, saw this as an encroachment into areas in which they were the dominant community and a blatant attempt to change the demographic balance.

The second threat came, as we have seen, from the state's language policies, which obstructed an important traditional path to advancement in government service and also relegated an ancient language with a rich cultural tradition to second-class status in a country in which it had a historical presence for millennia.

The third major threat was the regulations laid down for university admission in 1969 and retained until the Jayawardene government came to power in 1977. Tamils were disproportionately represented in the universities, reflecting the very strong educational system in place in the Jaffna peninsula and a well-developed work ethic. Mrs. Bandaranaike's government abolished admission based on merit to the universities and introduced a scheme (called "standardization") that required students taking the university entrance examination from Tamil districts like Jaffna to score significantly higher than students elsewhere in the island—in effect, a system of affirmative action for the Sinhalese majority.

The people who were most alienated by the state's treatment of its Tamil citizens were the Tamil middle classes, who saw their avenues for advancement closed off by these policies and their right to full and equal citizenship threatened. The promulgation of the 1972 and 1978 constitutions, in the shaping of which they, as a community, had no role, served to aggravate their alienation, and the state's repression of peaceful dissent led, eventually, to the violent campaign of various militant groups to carve out a separate Tamil state in Sri Lanka from the Northern and Eastern Provinces.

Like the insurgency of the Janatha Vimukthi Peramuna (People's Liberation Front), the Tamil insurgency, too, is the product of the same social frustrations and caste antagonisms that gave rise to the JVP, although an additional major factor was the deepening divide between the Sinhala and Tamil population. The leadership of the LTTE, for example, was largely drawn from the low-status Tamil caste known as the Karaiyar,[35] which has historically been subordinate to the Vellalas. Both these movements resembled each other in their ideologies (chauvinistic and reactionary Tamil nationalism, on one hand, its Sinhala counterpart on the other); their class base (lower-middle class, drawing their cadre primarily from impoverished educated youth, most of whom were unemployed and facing a deteriorating economic situation); and their tactics (the use of terror).

The LTTE lost the war in part because its leadership failed to understand the geopolitical context in which it was operating, especially after the attacks on the United States in September 2011. Its behavior during the cease-fire that lasted from 2002 to 2005 demonstrated to the international community that it was not a serious partner in the search for a peaceful resolution of the conflict, and by the time war broke out again in 2005, it had been banned by the EU and the United States, and most significantly, India. Its early successes against the Sri Lankan military had made it overconfident of its own abilities, as indicated by its evolution from a guerrilla organization to a conventional force, employing the tactics of conventional armies. Given the overwhelming superiority in firepower and men of the Sri Lankan state, this turned out to be a fatal mistake. It had made a number of serious strategic errors, of which by far the most important was the assassination of Rajiv Gandhi. India went from being a patron of Tamil militancy and a source of its weapons and training in the 1980s, to being an implacable enemy of the LTTE that cooperated with the Sri Lankan government to destroy it. In the end it had become the instrument of the megalomania of one man, the secretive Velupillai Prabhakaran, who refused to settle for anything less than a separate state that he believed he could wrest by the force of arms. With no allies to turn to, and confronted by a government that was determined to crush it once and for all whatever the cost in blood, treasure, and reputation, the LTTE met its end as a fighting force on the shores of a lagoon in Sri Lanka's remote northeast, fighting, as it had always done, behind a shield of the civilians it had claimed to protect.

WOMEN'S POWER AND KINSHIP
NETWORKS IN POLITICAL LIFE

Kinship, in Sri Lanka and elsewhere, has been an important pathway to political power. For most of independence, the leadership of Sri Lanka's two main political parties was dominated by two families, the Senanayakes of the UNP (who along with their collateral branches produced four of the country's prime ministers) and the Bandaranaikes of the SLFP (who produced three, and a president). With the rise of President Mahinda Rajapakse and his three brothers to power in Sri Lanka, a third major political dynasty is in the making. Kinship connections are important at lower levels of power as well, for both men and women.

Kinship connections through husbands (and in the case of Benazir Bhutto and Indira Gandhi, through fathers) have been the means through which women leaders in South Asia have achieved power. Sri Lanka produced the world's first woman prime minister, Sirimavo Bandaranaike, in 1960, and she was reelected twice to office. She was the head of government for twelve years, but her last stint as prime minister was during the presidency of her daughter Chandrika Kumaratunga, who had taken control of the party her father had founded. Mrs. Bandaranaike had had no public role in politics prior to her husband's assassination but very rapidly took control of the party after her husband's death and won the general election held ten months later. Chandrika, the widow of a charismatic movie actor and politician named Vijaya Kumaratunga, became prime minister in 1994 and soon after ascended to the presidency to govern Sri Lanka for twelve years. Her career trajectory, however, was more akin to that of a male politician from a politically notable family; her family background and political networks facilitated her rise to power, and she proved to be a far more skillful and adept politician than her brother Anura, who had also harbored ambitions of being leader of the SLFP.

Chandrika Kumaratunga became involved in the SLFP, the party founded by her father, in various minor capacities upon her return from France, where she had been a student at the Sorbonne. In 1984 she and her husband left the SLFP to form the Sri Lanka Mahajana Pakshaya (Sri Lanka People's Party, SLMP), which was notable for being one of the few Sinhala-dominated parties to show real commitment to ethnic reconciliation. Following the assassination of her husband by the JVP in 1988 (which killed him because of his strong support for the Indo-Lanka Accord), she left the country for England and did not return until 1993, when she reentered politics as the SLFP's candidate for chief minister of the important Western Province, home to the capital city Colombo and the most urban and industrialized part of the country. She won by a landslide, a victory that immediately catapulted her to the forefront of Sri Lankan politics.

Despite the presence of these two very prominent women at the helm of Sri Lankan affairs for much of its existence as an independent state, and although women have enjoyed the right to vote for as long as men have (since 1931), women play remarkably little role in the politics of the country at any level. However, unlike much of the rest of South Asia, other than those peripheral areas such as northeast India that have been historically matrilineal, women in Sri Lanka have enjoyed relatively high status. The economist Bina Agarwal attributes this to the bilateral inheritance patterns of the island, which allow both men and women to inherit family land.[36] Although gender relations in Sri Lanka among all ethnic communities are patriarchal (more so among Tamils and Muslims and relatively less so among Sinhalese), the social indices for Sri Lankan women are much in advance of those of women on the subcontinent. There is gender parity in enrollment in education from primary through tertiary levels, women are well represented in the professions such as law and medicine, and they are active in civil society and the NGO sector. Women also comprise the major part of the labor force in three vital components of the national economy: in the tea plantations, in labor migration to the Middle East, and in the garment factories. But one area from which women are conspicuously absent is politics.

Women are systematically and significantly underrepresented at every level of government, from local administration to Parliament. Until 1981, women constituted at most 3.2 percent of candidates and 4 percent of members elected to Parliament. Little has changed since then. Women who do enter national politics tend to come, far more than men who do, from the higher strata of society, and to be generally better educated or at least to have gone to prestigious private schools. Because few women are elected (or in the days of the Senate [1948–1972] appointed) to Parliament, there have been correspondingly few women cabinet members. No women served in the cabinet at all between 1947 and 1960 and again from 1965 to 1970, while in other years, only a handful have served.

Cultural assumptions about the proper role of women no doubt have something to do with this anomaly; no less a personage than Sirimavo Bandaranaike observed on the occasion of International Women's Year in 1975 that it was her firm belief that "we should make it a point not to forget the very important place women are occupying in family life and in bringing up their children properly."[37] On the other hand, women occupy positions of public importance in civil society, and even in rural areas may be active in organizations such as Sarvodaya. Another possible explanation for the lack of women in politics advanced by Kearney is that it is primarily urban women who have the kind of life experiences that might interest them in a political career, and not women in the rural areas that are the jumping off point—via participation in local government—for national politics for many male politicians. There are also relatively few women in the state bureaucracy at higher levels; this too is an entry point into politics. The high levels of violence and intimidation that have come to characterize Sri Lankan politics in recent decades is also a significant factor discouraging women from political careers.

According to Kearney, when women do contest elections, they stand a better chance of being elected than men. Women who contest tend to do so as candidates of the major parties, while large numbers of men contest as independent candidates who, given Sri Lanka's strong party system, are doomed to defeat. When the party does well, so do all its women candidates, even though their numbers are few. Kearney also points out that the wife or daughter of a politician becomes familiar with political work by working in the constituency, and so is well placed to take over from him should the need arise. Sons, however, are more likely to engage in politics than daughters.

However, recent work by Vidyamali Samarasinghe on the 2011 local government elections in the Kandy district challenges Kearney's argument. She found that women seeking nominations at the local government elections, mostly without connections to powerful families or politicians, have to navigate corruption (nepotism, cronyism, and the not uncommon practice of selling nominations to the highest bidder) and the threat of violence. Samarasinghe notes that "the fear of sexual assault deterred all but a very few women from seeking nomination." Women who do receive nominations are then listed low down on the slate, so that even when their party wins, they fail to get elected under the system of proportional representation. Unlike in South Asia generally, there are no quotas for women in politics, and female representation in any legislature in Sri Lanka is less than 10 percent.[38]

Almost all women candidates have come from the Sinhala community, a notable exception being Ferial Ashraff, who, following a common pattern in South Asia, entered politics on the death of her husband, the leader of the Sri Lanka Muslim Congress. Of the seventeen women who were elected to Parliament between 1947 and 1981, more than half entered Parliament to replace "a husband or father who had died or who was barred from contesting for legal infractions."[39] Some of these women never achieved a career of their own and soon disappeared from politics; others, however, like Mrs. Bandaranaike herself, went on to contest elections on their own and to develop a notable career independent of the male relative who was their initial means of entry into politics.

Women participated extensively in the LTTE, and formed a substantial proportion of its combat units, but no woman rose to a significant public leadership position in its ranks; their roles were largely limited to being officers in its women's wing. Indeed, the induction of women (and later of children) into the combat forces of the LTTE after the Indo-Lanka Accord of 1987 was due to the shortage of male fighters; it did not arise from an "ideological shift in thinking about women's empowerment."[40]

SOCIAL COSTS OF MILITARISM

Sri Lanka today is the most militarized state in South Asia (see table 4.3), and that militarization has come at a heavy economic and social cost. It was not always thus. For the first three decades after independence, Sri Lanka had a small and inconsequential military, poorly trained and armed with obsolete equipment. This did not matter very much because the military's role was to support the police on those rare occasions when it was called out to maintain order. The military once represented the ethnic makeup of the country and the officer corps was drawn from the elite schools of Colombo and the more important towns. Two events changed

Table 4.3. Militarization in South Asia

	Sri Lanka	India	Pakistan	Bangladesh	Nepal
Military personnel per million population	8,000	1,300	4,000	1,000	2,700
Military expenditure as percentage of GDP	4.1	2.5	3.5	1.5	2.5

Source: Semu Bhatt and Devika Mistry, *Cost of Conflict in Sri Lanka* (Mumbai: Strategic Foresight Group, 2006), 12, www.strategicforesight.com/publication_pdf/79052Cost%20of%20Conflict%20in%20Sri%20 Lanka.pdf.

this situation. The first was the JVP insurgency of 1971, which the military was unable to contain on its own; it required the support of a number of countries, including India, Pakistan, China, and Great Britain. The second was the explosion of civil war that followed the anti-Tamil pogrom of July 1983. These two factors contributed to a reorganization and expansion of the military; training was significantly upgraded and its equipment modernized. It is the largest organized institution in Sri Lanka today.

Militarization in Sri Lanka exceeds that of Pakistan, a country in which the military exercises an overweening influence (see table 4.3). The military does not, however, exercise the same role or influence in Sri Lankan affairs that it does in Pakistan. The militarization is directly related to the nature of the war: as the LTTE grew in sophistication and strength, the Sri Lankan security apparatus grew as well, and its influence infiltrated every aspect of civilian society. This was the case even more emphatically in areas controlled by the LTTE, where everyone over fourteen years of age was compelled by the LTTE to undergo military training.[41]

When Sri Lanka's civil war began in 1983, the country's army was a modest force of twelve thousand men. When the war ended on May 18, 2009, the military had become one of the most powerful institutions in the country with over two hundred seventy thousand men and women under arms. It had also undergone a social transformation. Where, at independence the officer corps had consisted of the English educated elite, with significant numbers of Tamil and Muslim officers, drawn from the elite schools in Colombo, it had become transformed during the war into an almost entirely Sinhalese institution, and the officer corps democratized to include men drawn from the nonelite Sinhalese middle classes.

Service in the military became and continues to be one of the few opportunities available to young men from Sri Lanka's impoverished rural areas, whose economies have come to depend to a great extent on military service. In 2000, an ordinary soldier could earn $120 per month, more if he served in a combat zone, a sum significantly higher than the salary of a teacher with twenty years of service—about $80.[42] For most of the civil war, the army had been plagued by high rates of desertion and difficulty in filling its ranks, but in the final phase of the war, responding to the success of the military campaign, recruitment swelled; thirty thousand joined in 2007 alone, allowing the army to raise a number of new divisions. The regime has continued to recruit men even though the war is over and the LTTE no longer poses a military threat of any sort, and defense expenditures have been maintained at approximately the same level as the last year of the war. Almost half of all defense expenditure goes for salaries (and pensions) for Sri Lanka's all-volunteer armed forces, which is the most highly paid in all of South Asia,[43] the balance going toward the acquisition of heavy weapons and munitions. Similarly, both the air force and the navy have increased in both size and sophisticated weaponry. The military has become a major actor in contemporary public life in Sri Lanka and is routinely deployed in law enforcement functions, including the policing of demonstrations and the eviction of the poor from urban areas slated for development (the Urban Development Authority, busily transforming the face of Colombo, is now located in the Ministry of Defense and Urban Development). The military is also actively engaged in businesses, including hotel developments, construction work, and tourism.

The cost of this expansion of the armed forces has been significant. The military budget was less than 0.5 percent of GDP until the early 1970s, and about 1 percent of GDP through the early 1980s.[44] In 1982, the year before the Tamil insurgency ballooned into full-scale war, defense expenditure consumed 1.4 percent of the budget (0.5 percent of GDP). In the last year of Eelam War I, it increased to 9.39 percent of the budget, and in 2001, shortly before the cease-fire agreement took effect, defense accounted for 13.63 percent of government expenditure (3.87 percent of GDP), down from a high of 17.4 percent in 1996.[45] One study estimated the combined expenditure on the war by both sides at the time of the 2002 cease-fire at 510 billion rupees in 2001 prices (or about $6.2 billion). Expenditure on the military in 2001 exceeded both government expenditure on health (1.3 percent of GDP) and education (2.0 percent), both of which had been the main items in government budgets until the war escalated, and which have been negatively impacted by the rise in defense costs.

The cost of the war, however, goes well beyond the economic statistics. No one will ever know the exact number of those who died, but it is well over a hundred thousand, including about sixty thousand combatants on both sides. This figure excludes the tens of thousands who died in the JVP insurgency of 1987–1988. The thousands of civilians who have died include those caught in the crossfire as well as those targeted deliberately by both sides. No proper accounting has been made of the civilians who died in the final push against the LTTE. Tens of thousands have been wounded or have suffered deep psychological trauma. Hundreds of thousands are internally displaced, and the war has created a Tamil diaspora several hundred thousand strong, scattered around the world and deeply alienated from the land of their birth. Many Tamils have settled in Europe, Australia, and North America, while others live in refugee camps in India. The loss of their labor and professional skills also represents a significant cost to society.

The social costs of militarization are to be found not simply in the numbers of the dead and wounded, and in the economic costs of the war, but also in the violence that has become endemic in Sri Lankan society and in the deterioration of the rule of law. Thousands of soldiers deserted over the period of the war, some with their weapons; some of these men have joined underworld gangs and contributed to the sharp rise in the rate of violent crime. Politicians routinely resort to violence to intimidate their opponents, and the chronic politicization of the police means that they are able to do so with impunity.

Militarism has infiltrated into every area of civilian life, including into Buddhism, the religion of the majority. Many Buddhist monks were among the most enthusiastic supporters of a military resolution of the war. A striking example of this militarization is the commercial greeting cards sent at Vesak, a sacred holiday for Buddhists that marks the date on which the Buddha was born, attained enlightenment, and died. In recent years, inserted into the traditional scenes of peaceful temples and serene representations of the Buddha are jarring images of soldiers in uniforms as protectors of the faith, a juxtaposition alien to the traditional ethos of Buddhism.

When coupled with the immense powers enjoyed by the Sri Lankan president, the demands of national security have facilitated the erosion of the democratic system in place in 1948. As we have seen, the constitution of 1978 centralized power in the executive while weakening Parliament, and the war created the conditions under which that power could be exercised with relatively few restraints. The Sinhalese majority, including their representatives in Parliament, tolerated the introduction of repressive legislation and antidemocratic practices because they were initially aimed at quelling Tamil dissent; once established, however, such laws and practices can and have been used to quell dissent among the Sinhalese themselves. Human and civil rights have been drastically eroded by draconian legislation such as the Prevention of Terrorism Act but also by extrajudicial means. Torture is routinely used, including by the police when dealing with ordinary criminal (i.e., nonpolitical) suspects.[46] The press has been effectively muzzled by a campaign of intimidation and murder whose most prominent victim was Lasantha Wickrematunga, the editor of the outspoken *Sunday Leader* newspaper; none of the many murders and disappearances of journalists since the Rajapakses came to power have been seriously investigated or solved by the police. Violence in democratic politics has become endemic, as the conditions created by the war have facilitated the expansion of violence in political life.

STRUGGLES OVER RIGHTS:
THE WOMEN'S MOVEMENT IN SRI LANKA

By Camena Guneratne

The women's movement in Sri Lanka is almost one hundred fifty years old, dating from the period of British colonial rule. It has to be viewed in a time frame of a precolonial society that, to a large extent, gave women an equal place through a century and a half of colonial rule and the changes brought about during that period, and continuing into more than sixty years of the postcolonial era. The latter period has been marked by ethnic and other forms of conflict, historical divisions of caste, class, ethnicity, and religion, together with a development paradigm that has increased social and economic inequalities and put extreme pressures on the democratic system of governance. The feminist movement and the experiences and responses of women have been colored by this history and environment.

The Early History of Women in Politics

Women's activism in the public sphere has been dated to the latter half of the nineteenth century. This period has varied impacts on women, some of whom suffered economic exploitation, while others benefited from the expansion of women's education and employment. From this period through to the early twentieth century, women gained employment as unskilled workers in both plantations and urban areas, as well as in skilled jobs such as nursing, teaching, and secretarial work. These experiences largely depended on class and ethnicity.[47]

These varied experiences of women gave rise concurrently to an increased political awareness among them, including on women's rights. This manifested itself in the formation of organizations in the first half of the twentieth century such as the Ceylon Women's Union, the Ceylon Women's Association, the Young Women's Christian Association, the Lanka Mahila Samiti, the Women's Political Union, the Eksath Kantha Peramuna, and the Ceylon Women's Franchise Union. The last organization, formed in December 1927, was instrumental in campaigning for and obtaining adult female suffrage.

However, the involvement of women in politics in this period was not broad based and was mainly confined to the middle-class elite. These women were characterized by high levels of education, class position, and the influence of husbands and other male relatives. They did not confine themselves to demands for the franchise and also championed claims for social equality, child welfare, and the rights of minorities and marginalized groups.[48] As Jayawardena and de Alwis comment, given the context of the times, such activism predominantly reflected nationalist or anticolonial sentiments.

Political Participation of Women in the Post-Independence Era

Although women, as we saw above, have not been prevalent in the mainstream political process, this does not mean that they are completely detached from the country's politics. Their involvement has been more visible from outside the political system, and there have been instances of women mounting successful challenges to the establishment. Examples of this phenomenon are the two Mothers' Fronts, of the north and south of the country, which arose in the late 1980s and the early 1990s in the context of the conflicts and armed struggles that prevailed in both areas. Both movements were a response to state-instigated terrorism, when husbands, sons, brothers, and other male relatives were arrested, tortured, and killed. In the north this took place in the context of the separatist war, and in the south in the context of a bloody youth insurrection. Women mobilized in protest, holding marches, public meetings, and interviews to voice their concerns, expose the activities of the state, and enforce their rights.

Both movements achieved their purpose in that in both north and south the repressive activities of the state were curtailed or ended. However, in both instances the movements died out as the separatist organizations in the north and opposition political parties in the south attempted to take control of and manipulate them for their own political ends. Having lost their autonomy and their purpose, women left the movements, which ultimately fizzled out.[49]

The Women's NGO Movement

Nongovernmental organizations (NGOs) have become a significant force in Sri Lanka in the last three decades and this includes what can be loosely termed women's organizations. Many NGOs dating from this time claim some specific features, which, however, are sometimes ambiguous. They generally claim to be voluntary; not for profit; and working in areas such as development, human rights, environment, and gender. At a later point of time, in the context of the recently ended war, humanitarian issues and peace building became a theme for NGOs, moving on to more political organizations that actively confront the state on issues such as good governance, legal reform, and integrity of elections. NGOs with a specific feminist focus emerged in the 1970s, a period in which the United Nations had declared 1975 as the International Year of Women and 1976–1985 as the UN Decade for women.[50] In addition, many NGOs that do not claim to be specifically "women's organizations" have also been working on issues of women's rights, for example, in areas of land ownership, labor, political participation, and violence against women.

Several reasons have been suggested for the emphasis on women and gender as a focus for both categories of NGOs. One is that it is largely donor driven and the other is that it is a response to current development trends. Three types of women's organizations operating in Sri Lanka have been identified as nongovernmental organizations (NGOs), private voluntary organizations (PVOs), and community-based organizations (CBOs). The early organizations were PVOs run by volunteers, depending on funds generated by fund-raising activities and membership fees, while NGOs are modeled on other development organizations run by full- or part-time staff raising money from donor agencies. The CBOs operate in much the same way but are located within the communities they work in with staff from that same community.[51] These organizations engage in a wide variety of activities ranging from antipoverty programs and problems of women in particular spheres such as plantations, free trade zones, and the Middle East to problems of violence against women.

NGOs, both women specific and otherwise, have been working on a range of issues affecting women. These include income generating and poverty alleviating projects and provision of basic needs including shelters for battered women. NGOs have also advanced the women in development discourse, furthering projects on economic empowerment, entrepreneurship, and skills training. More important, these organizations have engaged the state on issues of women's rights and equality with a high degree of success. Largely due to the lobbying efforts of women's NGOs, the Women's Bureau was founded in 1978, followed by the Women's Affairs Ministry in 1983. Further campaigning resulted in Sri Lanka signing the UN Convention for the Elimination of All Forms of Discrimination against Women (UNCEDAW) in 1981. In 1992 a Women's Charter was drafted based upon the provisions of the Convention through a consultative process between women's groups and government agencies. The National Committee of Women (now the National Commission on Women) was established in 1994. Further advocacy over the years has resulted in amendments to the penal code on violence against women, including the enactment of a Domestic Violence Act and strengthening of rape laws. Ad hoc campaigns have also taken the form of protests on specific issues, particularly during the period of conflict, on state-instigated violence against female victims. These campaigns have been supported to a great extent by organizations engaged in in-depth feminist research.[52]

Conclusion

The critique of the women's movement in Sri Lanka has focused on several issues, and these have been articulated by Carmen Wickramagamage.[53] One such criticism relates to the method of engagement of women's organizations with the state. Wickramagamage takes the view that the relationship between the two is one of collaboration and cooperation. While this has paid dividends to some extent, she also questions such a conciliatory approach. She attributes this method, to begin with, to the fact that Sri Lankan women, unlike their Indian counterparts, did not have to fight hard to achieve certain objectives, due to a more positive social environment and lack of overt oppression. As a result, organizations tended to rely on the goodwill of the state to achieve their goals. Nevertheless some much-needed reforms have not taken place due to the apathy of both the governmental and nongovernmental sectors. Further, when women's interests clash with those of other political interests, they are often subsumed by the latter. For example, attempts to amend discriminatory or women-unfriendly laws among certain ethnic groups have not progressed due to a greater interest in maintaining ethnic harmony.

Wickramagamage also notes that even where laws may guarantee equal rights, this has not often translated into true equity and equality for women due to social and cultural constraints. There are instances where gender equality cannot be achieved by legal amendments or state intervention alone, and a more vocal, activist approach is needed to change social and cultural norms. The women's movement in Sri Lanka has, in general, not adopted such an approach for varying reasons. These range from the desire not to appear radical, to the fact that the "movement" is not sufficiently broad based and cohesive. These factors, together with women's disengagement from party politics and the class and urban/rural divide among women's organizations have necessarily limited the movement's effectiveness and the range of its impact.

The women's movement in Sri Lanka has a mixed record. Although it has achieved many things for women, particularly as regards rights-based issues, it has tended to focus on matters that are of exclusive concern to women. As a movement it has not united to address matters of national concern such as the ethnic conflicts and youth insurrections that the country has experienced in the last few decades, nor the development paradigm that is increasing economic inequalities and furthering social injustice. It has thus played a limited role and has not realized its full potential as a social movement.

NOTES

1. Robert N. Kearney, *The Politics of Ceylon (Sri Lanka)* (Ithaca, NY: Cornell University Press, 1973), 44.

2. The role of the governor-general is discussed in A. Jeyaratnam Wilson, "The Role of the Governor-General in Ceylon," *Modern Asian Studies* 2, no. 3 (1968): 193–220.

3. E. F. C. Ludowyk, *The Story of Ceylon* (New Delhi: Navrang, 1985), 278–79.

4. Dilesh Jayanntha, *Electoral Allegiance in Sri Lanka* (Cambridge: Cambridge University Press, 1992).

5. Amita Shastri, "Estate Tamils, the Ceylon Citizenship Act of 1948 and Sri Lanka Politics," *Contemporary South Asia* 8, no. 1 (1999): 66.

6. K. M. de Silva, *Reaping the Whirlwind: Ethnic Conflict, Ethnic Politics in Sri Lanka* (New Delhi: Penguin Books, 1998), 52.

7. Calvin A. Woodward, *The Growth of a Party System in Ceylon* (Providence, RI: Brown University Press, 1969), 135.

8. James Manor, *The Expedient Utopian: Bandaranaike and Ceylon* (Cambridge: Cambridge University Press, 1989), 316.

9. Ibid., 327.

10. T. D. S. A. Dissanayaka, *Dudley Senanayake of Sri Lanka* (Colombo: Swastika Press, 1975), 71.

11. The Tamils constituted 86.35 percent of the population of the Northern province in 1981. In the Eastern province, they were 41 percent, but when Tamil-speaking Muslims (32 percent) were included, the proportion of Tamil-speaking people in the Eastern Province rose to 73 percent of the total. The Muslims, however, do not regard themselves as ethnically Tamil and adhere to a distinct identity based on their religion. As a community, they have stayed aloof from the Tamil struggle for a separate state.

12. South Asia Terrorism Portal, "Vaddukoddai Resolution," www.satp.org/satporgtp/countries/shrilanka/document/papers/vaddukoddai_resolution.htm (accessed March 17, 2010).

13. A. Jeyaratnam Wilson, *The Gaullist System in Asia: The Constitution of Sri Lanka (1978)* (London: Macmillan, 1980), xiii.

14. It was possible to adopt this amendment only because of a crisis precipitated by the withdrawal of the Sri Lanka Muslim Congress from President Kumaratunga's government in 2001. The JVP, which had ten seats in Parliament, then agreed to support the government on condition that the amendment, to which the opposition had agreed, was adopted.

15. See Basil Fernando and Sanjeewa R. Weerawickrame, *A Baseline Study on Torture in Sri Lanka* (Hong Kong: Asian Human Rights Commission, 2009) (available at http://www.ahrchk.net/pub/mainfile.php/books/327/); and Kishali Pinto-Jayawardena, *Post-War Justice in Sri Lanka: Rule of Law, the Criminal Justice System and Commissions of Inquiry* (Geneva, Switzerland: International Commission of Jurists, 2010) (available at http://reliefweb.int/report/sri-lanka/post-war-justice-sri-lanka-rule-law-criminal-justice-system-and-commissions-inquiry) for discussion of the use of torture and the violation of human rights by state forces, and the failure of the criminal justice system to address these violations.

16. W. A. Wiswa Warnapala and L. Dias Hewagama, *Recent Politics in Sri Lanka: The Presidential Election and the Referendum of 1982* (New Delhi: Navrang, 1983).

17. *Economic Review* (People's Bank, Sri Lanka), April–May 1988, 41.

18. Asoka Bandarage, "Women and Capitalist Development in Sri Lanka, 1977–87," *Bulletin of Concerned Asian Scholars* 20, no. 2 (1988): 77–78.

19. "Ranasinghe Premadasa." *Encyclopedia of World Biography*, 2nd ed. (Detroit: Gale, 2004), 12:437–39.

20. Secretariat for Coordinating the Peace Process, Sri Lanka, www.peaceinsrilanka.org/negotiations/slmm-statistics (accessed March 17, 2010).

21. Henry Chu, "Ruling Sri Lanka Is a Family Affair," *Los Angeles Times*, August 5, 2007, http://articles.latimes.com/2007/aug/25/world/fg-brothers25.

22. See Lasantha Wickrematunge, "And Then They Came for Me," *Sunday Leader*, January 11, 2009, www.thesundayleader.lk/archive/20090111/editorial -.htm. This is a posthumous indictment of the government for his murder.

23. Lakshman Yapa, "The Poverty Discourse and the Poor in Sri Lanka," *Transactions of the Institute of British Geographers*, New Series 23, no. 1 (1998): 96–97.

24. Quoted in Satchi Ponnambalam, *Dependent Capitalism in Crisis: The Sri Lankan Economy, 1948–1980* (London: Zed Press, 1981), 24.

25. Ronald Herring, "Economic Liberalization Policies in Sri Lanka: International Pressures, Constraints and Supports," *Economic and Political Weekly* (India) 22, no. 8 (1987): 325–33.

26. Ponnambalam, *Dependent Capitalism in Crisis*, 23.

27. G. Chris Rodrigo, "Manufacturing Industry," in Ajitha Tennakoon, ed., *Sri Lankan Economy in Transition* (Colombo: Vijitha Yapa Publications, 2009), 9.

28. H. Nakamura, P. Ratnayake, and S. M. P. Senanayake, "Agricultural Development: Past Trends and Policies," in W. D. Lakshman, ed., *Dilemmas of Development: Fifty Years of Economic Change in Sri Lanka* (Colombo: Sri Lanka Association of Economists, 1997), 250.

29. Rodrigo, "Manufacturing Industry," 8.

30. Nimal Sanderatne, "Agricultural Development: Controversial Issues," in Saman Kelegama, ed., *Economic Policy in Sri Lanka: Issues and Debates* (New Delhi: Sage, 2004), 200–201.

31. Rodrigo, "Manufacturing Industry," 11.

32. John M. Richardson, "Violent Conflict and the First Half Decade of Open Economic Policies in Sri Lanka: A Revisionist View," in Deborah Winslow and Michael D. Woost, eds., *Economy, Culture, and Civil War in Sri Lanka* (Bloomington: Indiana University Press, 2004), 48.

33. David Dunham and Sisira Jayasuriya, "Liberalisation and Political Decay: Sri Lanka's Journey from Welfare State to a Brutalised Society," International Institute of Social Studies Working Paper 352, p. 11 (http://repub.eur.nl/res/pub/19097/wp352.pdf).

34. Qadri Ismail, "Unmooring Identity: The Antinomies of Elite Muslim Self-Representation in Modern Sri Lanka," in Pradeep Jeganathan and Qadri Ismail, eds., *Unmaking the Nation: The Politics of Identity and History in Modern Sri Lanka* (Colombo: Social Scientists' Association, 1995), 67.

35. Bryan Pfaffenberger, "Crucible of Violence: The Social, Economic, and Political Roots of Tamil Militancy in Northern Sri Lanka" (paper presented at the 17th Annual Conference on South Asia, Madison, WI, 1988).

36. See the discussion in Agarwal's *A Field of One's Own: Gender and Land Rights in South Asia* (Cambridge: Cambridge University Press, 1994), especially 120–32 on Sri Lanka.

37. Quoted in Robert N. Kearney, "Women in Politics in Sri Lanka," *Asian Survey* 21, no. 7 (1981): 745.

38. Vidyamali Samarasinghe, "Impact of Corruption on Women's Political Participation in Sri Lanka" (paper presented at the 41st Annual South Asia Conference, Madison, WI, October 12, 2012).

39. Quoted in Kearney, "Women in Politics in Sri Lanka," 737.

40. Radhika Coomaraswamy, "Women of the LTTE: The Tigers and Women's Emancipation," *Frontline* (Madras), January 10, 1997, 62.

41. An excellent discussion of the impact of militarization on popular culture is Neloufer de Mel, *Militarizing Sri Lanka: Popular Culture, Memory and Narrative in the Armed Conflict* (New Delhi: Sage Publications, 2007).

42. Michele Gamburd, "The Economics of Enlisting: A Village View of Armed Service," in Deborah Winslow and Michael D. Woost, eds., *Economy, Culture and Civil War in Sri Lanka* (Bloomington: Indiana University Press, 2004), 159.

43. "Pak-Army More Professional Than India, Sri Lanka Despite Less Salary," *Frontier Star*, June 21, 2009, http://tinyurl.com/nyg5zgp.

44. Nira Wickramasinghe, *Sri Lanka in the Modern Age* (Honolulu: University of Hawai'i Press, 2006), 316.

46. National Peace Council of Sri Lanka, *The Cost of War: Economic, Social, Human Costs of the War in Sri Lanka* (Colombo: Author, 2006), 7.

46. "Torture Endemic in Sri Lanka Police—Rights Group," Reuters, June 5, 2008, http://in.reuters.com/article/2008/06/25/idINIndia-34230920080625.

47. Kumari Jayawardena and Malathi de Alwis, "The Contingent Politics of the Women's Movement in Sri Lanka after Independence," in Swarna Jayaweera, ed., *Women in Post-Independence Sri Lanka* (New Delhi: Sage Publications, 2002).

48. Selvy Thiruchandran, *The Politics of Gender and Women's Agency in Post-Colonial Sri Lanka* (Colombo: Women's Education and Research Centre, 1997).

49. Thiruchandran, *The Politics of Gender*.

50. Udan Fernando, *NGOs in Sri Lanka: Past and Present Trends* (Kohuwala, Sri Lanka: Wasala Publications, 2003).

51. Fernando, *NGOs in Sri Lanka*; Carmen Wickramagamage, "Sri Lankan Organisations for Women: A Critical Appraisal," in Sirima Kiribamune, ed., *Women and Politics in Sri Lanka: A Comparative Perspective* (Kandy, Sri Lanka: International Centre for Ethnic Studies, 1999).

52. Jayawardena and de Alwis, "The Contingent Politics of the Women's Movement."

53. Wickramagamage, "Sri Lankan Organisations for Women."

SUGGESTED READINGS

De Votta, Neil. *Blowback: Linguistic Nationalism, Institutional Decay, and Ethnic Conflict in Sri Lanka*. Stanford, CA: Stanford University Press, 2004.

Manor, James. *The Expedient Utopian: Bandaranaike and Ceylon*. Cambridge: Cambridge University Press, 1989.

Spencer, Jonathan. *Sri Lanka: History and the Roots of Conflict*. London: Routledge, 1990.

Tambiah, Stanley Jeyaraja. *Sri Lanka: Ethnic Fratricide and the Dismantling of Democracy*. Chicago: University of Chicago Press, 1986.

Wickramasinghe, Nira. *Sri Lanka in the Modern Age: A History of Contested Identities*. Honolulu: University of Hawai'i Press, 2006.

Winslow, Deborah, and Michael D. Woost, eds. *Economy, Culture, and Civil War in Sri Lanka*. Bloomington: Indiana University Press, 2004.

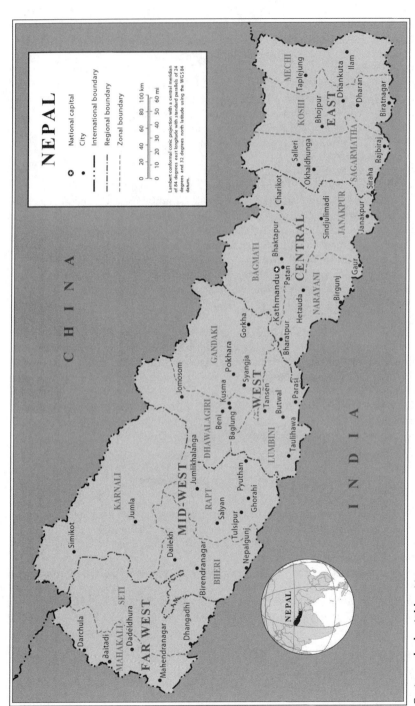

Cartography by Ashley Nepp

5

٭

Nepal

Pratyoush Onta and Seira Tamang

The territorial state of Nepal as we know it today was largely in existence by the second decade of the nineteenth century. Nepal was not
part of the British Empire in South Asia and thus never experienced an
anticolonial movement leading to independence as was the case for the
other countries in the region. However, it did experience a pro-demo-
cratic movement against a set of domestic autocratic rulers—known as
the Ranas—during the late 1940s. When this movement succeeded in
overthrowing that regime in 1951, a new era began in the modern history of Nepal. Hence the period of Nepali history covered in this chapter
roughly coincides with the postindependence period of the other states
in South Asia.

POLITICAL HISTORY

Territorial Consolidation and Rana Rulers

In the early part of the eighteenth century, the central Himalayan region
was home to several small kingdoms. Gorkha, a relatively poor kingdom governed by the Shah kings, was one of them. Its fortunes began to
change under the leadership of King Prithwinarayan Shah (r. 1742–1775),
who set out to expand the territory under his control through a process
of conquest. Over the course of the next seventy years, Gorkha annexed
territories five hundred times larger than itself.[1] When Gorkha lost the
Anglo-Gorkha war of 1814–1816 and had to give up a substantial part
of its territories to the British East India Company under the terms of

TIMELINE: NEPAL

1949	Formation of the Communist Party of Nepal (CPN)
1950	Formation of the Nepali Congress (NC) Party
February 1951	End of the Rana oligarchic regime following armed rebellion led by NC and the formation of the Rana-NC government
March 1951	Interim Government of Nepal Act, 1951, promulgated
November 1951	M. P. Koirala becomes the prime minister
March 13, 1955	King Tribhuvan dies and King Mahendra assumes full control
November 1957	King Mahendra rules Nepal directly
1958	King Mahendra announces elections for a bicameral legislature; committee to draft a new constitution of Nepal is appointed; government to prepare for the general elections formed under the chairmanship of Subarna Shamsher
February 12, 1959	The Constitution of Nepal, 1959, promulgated
February–April 1959	First general elections held; NC wins a majority in the House of Representatives (HOP)
May 1959	NC leader B. P. Koirala becomes the prime minister; King Mahendra forced to share the political stage with popularly elected politicians
October 1959	*Birta* system of land tenure abolished
December 15, 1960	King Mahendra dismisses the Koirala-led government, dissolves the Parliament, and assumes all executive powers; Koirala and his associates are jailed
1961	NC begins its armed opposition to King Mahendra's regime
1962	The Constitution of Nepal, 1962, promulgated and with it the Panchayat system is formally established; NC halts its armed opposition
1967	First Amendment to the 1962 Constitution
1968	B. P. Koirala freed and goes into self-exile in India
1972	King Mahendra dies; Birendra succeeds as king

1975	Second Amendment to the 1962 Constitution
1976	B. P. Koirala returns to Nepal with a policy of "National Reconciliation"; is arrested and tried for treason
April 1979	Student-led protests begin
May 24, 1979	King Birendra announces a national referendum on the future of the Panchayat system
May 2, 1980	Referendum held; a "reformed" Panchayat sytem wins
December 1980	Third Amendment to the 1962 Constitution
1981	Direct elections to the National Panchayat, the highest tier of the Panchayat system, held
1985	NC-led movement of noncooperation, satyagraha, is launched against the Panchayat system; explosions in Kathmandu and elsewhere by the Janabadi Morcha led by the Ramraja Prasad Singh; satyagraha called off
1986	Second direct elections to the National Panchayat held
1989	Trade and Transit Treaty with India lapses and India executes an economic blockade-like situation
1990	*People's Movement I* puts an end to absolute monarchy and the Panchayat system
April 19, 1990	An interim government with NC's Krishna P. Bhattarai as prime minister is formed
November 9, 1990	The Constitution of Nepal, 1990, is promulgated; constitutional monarchy is formally established but Nepal is retained as a "Hindu" kingdom
1991	National elections to the HOR are held; NC forms a majority government with Girija Prasad Koirala as prime minister
1994	Mid-term polls held; CPN (Unified Marxist and Leninist) emerges as the largest party without a majority and forms a new government with Man Mohan Adhikari as prime minister
1995	CPN-UML-led government is brought down and an era of coalition politics begins and lasts until 1999
1996	CPN (Maoist) launches its armed insurgency under the leadership of Prachanda

1999	National elections are held; NC wins majority and leads the government
2001	King Birendra and several members of his royal family are killed inside the royal palace; his brother Gyanendra becomes the new king
2001	Unsuccessful first cease-fire and talks with the CPN (Maoist)
2002	HOR dissolved and fresh call for national elections is made
October 2002	King Gyanendra assumes direct control and rules Nepal extra-constitutionally
2005	Citizens' Movement for Democracy and Peace begins to organize mass rallies and meetings in different parts of the country
November 2005	Twelve-point agreement reached between the CPN (Maoist) and the Seven Party Alliance in New Delhi
April 2006	*People's Movement II* ends King Gyanendra's direct rule
May 18, 2006	Nepal declared a secular state
November 21, 2006	Comprehensive Peace Agreement (CPA) signed between the government of Nepal and the CPN (Maoist)
January 15, 2007	The Interim Constitution of Nepal, 2007, promulgated
April 10, 2008	Elections to the Constituent Assembly (CA) held with a two-year mandate to write a new constitution; CPN (Maoist) emerges as the largest party
May 2008	Nepal is declared a republic by the first meeting of the CA
August 15, 2008	CPN (Maoist)–led government with Prachanda as prime minister is formed; it resigns on May 4, 2009
May 23, 2009	CPN-UML-led government with Madhav Kumar Nepal as prime minister is formed
2010	The tenure of the CA is extended as the parties are unable to write the new constitution by the original deadline
2010	Another CPN-UML-led government with Jhala Nath Khanal as prime minister is formed

August 2011	CPN (Maoist)–led government with Baburam Bhattarai as prime minister is formed
May 2012	The tenure of the CA expires after the Supreme Court rules against its further extension; political uncertainty reaches a new height
March 2013	Baburam Bhattarai–led government is replaced by a government led by the chief justice Khil Raj Regmi; it is given the task to hold elections to the second CA

the Treaty of Sagauli, its size was more or less reduced to today's Nepal. Gorkha's territorial conquest was one of the most remarkable political achievements during the eighteenth century in South Asia.

Despite the phenomenal growth in the size of the Kingdom of Gorkha, its leadership continued to come from a small set of families from its heartland. Members of this class, however, did not have an independent source of power and relied upon the king's generosity for their economic security. This was the situation in the first half of the nineteenth century when one family in the royal court, the Kunwars, usurped power in 1846 and retained it for a century. By eliminating his rivals, Jang Bahadur Kunwar was able to relegate the Shah king to the margins of everyday politics and retitle his clan as the Ranas.

The twentieth century began with Nepal under the firm grip of Rana premier Bir Shamsher and his brothers. In the fifteen years since usurping power by murdering their uncle Ranaudip (Jang Bahadur's younger brother and successor), the Shamsher brothers had consolidated their rule. They were the chief beneficiaries of the increasingly efficient extractions of a pan-Nepal agrarian bureaucracy. After Bir Shamsher's death in 1901, his four younger brothers and two nephews ruled Nepal until 1951. Among them, Chandra Shamsher (r. 1901–1929) and Juddha Shamsher (r. 1932–1945) ruled for particularly long periods. During Chandra Shamsher's reign, opposition to Rana rule emerged among Nepalis living in India. At home, Chandra Shamsher ruthlessly prosecuted anybody who talked about political freedom. Modern schools, libraries, and media outlets were largely nonexistent during his reign.

In the 1930s, political activists inside Nepal began to organize against the regime, and in the early 1940s, many of them were arrested by the Rana regime. Four were executed, and others were given long prison terms. Instead of extinguishing opposition to the Ranas, this action generated anti-Rana feelings among a new cohort of political activists. In 1947, several of them came together in the Indian city of Calcutta to form the Nepali Rashtriya Congress party. In March 1947, when mill workers in the southeastern city of Biratnagar went on strike, its party members joined the strike. The Ranas responded with the ruthlessness they were known for and several of the party workers were arrested. The party's subsequent call for a civil disobedience movement was responded to by people in various cities of southern Nepal. [2] Meanwhile, with British withdrawal from India in August 1947, the Ranas lost one of their chief external supporters. To show that the Rana regime was capable of reforms, Padma Shamsher promulgated the Government of Nepal Act in January 1948, despite the opposition of more hard-line Ranas led by his cousin and successor Mohan Shamsher. The act, which retained the hereditary right to succession both for the king and the Rana premier of Nepal, introduced a façade of democracy while real power continued to rest with the Rana premier. Since Padma Shamsher was forced out of office shortly thereafter, this act remained valid only on paper.

In the meantime, another political formation, the Nepal Prajatantrik Congress, came into existence in August 1948, advocating force to end the Rana regime. Subarna Shamsher and Mahabir Shamsher, two erstwhile members of the Rana oligarchy who had fallen out with their relatives, formed this party in Calcutta. The two Congress parties merged in April 1950 to become the Nepali Congress (NC) party. In fall 1950, the NC decided that an armed struggle was necessary to end Rana rule. Those who could not fit into the political folds of the NC formed the Communist Party of Nepal in 1949.

Armed NC activists defeated Rana forces in several towns in late 1950. In the last stages of the anti-Rana movement the then Shah monarch, King Tribhuwan, along with most members of his family, went to Delhi. Talks between him, the Ranas, and NC leaders were brokered by the Indian state with terms set by the latter.[3] The reality and perception of Indian interference in Nepali politics has been a constant feature in the national political debate ever since. The Ranas finally capitulated in February 1951. A few years after the rest of South Asia had emerged from colonial rule, Nepal opened a new chapter in its history.

The Political Experiments of the 1950s

In February 1951, King Tribhuwan returned to Nepal from India and announced that a new constitution would be framed by an elected Constituent Assembly (CA). The first government of post-Rana Nepal was largely a Rana-NC coalition government and was led by the last Rana prime minister himself. It did not even last for a year and was replaced by a new cabinet in November 1951, headed by a Congress leader, M. P. Koirala.

At the end of March 1951, the "Interim Government of Nepal Act" came into force. Although certain rights, such as freedom of speech and peaceful assembly, freedom to form associations, and freedom to practice any occupation were recognized, executive power was vested in the king, who could exercise it directly or through a prime minister nominated by him. The king was also given ultimate legislative power and was declared the supreme commander of the security forces. The act provided for an independent judiciary, a Public Service Commission, and an Election Commission. Nevertheless, the main purpose of the Interim Act was to allow the Shah monarch to consolidate his position following the demise of the Ranas.

During the first half of 1952, the relationship between Prime Minister M. P. Koirala and his half-brother and NC party president B. P. Koirala deteriorated. The former was seen by the latter to be too accommodative of the interests of the conservative camps in Nepal and not firm in pursuing the socially more progressive programs of NC. Intraparty wrangling led to the fall of the Congress government in August 1952. King Tribhuwan decided to rule directly with the help of a group of six royal councilors.[4]

This government lasted until June 1953 when Tribhuwan again asked M. P. Koirala to form a new government. A couple of months earlier, M. P. Koirala had formed a new party, the National Democratic Party. The second premiership of M. P. Koirala lasted until March 1955 but the shape of his cabinet changed several times during this period. This is noteworthy for several reasons. First, politicians from various parties could not learn to work with each other. Inter- and intraparty feuds prevented them from collectively promoting a democratic system in Nepal. Second, as the health of his father, Tribhuwan, deteriorated, Crown Prince Mahendra emerged as the power center in Nepali politics (see box 5.1). Third, the absolute powers of the executive branch of the government were enhanced by the amendment of the Interim Government of Nepal Act in 1954. The independence of the judiciary provided for in the original act was ended, and the judiciary was no longer allowed to question the activities of the executive, now headed by the King. When King Tribhuwan died on March 13, 1955, the elections to the CA had still not taken place.

King Mahendra's intent to further consolidate the power of the monarchy was made clear from the kind of politics he pursued. His refusal to hold elections to the CA showed his disdain for institutionalizing representative democracy. For the next four years, he either ruled Nepal directly or he nominated prime ministers with limited authority to govern. During this period, some of the main parties were focused on either forcing the king to grant room to cultivate democratic governance or engaging in crass opportunism to be in his favor. In early August 1955, King Mahendra announced that the general elections would be held in October 1957. During most of the fall of 1955, he engaged in several rounds of political negotiations with various parties, with the intention

Box 5.1. King Mahendra Bir Bikram Shah Dev (1920–1972)

King Mahendra was born in June 1920 in Kathmandu as the first son of King Tribhuwan and his wife Kanti Shah. He was educated within the palace compound by private tutors. He married Indra Rajyalakshmi, a granddaughter of the then reigning Rana prime minister, Juddha Shamsher, in May 1940. He had six children with her. After her death in 1950, he married her younger sister, Ratna Rajyalakshmi.

King Mahendra became the king of Nepal in March 1955. He consolidated the Shah monarch's hold on Nepali politics by continuously postponing the elections to a constituent assembly that would have written a new constitution of Nepal. In 1959 he promulgated a constitution for a multiparty parliamentary setup under an all-powerful monarch. He grudgingly accepted the outcome of the first national elections held that year but dismissed the B. P. Koirala–led government and representative democracy in December 1960.

King Mahendra then established the Partyless Panchayat System, which revolved around the undisputed authority of the king. He established diplomatic relations with many countries around the world. He traveled extensively within Nepal to gain firsthand recognition of his people, wrote poetry, and patronized the arts. He died of a heart attack in early 1972.

of forming a new government. These were futile exercises because he wanted the parties to come to power under terms of reference he had set. In early October 1957, it was finally confirmed that the general elections could not be held then. No new dates were announced. In mid-November 1957, King Mahendra dismissed the government and began to rule Nepal directly. When the king continued to engage in delaying tactics, oppositional politicians launched a noncooperation movement in December 1957. Subsequently, King Mahendra proclaimed that the elections would be held in February 1959.

In February 1958, King Mahendra announced that the election would be for a bicameral legislature and not to the CA. He also added that it would be held according to the terms of a constitution that had not yet been drafted at the time of his announcement. In March 1958 a committee to draft the constitution was appointed and two months later, in May, he announced the formation of a government to prepare for the general election. This government consisted of representatives from four political parties and two independents. There was no prime minister but the NC's Subarna Shamsher was the chairman of this council of ministers. This government immediately passed acts related to the election and the political parties began to prepare their campaigns accordingly.

The 1959 Constitution and National Elections

On February 12, 1959, the new constitution was promulgated by King Mahendra superseding the Interim Government of Nepal Act. Instead of the constitution emerging from a body of representatives (a constituent assembly), the people of Nepal were "given" a constitution by the king evoking his traditional rights to do so. The 1959 Constitution guaranteed personal and political rights to the people of Nepal. A bicameral legislative body with a lower house (called the House of Representatives, HOR) consisting of 109 elected representatives and an upper house (Senate) consisting of 36 elected and nominated members was envisaged as the Parliament. The party with a majority of representatives in the lower house would form the government. The cabinet was to be headed by a prime minister. A Supreme Court was also envisaged and was assigned the responsibility of making the final interpretations of the same document.

However, this constitution vested the king emergency powers that allowed him to suspend the entire constitution and assume all powers otherwise vested in the Parliament or any other governmental body.[5] The king was also the supreme commander of the army. In short, this constitution guaranteed a powerful monarchy with a multiparty parliamentary democracy. Several leading politicians were not happy with the Constitution but thought it better to work with it than risk another showdown with the king.[6]

The elections were held in several phases between February 18 and early April 1959. The NC and other parties campaigned over the country with their election manifestoes. This was the first occasion for Nepalis living in far corners of the country to taste competitive party-based politics. The NC's election manifesto emphasized agrarian reforms, promising to preserve the rights of the peasants and the tillers over the land by ending feudal exploitation and to increase the productivity of the land using scientific means. It also made the village the fulcrum of its policies on decentralization. Also on the NC's agenda was the promotion of industries. Apart from promoting the use of the Nepali currency throughout Nepal (at that time the Indian currency was as widespread as the use of Nepali currency), the NC promised to promote small industries on the principle of cooperatives, middle-size industries by supporting private investment, and large-size industries through state investment or state-invited foreign investment. In the elections, the NC won a majority of 74 of the 109 seats in the HOR. The rightist party Gorkha Parishad, United Democratic Party, and the Communist Party won 19, 5, and 4 seats, respectively. Many of the major leaders of the other political parties failed to be elected. Almost twenty years after the elections, B. P. Koirala attributed the NC's success to its national network of active workers.[7]

The NC Government and the Royal Coup

B. P. Koirala (see box 5.2) became prime minister in late May 1959. For the first time since the end of Rana rule, the monarch was forced to share the political stage with popularly elected politicians. Koirala became the emblem of the hope that the search for a new democratic post-Rana Nepal had finally found its track. Once in office, the NC government set out to

---

Box 5.2. Bishweshwar Prasad Koirala (1914–1982)

Bishweshwar Prasad Koirala, better known as B. P., was born in September 1914 in Varanasi, India, as the first son of Krishna Prasad Koirala and his third wife, Dibya Koirala. The senior Koirala was a successful businessman based in the Nepali southern city of Biratnagar. When B. P. was barely three, Rana premier Chandra Shamsher confiscated the family's property. The Koiralas spent the next twelve years in impoverished exile in India. B. P. studied at the Banaras Hindu University, and between 1938 and 1942, became involved in the Indian independence movement through the Congress Socialist Party. He spent the next three years in Indian jails.

In 1947 Koirala established the Nepali Rashtriya Congress, which became the Nepali Congress (NC) in 1950. The NC ousted the Ranas through the 1950–1951 armed rebellion. Koirala became the home minister for a few months in 1951. In May 1959, he became the first elected prime minister of Nepal. His political ideas were influenced by Gandhi and social democracy as interpreted by the likes of Indian political thinkers Rammanohar Lohia and Jayaprakash Narayan.

During the 1960s, while in prison, Koirala wrote several acclaimed literary works. After being released in October 1968, he went into exile in India from where he returned in 1976, only to be imprisoned again. He led the pro-multiparty camp during the 1980 national referendum. Before he died in July 1982 of cancer, Koirala recorded his oral autobiography, *Atmubrittanta*. He was survived by his wife Sushila, their three sons, and one daughter.

implement policies and programs that matched its preelection promises. It abolished the *birta* system of land tenure—land gifted by the state to individuals and one largely outside of the tax net—through a law passed in October 1959. In fall 1960, the NC government signed a new trade and transit treaty with India that provided greater independence for Nepal to import from third countries. It also introduced changes in the administrative machinery of the country. In the maintenance of law and order, the NC faced several challenges in the form of protests and disturbances by an array of individuals and organizations that were not happy with its programs.

It was Nepal's tragedy that the workings of an ambitious people's leader, B. P. Koirala, were read by an equally ambitious monarch as a direct threat to him. On December 15, 1960, using various pretexts as justification, King Mahendra used the emergency powers of the 1959 Constitution to dismiss Prime Minister Koirala's government, dissolve the Parliament, assume all executive power, and imprison most of the important leaders of all political parties. Koirala has claimed that he did not see this coming.[8]

Analysts have provided various reasons to explain King Mahendra's abolition of the multiparty political dispensation provided for in the 1959 Constitution of Nepal. Chatterji surmises that three factors might have propelled King Mahendra to take this decision: "(a) a feeling of uncertainty; (b) a desire for total political power; and (c) an obsession with destiny."[9] The three were related to each other. His feeling of uncertainty came in part from the growing popularity of B. P. Koirala, whose understanding of the location of monarchy in Nepali politics as a constitutional entity—that is, constitutional monarchy—threatened to render the position of the monarch as one without substantial power, as in the Rana-led days. King Mahendra, Chatterji notes, also saw the monarchy as the ultimate sovereign power in Nepal, the institution around which the rest of the power structure was to function. He adds, "To King Mahendra, Nepal was an idea, and none but he could realize what it was destined to be."[10] King Mahendra's move found support among the landowners who were opposed to the NC's land reform agenda, orthodox Hindu monarchists, oppositional leaders who had been wiped out from active politics in the 1959 elections, and, most important, the army.

The Panchayat Era under King Mahendra (1960–1972)

After dismantling the political infrastructure of a nascent representative democracy, King Mahendra sought to consolidate his hold over Nepali politics and society. Within three weeks after taking over, he engaged with the citizens of Nepal on three occasions through public addresses

or messages. In those texts, he emphasized the following four charges/
claims: (1) Leaders of the political parties had only indulged in personal
or party-specific interests that were detrimental to the welfare of Nepal.
(2) The NC government's misrule promoted corruption and stunted the
ability of the administration, resulting in a pervasive breakdown of law
and order in the country. Antinational elements flourished in this environment, and the unity of the country and nationalism was under threat;
since saving the unity of Nepal was ultimately the responsibility of the
monarch, he had undone the multiparty political setup. (3) Under his
leadership, the country would strive toward overall development and
since the political parties were an impediment in this process, they had
to be banned. (4) This process required a democratic system that could
strengthen its roots in the soil of Nepal, unlike the previous system, which
had been imported from elsewhere. This system, he claimed, was to be
built upon traditional Panchayats—councils of elders—found in many
parts of Nepal.

To consolidate his rule and prevent challenges to his authority, King
Mahendra jailed or exiled politicians belonging to the major parties who
did not support his action. Koirala and many of his close associates were
imprisoned for many years and when released in October 1968, they went
into self-exile in India. Those not opposed to Mahendra's rule were either
brought into the folds of the new political dispensation or allowed to live
quietly in the country. The king also worked to create intellectual justi-
fications for the Panchayat system. This consisted of disseminating propaganda making the case for why, in his view, a multiparty democratic
setup was inappropriate for Nepal. For such propaganda to succeed, the
media had to be tightly controlled. Media owned by the government such
as the newspaper *Gorkhapatra* and the only radio station, Radio Nepal,
was turned to the service of the regime. Newspapers were subject to censorship and editors who were critical of the king's regime were variously
punished.

The Panchayat Constitution of 1962

After his initial grip on power was ensured, King Mahendra promulgated the constitution of what was called the Panchayat system on
December 16, 1962. Nepal was declared "an independent, indivisible
and sovereign monarchical Hindu State" with Nepali as its national
language. All citizens were declared equal and protected from discrimination. It also guaranteed freedom of religion but active conversion was
prohibited. Rights to property and freedom of speech were also guaranteed. However, the 1962 Constitution did not guarantee the right to form
unions and associations. This was later included in the First Amendment

in 1967. The Constitution was also silent on the banning of political parties, a move that had already been realized via the king's proclamation on January 5, 1961.

The Panchayat Constitution devised a multitier political setup under the king with whom the sovereignty of Nepal was vested. All executive, legislative, and judicial power was ultimately derived from the king. It put village/town Panchayats at the bottom of the system, showcasing this feature as the proof of the decentralization of power. District Panchayats and Zonal Panchayats were the next tiers up with the National Panchayat (NP) at the apex of the system. Members of the NP were elected from the tier immediately below in the Panchayat hierarchy (ninety members) or by the so-called class and professional organizations (fifteen members).[11] NP members were also elected from among the university graduates (four members) and nominated by the king (sixteen members). The NP was mostly a legislative body. A Supreme Court was also provided for, with the king appointing its judges.

After the First Amendment in 1967, the adjective *partyless democratic* was added to the Panchayat system's name in the preamble of the Constitution. While adding the freedom to form unions and associations, the First Amendment explicitly stated that "no political party or any other organization, union, or association motivated by party politics shall be formed or caused to be formed or run." The ideal of participation of a maximum number of individuals in various tiers of the Panchayat system was central to its political logic and claims to being a democratic system. As two of its apologists put it, the Panchayat form of democracy was suitable to a country like Nepal, as it was "simple to understand, viable to maintain and elastically integrated."[12]

The multitier Panchayats, the class organizations, and the Ministry of National Guidance—responsible for propagating the Panchayat system and supervising the work of the various constituting elements of it—were already in place before the 1962 Constitution was announced. This ministry was the first to be set up (in February 1961), and its initial task was to commission and distribute propaganda supporting the king's coup and its aftermath. It later played a role in putting together the political infrastructure of the new system. Legislation establishing the village, town, and district Panchayats was passed between January and November 1962, but the ones dealing with the zonal and national Panchayats followed the 1962 Constitution. Although the multitier setup gave the impression that a large number of individuals were involved in Panchayat system politics and each member of the NP had reached that apex body via representative means of upward political mobility, this was not the case. One could become an NP member by securing the support of a tiny group of individuals working in the lower tiers of the system.[13]

The class organizations and the graduate constituency were designed to fill up some of the vacuum left behind by the banning of the political parties. The former was a mechanism to, at least in theory, coordinate class and professional interests in accordance with Panchayat values. Instead, they seem to have played a minor oppositional role within that system. The graduate constituency was a mechanism to secure the participation of college graduates in Panchayat politics at the NP level without having to deal with its lower tiers. It was eventually used by some candidates who did not believe in the tenets of the Panchayat system to expose its democratic pretensions and advocate for full restoration of multiparty democratic politics.[14]

With the forced demise of the multiparty political structure, competitive politics based on the values and visions of the political parties had come to an end in Nepal. For King Mahendra what mattered was simply the bureaucratic delivery of development that could be showcased as resulting from the Panchayat system under the king. Although the rhetoric of decentralization and people's participation in various tiers of the Panchayat were good for Panchayat propaganda, in reality, by closely controlling the mechanisms of popular participation and possibilities for political upward mobility, a system that was highly centralized around the monarch was put into place.

Panchayat Governments and the Opposition

After dismissing the government of B. P. Koirala on December 15, 1960, King Mahendra created a Council of Ministers under his chairmanship with five ministers and four assistant ministers. The new Panchayat Constitution was promulgated in mid-December 1962, and by 1963, with the constitution in place and elected Panchayat politicians occupying its various tiers, the new political system finally began to assume full shape. The opposition also became active. Beginning in the fall of 1961, NC workers in India, who were committed to armed opposition against the king's regime, attacked several locations in the southern Nepali plains known as the Tarai. In January 1962, the king's entourage was attacked in the town of Janakpur in east Nepal. The government responded by passing laws that gave it more power to control and detain Nepali citizens. Relations with India deteriorated, but when the Sino-Indian conflict started in the fall of 1962, the Indian establishment discontinued its tolerance of rebel NC activities. The NC leadership in exile in India decided to halt its activities in December 1962. Opposition to Panchayat rule from members of other political parties was not significant except for the merger of the Gorkha Parishad with the NC in late 1961.

The 1967 amendments to the Panchayat Constitution introduced further mechanisms through which the king controlled the whole system. During the same year, King Mahendra began another extra-constitutional experiment, the Back to the Village National Campaign (BVNC). This was another effort to emphasize that the focus of the Panchayat system was village Nepal, and those who hoped to be good Panchayat workers had to cut their political teeth in service to villagers.[15] But this campaign, too, was not effective. The dominant logic of the state expressed itself in a language of development and a call for service to the nation by all of its citizens through adherence to the "partyless" Panchayat system under the leadership of the king. Using foreign aid, King Mahendra launched several development infrastructure projects (especially roads and hydropower) and put into place various national and sector-specific development plans.

The Panchayat Era under King Birendra (1972–1990)

King Birendra succeeded his father after the latter's death in early 1972. Unlike his father, Birendra had been educated in some of the best universities in the world, and some critics even hoped that he would immediately restore full multiparty democracy. Instead, he continued on the same course of Panchayat politics that he had inherited. The Second Amendment to the Panchayat Constitution in December 1975 further enhanced central control of national politics. The most important change came with respect to the BVNC, which was made a constitutional body with the task of supervising those who were brought into the Panchayat fold and monitoring their activities. Its central committee consisted of nine members, all nominated by the king. Second, the size of the National Panchayat was increased from 125 members to 135. Although the number of elected members was increased from 90 to 112, the representation from the class organizations was repealed and the graduate constituency was abolished. This recognized that these arrangements had not worked to the benefit of the Panchayat system.

Koirala's Return and the National Referendum

As the changes introduced by the Second Amendment were being implemented, B. P. Koirala, then sixty-two years old, and his NC colleagues came back to Nepal from their self-imposed exile in India on December 30, 1976. This return, dubbed a move for "national reconciliation" by Koirala, was one that was supposed to reconcile differences between the Nepali Congress and the king. In an appeal published on the day of his return, Koirala explained that the crisis then faced by Nepal regarding its national existence emanated from the lack of national unity. He added: "National unity can only be achieved on the foundations of democracy."[16]

Despite his call for a national reconciliation, when Koirala arrived in Nepal, he was arrested but was subsequently allowed to leave the country for short durations for medical treatment. Leading members of the Panchayat establishment tried their best to make sure there would be no possibility of reconciliation between the king and Koirala. However, after he met King Birendra in late October 1978, Koirala seemed very optimistic about the possibility of change.[17]

In early April 1979, student-led protests began in Nepal. The initial protest was by a small group of students against the execution of the former prime minister of Pakistan, Zulfiqar Ali Bhutto, but when they were assaulted by police, the protests spread across the country. On May 23, 1979, a riot took place in the capital city of Kathmandu in which buildings, including the one that housed government-owned newspapers, were burnt. To defuse the crisis, the king announced a national referendum on the future of the Panchayat system on May 24, 1979, and relaxed controls over freedom of expression and assembly.[18] The people were asked to choose between a multiparty system and a suitably reformed Panchayat system. However, the regime did not specify just how the Panchayat system would be reformed, nor did it acknowledge the legality of political parties as they were still banned under the Panchayat Constitution. King Birendra announced in December that irrespective of the referendum's results, members of the legislature would be elected on the basis of universal adult suffrage, the legislature would recommend the appointment of the prime minister, and the cabinet would be responsible to the legislature.

Many politicians demanded that certain preconditions be met to ensure that the referendum was fair. These included the disbanding of the Panchayat government and the formation of an independent government to supervise the referendum. However, B. P. Koirala, who directly linked his call for national reconciliation to the king's decision to hold the referendum, did not agree with this view.[19] Koirala may have thought that if pressed with preconditions, King Birendra might rescind his decision to hold the referendum under pressure from his hard-liner relatives, who thought that there was no alternative to the Panchayat system.[20] For Koirala it was more important to use the occasion to reach out to the people after nineteen years in the wilderness.

The verdict of the referendum, held on May 2, 1980, favored the Panchayat system by a margin of about 400,000 votes. Many politicians and commentators who were critics of the Panchayat system said that the verdict was doctored. But B. P. Koirala described it as "inexplicable" and added that since the votes received by the multiparty side were massive, future democratic strategy had to be built "on the basis of this committed support."[21] In a speech he delivered to the Socialist International in Madrid in November 1980, Koirala blamed the lack of specificity in the choice given to the people, the misuse of governmental resources by the Panchayat side, and the use of state-owned radio to broadcast content against those championing the multiparty cause for the loss. He also added that the lack of resources in his party was also responsible.[22]

The Third Amendment

King Birendra announced the Third Amendment to the Panchayat Constitution in December 1980. This most important amendment included direct elections of the members of the National Panchayat (NP) through adult franchise, hence opening the process to the public at large. But there was a catch: election candidates still had to be members of one of the class organizations. The prime minister was to be appointed on the recommendation of the NP and the council of ministers was to be responsible to the NP. The role of the Back to the Village National Campaign (BVNC) as defined in the Second Amendment was eliminated, but another entity was instituted within the NP to perform some of its disciplining functions. The ban on political parties was continued. The king's powerful role in the Panchayat system was retained. These amendments were viewed as inadequate by most leaders in the multiparty fold. Their main criticism was focused on the fact that the referendum's verdict had favored an "improved Panchayat system" and they interpreted that to mean that its partyless character was no longer its foundational feature. In addition, they also stressed that the Third Amendment failed to adequately take into consideration the fact that over 45 percent of voters had favored a multiparty system in the referendum.

Elections to the NP were held in May 1981. While initially some sections of the opposition parties showed interest in taking part, by the time it was held, most of them had decided to boycott the elections. In the public domain, B. P. Koirala justified the NC's nonparticipation by saying that the party would be betraying the trust the people had reposed in it if it "accepted the constitution and fought the elections."[23] However, it is possible that the NC decided not to contest after field reports suggested that its candidates would lose in a humiliating fashion.[24] In the twenty-plus years since political parties had been banned, the NC leadership had shrunk due to death, retirement, state repression, and defection to the Panchayat side. No party-based or ideology-based competition was involved in the elections, and hence voters were influenced by the caste, personal links, and wealth of the candidates. In June 1981, the new NP recommended Surya Bahadur Thapa as the PM.

An era of Nepali politics that had begun with B. P. Koirala's return to Nepal thus came to an end. The four and half years between December 1976 and June 1981 were very interesting if only because King Birendra was forced to abandon the centrally controlled version of the Panchayat system. The students' movement and the referendum introduced degrees of political openness in Nepali society that had been denied by Panchayat leaders since 1960. Although parties were still banned, their space in Nepali society was ensured by the politics of these years.

Throughout the early 1980s, while the Panchayat politicians engaged in factional battles, the opposition was hardly visible. When B. P. Koirala died in July 1982, the NC did not seem to have a definite program of action. After the May 1981 elections, Koirala had not wanted the NC to engage in a struggle to overthrow the Panchayat system, but nor had he wanted his party to surrender to it. In so deciding, he had vetoed the position advocated by his NC colleagues, some of whom advocated launching a mass movement against the Panchayat system. Koirala opposed this for several reasons. His deteriorating health may have led him to believe that he could not physically lead such a movement, and he did not think that his deputies in the NC—Ganesh Man Singh, Krishna Prasad Bhattarai, and Girija Prasad Koirala—were capable of taking over the leadership from him on such a matter. He also thought that his party lacked the organization to launch such a movement. On the other hand, the various factions of the Nepali Communist movement were active in different parts of the country, but their strength too remained largely invisible. As part of the internecine struggle within the Panchayat fold, Surya Bahadur Thapa was dislodged as the prime minister in mid-1983 and succeeded by Lokendra Bahadur Chand, who held the post until a couple of months prior to the next national elections in May 1986.

Satyagraha and Panchayat's Swan Song

After four years of continuous party-building work across the country, in early 1985, the NC leaders had the confidence to call for a movement of noncooperation, satyagraha, against the Panchayat regime. In those years, apart from hardcore political activists, NC had successfully recruited teachers and other professionals into its fold. Protesting the ban on political parties and demanding a democratic system, thousands of NC party activists participated in various activities across Nepal. A chief form of protest included picketing in front of the chief district officer's office in each district as well as submitting petitions with demands. Political activists not associated with NC had also joined this peaceful movement in small numbers. By late spring 1985, several hundred political activists had been arrested. However, between June 19 and 22, explosions rocked

Kathmandu and some other cities, killing several persons and injuring many more. The NC said it had nothing to do with the bombings and suspended its satyagraha campaign. An organization called the Janabadi Morcha, led by Ramraja Prasad Singh, claimed responsibility for the explosions, which were described as the beginning of its efforts to make Nepal a democratic republic. These explosions gave the government further excuse to arrest more of its opponents. Many of the NC leaders were kept in jail through the summer of 1985.

In May 1986, the second national elections to the NP were held. Although NC and some factions of the Nepali left did not take part in these elections, some other leftist factions did. Six leftist political activists were elected to the new NP, where they made it a point to demand a multiparty system. In 1987, NC party activists did take part in the elections to local political bodies but did not succeed in the numbers that had been anticipated. In spring 1989, the trade and transit treaties with India came to an end. Facing an economic blockade-like situation, the government found itself to be the target of popular frustration with the system. This trade impasse, as well as worldwide uprisings against authoritarian regimes, provided the context for the origin, in the fall of 1989, of a decisive movement launched by the NC and the United Left Front (a coalition of different Nepal Communist Parties) against the Panchayat system. This *Jana Andolan* (People's Movement), lasting from January to April 1990, was led by NC leader Ganesh Man Singh. It resulted in the demise of the Panchayat system on April 16, 1990. Absolute monarchy in Nepal was significantly tamed.

By keeping Nepal's traditional power structure—revolving around the king, the army, and a bureaucracy controlled by high-caste Hindus—intact, the Panchayat system stunted the possibilities of democratic growth in Nepal. Certain levels of educational achievements as well as the gradual development of nongovernmental sectors of employment introduced some degrees of freedom in Nepali public life during the latter half of the Panchayat era. But these freedoms were severely policed and circumscribed. Dissenters spent long years in prisons or in self-exile. The judiciary on the whole did very little to protect the rights of dissenters. Professionals who refused to endorse the system suffered massively in terms of career dislocations. Because nongovernmental organizations (NGOs) were also policed by the state, the few NGOs that were allowed could hardly function as alternate sources of ideas and inspiration. Despite the platitudes of Panchayat apologists, Nepali society in general paid a heavy price for the ambitions of the two kings, Mahendra and Birendra. A political system that in 1960 harped on about creating an exploitation-less society left Nepal in 1990 as one of the poorest countries in the world.

The Multiparty Era (1990–2002)

After the Panchayat system was defeated, an interim government led by NC's Krishna P. Bhattarai was installed on April 19, 1990. It had two main political tasks: to oversee the making of a new constitution and to hold the first national elections.

The Constitution of 1990

The making of the 1990 Constitution was a tussle between a king who sought to retain as much of the executive and other powers formerly enjoyed by him and political parties that wanted to strip the monarchy of all executive power and place the army under the civilian government. After months of negotiations, the Constitution was finally promulgated on November 9, 1990, as a document of compromise that reflected the interests of the left parties, the Nepali Congress, and the king.

The 1990 Constitution of Nepal provided for a bicameral Parliament: a 205-member House of Representatives (HOR) elected from the same number of constituencies under the first-past-the-post system every five years and a 60-member National Assembly (NA). The HOR was the main legislative body. A piece of legislation became an act when it passed through both houses of Parliament and received the king's assent. As a constitutional monarch, the king's executive actions could now take place only on the recommendation of the prime minister or other constitutionally provided bodies. The army was placed under a National Defence Council (NDC), which consisted of the prime minister, the defence minister, and the chief of the army staff. The army could only be deployed by the king upon the recommendation of the NDC. This provision controversially ensured that the army was not under the direct control of the civilian government.

The party with a simple majority in the HOR would form the central government. A Council of Ministers led by the prime minister was the government's executive wing. It was responsible for the country's administration through a set of ministries and a civil service whose higher offices were filled through an entry-level selection process controlled by the Public Service Commission. The executive was also assisted by bodies such as the National Planning Commission (NPC), responsible for drawing up the country's development policies in the form of multiyear plans. Other constitutionally recognized bodies included the Election Commission (EC), the Public Service Commission (PSC), and the Commission for the Investigation of Abuse of Authority (CIAA). The Constitution provided for an independent judiciary consisting of the district courts, appellate courts, and the Supreme Court, which is the apex court of the country.

The 1990 Constitution was a landmark document for the guarantees of fundamental rights it provided to the citizens of Nepal. These included the right to freedom of expression, to the establishment of organizations, to information, and to protection from censorship. Article 18 provided for the cultural and educational rights of all Nepali citizens. The Directive Principles of the State mentioned the possibility of the state adopting affirmative action policies on behalf of historically marginalized population groups.

Compared to the 1962 Panchayat Constitution, the 1990 Constitution was progressive in its recognition of the multiethnic and multilingual nature of Nepali society. However, this Constitution also contained many elements that were discriminatory. Foremost in this list, as discussed below, was the assertion that Nepal was a Hindu kingdom. By making citizenship of the newborn dependent on the citizenship of the child's father, the Constitution also discriminated against all Nepali women.[25]

The 1991 Elections and Multiparty Politics (1991–2002)

The elections to the HOR were held in May 1991, with 65 percent of eligible voters participating. With 110 of its candidates elected to the 205-member HOR, the Nepali Congress was able to form a majority government. The Communist Party of Nepal–Unified Marxist and Leninist (CPN-UML)—which had given up on Maoism, won 69 seats. A formation of Maoist parties, United People's Front Nepal, won 9 seats. The Tarai-based Nepal Sadbhavana Party won 6 seats. The two factions of the party of former-Panchayat politicians, the National Democratic Party, won a total of 4 seats.[26] The campaigns of the two largest parties were noteworthy for their lack of specificity regarding the kinds of programs they would launch to meet the development and other needs of the Nepali people. This is understandable given that during the three decades of Panchayat rule, the single objective for politicians who opposed that regime was the realization of a multiparty democratic setup. However, given the lack of practice of governance, once that setup was available, broad rhetorical exercises were all that they had to offer in 1991.

In terms of its social base, the NC was a party backed by the urban wealthy classes and the rural landed elite.[27] Although democratic socialism was its mantra when the party was led by B. P. Koirala, by the early 1990s the party's economic policy was mostly oriented toward a market economy with state planning for the public sector. The CPN-UML claimed to represent the working classes, impoverished peasants, and industrial workers, but its support base mostly came from the middle peasantry and the petite bourgeoisie. It had a relatively more extensive grassroots organizational presence than the NC. Its economic policy placed a premium on the state's role but was also friendly to the private sector. However, at the time of the May 1991 elections its own commitment to multiparty democracy was suspect. The third-largest party in the HOR, United People's Front Nepal, was a loose coalition of Maoist parties committed to abolishing the monarchy and achieving a "people's democratic republic." They did not believe in the parliamentary system as defined in the 1990 Constitution but contested the 1991 elections to expose its inadequacies. The fourth-largest party, Nepal Sadbhavana Party, articulated the grievances of the Madhesi residents of Nepal's Tarai.

Factional fighting within the Nepali Congress (over party-government relationships and appointments to higher office) led the prime minister, G. P. Koirala, to dissolve the HOR in 1994 and call for mid-term polls. This time, no party won a majority in the HOR. The CPN-UML emerged as the largest party in the HOR with eighty-eight seats and NC had eighty-three.[28] The CPN-UML's Man Mohan Adhikari became the first elected Communist prime minister in South Asia and led a minority government that lasted from November 1994 to September 1995. It was brought down by a successful no-confidence motion proposed by the NC, National Democratic Party, and Nepal Sadbhavana Party. These three parties formed the next government under the leadership of NC's Sher Bahadur Deuba. Various coalitions ruled Nepal until the 1999 national elections returned NC as a majority party. However, between 1999 and October 2002 three NC politicians successively became prime minister—Krishna Prasad Bhattarai, Girija Prasad Koirala, and Sher Bahadur Deuba—again largely due to in-fighting within the party itself. This era was brought to an end when King Gyanendra sacked Sher Bahadur Deuba in October 2002, going beyond his constitutional prerogatives to do so. From then until April 2006, the king ruled extra-constitutionally until a mass movement prepared the stage for the end of monarchy.

After the successful holding of the 1991 elections, the Nepali people had expected the leaders of the new democracy to show a serious commitment toward the understanding of the problems that beset Nepali society. But that was not to be. Because of endless bickering between and among themselves, political parties devoted little intellectual energy toward clarifying the problems that confronted Nepal. They presented no program of action that described the hard choices Nepal needed to make in the early 1990s so that the country might have a viable future that could encompass even those Nepalis who have been victims of history for far too long. It was in the midst of this sense of hopelessness that the Maoist insurgency grew to rock the foundations of the Nepali state.

The Maoist Insurgency (1996–2006)

The Communist Party of Nepal (Maoist) (CPN [Maoist]) began its war against the Nepali state in February 1996. Its ultimate aim was to capture the state to make the country a "people's republic." Among its forty demands was that Nepal be declared a secular state and that where "ethnic communities are in the majority, they should be allowed to form their own autonomous governments." It also demanded that discrimination against the Tarai be ended, that land should belong to the tillers, that jobs be guaranteed for all, and minimum wages fixed for workers in industries and agriculture. The CPN (Maoist) also wanted poor farmers to be exempt from repaying loans and free and scientific health services and education to be available to all.

The dominant view of how the conflict began falls within what experts call the "grievance theory" of conflicts. It holds that economic and social inequalities are the fundamental causes behind the rise of the Maoists in Nepal.[29] Combined with the efficacy of organized activism of the far left in the mid-western hills and the ineptitude of successive governments in the 1990s in dealing with the initial demands of the Maoists, the proponents of this view conclude that structural inequalities in the system provided the fertile grounds for Maoism to grow. In other words, the perception of the rebellion as a conduit to rectify existing grievances and seek justice for Nepal's downtrodden informs the dominant view of how the conflict started and grew.

An alternate explanation first locates the conflict within the long history of theoretical battles for ideological purity in terms of revolutionary ideals.[30] Through a long process of ideological contestations, CPN (Maoist) emerged as the faction within the Communist movement in Nepal that asserted that "objective conditions" existed in Nepal for an armed revolution and hence it declared a war against the Nepali state in 1996. This idea was put forward mainly by a core group of Maoist ideologues and guerrillas led by Pushpa Kamal Dahal "Prachanda" (see box 5.3) for whom social justice in Nepal could only be obtained through an armed revolution. This explanation also holds that the growth of the Maoist insurgency was made possible by agencies (e.g., the king, political parties, Nepal Army, India, etc.) who, deliberately or otherwise, contributed to the reduction of risks for the Maoists with respect to the recruitment of guerrillas and finances needed to run their operation. Hence, while the strong formulation of the alternative "greed model" of conflicts (in which civil wars are motivated by the desire to acquire wealth especially in the form of natural resources) does not apply to Nepal, an argument can certainly be made for its weak formulation in which the opportunity for rebellion is tied to risks associated with accessing finances (domestic

Box 5.3. Pushpa Kamal Dahal "Prachanda" (1954–)

The chairman of the Communist Party of Nepal (Maoist), Pushpa Kamal Dahal, was born in December 1954 in a village in Kaski, a hilly district in central Nepal. He is the eldest son of Muktiram and Bhavani Dahal and is now better known by his nom de guerre, "Prachanda," which means "the fierce one." Muktiram was a poor farmer and his family migrated to Chitwan in south-central Nepal in 1962.

Prachanda was educated in a village school and married Sita Poudel when he was only fifteen. They have three daughters and a son. Prachanda became a committed Communist while studying for a BS in agriculture. Subsequently he briefly taught in several schools before becoming a full-time worker of the Communist Party of Nepal (CPN) in 1979. Two years later, he was already on the "wanted" list of the Panchayat police and thus went underground.

He quickly rose through the party ranks of the radical faction of the CPN, first siding with his mentor Mohan Bikram Singh and later with the faction led by Mohan Vaidya "Kiran." In 1989 Prachanda replaced Kiran as the general secretary of CPN (Mashal). After some intermediate permutations the party was renamed the CPN (Maoist) in 1995 when it decided to go for an armed struggle, which was launched in February 1996 under Prachanda's leadership. He emerged from underground politics in mid-2006, some weeks after the successful People's Movement II. The CPN (Maoist) was returned as the biggest party in the elections to the Constituent

and international) through the deployment of youth available in large numbers for recruitment. Put this way, the noninvolvement of the Royal Nepal Army in the Nepali state's responses to the insurgency before 2001 forces us to examine the post-1990 Nepali state as a constellation of not only inept political parties but also an obstructive monarchy with a tight hold on the use of the army as a credible state institution affecting the risk calculus of the insurgents. In this view, the success of the Maoist insurgency must be attributed to the ability of the leaders of CPN (Maoist) to exploit the weaknesses of and fissures in the Nepali state to its maximum advantage.[31]

By 2001, the Maoists had come to a position from where they could largely dictate the agenda for national politics in Nepal. The state's response until then had been to try to contain the insurgency through the use of the police force under the home ministry. On the evening of June 1, 2001, King Birendra and several other members of the royal family were killed by the crown prince Dipendra within the premises of the royal palace. Dipendra himself was found to be in a coma and died a few days later. This event made the erstwhile prince Gyanendra the king of Nepal. Long known for his dislike of the mainstream political parties, Gyanendra's arrival on the scene as the king further compounded the difficult relationship between the civilian government and the state army. The Maoists did their best to exploit the situation by stressing that Gyanendra should not be recognized as king. The army was also asked not to support the new king. Along with their rhetorical efforts, the Maoists continued their attacks on state forces. In attacks in early July 2001 in several districts, several dozen policemen were killed. A few days later, several dozen others were held hostage from a place called Holeri, and this act eventually precipitated the resignation of Prime Minister Girija Prasad Koirala when it became clear that the army, upon counter-orders from the Royal Palace, had not followed his orders to secure the release of the abducted policemen.

Koirala's resignation paved the way for the appointment of his fellow party member Sher Bahadur Deuba as the prime minister. Under Deuba, a cease-fire and the first round of talks between the government and Maoist rebels took place during the second half of 2001. The cease-fire lasted for about four months. However, the talks did not succeed, and following their breakdown, the government headed by Deuba quickly moved to mobilize the army against the Maoists for the first time, claiming there were no other alternatives. On November 26, Prime Minister Deuba's cabinet decided to impose a state of emergency in Nepal and asked King Gyanendra for the issuance of an order regarding this as provided in the 1990 Constitution. King Gyanendra obliged on the same day and also approved the mobilization of the Royal Nepal Army. He also promulgated the Terrorist and Disruptive Acts (Control and Punishment) Ordinance. Given the long list of rights that were suspended during the state of emergency, the environment in Nepal for the enjoyment of democratic rights by its citizens deteriorated abruptly. The level of violence went up significantly after that date, evident in the ever-increasing death toll of the conflict.

Deuba was known to be more pliable to the interests of the army and the Palace.[32] He was responsible for emphasizing the military solution to the conflict and creating the environment for the monarch to dispense with representative forms of government in fall 2002. When Deuba recommended that the elections due in 2002 be postponed, King Gyanendra dismissed him illegally on October 4, 2002, and started to rule Nepal arbitrarily. The parliamentary government provided for in the 1990 Constitution was abandoned and Panchayat-style royal absolutism was practiced by King Gyanendra. Party leaders were arrested and the media censored.[33] With the parties at a loss, the Citizens' Movement for Democracy and Peace, a loose group of civil society activists, organized several mass rallies and meetings in different parts of the country during 2005. These meetings provided a platform to voice opposition to King Gyanendra's rule and to prepare the people for a mass movement to end the royal misadventure.

People's Movement II and the Peace Process (2006–2012)

King Gyanendra's rule was brought to an end by what is called the second People's Movement during the spring of 2006. The movement was a by-product of the twelve-point agreement (facilitated by India) reached between the Maoists and a coalition of seven parliamentary parties called the Seven Party Alliance (SPA) in November 2005 in New Delhi.[34] The SPA resolved to end absolute monarchy in Nepal and to end the ongoing conflict by forming an all-party government and holding elections to a Constituent Assembly. The Maoists were not committed to the restoration of the Parliament but wanted to achieve the same goals.[35] The Maoists also committed themselves to a competitive multiparty system and recognized democratic rights. The two sides also agreed to mediation by international agencies to facilitate dialogue and to monitor the two armed forces during the process leading to permanent peace. They called upon all Nepalis to participate in the movement to dislodge the absolute monarch.

Nineteen days of continuous protests by unprecedented numbers of Nepalis in which eighteen people were killed and hundreds injured, forced the king to end his absolute rule on April 24, 2006. He restored the 1999 HOR and recognized that sovereignty was inherent in the people of Nepal. On April 30, Girija Prasad Koirala assumed office as the PM, and the SPA government and the Maoists declared a cease-fire. On May 18, the HOR amended the 1990 Constitution to declare Nepal a secular state, and virtually eliminated the power enjoyed by the king. His control over the Nepali army was revoked and the title "Royal" removed from the army's name. The erstwhile "His Majesty's Government" was renamed "Government of Nepal."

On June 16, the SPA and the Maoists signed an eight-point agreement to guide the peace process, according to which the UN would monitor the arms and armies of both sides, an interim constitution would be drafted to provide the basis for the political transition, and an interim government formed. After many months of negotiations, the interim constitution came into effect on January 15, 2007. In the meantime, after many months of public acrimony and behind-the-scenes negotiations, an understanding was reached between the SPA and the Maoists on November 8, 2006, regarding the monitoring of arms and the two armies, the contents of the interim constitution, and the schedule for the completion of these works as part of the peace process. It was agreed that the king would have no authority with respect to the governance of Nepal but the future of monarchy as an institution was left to be decided by the first meeting of the CA through a simple majority ruling.

The interim constitution was to be promulgated by the reinstated HOR but to be approved by the new interim legislature, which would be a single body consisting of 330 members including 73 Maoist-nominated members. Most of the members were to be members of the reinstated HOR and some 48 others to be nominated by mutual agreement, representing various professional and political organizations, oppressed communities, and regions. Those who had opposed the 2006 People's Movement were not to be members of the interim legislature even if they were members elected to the HOR in 1999. Once the interim legislature came into effect, the parallel government and judiciary units established by the CPN (Maoist) would be dismantled. An interim government would be formed from the interim legislature through consensus and it would be responsible for holding the constituent assembly elections by mid-June 2007. It was agreed that a mixed electoral system would be in use for the CA elections: 205 members were to be elected on the basis of the first-past-the-post system (FPTP) and 204 on the basis of proportional representation (PR) with reference to the votes received by the various parties. Candidates in the PR list would include representatives from all oppressed communities and regions, and Madhesis, women, and Dalits (formerly untouchables in the caste hierarchy). Sixteen nationally prominent personalities were to be nominated for the CA, which would therefore have a total of 425 members.

The November 8 understanding formed an integral part of the Comprehensive Peace Agreement (CPA) signed between the Government of Nepal and the CPN (Maoist) on November 21, 2006, and ended the armed rebellion. In addition to the agreements reached in the November 8 understanding with reference to the management of the arms and two armies, terms of the permanent end of hostilities were elaborated, and mechanisms to both execute and monitor the CPA were mentioned in broad terms. It spelled out the policies to be pursued to ensure a forward-looking political, economic, and social transformation of Nepal. Commitment to fundamental human rights and freedoms were reiterated. Commitments were also made to address justice-related concerns of those disappeared, killed, displaced, or otherwise violated by both sides during the course of the conflict. For that, two commissions were to be formed: a national peace and rehabilitation commission and truth and reconciliation commission. A further detailed agreement on the management of the arms and armies was signed on November 28, and a revised final version was signed on December 8 with the United Nations as a witness.[36]

The Interim Constitution and Constituent Assembly Process (2007–May 2012)

On January 15, 2007, the interim constitution (IC) was promulgated by the reinstated HOR, which was then immediately dissolved. The 330-member interim legislature—officially named Legislature-Parliament—was then formed. The IC is a document that facilitates the political interim between the 2006 People's Movement and the completion of the writing of the new constitution by an elected CA. The IC declared Nepal to be a secular state and suspended the monarchy. It provided for extensive coverage in the form of fundamental rights and freedoms for the citizens of Nepal. In the three branches of the government provided for by the IC, the executive is relatively more empowered, with more power vested with the prime minister. The IC called for the elections to a CA by mid-June 2007. At least one-third of all the candidates proposed by the parties for the CA elections had to be women. All Nepalis of age at least eighteen on December 15, 2006, would be eligible to vote in the CA elections. In response to various political situations, the IC was revised three times in 2007 in the months of April, June, and December. After the CA elections took place in April 2008, it was revised a further three times in the months of May, July, and December 2008. The first two revisions were caused by the Madhes rebellion, discussed below, which had engulfed much of the eastern and central southern plains of Nepal during early 2007, and the 2008 revisions were required mainly by the interparty dynamics following the results of the CA elections.

When developments delayed the political process, the Election Commission concluded that it did not have enough time to conduct the CA election in June. It was then moved to November 2007. That deadline was also missed due to lack of political consensus on the electoral system and some other issues. These two postponements were responsible for generating skepticism regarding the entire peace process among the public at large and hence even days before the CA election was finally held on April 10, 2008, widespread uncertainty about it persisted. By the time the CA elections were held, its size had been revised to a 601-member body: 240 from FPTP, 335 from PR, and 26 nominated. Nearly 62 percent of the voters showed up to cast their votes. There was some violence in the run-up to the elections and on the election day itself.

Surprising everyone, the Maoists did spectacularly well. The Maoists won 120 of the total 240 seats allocated on the FPTP system. The other two main parties did not do as well as expected: NC won 37 seats and CPN-UML won 33. Of the Madhes-based parties, the Madhes Janadhikar Forum (MJF) won 30 seats, Tarai Madhes Loktantrik Party (TMLP) won 9, and Nepal Sadbhavana Party (NSP) won 4. Three small left parties won a total of 5 seats. The seats allocated by proportional representation were as follows: CPN (Maoist) 100; NC 73; UML 70; MJF 22; TMLP 11; NSP 5. When the 26 nominated seats were also divided among nine of the parties present in the CA, the biggest parties emerged as follows with their total seats in the 601-member CA: CPN (Maoist) 229; NC 115; CPN-UML 108; MJF 54; TMLP 21, NSP 9; CPN (M-L) 9; Jana Morcha Nepal 8; Rastriya Prajatantra Party (RPP) 8.[37]

The CA results showed, not unexpectedly, the decline of the pro-monarchy forces in Nepal. They failed to win even a single seat in the FPTP part of the CA elections. The centrist party, the NC, had a total of 115 seats, half of the showing of the CPN (Maoist). According to Hachhethu, the NC's poor showing could be attributed to the decline in the political influence of local traditional elites who had joined the NC party in the 1990s, its bad record of governance during the 1991–2002 period, and the fact that none of the major issues in contemporary Nepal—republicanism, federalism, secularism—had been the NC's own agenda.[38] In addition, in the two-year period between the April 2006 uprising that tamed monarchical absolutism and the April 2008 CA elections, the NC party was not restructured to meet new challenges. The left parties obtained over 56 percent of the popular vote, which is much higher than what they had obtained in the three national elections to the HOR during the 1990s.[39] The most radical among the left parties, the CPN (Maoist) benefited the most, whereas CPN-UML took a beating with a total of just 108 seats in the CA. Prior to the elections the CPN-UML had believed that it would come out on top, but most of its leaders, including its then general secretary, lost in the CA elections. Overconfidence, deficient grassroots mobilization in the months leading to the CA elections, and failure of the left parties to agree on a consensus candidate in specific constituencies were some of the reasons behind CPN-UML's poor showing. It was also the victim of aggressive CPN (Maoist) tactics in some constituencies. On the other hand, perhaps a combination of the seduction to CPN (Maoist)'s slogans of creating a new and more socially just Nepal among the working and downtrodden classes, a desire for change partially emanating from a fatigue with the erstwhile parliamentary parties, and the overwhelming desire to keep the CPN (Maoist) in the peace process on part of the voters—the fear being that if it did not do that well in the CA elections, it would return to insurgency—were factors behind its success. Also to be noted was the rise of the Tarai-based regional parties which had a total of 87 seats in the CA. This showing was a direct result of the gains obtained from the rebellion in the Tarai during the early months of 2007.

The CA results were interesting from another perspective as well. The percentage of hill Hindu high castes in the CA had shrunk by half compared to their presence in the HOR elected in 1994 or 1999. Madhesi representation had gone up from about 20 percent in the past to about 34 in the CA. Similarly the Janajati (indigenous nationalities) representation had gone up from about 25 percent to about 35 percent. The Dalit participation had increased from under 1 percent to about 8 percent. One-third of the CA members were women. One analyst cited these data as evidence of a "transformation of identity movement into political power."[40] Official caucuses were ruled out in the CA, but unofficial caucuses of women, Janajatis, and Dalits did come into existence even as they were not very functionally effective.

When it became clear that due to its unexpected good showing the CPN (Maoist) would lead the government, the other parties jockeyed for two revisions in the interim constitution. One was to change the provision regarding the formation and dismissal of government by simple majority instead of the two-thirds majority provisioned in the IC. The second was to create the position of a president. It took two weeks to sort out the first of these and until almost the third week of July 2008 for the presidential office to be filled. Because the CPN (Maoist) did not have a simple majority, it had to form a coalition with the CPN-UML and MJF and only on August 15 was the Maoist leader Pushpa Kamal Dahal "Prachanda" elected prime minister. It took until November to finalize the procedural rules regarding the operation of the CA. Delays were also caused by other factors. For instance, no prior plan had been made to process the suggestions received from the public regarding the contents of the new constitution.

In the meantime, citing differences with its coalition partners over its decision to fire the chief of the Nepal Army, the CPN (Maoist)–led government resigned on May 4, 2009. Prime Minister Dahal claimed that "civilian supremacy" had been sacrificed by the failure of his government to implement its decision to fire the army chief when the president intervened to reinstate him. The PM's position was filled on May 23, by CPN-UML's Madhav Kumar Nepal, who headed a coalition government with the NC, MJF, and other parties. The CPN (Maoist) blocked all work in the legislative-parliament side of the CA for several weeks demanding that action be taken against the president for his "unconstitutional" intervention. While the business of the CA was not totally interrupted, it was partially delayed. The Madhav Kumar Nepal–led government lasted until June 2010 and it was eventually succeeded by a government led by a leader of the same party, Jhala Nath Khanal. The Khanal-led government was replaced by a government led by the CPN(Maoist) Party with Baburam Bhattarai as the prime minister in August 2011. The latter lasted until March 2013 when it was replaced by a government headed by the chief justice, whose primary job was to hold elections to the second CA.

The very diverse CA body turned out to be no guarantee that the constitution-writing process would be finished on time. Drafts of various thematic parts of the Constitution were prepared by twelve committees consisting of various CA members following intense and sometimes acrimonious deliberations. However, even after the original two-year mandate of the CA was extended several times for a total of two additional years, its full body was unable to deliver a new constitution for Nepal when its last deadline expired in May 2012. Several reasons could be attributed for this failure. First, the major parties had very different initial positions on key constitutional issues such as the desired form of government, electoral system, number of federal units (and the bases for their creation), and the kind of economic policies Nepal should pursue. While many of these differences were eventually narrowed down or eliminated through repeated rounds of deliberations, at the end there was no consensus on the number and names of the federal units. Second, the first problem was compounded because the CA was dominated by the large parties and its dynamics were controlled by politics based along party lines. Theoretically, if the CA was a national body for deliberation, each individual member should have been able to vote along the lines of her conscience instead of having to obey the party whip and discipline. But silence on this issue was maintained in the CA rules and regulations. Following the initial euphoria of having the "most representative body" in Nepal's history, it soon became clear that novices as well as old party hands were being forced to toe party lines and hierarchy within the CA. For all their initiatives, the caucuses (Janajati, Dalit, and women) and party wings of excluded groups, remain peripheralized. Major decisions were made by party leaders outside of the CA and very little debate took place in the full CA body where many of the elected leaders of the major political parties were often absent.[41]

Further embedding the complexities and dilemmas within the Nepali context, the peace process in Nepal, as in other countries, has been elite driven. This stems from concerns to prevent "spoilers" and preserve the peace process. The focus has thus largely been on building trust and reaching agreements among these elites. However, the lack of trust and meaningful consensus has translated into a prolonged transition period, which has legitimized the capturing of political space by political party elites, and the marginalization of civil society and citizens. This is most evident in the monopoly held by political parties over key decision-making processes and the functioning of various all-party mechanisms at the national and local levels. This, in turn, has created a permissive environment for the expansion and strengthening of political party patronage networks, corruption, and criminal/political nexus. Impunity is rife in the country, and importantly, those responsible for violations in the past are politically, financially, and institutionally stronger than they were when their crimes were committed. Justice for victims has not been achieved as part of the peace process.[42] The institutions that are supposed to protect Nepali citizens—the National Human Rights Commission (NHRC), the police, and the judiciary—continue to be largely dysfunctional.

POLITICAL ECONOMY

Nepal's economy has been primarily based on agriculture. Post-1951 governments have tried to implement measures to enhance agricultural production, without much success, and to implement national periodic plans to develop the economy under severe geopolitical and financial constraints. Landlocked on three sides by India, Nepal is dependent on India's generosity for international trade exchanges. Similarly, since domestic resources are inadequate to cover its development needs, Nepal has sought foreign aid since the early 1950s. The public sector has been prioritized in the national economy all along. However, after the political and economic liberalization of the early 1990s, the private sector has grown in some sections of the economy and nongovernmental organizations (NGOs) have taken a significant role in the delivery of certain types of services.

The Failure of Land Reforms

Until the demise of the Ranas in 1951, agriculture was the mainstay of economic activity. The Ranas used the state bureaucracy as a rent-seeking machine to support their lavish lifestyles. The main agricultural lands in the southern Nepali plains, the Tarai, and whatever useful lands that were available elsewhere were used for political patronage in Rana Nepal. The rulers had very little incentive to invest any part of what they were collecting from the peasants to increase the productivity of the land. Because what was left from the land (after the rent had been paid) was not enough to feed many families in the hills, able-bodied men began to migrate to India in search of work. Many joined the Gurkha battalions of the British Indian army.[43] Those who could not meet their economic needs, even with family members engaged in off-farm work, migrated to the Indian hills and elsewhere.

In post-Rana Nepal, agriculture has continued to be neglected. While each regime has talked about land reform, no substantial reform has happened. The abolition of the *birta* tenure system in 1959 is often described as a measure of land reform in the sense that it put an end to a type of privileged tenure category. However, the real objective of the abolition was to enable the then government "to widen the land tax base."[44] Even though tenancy rights had been part of the political discourse since the early 1950s, legislation to protect the rights of the tenants was enacted in the form of the Lands Act only in 1957. Providing financial security to the tenant by fixing the maximum rent on the land at 50 percent of the total annual produce (or lower if that was the existing arrangement) and protecting him from eviction were essential steps in increasing agricultural production. However, this act also allowed landowners to resume lands up to a certain limit for purposes of personal residence, thus creating a condition for eviction of the tillers. In addition, at the grassroots level, there was no machinery to effectively enforce the new rent-control measures.

In the late 1950s, all the political parties advocated a ceiling on land ownership and the redistribution of land that was in excess of the declared ceilings. But this policy decision had to wait until late 1964 when King Mahendra brought it in to buttress the "progressive and modern" image of his kingship and his Panchayat system.[45] This act required that lands in excess of declared ceilings to be redistributed over a three-year period. According to one evaluation done in 1971, this program had little success. Only about 9,100 landowners were affected and only something like 34,700 hectares (ha) of land was acquired as over-the-ceiling excess land, less than 3 percent of Nepal's agricultural lands. About 70 percent of that land was redistributed to about ten thousand five hundred households.[46] In subsequent decades, no substantial land reform initiative has been implemented. As two recent studies have suggested, the lack of will to reform and the commitment to implementation explain why land reform measures have failed in Nepal.[47]

In 2009, the distribution of land ownership remained very unequal. According to one study, "47 percent of land-owning households own only 15 percent of the total agricultural land with an average size of less than 0.5 ha, while the top 5 percent occupies more than 37 percent of land."[48] Only 10 percent of women own land, with average holdings being less than 0.1 ha. The corresponding figure for men is 1 ha/man. The 1996 amendment to the Land Act brought an end to the formal arrangement of tenancy. Registered tenants were given their share of the land but some half a million unregistered tenants were reportedly negatively impacted.[49] There has been a land rights movement in Nepal but its cumulative impact is yet to be felt.[50]

Overview of the Economy

Although never colonized, Nepal's politics and economy have been greatly influenced first by the British Raj, and then independent India. After the Anglo-Nepal war between 1814 and 1816, which ended with Nepal's defeat and the Treaty of Sagauli, the British imposed many restrictions on Nepal including territorial loss. By the beginning of the twentieth century, Nepal had begun to be integrated into the economy of the British Raj as a "semi-colony" with all the ills of colonial occupation and without the "modernizing" benefits such as investments in infrastructure, administration, and industry.[51] A trade treaty signed in 1923 permitted unrestricted import of British goods to Nepal, thereby helping the British and Indian economy to grow at the expense of Nepal's. By the middle of the twentieth century, domestic industries such as cotton production and metalware manufacturing and armaments were destroyed and the manufacture of commodities and the trade and exchange systems, which formed integral elements of the social economy of the hills, gradually declined.[52]

Consequently, although not colonized, like many underdeveloped postcolonial countries, Nepal's integration into the world economy was very much dictated by the legacy of the colonial economic structure. By the time of British departure from India in 1947, Nepal had already been deeply integrated into the capitalist economy of India as the periphery to India's core and as "an economy which not only provides a market, however small and peripheral, for its manufactured goods but which at the same time is able to provide labor and primary products for the Indian economy."[53] Overall, postcolonial India's interventions in Nepal have been structured to retain Nepal under India's security, economic, and political influence. In terms of the trade, the history of Nepal's trade and transit treaties with India has been fraught with tension and turmoil. The 1950 Treaty of Trade and Commerce continued trade links of primary products from Nepal to India, and manufactured products from India to Nepal. Successive treaties have followed the same mold, and although Nepali state policies and actions have not been blameless, despite special concessions on Nepali manufactured materials, the nature of the economic relationship works to the favor of India.

Under these politico-economic constraints, Nepal has tried to develop its economy in a planned manner since the mid-1950s. The orientation of these successive plans until the early 1990s favored a major role for the state sector in agriculture, industry, education, health, and in infrastructure development, especially the building of roads and communications. Agriculture involves over 60 percent of the labor force but its contribution to the national GDP is only about 40 percent. Once a food-sufficient country, Nepal's food output can no longer feed its population of 26.6 million as reported in the 2011 census. Those families that still rely on agriculture have now resorted to the time-tested two-pronged strategy: doing subsistence agriculture at home and sending off at least one able-bodied member to labor abroad, preferably beyond South Asia's borders. Since the mid-1990s, the more desired destinations for such people have been countries in Southeast Asia (South Korea, Japan, and Malaysia in particular) or the Gulf Region. Preliminary analysis of the 2011 census data recorded the absentee population at 1.92 million. In the 2001 census this number was only 0.76 million. Over three hundred fifty-four thousand work permits were issued by the Nepal government during the fiscal year 2010–2011.[54] Unofficially it is thought that the total number of Nepali migrant workers is larger than the reported absentee population. For instance, in Qatar alone, it is estimated that there were three hundred thousand Nepali workers in 2012. The remittances sent back to Nepal by workers abroad is one of the largest foreign exchange earners and were estimated to be about 20 percent of the country's GDP in 2011. Many believe that remittances hold the Nepali economy together.

Since the early 1970s, tourism has been one of the major hard-currency earning industries in Nepal. After reaching the half-million mark in the late 1990s, tourist arrivals dropped between 2001 and the signing of the comprehensive peace agreement in 2006 as the internal conflict enveloped Nepal. Since then the numbers have gone up with tourist arrivals reaching over 700,000 during the calendar year 2011, which had been declared as "Nepal Tourism Year" by the government with the goal of bringing a million tourists to Nepal. Although that goal was missed, tourism's future looks good provided there is relative peace in the country.

In the early 1990s, the NC government liberalized the economy by opening sectors such as banking, insurance, hydropower, finance companies, and airlines to the private sector.[55] Exports of carpets and garments to Euro-American markets recorded moderate successes, crossing the $300 million mark for the fiscal year 1993–1994. However, subsequent stagnation in these export industries has tempered the earlier euphoria regarding how such trade might lift Nepalis out of poverty. When intra-party conflict led to the downfall of the NC government in 1994 and it was followed by a series of short-lived governments led by political parties of all colors, the economic growth rate of the early 1990s could not be sustained. Subsequently, the passing of pro-labor laws, the militancy of labor unions, political corruption in state-owned enterprises, and the Maoist conflict squandered what looked like a promising economy in the early 1990s.

Many Nepalis believe their country to be "rich" in hydropower. But that is hardly the case. The total installed capacity of all hydropower plants in Nepal in mid-2012 does not even reach 1,000 MW even as state propaganda continues to stress that the potential total could be as high as 83,000 MW. It is certainly the case that Nepal is rich in terms of rivers, but falling water is not a resource by itself. The relatively successful construction of small hydropower projects with Nepali money and expertise in recent years gives hope that someday in the future a whole set of industries based on electricity and having both forward and backward linkages will come into operation in Nepal. However, during the winter of 2011–2012, that remained a pipe dream as the total demand for electricity far exceeded the available supply. About 40 percent of the population that has access to electricity suffered scheduled "loadshedding" of some twelve to fourteen hours a day.

Foreign Development Assistance

The downfall of the Rana regime and the consequent "opening up" of Nepal saw the entrance of development donors in 1950. Nepal was seen by Western development workers as "a laboratory" for development, "*particularly* desirable" given the fact that Nepal was free of the complications caused by colonization.[56] The massive entry of foreign aid into Nepal during the Panchayat period served to centralize the state and to extend its ideological apparatus into parts of the country hitherto left untouched by the Rana rulers who had focused only on the collection of taxes and law and order. Donor aid was thus key in enabling and legitimizing Panchayat-defined nation-state building and the concomitant creation of "the Nepali" political community in all its exclusionary forms.

Furthermore, while much has been made of Nepal's poor governance systems, embedding them in the history of governance and bureaucracy in Nepal reveals the important role of foreign aid in the structuring of certain key dynamics. For example, scholars have noted the pressure put on the human and financial resources of the country in the early years of development as a result of the uncoordinated entrance of foreign aid projects.[57] The Rana administration had never produced a budget, and it was over eighteen months before the Finance Ministry of the post-1951 administration could guess national revenues and expenditures. Projects were determined and decided according to donors' priorities.[58] Apart from China, all donors in the early 1960s rejected a proposal to make contributions in cash, which would have allowed the Nepali ministry of planning to apply a master plan.

Indeed, it has been argued that it is the continued influx of foreign aid that has obstructed the development of a coherent, capable, and effective state-system in Nepal.[59] Indeed, Nepal's first official foreign aid policy was formulated only in 2002 although the changes have, however, only remained on paper. Furthermore, despite the fact that the auditor-general has raised the issue for several years, more than one-third of foreign aid projects do not come under the orbit of national auditing.[60] Estimating the total volume of aid to Nepal is made difficult because of the various sources and the different amounts stated by such sources as UNDP, the government's own Economic Survey, and the Social Welfare Council, which tracks funds that flow to the not-for-profit sector.[61] A review of foreign aid estimated that the officially assessed foreign aid amounts to just over half of the total aid given.[62]

Despite these criticisms, foreign aid has been the mainstay of resources used for physical and social infrastructure development in Nepal since 1950. During the 1950s, the United States and India were Nepal's major aid donors, with the UK, Switzerland, China, and the United Nations entering Nepal in the 1960s.[63] In the 1970s, West Germany and Japan entered the picture, while in the 1980s, India was the dominant donor followed by the UK, China, and the United States.[64] This was also the period in which multilateral agencies entered in Nepal. Trends in foreign aid show that multilateral assistance is gradually replacing bilateral assistance as major sources of funds. In recent years, an average of over 60 percent of Nepal's development budget has been covered by foreign aid. Such aid has helped to make a little over 60 percent of the Nepalis literate, improve their average life expectancy to about sixty-four years, provide better health care facilities to a part of the population, and build infrastructure such as schools, roads, and power plants. But such aid has also created a culture of dependency, one in which modes of operationalizing domestic resources—savings and remittances—in productive sectors of the economy remain largely immature.

The Growth of NGOs

Nepal has seen a rapid growth in the number and activities of nongovernmental organizations (NGOs) since 1990. A study published in 1998 estimated the existence of about 15,000 NGOs then,[65] but the number in 2012 is probably closer to 50,000. This proliferation must be seen as the result of two developments. First, it is the manifestation of Nepali citizens exercising their fundamental rights to form associations in accordance with the post-1990 constitutions of Nepal. The opening of an NGO during the illiberal Panchayat system was all but impossible for the common person. Second, the regime change of 1990 coincided with the shift in international foreign aid assistance to "civil society" actors. In the then newly democratic Nepal, this assistance was channeled into supporting the activities of NGOs. Such funding priorities were in keeping with the then global trends in political and economic liberalization. Nepali NGOs functioned—or so it was believed—as relatively more efficient service providers in the "New Policy Agenda" pursed in the 1990s by bilateral and multilateral organizations. Although questions of transparency, dependency on donor contributions, and public monitoring (of services and products for quality) of NGO activities remain, NGOs have undoubtedly expanded the realm of service delivery in Nepal. Even though this mode is still dominant, advocacy NGOs have also emerged. In that sense the NGO movement is not only growing in size but also becoming increasingly differentiated in terms of functions.

Many of the most prominent NGOs work in the mainstay of development in terms of the delivery of services, but others have worked in nondevelopment sector as well. As the Maoist-state conflict escalated in Nepal, many NGOs also began to work on more politically charged turf, such as conflict mitigation and the recording of human rights violations by armies of both sides. Sometimes such work was done in collaboration with international organizations such as Amnesty International and Human Rights Watch. Many lobbied for the establishment of the National Human Rights Commission and the setting up of the Office of the United Nations High Commissioner for Human Rights (OHCHR) in Nepal. After the people's movement of 2006, many have been involved in the peace process, electoral education with respect to the CA elections, and the writing of the new constitution. NGOs have also worked in some vital areas of strengthening democracy in Nepal. For instance, by actively searching for information about development projects that had been shrouded in governmental secrecy and by filing cases of public interest litigation (PIL) in the Supreme Court of Nepal that has forced the Court to make decisions impacting the citizen's right to know, NGOs have contributed to the legal and social opening up of Nepali society. Others have also been at the forefront of critical exercises—in the form of research, publication, public hearings, debates, training, etc.—related to the enjoyment of fundamental rights of relatively disenfranchised sections of Nepal's population or in producing academic knowledge. In the sector of media, some NGOs have produced critical content for both print and electronic media, and many have operated radio stations, since licenses for the same were made available to non-state actors from 1997.

NGOs have also worked in collaboration with various social movements. NGOs have made important contributions to women's, Dalit, and Janajati movements as well as the movement to free bonded laborers, known as *kamaiyas*. In the case of women, NGOs have provided access to health, education, and literacy and to economic savings and credit activities; they have also been involved in voter education and national-level lobbying for women's rights. Feminist NGOs, although few in number, have been at the forefront of legal battles for equality for women as well as being involved in critical areas of intervention such as producing feminist magazines, books, media literacy, and much more. The massive participation of women in the April 2006 movement and the significant presence of rural women in the Maoist armed struggle have been interpreted as outcomes, in part, of the work that was done by mainstream service-delivery NGOs in fields of literacy and "empowerment."[66] NGOs have also played a part in the movement of indigenous nationalities, the movement to free bonded laborers and the Dalit movement.[67] The limited public sphere that Nepal inherited as a legacy of the Panchayat era has been stretched by a significant degree by collaborative work between movement activists, media practitioners, academics, and legislators.

It is important to note the phenomenal growth in NGOs funded by donors since 1990 for two reasons. One is the consequences that external interventions have had on the reinforcing of social inequalities. In Nepal analysts have argued that historical privileges have enabled a certain caste and class group by virtue of their education to take advantage of the opportunities offered by the development world.[68] Others have raised questions as to how much information elite Bahuns and Chettris and some Newars "sieve" before presenting it to donors as "facts" and "realities," which then guide funding decisions, and the impact this has for Janajati and Dalit groups and their ability to have their views and concerns heard and acted upon.[69] The historical role of the donors in perpetuating structured inequalities in Nepal has yet to be fully analyzed for its implications.

Second, donor aid to NGOs, equated as civil society, has ramifications for the structuring of democratic institutions and spaces. As theorists have made clear, financing "civil society" affects the manner in which the two key components of civil society—horizontal ties and the norm of reciprocity—function. This is clear in Nepal's case.[70] As in most countries, groups that have received aid are not more likely to develop networks of accountability to citizens as well as to the state, which are crucial from the perspective of governance. Critics have noted the manner in which NGOs are not publicly subject to monitoring except perhaps to stakeholders in the North.[71] Neither are they more likely to be embedded in more dense networks of association with other civil groups. Their use of global language obscures the way in which these NGOs are closer to their transnational partners than "the people" that they claim to represent.

In addition, the material gains from grants provide incentives for groups to engage in activities counter to the ethos of building social capital. Rather than building networks, most Nepali NGOs retain small memberships and engage in uncooperative behavior with other civic groups. This obviously is not to argue that all Nepali civic activists are financially driven, selfish actors but to point out the manner in which the "funding game" structures and influences these sorts of behavior.

IDENTITY POLITICS

The political ideology of the Nepali polity in the pre-1990 period revolved around the monarchy, a *bir* (brave) history, state-backed Hinduism, Nepali language, and a hill-centric cultural ethos.[72] Among these five elements, the last three are relatively more important for the present discussion and without a clear understanding of them, one cannot have a good grasp of the exclusive nature of dominant Nepali identity as was developed since the middle of the nineteenth century. Many of the current formations of identity politics in contemporary Nepal have reacted against these exclusions. This is especially so in the case of the women's movement for gender equality; the Madhesi movement, which seeks respectable citizenship for the residents of the southern Tarai belt; the Adivasi Janajati (indigenous nationalities) movement, whose goal is inclusion and empowerment for almost 40 percent of the national population; and the Dalit movement, which hopes to end discrimination against the so-called "untouchables" of Hindu society. State-backed Hinduism and the politics of language are discussed in this section whereas hill-centric cultural ethos is discussed as part of the case study on the 2007 Madhes rebellion presented below.

Religion in Politics: A Hindu Kingdom and Its Demise

Census data for 2011 show that of Nepal's population, 81.3 percent are Hindus, 9 percent are Buddhists, and 4.4 percent are Muslims. Three percent follow Kiranti religion, and 1.4 percent are Christians.[73] However, it should also be noted that many social activists question the veracity of these data because they claim that functionaries of the state involved in the census exercise have over-recorded the percentage of the population that is Hindu. Nevertheless, all agree that Hindus are not just a numerical majority in Nepal. Their religion, Hinduism, has been state-supported for ages.

In the medieval period (thirteenth/fourteenth to eighteenth centuries), there were two dominant models of statecraft linking Hinduism to kingship. The first was practiced in the Newar Malla kingdoms of the Kathmandu Valley and the second in the scores of kingdoms located in the central hills, one of which was Gorkha. The first was "tolerant, liberal, pluralist," whereas the "second was exclusive, intolerant, orthodox as far as the Brahmanical values were concerned." In the second model, "Hinduism was politicised in a much more decisive manner than among the Newars."[74] By the late medieval period, the kings of these small kingdoms in the central hills had begun to view themselves as protectors of pure Hinduism, as in their opinion the Indian plains had been defiled first by the Moghuls and then by the Westerners. After Prithvi Narayan Shah conquered the Kathmandu Valley in 1768–1769, Gorkha's version of what it meant to be a Hindu kingdom was extended to all the territories brought under its sovereignty.

State-backed Hinduism was most importantly manifested during the nineteenth century in the codification and practice of caste-based differentiation through the provision of national laws known as Muluki Ain. The original Muluki Ain of 1854 propagated by the first Rana premier Jang Bahadur provided a Hindu ideological base for the state of Nepal. It legalized a five-tier national caste hierarchy in which the people of Nepal were divided into the following categories according to ascribed ritual purity: wearers of the holy cord, non-enslavable alcohol-drinkers, enslavable alcohol-drinkers, impure but touchable castes, and impure and untouchable castes.[75] The high-caste hill Hindus (Bahun, Thakuri, and Chhetri) were placed at the top. Below them were the traditionally non-Hindu groups broadly corresponding to today's adivasi janajatis (indigenous nationalities) under the rubric of *matwali* (alcohol-drinker). The non-enslavable matwali contained those that were relatively close to the rulers such as Gurung, Magar, and Newar, and enslavable matwali contained relatively peripheral groups such as Bhote, Chepang, Gharti, and Tharu.[76] Hindu castes that were said to be impure but touchable along with Muslims and Christians were ranked one above the bottom, and Hindu castes deemed as impure and untouchable (namely, today's Dalits) were placed at the bottom. The national caste hierarchy provided the foundation for Hinduization of the polity. One implication of this scheme was that the state guaranteed inequality based on one's caste. For instance, the punishment for the same crime committed by a Bahun man and an untouchable man was sometimes vastly different.[77]

Neither the Muluki Ain nor any of the constitutions before 1962 formally declared Nepal to be a Hindu kingdom. However, the Hinduness of the kingdom was manifested by the fact that the monarch was a Hindu and the bureaucracy was dominated by Nepali-speaking male high-caste Hindus of hill origin. Given this nature of the ruling elite, the cultural ethos of the nation was projected in terms of the religious and cultural motifs of the dominant Hindu hill groups. This was not only the case, for instance, with respect to the rituals that produced legitimacy for the King's reign but also with respect to the general orientation of the laws governing many aspects of societal interaction. Cow slaughter was proscribed. Hindu festivals, especially Dashain, were celebrated as national holidays. It was only in the 1962 Constitution that inaugurated the Panchayat system that Nepal was first declared "Hindu." However, the logic of caste hierarchy was abandoned by its guarantee of equality to all citizens. The Muluki Ain itself was thoroughly revised in 1963, assuring equality before the law irrespective of one's caste. Nevertheless the state's patronage of Hinduism continued. During the Panchayat era, proponents of various religious or linguistic minority group rights were accused of being "communal" or "anti-national."[78]

After the end of the Panchayat system, the Constitution Recommendation Commission received many suggestions saying Nepal should be declared a secular state. These came, in part, from the Communists, who believed in secularism, but also from Buddhists and practitioners of other religions who thought that their respective religious beliefs were better protected if the state was declared secular. Janajati activists, liberal intellectuals, and politicians who had been influential in the regime change of 1990 were also in favor of declaring Nepal as a secular state. Advocates of keeping Nepal a Hindu kingdom even used the Bharatiya Janata Party of India to support their argument. They also played with the dominant Hindu community's fear that in a secular state, religious conversion, especially into Christianity, would be widespread. The 1990 Constitution ended up declaring the kingdom as Hindu.

Critics of this provision argued that this declaration negated the right guaranteed by Article 11.3, which prohibited state discrimination among citizens on the basis of religion. The Janajatis, in particular, claimed that in a constitutionally declared Hindu kingdom, all the other religions would face discrimination. Hence one of the fundamental demands of the Janajati movement from its inception had been that Nepal should be declared a secular state in which the state treats all religions equally.[79] As noted previously, a few weeks after the successful completion of the second People's Movement in April 2006, the restored HOR declared Nepal to be a secular state and suspended virtually all the political powers of the king. This secular status was reiterated when the Interim Constitution was promulgated in January 2007. Nepal was declared a republic on May 28, 2008. In this sense the end of monarchy in Nepal and the beginning of a secular state happened almost simultaneously.

However, to practice secularism in Nepal will be quite a challenge. Under one model of secularism, there should be a clear separation of the state and religion and no state-resources should go to support any activity that could be construed as religious. Under the second model, the state is declared secular to mean that all religions will be treated equally by the state. Although there is a lack of details regarding which model of secularism has been committed to in the Interim Constitution, the interim state has already funded religious activities, suggesting that it is the second model that works here. This implies that if state-resources are to be provided to support religious programs, they will have to be distributed equitably to all religions. However, defining what an equitable distribution means is not going to be easy. This is so because such support will be sought most probably not in the name of religion but in the name of culture or ethnicity, which in many an instance it will be very hard to distinguish from religion.

This difficulty will be even greater because the logic of proportional representation has already been written into the IC and will most likely emerge as a permanent feature of the new constitution when it is finally written. This logic recognizes that representation in the state machinery should tally with the size of various types of communities based on gender, ethnicity, caste, or regional origins and will also apply to questions related to the distribution of state-resources. Religion could easily enter this turf through the back door as part of one's ethnicity.

Language Politics: The Continued Dominance of Nepali

Nepali, which was previously called *Khas Kura* (the language of the Khas) or Gorkhali (language of the residents of Gorkha), spread from the western part of Nepal throughout its present territories over the course of many centuries through migration of its speakers and political conquest. This spread was especially strengthened by the military campaigns of Gorkha starting from the mid-eighteenth century. In the beginning of the twentieth century, more than one hundred twenty languages were spoken by the residents of Nepal. However, the deliberate promotion of Nepali, the mother tongue of the high-caste Hindus of hill origin, as the official language of the state from the early decades of that century, meant that its growth was achieved at the cost of the debilitation of the other languages. In the national education system developed in the 1950s, the state claimed that the use of Nepali as the language of instruction in schools would ensure that the other languages would die away and national unity be promoted. The Panchayat system instituted a Nepali-only policy in other spheres of public life as well, leading to discrimination against speakers of other languages.

In the three censuses conducted during Panchayat rule, the number of languages recorded saw a decline from 36 (in the 1961 census) to 17 (in 1971) and 18 (in 1981). The number increased quite dramatically in the first three censuses done after the regime change of 1990. The number of reported languages rose to 31 (in 1991), 92 (in 2001), and 123 (in 2011). These increases have all to do with the politics of census taking under two different regimes: one that wanted to project Nepal unified around the Nepali language and the other that acknowledged diversity within the Nepali nation. In the 2011 census, 44.6 percent of the population reported Nepali as their mother tongue. The five main languages spoken by population groups exceeding a million are Nepali, Maithili, Bhojpuri, Tharu, and Tamang. Together they account for 73.2 percent of the population. Thirty-seven of the 123 reported languages had speaker populations between one thousand and ten thousand individuals and another 37 languages had speaker populations under one thousand.[80] Out of the 123 languages, the first 19 in terms of the number of speakers make up almost 96 percent of the population, confirming what Malla wrote: "The most striking feature of Nepal's multilingualism is that it has *many languages* with very *few speakers*."[81] Nepali is understood as a second language by a majority of Nepal's population.

The 1990 Constitution guaranteed against discrimination based on religion, caste, sex, and ideology but not language. By declaring the Nepali language as the "language of the nation" and Nepal's "official language" and calling all other mother tongues spoken within Nepal "national languages," the Constitution gave at most a secondary status to these other languages. Based on this discrimination, the Supreme Court of Nepal ruled in 1999 against the use of local languages as a second official language in local offices with elected representatives. Against such practices, it has been argued that the state has the obligation to treat all languages equally.[82] In the Interim Constitution 2007, the provisions listed in the 1990 Constitution were listed with the addition of a sub-clause in the form of Article 5.3, which states, "The use of one's mother tongue in a local body or office shall not be barred. The State shall translate the language used for such purposes into the language of official business for the record." Janajatis have demanded that the state has to adopt a three-language policy in education and administration: mother tongue, a second Nepali language (in most cases, Nepali itself), and an international language. These demands for linguistic rights have been an integral part of the Janajati movement from day one.

After the political change of 1990, the democratic governments constituted several committees, commissions, and task forces to study and recommend policies that address issues in language politics. For instance, the National Language Policy Recommendation Commission (NLPRC), formed in May 1993, recommended among other things that a survey of national languages should be commissioned to produce reliable knowledge about the state of different languages of Nepal. It also recommended various activities to strengthen the different national languages, particularly those that were endangered or lacked a written tradition.[83] The Nepal government has commissioned a linguistic survey of Nepal from March 2009, and its results were not yet available in early 2013. The Committee to formulate suggestions for news broadcast in national languages over Radio Nepal was formed in February 1994. This committee recommended that Radio Nepal broadcast news in eight additional national languages along with the five in which it was already broadcasting news. A language was included in the recommendation for broadcast if the number of its speakers exceeded 1 percent of the entire population of Nepal according to the census of 1991.[84] Radio Nepal implemented the recommendations of this committee.

Also as a result of language-focused social activism in the post-1990 period, speakers of many of the languages other than Nepali have produced pamphlets, bulletins, journals, and books in their languages. Some have produced textbooks for formal inclusion in school curricula. Others have produced textbooks for informal education and literary works in languages in which none existed a generation ago. Still others have produced media contents in the form of magazines and newspapers and programs in various languages for the radio and television. Others have produced popular culture items such as music compact discs and films in various languages. Consequently the linguistic diversity available in the public sphere has certainly increased in the last fifteen years and the growth of independent FM radios has been very crucial for this. In a country where almost half of the population is not literate, radio has a distinct advantage. Since various FM radios are broadcasting programs in languages spoken by different ethnic and caste groups, even those who cannot understand Nepali have begun to have access to FM radio contents in many parts of Nepal.

WOMEN'S POWER AND KINSHIP
NETWORKS IN POLITICAL LIFE

Women's lives in Nepal have been greatly impacted by the cultural values of high-caste Hindu men. These cultural values, which have also dominated state structures, politics, and public life, have, for the most part, constrained women's participation in formal politics. Two foundational features of these cultural values "are the patrilineal inheritance system and the concern over the purity of the female body, which result in severe limits on women's mobility and various forms of female seclusion."[85] The inheritance system discriminates against women even as many of its most oppressive features have been tamed in the recent past. As Meena Acharya, a pioneer Nepali feminist scholar, notes, to "engage in politics, a woman must have a secure economic base, which present laws deny her."[86] The obsession over the purity of the female body is a part of the dominant patriarchal structure that controls the possibilities of formal and public political engagement for women in Nepali society.

Given the strong dominance of these cultural values, very few women have participated in formal politics in Nepal. In the last National Panchayat of the late 1980s under the Panchayat system, only 8 of the 140 members were women. Of them only 3 had been elected and the remaining 5 nominated by the then king. The presence of women in that system's subnational bodies was negligible. The Constitution of 1990 required all political parties to ensure that at least 5 percent of their candidates for the elections to the HOR be women. In the 1991 national elections to the 205-member HOR, only 7 women were elected.[87] In the 1994 elections, the five largest parties fielded a total of 37 women candidates out of which only 7 won.[88] In the HOR formed after the 1999 general elections less than 6 percent—12 out of the total 205 representatives—were women. Overall, one 2007 study on the status of women in political parties stated that only 9.1 percent of the central committee members of major political parties were women.[89] In other words, progress on this front has been very slow even during the relatively open political environment since 1990.

The Constituent Assembly formed after the April 2008 elections with 601 members, which also functioned as Parliament, had about 33 percent representation of women. This was ensured by the Interim Constitution of 2007, which required all political parties to name at least one-third women in the total number of their candidates for the mixed (first-past-the-post and proportional representation) elections to the CA. Most of these women (161) were allocated seats through the proportional representation system, while 30 were directly elected through the first-past-the-post system. These women were also more diverse (in terms of class, caste, ethnicity, age, and religion) than the elite women who have historically come to the forefront politically. However, as with other marginalized groups who had entered the CA in historic numbers, women were mostly sidelined in the constitution-making process within the CA, with political party loyalties and control dominating the agendas. The CA had also provided an opportunity for women who were primarily involved in the women's movement via the important nongovernmental organization (NGO) sector to be directly politically active. It is still unclear yet what impact erstwhile NGO activists had on structuring women's rights priorities across the political spectrum.

Nepal shares the dismal record of women's very low presence in formal politics with all of its neighbors in South Asia. However, Nepal stands out as an exception to the phenomenon of the rise of women to be head of state in every country in South Asia. The highest state position reached by a woman in Nepal has been deputy prime minister. However, overall, kinship ties have had some impact on the high positions reached by the few women both within the parties and in certain government positions. For example, the late Shailaja Acharya of the Nepali Congress, who became the deputy prime minister in the late 1990s, was the niece of B. P. Koirala. NC leader G. P. Koirala's daughter, Sujata Koirala, was nominated as foreign minister in the CPN-UML-led government in mid-2009.

It was with his direct intervention and pressure that she was placed in that position, despite heavy resistance and outcry from within the party. Other prominent women politicians in the NC fold have also been close relatives of men who held leadership positions in party politics.

Among left politicians, Sahana Pradhan—the first female foreign minister of Nepal (in the government following the April 2006 people's movement)—was married to the late Pushpa Lal Shrestha, one of the founders of the Nepal Communist Party. Pushpa Lal died in 1978 and Sahana Pradhan continued to hold major positions within the Communist formations that eventually became the CPN-UML. Bidhya Devi Bhandari—who became the defense minister in late May 2009—was married to the late Madan Bhandari, then general secretary of the CPN-UML and a member of the HOR. In the by-election that followed Madan Bhandari's accidental death in May 1993, Bhandari was fielded as a candidate by the CPN-UML and won—a victory interpreted by many as a result of the sympathy factor. But she also won in the following two elections to the HOR in 1994 and 1999.

What explains the manifestation of kinship networks for women in politics in Nepal? While these women share the economic, caste, and class standing of their male relatives, the relative relaxation of gendered control dynamics at home has helped them to make a mark for themselves in national politics. However, it would be wrong to say that all women in Nepali politics are there because of their relations to prominent male politicians. In 2008, for instance, Ramkumari Jhankri became the president of the student wing of CPN-UML, the first woman to head any national student body. Jhankri is not a daughter of any nationally prominent politician and was single then.

Much of the writing about women in Nepal since the mid-1990s has focused on women and the Maoists. Coverage on the "People's War" in Nepal by journalists, accompanied by photos of young, gun-toting guerrilla women in combat fatigues, highlighted the CPN (Maoist)'s claim of 30–50 percent female participation. Since the early 2000s, doubts on the veracity of high levels of female participation have been expressed. According to the United Nations Mission in Nepal (UNMIN), women made up only about 18 percent of registered combatants.[90] While the numbers of female combatants may have been exaggerated, it is clear that the Maoists have been able to attract considerable numbers of women, much more than any other political party in Nepal. However, even in this party, there were only two women in its politburo at the time of its split in mid-2012. The CPN (Maoist) has from the outset stated that gender transformation is part and parcel of its larger program for radical economic, political, and social transformation, although it is also well known that the CPN (Maoist) declares that the oppression of women cannot be addressed without first addressing issues of class, relegating women's issues to secondary importance. Furthermore, apart from the fact that the CPN (Maoist) had the largest number of women in the CA, many analysts have acknowledged that the Maoists have had a positive effect on empowering women in the social, cultural, and political realm, although these may be more unintended than intended consequences of overall Maoist strategies.[91]

SOCIAL COSTS OF MILITARISM

The issue of militarization in Nepal has come to the forefront as a direct result of the Maoist conflict. The question of mobilizing the army against the Maoists had always been raised, especially given poor police performance. However, it had been controversial because not only had the army been used by the former King Mahendra in the 1960 coup that ended Nepal's first experiment with multiparty democracy, but also the king continued to control the army despite constitutional provisions for a National Defense Council, and there was distrust of royal motives. Analysts have long pointed out that there is a history of distrust between politicians and the military, with the military leadership held by elite clans, under the protective umbrella of the palace.[92] Overall, civilian control of the military has been tenuous at best.

Before the escalation of the Maoist conflict, the Nepal Army (NA) had been a largely ceremonial army of around forty-six thousand individuals. Especially after 2001, with aid from the United States, the UK, and India, military spending escalated.[93] With generous military aid and the prioritization of militarized security, the size of the military was more than doubled to about ninety-six thousand men. Along with its professional and military deficiencies, one military analyst has highlighted the growing corruption within the NA, as well as business investment ventures that remain outside the accounting purview of the state.[94] This has meant the exponential growth of an institution, now increasingly more powerful, with vested interests of its own and still not internally restructured to face up to its new role of being accountable to a civilian-elected government.

The effect of the new dynamics were almost immediate on domestic politics. In the years of active conflict, the illusion that the Nepali state could defeat the Maoists militarily was "fueled in large part by an avalanche of modern weaponry, plus military training that [had] poured into the country from India, the US and Britain."[95] Amnesty International has long pointed out the impunity enjoyed by the NA.[96] The United Nations Working Group on Enforced and Involuntary Disappearances announced that in both 2003 and 2004 it had received more new reports of "disappearances" from Nepal than from any other country.[97] While it had become increasingly apparent that the war could not be won militarily by either side, the militarization process continued and had real democratic and social costs for the Nepali people.

Although the issue of the security sector reform has been raised since 2005 there has been limited progress to date. One reason is the fragile nature of the current peace process. In the context of underlying doubt and suspicion of Maoist intentions, alienating the army by undertaking much-needed security sector reform is not a priority for Nepal's other political parties. They have, in effect, supported the NA as their last bastion against Maoist authoritarianism. The insecurity has not been aided by the fact that despite assurances from the Maoist leader Pushpa Kamal Dahal ("Prachanda"), Maoist cadres continue to extort money and use violence, and they have yet to return seized property and continue to threaten to continue their struggle to capture the state. Most damaging for the CPN (Maoist) has been the public release of a video in early May 2009 in which Prachanda speaks to his troops admitting that the number of UN-verified Maoists was inflated. The release of the video had immediate political and social ramifications. At the political level there was increased distrust of the Maoists. Social and development costs are also involved inasmuch as the World Bank withdrew funds (estimated at $50 million) originally assigned in the Emergency Peace Support Project for the payment of ex-Maoist combatants in cantonments as allowances.

During 2009–2010, the expenses of the NA were budgeted at $203 million.[98] In 2008–2009, the budget of the Nepal government's defense ministry was $159 million and it accounted for over 5 percent of total government spending.[99] This amount did not include the expenses incurred in running the cantonments for about nineteen thousand ex-People's Liberation Army (PLA) combatants of CPN (Maoist) and their stipends, which were covered from a separate grant made to the Nepal government by international donors. Some analysts have suggested that the size of the NA should be reduced to its pre-insurgency strength or lower, but this suggestion was not been taken up for discussion in the Constituent Assembly. There continue to be large social and development costs to maintaining both the army and cantonments in post-conflict Nepal where basic infrastructure—including village development committee (VDC) buildings as well as health posts, schools, and roads that were destroyed during the years of active conflict—are yet to be rebuilt. Apart from the financial strain, there are other social costs of increased militarism. Given the reluctance to reduce the strength of the Nepal Army and the delay in managing the future of the PLA combatants (either through integration in NA or through retirement and rehabilitation), justice for conflict victims remains entangled in the larger politics of the peace process. This has been most evident by the lack of progress on the establishment of the

disappearance commission and the truth and reconciliation commission
to which political parties committed themselves in the Comprehensive
Peace Agreement (CPA) signed in November 2006.

STRUGGLES OVER RIGHTS: THE 2007 MADHES REBELLION

In January–February 2007, an unprecedented rebellion took place in Nepal's southern plains, known as the Tarai or Madhes (used interchange-
ably in this chapter), home to about 50 percent of the country's population. Protestors took to the streets to demonstrate against the dominance
of a hill-centric state and its implications for the daily lives of millions of
Madhesis. Depending upon whose definition you accept, there are two
ways to define the population of the Tarai/Madhes. The first places the
population of the region into two categories, the group of Madhesis including indigenous nationalities who speak various plains languages and
the relatively recent migrants of hill origins. In the second, there are Madhesis; indigenous nationalities such as the Tharu, who claim to be the first
residents of the plains; and hill migrants. Those in caste groups as well as
Muslims have identified themselves as Madhesi, while aboriginal groups
such as the Tharu and others have preferred to identify themselves as
Janajatis (indigenous nationalities).[100] In other words, who is or is not a
Madhesi in today's Nepal is itself a highly contested issue. Coming on
the wake of the massive people's movement of 2006, the rebellion in the
Madhes sought both respect and justice for the Madhesis, an equitable de-
signing of political constituencies, an end to discrimination perpetuated
by a unitary state in language, and distribution of citizenship certificates,
and representation in state structures.

Hill-Centric Cultural Ethos and Discrimination
against Madhesis: A Capsule History

Given that the members of the ruling elite since the Gorkha conquest have
come, for the most part, from a limited circle of upper-caste hill-origin
Hindu families, Madhesis have had to face discrimination in many sectors. Through the middle of the twentieth century, the Madhes was internally colonized by the rulers in Kathmandu. Because the Tarai is where
most of the food is grown, control over its land was the chief priority for
Nepal's rulers.

Until the mid-1950s, hill people (*pahadis*) did not settle in the Tarai for
fear of malaria. After the malaria control activities of that decade, migration to the Tarai increased dramatically, due to both planned resettlement on the part of the state and voluntary or forced migration of those

in search of better lives. Between the early 1950s and the census of 2001, the Tarai population increased fourfold, twice the rate of growth in the hilly region. When this growth was disaggregated, it was found that those with origins in the hills grew by almost twenty-nine-fold, while Madhesi population growth was less than fourfold. This fact has now been deployed to argue that the post-Rana Nepali state has consciously tried to establish hegemony of pahadis in the Tarai.[101]

Approximately half of Nepal's population now lives in the Tarai, of which about two-thirds are of plains origin. In the total population of the country, about 32 percent are Madhesis, including Janajatis of plains origins. The ancestors of many of the Madhesi caste groups came from India, and their physical appearance is similar to those of residents in the Gangetic plains of northern India with whom the Madhesis engage in various cultural exchanges today. Due to the particular construction of Nepali national identity and nationalism imbued in a hill-centric cultural ethos, especially during the Panchayat era, the loyalty of Madhesis to the Nepali state remained suspect.

Laws relating to acquired citizenship enacted during the early days of the Panchayat system required that applicants be able to speak and write Nepali, had a provision that referred to individuals who were of "Nepali origin" and gave chief district officers or zonal commissioners the authority to interpret the latter term. Although meant for foreign individuals who were seeking Nepali citizenship, these clauses were abused by Panchayat officials to deny citizenship to several million Madhesis who did not speak Nepali. Since the official certificate of citizenship was a prerequisite for legal ownership of land and other properties, it has been argued that the bureaucratic denial of citizenship was a means to prevent Madhesis from owning property. Not much progress was made in terms of revising these provisions after the 1990 regime change. After the People's Movement of 2006, the reinstated HOR passed a new citizenship law in late November 2006 that made it easier to acquire this certificate. By mid-2007, some one million additional individuals had acquired their citizenship in the Tarai.

Fighting for Madhesi Rights

The denial of both cultural membership in the Nepali nation as well as citizenship also contributed to large-scale poverty among Madhesis. These factors were also responsible for large-scale non-inclusion of Madhesis in the civil service and the army and created the environment in which Madhesis were socially harassed in most parts of the hills including the Kathmandu Valley. The discrimination faced by the Madhesis had been the focus of political activism by Madhesis since the regime change of 1951. The Nepal Tarai Congress (NTC), launched in 1951, demanded an autonomous Tarai state, recognition of Hindi as a national language, and adequate jobs in the civil service for Tarai residents.[102] The NTC was most active during the mid-1950s over the demand to make Hindi a national language and in opposing the government's October 1957 move to impose Nepali as the language of instruction in schools. However, it had little support.

After 1990, the Madhesi cause was mostly advocated by the Nepal Sadbhavana Party (NSP). Electoral success eluded the NSP and it managed to win only a handful of seats in the HOR in the 1990s. While it vigorously advocated for Hindi as a national language, it failed to champion the cause of citizenship for Madhesis in the same manner. This is perhaps because of the elite class background of the NSP leadership, which was content to be a promoter of Madhesi causes without actually emphasizing the concerns of the Madhesi poor and working classes.

The Madhes Janadhikar Forum (MJF) had been formed in the mid-1990s as a loose forum of politicians from various parties who wanted to highlight Madhes-related issues in mainstream national politics. Its founding chairperson was Upendra Yadav, an erstwhile CPN-UML politician, and it attracted members who were affiliated to various left parties until the latter parties decided to organize their own Madhes-related fronts. In the run-up to the promulgation of the Interim Constitution, the MJF and other Madhes-related parties had complained that the determination of the constituency map for the entire country with respect to the FPTP elections to the CA should not remain the same as that used in the elections to the HOR in the late 1990s. In particular, they had argued that the average population in each of the Tarai constituencies was much bigger than the corresponding number for most of the hill and mountainous regions. As a way to correct this imbalance, they had demanded additional constituencies for the Tarai and had even claimed that the CA elections should be held fully on the basis of proportional representation. They had also demanded that Nepal be a federal state.

When the full draft of the IC came into circulation in mid-December 2006, it became clear that these demands had been ignored. In response, the NSP called for a *bandh* (strike) on December 25, 2006. In the western Tarai town of Nepalgunj, the bandh became an excuse to create a communal riot, first along Madhesi-Pahadi division and then along Hindu-Muslim divisions. It is suspected that Hindu fundamentalists who have a strong organizational presence in Nepalgunj had carefully executed this riot to create a situation where the Interim Constitution could not be promulgated and the larger peace process would be derailed.

The Madhes Rebellion and Its Aftermath

The initial version of the IC retained the 205 constituencies for the Constituent Assembly based on the first-past-the-post system and made no commitments toward federalism. The day after the IC was promulgated, copies of it were burnt in Kathmandu by MJF leaders. Several of them including Upendra Yadav were arrested. Some days later, MJF activists and Maoists clashed in Lahan, a town in eastern Tarai where one MJF activist was killed. This prompted the Madhesi activists to call a general strike in most districts of the eastern Tarai and some elsewhere. The MJF called for amendments in the IC and the protests continued for three weeks. It was most intense in the central-eastern districts. Madhesi protestors attacked government institutions, media outlets, and offices of national political parties. They blocked highways leading to Kathmandu, thus preventing supplies from reaching the capital.[103]

In the state response that followed, some thirty-plus people were killed and hundreds injured. The MJF-led movement was brought to a halt after the then PM Girija P. Koirala made two public addresses, inviting the protesting Madhesi groups for talks and "promising electoral representation and inclusion of marginalized groups in state bodies on a proportional basis."[104] Such promises were interpreted by Madhesi advocates as the failure of those who ruled in Kathmandu to "understand the true nature of the Madhesi movement: that the protests are not about a few additional electoral seats or token representation. Rather, the Madhes struggle is one for *samman* and *nyay*, respect and justice."[105]

The IC was first amended in April 2007 to address the demand for the increase in constituencies in the Tarai, but the actual number was left to be determined by a commission constituted to study the redrawing of the electoral constituencies. The new clause added as Article 63.3A recognized that the "number of constituencies in the administrative districts in Madhes shall be increased in order to ensure that those constituencies are in proportion to the percentage of population." By the Third Amendment to the IC, done on December 28, 2007, the CA's 601-member size was fixed. The proposed federal structure was also written into the IC through the Fourth Amendment passed on May 28, 2008, the day monarchy was formally abolished from Nepal. The federal component was introduced as a way to preempt the work of the CA without specifying the number of the federal units or the bases on which they will be created.

The MJF registered as a separate party in spring 2007 and other Madhes-based politicians formed the Tarai-Madhes Loktanrik Party (TMLP) in late 2007. Building on the mood of the rebellion, the Madhes-based parties did much better than expected in the CA elections in April 2008. As mentioned earlier, Madhesi representation had gone up from about 20 percent in the past HORs to about 34 percent in the CA.[106] The rebellion had significantly eaten away the traditional support bases of the two national parties, NC and CPN-UML, in the eastern Tarai, and both have been anxious to regain lost ground. The rebellion had also seriously cut the dominance of the CPN (Maoist), whose inability to respond appropriately to the Madhes uprising was telling evidence that despite its revolutionary rhetoric, it lacked the finesse to deal with a set of protestors not under its control. Like the NC and UML, the Maoists, too, are trying to revitalize their organizational base in the eastern Tarai, but this has not been easy for internal reasons. One of their key Madhesi leaders, Matrika Yadav, left the party, criticizing its leadership for having lost its revolutionary edge, and a significant chunk of national and lower-level leaders formed a separate Maoist party in mid-2012. In addition to all this, the Tarai has also seen the rise of several armed groups, some of which have a political objective but many that are using politics as a façade for their criminal work.

Madhes-based parties were part of the ruling coalitions formed after the 2008 CA elections. In that sense, both with respect to representation in the CA when it existed and in the various ruling permutations of parties, Madhesi parties and leaders have done well since the rebellion of 2007. In other words, Madhesi power as demonstrated on the streets in 2007 was first utilized to amend the Interim Constitution of 2007, then used to organize political parties such as the MJF and TMLP and subsequently to send Madhesi politicians to the CA and ruling coalitions. Given this record, it is now certain that the new constitution of Nepal will not be written without taking into serious consideration Madhesi sentiments and desires for both respect and justice and the double agenda of inclusion and federalism. Hence demonstrations of street power and leverage in constitution making have become part of the strategy of Madhesi success since 2007, although use of this combination is not unique to the Madhesi community alone.

However, two issues have often been discussed in this connection. First is the multiple splits recorded by all Madhes-based parties and how we may understand them. For instance, the NSP had seen eight splits, the MJF had experienced four splits, and the TMLP had been divided twice by early 2011.[107] In mid-2012, there were more than a dozen Madhes-based political parties. While factors such as "caste, ethnicity, ideology, the differing political background of the leaders, conflicts over resource-sharing, India's role and willingness to create and split Madhesi parties . . . have played a crucial role" in these splits, they are ultimately "driven by the individual leader's calculation that the benefits of forming a splinter outfit—by way of a (ministerial) portfolio, a party position, increased prestige, autonomy or just more money—outweigh the risks."[108] In other words, the Madhes-based parties remain very much person-centric political formations highly susceptible to opportunistic politics of the day.

They are also "exclusivist and discriminatory" in their structure since Dalits, Muslims, women, and Janajatis who live in the Tarai are largely absent in their internal party structures.[109]

Second, what difference has the rise of Madhes-based parties made to the everyday life of Madhesis some five-plus years after the rebellion? This is a more difficult question to answer. According to an influential political analyst, the "tenant and farmhand of Tarai-Madhes have not been able to benefit from the good fortunes of Madhes-based parties."[110] The downtrodden of the region have not been the targeted beneficiaries of any special governmental program introduced after 2008, even when Madhesi politicians have been in government. There is said to be rampant corruption in the expenditure of resources made available to the local governmental bodies in the Madhes, and Madhesi youth continue to find themselves outside of the national mainstream in politics and other spheres of Nepali society. Given this situation, some have now even suggested that the current leadership of Madhes-based parties will be "the first target of the masses' ire" when the next uprising happens in the region.[111]

NOTES

1. Mahesh C. Regmi, *Kings and Political Leaders of the Gorkhali Empire* (Hyderabad: Orient Longman, 1995).

2. Anirudha Gupta, *Politics in Nepal: A Study of Post-Rana Political Developments and Party Politics* (Bombay: Allied, 1964).

3. Bhola Chatterji, *Nepal's Experiment with Democracy* (New Delhi: Ankur, 1977).

4. This and the following three paragraphs are based on Gupta, *Politics in Nepal*.

5. Bhuwan Lal Joshi and Leo E. Rose, *Democratic Innovations in Nepal: A Case Study of Political Acculturation* (Berkeley: University of California Press, 1966).

6. B. P. Koirala, presidential address (delivered at the seventh annual session of the Nepali Congress at Kathmandu, May 7, 1960).

7. Bhola Chatterji, *Palace, People and Politics: Nepal in Perspective* (New Delhi: Ankur, 1980).

8. Chatterji, *Palace, People and Politics*, 116.

9. Chatterji, *Nepal's Experiment with Democracy*, 108.

10. Ibid., 110.

11. Initially there were five class and professional organizations: the Nepal Peasants Organisation, the Nepal Youth Organisation, the Nepal Women's Organisation, the Nepal Labour Organisation, and the Nepal Ex-Servicemen's Organisation.

12. M. Mohsin and Pashupati S. J. B. Rana, *Some Aspects of Panchayat System in Nepal* (Kathmandu: Department of Publicity, Ministry of Information and Broadcasting, HMG/Nepal, 1966), 13.

13. Rishikesh Shaha, *Nepali Politics: Retrospect and Prospect*, 2nd ed. (Delhi: Oxford University Press, 1978).

14. Lok Raj Baral, *Oppositional Politics in Nepal* (New Delhi: Abhinav, 1977).

15. Baral, *Oppositional Politics in Nepal*, 201–4.

16. B. P. Koirala, Desbasika nauma apil [Appeal to the people], December 30, 1976.

17. Chatterji, *Palace, People and Politics*, 176.

18. Rishikesh Shaha, *Politics in Nepal 1980–1991: Referendum, Stalemate and Triumph of People Power*, 3rd ed. (New Delhi: Manohar, 1993).

19. Lok Raj Baral, *Nepal's Politics of Referendum: A Study of Groups, Personalities and Trends* (New Delhi: Vikas, 1983).

20. Based on personal communication with C. K. Lal, July 16, 2009.

21. Quoted in Baral, *Nepal's Politics of Referendum*, 104.

22. B. P. Koirala, speech delivered to the meeting of the Socialist International, Madrid, Spain, November 1980.

23. Bhola Chatterji, *B. P. Koirala: Portrait of a Revolutionary* (Calcutta: Minerva, 1990), 111.

24. Based on personal communication with C. K. Lal, July 16, 2009.

25. Krishna Bhattachan, "Minority Rights in the Predatory Nepalese State," in Sumanta Banerjee, ed., *Shrinking Space: Minority Rights in South Asia* (Kathmandu: South Asia Forum for Human Rights, 1999); Mahendra Lawoti, *Towards a Democratic Nepal: Inclusive Political Institutions for a Multicultural Society* (New Delhi: Sage, 2005).

26. John Whelpton, "The General Elections of May 1991," in Michael Hutt, ed., *Nepal in the Nineties* (Delhi: Oxford University Press, 1994).

27. This paragraph is based on Whelpton, "The General Elections of May 1991."

28. Lok Raj Baral, "The 1994 Nepal Elections: Emerging Trends in Party Politics," *Asian Survey* 35, no. 5 (1995): 426–40.

29. Deepak Thapa, with Bandita Sijapati, *A Kingdom under Siege: Nepal's Maoist Insurgency, 1996 to 2003* (Kathmandu: The Printhouse, 2003).

30. Chaitanya Mishra, "Locating the 'Causes' of the Maoist Struggle," *Studies in Nepali History and Society* 9, no. 1 (2004): 3–56.

31. Arjun Karki and David Seddon, eds., *The People's War in Nepal: Left Perspectives* (Delhi: Adroit, 2003); Michael Hutt, ed., *Himalayan "People's War": Nepal's Maoist Rebellion* (London: C. Hurst and Co., 2004).

32. Hari Roka, "Militarisation and Democratic Rule in Nepal," *Himal* 16, no. 11 (2003): 56–61.

33. Binod Bhattarai, "Censored: Nepal's Press under King Gyanendra's Regime," *Studies in Nepali History and Society* 10, no. 2 (2005): 359–401.

34. S. D. Muni, "Bringing the Maoists Down from the Hills: India's Role," in Sebastian von Einsiedel, David M. Malone, and Suman Pradhan, eds., *Nepal in Transition: From People's War to Fragile Peace* (New York: Cambridge University Press, 2012).

35. International Crisis Group (ICG), *Nepal's New Alliance: The Mainstream Parties and the Maoists*, Asia Report No. 106, November 28 (Brussels/Kathmandu: ICG, 2005).

36. The full text of this agreement was attached to the Interim Constitution of Nepal, 2007, as part of its schedule 4. Its text and its English translation can be

found in United Nations Development Program (UNDP), *The Interim Constitution of Nepal 2063 (2007) as Amended by the First to Sixth Amendments* (Kathmandu: UNDP, 2009).

37. Krishna Hachhethu, "An Observation on Contemporary Nepali Politics" (paper presented to a seminar on Social Inclusion Policies in South Asian States organized by the Centre for Nepal and Asian Studies [CNAS] and the Social Inclusion Research Fund [SIRF] in Kathmandu, June 25–27, 2009); International Crisis Group, *Nepal's New Political Landscape*, Asia Report No. 156, July 3 (Brussels/Kathmandu: ICG, 2008).

38. Hachhethu, "An Observation on Contemporary Nepali Politics."

39. Ibid.

40. Ibid., 7.

41. Martin Chautari, "Attendance and Participation in the Constituent Assembly," Policy Paper no. 4 (2010), martinchautari.org.np/files/policypaper4_eng .pdf.

42. International Crisis Group, *Nepal: Peace and Justice*, Asia Report No. 184, January 14. (Brussels/Kathmandu: ICG, 2010).

43. Mary Des Chene, "Relics of Empire: A Cultural History of the Gurkhas, 1815–1987" (PhD diss., Stanford University, 1991).

44. Mahesh Regmi, *Land Tenure and Taxation in Nepal* (Kathmandu: Ratna Pustak Bhandar, 1978), 361.

45. Peter Gill, "The Politics of Land Reform in Nepal, 1951–1964," *Studies in Nepali History and Society* 14, no. 2 (2009): 217–59.

46. M. A. Zaman, *Evaluation of Land Reform in Nepal* (Kathmandu: Ministry of Land Reforms, His Majesty's Government of Nepal, 1973).

47. Gill, "The Politics of Land Reform in Nepal, 1951–1964"; Liz Alden Wily, with Devendra Chapagain and Shiva Sharma, *Land Reform in Nepal: Where Is It Coming from and Where Is It Going?* (Kathmandu: Authors, 2009).

48. Jagannath Adhikari, *Land Reform in Nepal: Problems and Prospects* (Kathmandu: Nepal Institute of Development Studies and ActionAid Nepal, 2008), 6.

49. Jagat Basnet, "Unregistered Tenants as Prominent Issue in Land Rights Movement" (Community Self Reliance Centre, 2008) available at http://www .csrcnepal.org/issues_prominent.htm.

50. Jagat Basnet, "Overview of Land Rights Movements in Nepal," in Bishnu Raj Upreti, Sagar Raj Sharma, and Jagat Basnet, eds., *Land Politics and Conflict in Nepal: Realities and Potentials for Agrarian Transformation* (Kathmandu: Community Self Reliance Centre [CSRC], South Asia Regional Coordination Office of NCCR North-South and Human and Natural Resources Studies Center, Kathmandu University, 2008).

51. Piers Blaikie, John Cameron, and David Seddon, *Nepal in Crisis: Growth and Stagnation at the Periphery* (Delhi: Oxford University Press, 1980).

52. Stephen L. Mikesell, "Cotton on the Silk Road: Subjection of Labor to the Global Economy in the Shadow of Empire (or the Dialectics of a Merchant Community in Nepal)" (PhD diss., University of Wisconsin, Madison, 1988).

53. Blaikie et al., *Nepal in Crisis*, 84.

54. Bandita Sijapati and Amrita Limbu, *Governing Labour Migration in Nepal: An Analysis of Existing Policies and Institutional Mechanisms* (Kathmandu: Himal Books, 2012).

55. Sujeev Shakya, "The Squandering of a Promising Economy," in Kanak Mani Dixit and Shastri Ramachandaran, eds., *State of Nepal* (Lalitpur, Nepal: Himal Books, 2002).

56. Tatsuro Fujikura, "Technologies of Improvement, Locations of Culture: American Discourses of Democracy and 'Community Development' in Nepal," *Studies in Nepali History and Society* 1, no. 2 (1996): 271–311.

57. Tatsuro Fujikura, *Discourse of Awareness: Development, Social Movements and the Practices of Freedom in Nepal* (Kathmandu: Martin Chautari, 2013).

58. Joel Isaacson, Christa A. Skerry, Kerry Moran, and Kay M. Kalavan, *Half-a-Century of Development: The History of US Assistance to Nepal 1951–2001* (Kathmandu: United States Agency for International Development, 2001).

59. Fujikura, *Discourse of Awareness*.

60. Dilli Raj Khanal, Laxman Acharya, and Dilli Ram Upreti, *Role and Effectiveness of Foreign Aid under PRSP in Nepal* (Kathmandu: ActionAid Nepal and IPRAD, 2008), 68.

61. Sudhindra Sharma, "Half a Century of Aid," in Eugene Bramer Mihaly, *Foreign Aid and Politics in Nepal*, 2nd ed. (Kathmandu: Himal Books, 2002).

62. Citizen's Poverty Watch Forum (CPWF) and ActionAid Nepal (AAN), *A Review of Foreign Aid in Nepal 2003* (Kathmandu: CPWF and AAN, 2003), 34–35.

63. Eugene Bramer Mihaly, *Foreign Aid and Politics in Nepal: A Case Study* (Kathmandu: Himal Books, 2002).

64. Sharma, "Half a Century of Aid," xxx.

65. Bishwa Keshar Maskay, *Non-Governmental Organizations in Development: Search for a New Vision* (Kathmandu: Centre for Development and Governance, 1998).

66. Rita Manchanda, "Maoist Insurgency in Nepal: Radicalizing Gendered Narratives," *Cultural Dynamics* 16, nos. 2–3 (2004): 237–58; Lauren Leve, "'Failed Development' and Rural Revolution in Nepal: Rethinking Subaltern Consciousness and Women's Empowerment," *Anthropological Quarterly* 80, no. 1 (2007): 127–72.

67. Pratyoush Onta, "The Growth of the *Adivasi Janajati* Movement in Nepal after 1990: The Non-Political Institutional Agents," *Studies in Nepali History and Society* 11, no. 2 (2006): 303–54; Tatsuro Fujikura, "The Bonded Agricultural Labourers' Freedom Movement in Western Nepal," in Hiroshi Ishii, David N. Gellner, and Katsuo Nawa, eds., *Social Dynamics in Northern South Asia, vol. 2: Political and Social Transformations in North India and Nepal* (Delhi: Manohar, 2007).

68. Kanak Mani Dixit, "Foreign Aid in Nepal: No Bang for the Buck," *Studies in Nepali History and Society* 2, no. 1 (1997): 173–86; Seira Tamang, "The Politics of 'Developing Nepali Women,'" in Kanak Mani Dixit and Shastri Ramachandaran, eds., *State of Nepal* (Kathmandu: Himal Books, 2002).

69. Krishna B. Bhattachan, "(I)NGOs and Disadvantaged Groups in Nepal," in Krishna Bhattachan, Dev Raj Dahal, Sheetal Rana, Jyoti Gyawali, Min Bahadur Basnet, Kashi Ram Bhusal, and Ram Raj Pokharel, eds., *NGO, Civil Society and Government in Nepal: Critical Examination of Their Roles and Responsibilities* (Kathmandu: Central Department of Sociology and Anthropology, Tribhuvan University and Friedrich-Ebert-Stiftung, 2001).

70. Sarah L. Henderson, "Selling Civil Society: Western Aid and the Nongovernmental Organization Sector in Russia," *Comparative Political Studies* 35, no. 2 (2002): 139–67; Seira Tamang, "Civilizing Civil Society: Donors and Democratic Space," *Studies in Nepali History and Society* 7, no. 2 (2002): 309–53.

71. Chaitanya Mishra, "New Predicaments of 'Humanitarian' Organization," in Bhattachan et al., *NGO, Civil Society and Government in Nepal*.

72. *Bir* history is a narrative of the nation steeped in an ethos of bravery. See Pratyoush Onta, "Creating a Brave Nepali Nation in British India: The Rhetoric of *Jati* Improvement, Rediscovery of Bhanubhakta and the Writing of *Bir* History," *Studies in Nepali History and Society* 1, no. 1 (1996): 37–76.

73. Pitamber Sharma, "Some Aspects of Nepal's Social Demography: Update 2011," *Studies in Nepali History and Society* 17, no. 2 (2012): 333–72.

74. Gérard Toffin, "The Politics of Hinduism and Secularism in Nepal," *Studies in Nepali History and Society* 11, no. 2 (2006): 219–40.

75. András Höfer, *The Caste Hierarchy and the State in Nepal: A Study of the Muluki Ain of 1854* (Innsbruck, Austria: Universitatsverlag Wagner, 1979).

76. Harka Gurung, "Janajati and Dalit: The Subjugated in Governance," in Mukti Rijal, ed., *Readings on Governance and Development*, vol. 2 (Kathmandu: Institute of Governance and Development, 2003).

77. Tulasi Ram Vaidya and Tri Ratna Manandhar, *Crime and Punishment in Nepal: A Historical Perspective* (Kathmandu: Bini Vaidya and Purna Devi Manandhar, 1985).

78. Chaitanya Subba, *Adivasi/Janajatis in National Development: Major Issues, Constraints and Opportunities* (Plan of Action proposed for the Tenth Plan, 2003–2007). Report prepared by the Institute for Integrated Development Studies (IIDS) for the National Planning Commission (NPC), 2002.

79. Harka Gurung, Malla K. Sundar, Krishna Bhattachan, and Om Gurung, *Development of Nationalities: A Strategy Paper* (Kathmandu: Nationalities Development and Coordination Center, 2004).

80. Pitamber Sharma, "Some Aspects of Nepal's Social Demography: Update 2011."

81. Kamal P. Malla, "Language and Society in Nepal," in Kamal P. Malla, ed., *Nepal: Perspectives on Continuity and Change* (Kirtipur: Centre for Nepal and Asian Studies, Tribhuvan University, 1989), 451; emphasis in the original.

82. Nepal Federation of Indigenous Nationalities (NEFIN), "Janajatika sawalma vartaman sambhidhan samsodhan garna garieka sifaris," reprinted in 2001 in P. Onta, K. Yatru, and B. Gautam, eds., *Chapama Janajati* (Kathmandu: Ekata Books, 2000).

83. Narahari Acharya, *Radio Nepalbata rastriya bhasaharuma samacar prasaran garne bare sujhau samitiko pratibedan* [Report submitted by the committee to formulate suggestions for news broadcast in national languages over Radio Nepal to His Majesty's Government of Nepal], May 8, 1994.

84. Selma Sonntag, "Ethnolinguistic Identity and Language Policy in Nepal," *Nationalism and Ethnic Politics* 1, no. 4 (1995)): 108–20.

85. Meena Acharya, "Political Participation of Women in Nepal," in Barbara Nelson and Najma Chowdhury, eds., *Women and Politics Worldwide* (Delhi: Oxford University Press, 1997), 480.

86. Ibid., 481.

87. Ibid.

88. Baral, "The 1994 Nepal Elections."

89. Jagaran Nepal, *Status of Women in Political Parties: A Research Report* (Kathmandu: Jagaran Nepal, 2007).

90. See United Nations Mission in Nepal, www.unmin.org.np/downloads/publications/UNMIN_Newspaper_3_ENG.pdf (last accessed September 2008).

91. Seira Tamang, "The Politics of Conflict and Difference or the Difference of Conflict in Politics: The Women's Movement in Nepal," *Feminist Review* 91 (2009): 61–80.

92. Dhruba Kumar, "The 'Royal' Nepal Army," *Himal Southasian* 18, no. 5 (2006): 36–39.

93. Dhruba Kumar, "Consequences of the Militarization of Conflict and the Cost of Violence in Nepal," *Contributions to Nepalese Studies* 30, no. 2 (2003): 167–216.

94. Ashok Mehta, *The Royal Nepal Army: Meeting the Maoist Challenge* (New Delhi: Rupa, 2005).

95. Conn Hallinan, "Nepal—Nursing the Pinion," *Foreign Policy in Focus*, February 15, 2005 (available at http://fpif.org/nepal-nursing_the_pinion/).

96. Amnesty International, *Nepal: A Deepening Human Rights Crisis*, December 19, 2002 (available at www.amnesty.org/en/library/info/ASA31/072/2002).

97. Sam Zia-Zarifi, "Army's Violent Abuses Worsen Nepal's Crisis," *International Herald Tribune*, March 8, 2005.

98. International Crisis Group, *Nepal's Future: In Whose Hands?* Report No. 173, August 13 (Brussels/Kathmandu: ICG, 2009).

99. International Crisis Group, *Nepal's Faltering Peace Process*, Asia Report No. 163, February 19 (Brussels/Kathmandu: ICG, 2009), 18.

100. Arjun Guneratne, *Many Tongues, One People: The Making of Tharu Identity in Nepal* (Ithaca, NY: Cornell University Press, 2002).

101. This and the following two paragraphs are based on Bhaskar Gautam, "Parityakta Madhes: likhatdwara kaid Nepali rastriyata," *Studies in Nepali History and Society* 13, no. 1 (2008): 117–46.

102. Frederick H. Gaige, *Regionalism and National Unity in Nepal* (Berkeley: University of California Press).

103. For details about the rebellion, see Bhaskar Gautam, ed., *Madhes Bidrohako Nalibeli* (Kathmandu: Martin Chautari, 2008).

104. International Crisis Group, *Nepal's Troubled Tarai Region*, Asia Report No. 136, July 9 (Brussels/Kathmandu: ICG, 2007), 13.

105. Prashant Jha, "Madhes Rises," *Himal Southasian* 20, no. 8 (2007): 33.

106. Hachhethu, "An Observation on Contemporary Nepali Politics."

107. Jayaprakash Gupta, "Madhes Party bivajan: ko doshi?" *Kantipur*, January 4, 2011, 7.

108. Prashant Jha, "Big Madhesi Politics," *Nepali Times*, January 7, 2011, 3.

109. Prashant Jha, "Three Years Later," *Nepali Times*, January 22, 2010, 3.

110. C. K. Lal, "Five Years On," *República*, January 23, 2012, 6.

111. Ibid.

SUGGESTED READINGS

Brown, T. Louise. *The Challenge to Democracy in Nepal: A Political History*. London: Routledge, 1996.

Dixit, Kanak Mani, and Shastri Ramachandaran, eds. *State of Nepal*. Lalitpur, Nepal: Himal Books, 2002.

Hachhethu, Krishna. *Party Building in Nepal: Organization, Leadership and People*. Kathmandu: Mandala Book Point, 2002.

Hangen, Susan Irene. *The Rise of Ethnic Politics in Nepal: Democracy in the Margins*. London: Routledge, 2010.

Joshi, Bhuwan Lal, and Leo Eugene Rose. *Democratic Innovations in Nepal: A Case Study of Political Acculturation*. Kathmandu: Mandala Book Point, 2004. Originally published by the University of California Press, 1966.

Lawoti, Mahendra. *Towards a Democratic Nepal: Inclusive Political Institutions for a Multicultural Society*. New Delhi: Sage, 2005.

Lawoti, Mahendra, and Anup K. Pahari, eds. *The Maoist Insurgency in Nepal: Revolution in the Twenty-First Century*. London: Routledge, 2010.

Parajulee, Ramjee P. *The Democratic Transition in Nepal*. Lanham, MD: Rowman & Littlefield, 2000.

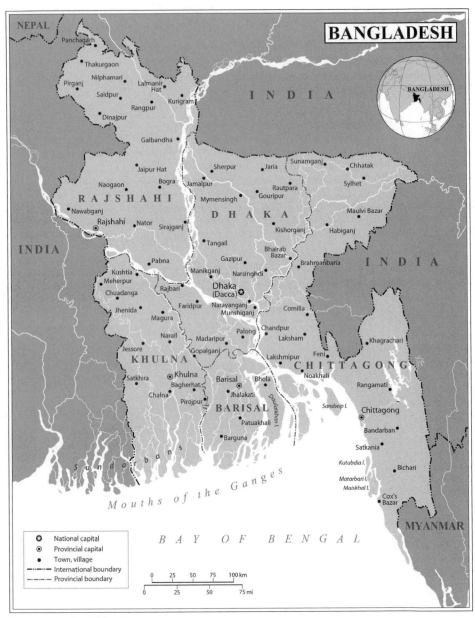

Cartography by Ashley Nepp

6

ॐ

Bangladesh

Haroun er Rashid

POLITICAL HISTORY

The politics of a country is deeply influenced by its cultural history and geography. The roots of the politics of Bangladesh stretch back to the beginning of the colonial years and even beyond. Bangladesh is said to be a new country, but it is so only in its legal framework. Certain aspects of its culture stretch back two thousand years or more.[1] During the medieval period (ca. seventh to thirteenth century CE) the Bangla language area known to Europeans as Bengal and to Asians as Bangala, began to coalesce into a single political domain.[2] Whereas the dominant religion in the medieval period was Buddhism, it faded away and the Muslims became increasingly numerous. The modern period (ca. fourteenth century to present) saw the cultural space divided between Islam and Hinduism, a divide far more strongly delineated than had possibly been the case between Buddhism and Hinduism in the earlier period.

Bangladesh means land of the Bangali (Bengali), the people who speak Bangla as their mother tongue. Cultural Bangladesh, therefore, covers a large area on the eastern part of South Asia.[3] Political Bangladesh covers only half of this area. Obviously one affects the other and has important ramifications on the social politics of this large tract and its neighboring territories. To the west of Bangladesh there is only one political entity, the state of West Bengal in India. To the northeast and east are a number of states of India and also Myanmar. On the borders of Bangladesh are the Indian states of Assam, Meghalaya, Tripura, and Mizoram. Not far away are Nagaland and Manipur. Each of these small parts of India has

TIMELINE

March 7, 1971	Mujibur Rahman declares campaign for independence
March 26, 1971	Pakistan army crackdown on Bangladeshis
December 16, 1971	Liberation of Dhaka city from Pakistan forces
January 10, 1972	Return of Mujibur Rahman to Dhaka
March 7, 1973	Elections to the first Jatiya Sangshad (National Assembly)
September 17, 1974	Bangladesh admitted to the United Nations
August 15, 1975	Assassination of Mujibur Rahman and his family members
November 29, 1976	General Zia Ur Rahman takes over as chief martial law administrator
April 20, 1977	Zia Ur Rahman nominated as president
September 1, 1978	Bangladesh National Party (BNP) finally launched
February 18, 1979	Election to the second Jatiya Sangshad
May 30, 1981	Assassination of President Zia Ur Rahman
November 15, 1981	Election of Justice Sattar as president
March 24, 1982	General H. M. Ershad takes over as chief martial law administrator
January 1, 1986	Jatiya Party (JP) formally launched
May 7, 1986	Elections to the third Jatiya Sangshad (National Assembly)
October 15, 1986	Ershad elected president
March 3, 1988	Elections to the fourth Jatiya Sangshad (National Assembly)
March 1, 1989	Parliamentary bill provides for Local Government Council in Chittagong Hill Tracts
December 4, 1990	President Ershad resigns
February 27, 1991	Elections to the fifth Jatiya Sangshad (National Assembly)
October 22, 1991	Government announces amnesty for Shanti Bahini members
February 15, 1994	First group of Chakma refugees return from India
February 15, 1994	Elections to the sixth Jatiya Sangshad (National Assembly)
March 28, 1996	Thirteenth Amendment to the Constitution providing for elections under caretaker government passed

June 12, 1996	Elections to the seventh Jatiya Sangshad (National Assembly)
December 12, 1996	Signing of the Ganges water sharing treaty with India
December 2, 1997	Signing of the Peace Accord with the Shanti Bahini (CTG Hill Tracts)
October 10, 2001	Elections to the eighth Jatiya Sangshad (National Assembly)
August 21, 2003	Attempted assassination of Hasina
January 11, 2007	Emergency declared under caretaker government
December 29, 2008	Elections to the ninth Jatiya Sangshad (National Assembly)
April 2009	Border Guard uprising and suppression
May 2009	Start of War Crimes Tribunal
June 2012	Fifth Amendment to the Constitution
February 2013	First verdicts of War Crimes Tribunal
March 2013	Outbreak of violence on Sayeedes' verdict
May 2013	Hefazat-i-Islam suppressed
January 2014	Scheduled first sitting of the tenth Jaytia Sangshod (National Assembly)

its own political and social dynamics, which are usually confined to its own political space but sometimes spill over. This has been of considerable concern from time to time, especially with regard to Myanmar. Nepal is only twenty-five kilometers from the northwest corner of Bangladesh, and Bhutan is barely fifty-five kilometers from the northern border. The geostrategic position of Bangladesh is thus quite obvious.

In 1971 the legal, political entity of Bangladesh was created after a bitter War of Liberation, but to understand the complicated political forces of today the search must begin earlier. The politics of any country are dependent on its power structure, which in turn is dependent on the fabric of its society. In some form or other, society in large, literate populations has to be hierarchical. Modern democracy tends to reduce the hierarchy, but in several traditional societies the differentiation is deliberately accentuated. In these societies the power structure is a pyramid that is congruent with the social pyramid. In other words those higher up on the pyramid have disproportionately more power.

Politics is a power game. Whether it does good or otherwise to the nation is dependent on the personalities who wield that power. The rules of play are defined by the legal framework, which itself is drawn up by those in power. This may result in a framework that is inherently weak and therefore can be shredded by those who feel they have sufficient power to change the rules. In countries with weak democratic institutions it is possible for a few persons or a small group to arrogate power in disproportion to their numbers because of the huge disparity in wealth between the rich and the poor. This situation in all poorer countries makes it impossible to bring about meaningful political changes without substantial socioeconomic changes. The most important factor of wealth in Bangladesh is land. This holds true for both rural and urban areas. Land ownership is considered to be the basis of all economic strength. Land holdings are small in comparison to many other regions of South Asia, but in relative terms, one who holds even five acres completely overshadows those who own half an acre or less. Over half the rural population lives below or close to the poverty line, a very abstract concept that tries to distinguish those merely poor from those who are abjectly poor. Being poor means having less food, clothing, and amenities than those who have several acres. It also means less education and less health care. All this adds up to an almost certain dominance of the landed over the landless. It also means much less chance for the poor to have a dignified role in the society.

The majority Muslim population of Bangladesh can be classed into two groups: the asset-owning patrons and the lower-income clients. These two groups have a slight overlap when scions of a rentier family becomes so poor as to take up a plough or pull a rickshaw, or someone from a poorer family moves into the rentier group by acquiring assets. The Hindus have greater fragmentation because of the caste system but can be arranged into three groups, the asset-owning upper class, the fishing and cultivating lower class, and the artisans in between.

Events Pre-1947

The story of Bangladesh may be traced back to the events of 1757 when the British outmaneuvered the Muslim dynasty then ruling Bengal (Subah-e-Bangalah). A scion of this dynasty apparently ruled this large country for another seven years, but by 1765 the charade was over and the British took over completely. The Muslims of Bengal, which in those days included Bihar, Orissa, and Assam, were greatly aggrieved at losing control over their destiny. In the true colonial manner, the British began to encourage the other large community, the Hindus, to manage all subordinate posts and replace Muslims in local-level administrations. This aggrieved the Muslim community even more. They were forced to withdraw into a cultural shell, as the languages of learning were Urdu, Persian, and Arabic. In other words, they clung to the past. The Hindu upper class lost no time in learning English and acquainting themselves with Western science and technology. In northern India, the heartland of the Mughal Empire, the grievances of the Muslims were even greater, and they rose up, along with many Hindus, in the first war of Independence in 1857. This was suppressed by the British, with their better-trained army and the assistance of several Indian rajas; however, they realized not only that the Muslims could once again challenge them in the future but that a popular Hindu revolt could end their exploitation. For the next ninety years the British played the two major communities against each other. Since the Hindu community had become more organized and vocal, the British leaned more toward the Muslim upper class, who cooperated with them. In 1885 the Indian National Congress was founded. Ostensibly noncommunal, it was increasingly seen by the Muslims as a Hindu-dominated organization. The leaders of the Muslim community, mostly large landlords, set up the All India Muslim League in 1905. The founding meeting was in Dacca (Dhaka), the choice of place portending the future. In that same year the British had created the province of East Bengal and Assam, an area with a Muslim majority. This was clearly a riposte to increasing calls from nationalists, mostly Hindus, for independence. From about the third quarter of the nineteenth century to the first quarter of the twentieth, there was a flowering of Bengali literature and arts that came to be known as the Bengal Renaissance. This was India's first response to the challenge and stimulus of the Western civilization. It was entirely the creation of the Hindu upper classes. Its ethos was the revival of Hinduism, in various forms, underlying which was a demand for the end of colonial rule and establishment of Hindu rule. This led the poorer and less literate Muslim community in Bengal to demand a province that had a substantial Muslim majority and was detached from the dominant Hindu society centered in Calcutta.

The creation of the East Bengal and Assam province with Dacca as its capital led to a storm of protests in India, particularly in Calcutta, which was, until 1912, the capital of the British Indian Empire. The colonial government reversed its decision in 1912. Understandably, this emboldened the Hindu-dominated Congress Party and infuriated the Muslim League. However, the Muslims did not want the British to abandon them to majority decisions within a united India, because they felt this would mean subservience to Hindu rule. As a group they shunned the politics of the *bhadralok*, the Hindu upper classes,[4] but after the Khilafat movement (to restore the Caliphate in Turkey) in the early 1920s they felt an increasing need to band together behind the Muslim League. This was true more for the Muslim gentry than for the cultivators, who tended to support the slightly socialistic Krishak Sramik Party. Since 1905 there had been increasing animosity between the Muslims and the Hindus, and in 1921 there was large-scale rioting between the two communities in Dhaka. The communalization of politics became very marked in the early 1930s. In 1940 at the annual conference of the All India Muslim League in Lahore, a resolution was passed stating that the areas in which Muslims were numerically a majority, meaning the Northwestern and Eastern Zones of India, should be grouped to constitute states that would be autonomous and sovereign.[5] Initially the Zones, as these areas were called, were thought of as being separate sovereign states. With the impending departure of the British, some of the politicians of Bengal, both Hindus and Muslims, began negotiations to create an independent Bengal. This effort to create an independent Bengal failed, and the British signaled that they would partition Bengal and Assam and create what was to become the province of East Bengal within Pakistan in 1947. Twenty-three years later, this country became Bangladesh after a War of Liberation to free it from Pakistan. It is ironical that had Pakistan not separated from India, Bangladesh may not have come into being.

Events Post-1947

The province of East Bengal included most of the Sylhet district of Assam and was very similar in area to East Bengal as defined in the earlier "partition" of 1905. However, this did not meet the territorial demand of the Muslim League, which wanted the whole of Bengal and Assam provinces in the Eastern Zone. They clutched at the straw of an independent Bengal, but negotiations broke down on the issue of power sharing between Hindus and Muslims.

In the all-India general elections in late 1945 to early 1946 the largest number of seats won by the Muslim League was in Bengal. It won 113 seats in Bengal, 73 in Punjab, and only 54 in the United Provinces (now Uttar Pradesh).[6] The British took this result to be in support of the Muslim League's idea of the partition of India. It is therefore often said that the Muslims of Bengal were responsible for creating Pakistan.

Within a year of its formation the province of East Bengal in Pakistan saw growing agitation for declaring Bangla (Bengali) as one of the national languages, the other being Urdu. The politicians of the Western province of Pakistan, many of them refugees from India, would not countenance this. They thought Urdu was the proper medium for Muslims, since it was written in Persian script and contained many more Persian and Arabic words. Moreover, it was the language of the Muslims in the United Provinces, who tended to dominate the government of Pakistan in the early years. The alienation of the two widely separated parts of Pakistan began as a cultural issue, and the lack of development became an issue much later. Though the Muslims of Bengal had supported the formation of Pakistan, they were not prepared to lose their cultural identity.[7] To their dismay, the leadership of the Muslim League did not support the Language Movement, which was the name given to the agitation for Bengali (Bangla) as a national language.

In 1949 Maulana Bhashani, a popular leader, broke away from the Muslim league to form the Awami Muslim League, which Mujibur Rahman joined. In the 1954 general elections the Muslim League was crushed by this new party, the Awami Muslim League, led by Suhrawardy, a former Muslim League leader. The word *Muslim* was dropped in 1955 at the insistence of the left. Mujibur Rahman played a prominent role in these elections. Later he assumed a pivotal role in the creation of Bangladesh. He was entirely a product of his early upbringing in village and small-town settings. It is said that his mentality was that of a petit landlord, a middle-class patron. The title reflects his agrarian origins,[8] and he was supposedly rooted in rural politics. He entered BM College in Barisal and then moved to Islamia College in Calcutta, where he became deeply involved in politics and was made the leader of the Muslim League Students Federation and worked closely under Husain Shahid Suhrawardy. In the fighting between Muslims and Hindus in Calcutta in 1946 he was in the forefront, displaying personal bravery. After the creation of Pakistan, an event known as the Partition of India, he moved to Dacca (Dhaka). In 1952 there was an upsurge in the protests over language, and five student demonstrators were shot dead on February 21, 1952. This led to the Language Movement. The general elections of 1954 brought Mujib into power as a provincial minister but only for two months. The central government, then based in Karachi, abrogated the Constitution and imposed governor's rule. Two years later the national legislature began to function again, but the military watched rising nationalism in East Bengal with apprehension. Just two more years later the democratic process was crushed by an army takeover under General Ayub Khan. Incidentally, East Bengal was then renamed East Pakistan and Bengali was accepted as one of the two official languages of Pakistan. Despite this triumph of the Language Movement, the political history of the next twelve years was essentially the sharpening of the conflict between East and West Pakistan. Overtly it was a struggle between two widely separated regions, but at the core it was a struggle between Muslim and Socialist ideologues. The former viewed opposition to Pakistan as undermining the aspirations of Muslim Bengalis, whereas the latter saw it as a class conflict with the upper class (patrons) in the East allying themselves with the military-civil bureaucrats of West Pakistan. By 1965 the Awami League (AL) openly asked for autonomy. They issued a six-point demand and challenged the national government to hold free and fair elections. The six points were (a) federal government with a directly elected Parliament, (b) only defense and foreign affairs to be with the federal government, (c) separate currencies and separate fiscal policies for the two parts of the country, (d) taxes to be levied separately by East and West Pakistan, (e) each of the two parts (federal states) would control the foreign exchange they earned, and (f) each of the two states would be entitled to have their own militia or a paramilitary force.[9]

General Ayub Khan's regime from 1958 to 1969 projected West Pakistan's economy into a take-off mode, but that of East Pakistan stagnated. Population growth in the 1960s and 1970s was very high, at close to 2.7 percent per year in both parts of the country. West Pakistan could cope with it because many development projects were coming into fruition, but in the East there was desperation. The cities did not draw the rural people because there were no employment opportunities, and the villages became ever more crowded and poorer. The difference in per capita income increased to 61 percent between the two parts of the country. The economic malaise quickly became an even more volatile issue than that of language. With increasing unrest in East Pakistan and parts of West Pakistan, Ayub Khan was forced out of the presidency in 1969 and General Yahya Khan took over. The military establishment had no intention of giving up power, and it received full support from the United States. Yahya Khan, having seen the debacle of Ayub Khan's regime, seemed to be amenable to a political settlement. Though he negotiated with Mujib and with Bhutto, the leader of the majority party in West Pakistan, it must be remembered that he was first and foremost a military man. What happened in the next three years clearly showed that the military establishment would not countenance a civilian regime that could make them subservient.

Political pressure in both parts of Pakistan and almost continuous unrest among the college and university students forced Yahya to call for elections in 1970. The student groups of various parties were in the vanguard of the movement to clear the deck of traditional politicians and even bring in a socialist system.[10] These leftist tendencies were strong, but they lacked a charismatic leader. Moulana Bhashani of the National Awami Party was a populist leader who often showed left tendencies but was not a doctrinaire socialist. Sheikh Mujibur Rahman realized that the Awami League needed the support of the Bengali middle class, and he wooed the rising urban entrepreneurial class. He was arrested, released, and then arrested again and charged along with twenty-eight others with treason, for conspiring with India to separate East and West Pakistan. In 1969 the Agartala Conspiracy case, as it became known, turned into a cause célèbre. The Pakistan government alleged that the conspirators had drawn up the plan in Agartala, the capital of Tripura in India, just ten kilometers from the eastern border.

With Mujib in jail, the movement to secure greater rights for East Pakistan was carried out even more vigorously by the East Pakistan Student Action Committee. Their agitation resulted in paralyzing the government and securing the release of Mujib. This show of solidarity and strength no doubt convinced the West Pakistan-dominated military that East Pakistan would break away at the first chance. On their part the Awami League leadership realized they could use the working class to further the interests of the petite bourgeoisie.[11] The students who led the 1969 movement were mostly from the landowning class, since only they could afford higher education. They had joined hands with the growing middle class in urban areas to realize greater economic opportunities in an East Pakistan that was expected to have autonomy in a federated Pakistan. Lacking a leader of Sheikh Mujib's stature, the left-leaning students began to gather around him and convince him that without independence East Pakistan would not achieve its economic and cultural goals. These student leaders time and again steered him away from compromise and toward confrontation.

The 1970 election results were a shock for Yahya and Bhutto. The Awami League won 167 out of 169 seats in East Pakistan and thus gave a resounding approval to the six-point program. Elated at this victory, Sheikh Mujib demanded that he should be installed as the prime minister of Pakistan. Bhutto objected, citing his party's winning of the majority of seats in West Pakistan and the Awami League's failure to win a single seat there. Yahya stalled, time and again delaying the convening of the National Assembly. Several rounds of negotiations took place between Sheikh Mujib, Bhutto, and Yahya. Sheikh Mujib insisted that as leader of the party that had won the largest number of seats he should form the government. With hindsight it seems that protracted negotiation, leading to months of delay, was deliberately fostered by Yahya to allow the military to build up their strength in the East. Much of what went on in the negotiations was kept secret and the public was led to believe that a compromise solution would be announced and the National Assembly called on March 25, 1971. General Yahya, who was in Dhaka at that time, suddenly flew back to Karachi on March 25, and a brutal military crackdown began late that very evening.

As soon as the army struck without warning, East Pakistan ceased to exist in the hearts of the people and an independent Bangladesh had come into being. On March 26, a faint broadcast by Major Zia Ur Rahman from Radio Chittagong was heard proclaiming the independent state of Bangladesh. Sheikh Mujib had refused to flee on March 25. He was arrested and later charged with sedition. The fire of the army was on the students, who were killed by the hundreds on that night alone. From then on, massacres big and small were perpetrated every day as the army spread throughout Bangladesh to crush the will of the people. The War of Liberation lasted from March 25 to December 16 of 1971. The people were very relieved it was over within the year, though at one time it looked as if it would drag on, possibly as guerrilla warfare, for many years. The resistance fighters, known as Mukti Bahini, and Bengalis from the Pakistan army had fought the Pakistanis from the very first day and had created small pockets of liberated areas in different places. The entire Awami League leadership, other than Sheikh Mujib, had escaped to India and had set up a government with the full backing of the government of India. The fiction was that the beleaguered government of Bangladesh operated from Mujibnagar, a village in Bangladesh close to the border of India. In reality it operated from Calcutta (Kolkata) and quite openly, too.

For many months before the brutal crackdown the U.S. government had tried to broker a solution between Sheikh Mujib, Bhutto, and Yahya, because in those Cold War years Pakistan was a major player in U.S. foreign policy. After the Mujibnagar government was set up, Washington backed the unity of Pakistan over the vociferous condemnation of Bengalis everywhere and also of many Americans.[12] India was not deterred in its policy of weakening Pakistan at every opportunity. It may be recalled that the Congress Party had never reconciled itself to the very formation of Pakistan. India was at that time quite close to the USSR, though nowhere near to being a socialist economy. The Liberation war had squarely aligned the United States with Pakistan and the USSR with India.

Around September, India seems to have decided to openly assist in the Liberation war. Two factors had tipped the balance. First, the radical left forces, essentially the Naxalites, had begun to gain ground in India, even in urban areas. The leftist students and workers in Bangladesh were sharply radicalized by the brutality of the Pakistan army, and there was the distinct possibility that they would join the Naxalites. This would have been a grave internal threat to India, because anything faintly resembling an all-Bengal movement remained an anathema to the politicians of northern India. Even more threatening was the possibility of radical left thought and action undermining the essentially capitalist economy of India. Second, on a much lower order of seriousness, there was a growing torrent of refugees, mostly Hindus, from Bangladesh, which affected West Bengal socially by opening up old wounds. Much of the terror unleashed by the Pakistan army was against Hindus, since they were supposed to be pro- India instinctively. This raised the specter of communal riots in India if Hindu extremists retaliated. In order to thwart these two possibilities India decided to invade and install the Mujibnagar government in Dhaka. The official line is that India invaded to assist the Mukti Bahini. They began the operations on November 19, 1971, and quickly reached Dhaka, assisted along their routes by the Mukti Bahini. The Pakistani army did not sally out, displaying a bunker mentality. The U.S. government sent the aircraft carrier *Enterprise* into the Bay of Bengal, probably to help the Pakistanis if they put up a stiff fight. This they did not do, surrendering unexpectedly and suddenly on December 16.

Bangladesh celebrates December 16 as Victory Day, remembering Indian assistance with mixed feelings. Indian participation in the Liberation war was for their own interests. India did not ask the newly formed government in Dhaka, with Bangabandhu Sheikh Mujibur Rahman at its head, about the disposal of the military hardware captured from the Pakistan army. It was all taken to India. They also began installing military and civil officers to "assist" the bureaucracy, though no such assistance was sought. Bangladeshis had developed repugnance for Pakistan, but it did not mean they wanted the Indians to stay on. Very soon voices were raised questioning why the Indians were staying on when Bangladeshis were quite capable managing their own affairs. Sheikh Mujib had returned from imprisonment in Pakistan less than a month after the liberation of Dhaka. He had not trusted the Congress since his college days and never forgot the armed confrontations with the Hindu Mahasabha cadres in 1946. Now he took advantage of the rising anti-India feelings to ask Indira Gandhi, then prime minister of India, to withdraw the Indian army. To everyone's surprise she did. Most likely, Indira Gandhi wanted to avoid bad publicity and the possibility of an insurgency. The withdrawal of Indian troops greatly enhanced the stature of Sheikh Mujib, who had earlier been honored with the title of Bangabandhu (Friend of Bengal) by his Awami League admirers.

The Sheikh Mujib Period (1972–1974)

From January 1972 to August 1974, when he was assassinated, Mujib tried hard to control a country wracked by suspicions, torn by factionalism, and bled by corruption. To make matters worse, population growth outstripped food production. It was to be expected that the nightmare of the Pakistan army's terror would leave a traumatized nation. The terror campaign had been aided by Bengalis who believed that the quest for Bangladesh was a Hindu plot to undo Muslim Pakistan. Some of them formed into an auxiliary of the Pakistan army known as Razakar. They informed on Mukti Bahini supporters, often assisting in murders and rapes. Their heinous role has left a deep scar on the soul of the nation. It has also created an abiding deep dislike of Muslim extremism among the secular intellectuals.

Not everyone participated in the armed struggle, and those who did had many different motives. With Liberation they began to blame each other of acting mala fide. Not only did the various left-leaning parties blame the Awami League for not following a socialist policy but the Awami League itself was factionalized.[13] Sheikh Mujib had sufficient charisma and following to keep the party together, but the factions blamed each other openly. Some Awami League leaders had vaulted from very modest means to positions of power controlling considerable wealth. Some of them and their cronies amassed wealth, whereas others got little of the spoils. The industries and land belonging to West Pakistanis was seized and given to the chosen few to manage. This generally meant expropriation for personal benefit. The pattern was familiar from rural situations where patrons are expected to grab newly formed land and distribute parts to staunch supporters.

This system of political patronage was opposed by only a few, the most prominent among them being Tajuddin Ahmed, the general secretary of the Awami League. Despite his political acumen and honesty, he did not have the following in the party to rival Sheikh Mujib. Deep in organizational work, and later as minister for planning for a mixed economy, he had not built up a popular following. He was staunchly leftist but not far from the center. He had persuaded Sheikh Mujib to nationalize many industries and possibly also to set up one-party rule. There were many opposed to him. Whereas Tajuddin wanted to shun America, many others wanted to court her. They generally kept quiet because the leftist student groups were armed and aggressive.

Sheikh Mujib himself arrogated more power by forming paramilitary units such as the Rakkhi Bahini, the Chhechha Sevak Bahini, and the Lal Bahini. The ostensible reason for these three Bahini (forces) was to combat the spread of lawlessness in rural areas by radical leftists who thought the Bangladesh "revolution" had been betrayed.[14] Other groups whose main aim was banditry took advantage of the situation. The government had to use the Bangladesh Rifles, Bangladesh police, Ansars, and the three Bahinis to keep some semblance of order. This was achieved, but at considerable social cost created by the three Bahinis.

A day after his return, Sheikh Mujib announced the Provisional Constitutional Order, which was followed up by a Constitution in December 1972. In March 1973 national elections were held and the Awami League received 291 out of 300 seats, even though they received 73 percent of the votes. This lopsided victory was due to a number of reasons, among the foremost being the strong-arm tactics of the Awami League. The election results directly affected the landlord instincts in Sheikh Mujib. He felt that what was good for him was good for the country. In this attitude he was greatly encouraged by all within his party, which was wracked by several factions, of which two, Jubo Dal led by Sheikh Moni and the Shramik League led by Abdul Mannan, became very powerful. These two young leaders often spoke in the name of Sheikh Mujib and threatened publicly that if Sheikh Mujib gave the order they would "cleanse and purify" the party, the civil administration, and the rest of the country of corrupt and unpatriotic elements. This must have been disquieting, if not alarming, to many in party and bureaucracy and most likely in the armed forces, too.

During the 1960s, dependence on imported food grains had steadily increased and by the mid-1970s the food situation was quite desperate. Population growth was high, but growth in rice production was slow. The United States provided wheat under Public Law 480, and this saved the poor people from near starvation. The food gap was such that it was described as being "ship to mouth"; any delay in shipments resulted in serious food shortages in rice-deficit areas. In 1974 Bangladesh tried to export jute bags to Cuba and was immediately rebuffed by the U.S. government, which delayed shipments of PL 480 wheat. Just at that time, floods damaged the rice crop in the north (mainly Kurigram). Relief could not be provided, and soon there were famine conditions in the northern parts of the country. This was a great blow to Sheikh Mujib's government and his own prestige. The famine and political disturbance in the countryside, the government's inability to improve the economy, factional infighting in his own party, and his desire to be the center of all power, all of these and other reasons contributed to a change in Mujib's mind about how the country should be governed.

There were discussions about necessary changes within the Awami League with the left-leaning political leaders looking to India and the USSR for a model. It seems the powerful elites within the Awami League had always been loath to work within a parliamentary system where opposition parties would be able to represent different points of view. In January 1975 the National Assembly passed an amendment to the Constitution that changed it entirely. The form of government was changed from parliamentary to presidential, the multiparty system was replaced by a single-party system, and civil liberties and the power of the courts were restricted. None of these went down well with the mass of civilians or the armed forces. The AL had avowedly taken the Indian style of democracy as its model, but that had not worked. It had also tried to impose secularism as the state ideology, but the masses moved away from it toward the Muslim Bengal ideal of earlier years. Rounaq Jahan has stated that Liberation "was followed by a very rapid rise in anti-India feelings among the masses and the secular ideology become unpopular."[15]

A month after Sheikh Mujib changed the Constitution, which he called the "second revolution," he announced the launching of the Bangladesh Krishok Shromik Awami League (BAKSAL), the party which alone would govern the country. This radical move seems to have been steered by the left wing of the Awami League, led by Tajuddin Ahmed. Members of all the civil bureaucracy and armed forces were also asked to join. What

Mujib thought was that a new system would emerge, though there was no attempt at changing the patron-client power base. Sheikh Mujib had always felt uneasy with the civilian bureaucracy and he wanted to bring it down from its pedestal. A few months into his experiment he said, "The system we find today is the British Colonial system. . . . I want to smash the old moth-eaten administrative system. I want to smash the moth-eaten legal system and create a new one. This new system of mine is the revolution."[16] He was right in thinking that change was needed, but given his strong patron bias there was no chance of a radical change.

His actions and statements had alarmed not only the powerful civilian bureaucrats but, more significantly, the armed forces also. By asking them to join BAKSAL he was striking a major blow at their internal discipline. He had earlier demoralized them by creating the Rakkhi Bahini, and now he seemed to take them on directly. On August 15, 1975, a small group of officers and soldiers attacked Sheikh Mujib's house and assassinated him and several members of his family, including his nephew Sheikh Moni. There was strong public resentment against Sheikh Mujib's extended family because they were considered to be corrupt. Their corruption had apparently aggravated the economic hardship of the common man. In fact, there was not a single large demonstration against the coup.

The Khondakar Mushtaq Ahmed Interregnum (1975–1977)

Though led by a small group of junior army officers this was a violent shift from the leftist trend to a clearly rightist trend. Khondakar Mushtaq Ahmed, who took over the helm of the government with the support of the coup leaders, was known to lead the right wing of the Awami League.[17] Pakistan quickly recognized the new regime. Saudi Arabia and China had both refused to recognize Bangladesh earlier, but now they did so. The left predictably charged that the CIA had a hand in engineering the overthrow. A definite change in state ideology and toward Muslim symbols was discernable. The Bengali slogan "Joi Bangla" (Victory to Bangla) was replaced by "Bangladesh Zindabad," the Persian/Urdu word *zindabad* being distinctly Muslim Bengali (though also used in Hindi).

Khondakar Mushtaq Ahmed made General Zia ur Rahman (popularly known as Zia) the chief of staff after removing the one who had held that post, clearly indicating that Zia was trusted by the right. Yet he was close to Colonel Abu Taher, who headed the radical leftist group within the army, self-styled as Biplobi Gono Bahini (Revolutionary Peoples Force). On November 3 there was another coup, this time by General Khaled Mosharraf, and Zia was put under house arrest. Earlier, several senior AL leaders, including Taj Uddin Ahmed, had been jailed pending charges. They were assassinated in the jail. Rumors at that time had it that Mosharraf's coup was backed by the Awami League and India. This inflamed feelings among the military and public against Mosharraf. Colonel Taher led the counter-coup when there was an uprising in the army on November 7. This led to the death of Mosharraf and the freeing of Zia, who was reinstalled as chief of staff. Taher may have thought he could utilize Zia's popularity in the army, but he was very wrong. The Gono Bahini issued a twelve-point demand, essentially asking for a classless revolutionary army. Zia moved swiftly to consolidate his position by garnering rightist forces. On November 15 he promulgated a martial law regulation prescribing death for any future mutineer, which showed he was ready to tackle the Gono Bahini. Just nine days later, on November 24, he had Taher arrested. Though Zia was now the most powerful person in the country, able to dictate to the president, Abu Sadat Mohammad Sayem, he still had to contend with mutinies by various army units, demands by political parties for early elections, and a power play by Air Vice Marshal Tawab, who along with Zia was one of the two deputy chief martial law administrators. Zia crushed the mutinies ruthlessly and had Colonel Taher executed in July 1976. As for the political parties, he deftly played around them for more than three long years. A day after he was freed a presidential proclamation dissolved Parliament and continued martial law. It also pledged a general election by February 1977. In April 1976 Zia forced Tawab to resign and go into exile. This allowed him to maneuver freely since President Sayem carried out all his requests.

That there was a complete turnaround from Mujib's years was evident from the appointment as minister or adviser persons such as M. N. Huda, Anwarul Haq, Hafizuddin, Colonel (retd.) M. M. Haq, and Professor Shamsul Haq, all of whom had held high posts in the Ayub Khan or Yahya Khan regimes. This open flouting of pro-leftist policy was possible because many active party workers of the two major opposition parties, the Awami League and JSD, had been imprisoned. Since martial law was in force, many other forms of coercion could be used. Zia's government began to get a bad name in the U.S. press and questions were asked about human rights abuses in U.S. Congress. In July 1976, soon after the openly pro-U.S. Tawab had been pushed out, the Political Parties Regulation (PPR) was issued. This allowed the political parties to petition the government to be given permission to function. The president increasingly relied on the civil bureaucracy, most of whose senior officers had been in the Pakistan Civil Service.

In November 1976 President Sayem announced that general elections would not be held in February 1977, that elections to the Union Parishads (local councils) would be held in January 1977 and that elections to the Pourosabhas (municipalities) and Zila Parishads would be held in stages thereafter. The Union Council elections, and the following ones, brought to local level power the age-old landowner-patrons and their kin.

Ziaur Rahman's Presidency (1977–1981)

Nine days after Sayem's announcement, Zia became the chief martial law administrator, which in fact was a dictatorial position. Less than five months later, on April 20, 1977, Zia assumed the post of the president. He announced that national elections would be held in December 1978, but before that he would seek people's support of his policies in a referendum on May 30, just forty days away. Next he changed two of the four principles of state ideology in the Constitution. These four had been nationalism, democracy, socialism, and secularism. The amendments affected secularism, socialism, and nationalism. Secularism was deleted and Islam was put in its place by asserting "absolute trust and faith in Almighty Allah." The deep-seated feelings for Muslim Bengal had repulsed a pull toward the left, and this seemed to find favor with the majority. Socialism was curbed by defining its purpose as the achievement of "economic and social justice." Moreover expropriation of property without compensation was annulled and henceforth acquisition for nationalization could be only with compensation. This assertion of the rights of property owners greatly reassured the middle class. The earlier provision was there not so much to humble the propertied class as to put nationalized property into the hands of Awami Leaguers. As regards nationalism there was a small but significant change. Whereas the 1972 Constitution called all citizens of the country "Bengali," this amendment said they were "Bangladeshi." Many Muslims felt the former term appeased the Bengalis of India and were pleased with the change because they felt Bangladesh must not be confused with any part of India.

Zia was assassinated in a military coup on May 30, 1981. Throughout his years in control of the country he could not reconcile the different elements in the army, in particular, those who had participated in the Liberation war (the "freedom fighter") and those who had returned from Pakistan.[18]

The Ershad Regime (1982–1990)

Though Zia was assassinated by a faction of the army, the government remained civilian in form until Lieutenant General Hussain Muhammad Ershad took over as chief martial law administrator ten months later. In these months the Bangladesh Nationalist Party (BNP) government remained and Justice Abdus Sattar, the civilian vice president, took over as president. The army officers demanded a greater say in the government.

The civilians tried to resist, but then agreed to a National Security Council with the president, vice president, prime minister, and the chiefs of the three military services as members. This did not satisfy the ambitions of the senior military officers. On March 24, 1982, Ershad took over as chief martial law administrator after declaring martial law, suspending the Constitution, dismissing Sattar and his cabinet, and dissolving the Jatiya Sangshad (National Assembly). He appointed the air and navy chiefs as his deputies. Thereafter he ruled the country under military law until 1986.

Ershad took an even more rightist path than Zia, vigorously promoting capitalist policies and paying lip service to Islamic ideals. Zia had begun to undo the state capitalism of the Mujib years. Ershad pushed even more for disinvestment of industries to private ownership. The major donors were pleased with his policies and increased their loans. In return, he tried to implement a structural adjustment program. Fortuitously the RMG industries began to mushroom in these years, and the availability of increasing employment blunted political discount. Like Zia he relied on a chosen group of civil bureaucrats and many retired military officers. He floated a party named Jana Dal (People's Party) in 1983, but it did not do too well. Then in 1986 he formed the Jatiya Party (National Party), which consisted mostly of defectors from other political parties, mainly from the BNP. State patronage made sure it would survive and flourish.

Ershad abolished the system of Gram Sarker (village government) set up under Zia (but never really implemented) and turned all the 460 Thanas (police stations) into Upazilas (subdistricts). Under the new system the Upazilas Parishad (subdistrict council) would be headed by a democratically elected chairman, a move thoroughly disliked by the civilian bureaucracy, since senior officers posted to the Upazila were made accountable to the Parishad. The Upazilas were made the focal points for local administration and development. However, the system did not work well, with considerable infighting between the elected members and the bureaucrats. It has been said that "the Upazila become a den of corruption and misuse of public money in which both elected Chairman and appointed officials were involved."[19]

The aping of Zia's policies by Ershad is quite clear. In 1984 he held local elections, so that the Union Council members could be patronized to support the Jatiya Party (JP). He also held a national referendum in 1985 both to test the water and to gain more time. In 1986 elections were held both for the post of president, which he of course won, and for a National Assembly. In his search for a power base there were elections for the National Assembly once again in 1988.

During Ershad's time, enhanced aid flow allowed considerable growth in infrastructure, particularly roads. It had become quite apparent in the early 1980s that poor infrastructure inherited from East Pakistan times and merely patched up since then was hopelessly inadequate for growth that could be generated by the private sector. To a large extent, the form and content of development was guided by the World Bank. Since Ershad had embraced the Western powers and capitalism wholeheartedly, the path of economic development was clearly toward foreign market dependency. There was also a big change in the delivery system of development assistance. A few nongovernmental organizations (NGOs) for development work had been set up in the early 1970s, but their numbers suddenly grew exponentially in the 1980s when donors found their service delivery was more prompt than the government routing. Moreover the NGO personnel were more amenable to donor aims and controls than government officials. The donors found large NGOs such as BRAC, PROSHIKA, RDRS, and ASA so suitable for their aim of privatizing the service functions of the government that at one time nearly a third of all assistance to the country was channeled through NGOs. Ershad did not protest these moves. He was busy maneuvering the Upazila system to bolster his Jatiya Party.

Public opinion turned against him when they found that he was not sincere when he promised a corruption-free system. In fact corruption increased by leaps and bounds and he was himself implicated in corrupt practices. Khaleda Zia thought he may have had a hand in the assassination of Ziaur Rahman, and she stumped the country tirelessly to speak out against his policies and his corrupt government (see box 6.1). Massive protests on the streets, *hartals*, and noncooperation by all sections of the civil society forced him to resign on December 5, 1990. He left the helm of government to Chief Justice Shahabuddin Ahmed, who gave up his post to become the acting president.

Box 6.1. Khaleda Zia (1945–)

Khaleda Zia is the widow of President Ziaur Rahman, who was assassinated in 1981. After the death of her husband she became very active in politics, and campaigned tirelessly against the corrupt rule of General Ershad. In the first free and fair election in the country, in 1991, she became the prime minister for a five-year term. During this period she introduced compulsory free primary education and free education for girls up to grade 10. She became prime minister once again for the period 2001–2006. The military-backed Caretaker Government has detained and charged her with acts of corruption. She has campaigned tirelessly against Sheikh Hasina's second term of office (2008–present).

The First Khaleda Government (1991–1996)

Acting President Shahabuddin Ahmed's task was to organize a free and fair election, and this government managed to do so. Within ninety days elections were held and it was no surprise that the BNP emerged the winner with 140 of the 300 seats. Khaleda Zia had opposed Ershad from the very beginning and steadfastly refused to join in any of the elections held by him. By participating in the 1986 elections AL had lost a good deal of their prestige, and they came second with 88 seats. The Jatiya Party was strong only in Ershad's home base of Rangpur, but they won as many as 35 seats. The Jama'at-i-Islami surprised many by winning 18 seats, and significantly many of these were along or near the western border. The BNP had to join with the Jamaat to form a government, and this gave the Jamaat the chance to build up their base.

After taking over, the BNP worked with the AL to change the form of government from presidential to parliamentary. Cooperation between the two big parties lasted for about two years. Thereafter cooperation gave way to continuous street agitation by AL workers and frequent clashes between the workers of the two parties. In 1994 a by-election in Magura was won by the BNP candidate but the AL charged that the result was a fraud. This led to many shutdowns, with the AL demonstrating that they controlled the streets in the urban areas. Despite work stoppages and prolonged closure of Chittagong port, the economy did not collapse, though it was a close call. That imports and exports were able to move is a testament to the extent to which the private sector had transformed the economy. Khaleda had continued the pro-Western policies of Zia and Ershad and privatized many state-controlled industries. Big business became a major factor in national politics.[20] She had reversed the Upazila system to the earlier Thana system and allowed the senior bureaucrat, the thana nirbahi (executive) officer (TNO) to take control of administration and development.

When her term was nearly over in February 1996 a national election was held, but very few voted because of AL control of the streets and the threat of physical violence. Despite the very low turnout a fairly large vote was declared. This was pounced upon by AL as the type of fraud to be expected unless caretaker governments supervised national elections. The concept of caretaker governments is uniquely Bangladeshi and reflects the tendency of the nation to polarize on major issues. A caretaker government is expected to take over at least three months before national elections, hold the elections, and then hand over power. This was thought necessary to prevent the ruling party from rigging the elections. Ershad had handed over to a caretaker president and set a precedent. After the February elections even senior bureaucrats began to speak out openly, and some of them openly canvassed for AL. Donors, always powerful since they control aid, advised her to hand over to a caretaker government. The February National Assembly met once only to pass an amendment to the Constitution allowing for caretaker governments for ninety days only. The members of the Assembly, including Khaleda, then resigned. The head of the caretaker government had been agreed upon by both parties and his neutral stand alleviated many fears. The election in June 1996 gave the AL 146 seats, the BNP 116, the Jatiya Party 32 seats, and the Jamaat a mere 3 seats. It was said that the BNP could have won had they refrained from the February elections and gone in for a caretaker government. As for the rout of the Jamaat it was said that the people had seen through their personal agenda, which was cloaked in a religious garb. The AL that won handsomely, headed by Sheikh Hasina, was certainly not the party of the early 1970s (see box 6.2). They had given up their socialist ideology and committed to the free market economy. They had wooed the civil bureaucrats and even the military. Most revealingly, Hasina had gone out of her way to demonstrate that she was a believing Muslim by going on the haj and wearing hijab for a while.

Box 6.2. Sheikh Hasina (1947–)

Sheikh Hasina is one of the major political figures in Bangladesh. She is the daughter of Sheikh Mujibur Rahman. When he was assassinated with his family she was in Germany and thus was spared. She was active in student politics in her college and university days, but after her marriage she stayed out of politics until the Awami League party implored her to come back as its head. In 1982 she was the first to raise the voice of protest against an assumption of state-power through military coups d'état. During the Ershad regime she was put under house arrest several times for protesting against his arbitrary actions. She was prime minister from 1996 to 2001. During this period her two main achievements were the signing of the Peace Accord for the Hill Tracts and the signing of the thirty-year Ganges Water Sharing Treaty. In 2006 she was again put under house arrest by the military-backed caretaker government, which charged her with corruption. She returned to power as prime minister in 2009.

The Hasina Government (1996–2001)

Over the past five years the AL had cultivated the civil bureaucracy and the military officers. Most important they had assured the powerful industrialist and trader group that they had no problems with big business and free market economy. In fact several of the AL bigwigs were already in that group. Several retired military and civil officers contested and won seats on the AL ticket. Though they apparently fought tooth and nail on the public stage, in reality the AL and the BNP had come a lot closer over the years in their views about the economy and the patron-client relationship. Their views on international relations were, however, dramatically opposed. Whereas the AL favored closer ties with India, the BNP did not.

The two big achievements of this government were the 1996 Ganges Water Sharing Treaty with India and in 1997 the Peace Accord with the tribal rebels in the Chittagong Hill Tracts area. Ever since India constructed a barrage across the Ganges at Farakka, Bangladesh had accused India of diverting most of the flow during the critical months of March to May when flow was at its lowest.[21] It is to Hasina's credit that she could persuade India to be fair and allocate a reasonable amount of flow during the low water season. There had been an agreement during Mujib's time, which was not renewed during the rule of the generals, but this thirty-year treaty was considered fair to Bangladesh.

The other big achievement was a Peace Accord with the Shanti Bahini, the guerrilla group (mainly Chakma) who had rebelled against the settlement of Bangalis in the Chittagong Hill Tracts. This accord granted the tribal people indigenous to that area some local autonomy but allowed the settlers to remain. The BNP saw the accord as a sellout, but it did bring peace to that area and a fair measure of development.[22]

Hasina called for a national consensus government, but the BNP declined to join. The Jatiya Party and JSD did join and gave the government a majority in the National Assembly. She formed several commissions to suggest changes in education and health policies and the mechanism of local government and civil administration. The commissions' membership included people from all walks of life including the now powerful NGO sector. The industrialists had become the most influential lobby, given the vast amounts of money they had made, particularly in the RMG sector and also through land speculation. An industrial policy document was approved to their satisfaction. AL wanted closer economic ties with India, but the terms seemed to be very much in favor of the bigger partner. India's rapid industrialization had pushed up its fuel needs and it wanted to tap into Bangladesh's fairly rich natural gas potential. India also wanted transit rights to reach the northeastern states (with rebellions in all of them) and for the shipment of goods. The AL and its allies seemed to be split on these terms, and the BNP was vehemently opposed. Their vehemence and the anti-India mood of the public made it impossible for the Hasina government to sign these deals, both in the 1990s and more recently (2008–2014).

On the administration front, though a revamping of the government structure was talked about, only Union Parishad–level elections were held. Unlike in earlier years the AL did not mind the civil bureaucrats and technocrats running the administration. The major problem the AL faced with the public was its pro-India leanings. When elections were held in 2001 the AL secured 40 percent of the vote but only 62 out of 300 seats. In many constituencies they lost to the opposition candidate, mainly the BNP, by just a few thousand votes. The BNP led a coalition of BNP, Jatiya Party, Jamaat, and Islami Oikya Jote (Islamic Unity Front), which won 46 percent of the votes and a windfall of 225 seats, of which the BNP candidates won 192 seats, and the Jamaat, which had once been written off, bounced back by winning 17 seats for its nominees.

Khaleda Zia's Second Term (2001–2006)

The result of the 2001 election stunned the AL, but it was a free and fair election according to national and international observers. The pendulum swing of the nonparty independent and nationalist voters seemed to have swung away from the AL because of their pro-India pronouncements. Though the BNP spoke against the Ganges Treaty and the Hill Tracts Accord, they realized they were realistic and did not unravel them. However, the BNP-led alliance government did move against AL party workers in many constituencies. Since the AL had a solid core of support in the Hindu community, there were many instances of repression against them, particularly in the southwest. Most of these cases of communally targeted crime were instigated by local politicians aided by local criminals. They do not seem to have had the backing of the government, but their tardy response, perhaps influenced by the Jamaat and Islami Oikya Jote, was tantamount to moral support. The law and order situation, which had deteriorated during the previous government, went from bad to worse. To some observers this was a natural consequence of the jostling between the newly super-rich, particularly for grabbing government-owned land. Khaleda deployed the army in Operation Clean Heart, and many alleged criminals were eliminated. Later she had to deploy the Bangladesh Rifles in Operation Spider Web to ferret out drug smugglers and other antisocial elements. Several custodial deaths, euphemistically said to be due to "crossfire," raised serious concerns about Human Rights. Yet there was general consensus that the victims were gangsters, and their violence did go down dramatically. However, violence of another type grew suddenly. Extreme Islamists, mainly those in the Jamat-ul-Mujahideen Bangladesh (JMB) group, began to openly criticize the pro-West tilt of the government and the society. In 2003 there was a grenade attack by them on a political rally by Sheikh Hasina, but she luckily escaped unhurt. In 2005 they set off four hundred small explosive devices in various parts of the country within an hour. This, and instances of them lynching alleged leftists and an attempt at suicide-bombing, raised a major alarm. Members of various extreme groups were put on trial and several of them were hanged for murder.

Despite the alliances with openly "Islamist" parties, foreign aid doubled. There was also a sharp rise in remittance by Bangladeshi workers who had gone abroad. Both of these sources of financing buoyed up the economy, increasing industrial employment and spending on development projects.

On the political side, this government had much less success. The AL boycotted the National Assembly and several by-elections. This did nothing to build up a parliamentary tradition. Lacking opposition in the National Assembly, or Jatiya Sangshad (JS), the four-party alliances felt they could do whatever they wanted in their own interest. Most significantly the Jamaat began to give employment to its dedicated workers in various government organizations that they dominated by virtue of the ministries they controlled. This was viewed with great alarm by all other groups. The affluent middle class wanted a moderate, centrist line on all matters, but the newly super-rich, some of whom earned the epithet of "godfather," were not to be thwarted in seizing whatever they could. To make matters worse there was infighting between the Alliances parties and within the BNP, too. Khaleda Zia's son Tareq became the power behind the throne and was accused by detractors of having amassed enormous wealth and of distributing favors. He appeared to be inclined to a dynastic takeover, and by 2005 all major decisions seemed to be made by him, even though he was not in the government in any capacity. In 2004 the AL announced it wanted the government to resign or else it would topple it through agitation, as it did in 1996. The specters of shutdowns and road closures were by now dreaded by industrialists, whose assets had increased considerably over a decade. It was also disliked by the bigger farmers, since they had moved into the Green Revolution and needed inputs like diesel fuel and fertilizers in seasonal peak periods. Nevertheless the AL felt that for the greater good of the country some sacrifice had to be made. The mood of the majority was not quite that of a decade ago, and the country was not brought to a standstill. The threat of economic and social disruption was sufficient to make many in the civil society (bureaucrat, NGO personnel, affluent farmers, and teachers) and in the military discuss ways out of a polarizing politics that periodically paralyzed the country. Matters were brought to a head when the Alliances announced they would hold the next national election while they were in office, and would not need a caretaker interregnum. This created a furor in the opposition. Such was the level of concern that even donors and embassy personnel became vocal. It was reported that the U.S. ambassador hinted at a "Third Force" unless the two major parties found a parliamentary solution. Several meeting to discuss the political deadlock were reportedly held by the various bilateral and multilateral donor agencies, and they pressured the BNP and AL to hold talks about the appointment of the caretaker government. There was a deadlock over the appointment of the chief election commissioner and much to and fro of political negotiators. The term of the Alliances government ended in December 2006, and, not unexpectedly, the military intervened a month later to create a new caretaker government known popularly as One-Eleven, because the change was effected on January 11 (2007).

The One Eleven Caretaker Government (2007–2008)

The installment of this caretaker government had many ups and downs when the Alliances tried to maneuver the incumbent president, Iajuddin Ahmed, into appointing someone of their choice. The military tired of their twists and turns and forced Iajuddin himself to be the caretaker president with advisers chosen by them. The public accepted this move, which made the military the guarantor of future democratic rule. Corruption has been a big issue right from the early 1970s, but since the parties needed big funding no real move to reduce it was made. There was known corruption by petty officials and technocrats in many government organizations, but they were only tapped for funding and never indicted. Their corruption had cut into the efficiency of government-owned organizations, such as Titas Gas Distribution Company, and departments, such as the Forest Department. All this affected the utilization and returns from donor funding, which made them vocal about reducing corruption. In a very bold move, the military-backed caretaker government indicted many prominent politicians and businessmen for corruption and locked them up for trial. Among the politicians indicted were Sheikh Hasina and Khaleda Zia. Several businessmen-politicians were given long-term punishments. What bothered observers most is that while some of the corrupt were indicted and tried, others remained free. Some of the issues that had been raised since 1994, such as transparent ballot boxes and identity cards for all voters, were quickly accepted and implemented.

Sheikh Hasina's Second Term (2008–2013)

The AL charged the BNP with three major misdemeanors: packing the Election Commission with persons supporting them; posting officers in the districts with known BNP leaning; and worst of all, creating a million bogus voters by listing them on electoral rolls. None of these allegations were proved, but in the preelection charged atmosphere they were damaging. Some constituencies had their borders redrawn at AL insistence. In the elections that followed the BNP lost many seats by narrow margins and the result was lopsided, mirroring the 2001 results. The AL won by a landslide, receiving 230 seats out of 300, with the BNP getting only 30 seats, despite its 30 percent of the vote. This lopsided result again revived demands for seats to be allocated by proportion of votes received.

Soon after being elected, Sheikh Hasina moved quickly to charge Jamaat leaders with anti-Liberation sentiments and crimes committed during the Liberation struggle, and placed them on trial. This pleased the extreme leftists and the Hindus, who had suffered grievously at their hands. She actively pursued Indian calls for a treaty to allow for transit through Bangladesh to its northeastern states, and also promoted Hindu officers to many high posts, often over the heads of more senior officers. This was greatly resented by many, including many in the AL itself. On the other hand, she resisted calls to de-Islamicize the Constitution. There was also the Yunus affair, where she removed Muhammad Yunus (see box 6.3), the Nobel Peace Prize winner, from the chairmanship of

---

Box 6.3. Muhammad Yunus (1940–)

Muhammad Yunus was born in Chittagong, the major seaport in Bangladesh. After he became a faculty member of the economics department in Chittagong University, he was awarded a Fulbright Scholarship to study at Vanderbilt University. He took a very active part in campaigning for the liberation of Bangladesh in 1971. Later he returned to Chittagong University and became head of the Economics Department. He became well known for his micro credit program, wherein loans are given to entrepreneurs too poor to qualify for traditional bank loans. He is the founder of Grameen Bank. In 2006, Yunus and the Grameen Bank were jointly awarded the Nobel Peace Prize, "for their efforts to create economic and social development from below."

Grameen on the grounds that he had been appointed by Bangladesh Bank and, therefore, like all government appointees, could not serve beyond his sixty-fifth year. Yunus was seventy-one then. Yunus took his case to the Supreme Court, and lost. His removal was widely regarded as a move to eliminate a major political opponent. Yunus had tried to form a political party in 2006 and failed, but the rumor was that the BNP or maybe the next caretaker would offer him the presidency. Now he faces an inquiry as to how he set up fifty-two subsidiaries in Grameen's name but entirely under his control. Among these is Grameen Phone, worth billions of dollars.

Hasina's second term is about to finish, with positive and negative elements evenly balanced. Her future will be decided by rising food prices, declining overseas employment, her handling of India's demand for free and unfettered transit to their troubled Northeast, her response to the sentences passed by the War Crimes Tribunal, and above all by the AL's response to the demand by all other major parties to reinstate the caretaker government system. About rising food prices she can do little, since much of it is due to globalization, but so far the AL government has held down the rice prices. The crisis of declining overseas employment is due to the adverse reaction by Kuwait, Saudi Arabia, and UAE, which are major destinations for Bangladeshi labor, to her attitude toward the Jamaat. Malaysia has opened its doors wider, but she has to tackle this carefully. The War Crimes Tribunal, which was criticized by Human Rights Watch and by a Turkish Human Rights organization, has tried and condemned several members of Jamaat to very long jail sentences or to be hanged for war crimes.

Hasina has become more hardline on relations with India, after the Tista river agreement was scuttled by Momota Banerjee, chief minister of West Bengal. India's Border Security Force (BSF) has always had a hard line on border crossing, and hundreds of Bangladeshis have been killed attempting to cross the closely guarded border into India.[23] The Tipaimukh Dam in the Northeast of India is being disputed and many are questioning India's motives. Free and unfettered transit across Bangladesh for India has been put on the back burner.

As for the caretaker government issue, this is one for the legislature to resolve. It passed a bill providing for the election to be held under the ruling government, as is done in most democracies. The opposition counters that this will lead to widespread corruption by the administration and undue pressure on the electorate. They want a caretaker government to supervise the elections and, therefore, another legislative response is awaited. The opposition is also pushing to reconstitute the Election Commission, to make it stronger and more impartial.

MAJOR POLITICAL PARTIES

Over the years four political parties have survived and slowly but surely carved out their political space. Other than these big four, there have been eighty smaller parties, some of which came and went and made no impression and others that have waxed and waned. Among the small ones that have polled 1 percent or more of the total votes on one or more of four relatively fair elections (1991, 1996, 2001, 2008) are the Jatiyo Samajtantrik Dal (JSD, National Socialist Party), the Communist Party of Bangladesh (CPB), Islami Oikya Jote (IOJ, Islamic Unity Front), and the Bangladesh Krishok Shromik Awami League (BAKSAL). The National Awami Party (NAP) played a significant role in the 1960s and 1970s but faded away after the June 1996 elections. The four major parties are the Awami League (AL), the Bangladesh Nationalist Party (BNP), the Jatiya Party (JP), and the Jama'at-i-Islami (Jamaat). Their political history could be an indicator of what role they will play in the political future of the country.

Awami League (AL)

This party seems to have solid support of almost 40 percent of the population. In the 1991 elections they won 30 percent of the votes, increased this support to 37 percent in 1996, improved their showing in 2001 by getting 40 percent, and did impressively in 2008 by getting 49 percent of the votes cast. After the debacle of the BNP in 2006–2007 there has been an increasing groundswell of support for the AL. The AL is a populist party in the sense that it appeals strongly to a wide spectrum of the society from small farmers and rickshaw pullers to lower- and upper-middle-class businessmen and office workers. Bangalis are an emotional people and they are swayed again and again by slogans, exhortations, and emotional appeals. The AL workers observe various anniversaries of the pre- and post-Liberation periods (1969–1973), and meticulously pay homage to the memory of Bangabandhu Sheikh Mujibur Rahman.

Indeed they have created an aura of martyrdom around Sheikh Mujib and have used this to create a sense of mission among party workers. The AL has a host of senior party workers from the 1960s, but in the natural course of events their numbers are dwindling. This party can be labeled left of center, but it also contains members who are quite far left and right of center. The central theme is nationalism as it was said to be propounded by Sheikh Mujib. Some think it encompasses secularism and socialism. Others think these are not a part of Bengali Nationalism. In any case these words have effectively been dropped from the credo since the 1980s. It is to their credit that all minority groups, both Bangali and non-Bangali, tend to support the AL rather than any other party.

Members of opposition parties often accuse the AL of being pro-India, thereby implying that they listen to Indian political leaders and favor Indian business interests. Their success at negotiations with India, for example, in sharing Ganges water, seems to imply that Indian politicos understand their concerns better than those of the other parties. It cannot be denied that there are ties that go back to the Liberation struggle. Moreover, given the trust that the Hindu community reposes in the Awami League, there is a greater empathy with Indian politicians, bureaucrats, and businessmen. Over the years the AL has, however, learned that India will always give its own interests absolute priority, and the party cannot alienate its own people for the sake of being friendly with India.

Bangladesh Nationalist Party (BNP)

When General Zia Ur Rahman started a new party in February 1978 he began with a patched-together group of politicians from various other parties. This party was called Jatiyatabadi Gonotantrik Dol (JAGODAL), but he was not quite happy with its composition or its name. In September of the same year he created the Bangladesh National Party (BNP) after members of rightist and leftist parties and various retired military civil bureaucrats fell in behind him. Zia had begun the process of turning the country to the right even before he created BNP. The new party obviously became the focal point for right-of-center politicians, businessmen, and bureaucrats. Over the years, BNP became the party of the middle class, particularly the upper echelon. In the countryside, the land holding/patron class became divided between the AL and the BNP, with clients generally following their patrons. Zia's move to remove socialism and secularism and replace them with Islamic symbols and rhetoric proved very popular with both middle- and the working-class Muslims. However, this very move alienated most of the ethnic and religious minorities. Khaleda Zia led the party after Zia Ur Rahman's assassination, steadfastly remaining true to the orientation given by him. The BNP has supported the process of disinvestment and so-called free-market economy all through. It has always been quite suspicious of India and frequently sought guidance from Saudi Arabia. In the 1991 elections the BNP secured nearly 31 percent of the votes and in the 1996 elections improved that to 33 percent. In the 2001 elections the BNP worked in alliance with the Jamaat, the JP, and the IOJ. In the constituencies where any one of the other parties was strong the BNP did not put up a candidate. It is therefore difficult to estimate the percentage of votes the BNP alone would have received. On the basis that BNP candidates won 192 seats, it is estimated that they received about 40 percent of the total votes cast. In the 2001 elections they received

30 percent of the votes but were so fragmented that it resulted in a mere 30 seats out of 300, 10 percent of the total.

Jatiya Party (JP)

General Hussain Muhammad Ershad had to try twice to float his own new party. In 1983 he formed the Jana Dal, but three years later he transformed it into the Jatiya Party. The core area of support of the JP is the northern part of the country, particularly in the districts of Rangpur and Dinajpur. The people of northern Bangladesh (often known as north Bengal) have for years resented the apparent neglect of their area by government planners and private-sector investors. Ershad, who hails from Rangpur, harped on the lack of investments and employment and became a local hero. The JP has retained its support in many areas of the north over the past two decades. In terms of political and economic orientation the JP is so similar to the BNP that punsters have often called them the B-team. The JP receives solid support among landowners and their clients by supporting privatization programs and promoting Islamic symbolism. One reliable estimate is that the JP has the support of less than 10 percent of the electorate at present. In the 1991 elections the JP received nearly 12 percent of the votes and in the 1996 elections they got 15 percent.

Jamaat

The Jama'at-i-Islami is an avowedly Muslim-oriented party and the most controversial of the big four. Controversial because it is said to have members who actively fought or killed Liberation fighters in 1971 and also because it promotes behavior that is intolerant not only of non-Muslims but also of Muslims who do not agree with it. Its sympathizers say that it is a political party advocating the incorporation of Islamic ideology into the governing system. The AL and all the left parties have been very critical of Jamaat. Yet in 1986 and again in 1994 the AL did not mind its support against the BNP. Many within the AL, and even the BNP, think most of the leadership of the Jamaat is tainted with pro-Pakistani activities during the Liberation war. During a TV interview in 2007 one of the Jamaat leaders blurted out that the conflict in 1971 was a civil war. Though this attitude of theirs was an open secret for years, its public admission shocked the nation and led to calls for a war crimes trial of the Jamaat leadership.

The genesis of the Jamaat is in the ideology articulated by Sayyid Abul Ala Maudoodi, an eminent Islamic scholar who migrated from India to Pakistan. The Jama'at-i-Islami in Pakistan is a completely separate party organizationally, but linked by ideology to the Jamaat in Bangladesh.

Both parties wish to set up governments that will strictly follow their interpretation of Shariat (Islamic law and governance).

The Jamaat was banned as soon as the Bangladesh government took over in 1971. Five years later, after the assassination of Mujib, a new party named the Islamic Democratic League (IDL) obtained permission to operate and Jamaat workers organized under this banner. In 1979 six Jamaat leaders were elected to the JS as IDL members. The JS then withdrew the ban on religion-based political parties. The Jamaat began to organize openly, and its militant student arm, the *Shibir*, began to terrorize all those who opposed them in the universities and colleges. They were brought under control only during Sheikh Hasina's regime (1995–2000). In 1986 the Jamaat participated in Ershad's first election and got 10 seats. However, they resigned a year later and soon joined the BNP in the anti-Ershad campaign. In 1991 the Jamaat got 12 percent of the votes and eighteen seats. This was their high point in popularity. In the next election, in February 1996, they did not take part along with most other parties. This was followed by the June 1996 elections where they got only 8.6 percent of the votes and a mere three seats. After this showing they entered into an alliance with the BNP and in the 2001 elections secured seventeen seats, but only due to the votes of BNP supporters since their alliance had put up one main candidate in all constituencies. Had the Jamaat fought the elections on their own they probably would not have received more than 5 percent of the votes.

None of the Jamaat's top echelon could be faulted for personal financial aggrandizement. Even a critical study of the Jamaat had to admit that the Jamaat leaders "have been able to avoid the temptation of personal corruption."[24] Like many of the radical Muslim organizations around the world, the Jamaat has shown that it has an apparently ethical leadership and that it can provide social services, such as low-cost medical and educational services, in many areas. Despite this favorable attribute there is a deep-seated distrust of them even among other Muslims, who seem to have an affinity for centrist, tolerant parties. The Jamaat may therefore not be able to garner more than 8–10 percent of the votes in the near future. Their influence will, however, be far greater than their share of the votes because the two major parties are apparently implacably opposed and evenly balanced in voter support, thereby unable to rule without forming coalition with smaller parties.

Elections

So far Bangladesh has held nine national elections to the Jatiya Sangshad (National Assembly), as shown in table 6.1.

Table 6.1.   Election and Majority Parties

Year	Largest party	Number of JS members Government	Others	Total	Period in office
1973	AL	306	9	315	2 yrs 6 months
1979	BNP	248	82	330	3 years
1986	JP	206	124	330	1 yr 5 months
1988	JP	252	48	330	2 yrs 7 months
1991	BNP	168	162	330	4 yrs 8 months
1996	BNP	319	11	330	120 days
1996	AL	175	155	330	5 years
2001	BNP	245	85	330	5 years
2008	AL	300	30	330	5 years

The JS had 300 elected members and 15 nominated women members in 1973. Thereafter the elected seats have remained the same, but the number of seats reserved for women, who are nominated by the ruling party, was increased to thirty. During the 1973 elections under Mujib fourteen parties contested, but the pressures from the AL government were such that the AL won 291 of the 300 elected seats. In order to encourage more participation by women 15 seats were reserved for them. These were filled by election by the 300 members from a panel of nominated candidates submitted by the parties that had won the seats. Not surprisingly the AL nominees won all the seats, thus giving them a total of 306 out of 315 seats. The attitude of the AL, that they were the only patriotic party, did not serve them well in the long run. The next election was under the tutelage of General Zia in 1979. The newly formed BNP won 207 seats, with the AL winning 39 seats and various parties and independent candidates getting the rest. The BNP had received 44 percent of the votes and the AL 25 percent. In many constituencies the AL lost by a small margin. The number of seats reserved for women had been raised to 30 and the BNP received all of them. The BNP got the support of 41 members of the Muslim League, various small parties, and those elected as independent. The third national election was held in 1986, under circumstances that made it a farce.[25] Ershad needed an assembly that would ex post facto legalize his martial law rule. To this end he had the elections rigged and the JP became the ruling party with 153 elected seats and 30 women's seats. Ershad had financed several small parties and many independent candidates, and they voted for the Seventh Amendment, which legalized all political actions taken by Ershad between 1981 and 1986. The BNP had refused to take part in any election under Ershad but the AL had taken part. However, when they won only 76 seats the result was rejected and the AL did not sit in the JS. Later in the same year Ershad had himself elected as president, though very few cast votes. He was aware that the nation seriously questioned his legality and authority and tried to rectify the situation by dissolving the JS and holding another national election in early 1988. Both the BNP and the AL boycotted this election and the next JS totally lacked popular support. Ershad had funded and encouraged the Jatiyo Samajtantrik Dal (JSD) to become the major opposition party with 35 seats. The JSD was a respected leftist party in the 1970s but when the left fragmented on personality lines the JSD became opportunistic and participated in the 1988 election, which was the worst one the country had yet seen. These corrupt elections were followed in 1991 by the best one so far. The political parties and the public had been so chastened by nine years of increasingly corrupt governance that everyone came together to make this election exemplary. It was little surprise that the BNP won most seats. Khaleda had worked tirelessly to bring down the Ershad regime and her party won 140 elected seats and 28 of the women's seats. The AL won 88 elected seats, the JP 35 seats, and the Jamaat 18 elected seats and 2 women's seats. This marked the beginning of the Jamaat's role as a major factor in national politics.

The next national election in February1996 was marred by a return to the pressure tactics of the Ershad regime, and this time the AL bore a big share of the blame. Three major parties—the AL, the JP, and the Jamaat—boycotted the elections because it was not held under a caretaker government. They called a *hartal* (protest demonstration) on election day and in many constituencies voters were intimidated from going to the polling booths. The BNP won a hollow victory and secured 289 seats. One seat was won by the small Freedom Party and 10 were won by independents. This JS did not even have the opportunity to elect nominated women members. There was a big national campaign against this JS by the three parties (AL, JP, and Jamaat) alliance.[26] The elected JS met only once, and that only to pass the Thirteenth Amendment to the Constitution, which made it mandatory henceforth for all national elections to be held under caretaker governments.

The way was cleared for the next national elections in June 1996. The election campaign was bitter and every constituency was contested by all four of the major parties. The Election Commission found irregularities in twenty-seven constituencies and there was repolling. The AL came out as the winner, but they had to form an alliance with the JP to get a majority, which naturally took all the women's seats. The alliance governed for five years. It may be recalled that soon after the 1991 election AL declared noncooperation with the BNP government and agitated for four years. In the same vein, as soon as the 1996 JS convened, the BNP began a concerted campaign to oust the AL-JP government. Within nine months the BNP called its first *hartal* when the Jamaat began to openly support them. Several petty provocations to the BNP brought down the image of the AL, and when in 1997 the Chittagong Hill Tracts Accord was signed without adequately explaining its provisions to the people, the AL seemed to lose ground. By the time the next national elections were due, the BNP had made up for the loss in popularity that it had suffered in 1996.

The 2001 elections were duly held under a caretaker government and the BNP won a stunning victory. National and international observers affirmed that the elections were free and fair. The BNP had contested them in alliance with the Jamaat, IOJ, and the Naziur faction of JP. The alliance won 215 seats as against only 62 seats won by the AL. In nearly a hundred constituencies the AL candidate lost by less than 2 or 3 percent of the total votes cast. Though the AL received 40 percent of the votes, they won only 21 percent of the seats. It is alleged that the BNP candidates received all the alliance votes, while the AL had to rely on their own followers. Whatever the case, BNP candidates won 192 seats and Jamaat 17 seats. They got their nominated 30 women elected to the JS.

There was no election in 2006 when the Khaleda-led government of four party alliances ended. A caretaker government was hammered out with great difficulty because at least the two major parties had to agree to the selection of the chief election commissioner. Whoever was suggested by the BNP was rejected by the AL. The decades-old rivalry would allow no compromise. The country remained under president's rule until, in exasperation, the army stepped in and appointed a chief adviser to head the caretaker government. The military-civil caretaker government held an election in 2008 and the new Hasina government took over at the very end of the year.

A leading political scientist has blamed the majority of politicians for arrogance, cowardice, and selfishness and thereby distorting the election process and thwarting the growth of democracy.[27] The JS has been a forum for one-party rule and not a place for dialogue and negotiation between politicians. Rounaq Jahan has very correctly diagnosed that politics "has degenerated into a deadly confrontation because the stakes of winning or losing control of state power is too high for the personal and political fortunes of the competing leaders and their parties."[28]

POLITICAL ECONOMY

Bangladesh's economy has come a long way from what was inherited in 1971. Today it is considered to be a successful economy among the poorer nations and even to have the prospect of becoming a middle-income economy in the next five to ten years. If there is a success story in

Bangladesh it is about how the economy has been salvaged from the desperate years of 1970s.

At the time of Liberation, Bangladesh had just started the process of industrialization. Industry as an economic sector accounted for only 7 percent of GDP, with factory industries accounting for less than half the product. The rest of it was from artisanal industries from various rural areas. The agriculture sector provided 30 percent of GDP. Crop agriculture stagnated, and domestic food supply could not keep up with population growth. The food gap kept increasing each year, necessitating ever larger cereal imports. These imports consisted in the smaller part of rice bought abroad by the government. The larger part was wheat from the United States, sold to the government at very concessional rates under U.S. Public Law 480. The fund realized from the sales of wheat could be used by the government for development work. This enabled the economy to tick over and feed the people. It also made the government totally dependent on the United States.

In this same period there was an international effort, spearheaded by the United States, to evolve high-yielding hybrid rice, maize, and wheat that could meet the needs of the rapidly increasing world population. The International Rice Research Institute (IRRI) was established at Los Banos in the Philippines. IRRI set up cooperating institutions in various countries, the one in Bangladesh being known as BRRI (Bangladesh Rice Research Institute). After a breakthrough in producing what has been called the "miracle rice" in 1972, these two institutions produced a steady stream of high-yielding varieties that completely changed the food grain production scenario. The leader of the team that ultimately saved billions of people from starvation, Dr. Norman E. Borlaugh, won the Nobel Prize for peace, an award he richly deserved. These high-yielding varieties (HYV) need certified seeds, large doses of fertilizer, and a controlled water supply. To save the large yields, increased amounts of pesticides are also necessary. This package of inputs brought about what is known as the Green Revolution. Bangladesh benefited greatly from it. Rice production shot up from seven million tons in 1975 to twenty million tons in 2000. The main rice crop used to be Amon, which grows in the rainy season and is therefore susceptible to floods. This was overtaken by the Boro crop, which grows in the drier half of the year. To supply irrigation water in the dry season low-lift pumps (LLP), deep tube wells (DTW), and shallow tube wells (STW) were necessary. Once again USAID and U.S. funding played a big part in the Green Revolution. Industrialization was boosted by the discovery of natural gas in a half dozen locations. To supply the urea fertilizer needed by HYV rice, a large factory was first set up at Fenchuganj, then one at Ghorashal and later another larger one near Chittagong.

An even more fundamental development took place in the early 1980s. Jute, a fiber from a seasonal plant, had dominated the cash economy for over a century. At the time of Liberation large-scale industrial production was concentrated in jute processing. In the early 1970s there was both expansion and diversification, but government-owned factories ratcheted up huge losses due to corruption and mismanagement. In these very years petrochemical polymers (polyethylene, polyvinyl, etc.) began to massively replace jute in the packaging industry. The Bangladesh economy was saved from dire straits by the sudden growth of the Readymade Garments (RMG) industry.[29] The number of such factories increased from 9 to 2,726 in twenty years, and the value of RMG exports from less than US$1 million to US$3.7 billion in that period. These are total export values, and it should be remembered that value added is only 15 percent. Nevertheless it ushered in two welcome changes: the employment of large numbers in factory industries and the employment of women in industrial activity. Politicians had to cope with the expectations of a fast-rising industrial population, at least half of whom were women.[30]

Bangladesh was fortunate to be given liberal imports quotas by the United States, and in the first fifteen years of the RMG growth America was the primary market. Problems arose when the Harkin Bill required all exporting industries not to employ child labor. Many of the owners of the industries tried to circumvent it, but the various Chambers of Commerce exhorted them to comply. They had no choice when the U.S. government, and the European Commission, sent inspectors to find out which enterprises had complied.

The path to economic liberalization was not easy. The industrialists and exporters had been used to import protection and/or export subsidy for over a generation. Changeover was neither wanted nor easy. Understandably, there was widespread resistance. Most of the arguments were of the infant-industry protection nature, even when the enterprise or industry was fifteen or twenty years old. A large part of their problems arose from corruption and inefficiency in the government machinery. Whereas corruption both benefited and thwarted the private sector, growing inefficiency benefited no one.

As explained in the historical overview, the left-leaning students, workers, and politicians were numerous and active in the years before and after the Liberation. Their ideology pushed the Sheikh Mujib regime toward socialism. It should be remembered that in the 1960s and 1970s the Soviet economic system was still considered a viable alternative to that of the West. The Vietnam War had generated anger, particularly among the younger generation. The ideal of a nonaligned Third World was still inspiring many intellectuals who wanted an alternative to the two systems that dominated the world. It was considered quite natural for a food-deficient, very poor country to take the socialist path for rapid development. None of the planning commission members were socialist, and yet they advocated state ownership of banks and industries.

With the coming of Zia to power there was a sudden change in direction. During the fifteen years of military domination almost all the nationalized banks and industries were sold to private ownership. This turn to the right has been termed *liberalization,* which has had a positive effect on employment, foreign-exchange earnings, donor lending, and economic growth, but a negative effect on fair play and equity. Even after the return to an electoral system the change to economic liberalization was neither halted nor reversed. In twenty-five years, the economy had quadrupled and the industrial sector had increased to 15 percent of the economy. The AL government (1996–2001) did not feel they could back go to state capitalism in the name of socialism.

The efforts of the World Trade Organization (WTO) to completely open up all economies to world market forces has been resisted by nearly all least-developed countries (LDCs), and Bangladesh is no expectation. It is argued that under the full WTO system the rich would swallow up the poor economies or exploit them for short-term gain. The 1997 Asian Financial Crisis has been cited as an example of the uneven playing field in a fully globalized economy. The globalization issue generated heated debates in the late 1990s and early 2000s. The campaigns of Indian activists, such as Vandana Shiva, had created awareness of the contentious issues, mainly among academics and in the NGO community.[31] Unlike the public and the politicians, NGOs' activities in Bangladesh and India are closely allied in vision. In both countries, NGOs are highly critical of their government's bureaucracy and they are very distrustful of multinational corporations (MNCs). The issue that really agitated them was trade-related intellectual property rights (TRIPs). They allege that thirteen major MNCs used the U.S. government to pressure GATT (General Agreement on Tariffs and Trade, based in Geneva) into accepting TRIPs as a binding international treaty. The definition of intellectual property rights was expanded to include all life forms. This raised a storm of protests. Several well-known Indian and Pakistani products such as basmati rice and all products of the neem tree (*Azadirachta indica*) came up for patenting by MNCs. Most NGOs of all South Asian countries joined hands to resist this crude form of capitalism. Both the rice and the neem were saved for the time being, but patented hybrids of rice, wheat, and maize have been introduced on a large scale, ironically through a few large NGOs who have grown so large that their ethos has become more like that of MNCs.

It is said that there are three types of NGOs: the visionary, the missionary, and the mercenary. The visionary are very few and they usually do not solicit funds from the donors. They are advocacy groups who do not mouth whatever the donors or political parties or business groups want to tell the public. By their very nature they have small membership and lofty objectives and therefore find it difficult to make their views known. The missionary ones are many more and the nature of their work makes them public and often controversial. Most of them advocate Christianity and raise their funds abroad. Some of them promote Islam and are usually funded from Saudi Arabia. By far the largest numbers of NGOs are engaged in development work. To brand all of them as mercenary would be unkind, but there are many which seem to be more interested in their own well-being than in pro-poor programs. Within the ranks of development NGOs half a dozen are very large, another hundred or so are medium sized, and then there are thousands that are small. These small NGOs are usually registered in district towns, whereas the large and medium ones have their head offices in Dhaka. Some of the large and medium NGOs such as Grameen, BRAC, and PROSHIKA are well known internationally and their funding runs into millions of dollars. BRAC is said to be the largest NGO in the world, and it owns the BRAC Bank. In contrast hundreds of small NGOs operate on the equivalent of a few thousand dollars a year, which makes most small, and even medium-size NGOs, look toward the large ones for survival. This situation again reproduces the patron-client relationships that are so typical of the country.

The large NGOs have been used by their donors to carry out development work. The argument is that government agencies are inefficient and corrupt and that the NGOs can get the work done better and quicker. The results have varied over time and place. During Ershad's regime a big chunk of development funds was channeled through NGOs. In the next government NGOs were curbed due to the influence of the Jamaat. Donors also found out that the initial enthusiasm and efficiency of NGOs had tapered off and that government officers could deliver the goods provided they received as much financial and logistical support as the NGOs. Subsequently governments have limited the extent to which development work is dependent on NGOs. Possibly the turning point was widespread agitation against NGOs by the Jamaat and Islamic groups in 2002.

The NGOs have also become wiser and less confrontational. Qazi Farooque Ahmed, chairman of PROSHIKA, one of the large NGOs, openly sided with the AL in the Hasina period and politicized most of the paid workers. They held public meetings against the "Islamization" policy promoted by the Jamaat and similar organizations. As soon as the BNP came back to power in 2001 Qazi Farooque was arrested along with many PROSHIKA workers and charged with corruption, but was later released. The work of that NGO has been reduced quite a bit. Of the other major NGO leaders only Muhammad Yunus participated openly in politics;

others who did not have not been tarnished. The obvious lesson for all NGOs has been to stay clear of politics.

Whereas the development NGOs are now keeping clear of any open connection with politics, the civil society has become increasingly vocal. The rise of the civil society as a factor in national politics has been due to greater involvement of a growing professional class, growth of print and television media, and increasing fear of radical Islamists. The role of television is particularly interesting. In the early 1990s few families owned televisions and there was only one TV channel. For international channels expensive dish-antennas had to be put up. After a few years, more television stations were set up and customers could get cable channels. With the assembly of cheaper sets in Bangladesh the audience increased rapidly. In the early 2000s import of Chinese television sets virtually halved costs. Since then the number of TV stations has increased to sixteen and cable TV has made another sixty channels available. Thus, in just over a decade television media has become possibly the single most important forum for politicians. Civil society has used this media adeptly and extensively. The print media has been surprisingly open and critical of curbs on basic rights, particularly since the mid-1980s. This, too, has helped the civil society to vent their feelings and suggest viable courses of action by the politicians.

IDENTITY POLITICS

As explained earlier, the history of the area that is now Bangladesh clearly shows that both language and religion are important in Bangladesh identity. It is said that Bangladesh is the first postcolonial nation to have been formed on the basis of language, and therefore Bangla language unites all religious groups. This is true, but not entirely. The Bangla language used by Muslims and Hindus differs significantly in greetings and kinship terms. This may not seem like much, but it does set them slightly apart, more so because Muslims use many Arabic and Persian words. Yet educated Muslims do admire the literature and songs written by Hindus, even when there are allusions to Hindu gods and goddesses. Not only is there a thin fault line among Bangla speakers, there is rejection of Bangla itself, at least as a mother-tongue, by many small groups, such as the Chakmas and Tripuras, who are not Bangali. In 1978 Zia ur Rahman changed the Constitution to name the people of the country "Bangladeshi," which was slightly less offensive to them, but they protested again. While language more or less unites 99 percent of the citizens, religion creates a much deeper fault line. At the time Pakistan was created (1947) an estimated 30 percent of the people were of the Hindu community. After serious communal riots in West Bengal, India, in 1950, a large number of Muslims immigrated into East Bengal and an even larger number of Hindus emigrated to India. Another wave of immigration took place after the 1965 Indo-Pakistan War. Then another outflow happened in 1971. The proportion of Hindus thereby dropped to 20 percent at Liberation, and due to a fairly steady flow thereafter, the 2001 census showed that they were only about 12 percent of the population. Much of the immigration was due to better economic opportunities in India and also the pull of kinship groups. A big part was admittedly due to actual or anticipated animosity with Muslims. Most political parties profess to be neutral about religious issues, but their local cadres in the villages and small towns often display a marked bias. The avowedly "Islamic" parties are of course openly for Muslims only, but that does not mean they always incite discrimination. In areas where there are relatively few Hindus, communal feelings are uncommon, except when there are major communal incidents in India, such as the destruction of Babri mosque in 1992 and riots in Gujerat in 2002.

Communal feelings can be deliberately aroused when there are impending elections and Hindu voters can swing the results toward the AL, which has been the party of choice for the majority of Hindus since the 1950s. Voters of the Hindu community were set upon, and in a few instances houses were set on fire in several constituencies where the BNP candidates thought the AL would win with Hindu votes. The tendency of the Hindu community in areas where they are a large (over 15 percent) minority to vote almost en bloc for the AL is a political phenomenon that irritates parties that have few Hindu supporters. The Hindu community had by and large supported the Indian National Congress before Partition (1947). After the formation of Pakistan they found that the AL avowal of secularism and socialism was similar to that of the Congress Party. By backing the AL wholeheartedly, they have at times secured important posts in the party and in the government, including ministerial positions. In contrast the BNP has been lukewarm toward the Hindu voters and the Jamaat has ignored them.

For the AL, Hindu community votes are of crucial importance. They had large minorities in all the constituencies of the southwest. In several elections the AL has generally secured all those constituencies. This has made the Hindu community, particularly in the southwest, suspect in the eyes of BNP voters. As for the Jamaat, this is grist for their mill and they use this bogey to arouse extremism in the areas bordering India. Whereas language is a binding factor between the two communities, religion divides. Normally this division does not create friction and the numbers of communal riots have been remarkably low. However, the potential for mischief exists.

The BNP is essentially a part of the middle class, both urban and rural, with a philosophy that derives from the Muslim Bengal idea of past generations. It is supported by those who think the AL is susceptible to pro-Indian decisions because of its Hindu community backing. The Jamaat is clearly for Muslims only and it has its strongest backing along the western border, where large numbers of Muslim refugees settled after the 1950 riots in India.

The four principles of the AL ideology are nationalism, democracy, socialism, and secularism. These were written into the 1972 Constitution but were changed only five years later by President Zia ur Rahman in 1977. Nationalism was redefined, the aims of socialism were made compatible with middle-class aspirations, and secularism was replaced by Islam. When the AL came to power once again, eighteen years later, they did not try to go back to the 1972 formulation of the national ideology. Like any large party embracing middle- and working-class supporters and the greater part of the voters of all minority communities, it has groups that often do not see eye to eye. One group was insistent on a return to socialism and secularism, but the opposing and larger group feels that the majority in the Muslim community are satisfied with the changes made in 1977. It seems that the AL has learned from the turbulent political history since Liberation.

A seemingly intractable identity problem concerns the minority groups whose mother-tongue is not Bangla. Such groups totaled about a million in the 2001 census, or less than 1 percent of the total population. Many of these groups live as small communities scattered over western and northern areas. In the hill country of the southeast, however, they form fully half the population. East of the large city of Chittagong there are three hill districts (Bandarban, Rangamati, and Khagrachhari) with a total population of only one million, a seemingly empty area at the edge of a densely populated plain. Bangalis have gone into this area for centuries to trade and extract forest produce. As the plains began to fill up with people, a small but increasing number of Bangalis began to settle permanently in the valleys at first and then on the low hills. Between 1957 and 1962, the government of Pakistan built a large dam at Kaptai, on the biggest river of the hills, the Karnaphuli. The objective was to generate electricity and save on imported coal from India. The Karnaphuli valley was, and still is, the core homeland of the Chakma, who are Buddhists and now number a quarter of a million in Bangladesh. They protested very strongly at the impending loss of their ancestral land, but the government went ahead with American funding and engineering. It was said in those times that development has a clear precedence over sentiments. Many of the displaced Chakma migrated as far as the northeast frontier of India. Some settled in Tripura and Mizoram, also in India. The great majority moved into nearby hills, where the soil was much poorer than in the valley. At the same time they saw equally poverty-stricken Bangalis come in numbers and settle in the areas not flooded by the lake. Alarmed at the prospect of losing their land, and their culture, they revolted and formed a guerrilla force known as the Shanti Bahini. Some Tripuras and Marmas joined the Chakmas, but not many. The army moved in and tried to suppress them. Massacres were perpetrated by both sides and there was great unrest throughout the hills for twenty long years. The military dominated the governments of Zia and Ershad, and the BNP government of Khaleda was loath to concede much to the Shanti Bahini. It was said that as long as India encourages the Shanti Bahini there cannot be peace. Nevertheless the bill for formation of local government councils in the Chittagong Hill Tracts was passed in 1989 and the Chakmas who had taken refuge in India began returning in 1994. As soon as Hasina formed her AL government in 1996 progress was made in reaching an agreement. In reality both the Bangladesh army and the Shanti Bahini had realized that outright victory was unlikely for either side even though the army seemed to have the upper hand. The Chittagong Hill Tracts Peace Accord was signed in December 1997, and, on paper at least, a curb was put on Bangali settlement. It is significant that every constituency in the three hill districts have voted in AL candidates over the past thirty years. Khaleda Zia strongly protested against the provisions of the Peace Accord and called it a sellout to India. Later she led a protest motorcade from Dhaka to Chittagong to publicize what she called a blow to the sovereignty and integrity of the country.[32] This illustrates the diametrically opposed views of the two major parties, which of course makes any dialogue between them difficult. Less than four years later Khaleda was back in power and implementation of the provisions was put on the back burner. Not that the AL government had done much to hasten a change. They were conscious of the growing voice of the Bangali settlers, who had become the majority in Banderban and Rangamati districts and the single biggest ethnic group in Khagrachhari district. The different tribal ethnic groups have, however, become conscious of their heritage and have promoted a revival of their languages, music, songs, and dances. Many books are being printed in Chakma and other tribal languages. New kyangs (temples) are being built. This gives some hope to the Chakma and other groups that they will not be imminently overwhelmed culturally.

WOMEN'S POWER AND
KINSHIP NETWORKS IN POLITICAL LIFE

For the last twenty years the two most powerful persons in Bangladesh politics have been women. They came into this position through kinship links but have retained their power by judicious use of patronage. Even during their house arrest in 2007 by the caretaker government these two women remained powerful. That women can be so preeminent in a Muslim-majority country astonishes those who do not know this country. In the West it is readily assumed that in Muslim communities women are secluded, deprived of basic needs, denied basic rights, and all too often oppressed. The media, particularly television, has played a major role in this stereotyping. These images are mentally contrasted with the freedom Western women have, or think they have. No two cultures are the same, or need to be so. Indeed even within larger cultures there often are sub-cultures. So it is in Bangladesh where Bangali Muslims, Christians, Hindus, and Buddhists have similar but not exactly the same culture. Even Muslims in different parts of the country have noticeably different culture norms. As for the various tribal groups, their cultures are usually quite different from those of the Bangali communities.

In all the different communities of Bangladesh the nuclear component is the family and in the family the mother is the kernel. She is respected and protected. The exclusion and deprivation of rights that Westerners allege are seen in quite a different light by the Bangladeshi. However, it is true that this idealized norm may break down when there is grinding poverty or rapidly changing lifestyles in an urbanizing situation. In the former case the breakdown is explained by the sheer pressure for survival. In the latter case the explanation is Westernization of the consumer society type. By and large, Bangladeshis consider the role of women as being within the extended family system and therein they are empowered. Outside those limits women have to struggle hard to create their social space. It is against this background that one has to evaluate the existence of women's power.

That women are suppressed is all too true, but it is general in nature and not individually targeted. An in-depth case-by-case analysis is likely to show that poverty is at the root of most cases of suppression. The wretchedness of poverty exacerbates a social construct, which is male dominated, like in most other societies in the world.

The politicians have been aware of the disadvantages suffered by women but seem to have taken measures only when pressured by women activities. The Convention on Elimination of All Forms of Discrimination against Women (CEDAW) was passed by the UN General Assembly on December 18, 1979. Due to pressure from UN bodies, NGOs, and women's groups it was ratified by Bangladesh on November 6, 1984, with reservations on Articles 2, 13.1 (a), 16.1 (c), and (f) on the basis of religious sentiments. In most Muslim countries not only CEDAW but also other international moves to empower women have been seen as attempts to Westernize the society. They have therefore been opposed by the conservative Muslims, both men and women. Over time, Muslim society has seen that the effects can be progressive provided family values remain intact.

It is interesting that it was during the Ershad regime that CEDAW was ratified, a Directorate of Women's Affairs was set up (1984), and Family Courts Law (1995) was enacted. During the first BNP government, the Muslim Family Law (Amendment) Ordinance was passed in 1992. Compulsory primary education for girls was also declared in 1992, followed by funding schooling for girls up to grade 8 without tuition fees in 1993. Four years later the AL government enacted that women could compete in direct election for 3 reserved seats in all Union Parishads and also passed the Women and Children Repression Prevention Act in 2000. Two years later during the BNP Alliance Government, the Acid Crime Prevention Act and the Acid Control Act were passed. In 2004, under the Fourteenth Constitution Amendment Bill, the number of seats in the JS reserved for women was increased to 45 and they were to be allotted to the different parties in proportion to the number of seats the party has in the JS. It is clear that all governments have assisted in passing legislation that could empower women and reduced their repression. They have also taken measures to greatly encourage the education of girls. This has been so successful that girls now outnumber boys in the primary schools. Many surveys show that this has greatly helped in empowering women in the rural areas.

Recently the Bangladesh Mohila Parishad (Women's Forum) has begun a movement to increase the number of seats reserved for women in the JS and also to fill them by direct election and not by nomination. The latest caretaker government said it intends to legislate that in all local government bodies 40 percent of the seats are to be contested by women only. Anything like this could bring about a sea change in the political scene.

On paper at least there is no dearth of action or legislation for girls and women. Implementation of the provisions of these acts, ordinances, and executive orders is quite another matter. It is to be expected that the majority of men will be reluctant to bring about change, particularly when the prospects for their (or their family's) economic betterment is seen to be very limited.

Kinship Networks

Since the political institutions of a country are largely shaped by the nature of their social institutions, it is necessary to review the social structures that affect politics. Bangladesh society in the villages is dominated by landowners, some with quite large holdings, and others with a few plots. Since two-thirds of the people are landless or near landless this creates a large client group dependent on a much smaller number of patrons. The patrons are, or have to be, predatory. This is how they, or their ancestors, acquired land and increased their share of the village economy. In the new scheme of things being predatory is considered to be corrupt, but this is not how they see it. They consider it their natural right to keep the flow of resources to and from their villages under their control. There is a hierarchy among the patrons with wealth, with position and power highly skewed. It is not uncommon for the wealthier patrons to keep musclemen in their service. Known as *lathials* (stave wielders) in the more remote villages and as *mastans* in the urban and peri-urban areas, these musclemen keep not only the clients, but also the lesser patrons, in line. In many areas the big patron has undisputed control, at least for a number of years, but in other areas there is constant jostling for power. This system, if it can be called that, can be seen in its most raw form along the large rivers and in the deltaic islands accreting progressively to the *south and the southeast.*[33]

The process of land building was of vital interest to potential patrons. The deposition of sediments along or in the stream bed of the larger rivers is known as alluvion, and it forms river islands known as char or adds new land to the sides, which is known as diara. Such new land forms all the way down into the delta and out into the near shore of the Bay of Bengal. Alluvion also leads to diluvion, whereby these new areas are broken up or washed away altogether. Over the past six thousand years accretion has exceeded erosion and the land area of Bangladesh has increased considerably.

It is thought that significant numbers of people began to settle in Bangladesh about three thousand years ago. No doubt since those earliest times, the various tribes who lived in this land and later coalesced into the linguistic group known as Bengali struggled to exploit and possess the ever-shifting deltaic islands. Even today these areas are dominated by large patrons, buttressed by close relatives, many of whom are smaller patrons, and strongly supported by retainers who are lathials. There is almost constant jostling between the large patrons, since new lands appear and disappear, and also because the predatory habit has become entrenched.

The extent of urbanized life has waxed and waned over the medieval and modern period. Dhaka was a large city in the late seventeenth century but shrunk to a small town by the late nineteenth century. The urban centers shrank after the coming of the British as rulers in the mid-eighteenth century, mainly due to the funneling of resources to Calcutta (Kolkata). In the 1950s only 5 percent of the population was urbanized, one of the lowest proportions in Asia. After the formation of political Bangladesh in 1971 there was great impetus for urban growth. Though total population has doubled since then, the proportion of people living in urban areas has increased to 25 percent. Thirty-five million people now live in urban areas, but they cannot be said to be truly urbanized. The majority of them are the landless poor of the villages who have come to seek employment. These are the poverty refugees. Their numbers are swelled by those who have been totally dispossessed of fixed assets by riverbank erosion, which is a major scourge for those living within a couple of kilometers of the large rivers. These are environmental refugees. Nearly all of these poor people have relatives in the villages, so that in the cities they are not cut off from rural culture and rural patronage. They save up to visit their villages once or twice a year and if they find good employment they save up to buy land in the village and build a substantial hut. In mode of thinking and personal lifestyle they remain rural. Many of their village patrons have also moved to the urban areas, and it has been easy for them to recreate the rural patronage system. The poor do not always want to shrug off the system. Rather, they often seek it out, because it offers security among familiar groups from their area (*elaka*) of the country.

Bangladeshi society is deeply rooted in the rural structure of patrons and clients. Inequity is accepted as inevitable and nepotism as the desirable norm. The patrons are expected to sustain society on this basis. Land ownership is the foundation of the patrons' place in rural society and since half of the villagers have extremely little or no land there is a huge pool of clients. Some of the landless clients work directly for large landlord patrons. Most of them are dependent on smaller landholders, who are in turn dependent on the large landlords. This dependency is critical to the functioning of the patron-client system. The small landholder's relationship to the large landlord is not always dependent on lease of land for cultivation. Very often it is social dependency through marriage ties, which may frequently be quite distant. There is also the network of a quasi-religious nature whereby big donors to mosques and madrasas are considered of higher social status than others who use those mosques and madrasas. The patrons thereby dominate not only the financial and kinship groups but also the religious establishments.

These attitudes, formed by history and inequities, have shaped the social fabric. People who have power almost invariably think they are above the law. Those who have position think they do not have to abide by set rules. Everyone seems to think their first, and often their only, loyalty is to their extended family and their friends. To the landed patron class, the kinship network is the only social reality. In the cities the network necessarily extends beyond the family group to those who are from their elaka. To the politicians, and even bureaucrats, this very often means that people of their part of the country can demand their patronage. To this extent there are vestiges of tribalism in Bangali society. When only a small fraction of the population, possibly only 5 percent, controls more than half the resources of the country, democracy can be a sham and social justice is almost impossible for the poor.

Power flows from land ownership. This holds true even in the cities. Land means money— to purchase, bribe, intimidate. It means assets that can be the collateral for large loans from banks. These loans can be used to set up housing or industrial assets, which in turn make it possible to get huge loans to buy more land, construct shopping malls, dredge sand to fill in lowland, and sell house plots to the aspiring middle class. Others go in for trading and profiteering in a quasi-monopolistic economy. This is where corrupt practices can lead to big dividends. Where import or export is dependent on government permission, the concerned officials can be bought off. If there is unexpected competition, the stevedore union or the transport union can be bribed to block or delay the movement of their goods. As a last measure, the various wholesaler associations can be used to refuse to handle the competitor's merchandise. Both money and the tribalism of regional connection can be used to prevent a corrupt system from getting any better.

SOCIAL COSTS OF MILITARISM

The military has played a major role in Bangladesh throughout its short history. Some units of the Pakistan army stationed in East Pakistan had Bangali officers and *jawans* (servicemen). Most of them decided in favor of Bangladesh after March 26, 1971, when they found that their West Pakistani compatriots were planning to disarm and eliminate them. Some of the units managed to march out of the cantonments (army camps) while others had to fight to get out. They were greatly outnumbered by the West Pakistani troops and had to retreat to safe areas in India, along the Bangladesh border. They were deployed in three sectors on the northern and eastern borders and carried out occasional raids until November, when they marched in with the Indian army. These units formed the core of the new army. They were joined in 1972 by those Bangali soldiers who were stranded in Pakistan when the breakup happened. Many of them were retired soon so that the existing structure of the new army would not be compromised. With the creation of Rakkhi Bahini, Sheikh Mujib sent a clear signal that he would not rely very much on the loyalty of those who had once served in the Pakistani army. This created considerable discontent. Then again the Awami League's choice of symbols and slogans offended the generally conservative Muslim *jawans*. Formation of the one-party BAKSAL government and the talk of subordinating the army officers to it precipitated the coup in which Sheikh Mujib and his family members were assassinated. The senior officers soon took charge of the government but denied prior knowledge of the coup. That was the beginning of de facto military control of the government for fifteen years (1975–1990).

The reasons for the power of the military are many. Some of these are divisiveness among politicians, weakness of the bureaucracy, and arrogance of the military officers. The politicians by and large make their living from politics. The single biggest group is made up of those with a legal education. Among them are many small-town lawyers, often briefless. Coming into power is their main aim in life, and through this power to make enough money to be able to join the affluent middle class. They squabble for the smallest spoils and dig in their heels on the smallest issues. During the Sheikh Mujib years the politicians were those inherited from the struggle for Liberation. Some of them and their associates, the so-called briefcase walas, made fortunes from government permits for imports or exports. In impoverished East Pakistan there had never been so much visible wealth. The new millionaires could afford to garner support from the politicians by bankrolling them. The trend continued in the Zia years and the pool of millionaires able to fund politicians increased. During Ershad's time corruption rose to new heights and most of the politicians were found to be in need of funding. Since there could not be enough for everyone there was constant jockeying and bickering. The military watched this spectacle with distaste, though some say they also participated. With the coming of Khaleda the divisiveness of the politicians increased because neither the BNP nor AL would give an inch. This intransigence and growing levels of corruption marked the political sphere right up to the end of Khaleda's second term in 2006.

As for the civil bureaucrats, they have a mixed record. Some of them had become politicized before Liberation. Others stayed away from politics even when compelled to join BAKSAL in 1975. A few even refused to join it. The Sheikh Mujib regime tried hard to break the so-called "colonial" bureaucracy. It went so far as to rescind the Civil Service Rules, which ensured the right of officers to be able to differ and to present their views. Sheikh Mujib wanted them to do the bidding of the politicians. Even though he himself relied heavily on a few civil servants, he wanted the backbone of the civil bureaucracy to be broken. General Zia was an army officer and he, too, could not tolerate the idea of a powerful civilian bureaucracy. Under his one-man rule he used them skillfully but curbed their freedom to act. The next regime of General Ershad was openly not pleased with the civilian bureaucracy. They gained influence once again in Khaleda's first term, even though a serious breach of service discipline occurred when senior bureaucrats openly campaigned for Hasina. When Hasina came to power the pro-AL set of officers gained ascendancy. The

civilian bureaucrats had finally lost their former prestige and became
lesser politicians. The same happened in Khaleda's second term but with
a different set of officers. This difference between politicians and civilian
bureaucrats has narrowed in the past twenty years, to the detriment of
their administrative capability.

The third factor is the natural arrogance of the military vis-à-vis the
politicians and bureaucrats. In an undisciplined country the military is
often the most disciplined entity, and thereby it attracts respect. From the
early years the politicians, and from 1994 onward the civilian bureaucrats,
had lost the respect of the people. In this context the discipline of the military has often been looked upon favorably by the people. On their part
the military, particularly the officers, have always made it known that
they are intrinsically superior to anything civilian. This is not of much
concern until they step into the civilian realm, which they have done time
and again. To the military these interventions were necessary because of
chaotic politics and the inefficiencies of the bureaucracy. All these factors became apparent during Zia's regime and guided the first part of
Ershad's regime. Military efforts to rule civilian government inevitably
end in disgust on both sides. Military and civilian ways of governance
are by definition different. Due to the often chaotic nature of politics, the
military have always received public approval at first, but in less than a
year public opinion changed and there was growing restiveness thereafter. It is said that in the first few weeks of direct military intervention the
military are very disciplined. Thereafter they learn the ways of corruption
in the much more vibrant civilian life. Daily contact reduces the difference in behavior. Whenever direct military contact with civilian life has
continued for a year or more, the effectiveness of military intervention
has vanished. Both Zia and Ershad seemed to be acutely aware of this
when they tried to convert their military rule into a constitutional one.
Each time the politicians only murmured at first, but their voices grew
ever louder as time passed and the public gauged the limits to which the
military were willing to go.

There were two occasions when the military really showed their teeth.
The first of these was during Zia's time when they mercilessly killed the
extreme leftists in the military cantonments and in the villages. These
cadres had grown up under Naxalite influence, deepened their bases during the Liberation war, and spread their doctrine into the Mukti Bahini
and then into the Bangladesh army. A small but dedicated extreme-left
formed in the army and air force. They were instrumental in rescuing Zia
on November 7, 1975, when he was under house arrest. This was their
fatal move, because Zia subsequently turned on them. When they muti-
nied in the cantonments they were systematically eliminated. When the
cadres tried to oppose his regime in the countryside he suppressed them

ruthlessly.[34] One of the longest campaigns was in Rajshahi district in the west, where the leftist cadres had long had direct contact with Naxalites in India.

The other occasion was in the Hill Tracts when tribal people (mainly Chakma) demanded autonomy amounting to independence. This twenty-year-old conflict was discussed above in the "Identify Politics" section. The two sides fought to a standstill. The army is said to have found the virulent strains of malaria in the forested hills a greater danger than the Shanti Bahini. Since the Peace Accord was signed in 1997, the army has reduced the number of camps but is said to have increased the size of major cantonments. The Shanti Bahini is alleged to have been trained and armed by the Indian army, and therefore it was felt that a strong presence should be maintained for reasons of national security.

The military-steered civilian caretaker government that took over on January 11, 2007, has been discussed elsewhere. The social costs of that coup have been mixed. On the one hand several corrupt super-rich were caught, exposed, and jailed. Top bureaucrats and politicians were asked to submit statements about their assets in the hope that public scrutiny would reduce inordinate financial corruption. On the other hand, many suspected that corrupt, super-rich members of the elite were not even interrogated, let alone punished. Moreover, legitimate politics was stifled. It has surprised many observers that the public did not react strongly either way.

STRUGGLES OVER RIGHTS: THE NAGORIK COMMITTEE INITIATIVE

Given the colonial background of the government apparatus and the long period under direct and indirect military rule, the fight for basic rights has been a steeply uphill task. The constitution of the Republic of Bangladesh contains all the necessary Human Rights. However, the social fabric, with dominance of the landed patrons and the very quick growth of super-rich families, does not favor the growth of democracy and the protection of Human Rights. From time to time every one of the various governments since 1971 have infringed upon basic human rights. The list of violations is a long one and none of them are exhaustive.[35] A large number of violations pertain to women, followed by those against minorities. Organizations such as Ain O Salish Kendra have played a yeoman role in tracking down such violations and referring them to the courts. Many NGOs have also assisted in this effort. However, this is a difficult task, mainly due to the cultural effect of centuries of patron-client relationships where the powerful are expected to have the law in their hands. Most politicians are patrons, either through kinship networks or through recently acquired wealth. This makes political solutions all the more difficult.

The person or party in power assumes the law to be in their favor. The power of the police is excessive and it is used to bolster political strength. The Special Powers Act, a repressive law, has been used frequently to snuff out democratic sentiments and appeals to constitutional guarantees of basic rights. The AL, BNP, and JP all have used repressive measures when they deemed it necessary to preserve their dominance. There has, therefore, long been a great deal of concern in the civil society.

The South Asian Association for Regional Cooperation (SAARC), which is the regional body for promoting cooperation between countries of South Asia, has by this time prepared citizens' social charters for the member countries through its South Asian Centre for Policy Studies (SACEPS). These charters voice concerns about the right of the people.[36] When, by 2006, it was evident that the two major parties would stay locked in personal animosities, retarding the growth of democracy with guarantee of basic rights, deep concern was voiced about the very future of the nation. The civil society began to look for a "third force" and also to come to a consensus about the future makeup of the nation's social and political structure. The Nagorik (citizens) Committee 2006 was formed by members of concerned groups, mostly allied to the AL and left-of-center parties, and they drafted *Vision 2021* for Bangladesh. This vision was composed of eight interrelated goals.

1. To Become a Participatory Democracy

This included several demands, among others: a credible election process, members of the JS to be publicly accountable, widely implemented Right to Information Act, and an independent, decentralized and corruption-free judiciary. Interestingly enough there was also a demand for a non-partisan and professional public administration system. Surprisingly, an elected president with *increased* discretionary power was also sought.

2. To Have an Efficient, Publicly Accountable, Transparent, and Decentralized Government

Among the detailed proposals were demands for a transparent govern-ment procurement system, mandatory asset disclosure for members of the JS and civil service professionals, an effective anti-corruption com-mission, and an independent Bangladesh Bank (equivalent of the Federal Reserve). The first demand was necessary because the government system of procuring (buying) abroad had been used by all governments to siphon off funds. There were allegations in both Hasina and Khaleda's time of military purchases that were greatly overpriced. As for mandatory asset disclosure, it has been evaded every time the media and the civil society have asked for it. The few disclosures of 2007 showed how much more unearned wealth would be discovered and recovered if asset disclosure was made mandatory. It was feared that politicians had used the Bangladesh Bank to open commercial banks that funded illegal acquisitions.

3. To Become a Poverty-Mitigated Middle-Income Country

This social-economic goal included demands for an improved investment climate, increased global market access by Bangladesh firms, and a diversified export base. Since agricultural productivity had virtually stagnated in the past decade, one of the demands was for greater productivity, diversification, and commercialization of agriculture. Most interestingly, two other demands were effective urban planning and the development of small-town growth hubs via rural nonfarm industries and services. These demands directly addressed the social and economic problems being created by the continued growth of Dhaka as a megacity and the drain of human and financial resources to it from all parts of the country. The government has tried to partially address this problem through a project for developing growth centers, but this has hardly created a ripple. Now it is considering the building of many Compact Towns to spread the benefits of urbanization to all parts of the country.

4. To Have a Health-Endowed Nation

Here some of the demands were to achieve a replacement level of fertility, reduced neonatal and maternal mortality, and reduction of malnutrition in children. These relate to health education and services, which are woefully inadequate. Bangladesh still has high neonatal and maternal mortality. One of the demands was for prevention of food adulteration and lowering the incidence of food-related diseases. This has indeed been a sore point with the public for many years. Adulteration of cooking oil has been the main complaint. It has been alleged that industrial-grade palm oil is mixed with the lighter edible grade, resulting in serious liver problems. Roadside food stalls and cheap restaurants have often been caught using industrial oil and even electrical transformer oil, which is highly carcinogenic. Apart from sporadic checking, nothing systematic to prevent this happening on a regular basis has been undertaken.

5. To Have a Skilled and Creative Workforce

Most of the demands under this goal relate to education. It was proposed that there should be universal access to education up to the secondary level and free tertiary education for the best students. A decentralized education system free from party-based politics was one of the demands. This is extremely interesting because of the extent to which all parties have depended on students to mobilize public opinion. During the Pakistan years the students spearheaded the language and national movements. After Liberation they became affiliated to different political parties and lost their nation-building role. This demand shows that many in the civil society had at last realized that it was very damaging for the future of the country to have them involved in the politics of power. Another demand was for developing a culture of Corporate Social Responsibility for resource mobilization. This goes to the heart of the accusation that big business seems to direct political decision making. Possibly more should have been demanded of the big industrialists and traders. Many outbreaks of unrest by workers of RMG industries in 2005 and 2006 showed that discontent is simmering. The quasi-civilian caretaker government moved in 2007 to curb trade union activities in the RMG sector and quiet the discontent, but not to assuage it.

6. To Become a Globally Integrated
Regional Economic and Commercial Hub

The demands to achieve this goal are a curious mix of projects and policies. Foremost among the projects was for the establishment of a mega port along the Chittagong coastline, with an international airport, and with a superhighway and a railway system connecting it to Dhaka. This demand has grown out of the fact that most of the near shore is affected by the huge sediment discharge of the large rivers and the Bay of Bengal is shallow for a long distance from the shore. Only two locations have been identified for a relatively deep seaport and both are along the Chittagong region coastline. The existing Chittagong port can barely handle the present volume of trade, partly because of administrative problems.[37] It cannot cater to future demand, which could include the external trade of the seven states in India's northeast. The traders are acutely aware of this and they have demanded the establishment of a "mega port." The shortage of electricity and natural gas leads to frequent power shortages, which affect trade and industries particularly, and therefore another of the demands is for ensuring uninterrupted power and gas supply all over the country. Most interestingly, one of the demands is for integration into the regional energy market. This has been an explosive issue since the BNP and Jamaat have been vehemently against export of natural gas to India, on the ground that there is not enough for Bangladesh's foreseeable future needs. This fear of being an unequal partner with a much more economically powerful neighbor definitely affects political thinking.

7. To Be Environmentally Sustainable

From time to time environmental issues have come to the forefront. The environment movement began in earnest in the mid-1980s with palpable growth of industries and urbanization. The World Conservation Union, known as IUCN (International Union for Conservation of Nature and Natural Resources), published *Caring for the Earth* in 1982 and followed up by assisting many countries, including Bangladesh, to formulate their National Conservation Strategy (NCS). It took nearly five years, and fourteen national seminars, to draft the NCS and get it approved by the government.

The long, drawn-out process made the civil society aware of urgent environmental issues, and many NGOs oriented their efforts to these. With greater dissemination of information and more field-oriented research it became apparent that the proverbially rich inland-water fisheries were rapidly declining, the forests were becoming depleted, soils in many areas were losing their fertility, and both air and water pollution in rapidly growing urban areas had become major menaces to health. The government of General Ershad moved to set up the Ministry of Environment and Forest and the Department of Environment. Two international conferences on environment were held and the president attended both.

With the change of government in 1991 the environment took a back seat. Though invited to the Rio Conference in 1992 Khaleda Zia chose not to attend it. However, the NGOs were committed to ameliorating the rapidly deteriorating situation and pushed the government to draft some basic legislation. Having accepted the Convention on Bio-diversity (CBD) and Convention on Climate Change (CCC), both agreed upon at the 1992 Rio Conference, the government was compelled to legislate more for environment improvement. In 1995 the Environment Conservation Act (ECA), and in 1997 the Environment Conservation Rules (ECR) were passed, but the deterioration of natural resources continued. These broad legislations did not make much difference. By 1998 air pollution in Dhaka was considered one of the worst in the world. Thousands of motor scooters with two-stroke engines created a permanent haze in parts of the city and reportedly caused a rise in heart problems and deaths. To make matters worse the city's natural drainage system was filled in for ill-conceived housing and the remaining outlets were clogged by cheap polyethylene shopping bags that were used and thrown away by the million.

The Bangladesh Poribesh Andolon (BAPA) and the Bangladesh Environment Network (BEN) were two leading groups that campaigned for a better environment. The media were also very active in the campaign to reverse the deteriorating situation. The Hasina government drafted ordinances and the Khaleda government finalized and promulgated them in

2002 to ban two-stroke engines in Dhaka and lightweight polyethylene bags throughout the country. Motor scooters with four-stroke engines were imported to meet the transportation demanded. The improvement of Dhaka's air quality was dramatic and there was a marked decline in clogging of drainage outlets. These are sporadic improvements and very often conditions go back to unacceptable levels. Nevertheless it does show that people tend to obey laws if the authorities show they are serious. Unfortunately the breach comes from the top, when influential persons circumvent or even openly defy the law and are allowed to get away with it because of wealth or family or connections.

Among the demands of the Nagorik Committee were reduction of air and water pollution, better household waste management, and mandatory treatment of industrial and hospital waste. Due to lax enforcement of laws, industries dispose of wastewater into rivers and seasonal lakes. Ultimately this affects drinking water sources. Hospital waste is a major hazard in all urban areas, and the media often carries articles about it, but little is done. UNFPA has made an effort to make professionals and NGOs aware of this particular hazard. The politicians are usually silent about it probably because it is not the type of issue that will affect the unaware electorate.

There were also demands for improvement of the agricultural sector, through *reduction* of the use of chemical fertilizers and pesticides. Here one sees the effect of research directed by the Bangladesh Agricultural Research Council (BARC). It is said that the use of unbalanced doses of chemical fertilizers, without commensurate applications of green manure, has reduced essential micronutrients in the soil. This is held to be largely responsible for the stagnation of rice yields since the 1990s. The four-cow model, generating milk, biogas, and organic manure, is said to be the solution, and is increasing in popularity. Other demands were for preservation of wetlands to maintain the ecosystems, protection of designated forest areas, disaster insurance schemes, and increased use of alternative sources of energy. Bangladesh had once been a country full of wetlands, but their conversion to rice farming has seriously affected freshwater fisheries and the diet of the poor people. The drying up of many wetlands has also adversely affected natural ecosystems of the floodplains. As for forest areas, many of them were decimated for urban housing, biomass fuel use, and a steep rise in the demand for furniture, architraves, and doors by the newly rich. Some of the best forested areas of Chittagong and the Hill tracts were denuded, and collusion by officials of the Forest Department was proved when in 2007 the latest caretaker government found a huge amount of cash hidden in the residence of the head of the department. This denudation of the forest has severely affected wildlife, and greatly increased soil erosion, which in turn has filled the riverbeds and aggravated seasonal floods. Many local and some national politicians were known to have either encouraged or abetted those who destroyed big swathes of forest. Much was said about bringing them to book during Hasina's first government, but some visible action was taken only in the first year of the "one-eleven" caretaker government.

Bangladesh is prone to a host of natural disasters (floods, cyclones, river bank erosion, etc.), and annually large numbers of families become destitute because of them. The local-level politicians have always demanded greater attention to disaster-mitigation projects, and community-based organizations (CBOs) have campaigned for insurance schemes. Most of the influential national-level politicians live securely in large cities and pay scant attention to such ideas. Regarding alternative sources of energy, the demand was for renewable sources. Very little donor resource is being put into this and it is at the very margin of politicians' interest, because they would rather deal with the very big funds for the development of natural gas and coal resources.

8. To Be a More Inclusive and Equal Society

This is actually the core of the struggle for rights. The seven demands were greater access to opportunities for the poor through scholarships, training, and targeted programs; reduced regional inequality through local economic development; minimum employment guarantee for all; increased opportunities for women and no discrimination against women; reduced violence against women; no discrimination against ethnic and religious minorities; and social security for the elderly, the disabled, widows, orphans, and the chronically ill.

As discussed earlier, the poor, women, ethnic minorities, and religious minorities are four sections of the nation who have often complained about feeling insecure. The patron-client nature of the society and the unbridled capitalist nature of the newly rich preclude sympathy for the underprivileged. On the other hand many CBOs, NGOs, charitable institutions, and social organizations are working to achieve these goals. Politicians are not prominent in this work. However, both Khaleda and Hasina did promote greater roles and rights for women. The few politicians who have spoken up for these demands for many decades are in the leftist parties. They have not had a sizeable following since the 1970s and therefore have not been able to push the two major political parties to do more for a just society.

NOTES

1. Niharranjan Ray, *History of the Bengali People*, J. W. Hood trans. (Calcutta: Orient Longman Limited, 1994).

2. Ibid.

3. Joseph E. Schwartzberg, ed., *A Historical Atlas of South Asia* (Chicago: University of Chicago Press, 1978); Haroun er Rashid, *Geography of Bangladesh* (Dhaka: The University Press Limited, 1991); Nitish K. Sengupta, *Bengal Divided: The Unmaking of a Nation (1905–1971)* (New Delhi: Penguin, Viking, 2007).

4. Joya Chatterji, *Bengal Divided* (Cambridge: Cambridge University Press, 1996).

5. Moudud Ahmed, *South Asia, Crisis of Development: The Case of Bangladesh* (Dhaka: The University Press Limited, 2002).

6. Chatterji, *Bengal Divided*.

7. Aminur Rahim, *Politics and National Formation in Bangladesh* (Dhaka: The University Press Limited, 1997).

8. David E. Sopher, "The Geographic Patterning of Culture in India," in *An Exploration of India: Geographical Perspectives on Society and Culture* (Ithaca, NY: Cornell University Press, 1980).

9. Rahim, *Politics and National Formation in Bangladesh*.

10. Rahim, *Politics and National Formation in Bangladesh*; Rounaq Jahan, *Bangladesh: Politics, Problems and Issues*, new expanded ed. (Dhaka: The University Press Limited, 2005).

11. Rahim, *Politics and National Formation in Bangladesh*, 241.

12. A. M. A. Muhith, *American Response to Bangladesh Liberation War* (Dhaka: University Press Limited, 1996).

13. Jahan, *Bangladesh: Politics, Problems and Issues*; Rounaq Jahan, ed., *Bangladesh: Promise and Performance* (Dhaka: The University Press Limited, 2000).

14. Lawrence Lifschultz, *Bangladesh: The Unfinished Revolution* (London: Zed Books, 1979).

15. Jahan, *Bangladesh: Promise and Performance*, 151.

16. Jahan, *Bangladesh: Politics, Problems and Issues*, 134.

17. Lifschultz, *Bangladesh: The Unfinished Revolution*; Jahan, *Bangladesh: Politics, Problems and Issues*.

18. Moudud Ahmed, *Democracy and the Challenge of Development* (Dhaka: The University Press Limited, 1995).

19. Jahan, *Bangladesh: Politics, Problems and Issues*, 119.

20. Stanley A. Kochanek, "The Rise of Interest Politics in Bangladesh," *Asian Survey* 36, no. 7 (July 1996): 704–22.

21. Haroun er Rashid and Babar Kabir, "Water Resources and Population Pressures in the Ganges River Basin," in Victoria Dompka, ed., *Water and Population Dynamics: Case Studies and Policy Implications* (Washington, DC: American Association for the Advancement of Science, 1996).

22. Willem Van Schendel, "Bengalis, Bangladesh and Others: Chakma Visions of a Pluralist Bangladesh," in R. Jahan, ed., *Bangladesh: Promise and Performance* (Dhaka: The University Press Limited, 2000); Moudud Ahmed, *South Asia, Crisis of Development: The Case of Bangladesh* (Dhaka: The University Press Limited, 2002).

23. See Human Rights Watch, "India/Bangladesh: Indiscriminate Killings, Abuse by Border Officers," available at http://tinyurl.com/nxd5vt3.

24. Akhtar Hossain and Salim Rashid, *In Quest of Development* (Dhaka: The University Press Limited, 1996), 30.

25. Ahmed, *South Asia, Crisis of Development*.

26. Syed Serajul Islam, "Elections and Politics in the Last Decade of the Twentieth Century in Bangladesh," in M. H. Chowdhury, ed., *Thirty Years of Bangladesh Politics* (Dhaka: The University Press Limited, 2002).

27. Ibid.

28. Jahan, *Bangladesh: Politics, Problems and Issues,* 293.

29. Munir Quddus and Salim Rashid, *Entrepreneurs and Economic Development* (Dhaka: The University Press Limited, 2000).

30. Salim Rashid, *The Effect of the Women Quota on Bangladesh Politics* (Working Paper for the National Bureau for Asian Research, Seattle, WA, 1999).

31. Vandana Shiva, *Protect or Plunder?* (London: Zed Books, 2001). See also Arundhati Roy's *Power Politics* (Cambridge, Mass.: South End Press, 2001).

32. Van Schendel, "Bengalis, Bangladesh and Others."

33. Haroun er Rashid, "Land and People: Changing Environmental Conditions," in Sufi Mustafizur Rahman, ed., *Archaeological Heritage* (Dhaka: Bangladesh Asiatic Society, 2007, in Bangla; English edition, 2008).

34. Ahmed, *Democracy and the Challenge of Development.*

35. Ain O Salish Kendra et al., *Human Rights in Bangladesh 1997* (Dhaka: The University Press Limited, 1998).

36. Rehman Sobhan, ed., *A Citizen's Social Charter for South Asia* (Dhaka: The University Press Limited, 2005).

37. Haroun er Rashid, *Economic Geography of Bangladesh* (Dhaka: The University Press Limited, Dhaka, 2006).

SUGGESTED READINGS

Given the relative paucity of materials on Bangladesh and the difficulty of obtaining them in the United States, we give below an extended annotated list of books and articles on Bangladesh that elaborate on the points raised in this chapter.

Ahmed, Moudud. *Democracy and the Challenge of Development.* Dhaka: The University Press Limited, 1995. An insider's view of Bangladesh politics. Details events during Zia's and Ershad's rules. Analyzes the role of the military, their relationship with the civil bureaucracy, and the critical future of democracy in the country.

———. *South Asia, Crisis of Development: The Case of Bangladesh.* Dhaka: The University Press Limited, 2002. Discusses the setting of Bangladesh in South Asia, and details many instances of political and legal maneuvering in the 1975–2000 period.

Ahmed, Rafiuddin. *The Bengal Muslims 1871–1906: A Quest for Identity.* Delhi: Oxford University Press, 1981. This is a much-cited work. Presents arguments that Muslim Bengal does not have deep roots.

Ahmed, Sufia. *Muslim Community in Bengal 1884–1912.* 2nd ed. Dhaka: The University Press Limited, 1996. Presents arguments that Muslim Bengal has deep roots and it reflects the aspirations of the majority. Counters arguments in Rafiuddin Ahmed (1981).

Ain O Salish Kendra, et al. *Human Rights in Bangladesh 1997*. Dhaka: The University Press Limited, 1998. An exhaustive list of violations and the efforts of the Human Rights groups.

Anisuzzaman, M. "Identity Question and Politics." In Jahan, *Bangladesh: Promise and Performance* (pp. 45–64). Reviews the question of Bengali Muslim identity and how it affects politics. Discusses the Constitutional changes made by President Zia ur Rahman and some of the reasons why the AL and the BNP are divided.

Blair, Harry W. "Civil Society, Democratic Development and International Donors." In Jahan, *Bangladesh: Promise and Performance* (pp. 131–217). Attempts to define civil society and how the bigger farmers (patrons) reinforce the elite stratum by their linkage to the military, senior bureaucracy, and political leaders.

Chatterji, Joya. *Bengal Divided*. Cambridge: Cambridge University Press, 1996. Of great importance in the continuing debate about why Bengal divided and ultimately Bangladesh was formed. Her work supports arguments that Muslim Bengalis had a genuine grievance and that Partition was not the work of only a few leaders.

Chowdhury, J. A. *Essays on Environment*. Dhaka: Botomul, 2007. Reviews the conventions, treaties, and protocols that affect Bangladesh. Material not readily available elsewhere.

Chowdhury, M. H. (ed.). *Thirty Years of Bangladesh Politics*. Dhaka: The University Press Limited, 2002. Contains a number of articles (cited here) of great interest to the student of Bangladesh politics. Argues for the basic requirement of good governance. Presents the center-right view.

Feldman, Shelley. "NGOs and Civil Society (Un) Stated Contradictions." In R. Jahan, *Bangladesh: Promise and Performance* (pp. 219–43). Discusses the growing importance of NGOs in the political discourse and the charges made by the Jamaat to meet what it sees as a challenge. Raises the important issue as to who has access to private sector resources distributed by NGOs.

Gain, Philip (ed.). *Bangladesh Environment: Facing the 21st Century*. Dhaka: Society for Environment and Human Development, 2002. A useful selection of articles on various environmental issues that affect the social and economic development of the country.

Ghosh, Shyamoli. *The Awami League 1949–1970*. Dhaka: Academic Publishers, 1970. A detailed study of the party up to 1971. Useful for tracing the various social situations that shaped its political stance.

Hossain, Akhtar, and Salim Rashid. *In Quest of Development*. Dhaka: The University Press Limited, 1996. Compares the development of Bangladesh, Pakistan, India, and Sri Lanka to arrive at answers regarding the necessary conditions for economic growth.

Huda, Sigma. "Women through the Decades 1972–1992." In *Bangladesh: The Past Two Decades and the Current Decade*, edited by Q. K. Ahmad (pp. 407–29). Dhaka: Bangladesh Unnayan Parishad & Academic Publishers. An important review of the women's movement in the first two decades of Bangladesh, and their difficulties and successes. Written by one who was in the movement.

Islam, Syed Serajul. "Elections and Politics in the Last Decade of the Twentieth Century in Bangladesh." In Chowdhury, *Thirty Years of Bangladesh Politics* (pp.

133–48). A good review of the politics of the 1990–1998 period, with a rather pessimistic conclusion about the future of democracy in Bangladesh.

Jacques, Kathryn. *Bangladesh, India and Pakistan: International Relations and Regional Tension in South Asia.* New York: St. Martin's Press Inc., 2000. A useful study on South Asia but only up to 1990. Interesting piece on the Chittagong Hill Tracts problem. She refers to the hill people as Montagnards, a term not used in South Asia.

Jahan, Rounaq. *Bangladesh: Politics, Problems and Issues.* New expanded ed. Dhaka: The University Press Limited, 2005. An excellent account of the Mujib era and of the Zia regime. The new expanded edition adds analyses of two years of the BNP Alliance government. This work is essential reading for the student of Bangladesh politics.

Jahan, Rounaq (ed.). *Bangladesh: Promise and Performance.* Dhaka: The University Press Limited, 2000. Contains a number of in-depth articles about different aspects of the country's politics and governance. Chapters by Stanley A. Kochanek, Harry W. Blair, and Shelly Feldman are recommended reading.

Jansen, G. H. *Militant Islam.* London: Pan Books, 1979. This early study remains one of the best about the roots of Muslim radicalism. For a deeper understanding of the Jamaat, and the parties to their right, this is a good beginning.

Kabir, Bhuian M. Monoar. "Islamic Politics in Bangladesh: Internal and External Contexts." In Chowdhury, *Thirty Years of Bangladesh Politics* (pp. 149–202). A nonpartisan view of the rise of the Islamists. Recounts opposition to them by the AL and the Indian government and why they came into an alliance with the BNP in 1997.

Kochanek, Stanley A. "The Growing Commercialization of Power." In Jahan, *Bangladesh: Promise and Performance* (pp. 149–79). An essay on how for the first time the business community played an active role in national politics in the period 1994–1996. Given their subsequent major role in politics this article is of particular importance.

———. "The Rise of Interest Politics in Bangladesh." *Asian Survey* 36, no. 7 (July 1996): 704–22. Outlines the increasing role of the business community in the largely patrimonial, patron-client political process.

Lifschultz, Lawrence. *Bangladesh: The Unfinished Revolution.* London: Zed Books, 1979. Details events in the mid-1970s and is critical of Zia's "betrayal" of Taher. Furnishes the left's view of the fateful times when it struggled for supremacy with rightist forces.

Mohsin, Amena. "State of Indigenous Communities in Bangladesh: An Overview." In *Indigenous People of Bangladesh*, edited by A. Ahsan and A. S. Abbasi. Dhaka: Independent University Bangladesh, 2005. A sympathetic account of the small tribal groups and their problems of economic and cultural survival.

Munshi, M. B. I. *The India Doctrine.* Dhaka: The Bangladesh Research Forum. Openly critical of India's role in agitations in neighboring countries. Discusses the AL relations with India, and also the Chittagong Hill Tracts problem.

Murshid, Tazeen M. *The Sacred and the Secular: Bengal Muslim Discourses 1871–1977.* Dhaka: The University Press Limited, 1996. Discusses the formation of a separate identity by the Muslims of Bengal and how this led to East Pakistan and then Bangladesh.

Quasem, Muhammad A. *Development Strategies and Challenges Ahead of Bangladesh.* Dhaka: Polok Publishers, 2008. Presents data from many sources to argue that there is a high degree of correlation between corruption control indicators and those of governance effectiveness and the rule of law.

Quddus, Munir, and Salim Rashid. *Entrepreneurs and Economic Development: The Remarkable Story of Garment Exports from Bangladesh.* Dhaka: The University Press Limited, 2000. The subtitle of the book succinctly describes the contents. Explains multi-fiber arrangement (MFA) quotas, use of child labor, and the effect of national politics on the growth of this industry.

Rahim, Aminur. *Politics and National Formation in Bangladesh.* Dhaka: The University Press Limited, 1997. A deeply introspective study of how society has shaped politics in Bangladesh. Explains the patron-client relationship. Much material on pre-Bangladesh events.

Rahman, Hasibur. "Governance and Election under Military Backed Caretaker Government in Bangladesh." *Asian Studies, Journal of the Department of Government and Politics,* no. 29, June 2010. A detailed account of quasi-military government, the election they held, and the politics associated with it.

Rashid, Haroun er. *Economic Geography of Bangladesh.* Dhaka: The University Press Limited, 2006. A concise account of the various sectors of the Bangladesh economy. Chapter 2 recounts the significant changes in the society and the economy since 1971.

Rashid, Haroun er. *Geography of Bangladesh.* Dhaka: The University Press Limited, 1991. Provides essential background information. Relevant chapters are "Historical Background," "The People," and "Population and Environmental Issues."

Rashid, Haroun er. "Land and People: Changing Environmental Conditions." In *Archaeological Heritage,* edited by Sufi Mustafizur Rahman (in Bangla). Dhaka: Bangladesh Asiatic Society, 2007. English edition in 2008. Outlines briefly the changes in the physical and social environment in Bangladesh over the past ten thousand years (i.e., from the end of the last Ice Age). Shows that environmental concerns have been critical for a long time.

Rashid, Haroun er, and Babar Kabir. "Water Resources and Population Pressures in the Ganges River Basin." In *Water and Population Dynamics: Case Studies and Policy Implications,* edited by Victoria Dompka. Washington, DC: American Association for the Advancement of Science. Discusses the plight of the people in the lower Ganges Basin due to population pressure and the Farakka Barage in India, and the politics associated with it.

Rashid, Mamun Ur. "Sustainable Environment Management Program." In S. Rashid, *Rotting at the Head.* A case study of how donors maneuvered to favor certain NGOs and their lack of transparency in dealing with the government. Raises questions about lack of transparency in donor activities and funding, and what effect this has on the climate of corruption.

Rashid, Salim. *The Effect of the Women Quota on Bangladesh Politics,* Working Paper for the National Bureau for Asian Research, Seattle, WA. Discusses the effect of the women quota and finds it to have been externally driven and therefore not very effective.

Rashid, Salim (ed.). *Rotting at the Head.* Dhaka: The University Press Limited, 2004. Presents arguments and case studies that donor agencies (bilateral and multilateral) can be complicit in corruption in less developed countries and that a small number of bureaucrats and politicians are in league with them.

Rashiduzzaman, M. "The CHT and National Security for Bangladesh." In Chowdhury, *Thirty Years of Bangladesh Politics* (pp. 77–88). An interesting presentation of the tribal vs. settler dichotomy. Mentions the externalization of the problem due to the presence of Christian missionaries.

Razia, Akter Banu. "Jamaat-i-Islami in Bangladesh: Challenges and Prospects." In *Islam, Muslims and the Modern State*, edited by H. Mutalib and T. I. Hashmi. London: Macmillan, and New York: St. Martin's Press, 1994. Describes the formation and prospects of the party, and discusses relevance in the modern world.

Schwartzberg, Joseph E. (ed.). *A Historical Atlas of South Asia.* Chicago: University of Chicago Press, 1978. A major contribution to South Asian studies. Maps information on historical and social changes in a geographical setting. Provides a South Asian background to Bengal and Bangladesh.

Sengupta, Nitish K. *Bengal Divided: The Unmaking of a Nation (1905–1971).* New Delhi: Penguin, Viking, 2007. Narrates the recent story of Bengal from the Indian point of view. The subtitle refers to the romantic view that West Bengal and Bangladesh could have been one country, ignoring the resentment between Muslims and upper-caste Hindus. Particularly good when narrating events that led to Partition in 1947.

Sobhan, Rehman. *Bangladesh: Problems of Governance.* Dhaka: The University Press Limited, Dhaka, 1993. An indispensable work by one who was in a ministerial rank and an insider for many years. The author is chair of the Centre for Policy Dialogue in Dhaka.

Sobhan, Rehman (ed.). *A Citizen's Social Charter for South Asia: An Agenda for Civic Action.* Dhaka: The University Press Limited, 2005. This is a landmark document. Prepared jointly by the South Asia Centre for Policy Studies (SACEPS) and Centre for Policy Dialogue (CDP), it outlines Citizens Social Charters for Bangladesh and other South Asian countries.

Sopher, David E. "The Geographic Patterning of Culture in India." In *An Exploration of India: Geographical Perspectives on Society and Culture*, edited by David E. Sopher. Ithaca, NY: Cornell University Press, 1980. Very interesting analysis of the patterning of Muslim groups, and the origin of the Sheikhs in Bangladesh.

Umar. B. *The Emergence of Bangladesh: Class Struggles in East Pakistan 1947–1958.* Karachi: Oxford University Press, 2004. Indispensable for understanding the patron-client society and the part played by the left in the formation of Bangladesh.

Van Schendel, Willem. "Bengalis, Bangladesh and Others: Chakma Visions of a Pluralist Bangladesh." In Jahan, *Bangladesh: Promise and Performance* (pp. 65–105). Reviews cogently the existence of Bengali nationalism and its impact on non-Bengali groups. Argues for a pluralist approach to the question of culture. See also Moudud Ahmed (1995, 292–98).

White, C. Sarah. "NGOs, Civil Society, and the State in Bangladesh: The Politics of Representing the Poor." *Development and Change* 30, no. 2 (1999): 307–26. Examines the role of the government and the NGOs as development agents. Raises questions whether they really reflect the interests of the poor.

Index

414   *Index*

Pakistan independence:
  constitutionalism and, 176–179;
  development of, 79, 81–90;
  ideologies of, 175; Islam and, 175–
  179; Objectives Resolution of the
  Constituent Assembly of Pakistan,
  176, *178*; Two Nations Theory,
  83–84, 196; violence and, 88–91
Pakistan political history: Baluchistan
  and, 172–173, 192–194, 197, 198,
  200–206; Bhutto, Benazir, 12, 122,
  183–185, *184*, 188–190, 213; Bhutto,
  Zulfiqar Ali, 115, 180–182, 190,
  204, 298; Chaudhry, Chief Justice
  Iftikhar Muhammad, 188, 190; civil
  society in, 174, 185; constitutional
  development, 176–179, 181–183,
  186–189, 207, 212–216; East Pakistan,
  176, 180, 196–197, 207; economic
  development and, 181, 191–196;
  Islam and, 177, 182–183, 187,
  218–221; Islamization, 182–183, 196,
  212, 221nn10–11; Jama'at-i-Islami,
  Pakistan 116, 187, 191, 205, 213,
  223n40; Jinnah, Muhammad Ali,
  173–176, *174* 191, 216; Kashmir,
  173, 179, 181, 185, 197, 206–207,
  216–217; Khan, Muhammad Ayub,
  179–181, *180*, 192, 219, 351–352, 359;
  land reform and, 181; military and,
  177, 179, 180, 182, 185, 216–218;
  Musharraf, Pervez, 184–190, 214,
  224n45; Muttahida Majlis-i-Amal
  (MMA), 187, 205–206, 223n40,
  224n51; Nawaz, Sharif, 183–185,
  189–191, 213, 217; nuclear weapons,
  185; Pakistan's Peoples Party (PPP),
  179, 181–183, 190–191, 195, 215;
  political development of, 179–183,
  186–194, 222n17; regionalism, 196–
  207; relationship with the United
  States, 173, 183; ul-Haq, Muhammad
  Zia (1924–1988), 169, 181–183, 196,
  204, 212–213, 216, 221nn10–11; wars
  with India, 176, 179–180, 197, 207,
  216; women rights, 182, 202, 212–
  216, 224n46, 224n50

Pakistan state: civil-military relations,
  216; constitution and, 176–179,
  181–183, 186–189, 207, 212–216;
  Islam and, 177, 182–183, 187,
  211–215; military and, 180, 182, 185,
  216–218; presidential power and,
  189; regionalism, 172, 217; terrorism
  and, 172, 185–187, 190, 217–218;
  women's rights and, 182
Pakistan's People's Party (PPP), 179,
  181–183, 190–191, 195, 215
partition (1947), 75–76, 83, 85, 87,
  89–91, 109, 144, 147, 173–175, 196,
  199, 216, 350–351, 383
Premadasa Ranasingh (1924–1993),
  246–247, 249, 251, 253, 262, 279
Phule, Mahatma Jyotirao (1827–1890),
  54

Rahman, General Zia Ur (1936–1981),
  353, 358–361, 363, 372. 375, 380, 382,
  384, 391
Ram Mohan Roy (1772–1833), 47
Ranade, Mahadev Govind (1842–
  1901), *56*

Savarkar, Vinayak Damodar (1883–
  1966), 67
Senanayake, Don Stephen (1884–1952),
  75, 233, 257, 266
Senanayake, Dudley (1911–1973), 75,
  233, 235–238, *238*, 240, 257, 259, 261,
  266
September 11, 2001, 127, 185–186, 217,
  248, 267
Sheikh Hasina, 13, 364–365, *364*, 367–
  370, 377, 381, 385, 391, 394, 397
Sinhala: colonial history of, 265;
  cultural types, 264; JVP and,
  238, 240, 243, 245–246; political
  development of, 227, 230–231, 234–
  235, 237–240, 248–254
South Asian Association for Regional
  Cooperation (SAARC), 16–17, 18n3,
  394
Sri Lanka: Bandaranaike, Sirimavo,
  12, 236–240, *236*, 243, 247, 257, 259,

About the Contributors

Arjun Guneratne received his PhD from the University of Chicago, and is professor and chair of anthropology at Macalester College in Saint Paul, Minnesota. He is the author of *Many Tongues, One People: The Making of Tharu Identity in Nepal* (2002) and editor of *Culture and the Environment in the Himalaya* (2010), *Ethnicity, Inequality and Politics in Nepal* (2010, with Mahendra Lawoti), *Dalits of Nepal: Towards Dignity, Citizenship and Justice* (2010), and *The Tarai: History, Society, Environment* (2011). He was formerly the editor of *Himalaya*, the journal of the Association for Nepal and Himalayan Studies, and is on the editorial board of PoLAR, the *Political and Legal Anthropology Review*. He serves on the board of directors of the American Institute for Sri Lankan Studies. His current projects include a reader on the culture, politics, and history of Nepal and a book on wildlife and biodiversity conservation in Sri Lanka.

Christophe Jaffrelot received his doctorate in political science from the Institut d'Études Politiques (IEP) in Paris, as well as other degrees from the Université de Paris-I Panthéon-Sorbonne and of the Institut National des Langues et Civilisations Orientales (INALCO). He is Senior Research Fellow at CERI-Sciences Po/CNRS in Paris, professor at the King's India Institute, and Princeton Global Scholar. He teaches South Asian politics at Sciences Po, Princeton, and King's College (London). He is the author of *The Hindu Nationalist Movement and Indian Politics, 1925 to the 1990s* (1996, 1999); *India's Silent Revolution: The Rise of the Lower Castes in North India* (2003); *Dr. Ambedkar and Untouchability: Analysing and Fighting Caste* (2005); and *Religion, Caste and Politics in India* (2010). Among his most recent edited volumes are *Pakistan: Nationalism without a Nation?* (2002), *A History of Pakistan and Its Origins* (2004), *Hindu Nationalism: A Reader* (2007), with L. Gayer, *Armed Militias of South Asia: Fundamentalist, Maoists and Separatists* (2009), and with L. Gayer, *Muslims of India's Cities: Trajectories of Marginalization* (2012). His forthcoming book is titled *The Pakistan Paradox: Instability and Resilience.*

Pratyoush Onta has a PhD in history from the University of Pennsylvania (1996). He has written on Nepali nationalism, Gurkha history, institutions, area studies, knowledge production, and media. His articles have been published in journals such as *Anthropology Matters, Contributions to Nepalese Studies, Dhaulagiri Journal of Sociology and Anthropology, Economic and Political Weekly, European Bulletin of Himalayan Research, Media Adhyayan, Nepali Journal of Contemporary Studies, Rupantaran, Seminar,* and *Studies in Nepali History and Society (SINHAS).* He has written, edited, or coedited several books including *Nepal Studies in the UK* (2004); *Social History of Radio Nepal* (2004, in Nepali); *Social Scientific Thinking in the Context of Nepal* (2004, in Nepali); *Radio Journalism: News and Talk Programs in FM* (2005, in Nepali); *Growing up with Radio* (2005, in Nepali); *Mass Media in Post-1990 Nepal* (2006); *Ten Years of Independent Radio: Development, Debates and the Public Interest* (2008, in Nepali); and *Socially Inclusive Media* (2008, in Nepali). He is also the founding editor of the journals *Studies in Nepali History and Society* and *Media Adhyayan* (in Nepali). He has been associated with the research institute and public forum Martin Chautari in Kathmandu since 1995 and is currently its chair.

Haroun er Rashid received an MA in geography from Cambridge University and an MA in economics from the Center for Development Economics, Williams College. He is professor of geography and chair of the School of Environmental Science and Management at the Independent University, Bangladesh, in Dhaka. He is the author of *The Geography of Bangladesh* (1977/1991), *Conflicts of Culture: Lessons from Bosnia* (1998), and *Economic Geography of Bangladesh* (1981/2005). He has also written on recent conflicts with extremists in "Huntington's Prediction Refuted" in the *Journal of the Historical Society* (2002) and in "Muslims and the West" in *Islam and the West: Critical Perspectives on Modernity* (edited by Michael Thompson, 2003). He is associated with the Higher Education Consortium for Urban Affairs (HECUA), a St. Paul, Minnesota, based organization that sends students every year to Bangladesh to study community and development. This project earned the Heiskell Award from the Institute of International Education in 2006. He is also associated with the Wildlife and Nature Conservation Society of Bangladesh (WNCSB), which works on biodiversity conservation and has been working with other biodiversity groups trying to save tigers, elephants, hoolocks, and other species. He runs Green Education for underprivileged children, especially with the children of Tea Garden laborers.

Seira Tamang has a PhD in International Relations and her research interests have focused on gender, state, foreign aid, and democracy. She is the author of numerous articles in English and Nepali in edited volumes and has published in journals such as the *Feminist Review, Citizenship Studies, International Journal on Minority and Group Rights, Studies in Nepali History and Society (SINHAS)*, and *Nepali Journal of Contemporary Studies*. She is also the primary author of policy briefs published by the research and policy institute Martin Chautari (MC) on the Constituent Assembly process in Nepal. She is based in Nepal and has been affiliated with MC in Kathmandu for over a decade, serving as its chair for the period 2008–2012. She is also a coeditor of the journal *SINHAS*, an international, peer-reviewed academic journal published from Nepal. She has made interventions in the development field, working with various foreign aid donors and civil society organizations, particularly in researching dimensions of social exclusion and in promoting practices and policies of good governance at national and local levels. She has received various academic awards and research fellowships at various institutions including at the Graduate School of Asian and African Studies (ASAFAS) at Kyoto University, Japan, and the Asian Scholarship Foundation (ASF) in Thailand.

Shabnum Tejani received her doctorate in history from Columbia University and now teaches modern South Asian history in the History Department at the School of Oriental and African Studies, University of London. Her publications include *Indian Secularism: A Social and Intellectual History, 1890–1950* (2007); "Reflections on the Category of Secularism in India: Gandhi, Ambedkar, and the Ethics of Communal Represenation, c. 1931" in *The Crisis of Secularism in India* (edited by A. D. Needham and R. S. Rajan, 2007); "Reconsidering Chronologies of Nationalism and Communalism: The Khilafat Movement in Sind and Its Aftermath, 1919–1927" in *South Asia Research* (2007); and "Music, Mosques and Custom: Local Conflict and 'Communalism' in a Maharashtrian Weaving Town, 1893–1894" in *South Asia: Journal of South Asian Studies* (2007). Her new project is a social history of wealth in twentieth-century Bombay.

Anita M. Weiss received her doctorate in sociology from UC Berkeley and is now professor and head of the Department of International Studies at the University of Oregon. She has published extensively on social development, gender issues, and political Islam in Pakistan. Her books include *Development Challenges Confronting Pakistan* (coedited with Saba Gul Khattak, 2013); *Power and Civil Society in Pakistan* (coedited with Zulfiqar Gilani, 2001); *Walls within Walls: Life Histories of Working Women in the Old City of Lahore* (1992, republished 2002); and *Culture, Class, and Development in Pakistan: The Emergence of an Industrial Bourgeoisie in Punjab* (1991). Recent publications include "Crisis and Reconciliation in Swat through the Eyes of Women" in *Beyond Swat: History, Society and Economy along the Afghanistan-Pakistan Frontier* (edited by Magnus Marsden and Ben Hopkins, 2012); *Moving Forward with the Legal Empowerment of Women in Pakistan* (USIP Special Report 305, 2012); and "Population Growth, Urbanization and Female Literacy" in *The Future of Pakistan*, edited by Stephen P. Cohen and others (2011). Her current research project is analyzing how distinct constituencies in Pakistan, including the state, are grappling with articulating their views on women's rights and is titled *Interpreting Islam, Modernity and Women's Rights in Pakistan* (forthcoming). Professor Weiss is a member of the editorial boards of *Citizenship Studies* and *Globalizations*, is on the editorial advisory board of Kumarian Press, is a member of the Research Advisory Board of the Pakistan National Commission on the Status of Women, and is the vice president of the American Institute of Pakistan Studies (AIPS).